Dictionary of Literary Biography

Dictionary of Literary Biography Documentary Series

Dictionary of Literary Biography Yearbooks

1980 edited by Karen L. Rood, Jean W. Ross, and Richard Ziegfeld (1981)

1981 edited by Karen L. Rood, Jean W. Ross, and Richard Ziegfeld (1982)

1982 edited by Richard Ziegfeld; associate editors: Jean W. Ross and Lynne C. Zeigler (1983)

1983 edited by Mary Bruccoli and Jean W. Ross; associate editor Richard Ziegfeld (1984)

1984 edited by Jean W. Ross (1985)

1985 edited by Jean W. Ross (1986)

1986 edited by J. M. Brook (1987)

1987 edited by J. M. Brook (1988)

1988 edited by J. M. Brook (1989)

1989 edited by J. M. Brook (1990)

1990 edited by James W. Hipp (1991)

1991 edited by James W. Hipp (1992)

1992 edited by James W. Hipp (1993)

1993 edited by James W. Hipp, contributing editor George Garrett (1994)

1994 edited by James W. Hipp, contributing editor George Garrett (1995)

1995 edited by James W. Hipp, contributing editor George Garrett (1996)

1996 edited by Samuel W. Bruce and L. Kay Webster, contributing editor George Garrett (1997)

1997 edited by Matthew J. Bruccoli and George Garrett, with the assistance of L. Kay Webster (1998)

1998 edited by Matthew J. Bruccoli, contributing editor George Garrett, with the assistance of D. W. Thomas (1999)

1999 edited by Matthew J. Bruccoli, contributing editor George Garrett, with the assistance of D. W. Thomas (2000)

2000 edited by Matthew J. Bruccoli, contributing editor George Garrett, with the assistance of George Parker Anderson (2001)

Concise Series

Concise Dictionary of American Literary Biography, 7 volumes (1988–1999): *The New Consciousness, 1941–1968; Colonization to the American Renaissance, 1640–1865; Realism, Naturalism, and Local Color, 1865–1917; The Twenties, 1917–1929; The Age of Maturity, 1929–1941; Broadening Views, 1968–1988; Supplement: Modern Writers, 1900–1998.*

Concise Dictionary of British Literary Biography, 8 volumes (1991–1992): *Writers of the Middle Ages and Renaissance Before 1660; Writers of the Restoration and Eighteenth Century, 1660–1789; Writers of the Romantic Period, 1789–1832; Victorian Writers, 1832–1890; Late-Victorian and Edwardian Writers, 1890–1914; Modern Writers, 1914–1945; Writers After World War II, 1945–1960; Contemporary Writers, 1960 to Present.*

Concise Dictionary of World Literary Biography, 10 volumes projected (1999–): *Ancient Greek and Roman Writers; German Writers; African, Caribbean, and Latin American Writers; South Slavic and Eastern European Writers.*

Dictionary of Literary Biography® • Volume Two Hundred Fifty-Eight

Modern French Poets

Dictionary of Literary Biography® • Volume Two Hundred Fifty-Eight

Modern French Poets

Edited by
Jean-François Leroux
University of Ottawa

A Bruccoli Clark Layman Book
The Gale Group
Detroit • San Francisco • London • Boston • Woodbridge, Conn.

Printed in the United States of America

The paper used in this publication meets the minimum requirements
of American National Standard for Information Sciences–Permanence
Paper for Printed Library Materials, ANSI Z39.48-1984. ∞ ™

Library of Congress Cataloging-in-Publication Data

Modern French poets / edited by Jean-François Leroux.
    p. cm.–(Dictionary of literary biography; v. 258)
"A Bruccoli Clark Layman book."
Includes bibliographical references and index.
ISBN 0-7876-5252-0 (alk. paper)
1. French poetry–20th century–Dictionaries. 2. French poetry–20th century–Bio-bibliography–
Dictionaries. 3. Poets, French–20th century–Biography–Dictionaries. 1. Leroux, Jean-François.
II. Series.

PQ441 .M63 2002
841'.9109'003–dc21   2002022119

10 9 8 7 6 5 4 3 2 1

*À Camille R. La Bossière, une âme véritablement
encyclopédique et un grand ami . . .*

Contents

Plan of the Series

. . . Almost the most prodigious asset of a country, and perhaps its most precious possession, is its native literary product—when that product is fine and noble and enduring.

Mark Twain*

The advisory board, the editors, and the publisher of the *Dictionary of Literary Biography* are joined in endorsing Mark Twain's declaration. The literature of a nation provides an inexhaustible resource of permanent worth. Our purpose is to make literature and its creators better understood and more accessible to students and the reading public, while satisfying the needs of teachers and researchers.

To meet these requirements, *literary biography* has been construed in terms of the author's achievement. The most important thing about a writer is his writing. Accordingly, the entries in *DLB* are career biographies, tracing the development of the author's canon and the evolution of his reputation.

The purpose of *DLB* is not only to provide reliable information in a usable format but also to place the figures in the larger perspective of literary history and to offer appraisals of their accomplishments by qualified scholars.

The publication plan for *DLB* resulted from two years of preparation. The project was proposed to Bruccoli Clark by Frederick G. Ruffner, president of the Gale Research Company, in November 1975. After specimen entries were prepared and typeset, an advisory board was formed to refine the entry format and develop the series rationale. In meetings held during 1976, the publisher, series editors, and advisory board approved the scheme for a comprehensive biographical dictionary of persons who contributed to literature. Editorial work on the first volume began in January 1977, and it was published in 1978. In order to make *DLB* more than a dictionary and to compile volumes that individually have claim to status as literary history, it was decided to organize volumes by topic, period, or

From an unpublished section of Mark Twain's autobiography, copyright by the Mark Twain Company

genre. Each of these freestanding volumes provides a biographical-bibliographical guide and overview for a particular area of literature. We are convinced that this organization—as opposed to a single alphabet method—constitutes a valuable innovation in the presentation of reference material. The volume plan necessarily requires many decisions for the placement and treatment of authors. Certain figures will be included in separate volumes, but with different entries emphasizing the aspect of his career appropriate to each volume. Ernest Hemingway, for example, is represented in *American Writers in Paris, 1920–1939* by an entry focusing on his expatriate apprenticeship; he is also in *American Novelists, 1910–1945* with an entry surveying his entire career, as well as in *American Short-Story Writers, 1910–1945, Second Series* with an entry concentrating on his short fiction. Each volume includes a cumulative index of the subject authors and articles.

Since 1981 the series has been further augmented by the *DLB Yearbooks,* which update published entries, add new entries to keep the *DLB* current with contemporary activity, and provide articles on literary history. There have also been nineteen *DLB Documentary Series* volumes which provide illustrations, facsimiles, and biographical and critical source materials for figures, works, or groups judged to have particular interest for students. In 1999 the *Documentary Series* was incorporated into the *DLB* volume numbering system beginning with *DLB 210: Ernest Hemingway.*

We define literature as the *intellectual commerce of a nation:* not merely as belles lettres but as that ample and complex process by which ideas are generated, shaped, and transmitted. *DLB* entries are not limited to "creative writers" but extend to other figures who in their time and in their way influenced the mind of a people. Thus the series encompasses historians, journalists, publishers, book collectors, and screenwriters. By this means readers of *DLB* may be aided to perceive literature not as cult scripture in the keeping of intellectual high priests but firmly positioned at the center of a nation's life.

DLB includes the major writers appropriate to each volume and those standing in the ranks behind them. Scholarly and critical counsel has been sought in deciding which minor figures to include and how full their entries should be. Wherever possible, useful references are made to figures who do not warrant separate entries.

Each *DLB* volume has an expert volume editor responsible for planning the volume, selecting the figures for inclusion, and assigning the entries. Volume editors are also responsible for preparing, where appropriate, appendices surveying the major periodicals and literary and intellectual movements for their volumes, as well as lists of further readings. Work on the series as a whole is coordinated at the Bruccoli Clark Layman editorial center in Columbia, South Carolina, where the editorial staff is responsible for accuracy and utility of the published volumes.

One feature that distinguishes *DLB* is the illustration policy—its concern with the iconography of literature. Just as an author is influenced by his surroundings, so is the reader's understanding of the author enhanced by a knowledge of his environment. Therefore *DLB* volumes include not only drawings, paintings, and photographs of authors, often depicting them at various stages in their careers, but also illustrations of their families and places where they lived. Title pages are regularly reproduced in facsimile along with dust jackets for modern authors. The dust jackets are a special feature of *DLB* because they often document better than anything else the way in which an author's work was perceived in its own time. Specimens of the writers' manuscripts and letters are included when feasible.

Samuel Johnson rightly decreed that "The chief glory of every people arises from its authors." The purpose of the *Dictionary of Literary Biography* is to compile literary history in the surest way available to us—by accurate and comprehensive treatment of the lives and work of those who contributed to it.

The *DLB* Advisory Board

Introduction

. . . il en est des révolutions de l'art comme des révolutions des sociétés: ce qu'elles renversent subsiste souvent dans la mesure même où elles se sont formulées et définies contre lui . . . . Ainsi ces adversaires dont l'étreinte est si violente qu'en se combattant ils s'imitent, et, à force de s'opposer, "déteignent" l'un sur l'autre, dans l'antagonisme des similitudes et la symétrie des antithèses.

(. . . it is with revolutions in art as with revolutions in society: what they overthrow often subsists to the very extent that they have formulated and defined themselves against it. . . . like those adversaries whose embrace is so violent that in fighting each other they imitate one another, and, by dint of opposing each other, "rub off" on one another, in the antagonism of similitudes and the symmetry of antitheses).

–Claude Roy, in his preface to *Anthologie de la poésie française du XXᵉ siècle,* edited by Michel Décaudin (1983).

Francis Ponge's educing, in his *Proêmes* (1948), of the exacting nature of poetic language from "Maître de Vie" (Master of Life) Georges Braque's painterly formula–"l'objet, c'est la Poétique" (the object is the Poetics)–would seem to make the task of introducing modern French poetry unnecessary. Rekindling the spirit of high inventiveness that has animated and presided over so much of modern classical French literature, thought, and art since Guillaume Apollinaire first evoked it, in his 1917 conference on the "esprit nouveau" (new spirit), as the marriage of order and adventure, logic and inspiration in an "ardente Raison" (ardent Reason), Ponge's equation also summons its perfect insularity. If every poet, seeking with him to fuse word and thing, prose and poetry, theory and practice in a "poésie pure" (pure poetry) analogous to the Cubists' "peinture pure" (pure painting), rewrites his or her *ars poetica* with every poem–"une rhétorique par poème" (a rhetoric by poem)–then any attempt to capture the Protean richness of this secular poetry must needs be, in the manner of anthologies, studies, and literary histories of the period, panoramic, inviting the reader to discover in every poet a separate and distinct itinerary. Whether aspiring with Stéphane Mallarmé to the encyclopedic "Grand Œuvre" (Great Work) that

would round out the world in a book, with André Breton and the Surrealists to "le point suprême" (the supreme point) or with René Char to "le poème pulvérisé" (the pulverized poem–to mention but a few of the hymns sung to its high metaphysical ambitions)– a large part of twentieth-century French poetry from Paul Valéry to Yves Bonnefoy remains necessarily inchoate, less a series of "œuvres" belonging to a coherent worldview than a constellation of idiosyncratic and often contradictory "épreuves," essays or approximations.

These approximations can be found scripted, for example, in the Surrealists' "Cadavres exquis" (Exquisite Corpses), collective creations in which one member of the group would write part of the text and pass it on for another member to write another section, and so on. The name of the technique is derived from the collage produced during one early session, "Le cadavre exquis boira le vin nouveau" (The exquisite corpse will drink the young wine). In 1960, some thirty-five years after the Surrealists first played their modified parlor game, the writer Raymond Queneau and the mathematician and chess player François Le Lionnais founded OuLiPo (Ouvroir de Littérature Potentielle; Workshop of Potential Literature); originally focused on the possibilities of combining mathematics and literature, OuLiPo advocated self-conscious experimentation in literature, including open-ended storytelling such as Queneau's "Un conte à votre façon" (A Story Your Way, 1967), in which the reader is presented with choices in reading a text and he or she determines the structure of the narrative through choosing which narrative line to follow.

In his *Exercices de style* (1942) Queneau declares "il n'y a plus d'écriture" (there is no more writing), while Roland Barthes elegizes on the nullity of writing as a system of formal conventions in *Le Degré zéro de l'écriture* (1953; translated as *Writing Degree Zero,* 1953), "il n'y a que des styles" (there are only styles). So conceived, along post-neosymbolist lines, every poem is its own introduction, defying canonical syntax, prosody, logic, and grammar and so challenging the newly enfranchised, inspired, or initiated reader to invent "sa propre rhétorique" (his own rhetoric), as Ponge states the aim both of his prose-poesy and that of Mallarmé's poetic art, which Albert Thibaudet described in 1913 as "des caractères juxtaposés, sans phrase, ni grammaire, où l'ordre syntaxique ne déformerait pas la pureté des mots, où l'esprit de la syntaxe serait chez le lecteur, non la réalité de la syntaxe sur le papier" (juxtaposed characters, without sentence, nor grammar, where the syntactic order would not deform the purity of the words, where the spirit of syntax would be that of the reader, not the reality of syntax on paper). Not surprisingly, given such promptings to free- and high-spirited reprise, this aesthetic, much like its postmodern, deconstructionist avatars, has been seen, by turns, as inherently democratizing and liberating and as fundamentally aristocratic and gnostic, depending on the spirit of the reader.

Cubism was itself, of course, the end result of a series of experiments in the second half of the nineteenth century, experiments that had conspired to create a new awareness of medium. Just as Mallarmé, in his now legendary riposte to an overzealous Hilaire Degas, had made it clear that "poetry is not written with ideas but with words," so, too, Paul Cézanne, it was said, had "showed that paintings were not pictures but *paint*." In the visual arts, that new awareness eventually gave rise to the cerebral geometry that first gave Cubism its name, but Cubism also generated, in a later phase of its development, the "simultaneism" of Robert Delaunay, Pablo Picasso, and those painters Apollinaire termed "orphic"; in both cases, the outcome was, in the words "Cubist" poet Pierre Reverdy used to define the poetic image in the March 1918 edition of *Nord-Sud,* which were subsequently adopted as part of the *Premier Manifeste du Surréalisme* (First Manifesto of Surrealism, 1924), "une création pure de l'esprit" (a pure creation of the spirit), an autonomous creation or "poème-objet" made up, as were Max Ernst's collages, of the synthesis or juxtaposition of disparate realities. "To paint, not the thing itself," Mallarmé had written, "but the effect it produces." Aiming at the perfect reciprocity of ends and means conducive to a poetical state of mind, the perfect poem, as Valéry points out in his remarks on Mallarmé and "la poésie pure," necessarily calls for a suspension of the reader's disbelief; it cannot be reduced to any didactic, prosaic statement, to the understanding or reason in the Kantian sense. Where Immanuel Kant saw the categorical imperative, as though written in the stars, there, Valéry contends, Mallarmé saw only the urgings of a poetics as richly enigmatic as the silent reaches of space.

Their eventual disenchantment with and dismissal of Valéry upon his election to the Académie Française in 1925 notwithstanding, the Surrealists found themselves in accord with him on this point at least, hostile as they were, in their initial definition of Surrealism in 1924, to any form of rational control and

so to "toute préoccupation esthétique ou morale" (any aesthetic or moral concern). Thus, while it encompassed a whole series of practices, excommunicated renegade members, and issued manifesto upon manifesto in its heyday between the world wars, the Surrealist movement never figured, in the eyes of its leading exponents, as a school, party, or church founded on the solid bedrock of a doctrine. Breton himself–the only truly "orthodox" Surrealist, according to some critics– preferred to speak of the movement as an "aventure spirituelle" (spiritual adventure); it was an adventure endowed, significantly, with an experimental, intuitive method which owed as much, if not more, to the venturesome, iconoclastic spirit evinced in Arthur Rimbaud's *Une Saison en Enfer* (1873; translated as *A Season in Hell,* 1931) and Apollinaire's "Onirocritique" (published in the review *La Phalange,* 1908) as to Sigmund Freud's *Die Traumdeutung* (The Science of Dreams, 1900). The term "Surrealism" itself is borrowed from Apollinaire, who had styled his 1917 play *Les Mammelles de Tirésias* (translated as *The Mammaries of Tiresias,* 1997) a "drame surréaliste." For the prototypical, avant-garde Surrealist intent on marrying dream and reality in the Surreal, as its apologists hasten to point out, poetry was an introduction or provocation to its own largely utopian ends, an attitude or way of being in accord with Apollinaire's Romantic injunction, at the outset of "L'Esprit nouveau et les poètes" (The New Spirit and the Poets, 1917), to celebrate life in all its manifestations ("exalter la vie sous quelque forme qu'elle se présente"). Everything–from billboards and street signs to the airplane, the world, the cosmos even–could now be subject matter for poetry. Not surprisingly, then, in terms of the development of twentieth-century French poetry, Surrealism has been valued primarily as a locus of influence and confluence, an invocation and convocation of the synthetic powers of the imagination at work in all modernist enterprises, rather than for its more doctrinaire statements. That influence or magnetism (the metaphor is unavoidable in a Surrealist context) has by no means been confined to its official members or to the period of its greatest creative output. Elegizing the movement in *La Part du feu* (Sacrifice to Save the Rest, 1949), Maurice Blanchot stated that, though Surrealism was moribund as a school, every one knew they might have belonged to it; and he testified to its abiding importance: "Il n'y a plus d'école, mais un état d'esprit subsiste" (there is no longer a school, but a state of mind remains). Marcelin Pleynet, in a 1986 interview, concurred, finding that state of mind pervasive in contemporary poetry, even the most "mallarméenne contemporaine" (contemporary Mallarméean).

For all the apparent inchoateness and incongruousness of this canon, then, Virginia A. La Charité's conclusion, in her *Twentieth-Century French Avant-Garde Poetry, 1907–1990* (1992), concerning its cohesiveness and its salient features seems apposite: "Non-conceptual in its conjunction of opposites and synthetic only in its inquiry into form," she writes, "the poem as practiced in this century has, nonetheless, discernible points of agreement and accord." Confronted first with the challenge to its traditional hegemony represented by the advent and consolidation of modes of communication and transportation rapidly ushering in a barbaric "ère du fait" (era of the fact), as Valéry put it, then with World War I and the disillusionment and totalitarianism it occasioned, twentieth-century French poetry appears under the guise of an impossible wager: to abolish or to provoke "le hasard" (fate) by the dice-throw of inspiration submitted to the rigors of technique. That "ascèse" (asceticism) could be directed either, as in Valéry and Paul Claudel, toward a reclamation of the past and a part of its cultural mystique (neoclassical in the first instance, Catholic in the second), or alternately, with the Surrealists, toward an assumption of "la modernité" (modernity), a word Apollinaire made fashionable.

The continuities of twentieth-century French poetry thus appear, in the view of La Charité as well as of critics of a decidedly more deconstructionist turn, under the aspect of diversity and controversy, crisis and solution. The drastic denuding of a preconceived reality and the juxtaposing of conflicting convictions, all agree, is prelude to a potential, albeit, by the same token, an endlessly postponed, reconciliation. And understandably so—for whereas there is considerable agreement that genres, norms, and values have been in a state of immanent crisis ever since Mallarmé notoriously pointed to a "crise de vers" (crisis of verse) and Valéry to a "crise de l'esprit" (crisis of the spirit), the solutions proposed are as varied and idiosyncratic as the poets under review. As the sheer amount of ink and vitriol expended on all sides in parodies, manifestos, polemics, broadsides, and apologias serves to suggest, the history of twentieth-century French poetry is fraught with antagonisms and cross purposes.

And yet, if they leave the reader more or less nonplussed, findings of positive value among critics kindly disposed to an aesthetics of contradiction (and so gladdened at the prospect of a modern Orpheus) relentlessly made to signify the "impasse" of a zero-sum game rhyme nicely with the other mythical figure in which La Charité sees an antitype of the student or scholar intent on "mapping out a reading journey through the literature of this century." It is that of Albert Camus's happy Sisyphus, in his *Le Mythe de Sisyphe* (1942; translated as *The Myth of Sisyphus,* 1955), which concludes "La lutte elle-même vers les sommets suffit à remplir un

cœur d'homme. Il faut imaginer Sisyphe heureux" (The struggle itself towards the heights is enough to fill a human heart. One must imagine that Sisyphus is happy). So it fares, at least, with those bent on "sanctifying the conjunction of contradictions." The reader who, for his or her part, does not care to go about his or her business in quite the same spirit of stoical indifference at self-contradicting toil, happily oblivious of the ever-sloping terrain, may benefit from a topography more attentive to the relief, the contrary push and pull, highs and lows, and the consequent returns, of twentieth-century French poetry. While by no means exhaustive, the following account attempts one such charting by focusing on the antagonism of similitudes and the symmetry of antitheses made salient in the war of words and wits between canonical patriarchs and prophets.

The turn of the century is celebrated by historians of Zeitgeist, or *mentalités,* as a "renaissance spiritualiste" (spiritualistic rebirth). Hearkening to a change in the national temper reflected in the popular press, poets, so goes their account, descended from the ivory towers of Symbolism to man the bulwarks of a renewed nationalism founded on an alliance between the qualities traditionally ascribed to the French genius—order, clarity, and harmony—and what Claudel, in his *Cinq Grandes Odes, suivies d'un Processional pour saluer le siècle nouveau* (Five Grand Odes, with a Processional to Salute the New Century, 1910; translated as *Five Great Odes,* 1967), personifies as its "cœur catholique" (Catholic heart). In his review of Joris Karl (Charles Marie Georges) Huysmans' *A Rebours* (1884; translated as *Against Nature,* 1959) for *Le Conditionnel,* Barbey d'Aurevilly had struck what became for many the keynote of the last decade of the nineteenth-century and the start of the coming century: "Après un tel livre" (After such a book), he wrote, "il ne reste plus qu'à choisir entre la bouche d'un pistolet ou les pieds de la croix" (all that is left is to choose between the mouth of a gun or the foot of the cross). Not only Huysmans, but Paul Verlaine, Jacques Maritain, Charles Péguy, Francis Jammes, Claudel, Charles Du Bos, Gabriel Marcel, François Mauriac, Max Jacob, and Reverdy, to name but a few, apparently arrived at the same conclusion, choosing the cross over pistol and ball. The German threat that came to a head in Tangier and the scandal brought about by the Dreyfus affair soon polarized opinion and thought in France, especially in the militantly nationalistic press of Charles Maurras and *L'Action française.* Max Simon Nordau's *Entartung* (1892; translated as *Degeneration,* 1895), translated from German into French by Auguste Dietrich in 1894 as *Dégénérescence,* epitomized the reaction against the disenchanted, *fin de siècle* attitudes of the decadents, the "beau dégout" (beautiful disgust) of

Rimbaud and the equally beautiful "suicide" of Mallarmé, detecting and condemning in them as in English Pre-Raphaelitism, Tolstoyism, and Wagnerism the same will to nothingness, the same lack of consecutive or purposive thinking. Coupled with a plea for lyrical simplicity and sincerity, Verlaine's witty rejoinder to Jules Huret in an interview of 1891 suggests just how embattled the Symbolist avant-garde had become and why: "Le Symbolisme? comprends pas. Ca doit être un mot allemand, hein?" (Symbolism? [I] do not understand. It must be a German word, eh?). Maurras, in an article that appeared in *La Plume* in July of the same year, essentially concurred, opposing the Northern or Germanic "barbares" to the Southern "romans"; following Mallarmé's election as Prince of Poets in 1896, he cited with approval Louis Baragnon's portrait of the master as one who "nourri de Hoffman et de Poe, pense en allemand, construit en anglais et par une plaisanterie suprême nous fasse l'honneur d'emprunter notre vocabulaire" (nourished by Hoffman and Poe, thinks in German, builds in English and by a supreme joke does us the honor of borrowing our vocabulary). Proust, for his part, adopted the middle way in an essay titled "Contre l'obscurité" (Against Obscurity) published in *La Revue blanche* in July 1896, soberly advising poets to study "la nature, où, si le fond de tout est un et obscur, la forme de tout est individuelle et claire" (nature, where, if the base of all is one and obscure, the form of all is individual and clear). As attested to by the various poetical movements that flowered in the first decade of the twentieth century—humanism, naturism, Fauvism, neo-Romanticism, neoclassicism, Unanimism—the poets who heeded that call or counsel found themselves, like Valéry's Jeune Parque, enamored of life. Valéry himself came to envision *La Jeune Parque* (The Young Fate), begun in 1913 and completed against the troubling backdrop of World War I, as "une sorte d'adieu à ces jeux de l'adolescence" (a sort of farewell to these games of adolescence), so designating his predominantly Symbolist- and Parnassian- inspired *Album de vers anciens* (Collection of Early Verses; published separately between 1890 and 1893; collectively in 1920). Beauty, he noted, had come out of fashion, at least as a watchword, to be succeeded by "le mot 'Vie'" (the word "Life"). And yet, he too had once professed with Verlaine his allegiance to the cult of the decadents—"le cloître des Nobles Inutiles, des raffinés, des Féminins" (the cloister of the Useless Nobles, the refined, the Effeminates), as he dubbed them in his letter to Pierre Louÿs of 2 June 1890—and had celebrated, in his first published article, "Sur la technique littéraire" (On Literary Technique, 1882), the "suprême Antithèse" (supreme Antithesis) offered to contemplation by the historical coexistence of "la grandeur barbare du moderne monde industriel" (the barbaric grandeur of the modern industrial world) and "les dernières élégances, les recherches des plus rares voluptés, et l'Alchimie de la Beauté" (the last elegances, the search for the rarest pleasures, and the Alchemy of Beauty) of the Symbolists.

Claudel's recollection of the *fin de siècle,* in his "Réflexions et Propositions sur le Vers Français" (Reflections and Proposals on French Verse) is even more bitter. Valéry, at least, could go on to erect columns to the Baconian idol of his intellect and so rival his master Mallarmé, just as Mallarmé had rivaled Baudelaire and Baudelaire in turn rivaled Victor Hugo in his analyses; for Claudel, who upon receiving Valéry's *Poésies* in 1942 could not help but note with some admiration, in his *Journal* (1968, 1969), their extreme "finesse," all while deploring the vanity of the poet's narcissistic endeavor, this idol was only one among many strewn across the wasteland of the pagan nineteenth century—"lande pleine de ruines et de fouilles" (moor full of ruins and excavations). Against these ruins the third of the *Cinq Grandes Odes* would marshal its song. So viewed and particularly, when set beside his "album de dessins minutieux" (album of meticulous drawings) or "livre d'exercices" (exercise book) *Connaissance de l'Est* (1900; translated as *The East I Know,* 1914), the achievement represented by the processional *Cinq Grandes Odes* is as much a farewell to the literary-philosophical adolescence imaged in nineteenth century as a hymn to the new. The twilight of that bygone era was haunted, in Claudel's imagination, by "grands hallucinés" (great hallucinators): Hugo, William Blake, Johann Wolfgang von Goethe, Jules Michelet, Henrik Ibsen, culminating in the self-consuming doubter Friedrich Wilhelm Nietzsche, "dévoré tout vivant par le monstre dont les autres n'étaient que poursuivies" (devoured alive by the monster by whom the others were only pursued).

Those ghosts would not so easily be laid to rest. Elegize as they might, Valéry and Claudel were forced to confess, tacitly and explicitly, their debt to the Symbolist milieu from which they had emerged. The omission of Rimbaud from Claudel's list of blind visionaries, for example, is at least as significant as the inclusions. As he recalled in his account of his conversion for the *Revue de la Jeunesse* (10 October 1913), the reading of *Les Illuminations* (1886; translated, 1953) and *Une Saison en Enfer* in 1889 had opened a breach in the "bagne matérialiste" (materialist penal colony) then imprisoning him, giving him his first vivid impression of the supernatural and so making way for his affirmation of the role of the *poet-vates* (poet-prophet) in the materialistic, technocratic society depicted in his play *La Ville* (1890; translated as *The City,* 1920). Just as significant is Claudel's singling out of Richard Wagner as "le premier éclairé d'un rayon rédempteur" (the first-enlightened of a redemptive ray). Wagner's name could stand at the head of a much different list consisting, for the most part, of those Nordau had dismissed as *illuminés* (visionaries of cranks) because they enlisted under the banner of some vague idealism–the English Pre-Raphaelites, the Russian novelists, and the Scandinavian dramatists–but also of the American Walt Whitman, then much translated and appreciated. These had all participated in some fashion in the "renaissance spiritualiste" that found its high point in the ambition voiced by Claudel *contra* Mallarmé–"le grand poëme de l'homme soustrait au hasard" (the great poem of man freed from chance)–an ambition shared by Christian poets descended from him to Pierre Emmanuel. And yet, part of the Claudelian legacy, and by no means the less abiding part, has been the early Claudel, the pagan poet of *Tête d'or* (Head of Gold, 1889; translated, 1919) and the mystical poet of the first *Partage du midi* (1906; translated as *Break of Noon,* 1960), whose verses have inspired poets as unchristian in orientation as Ponge and Saint-John Perse. It was not without reason, then, that Valéry, in the two 1919 letters addressed to the London *Athenaeum* as "The Spiritual Crisis" and "The Intellectual Crisis" and to *the Nouvelle Revue française* as "La Crise de l'Esprit," resorted to hyperbole to evoke the imbroglio of doctrines "in the air" by 1914. He compared the period to a blast furnace, in which, if the eye could see, it would see, according to the new theoretical physics, nothing, the light being equally diffused. The relative stability that followed the defeat of France in the Franco-Prussian War of 1870 had also allowed for the very "liberté d'esprit" that ceaselessly questioned its most cherished ideals and myths. Such a state of mind, in which one found "la libre coexistence des idées les plus dissemblables, des principes de vie et de connaissance les plus opposés" (the free coexistence of the most dissimilar ideas, of the most opposed principles of life and of knowledge), Valéry defined as eminently modern. His 1926 preface to, or digression on, Montesquieu's *Lettres persanes* (Persian Letters, 1721) left readers musing that never since the age of Enlightenment had the all-embracing, all-absorbing lucidity of the West burned so ardently, or blindingly, as it did now, when it was in danger of being snuffed out by the systematic conquest of the world through instrumental reason, which Valéry had described in *Une Conquête méthodique* (A Methodic Conquest, 1924), originally published in the January 1897 issue of the London *New Review* as "La Conquête allemande" (The German Conquest).

With his usual uncannily porous sensibility, Apollinaire captured something of the antithetical rhetoric and mood to which Valéry pointed. The four bombardiers in his poem "Exercice," collected in *Calligrammes, poèmes de la paix et de la guerre, 1913–1916* (1918; translated as *Calligrammes: Poems of Peace and War [1913–1916],* 1980), renounce the present in the hope that the past may persist through their sacrifice or "ascèse." But even as "L'Esprit nouveau et les poètes" militates, on one front, in favor of the classical "esprit critique" and against the influence of the colossal Romanticism of Wagner's Germany and the equally formidable anarchism of Italian and Russian Futurism that the poet had himself so deeply apprehended–his "Rhénanes" (Rhenishes) in his *Alcools, poèmes 1898–1913* (1913; translated, 1964) and *L'Antitradition futuriste: Manifeste-synthése* (The Futurist Antitradition: Manifesto-Synthesis, 1913) immediately come to mind–the lecture-essay is also, on another front, an apology for those poets who, like Apollinaire, had seen fit to resume the Romantic-Symbolist heritage. The elegiac poet of "Le pont Mirabeau" (Mirabeau Bridge) is also the poet who could write, in another mood, his "Adieu" to Romanticism, echoing the Symbolists and anticipating the Surrealists in singing the praises of the new: "La Victoire avant tout sera. . . . que tout ait un nom nouveau" (The Victory above all will be. . . . that all will have a new name). Part of the reason, indeed, for Apollinaire's vast appeal to historians of the period (he has been fitly hailed a "classique de l'avant-garde") is that he thus anticipates and attempts to reconcile the two apparently divergent tendencies that French poetry assumed in the interwar period: "Son tort et son mérite confondus" (His fault and his merit confused) in the balanced assessment of André Lagarde and Laurent Michard, "ont été . . . de n'avoir rien formulé dogmatiquement, ni rien choisi" (were . . . not to have formulated anything dogmatically, nor selected anything). Much the same might be said of Apollinaire's contemporary and fellow avant-gardist Blaise Cendrars. Spoken to quieting effect to the ingenuous Petite Jehanne and in the face of an absurdly prosaic reality–"un orage sous le crâne d'un sourd" (a storm under the cranium of a deaf person)–Cendrars' "Les inquiétudes / Oublie les inquiétudes" (Concerns / Forgets concerns) is a call to arms *avant la lettre,* evoking a Tolstoyian conflict of convictions aesthetically resolved, as *La Prose du Transsibérien et de la Petite Jehanne de France* (1913; translated as "The Trans-Siberian Express," 1968) builds to a crescendo, in the poet's deciphering and rendering of "une violente beauté" (a violent beauty). But, as with Apollinaire, Cendrars' very exuberance betrays a creeping nostalgia for a sense of order in an increasingly fragmented, decentered world: "j'ai perdu tout mes paris" (I have lost all my bets) is his telling pun, in which "paris" can mean either "bets" or the city Paris, his home. A new-age conquistador equipped, in lieu of sextant and compass, with the knowledge of "tous les horaires—tout les trains et leurs correspondences" (all the timetables—all the trains and their connections), his poetic voyage is the image of a vicious circling charting the shifting coordinates of his inner contradictions—the poet describes himself as turning "dans la cage des méridiens comme un écureuil dans la sienne" (in the cage of the meridians like a squirrel in his own)—and so ending, paradoxically, in stasis.

The living antithesis of Cendrars, staunch Catholic and patriot *homme du peuple* (man of the people) Péguy stands out as having led the most vigorous and uncompromising counter-offensive against such *dépaysement* (removal from one's country) in the shape of "les idées modernes" (modern ideas) and "une pensée toute faite" (a thought ready-made)—that is, the positivism and scientism which had become increasingly conspicuous in the disciplines of history and the new social sciences. Inscribing his own thought, rather, in the intuitionist tradition running from René Descartes through Michelet to his one-time teacher Henri Bergson, Péguy sought to preserve from such abstract or formal foreshortenings the "élan vitale" (vital impulse) that for him, as for Bergson, constituted the basis of any true religion, politics, or morality. Opposition to scientism and positivism, however, provided a common front for poets of all persuasions, thus tending to offset the reaction against the Romantic-Symbolist heritage. Indeed, the wide appeal and representative scope of Bergson's work (some critics have spoken, in this regard, of a "bergsonisme littéraire" analogous to the "cartésianisme littéraire" of the seventeenth century) may be explained through his contribution to the debate opposing realism to idealism. Artists, Bergson contends, will always be put in the idealist camp by virtue of their negative capability ("désintéressement innée"); but because art is also a cleansing of the doors of perception, breaking with established conventions and habits of mind—"les symboles pratiquement utiles, les généralités conventionnellement et socialement acceptées" (the practically useful symbols, the generalalizations conventionally and socially accepted—it operates a dialectical reconciliation of these conceptually opposed terms: "le réalisme est dans l'œuvre quand l'idéalisme est dans l'âme" (realism is in the work when idealism is in the heart), writes Bergson, "et . . . c'est à force d'idéalité seulement qu'on reprend contact avec la réalité." (and . . . it is only by dint of ideality that one renews contact with reality). In his emphasis on the allusive and elusive powers of art—"cet imprévisible rien qui est le tout de l'œuvre d'art" (this unforeseeable

nothing which is the whole of the work of art), in the words of *L'Evolution créatrice* (1907)—Bergson looks back to Mallarmé and the Symbolists and forward to the Surrealists. His reflections on the creative process invite comparison, in particular, with Valéry's analogous inquiry into the workings of his poetic art. By way of distinguishing between a predetermined, clockwork view of existence and a creative, spiritual one, Bergson likens the former to a child's game of patience, wherein the result or solution is pregiven, the latter with the task confronting the artist, wherein the invention or solution is part of "un processus vital," the thought evolving organically with the material. Similarly, Valéry's ideal of the pure poem is that of a musical fugue, "où *la transmutation des pensée les unes dans les autres paraîtrait plus importante que toute pensée,* où le jeu des figures contiendrait la réalité du sujet" (wherein *the transmutation of thoughts into one another would seem more important than all thought,* wherein the play of figures [tropes] would contain the reality of the subject).

Where Valéry parted ways with Bergson and so many of his contemporaries, as he made clear in the eulogy for Bergson that he delivered to the Académie Française on 9 January 1941, it was with regards to the religious significance and unifying force that the latter hypostatized as "esprit." Antagonisms, Valéry speculated in his eulogy, as the war raged on outside, were perhaps not foreign but native to humanity, and the spirit, he left his audience to surmise, was as destructive as it was creative. Additional confirmation of that theory had come to him in the form of several polemics, most notably the much publicized one initiated by his long-time friend the Abbé Henri Bremond in 1925. Whereas Valéry saw in the notion of "la poésie pure" a purely analytical concept, the phrase conjured for Bremond the coincidence of poetry and prayer. By necessity a stalemate, since the initial assumptions were so different on both sides, the debate is nonetheless noteworthy for what it reveal about the agonists and their secret affinities. For all his vaunted intellectualism in theory, Valéry, as Bremond astutely remarked and as criticism has since tended to bear him out, was no Cartesian in practice, untranslatable as were his "charmes," by his own definition, into Descartes' "idées claires" (clear ideas) Valéry was, rather, in Bremond's phrase, a "poète malgré lui" (poet in spite of himself), one of those "hallucinés de la technique" (persons deluded by technique) who, in an act of self-mystification, had found in Edgar Allan Poe's "The Philosophy of Composition" (1846), by way of Baudelaire, "une doctrine très séduisante et très rigoureuse" (a doctrine very tempting and very rigorous), as Valéry put it, "dans laquelle une sorte de mathématique et une sorte de mystique s'unissaient" (in which a kind of mathematics and a kind of mysticism united). The fact that this supposedly rigorous mathematico-mystical science was predicated on a hoax and devoid (as Mallarmé later conceded) of anecdotal substance did not escape the attention of Valéry's considerably more skeptical Anglo-American contemporaries, who were inclined to see in the purloining and apotheosizing of Poe by the Symbolists a hoax of even greater proportions. In *Symbolisme from Poe to Mallarmé* (1956), a study of influence prefaced by T. S. Eliot, Joseph Chiari prefers to trace the Symbolist lineage (as does Bremond) to the didactico-religious Thomas Carlyle of *Sartor Resartus* (1836). But for all the high seriousness they thus sought to impart to modern French poetry, such critics found themselves not a little disconcerted by its constant remarking of a narcissistic "impasse."

Lying at the heart of the debate over the nature of modern French poetry, the near-contemporary quarrel between Valéry and the Surrealists replays this close proximity between spirituality and *jeux d'esprits,* mystery and mystification, science and unscience, in a contest of aphorisms and antitheses. A case in point is Breton and Paul Eluard's deliberate parody of Valerian poetics in the review *La Révolution Surréaliste* (1929):

> Nous sommes toujours, même en prose, conduits et consentants à écrire ce que nous n'avons pas voulu et qui ne veut peut-être pas même ce que nous voulions.
>
> Perfection
> c'est *paresse.*
>
> (We are always, even in prose, driven and consenting to write that which we have not willed and which perhaps does not even want what we want
>
> Perfection
> is *idleness*).

Far from offering a clear antithesis, this parody only manages to duplicate the equivocation or aporia latent in the original:

> Nous sommes toujours, même en prose, conduits et contraints à écrire ce que nous n'avons pas voulu et que veut ce que nous voulions.
>
> Perfection
> c'est *travail.*
>
> (We are always, even in prose, driven and constrained to write what we have not wanted and which wants what we wanted.
>
> Perfection
> is *work*).

Breton and Eluard's parody is a coincidence or compounding of contradictions consecrated by Surrealism's ablest *automatiste* (automatic writer), Robert Desnos, in his "Réfléxions sur la Poésie" (Reflections on Poetry, 1944): "Il me semble qu'au-delà du surréalisme il y a quelque chose de très mystérieux à réduire, au-delà de l'automatisme il y a le délibéré, au- delà de la poésie il y a le poème, au-delà de la poésie subie, il y a la poésie imposée, au-delà de la poésie libre il y a le poète libre" (It seems to me that beyond Surrealism there is something very mysterious to reduce, that beyond automatic writng there is the poem, beyond poetry undergone, there is poetry imposed, beyond free poetry there is the free poet). Louis Aragon suggests much the same in his treatise on art *La Peinture au défi* (1930; translated as "The Challenge to Painting," 1990), and Breton himself, in his annotations to *Les Champs magnétiques* (1919; translated as *The Magnetic Fields,* 1985), distinguishes between a "rigueur apparente" (apparent rigor) and the "rigueur réelle" (real rigor) he detected in his collaborator Philippe Soupault and wished to effect through automatic writing, which he described, following Freud, as psychic "dictée" (dictation) or "pensée parlée" (spoken thought). But just as it redefined rigor and perfection to mean a freedom sometimes bordering on gratuitousness, the valorization of dreams and the unconscious so achieved virtually inverted one of the central tenets of Freudian psychology–that the unconscious life should be conquered by the ego.

Given this antagonism of similitudes and symmetry of antitheses, Surrealist aesthetics might be read with profit as an expression of the unconscious, irrational side of Valery's highly conscious poetics and vice versa. Significantly, Valéry's triumphal "Il faut tenter de vivre!" (We must attempt to live!) or "Eternal Yea" to existence comes at the end of a poem the larger part of which is dominated by a melancholy meditation on the Heraclitean flux of existence. That meditation culminates in an allusion to the arrow of Zeno the Eliatic, fatal to logical distinctions and so, finally, to the need for individuation. Mortally wounded, like his Jeune Parque, the poet of *Le Cimétière marin* (1920; translated as *The Graveyard by the Sea,* 1932) is tempted by a state of indifference and revery. The death instinct is vanquished only when Valéry-Parque renounces "cette forme pensive" (that pensive form) to submit to the charms of carnal existence. Valéry's assent, like that of his contemporary Perse, rests on a conception of life and spirit not at all that inconsistent, ultimately, with Tristan Tzara's 1918 manifesto proclaiming Dada-Life as anarchic freedom in the conjunction of contraries and contradictions: "Liberté: DADA, DADA, DADA, *hurlement des couleurs crispées, entrelacement des contraires et de toutes les contradictions, des grotesques, des inconséquences:* LA

VIE" (Freedom: DADA, DADA, DADA, *shrieking of shriveling colors, interlacing of contraries and of all contradicitons, of grotesques, of inconsequences:* LIFE). A year later in Paris and some time before they had rallied to Tzara's cause, Soupault and Breton wrote and published *Les Champs magnétiques.* This elegiac volume was dedicated to the memory of the indomitable Jacques Vaché, whose last "fourberie drôle" (droll deceit) had been his suicide by massive narcosis; he had literally disappeared in a cloud of opiated smoke. By coincidence or design (or perhaps by one of those "hasards objectifs" (objective accidents) which the Surrealists actively cultivated), the highly hallucinogenic *Les Champs magnétiques* end with a sort of mock suicide, titled "LA FIN DE TOUT" (THE END OF EVERYTHING) in which the authors leave their calling card–ANDRÉ BRETON & PHILIPPE SOUPAULT / BOIS & CHARBONS–signing, Breton later confessed, their desire to be obliterated, symbolically if not in fact. The joke, of course, is twofold: it not only suggests, as Breton points out, that he and Soupault wished to disappear into the comfortable anonymity conferred by a small boutique stocked in "bois et charbons" (wood and coal), but also, on a deeper, perhaps unconscious level, that in writing *Les Champs magnétiques,* they have provided their more lucid readers with the combustibles requisite to consume the work as they read it. Caveat emptor. Both Valéry and the Surrealists, then, skirted nihilism, thus heralding what Jean-Paul Sartre later calls, in an article published in *Les Temps modernes* in May 1947, "le retour de l'esprit de Négativité" (the return of the spirit of Negativity); but while Valéry, in the manner of a latter-day Montaigne, sought refuge in the necessary illusions that made up his "art de vivre" (art of life), the Surrealists ostensibly set out to transform the world, to bridge the gap between vision and reality.

Valéry was, in this respect, the more poetically orthodox of the two, as suggested by no less formidable or Surrealistic a poet than Rimbaud, in his evocation of his "Alchimie du Verbe" (Alchemy of the Word) in *Une Saison en Enfer:* "Je m'habituai à l'hallucination simple: je voyais très franchement une mosquée à la place d'une usine . . . un salon au fond du lac" (I was accustomed to simple hallucination: I quite frankly saw a mosque in the place of a factory . . . a salon at the bottom of the lake). The Symbolist artist either followed Mallarmé's advice and turned "l'épaule à la vie," seeking refuge from reality in the aestheticized realm of *voyance* (clairvoyance) and pure subjectivity or, like Rimbaud at the end of *Une Saison en Enfer,* abdicated poetry altogether. By contrast, the Surrealist artist, according to Sartre, in his 1947 article published in *Les Temps modernes,* "veut être perpétuellement sur le point de voir salon et lac" (wants to be perpetually on the point of seeing salon

and lake). The remark, of course, is part of Sartre's devastating indictment of the Surrealist "esprit" and its ambition, expressed in the *Position politique du surréalisme* (Political Position of Surrealism, 1935), of marrying the imperative of Karl Marx, "Transformer le monde" (Transform the world), to that of Rimbaud, "Changer la vie" (Change life). While it verges at times on the mere *boutade,* Sartre's critique is in fact far-ranging and thoroughgoing. Recalling Georges Politzer's (under his pseudonuym, Arouet) attack on Bergson's studied detachment in 1929 and likening the Surrealists' "poème-objets" and their "point *gamma*" to the aporias and the ataraxia of the Skeptics and the Stoics, Sartre's indictment focuses on the charge of *mauvaise conscience* (bad conscience). Because he ultimately does not elect between the idealism of Rimbaud and the dialectical and historical materialism of Marx, lacking, on the one hand, the admirable inconsequence of the Symbolists– "Du moins Rimbaud voulait-il voir un salon dans un lac" (At least Rimbaud wanted to see a salon in a lake)– and eschewing, on the other, any doctrine and any practice but that of poetic inspiration and imaginative skepticism, the Surrealist is condemned from the outset to historical bad faith. As if it were the formal realization of Zeno's arrow paradox, the Surrealist's poetic art works at cross purposes, aiming at the symbolical annihilation of painting through painting and of literature through literature, in the "le papillotement sans fin des contradictoires" (the endless flickering of self-canceling contraries). Capping off the attacks on Surrealism that followed several defections to the Communist camp (Eluard in 1926, and Aragon in 1930), Sartre's essay only ratifies the *fin de non recevoir,* or dead ending, between Breton and the Communist Party documented in *Odile* (1937; translated 1988), one-time Surrealist Queneau's satirical roman à clef:

> . . . Anglarès se fatigua très vite d'aller à sa cellule, une cellule de rue où il ne rencontrait que des concierges et des cafetiers qui regardaient avec suspicion le large cordon noir qui retenait son binocle, ses cheveux balayant ses épaules et sa vêture mi-salon de la rose-croix et mi-ère du cocktail. Et la grossièreté de ces gens allait jusqu'à ne pas se laisser impressionner par son regard. Aussi quand ils voulurent l'obliger à potasser la situation économique de l'Europe pour la leur expliquer, il préféra se retirer.

> (Angles tired rather quickly of going to his cell, a cell in a street where he met only concierges and café-owner who looked with suspicion at the long black string which held his binocle, his hair brushing his shoulders and his dress half-rosicrucian and half cocktail era. The crudeness of the people went so far as to not let itself be impressed by his gaze. Thus when they wanted him to

swot at the economic situation of Europe to explain it to them, he preferred to withdraw).

In the lecture he delivered at Yale University in December 1942, published in 1945 as *Situation du surréalisme entre les deux guerres* (Situation of Surrealism Between the Two Wars), Breton made it clear enough how far removed the ambitions of Surrealism were from those of historical materialism, identifying the movement with the antirationalist, idealistic tradition of coinciding opposites and imaginative dialectics running from Heraclitus through Meister Eckhart to Georg Wilhelm Friedrich Hegel. The defections of Aragon and Eluard were accented, of course, by a return to the cloak of Balzacian realism and Hugolian eloquence—that is to say, to a poetics engagé by virtue of its very commitment to standard rhetoric. But with the subsiding of wartime hostilities, the long-standing philosophical and moral dilemmas—between fate and freedom, being and nothingness—to which Sartre's critique pointed came once again to the fore, along with their attendant aporia. "Un philosophe à sa façon" (A philosopher in his way), to use his epithet for the Solomon-like Alfred in his novel *Les Derniers Jours* (1936; translated as *The Last Days,* 1990), Queneau has done his utmost to make plain the vanity of the wisdom purveyed by high modernist intellectual culture, including his own. His novels can be read as late neo-baroque improvisations burlesquing the much-rehearsed theme of *la vida es sueño* (life is a dream). Familiar to readers of Pedro Calderon, William Shakespeare, William Faulkner, and Claude Simon, that theme runs like a contrapuntal motif through the popular *Zazie dans le métro* (1959; translated, 1960): "Paris n'est qu'un songe, Gabriel n'est qu'un rêve (charmant), Zazie le songe d'un rêve (ou d'un cauchemar) et toute cette histoire le songe d'un songe, le rêve d'un rêve, à peine plus qu'un délire tapé à la machine par un romancier idiot (oh! pardon)" (Paris is but a dream, Gabriel is but a dream [charming], Zazie the dream of a dream [or a nightmare] and all this story the dream of a dream, the musing of a musing, little more than a delirium typed on the machine by an idiot novelist [oh! sorry]). Such lively wit is amusing, even charming (like Gabriel), but it is also, practically speaking, nightmarishly absurd (like Zazie), mere zigzagging among perpetual irresolvables and ineffables. Confronted with the fleeting nature of existence and happiness in a godless world, Queneau's characters, like those of Samuel Beckett, naturally tend to an immobility passively wise, an immobility that is perhaps only the mirror-image of Camus' antique modern Sisyphus, free to govern his own destiny and ken what meaning

in it he can. "L'homme dispose," as Breton would have us imagine—that is to say, "Il faut imaginer Sisyphe heureux."

—Jean-François Leroux

Acknowledgments

This book was produced by Bruccoli Clark Layman, Inc. Karen L. Rood is senior editor. Jan Peter F. van Rosevelt was the in-house editor.

Production manager is Philip B. Dematteis.

Administrative support was provided by Ann M. Cheschi, Amber L. Coker, and Angi Pleasant.

Accountant is Ann-Marie Holland.

Copyediting supervisor is Sally R. Evans. The copyediting staff includes Phyllis A. Avant, Brenda Carol Blanton, Melissa D. Hinton, Charles Loughlin, Rebecca Mayo, Nancy E. Smith, and Elizabeth Jo Ann Sumner.

Editorial associates are Michael S. Allen, Michael S. Martin, and Pamela A. Warren.

Permissions editor is Jason Paddock.

Database manager is José A. Juarez.

Layout and graphics supervisor is Janet E. Hill. The graphics staff includes Karla Corley Brown and Zoe R. Cook.

Office manager is Kathy Lawler Merlette.

Photography supervisor is Paul Talbot. Photography editor is Scott Nemzek.

Digital photographic copy work was performed by Joseph M. Bruccoli.

Systems manager is Marie L. Parker.

Typesetting supervisor is Kathleen M. Flanagan. The typesetting staff includes Patricia Marie Flanagan, Mark J. McEwan, and Pamela D. Norton. Freelance typesetter is Wanda Adams.

Walter W. Ross did library research. He was assisted by Pamela A. Warren and the following librarians at the Thomas Cooper Library of the University of South Carolina: circulation department head Tucker Taylor; reference department head Virginia W. Weathers; Brette Barclay, Marilee Birchfield, Paul Cammarata, Gary Geer, Michael Macan, Tom Marcil, Rose Marshall, and Sharon Verba; interlibrary loan department head John Brunswick; and interlibrary loan staff Robert Arndt, Hayden Battle, Barry Bull, Jo Cottingham, Marna Hostetler, Marieum McClary, Erika Peake, and Nelson Rivera.

Dictionary of Literary Biography® • Volume Two Hundred Fifty-Eight

Modern French Poets

Dictionary of Literary Biography

Guillaume Apollinaire

(26 August 1880 – 9 November 1918)

Camille R. La Bossière
University of Ottawa

BOOKS: *Mirely ou le petit trou pas cher* (N. p., 1900);

Les Exploits d'un jeune Don Juan, as G.A. (Paris, 1907; Philadelphia, 1944; London, 1949); translated as *Amorous Exploits of a Young Rakehell* (Paris: Olympia, 1953);

Les Onze mille verges, as G. . . . A. . . . (Paris, 1907); republished as *Les Onze mille verges, ou Les Amours d'un hospodar* (Paris, 1911); translated by Alexander Trocchi (as Oscar Mole) as *The Debauched Hospodar* (Paris: Olympia, 1953);

L'Enchanteur pourrissant, illustrated with woodcuts by André Derain (Paris: Kahnweiler, 1909);

L'Hérésiarque et cie (Paris: Stock, 1910); translated by Rèmy Inglis Hall as *The Heresiarch and Co.* (Garden City, N.Y.: Doubleday, 1965); translation republished as *The Wandering Jew, and Other Stories* (London: Hart-Davis, 1967);

Le Bestiaire, ou, Cortège d'Orphée, illustrated with woodcuts by Raoul Dufy (Paris: Deplanche, 1911; republished, with translations by Lauren Shakely, New York: Metropolitan Museum of Art, 1977);

Pages d'histoire—Chronique des grands siècles de la France (Vincennes: Les Arts graphiques, 1912);

Les Peintres cubistes: Méditations aesthétiques (Paris: Figuière, 1913); translated by Lionel Abel as *The Cubist Painters: Aesthetic Meditations, 1913* (New York: Wittenborn, 1944; revised edition, New York: Wittenborn, Schultz, 1949);

Alcools, poèmes 1898–1913, with a portrait by Pablo Picasso (Paris: Mercure de France, 1913); translated by William Meredith as *Alcools: Poems, 1898–1913,* introduction and notes by Francis Steegmuller (Garden City, N.Y.: Doubleday, 1964);

Guillaime Apollinaire, 1900

L'Antitradition futuriste: Manifeste-synthése (Milan: Direction du Mouvement futuriste, 1913);

L'Enfer de la Bibliothèque nationale; icono-bio-bibliographie descriptive, critique et raisonnée, complète à ce jour, de tous les ouvrages composant cette célèbre collection, avec un

Apollinaire's mother, Angeliska de Kostrowitzky

index alphabétique des titres et noms d'auteurs, by Apollinaire, Fernand Fleuret, and Louis Perceau (Paris: Mercure de France, 1913);

Les Trois Don Juan, L'Histoire romanesque (Paris: Bibliothèque des Curieux, 1914); translated by Harold Winner as *Three Don Juans* (Calcutta: Susil Gupta, 1944);

Le Poète assassiné (Paris: Bibliothèque des Curieux, 1916); translated, with a biographical notice and notes, by Matthew Josephson as *The Poet Assassinated* (New York: Broom, 1923);

Vitam impendere amori: Poèmes et dessins, with line drawings by André Rouveyre (Paris: Mercure de France, 1917);

Les Mammelles de Tirésias: Drame surréaliste en deux actes et un prologue (Paris: Editions Sic, 1918); translated by Maya Slater as *The Mammaries of Tiresius* in *Three Pre-Surrealist Plays,* introduction and notes by Slater (Oxford & New York: Oxford University Press, 1997);

Calligrammes, poèmes de la paix et de la guerre, 1913–1916 (Paris: Mercure de France, 1918); translated by Anne Hyde Greet as *Calligrammes, Poems of Peace*

and War (1913–1916), introduction by S. I. Lockerbie and commentary by Greet and Lockerbie (Berkeley & London: University of California Press, 1980);

Le Flâneur des deux rives, Collection des tracts, no. 2 (Paris: Editions de la Sirène, 1918);

La Femme assise (Paris: Editions de la Nouvelle Revue Français, 1920);

Le Verger des amours (Monaco, 1924);

Cortège priapique (Havana [i.e., Paris]: Au Cabinet des Muses [i.e., René Bonnel & René Picart], 1925);

Il y a, preface by Ramón Gomez de la Serna (Paris: Messein, 1925);

Anécdotiques (Paris: Stock, 1926);

Julie, ou la Rose (Hamburg, 1927); translated by Chris Tysh and George Tysh as *Julie or the Rose* (Deal, U.K.: Transgravity Press, 1978);

Ombre de mon amour, introduction by Pierre Cailler (Vésenaz, Switzerland: Cailler, 1947);

Couleur du temps, drame en trois actes et en vers, preface by Edouard Autant-Lara and Louise Autant-Lara (Paris: Editions du Bélier, 1949);

Que faire? Roman, edited by Noëmi Onimus-Blumenkranz; preface by Jean Marcenac (Paris: La Nouvelle Edition, 1950);

Casanova, comédie parodique, preface by Robert Mallet (Paris: Gallimard, 1952);

Le Guetteur mélancolique: Poèmes inédits, preface by André Salmon (Paris: Gallimard, 1952);

Textes inèdits: Guillaume Apollinaire, introduction by Jeanine Moulin, Textes littéraires français, no. 50 (Geneva: Droz / Lille: Giard, 1952);

Poèmes à Lou, with two texts by Rouveyre (Geneva: Cailler, 1955); enlarged as *Poèmes à Lou: précédé de Il y a,* preface by Michel Décaudin, Collection Poésie, volume 44 (Paris: Gallimard, 1969);

Chroniques d'art, 1902–1918, edited, with a preface and notes, by LeRoy C. Breunig (Paris: Gallimard, 1960); translated, and enlarged, by Susan Suleiman as *Apollinaire on Art: Essays and Reviews, 1902–1918* (London: Thames & Hudson, 1972; New York: Viking, 1972);

Les Diables amoureux, edited by Décaudin (Paris: Gallimard, 1964);

Œuvres complètes, 4 volumes, edited by Décaudin (Paris: Balland & Lecat, 1965–1966);

Apollinaire et La Démocratie sociale, edited by Pierre Caizergues, Archives des Lettres modernes, no. 101/ Archives Guillaume Apollinaire, no. 1 (Paris: Minard, 1969);

Le Bréhatine, Cinéma-drame, by Apollinaire and André Billy, edited, with an introduction, by Claude Tournadre, with a critical essay by Alain Virmaux, Archives des Lettres Modernes, no. 126/

Archives Guillaume Apollinaire, no. 5 (Paris: Lettres Modernes, 1971);

Œuvres en prose complètes, 3 volumes, edited by Décaudin and Caizergues, Bibliothèque de la Pléiade, nos. 267, 382, and 399 (Paris: Gallimard, 1977, 1991, 1993);

Petites merveilles du quotidien, edited, with an introduction and notes, by Caizergues (Montpellier: Fata Morgana, 1979)–comprises texts published from 1909 to 1912 in *L'Intransigeant* and *Paris-Journal;*

Soldes, poèmes inédits de Guillaume Apollinaire, edited by Gilbert Boudar, Caizergues, and Décaudin (Saint-Clément-la-Liviere: Fata Morgana, 1985);

Journal intime 1898–1918, edited by Décaudin (Paris: Editions du Limon, 1991);

L'Arbre à soie et autres échos du "Mercure de France," edited and annotated by Caizergues and Décaudin, Collection L'Imaginaire, no. 347 (Paris: Gallimard, 1996).

Editions and Collections: *Les Œuvres érotiques complètes de Guillaume Apollinaire,* 3 volumes (Paris: Barcelonnette, 1934)–comprises volume 1, *Poésies: Cortège priapique. Julie, ou la Rose. Le Verger des Amours;* volume 2, *Les Exploits d'un jeune Don Juan;* and volume 3, *Les Onze mille verges, ou Les Amours d'un hospodar;*

Choix de poésies: Guillaume Apollinaire, edited, with an introduction in English, by C. M. Bowra (London: Horizon, 1945)–comprises selections from *Calligrammes* and *Alcools;*

Il y a, preface by Paul Léautaud and illustrations by Edouard Goerg (Paris: Editions Grégoire, 1947);

Alcools, edited, with commentary and notes, by Tristan Tzara (Paris: Club du Meilleur Livre, 1955);

Calligrammes: Poèmes de la paix et de la guerre (1913–1916), edited and annotated by Michel Décaudin (Paris: Le Club du Meilleur Livre, 1955);

Œuvres poétiques, edited by Marcel Adéma and Décaudin, preface by André Billy, Bibliothèque de la Pléiade, no. 121 (Paris: Gallimard, 1956);

Le Poète assassiné, edited and annotated by Décaudin (Paris: Le Club du Meilleur Livre, 1959);

Le Dossier d'Alcools, edited, with introduction and notes, by Décaudin (Geneva: Droz / Paris: Minard, 1960);

Les Onze Mille Verges, afterword by Toussaint Médecin-Molinier (Paris: Cercle du Livre Précieux, 1963);

Alcools, edited, with an introduction and notes in English, by A. E. Pilkington (Oxford: Blackwell, 1970);

L'Enchanteur pourrissant, edited, with an introduction and notes, by Jean Burgos, Paralogue, no. 5 (Paris: Lettres Modernes, 1972);

Apolliniare's putative father, Francesco-Constantino-Camillo Flugi d'Aspermont

Alcools; et, Calligrammes, edited by Claude Debon, illustrated by Antonio Segui (Paris: Imprimerie Nationale, 1991);

Tendre comme le souvenir, preface by Madeleine Pagès (Paris: Gallimard, 1997).

Editions in English: *Selected Writings of Guillaume Apollinaire,* translated, with a critical introduction, by Roger Shattuck (New York: James Laughlin, 1948; London: Harvill, 1950);

Alcools, translated by Anne Hyde Greet, with a foreword by Warren Ramsey and commentary by Greet (Berkeley & Los Angeles: University of California Press, 1965);

Selected Poems: Apollinaire, translated, with an introduction, by Oliver Bernard (Harmondsworth, U.K.: Penguin, 1965); enlarged bilingual edition published as *Apollinaire: Selected Poems* (London: Anvil Press, 1986);

Debauched Hospodar and Memoirs of a Young Rakehell, introduction by David B. Lewis (Los Angeles: Holloway House, 1967);

The Poet Assassinated, translated by Ron Padgett, illustrated by Jim Dine (New York: Holt, Rinehart & Winston, 1968; London: Hart-Davis, 1968); republished as *The Poet Assassinated and Other Stories* (San Francisco: North Point Press, 1984; Manchester: Carcanet, 1985);

Apollinaire: Calligrams, translated by Greet, Unicorn French Series, volume 10 (Santa Barbara, Cal.: Unicorn Press, 1970)—comprises selections from *Calligrammes* in English and French;

Hunting Horns: Poems of Apollinaire, translated by Barry Morse (South Hinksey, U.K.: Carcanet, 1970)—comprises translations of poems from *Alcools* and *Calligrammes;*

Zone, translated by Samuel Beckett (Dublin: Dolmen Press/London: Calder & Boyars, 1972);

Les onze mille verges, or, The Amorous Adventures of Prince Mony Vibescu, translated by Nina Rootes, introduction by Richard N. Coe (London: Owen, 1976; New York: Taplinger, 1979);

Bestiary, or, The Parade of Orpheus, translated by Pépé Karmel (Boston: Godine, 1980);

Century of Clouds: Selected Poems from the French of Guillaume Apollinaire, translated by Geoff Page and Wendy Coutts (Canberra: Leros, 1985);

The Amorous Exploits of a Young Rakehell, translated by Reaves Tessor (New York: Blue Moon, 1994; Ware, U.K.: Wordsworth Classics, 1995);

Alcools: Poems, translated by Donald Revell (Hanover, N.H.: Published by University Press of New England for Wesleyan University Press, 1995);

Apollinaire, edited by Robert Chandler, translated by Chandler and others, Everyman's Poetry, no. 75 (London: Everyman, 2000).

PLAY PRODUCTION: *Les Mammelles de Tirésias,* Paris, Conservatoire Renée Maubel, 21 June 1917.

OTHER: Marquis de Sade, *L'Œuvre du Marquis de Sade: Zoloe. Justine. Juliette. La Philosophie dans le boudoir. Les Crimes de l'amour. Aline et Valcour; Pages choisies, comprenant des morceaux inédits et des lettres publiées pour la première fois, tirées des Archives de la Comédie-Française,* edited, with an introduction, notes, and bibliographic essay, by Apollinaire, Les Maîtres de l'amour, first series (Paris: Bibliothèque des Curieux, 1909);

Pietro Aretino, *L'Œuvre du divin Arétin,* 2 volumes, introduction and notes by Apollinaire, Les Maîtres de l'amour, first series (Paris: Bibliothèque des Curieux, 1909, 1910);

Andréa de Nerciat, *Julie philosophe, ou Le bon patriote; histoire à peu près véritable d'une citoyenne active, qui a été tour à tour agent et victime dans les dernières révolutions de la Hollande, du Brabant et de la France,* 2 volumes, edited, with an introduction, notes, and bibliographic essay, by Apollinaire, Le Coffret du bibliophile: Les Romans libertins, first series no. 4 (Paris: Bibliothèque des Curieux, 1910);

Giorgio Baffo, *L'Œuvre du Patricien de Venise, Giorgio Baffo: Sonnets, madrigaux, canzoni, capitoli: Traduction nouvelle,* edited, with an introduction, notes, and bibliographic essay, by Apollinaire, Les Maîtres de l'amour (Paris: Bibliothèque des Curieux, 1910);

L'Œuvre libertine des conteurs italiens, 2 volumes, edited, with an introduction, notes, and bibliographic essay, by Apollinaire, Les Maîtres de l'amour (Paris: Bibliothèque des Curieux, 1910, 1911);

John Cleland, *Mémoires de Fanny Hill, femme de plaisir; avec des documents sur la vie à Londres au XVIIIe siècle, et notamment la Vie galante d'après les Sérails de Londres,* edited, with an introduction, notes, and bibliographic essay, by Apollinaire, Les Maîtres de l'amour, first series (Paris: Bibliothèque des Curieux, 1910);

Ernest Feydeau, *Souvenirs d'une cocodette, écrits par elle-même,* edited, with an introduction, notes, and bibliographic essay, by Apollinaire, Le Coffret du bibliophile, second series no. 3 (Paris: Bibliothèque des Curieux, 1910);

Abbot Jouffreau de Lazerie, *Le Joujou des demoiselles: Le calembourg en action,* edited, with an introduction, notes, and bibliographic essay, by Apollinaire, Le Coffret du bibliophile (Paris: Bibliothèque des Curieux, 1910);

Honoré-Gabriel de Riquetti, comte de Mirabeau, *L'Œuvre du comte de Mirabeau,* edited, with an introduction, notes, and bibliographic essay, by Apollinaire, Les Maîtres de l'amour (Paris: Bibliothèque des Curieux, 1910);

Claude-Prosper Jolyot de Crébillon, *L'Œuvre de Crébillon le fils,* 2 volumes, edited, with an introduction, notes, and bibliographic essay, by Apollinaire, Les Maîtres de l'amour (Paris: Bibliothèque des Curieux, 1911, 1913);

Pierre Corneille Blessebois, *L'Œuvre de Pierre-Corneille Blessebois: Le Rut, ou La Pudeur éteinte. Histoire amoureuse de ce temps. Le Zombi du Grand-Pérou,* edited, with an introduction, notes, and bibliographic essay, by Apollinaire, Les Maîtres de l'amour (Paris: Bibliothèque des Curieux, 1912);

Louis Charles Fougeret de Monbron, *Le Canapé couleur de feu: Histoire galante par Fougeret de Montbron; suivie de La Belle sans chemise ou, Eve ressuscitée,* introduction by Apollinaire, Le Coffret du bibliophile (Paris: Bibliothèque des Curieux, 1912);

Etienne de Jouy, *La Galerie des femmes: Collection incomplète de huit tableaux recueillis par un amateur,* edited, with an introduction and bibliographic essay, by Apollinaire, Le Coffret du bibliophile, third series no. 6 (Paris: Bibliothèque des Curieux, 1912);

Parnasse satyrique du XVIIIe siècle, introduction by Apollinaire (Paris: Bibliothèque des curieux, 1912);

La Philosophie des courtisanes: Ouvrage imité de l'italien, edited, with an introduction, notes, and bibliographic essay, by Apollinaire, Le Coffret du bibliophile (Paris: Bibliothèque des Curieux, 1913);

Pierre Albert-Birot, *Trente et un poèmes de poche,* preface by Apollinaire (Paris: Editions "Sic," 1917);

Charles Baudelaire, *Les Fleurs du mal: Texte définitif avec les variantes de la première édition (1857), les pièces ajoutées dans les éditions de 1861, 1866, 1868, suivies des poèmes publiés du vivant et après la mort de l'auteur,* edited, with an introduction and notes, by Apollinaire, Les Maîtres de l'amour (Paris: Bibliothèque des Curieux, 1917);

Très plaisante et récréative hystoire du très preulx et vaillant chevalier Perceval le Galloys, jadis chevalier de la Table Ronde, lequel acheva les adventures de Sainct Graal, au temps du noble Roy Arthurs, edited by Apollinaire, Nouvelle Bibliothèque bleue (Paris: Payot, 1918);

Le Festin d'ésope: Revue des belles lettres, edited by Apollinaire and others (Geneva: Slatkine, 1971).

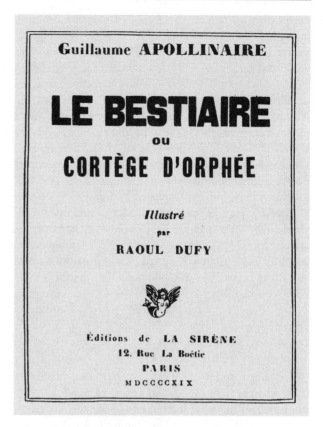

Title page for a posthumous edition of Apollinaire's 1911 poetry collection (from Blaise Cendrars, Jéroboam et La Sirène, *1992)*

Guillaume Apollinaire, poet, journalist, critic, editor, short-story writer, pornographer, dramatist, stockbroker, and bank clerk, achieved fame among his contemporaries primarily in his role of impresario, leading critic, and spokesman for avant-garde action in the arts. More enduringly, he has come to be recognized as a major artist in his own right, especially in his guise as a protean and syncretistic poet. The now-conventional casting of Apollinaire in the role of a Janus in whom a nineteenth-century Romantic sensibility and the modernist disposition to ambiguity, technical artifice, and experimentation met has assured him a niche among the dominant shapers of twentieth-century French literary culture. Perhaps understandably, though, the canonization of an Apollinaire "dieu bifrons" (double-faced god) simultaneously committed to the values of conservation and newness has not laid to rest the question of the degree of originality or inventiveness achieved in his poetry.

Wilhelm Apollinaris de Kostrowitzky was born in Rome on 26 August 1880. His exact given name is questionable, since his mother, Angeliska (or Angelica) Alexandrina Kostrowitzky, recorded his name in various official documents as Guillaume Albert Dulcigni,

Guglielmo Alberto Vladimiro Apollinaire de Kostrowitzky, Guglielmus Apollinaris Albertus de Kostrowitzky, and Wilhelm Albert Wladimir Alexandre de Kostrowitzky. Angeliska Kostrowitzky was the daughter of Michel-Apollinaire Kostrowitzky, a Polish aristocrat of the minor order who had found refuge in Italy after the January Uprising of 1863 was finally crushed by the forces of the Tsar and Poland was forcibly reincorporated into the Russian Empire in 1865. The father of Angeliska Kostrowitzky's son, so evidence would seem to suggest, was one Francesco-Constantino-Camillo Flugi d'Aspermont, army officer, inveterate gambler, bon vivant, and black sheep of an old Piedmontese family, some twenty-six years Angeliska Kostrowitzky's senior when their liaison began in the late 1870s. In 1882, shortly after the birth of Kostrowitzky's second, and last, child, Albert, Flugi d'Aspermont broke with his mistress, who then promptly decamped from Rome to the French Riviera and settled into a life of casino-playing and dalliance in the fashion of the beau monde. A dutiful mother, she found the means to have her children rejoin her and enrolled them in the Roman Catholic Collège Saint-Charles in Monaco. Guillaume de Kostrowitzky (nicknamed Kostro by his schoolmates) excelled in his studies there, made his First Communion (1892), and won a circle of friends enchanted by his personal dynamism and his stylish spinning of piquant, recherché tales about the secret lives of the legendary rich and famous. The overweight boy, inclined to write detailed appreciations of the delights of French and Italian haute cuisine, fared poorly in his studies, first at the Collège Stanilas in Cannes (1896–1897), then at the Lycée de Nice (1897–1899). He failed to graduate from the Lycée because he spent too much time writing poetry and dreaming over such tales of love, sex, and magic as he found in Giovanni Boccaccio's *Decameron* (1348–1353), and Breton lays of Merlin and Viviane. "I would have done better to have swotted at my maths . . . got a secure job. No, instead of working, I wrote poems, had dreams, occupied myself with literature, *merde, merde,*" as he laments in a notebook dating from 1898–1899, quoted by Margaret Davies in her *Apollinaire* (1964). But despite his poor grades he did continue to win friends and impress schoolmates by force of his enthusiastic personality and remarkable gift for telling enchantingly titillating stories.

After a series of financial embarrassments Angeliska Kostrowitzky, in the company of her lover, the impecunious financier Jules Weil (whom she passed off as a male relative), moved her family to Paris in 1899. There the young Apollinaire supported himself by doing odd jobs as a copyist, a secretary at a somewhat dubious investment agency, and a hack story-writer for the newspaper *Le Matin*. A serial contribution to that newspaper, *Que faire?* (What To Do?), provides an indication, as Davies puts it, of the "range of fantasy and invention" that later established him as a writer. Davies aptly sums up this novel, serialized from February to May 1900 and first published in book form in 1950: "There are duels and Duchesses and talking gorillas and a sort of de Sade hero, an expert criminal who violates the heroine while she is dying in a welter of blood, and a hilariously funny scene when the gorilla irrupts into a spiritualist seance." Omnivorous reading in works of gnostic, mystic lore (such as the kabbala), and the works of Jules Verne, H. G. Wells, and the symbolists, and the writing of occasional pieces across an uncommonly wide range, from stylish verses on contemporary life for Marius and Ary Leblond's *La Grande France* and notices for the small financial review *Le Tabarin,* to the spoofy pornographic novel *Mirely ou le petit trou pas cher* (Mirely or the Wee Hole Not Dear, 1900) and love poems dedicated to Linda Molina (the latest of the several ardently wooed girlfriends of his youth), additionally helped fill the gaps of his enforced leisure and prepared the way for his advancement as a man of letters, if not an affluent one. The revenue from the publication by *La Revue blanche* of his short story

"L'Enchanteur" (The Enchanter) some two years after its publication in 1899 did little to alleviate Apollinaire's pressing need for funds. Finding his chance of obtaining secure employment in Paris slim, he was quick to accept the position of private tutor to Gabrielle Holterhöff, the daughter of Elinor Holterhöff, vicomtesse de Milhau, when the opportunity presented itself in August 1901.

Apollinaire's year of service in the viscountess's household in the Rhineland afforded him time to grow as a writer, since the duties of his position took up barely two hours a day. He read extensively in Gothic ballads and romances, wrote stories attuned to the sexual predilections encompassed in the works of Leopold von Sacher-Masoch, Richard von Krafft-Ebing, and the Marquis de Sade (Donatien Alphonse François, comte de Sade), and composed dreamy yet muscular love lyrics—among them, "La Chanson du mal-aimé" (The Song of the Ill-Loved)—in tribute to the charms of Annie Playden, English governess and Sunday-school teacher likewise in his employer's hire. Making no bones of the nature of his regard for Playden, Apollinaire described her in a dithryambic letter, published in *Lettres à Lou* (Letters to Lou, 1969), as "L'Anglaise . . . épatante, blonde comme la lune, des tétons épatants, gros et fermes et droits, qui bandaient dès qu'on les touchait et la mettaient de suite en chaleur, un cul mirobolant énorme et une taille mince à ravir" (The Englishwoman . . . stunning, pale as the moon, with terrific breasts, big and firm and high, which arced when touched, making her hot, and with a gloriously wide backside and ravishingly thin waist). Nor, as the vigorous pleading of "La Chanson du mal-aimé" makes clear, did he demur from savoring the pain inflicted by Playden's rejection of his many offers of marriage. Apollinaire declined the viscountess's offer to renew his appointment, and in 1902 he returned to Paris and the lot of eking out a living with odd jobs in banking and the stock exchange.

Soon dissatisfied again with the meager returns of clerking, Apollinaire came increasingly to involve himself in literary and journalistic circles. In April 1903 Karl Boës introduced him to the Soirées de la Plume. These evenings afforded him the occasion to mingle with the veteran symbolists Jean Moréas and Alfred Jarry, the poets Stuart Merrill and René Ghil, the journalists Charles Henry Hirsch and Félix Fénéon, and to establish himself at the head of the group of up-and-coming young writers—among them André Salmon, Arne Hammer, Nicolas Deniker, Mécilas Goldberg, and Paul Géraldy—who were all keen to make names for themselves. Ever enterprising, Apollinaire somehow found funds to launch *Le Festin d'Esope* (1903–1904), a little magazine intended, as Davies quotes him

Page from the manuscript for "Le Pont Mirabeau," a poem in Apollinaire's 1913 collection, Alcools *(Bibliothèque Nationale, Paris)* as saying, "to publish works of every description, literature of the imagination and ideas." Sundry playful advertisements for phantom products and firms, a spicy monthly gossip column ("Notes du Mois"), and the serially published tale *L'Enchanteur pourrissant* (The Rotting Enchanter)—all of Apollinaire's own creation—figured prominently in the life of that magazine. *L'Enchanteur pourrissant* was published in book form, with woodcuts by André Derain, in 1909. His first business as editor having failed after nine issues, Apollinaire promptly went on to find financial backing for two further magazines, *La Revue immoraliste* and *Les Lettres modernes,* each of which failed to survive beyond one issue in 1905. He continued to supplement his scant income as a bank employee by trafficking in pornography. His parodic take on the writings of de Sade, *Les Exploits d'un jeune Don Juan* (The Exploits of a Young Don Juan; translated as *Amorous Exploits of a Young Rakehell,* 1953), and his erotic tale of a depraved Romanian nobleman's travels across Europe, *Les Onze mille verges* (The Eleven Thousand Rods; translated as *The Debauched Hospodar,* 1953), were both published in 1907. Although both works were frequently republished and are now considered classics of erotica, Apollinaire made little money from them.

But fame, if not material fortune, was not long in coming. Apollinaire's introduction to the painter Pablo Picasso and the world of modern art in 1904 opened a wide door of opportunity. Apollinaire's first article on Picasso, in *La Revue immoraliste* (1904), registers something of his readiness to profit from an oblique identification of himself with his promising subject: "Everything fascinates him and his incontestable talent seems to me to serve a fantasy which mingles the delicious and the horrible, the abject and the delicate." The charms of the painter Marie Laurencin, whose work he sometimes rated on par with the great Picasso's, lent added force to the attraction that his new-found milieu held for him. With his characteristic appetite for the unknown—his knowledge of painting at this time was minimal—the personable Apollinaire seized the opportunity to grow.

The accession of Apollinaire to the status of cultural impresario and leading apologist for avant-garde art after 1904 was almost meteoric. Salient events in the history of that rise include the arranging of Georges Braque's introduction to Picasso in 1907; the promotion of Cubism, in his capacity as art critic for the daily newspaper *L'Intransigeant* in 1911, as "the most elevated, the most sublime form of art," as he put it in his 1904 article in *La Revue immoraliste,* followed up in 1911 by his helping to organize the "cubist room 41" at the Salon des Indépendants; his launching of the influential monthly magazine *Les Soirées de Paris* and lecturing at

the Section d'Or exhibit, both in 1912; the publication the following year of his anecdotal *Les Peintres cubistes: Méditations aesthétiques* (translated as *The Cubist Painters: Aesthetic Meditations, 1913,* 1944); his resonant discourse for *Orphisme* (Orphism), the term he coined to describe the shimmering chromatic effects used by Cubist painters such as Robert Delauney, delivered on the occasion of a 1913 Delaunay show in Berlin and quickly published in Milan as *L'Antitradition futuriste: Manifeste-synthèse* (The Futurist Antitradition: Manifesto-Synthesis); and his writing of the program note for the premiere of *Parade* (1917), a ballet that combined the talents of Jean Cocteau (writer), Picasso (costume and set designer), Léonide Massine (choreographer), Erik Satie (music), and impresario Sergei Pavlovich Diaghilev's celebrated Ballets Russes. Apollinaire's coining of the term "Surrealism" in the program note for *Parade* assured him a niche in the history of criticism. The short-listing of his book of short stories *L'Hérésiarque et cie* (1910; translated as *The Heresiarch and Co.,* 1965), a collection that includes "Cox City," "La Rose de Hildesheim," and "Simon-Mage," for the Prix Goncourt in 1910, the considerable notice garnered by his 1916 collection of tales *Le Poète assassiné* (translated as *The Poet Assassinated,* 1923), which includes "La Favorite" (The Favorite), "La Fiancée postume" (The Posthumous Fiancée), and "Le Roi Lune" (The Moon King), and the success enjoyed by the 1917 production of his Surrealist play *Les Mammelles de Tirésias* (translated as *The Mammaries of Tiresias,* 1997) at once confirmed and lent additional luster to Apollinaire's reputation as a significant contributor to the cause of progressive art.

Apollinaire was ideally placed for advancement in the role of critical promoter and *éclaireur* (lighter; or scout). He had little difficulty attuning himself to the modernist spirit of eclectic fabrication and technological fantasy that found expression, for example, in Wellsian visions of future science, the Promethean poetics of the symbolists, the miming of mechanical movement in productions by Diaghilev and Igor Stravinsky, the ludic geometry of Cubist and Surrealist representations and, on yet another level, his own playful exercises in writing pornography. His name in conservative circles for being somewhat of a *fumiste* (con man) and dealer in shady goods (he was briefly imprisoned on suspicion of complicity in the 1911 theft of the Mona Lisa) naturally enough served to endear him to fellow exponents of the avant-garde as a leader in the way of artistry. The anecdotal and personality-driven nature of his reflections on art, as in *Les Peintres cubistes,* have led most later students of Apollinaire's achievement to rate his performance as critic less highly. The posthumous publication of the volume *Chroniques d'art, 1902–1918* (1960; translated as *Apollinaire on Art: Essays and Reviews, 1902–1918,* 1972),

Apollinaire (far right) with other patients and doctors at the military hospital where he recovered after being wounded in March 1916

though, heightened the interest literary theorists had in his aesthetic thinking.

For most of his readers, however, it is Apollinaire the poet of *Alcools, poèmes 1898–1913* (1913; translated as *Alcools: Poems, 1898–1913,* 1964) and *Calligrammes, poèmes de la paix et de la guerre, 1913–1916* (1918; translated as *Calligrammes, Poems of Peace and War [1913–1916],* 1980) who counts for more, retains lasting value for his questing, in his own words, "à la recherche d'un lyrisme neuf et humaniste à la fois" (in search of a lyricism at once humanist and new). By 1911, certainly, Apollinaire had made significant moves toward the realization of that quest. Signs of the appetite for a romantic humanism bound to make a religion of poetry are duly marked in his first book of verse, *Le Bestiaire, ou, Cortège d'Orphée* (1911). The work was translated by Lauren Shakely in a facsimile of the first edition published by the Metropolitan Museum of Art in 1977 and retranslated by Pépé Karmel as *Bestiary, or, The Parade of Orpheus* in 1980. In this work the poet aligns himself with suffering wonder-worker Jesus and his disciples—"Jésus . . . et les douze" (Jesus . . . and the dozen)—and master of the occult sciences Hermes Trismegistus:

Admirez le pouvoir insigne
Et la noblesse de la ligne
Elle est la voix que la lumière fit entendre
Et dont parle Hermès Trismégiste en son Pimandre.

(Admire the remarkable power
And the nobility of the line
It is the voice made heard by the light
And of which Hermes Trismegistus speaks in his Pimander).

The tribute to tradition paid in this address and many times redoubled in a book of new lyricism resonant with echoes of such antecedent poets as François Villon, Nicolass Boileau, Jean de La Fontaine, Alfred de Vigny, Charles Baudelaire, Arthur Rimbaud, Stéphane Mallarmé, and Moréas, bespeaks something of the conjunction of humility with ambition that dominates *Le Bestiaire*. Taking on the persona of a pygmied Prometheus and paltried Trismegistus, in "La Poulpe" (Octopus) the poet figures himself as a mere blood-sucking creature, like a vampiric octopus:

Jetant mon encre vers les cieux,
Suçant le sang de ce qu'il aime

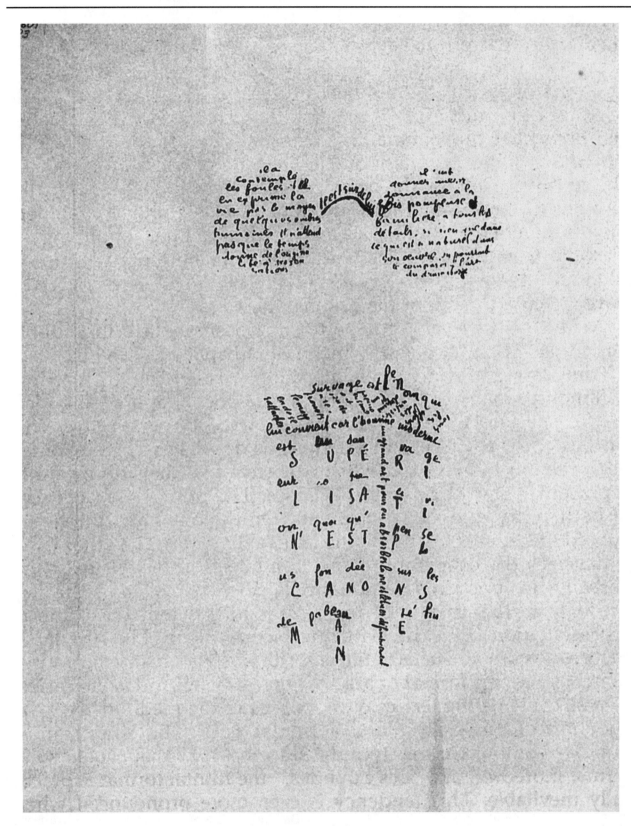

Manuscripts for "Les Lunettes" and "Le Livre" (left) and "La Femme," "La Fontaine," "Le Bouquet," and "La Jambe"
(exhibition catalogue, Galerie Bongard, 21–31 January 1917)

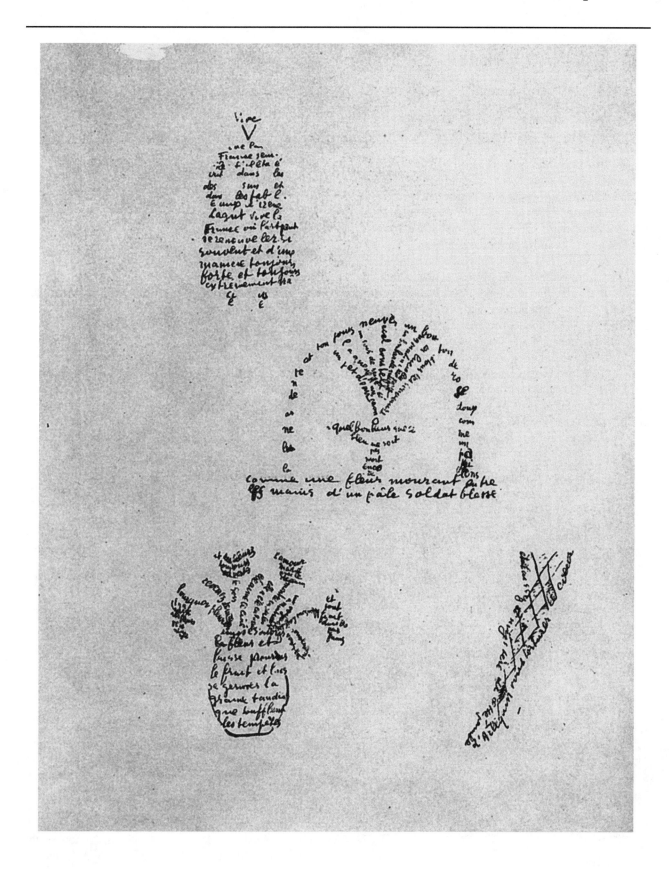

Et le trouvant délicieux,
Ce monstre inhumain, c'est moi-méme

(Squirting my ink towards the sky,
Sucking the blood of what he loves
And finding it delicious,
This inhuman monster, it's myself).

As the two large books of his poetry that Apollinaire assembled after *Le Bestiaire* indicate, he remained true to his talent for mixing audacity with deference.

The year 1913 was something of an annus mirabilis for Apollinaire. That year he published not only *Les Peintres cubistes* and *L'Antitradition futuriste,* but also his *Alcools*. Arranged as a sequence of reflections timed to a one-day promenade on the streets of Paris, the fifty poems of *Alcools* reflect the peripeties of a consciousness drinking in the contradictions that it reads in the places it traverses. The poetic persona of *Alcools* virtually becomes his milieu, a site where seaminess and splendor, beauty and ugliness, destitution and luxury, the high and the low, beggars and airplanes, prostitutes and the Eiffel Tower sit cheek by jowl. Apollinaire repeatedly strives to encompass his readers as well, by identifying "Tu" (You) with "Je" (I), as in "Zone":

Tu as fait de douloureux et de joyeux voyages
Avant d'apercevoir du mensonge et de l'âge
Tu as souffert de l'amour à vingt et à trente ans
J'ai vécu comme un fou et j'ai perdu mon temps
Tu n'oses plus regarder tes mains et à tous moments
   je voudrais sangloter
Sur toi sur celle que j'aime sur tout ce qui t'a épouvanté.

(You have made painful and joyful journeys
Before your becoming aware of lies and growing old
You have suffered for love at twenty and thirty
I have lived like a fool and I have wasted my time
You no longer dare look at your hands and at every
   moment I would burst into tears
Over you over she that I love over all which has terrified
   you).

Recollective as they are of their author's own bittersweet journeys in a hopeful yet futile, since endless, quest in search of the distinctive and whole "I" in "the Other"–according to the sad, riddling joking of "Cortège":

Un jour
Un jour je m'attendais moi-méme
Je me disais Gillaume il est temps que tu viennes
Pour que je sache enfi celui-la que je suis

(One day
One day in wait for myself
I said Gullaume it is time that you came
So that I might come to know what person I am).

The poems of *Alcools* depict the poetic persona in a nostalgic mood, deep in melancholy. That mood could be profound indeed, as in "Le Pont Mirabeau" (Mirabeau Bridge), in which the solitary poet dwells on the passing of his days of love with his former lover Laurencin:

Quand donc finira la semaine
Quand donc finiront les amours
Vienne la nuit sonne l'heure
Les jours s'en vont et je demeure.

(When then will the week end
When then will loves end
Come the night strike the hour
The days pass and I remain).

The question of what is truly original in Apollinaire's work remains unresolved. Readers familiar with Villon's "Allé s'en est et je demeure" (Time goes by and I remain), will find "Le Pont Mirabeau" not altogether fresh in conception, mood, or technique. And students of "Zone," the extensive liminary poem of *Alcools,* have long entertained the possibility of Apollinaire's having "lifted" the plan for his extended "poème-promenade" from Blaise Cendrar's 1912 poem of an Easter parade, "Pâques à New York" (Easter in New York). What does remain certain is that the poet of *Alcools* had a rich store of memories on which to draw and that he retailored a variety of materials from that store in a way designed to make them fit others and himself anew. "Je prétends être un des pionniers de l'art varié" (I aspire/pretend to be one of the pioneers of diversified art), as he promoted and confessed himself with due double-entendre in a letter of 1913, quoted by Marie-Louise Lentengre in her *Apollinaire: Le nouveau lyrisme* (Apollinaire: The New Lyricism, 1996).

For all of his productivity in 1913, though, Apollinaire soon came to find himself once again in straitened financial circumstances. On 28 June 1914 Archduke Franz Ferdinand, heir to the throne of the Austro-Hungarian Empire, was assassinated, and all of Europe became preoccupied in the diplomatic exchanges that led up to World War I. A Paris interested more with questions of war and mobilization of troops than with matters of advancement and mobility in the fine arts afforded Apollinaire little opportunity for journalistic endeavor. In September of 1914, with German forces menacing Paris, he departed for Nice, where he indulged in bouts of cocaine use with other non-nationals and savored the delights of his lover Louise de Coligny, comtesse de Pillot de Coligny-Châtillon, known as "Lou." Apparently depressed by Lou's abrupt cutting short of their intense liaison and his growing sense of separation from French friends at the front, Apollinaire enlisted in an artillery regiment at Nîmes in December 1914. Yet again, he

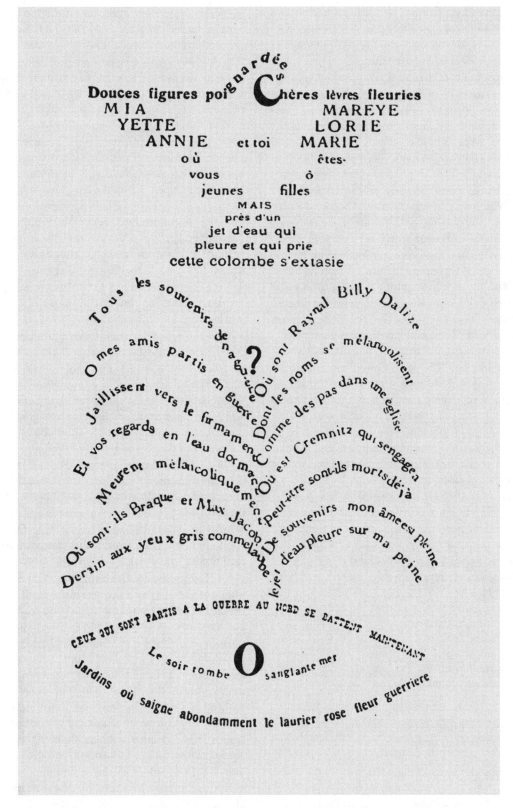

"La Colombe Poignardée et le Jet d'Eau" in the 1925 edition of Apollinaire's Calligrammes
(Thomas Cooper Library, University of South Carolina)

found the means to profit from parlous circumstances: his wartime experiences are reflected in *Calligrammes,* the third and, arguably, the most memorable of Apollinaire's books of poetry published in his lifetime.

The aestheticism of that book, with its highlighting of poems in the shape of "calligrammes" or "idéogrammes lyriques" (lyrical ideograms)–pictures limned by the arrangement of words on the page–remains remarkable, even notorious. War is "belle" (beautiful), "une chose charmante" (a charming thing), like poetry–"le Jeu supréme" (a grand game), so artillery officer Apollinaire reported in letters to friends well beyond the range of German guns. War surely figures as playful work in *Calligrammes,* where "obus" (artillery shells) are made to stand for women's breasts and where words in praise of the pleasures of cannon-fire find their visual analogue in the shape of a smoking cigar. "Vigoureux priapes" (Vigorous phalluses) designates the action and virtue of big guns in their ardor to search out the objects of their desire (as in the poem "A Nîmes" [To Nîmes]): "O Guerre / Multiplication de l'amour" (O War / Love multiplied), Apollinaire ecstatically proclaims in "Oracles." But he could also be domestic in his romanticizing: "Paysage" (Countryside), the first of his published lyrical ideograms, represents a bush, a smoking cigar, a copulating couple, and a house intact, while the last entry in *Calligrammes,* "La Jolie Rousse" (The Pretty Redhead), pays tribute to Apollinaire's latest love, Jacqueline Kolb, another recipient of his missives from the front. The few poems of *Calligrammes* informed by Apollinaire's experience of life in the trenches after his transfer to the infantry in April 1915 are understandably less glowing and romantic: "Quelle effroyable boue dans les effroyables boyaus" (What horrid muck in the horrifying trenches). André Breton and other Surrealists who kept their distance from those trenches later celebrated the play of nonsense in *Calligrammes,* especially as evinced in "Les Collines" (The Hills):

Un chapeau haut de forme est sur
Une table chargée de fruits
Les gants sont morts près d'une pomme
Une dame se tord le cou
Auprès d'un monsieur qui s'avale

(A high hat sits on
A table laden with fruit
Gloves sit dead next an apple
A lady wrings her neck
Next to a man who swallows himself).

Apollinaire's last major experience on the Western Front was less funny. On 17 March 1916 he was severely wounded by a piece of shrapnel that struck his right temple after piercing his helmet. He survived to find himself on his way back home to Paris.

Apollinaire yet again found the means to prosper from setbacks and pain. His head still bandaged, he was released from the hospital in August to renewed opportunity for avant-garde action in a Paris pregnant with hopes of armistice. He attended a banquet on 31 December 1916, which was arranged by friends in honor of his patriotic work. Apollinaire soon was able to publish a slim volume of poems of impending love, *Vitam impendere amori* (Life Hangs on Love, 1917). Returns from the production in June 1917 of *Les Mammelles de Tirésias,* his opera bouffe *Casanova,* and various articles for magazines such as *Sic* helped defray the expenses of his marriage to Kolb in May 1918. That prosperity and marriage, though, was short-lived. Some six months later, on 9 November 1918, two days before the armistice, Apollinaire died, a victim of the great Spanish influenza epidemic that swept across Europe that fall.

The many works by Apollinaire published after his death have kept interest in his writing alive. These works include *La Femme assise* (The Seated Woman) in 1920, *Le Verger des amours* (Love's Orchard) in 1924, *Il y a* (There Is) and *Cortège priapique* (Priapic Procession) in 1925, *Ombre de mon amour* (Shade of My Love) in 1947, *Couleur du temps, drame en trois actes et en vers* (Time's Hue, Drama in Three Acts and in Verse) in 1949, *Le Guetteur mélancolique: Poèmes inédits* (The Melancholic Lookout: Unpublished Poems) in 1952, *Poèmes à Lou* (Poems to Lou) in 1955, and *Journal intime 1898–1918* (Intimate Journal 1898–1918) in 1991. The publication of a volume of his collected poetry, *Œuvres poétiques* (Poetic Works, 1956), and three volumes of his prose *Œuvres en prose complètes* (Complete Works in Prose, 1977, 1991, 1993), in the prestigious Bibliothèque de la Pléiade series has assured his inclusion among the greats of French literature.

References to Guillaume Apollinaire by subsequent writers have confirmed his legendary status and the depth of the impression made by his achievement. For example, in his novel of love, war, machines, and dipsomania, *Under the Volcano* (1947), Malcolm Lowry drew on the poet of *Alcools* and *Calligrammes* for the character of M. Jacques Laruelle, an art collector, moviemaker, and "elderly aesthete" in exile, though not without a stroke of irony: "M. Laruelle had been in the artillery during the last war, survived by him in spite of Guillaume Apollinaire's being for a time his commanding officer." Postmodernist readers of Apollinaire's body of work have found a place for his enterprise in the progress of grammarless discourse and aesthetic self-reflection from Friedrich Nietzsche to Michel Butor, Jacques Derrida, Michel Foucault, and Jean-François Lyotard. As David Berry remarks in his 1982 study of Apollinaire's poetry, "It has a become a cliché in the criticism of twentieth-century

Apollinaire and his wife, Jacqueline, shortly after their marriage in May 1918

French poetry to point out that Guillaume Apollinaire represents the last of the traditional lyric poets and the first of the modern literary iconoclasts."

Letters:

Lettres à sa marraine, 1915–1918, edited, with an introduction and notes, by Marcel Adéma (Paris: Pour les Fils du Roi, 1948);

Lettres de Guillaume Apollinaire envoyées à Jane Mortier (Liège, Belgium: Editions Dynamo, 1950);

Lettres à Lou, edited by Michel Décaudin (Paris: Gallimard, 1969);

Guillaume Apollinaire, André Level: Lettres, edited, with an introduction and notes, by Brigitte Level (Paris: Lettres Modernes, 1976);

Six lettres d'Apollinaire: Avec des réponses de Saint-Georges de Bouhélier, Raymond de La Tailhède et André Fontainas, afterword by Décaudin (Muizon: A l'Ecart, 1982);

Correspondance avec son frère et sa mère: Guillaume Apollinaire, edited by Gilbert Boudar and Décaudin (Paris: José Corti, 1987);

Correspondance Guillaume Apollinaire, Jean Cocteau, edited by Pierre Caizergues, Décaudin, and Boudar (Paris: Jean-Michel Place, 1991);

Picasso/Apollinaire: Correspondance, edited by Pierre Caizergues and Hélène Seckel (Paris: Gallimard, 1992);

Guillaume Apollinaire. Corrispondenza I, edited by Lucia Bonato (Rome: Bulzone, 1992);

Correspondance Jules Romains/Guillaume Apollinaire, edited by Claude Martin (Paris: Jean-Michel Place, 1994);

Correspondance 1913–1917: Guillaume Apollinaire, Mireille Havet, edited by Dominique Tiry (Montpellier: Centre d'Etude du XXe Siècle, Université Paul-Valéry, 2000).

Bibliographies:

La Revue des Lettres Modernes, special Apollinaire issues, 1–14 (1962–1978);

Scott Bates, "Guillaume Apollinare," in *A Critical Bibliography of French Literature,* volume 6, *The Twentieth Century,* edited by Douglas W. Alden and Richard A. Brooks, part 2, *Principally Poetry, Theater, and Criticism before 1940, and Essay* (Syracuse, N.Y.: Syracuse University Press, 1980), pp. 882–907;

Carnets bibliographiques de La Revue des Lettres Modernes–Guillaume Apollinaire, edited by Peter C. Hoy (Paris: Minard, 1983).

Biographies:

André Billy, *Apollinaire vivant* (Paris: Editions de La Sirène, 1923);

Philippe Soupault, *Guillaume Apollinaire, ou, Reflets de l'incendie* (Marseilles: Cahiers du Sud, 1927);

Christian Fettweis, *Apollinaire en Ardenne* (Brussells: Henriquez, 1934);

Ernst Wolf, *Guillaume Apollinaire und das Rheinland* (Dortmund: Husen, 1937);

Louise Faure-Favier, *Souvenirs sur Guillaume Apollinaire* (Paris: Grasset, 1945);

Cecily Mackworth, *Guillaume Apollinaire and the Cubist Life* (London: Murray, 1961; New York: Horizon, 1963);

Francis Steegmuller, *Apollinaire: Poet among the Painters* (New York: Farrar, Straus, 1963; London: Hart-Davis, 1964);

Margaret Davies, *Apollinaire* (Edinburgh & London: Oliver & Boyd, 1964; New York: St. Martin's Press, 1965);

Pierre-Marcel Adéma, *Guillaume Apollinaire* (Paris: Editions de La Table Ronde, 1968);

Pierre Caizergues, *Apollinaire journaliste: Les Débuts et la formation du journaliste, 1900–1909* (Paris: Minard, 1981);

André Parinaud, *Apollinaire 1880–1918: Biographie et Relecture* (Paris: Editions Jean-Claude Lattès, 1994).

References:

Scott Bates, *Guillaume Apollinaire,* revised edition (Boston: Twayne, 1989);

Claude M. Bégué and Pierre Latigue, *"Alcools," Apollinaire: Analyse critique,* Profil d'une œuvre, no. 25 (Paris: Hatier, 1972);

David Berry, *The Creative Vision of Guillaume Apollinaire: A Study of Imagination* (Saratoga, Cal.: Anma Libri, 1982);

Madeleine Boisson, *Apollinaire et les Mythologies antiques* (Fasano, Italy: Schena/Paris: Nizet, 1989);

Claude Bonnefoy, *Apollinaire,* Classiques du XXe siècle, no. 100 (Paris: Editions Universitaires, 1969);

Laurence Campa, *L'Esthétique d'Apollinaire* (Paris: Société d'Edition d'Enseignement Supérieur, 1996);

Blaise Cendrars, *Jéroboam et La Sirène,* preface by Hughes Richard (Dole: Canevas, 1992);

Claude Debon, ed., *Les Critiques de notre temps et Apollinaire* (Paris: Garnier Frères, 1971);

Antoine Fongaro, *Apollinaire poète: Exégèses et discussions, 1957–1987* (Toulouse: Presses Universitaires du Mirail-Toulouse, 1988);

Raymond Jean, "L'Erotique de Guillaume Apollinaire," *Cahiers du Sud,* 386 (1966): 13–21;

James Lawler, "Music and Poetry in Apollinaire," *French Studies,* 10 (1956): 339–346;

Marie-Louise Lentengre, *Apollinaire: Le nouveau lyrisme,* revised edition (Paris: Jean-Michel Place, 1996);

Roger Little, *Guillaume Apollinaire* (London: Athlone, 1976);

Timothy Mathews, *Reading Apollinaire: Theories of Poetic Language* (Manchester: Manchester University Press, 1987);

Henri Meschonnic, "Apollinaire illuminé au milieu des ombres," *Europe,* 451/452 (1966): 141–169;

Catherine Moore, *Apollinaire en 1918: La poétique de l'enchantement* (Paris: Minard, 1995);

Peter Read, *Apollinaire et "Les Mammelles de Tirésias": La Revanche d'Eros* (Rennes: Presses Universitaires de Rennes, 2000);

Read, *Picasso et Apollinaire: Les Métamorphoses de la mémoire, 1905–1973* (Paris: Jean-Michel Place, 1995);

André Rouveyre, *Amour et poésie d'Apollinaire* (Paris: Seuil, 1955);

Pénélope Sacks-Galey, *Calligramme, ou, Ecriture figurée: Apollinaire inventeur de formes* (Paris: Minard, 1988);

Pierre Souyris, "Les Deux Versions du *Pont Mirabeau,*" *Le Flâneur des deux rives,* 7/8 (1955): 19–26;

Jean Starobinski, *L'Œil vivant: Essai* (Paris: Gallimard, 1961);

Stefan Themerson, *Apollinaire's Lyrical Ideograms* (London: Gaberbocchus, 1968);

Margareth Wijk, *Guillaume Apollinaire et l'esprit nouveau,* Etudes romanes de Lund, no. 36 (Lund, Sweden: C.W.K. Gleerup, 1982);

Sergio Zoppi, *Apollinaire teorico* (Naples: Edizioni Scientifiche Italiane, 1970).

Papers:

Manuscripts of Guillaume Apollinaire's works are held in the Fonds Jacques Doucet, Bibliothèque Ste-Geneviève, Paris.

Louis Aragon

(3 October 1897 – 24 December 1982)

Paul Matthieu St-Pierre
Simon Fraser University

See also the Aragon entry in *DLB 72: French Novelists, 1930–1960.*

BOOKS: *Feu de joie,* illustrated by Pablo Picasso (Paris: Au Sens Pareil, 1920);

Anicet, ou, Le Panorama (Paris: Editions de la Nouvelle Revue Française, 1921);

Les Aventures de Télémaque (Paris: Editions de la Nouvelle Revue Française, 1922); translated by Renée Riese Hubert and Judd D. Hubert as *The Adventures of Telemachus* (Lincoln: University of Nebraska Press, 1988);

Paris, la nuit: Les Plaisirs de la capitale, ses bas fonds, ses jardins secrets (Berlin, 1923);

Le Libertinage (Paris: Editions de la Nouvelle Revue Française, 1924); translated by Jo Levy as *The Libertine* (London: Calder / New York: Riverrun Press, 1987);

Une Vague de rêves (Paris: Hors Commerce, 1924);

Le Mouvement perpétuel, poèmes (1920–1924) (Paris: Gallimard, 1926);

Le Paysan de Paris (Paris: Gallimard, 1926); translated by Frederick Brown as *Nightwalker* (Englewood Cliffs, N.J.: Prentice-Hall, 1970);

Le Traité du style (Paris: Gallimard, 1928); translated by Alyson Waters as *Treatise on Style* (Lincoln & London: University of Nebraska Press, 1991);

Le Con d'Irène, anonymous (Paris: René Bonnel, 1928); republished, as Albert de Routisie, preface by André Pieyre de Mandiargues (Paris: Cercle du Livre Précieux, 1962); republished as *Irène,* as de Routisie, preface by Jean-Jacques Pauvert (Paris: L'Or du Temps, 1968); translated by Lowell Blair as *Irene* (New York: Grove, 1969);

La Grande Gaité, with two drawings by Yves Tanguy (Paris: Gallimard, 1929);

La Peinture au défi (Paris: Editions Surréalistes, 1930)– translated by Michael Palmer and Norma Cole as "The Challenge to Painting," in *The Surrealists Look at Art: Eluard, Aragon, Soupault, Breton, Tzara,*

Louis Aragon (New York World-Telegram and Sun Collection, Library of Congress)

edited by Pontus Hulten (Venice, Cal.: Lapis Press, 1990);

Persécuté persécuteur (Paris: Editions Surréalistes, 1931);

Eclairez votre religion: Aux enfants rouges (Paris: Bureau d'Editions et de Diffusions, 1932);

Hourra l'Oural: Poèmes (Paris: Denoël & Steele, 1934);

Les Cloches de Bâle (Paris: Denoël & Steele, 1934 [i.e., 1935]); translated by Haakon M. Chevalier as *The Bells of Basel* (New York: Harcourt, Brace, 1936; London: Davies & Lovat Dickson, 1937);

Pour un réalisme socialiste (Paris: Denoël & Steele, 1935);

Les Beaux Quartiers, roman (Paris: Denoël & Steele, 1936); translated by Chevalier as *Residential Quarter* (New York: Harcourt, Brace, 1938);

Le Crève-Coeur (Paris: Gallimard, 1941);

The Century Was Young, translated by Hannah Josephson (New York: Duell, Sloan & Pearce, 1941); censored French version published as *Les Voyageurs de l'impériale, roman* (Paris: Gallimard, 1942); Josephson's translation republished as *Passengers of Destiny* (London: Pilot, 1947); revised French-language edition (Paris: Gallimard, 1947);

Les Yeux d'Elsa, Les Cahiers du Rhône–Série Blanche, no. 3 (Neuchâtel, Switzerland: Editions de la Baconnière, 1942; New York: Editions de la Maison Française, 1942; London: Edition Horizon–La France Libre, 1943; Paris: Seghers, 1945);

Cantique à Elsa (Algiers: Editions de la Revue *Fontaine,* 1942);

Brocéliande: Poème, Les Poètes des Cahiers du Rhône, no. 3 (Neuchâtel, Switzerland: Editions de la Baconnière, 1942);

En français dans le texte, Ides Poétiques, no. 1 (Neuchâtel, Switzerland: Ides et Calendes, 1943);

Le Musée Grévin, as François La Colère (Paris: Editions de Minuit, 1943); enlarged as *Le Museé Grévin: Les Poissons noirs et quelques poèmes inédits,* as Aragon (Paris: Editions de Minuit, 1946);

France écoute (Algiers: Editions de la Revue Fontaine, 1944);

Le Crime contre l'esprit (Les Martyrs), as Le Témoin des Martyrs (Paris: Editions de Minuit, 1944);

Aurélien, roman (Fribourg, Switzerland: Librarie de l'Université, 1944; Paris: Gallimard, 1944); translated by Eithne Wilkins as *Aurelien* (London: Pilot, 1946; New York: Duell, Sloan & Pearce, 1947);

Contribution au cycle de Gabriel Péri (Toulouse: Comité National des Ecrivains, Centre des intellectuels, 1944);

La Diane française, Collection Poésie, no. 44 (Paris: Seghers, 1944); enlarged as *Le Diane française, suivi de En étrange pays dans mon pays lui-même* (Paris: Seghers, 1945);

Saint-Pol Roux, ou, L'Espoir (Paris: Seghers, 1945);

Servitude et grandeur des Français: Scènes des années terribles (Paris: Bibliothèque Française, 1945);

En étrange pays dans mon pays lui-même; En Français dans le texte; Brocéliande, précédés de De l'Exactitude historique en poésie (Monaco: A La Voile Latine, 1945);

Neuf Chansons interdites, 1942–1944, as La Colère (Paris: Bibliothèque Française, 1945);

Trois contes, as Saint Romain Arnaud (London: Burrup, Mathieson, 1945)–comprises "Les bons voisins," "Pénitent 43," and "Les Rencontres";

L'Enseigne de Gersaint: Hors-text de Watteau (Neuchâtel, Switzerland & Paris: Ides et Calendes, 1946);

Apologie du luxe, illustrated by Henri Matisse, Les Trésors de la peinture française. XX. siècle, no. 1 (Geneva: Skira, 1946);

L'Homme Communiste, 2 volumes (Paris: Gallimard, 1946, 1953);

Deux Poètes d'aujourd'hui, by Aragon and Paul Eluard (Lausanne, Switzerland: La Guilde du Livre, 1946; Paris & Lausanne, Switzerland: Clairefontaine, 1947);

Chroniques du Bel Canto (Geneva: Skira, 1947);

La Culture et les hommes (Paris: Editions Sociales, 1947);

Le Nouveau Crève-cœur: Poèmes (Paris: Gallimard, 1948);

Les Communistes: Roman, 6 volumes (Paris: Bibliothèque Française, 1949–1951);

La Lumière et la Paix: Discours prononcé au Congrès National de l'Union Nationale des intellectuels (U.N.I.) le 29 avril 1950 à Paris, à la Maison de la pensée (Paris: Editions des *Lettres Françaises,* 1950);

Hugo, poète réaliste (Paris: Editions Sociales, 1952);

Les Egmont d'aujourd'hui s'appellent André Stil (Paris: Editions des *Lettres Françaises,* 1952);

La Vraie Liberté de la culture, réduire notre train de mort pour accroître notre train de vie (Paris: Editions des *Lettres Françaises,* 1952);

L'Exemple de Courbet (Paris: Editions Cercle d'Art, 1952);

Le Neveu de M. Duval, suivi d'une lettre d'icelui à l'auteur de ce livre (Paris: Editeurs Français Réunis, 1953);

Mes Caravanes et autres poèmes (1948–1954), Collection le Phénix, no. 4 (Paris: Seghers, 1954);

La Lumière de Stendhal (Paris: Denoël, 1954);

Journal d'une poésie nationale (Lyons: Armand Le Henneuse/Les Ecrivains Réunis, 1954);

Les Yeux et la mémoire, poème (Paris: Gallimard, 1954);

Littératures soviétiques (Paris: Denoël, 1955);

Le Roman inachevé (Paris: Gallimard, 1956);

Entretiens sur le Musée de Dresde, by Aragon and Jean Cocteau (Paris: Editions Cercle d'Art, 1957); translated by Francis Scarfe as *Conversations on the Dresden Gallery,* foreword by Joseph Masheck (New York & London: Holmes & Meier, 1982);

La Semaine sainte (Paris: Gallimard, 1958); translated by Haakon Chevalier as *Holy Week: A Novel* (New York: Putnam, 1961; London: Hamilton, 1961);

Elsa: Poème (Paris: Gallimard, 1959);

L'Un ne va pas sans l'autre: Un Perpétuel Printemps, suivi de Paroles à Saint-Denis (Lyon: Armand Henneuse/ Ecrivains Réunis, 1959);

Il faut appeler les choses par leur nom, preface by Maurice Thorez (Paris: Parti Communiste Français, 1959);

J'Abats mon jeu (Paris: Editeurs Français Réunis, 1959);

Poésies: Anthologie 1917–1960, edited, with an introduction, by Jean Dutourd (Paris: Le Club de Meilleur Livre, 1960);

Les Poètes: Poème (Paris: Gallimard, 1960; revised, 1969; revised again, 1976);

Histoire parallèle, by Aragon and André Maurois, 4 volumes (Paris: Presses de la Cité, 1962)–comprises volume 1, *Histoire des États-Unis de 1917 à 1961,* by Maurois; volume 2, *Histoire de l'U.R.S.S. de 1917 à 1960–tome I, 1(janvier 1917–octobre 1917) à 5 (1929–1939),* by Aragon; volume 3, *Histoire de l'U.R.S.S. de 1917 à 1960–tome II, 6 (1ᵉʳ septembre 1939 au 1ᵉʳ janvier 1944) à 9 (de janvier 1954 à fin décembre 1957),* by Aragon; and volume 4, *Louis Aragon et André Maurois Histoire paralléle–tome IV–* comprises "Conversations avec quelques Américains éminents," by Maurois, and "Aperçus donnés par quelques Soviétiques éminents," by Aragon; republished as *Les Deux Géants: Histoire des Etats-Unis et de l'U.R.S.S., de 1917 à nos jours,* 5 volumes (Paris: Editions du Pont Royal, 1962–1964)–comprises volume 1, *Histoire des Etats-Unis, de 1917 à 1938* (1962), by Maurois; volume 2, *Histoire de l'U.R.S.S., de 1917 à 1929* (1963), by Aragon; volume 3, *Histoire des États-Unis, de 1939 à nos jours* (1963), by Maurois; volume 4, *Histoire de l'U.R.S.S., de 1929 à nos jours* (1963), by Aragon; and volume 5, *Conversations et aperçus* (1964), by Aragon and Maurois; volumes 2 and 3 of original French edition translated by Patrick O'Brian as *A History of the USSR from Lenin to Krushchev* (London: Weidenfeld & Nicolson, 1964; New York: McKay, 1964); Aragon's contributions partially republished as *Histoire de l'U.R.S.S.: 1917 à 1960,* 3 volumes (Paris: Union Générale d'Editions, 1972)–comprises volume 1, *Janvier 1917 à janvier 1923;* volume 2, *Janvier 1923 à janvier 1946;* and volume 3, *Janvier 1946 à janvier 1960 et au-delà;*

Le Fou d'Elsa: Poème (Paris: Gallimard, 1963);

Le Voyage de Hollande (Paris: Seghers, 1964); enlarged as *Le Voyage de Hollande et autres poèmes* (Paris: Seghers, 1965);

Il ne m'est Paris que d'Elsa: Anthologie, photographs by Jean Marquis (Paris: Laffont, 1964);

Œuvres romanesques croisées d'Elsa Triolet et Louis Aragon, by Aragon and Elsa Triolet, 42 volumes (Paris: Laffont, 1964–1974)–includes volume 4, revised edition of *Servitude et grandeur des Français: Nouvelles inédites* (1964); and volumes 23–26, revised edition of *Les Communistes: Roman,* 4 volumes (1966–1967);

Les Collages (Paris: Hermann, 1965);

La Mise à mort (Paris: Gallimard, 1965);

L'Art nouveau en Europe, Roger-H. Guerrand; Précédé de: Le Modern Style d'où je suis, par Aragon, by Aragon and Roger H. Guerrand (Paris: Plon, 1965);

Shakespeare, illustrated by Picasso (Paris: Cercle d'Art, 1965); translated by Bernard Frechtman as *Shakespeare Aragon Picasso* (New York: Abrams, 1966);

Elégie à Pablo Neruda, illustrated by André Masson (Paris: Gallimard, 1966);

Blanche ou l'oubli (Paris: Gallimard, 1967);

Aragon, edited by Georges Sadoul (Paris: Seghers, 1967);

Les Chambres: Poème du temps qui ne passe pas (Paris: Editeurs Français Réunis, 1969);

Je n'ai jamais appris a écrire, ou Les Incipit, Les Sentiers de la Création, no. 2 (Geneva: Skira, 1969);

Le Mouvement perpétuel, précédé de Feu de joie, et suivi de Ecritures automatiques, preface by Alain Jouffroy, Collection Poésie, no. 54 (Paris: Gallimard, 1970);

Henri Matisse: Roman, 2 volumes (Paris: Gallimard, 1971); translated by Jean Stewart as *Henri Matisse: A Novel,* 2 volumes (London: Collins, 1972; New York: Harcourt Brace Jovanovich, 1972);

Théâtre/Roman (Paris: Gallimard, 1974);

L'Œuvre poétique, 15 volumes (Paris: Livre Club Diderot, 1974–1981);

Celui qui dit les choses sans les dire (Paris: Maeght, 1975);

L'Essai Max Ernst (Paris: Editions Georges Visat, 1976);

Le Yaouanc, preface by Jean-Claude Pedrono and Carmen Martinez (Paris: La Pierre d'Angle, 1979);

Chroniques de la pluie et du beau temps, précédés de, Chroniques du bel canto (Paris: Editeurs Français Réunis, 1979);

Cantate à André Masson (Frankfurt, Berlin & Vienna: Propyläen Verlag, 1979);

Le Mentir-vrai (Paris: Gallimard, 1980);

Ecrits sur l'art moderne, preface by Jacques Leenhardt (Paris: Flammarion, 1981);

Les Adieux: Poèmes (Paris: Temps Actuels, 1982); enlarged as *Les Adieux et autres poèmes* (Paris: Temps Actuels, 1983);

La Défense de l'infini: fragments; Les Aventures de Jean-Foutre La Bite, edited by Edouard Ruiz (Paris: Gallimard, 1986); *La Défense de l'infini* revised and enlarged by Lionel Follet as *La Défense de l'infini: Romans* (Paris: Gallimard, 1997);

Pour expliquer ce que j'étais, introduction by Apel-Muller (Paris: Gallimard, 1989);

L'Œuvre poétique, 7 volumes, edited by Ruiz (Paris: Livre Club Diderot, 1989–1990);

Lautréamont et nous (Pin-Balma: Sables, 1992);

Projet d'histoire littéraire contemporaine, edited, with an introduction and notes, by Marc Dachy (Paris: Gallimard, 1994);

Anti-Portrait: Dessins et textes inédits, edited, with an introduction, by Hamid Fouladvind (Paris: Maisonneuve & Larose-Archinbaud, 1997);

Chroniques, edited by Bernard Leuilliot (Paris: Editions Stock, 1998–)—includes *Chroniques: I, 1918–1932.*

Editions and Collections: *Le Crève-coeur,* preface by André Labarthe and Cyril Connolly (London: Edition Horizon–La France Libre, 1942);

Aragon: ou, Les métamorphoses, photographs by Jean-Louis Rabeux, postface by Danièle Sallenave (Paris: Gallimard, 1977);

Choix de poèmes, edited by Michel Apel-Muller (Paris: Temps Actuels, 1983);

Œuvres romanesques complètes, 2 volumes, edited by Daniel Bougnoux, Philippe Forest, and Raphaël Lafhail-Molino (Paris: Gallimard, 1997–2000);

Hourra l'Oural: Poème, preface by Olivier Barbarant (Paris: Stock, 1998);

Les Communistes (février 1939–uin 1940): Roman, edited, with an introduction, by Bernard Leuilliot (Paris: Stock, 1998);

Non, Aragon n'est pas un écrivain engagé!: Textes inconnus ou méconnus, edited, with commentary, by Jean Albertini (Grigny: Editions Paroles d'Aube, 1998);

Le Con d'Irène, preface by Philippe Sollers (Paris: Mercure de France, 2000);

Feu de joie et autres chansons, illustrated by Nathalie Novi (Paris: Gallimard, 2000).

Editions in English: *The Red Front,* translated by E. E. Cummings (Chapel Hill, N.C.: Contempo Publishers, 1933);

Aragon, Poet of the French Resistance, edited by Hannah Josephson and Malcolm Cowley, introduction by Cowley and biographical essays by Peter C. Rhodes and Waldo Frank (New York: Duell, Sloan & Pearce, 1945); republished as *Aragon, Poet of Resurgent France* (London: Pilot, 1946);

Paris Peasant, translated, with an introduction, by Simon Watson Taylor (London: Cape, 1971; Boston: Exact Change, 1994);

The Exploits of a Young Don Juan; &, Irène, by Guillaume Apollinaire and Aragon, translated by Alexis Lykiard (London: Nexus, 1989); *Irène* republished as *Irene's Cunt* (London: Creation Books, 1996).

OTHER: Arthur Rimbaud, *Un Cœur sous une soutane: Intimités d'un séminariste,* preface by Aragon and André Breton (Paris: R. Davis, 1924);

Lewis Carroll, *La Chasse au snark: Une Agonie en huit crises,* translated by Aragon (Chapelle & Réanville: Hours Press, 1928);

Pablo Neruda, *L'Espagne au coeur, hymne à la gloire du peuple en guerre,* translated by Louis Parrot, preface by Aragon (Paris: Denoël, 1938);

Paul Vaillant-Couturier, *Enfance, souvenirs d'enfance et de jeunesse,* preface by Aragon (Paris: Editions Sociales Internationales, 1938);

Jean Cassou as Jean Noir, *33 sonnets composés au secret,* introduction by Aragon as François La Colère (Paris: Editions de Minuit, 1944);

Charles Péguy and Gabriel Péri, *Deux voix françaises: Charles Péguy. Gabriel Péri,* preface by Jean Bruller as Vercors, introduction by Aragon as Le Témoin des martyrs (Paris, 1944);

Daniel Decourdemanche, *Comme je vous en donne l'exemple: Textes de Jacques Decour,* edited by Aragon (Paris: Editions Sociales, 1945);

Alfred Gilbert-Dreyfus, *Gilbert Debrise. Cimetières sans tombeaux,* preface by Aragon (Paris: Bibliothèque Française, 1945);

Petrarch, *Cinq Sonnets de Pétrarque, avec une eauforte de Picasso et les explications du traducteur,* translated by Aragon (Vaucluse: Fontaine, 1947);

"Henri Matisse, ou le peintre français," in *Henri Matisse: Retrospective Exhibition of Paintings, Drawings and Sculpture Organized in Collaboration with the Artist* (Philadelphia: Philadelphia Museum of Art, 1948), pp. 17–23;

Victor Hugo, *Avez-vous lu Victor Hugo? Anthologie poétique commentée,* edited, with commentary, by Aragon (Paris: Editeurs Français Réunis, 1952);

Pierre Daix, *La Dernière forteresse: Roman,* preface by Aragon (Paris: Editeurs Français Réunis, 1954);

Eugène Guillevic, *31 sonnets,* preface by Aragon (Paris: Gallimard, 1954);

Introduction aux littératures soviétiques: Contes et nouvelles, edited, with an introduction, by Aragon (Paris: Gallimard, 1956);

Tchinghiz Aitmatov, *Djamilia,* translated by Aragon and A. Dmitriev (Paris: Editeurs Français Réunis, 1959);

Fernand Léger, *Contrastes,* preface by Aragon (Paris: Au Vent d'Arles, 1959);

Elsa Triolet, *Elsa Triolet: Choisie par Aragon,* edited by Aragon (Paris: Gallimard, 1960);

Andrée Paule Lafont, ed., *Anthologie de la poésie occitane, 1900–1960,* preface by Aragon (Paris: Editeurs Français Réunis, 1962);

Roger Garaudy, *D'un Réalisme sans rivages: Picasso, Saint-John Perse, Kafka,* preface by Aragon (Paris: Plon, 1963);

Giannes Ritsos, *Pierres, Répétitions, Barreaux: Poèmes,* translated by Chrysa Prokopaki, Antoine Vitez, and Gérard Pierrat, preface by Aragon (Paris: Gallimard, 1971);

Jean Ristat, *Le fil(s) perdu; suivi de Le Lit de Nicolas Boileau et de Jules Verne,* postface by Aragon (Paris: Gallimard, 1974).

Louis Aragon is a twentieth-century personification of Dada; he is a writer, poet, and critic who deconstructed the literature and politics of France, giving his Dada-shape to French literature and then projecting that *voix-et-image* (voice-and-image) of "Aragon-France" into his pacts with Surrealism and Communism and throughout the art world. His egalitarian body of work balances the equation "*œuvre=ouvré*" (work=wrought) in that his life's work is open to all readers: non francophone as well as francophone. This condition of author-reader equality is the essence of *Aragonesquerie,* the antithesis of Roland Barthes's assertion in "La Morte d'auteur" (1968; translated by Richard Howard as "The Death of the Author," 1986), that "the birth of the reader must be requited by the death of the Author."

In a literary career that spanned seven decades, Aragon published more than one hundred volumes of writing. More than a dozen additional volumes have appeared since his death, along with eight major full-length critical studies published in 1997, the centenary of his birth, alone; all these works form a corpus of knowledge that has changed the course of literary, artistic, and political history in France.

Louis Marie Alfred Antoine Aragon was born in the Beaux Quartiers arrondissement of Paris on 3 October 1897, to Marguerite Toucas-Massillon and Louis Andrieux Aragon. His twenty-four-year-old mother was single, and his fifty-seven-year-old father was already married. To conceal the circumstances of his birth, his parents arranged for him to be brought up as the adoptive son of his maternal grandmother, Claire Toucas. At the age of fourteen months he was reunited with his parents, though he was brought up to believe that his mother was his sister, his father was his guardian, and his grandmother was his adoptive mother. In 1899 Aragon's mother, Marguerite, opened a pension in Paris. Louis began reading (Leo Tolstoy and Friedrich Nietzsche) and writing (poetry) even before he started attending Madame Boucher's coeducational private school in 1906 and the Ecole Saint-Pierre in 1907, both at Neuilly. Precocious, he completed his first novel at age nine. In 1912 he went to the Lycée Carnot in Paris, receiving baccalaureate degrees in Latin and the sciences in 1914 and in philosophy in 1915. Three events in the following year changed his life: he enrolled in the Faculté de Médecine de Paris, he met André Breton at Adrienne Monnier's avant-garde bookshop, and his writing came to the attention of Guillaume Apollinaire. When Aragon published his first

Aragon in 1918, while he was serving as a medical orderly in the French army

article, "Alcide ou De l'Esthétique du Saugrenu" (Alcide, or, On the Aesthetic of Saugrenu), on Apollinaire, in the avant-garde journal *Sicoù* (1917); Apollinaire asked him to write a review of his play *Les Mammelles de Tirésias* (The Breasts of Tiresius, 1917), when it was in rehearsals.

In 1917 he was conscripted into the infantry, where he again met up with Breton, who had also been drafted to fight in World War I. The following year Aragon was three times "deconstructed" in the Dada sense: when he finally learned from his mother that his birth was illegitimate (and that she was in fact his mother and not his sister); when he was sent to the front as *un médecin auxiliaire* (an auxiliary doctor, or medical orderly), a deconstructed warrior; and when he was awarded the Croix de Guerre for bravery, a military medal that Dada appropriated as his first literary prize—the upright post of its cross denoting the survivor (the soldier left standing) and the transverse beam representing the lines of poetry that he wrote during the war. In the midst of battle he composed some of the poems that appear in his first collection, *Feu de joie* (Bonfire, 1920), and he began to write his first novel, *Anicet, ou, Le Pan-*

orama (Anicet, or, The Panorama, 1921), and the narrative *Les Aventures de Télémaque* (1922; translated as *The Adventures of Telemachus,* 1988). Aragon served in the military until 1919, taking part in the Allied military occupation of the Rhineland and Saar. In the spring of 1919 Aragon and Breton formed a Dada coterie dedicated to deconstructing traditionalist literature and art. In March 1919 Aragon, Breton, and Philippe Soupault co-edited the first issue of *Littérature,* an antitraditionalist journal that inaugurated the Surrealist movement from the trenches of war and from the hollow of Dada.

After his demobilization in September 1919, and the appearance the following year of his first book, *Feu de joie,* Aragon resumed his medical studies, pondered his literary career, and set out to establish Paris as a kind of off-center center for Dada. The poems in *Feu de joie* are quite intentionally artless—that is, the "antitheses of art"—as in "Le Chien qui parle" (The Talking Dog):

> Pauvres embrasses des rideaux votre affection n'est pas payée de retour. Vous ressemblez à mon chagrin: dès qu'on vous fixe vous devenez vulgaires

> (Poor curtain rings your affection is not paid in return. You resemble my grief: as soon as one stares at you you become vulgar).

This mix of absurdity ("the talking dog" of the title) and punning nonlinearity ("embrasses" [curtain loops] echoes "embrasser" [to kiss] and "retour" can mean either "winding" or "requited," as in *Payer de retour*) is the gist of Dada, marking the course of Aragon's artistic activity at the time.

Throughout 1920 Aragon, Breton, and Soupault joined others in staging Dada events at such venues for *nouveautés* (novelties) in art as the Salon des Indépendants, the Club de Faubourg, the Théâtre de l'Œuvre, the Salle Gaveau, and the Galerie La Cible. Amid the staged scandals of the anti-art art movement—at a show in Cologne in 1920, for example, spectators were provided with hatchets and invited to destroy the exhibits—and prompted by the November 1920 Soviet Congress, held at Tours, Aragon and his associates considered joining the French Communist Party but temporarily abandoned the idea.

The fiction that Aragon had begun working on while serving in the military now began to appear in print: *Anicet, ou, Le Panorama,* a metafictional deconstruction of the novel as a genre and even as a forum for iconoclasm, was published in 1921; and *Les Aventures de Télémaque* appeared in 1922, the same year as James Joyce's novel *Ulysses.* But whereas Joyce Dublinized Homer, Aragon Dadaized him, turning the classical archetype of Ulysses' son, Telemachus, and the narratorial technique of stream

of consciousness into a single lingering Telemachian utterance—the name "Eucharis" enunciated four hundred times: "Eucharis, Eucharis, Eucharis. . . ." As Aragon's antitype, Telemachus is a modern Everyman, but he also represents no one: "Télémaque se dressa sur le bord de la falaise; son vêtement tomba, et le corps nu, jeune et bien portant se précipita subitement dans le vide, tournoya, bolide oiseau mortel, tournoya pour s'abattre, sac d'os fracassés sur les rochers, devant les vagues qui ne sanglotèrent même pas" (Telemachus stood on the edge of the cliff; his clothing dropped; the naked body, young and healthy, suddenly dashed into the void, whirled, a mortal winged projectile, whirled before it crashed, a bag of broken bones, on the rocks, in front of the waves that did not even sob). In January 1922, having failed his second doctoral examination, Aragon decided to withdraw from medical studies and concentrate on his literary career. He started to publish individual short stories, such as "Lorsque tout est fini" (When All Is Ended), published in *Les Ecrits Nouveaux* (January 1922); "Les Paramètres"(Parameters), published in *Nouvelle Revue Française* (1 February 1922); "Asphyxies" (Asphyxiations), published in *Littérature* (1 April 1922); "L'Extra" (The Extra), published in *Nouvelle Revue Française* (1 July 1922); and "Le Grand Tore" (The Large Torus), published in *Littérature* (1 December 1922). These stories were later collected in *Le Libertinage* (1924; translated as *The Libertine,* 1987), a series of narratives, dramatic dialogues, maxims, and Dadaist "minims," such as the song of the clown from the Z. circus in "Asphyxies":

> Non, je ne rentrerai plus à la maison
> Non, je ne rentrerai plus à la maison
> Non, je ne rentrerai plus à la maison
> Non, je ne rentrerai plus à la maison
> Non, je ne rentrerai plus à la maison.

> (No, I won't go home again
> No, I won't go home again
> No, I won't go home again
> No, I won't go home again
> No, I won't go home again).

A holiday in Germany in September and October of 1922 led to Aragon's publishing in Berlin the volume *Paris, la nuit: Les Plaisirs de la capitale, ses bas fonds, ses jardins secrets* (Paris at Night: The Pleasures of the Capital, Its Underworld, Its Secret Gardens, 1923). In March of 1923 he became editor in chief of the weekly *Paris-Journal,* but he stayed in the position only one month, devoting himself instead to his novel *La Défense de l'infini* (The Defense of the Infinite, 1986), which, to rephrase the title of his posthumous work *Pour expliquer ce que j'étais* (To Explain What I Was, 1989), might have been subtitled "pour expliquer ce que je serai" (to explain what I will be) as a

Dadaists in April 1921: Jean Crotti, Georges d'Esparbès, André Breton, Jacques Rigaud, Paul Eluard, Georges
Ribemont-Dessaignes, Benjamin Péret, Théodore Fraenkel, Aragon, Tristan Tzara, and Philippe Soupault

comment on *la vie inédite* (the unpublished life), since the novel, like the human subject, survives only in fragments, as in Aragon's fragment titled "Je te déteste, univers" (I Hate You, Universe). During the summer of 1923 Aragon began exchanging love letters with Denise Lévy, whom he later identified as the model for Bérénice, the heroine of his novel *Aurélien* (1944; translated as *Aurelien*, 1946). *Lettres à Denise* (Letters to Denise, 1994) comprises twenty-one of his letters to her. During the years 1924 and 1925 Aragon worked with Breton and other writers and artists to promote the study and practice of Surrealism in Paris.

By the end of the 1920s Aragon had established himself not only as a poet, novelist, and essayist, but also as a "doctor of Dada," an anarchist "anti-leader" of Surrealism. His 1926 poem cycle, *Le Mouvement perpétuel, poèmes (1920–1924)* (Perpetual Motion: Poems [1920–1924]), was a poetics and a manifesto, enunciating the interface of words and time, much as Malcolm Lowry proposed to do in his projected but unrealized fictional cycle, "The Voyage That Never Ends," to be built around his novels *Under the Volcano* (1947), the posthumously published *Lunar Caustic* (1968), and the unpublished and lost "In Ballast to the White Sea." The poems in *La Grande Gaité* (High Spirits, 1929) and *Persécuté persécuteur* (Persecutor Persecuted, 1931) mark Aragon's literary transition from the anarchism of Dada into what he saw as the deliberateness of Surrealism. He tried to resist the Surrealist tendency toward automatic writing, although some of his slips have been documented in *Le Mouvement perpétuel, précédé de Feu de joie, et suivi de Écritures automatiques* (Perpetual Motion, Preceded by Bonfire, and Followed by Automatic Writ-

ings, 1970). His other novel of the 1920s is *Le Paysan de Paris* (1926), translated by Frederick Brown as *Nightwalker* (1970) and retranslated by Simon Watson Taylor as *Paris Peasant* (1971). Two additional narratives that Aragon composed in the 1920s appeared posthumously: *La Défense de l'infini*, based on fragments of the manuscript that Aragon burned in frustration in 1927, a praxis-aesthetics that complements the poetics of *Le Mouvement perpétuel;* and *Les Aventures de Jean-Foutre La Bite* (The Adventures of Jackass the Prick, 1986), whose plotted surreality supplements that of *Les Aventures de Télémaque.* In between the critical works *Une Vague de rêves* (A Wave of Dreams, 1924) and *La Peinture au défi* (1930; translated as "The Challenge to Painting," 1990), he published the most important work of criticism in his career, *Le Traité du style* (1928; translated as *Treatise on Style*, 1991), which in his view was as incisive as the Netherlands-based De Stijl movement, which sought to create art that took abstractionism to its logical extreme. His treatise is a lasting theoretical statement, which even in his later work he never refuted, as well as a "treaty" between Dada and Surrealism, in which he makes his definitive statement on Surrealist automatism, translated by Alyson Waters as

> There are ways, as shocking as it may seem, to discriminate among surrealist texts. By their power. By their novelty. And like dreams, they must be well written. . . . Writing well is like walking a straight line. But if you stumble, spare me that distressing spectacle. Hide. You should be ashamed.

He states his position in another form in *La Chasse au snark: Une Agonie en huit crises* (1928), his deliberate but surrealizing translation of *The Hunting of the Snark: An Agony in Eight Fits* (1897), by transforming Lewis Carroll's nonsense poem into an Aragonie.

The year 1928 is noteworthy for two other reasons: Aragon experimented with erotic writing, and he met Elsa Triolet, his soul mate and life partner. First published anonymously, the novel *Le Con d'Irène* was inspired partly by Aragon's preoccupation with his lover Nancy Cunard after their romantic relationship had ended. In 1962 the book was republished under the pseudonym of Albert de Routisie; republished (under the same pseudonym) in 1968 as *Irène,* the book was first translated by Lowell Blair in 1969 as *Irene* and was retranslated by Alexis Lykiard in 1989 as *Irène;* Lykiard's unexpurgated translation was republished in 1996 as *Irene's Cunt,* which is a literal translation of the original French title. *Le Con d'Irène* is a surrealist analysis of the body of woman as text, which can be seen as anticipating the *nouveaux romans,* or new novels, of such postmodern writers as different (from each other, and from Aragon) as Alain Robbe-Grillet and Kathy Acker. The narrative's gyneocentric imagery alternates between pornographic figuration-appropriation and pathetic fallacy. In one famous passage Aragon the Surrealist comes closest to acknowledging automatic expression, in his writing and in life generally:

Ce que je pense, naturellement s'exprime. Le langage de chacun avec chacun varie. Moi par exemple je ne pense pas sans écrire, je veux dire qu'écrire est ma méthode de pensée. Le reste du temps, n'écrivant pas, je n'ai qu'un reflet de pensée, une sorte de grimace de moi-même, comme un souvenir de ce que c'est. D'autres s'en remettent à diverses démarches. C'est ainsi que j'envie beaucoup les érotiques, dont l'érotisme est l'expression. Magnifique langage. Ce n'est vraiment pas le mien.

Lykiard translates this famous passage as

What I am thinking naturally expresses itself. Everyone's language differs each from each. I for example do not think without writing, which is to say that writing is my method of thinking. The rest of the time, not writing, I have only a reflection of thought, a sort of grimace of myself, like a memory of what it is. Others rely on diverse procedures. Thus I greatly envy the eroticists, whose eroticism is their expression. Magnificent language. It is not really mine.

This decidedly unerotic (but quotable) passage is perhaps the greatest expression of Aragon's repressed *poétique érotique* (poetic erotic) in the novel. Otherwise, its imagery is either titillating or predatory, depending upon the reader's perspective.

In November 1928 Aragon happened to meet the Russian poet Vladimir Mayakovsky at a Montparnasse café. The next day Mayakovsky introduced him to his sister-in-law, Elsa Triolet, with whom Aragon immediately fell in love, and stayed truly in love for the rest of his life. From then on, Triolet, his soul mate, was the inspiration for all his poetry, all his writing, and even all his political action. His output in the 1930s was an easy balance of poetry, such as *Eclairez votre religion: Aux enfants rouges* (Clarify Your Religion: With the Red Children, 1932) and *Hourra l'Oural* (Hurrah for the Urals, 1934); fiction, such as the novels *Les Cloches de Bâle* (1934; translated as *The Bells of Basel,* 1936) and *Les Beaux Quartiers* (1936; translated as *Residential Quarter,* 1938); criticism, such as *Pour un réalisme socialiste* (For a Socialist Realism, 1935), a collection of lectures delivered from February through June 1935—and his growing love and respect for Elsa. They married in February 1939 in Paris, then traveled to the United States, where they met with President Franklin Delano Roosevelt, who was then soliciting European perspectives on the threat of war.

Aragon had joined the French Communist Party in 1927. His commitment to communism became more intense after he met Triolet, herself a dedicated communist and award-winning novelist. In 1930 the couple traveled to the Soviet Union to attend the Second International Congress of Revolutionary Writers, and Aragon returned determined to combine his art and politics. His provocative poem "Front rouge" (translated as *The Red Front,* 1933), collected in his 1931 book of poetry, *Persécuté persécuteur,* earned him a suspended five-year prison sentence for allegedly inciting troops to mutiny and provocation to murder. During the early 1930s Aragon wrote for French Communist Party publications such as *L'Humanité, Commune,* and *Ce Soir.* His article celebrating the 1939 German-Soviet Nonaggression Pact, "Vive la paix!" (Long Live the Peace), published in the 23 August 1939 issue of *Ce soir,* provoked the French authorities into suspending and then shutting down the newspaper. Threatened by angry French veterans for what were seen as pro-German views, Aragon and Triolet sought refuge in the Chilean embassy on 26 August. There he finished his novel *Les Voyageurs de l'impériale* (The Passengers on the Upper Deck) which was first published in New York in 1941 in an English version translated by Hannah Josephson as *The Century Was Young* (republished in London in 1947 as *Passengers of Destiny*). A partially censored French version was published in December 1942, and the complete text was first published in October 1947.

By the early 1930s Aragon had started his major work of literature, the narrative series *Le Monde réel* (The Real World), a Surrealist vision of middle-class experience in France that is often rightly compared with Honoré de Balzac's *La Comédie humaine* (The Human Comedy, 1842–1846, 1848, 1855) series of the preceding century. *Le Monde réel* comprises the novels *Les Cloches de Bâle; Les Beaux Quartiers; Les Voyageurs de l'impériale; Aurélien;* the six-volume novel *Les Communistes* (The Communists, 1949–1951), which is sometimes published with *L'Homme Communiste* (Communist Man, 1946, 1953); and *La Semaine sainte* (1958; translated as *Holy Week,* 1961). The theoretical center of this series is the critical study, a cross between a communist manifesto and a kind of personal communist coming-out, *Pour un réalisme socialiste,* in which Aragon takes the literary principle of social realism and makes it a socialist principle of anti-bourgeois and post-bourgeois society. His polemical plea anticipates that of Robbe-Grillet in his critical study *Pour un nouveau roman* (1963; translated as *For a New Novel,* 1966). In fact, Aragon's *Le Monde réel* cycle mediates between two great movements in French literature: *La Comédie humaine* and Robbe-Grillet's super-Surrealist *nouveaux romans* of the 1950s and after; for example, *L'Année dernière à Marienbad* (1960; translated as *Last Year at Marienbad,* 1962).

The "real world" sequence began with *Les Cloches de Bâle,* in which Aragon, rather than invoking the formula of the roman à clef, mixes fictional characters (such as Diane de Nettencourt, the heroine of the first part of the novel), with composite renderings of people from his own life (such as Catherine Simonidzé, the heroine of the second part, whose character is drawn from Aragon's recollection of guests at his mother's pension), undisguised historical personages (such as Clara Zetkin, a founder of the German Communist Party and the heroine of the fourth part), and characters who seem to take on lives of their own (such as Diane, who appears in other novels in *Le Monde réel*). *Les Cloches de Bâle* might have been subtitled (anticipating the title of Luis Buñuel's 1972 motion picture) "Le Charme *in*discret de la Bourgeoisie" (the *in*discreet charm of the middle class) because it is an attack on middle-class values, particularly as they affect women. Through the story of Diane, a courtesan whose only opportunities for power are through her relationships with men, Aragon shows the oppression of French women within a class system that cannot be overcome by even the deconstructive spirit of Dada; only the classless system of communism seems capable of destroying it. In contrast to Diane, Catherine Simonidzé manages to step outside the bourgeoisie and outside patriarchy, largely through the influence of Clara Zetkin and the workers and anarchists with whom she associates in class struggle. Exploiting socialist realism, and with a nod toward the surreal, Aragon shows how a fictional character can be inspired by an historical per-

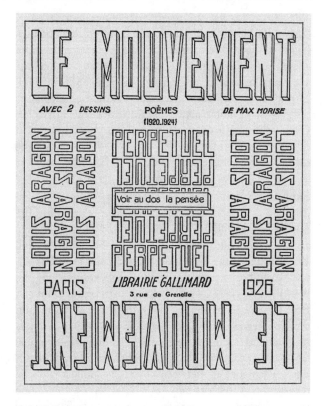

Title page for the collection of poems Aragon wrote at the height of his involvement with the Dada movement (from Le Mouvement perpétuel précédé de Feu de joie et suivi de Ecritures automatiques, *1970; Thomas Cooper Library, University of South Carolina)*

sonage. His optimistic conclusion, with Catherine set to follow the path of "la militante allemande" (the militant German woman) Clara Zetkin–"La femme des temps modernes est née, et c'est elle que je chante" ("The woman of modern times is born, and it is of her that I sing")–is not merely literary convention or romantic posturing, but an exemplar of political pragmatism, a call to action or arms.

In *Les Beaux Quartiers* Aragon fictionalizes the Parisian arrondissement in which he was born through the story of his protagonists, the brothers Armand and Edmond Barbentine, and gives the story polemical overtones by accusing the French class hierarchy of violating the natural law of *égalité* (equality). Class division separates the brothers, as Armand studies for the priesthood and Edmond studies to be a doctor. A wavy line (the river Seine) runs through Paris, demarking the class divisions of *rive droite* (right bank: Paris and right-wing politics) and *rive gauche* (left bank: Beaux Quartiers and left-wing politics), and thus forming a capitalist theater of war that serves as a forum for or backdrop to Aragon's ideas on the Communist movement. Aragon received the Prix Renaudot for this novel.

Les Voyageurs de l'impériale continues Aragon's discussion of the indiscretions of the bourgeoisie. The protagonist, Pierre Mercadier, is *une pierre du mercantilisme* (a rock of profiteering), who fragments when he shifts his allegiance from a capitalist meritocracy to an individualist plutocracy in which speculation is the highest observance. He gambles away his entire fortune in Monte Carlo, then returns to Paris to earn his living as a schoolteacher and to die an obscure death under the care of a brothel keeper.

The fourth volume of *Le Monde réel* is *Aurélien.* Published in 1944, it is a love story set against the backdrop of World War I, on the one hand, marking the end of civilization and so, too, the end of courtly love and other chivalrous traditions, and the Spanish Civil War, on the other hand, signaling a conflict of fascism and republicanism wider in its implications than the war in Spain itself. The barrier between the lovers, Bérénice and Aurélien, is absolutism: she seeks in him the apotheosis of transcendental love, whereas he is unable to concede that love, which for him is inseparable from existence, is anything but a distraction from absurdity. This conflict between love and politics can be resolved only theoretically, as in Aragon's two-volume essay collection, *L'Homme Communiste,* and in his six-volume documentary narrative, *Les Communistes,* a precursor of the cursor-driven metafiction of the postmodern period in the form of a multigeneric catalogue of Communist characters who debate the political and diplomatic ties of France and Russia and the nature of the class struggle of which war is a prelude:

> Armand regarde les hommes autour de lui, leurs figures graves, leurs traits émaciés, les marques de la vie. . . . Il sourit. Il se sentait à l'abri. Il avait confiance dans ces hommes. Oui, la guerre a changé de caractère. Maintenant, il s'agit *seulement* de créer l'enthousiasme pour la guerre nouvelle qui va commencer. Notre guerre à nous. Celle du peuple.

> (Armand looks at the men round him, their grave faces, their wasted features, the scars of life. . . . He smiles. He felt sheltered. He had faith in these men. Yes, the war had changed its character. Now, it's *only* a matter of creating enthusiasm for the new war which is about to begin. Our own war. The people's war).

This passage encapsulates Aragon's own transition from Dadaist to Surrealist to Communist. His struggle for artistic expression had become the struggle of all peoples oppressed by classism and capitalist materialism.

Le Monde réel takes French history through World War II into a theoretically postcapitalist age. In the final volume in the series, *La Semaine sainte,* published in 1958 and translated by Haakon Chevalier in 1961 as *Holy Week,* Aragon traces the pattern of French history through a flashback to Easter 1815, and the passionate concentration of events—a kind of secular Passiontide—between Napoleon's escape from the exile of his insular sovereignty on Elba and his hastily mounted assault on Paris to his eventual defeat at Waterloo by the Allied commanders Arthur Wellesley, first Duke of Wellington, and Gebhard Leberecht von Blücher, Prince of Wahlstatt. Of more immediate relevance to Aragon historically and narratorially is Louis XVIII's abandonment of Paris under the threat of Napoleon's attack, which event he focalizes through his protagonist, Théodore Géricault, a portrait-painter of the common people, the future proletariat, based on the painter who used ordinary people as models in his art. As a witness to historical spectacle, Géricault is both a spectator and, within the Christian paradigm of the novel, a martyr. Aragon concludes *Le Monde réel* by expressing his hope that post–World War II France will recover as it did after the Napoleonic Wars.

In 1958 his reasons for optimism were greater than during the war itself. Aragon was mobilized 3 September 1939, shortly after his inflammatory article on the Soviet-German Nonaggression Pact had appeared in *Ce Soir.* He was at first sent to the 220th Régiment Régional de Travailleurs, a labor battalion to which politically suspect individuals—communists, anarchists, White Russians, fascists, and so on—were assigned. On 25 February 1940 Aragon was put in charge of a unit of stretcher bearers attached to the 3rd Division Légère Mécanique, a newly created armored division. His division was stationed near the Belgian border when the German invasion of France began in May 1940. Aragon was mentioned in dispatches for his actions in treating and evacuating wounded soldiers during the Allied retreat to Dunkirk. He had the page proofs of *Les Voyageurs de l'impériale* in his rucksack, which he managed to keep with him despite it being "Un poids bien encombrant" (a quite cumbersome weight), as he wrote Jean Paulhoun in a letter dated 6 November 1940. Aragon's unit was evacuated to England on 1 June 1940, but it soon returned to France, landing in Brest. Captured by the Germans in Angoulême, Aragon led a daring escape, managing to get thirty men in six vehicles to freedom on 20 June 1940. A few days later, Aragon volunteered to rescue several wounded men who were pinned down by enemy fire. For this action, which took place on 22 June 1940—the same day that France capitulated to Germany—Aragon was subsequently awarded a second Croix de Guerre (with palm) as well as the Medaille Militairé.

Demobilized at the end of July 1940, Aragon rejoined Triolet in the unoccupied section of France

Page from the manuscript for Aragon's 1936 novel, Les Beaux Quartiers *(translated as* Residential Quarter, *1938), about two Parisian brothers (Bibliothèque Nationale, Paris)*

Cover of the 1975 paperback edition of Aragon's 1964 book of poems praising his wife, Elsa Triolet (Thomas Cooper Library, University of South Carolina)

and began working for the resistance, writing pamphlets, editorials, and other works for the Maquis, as well as editing the clandestine periodicals *La Drome en armes* and *Etoiles*. Some of his actions and sentiments in the face of the Nazi occupation are chronicled in his poetry of the period: *La Crève-coeur* (Heartbreak, 1941); *Les Yeux d'Elsa* (Elsa's Eyes, 1942); *Le Musée Grévin* (The Grévin Museum, 1943), published under the pseudonym François la Colère (François the Wrathful); and *La Diane française* (The French Reveille, 1944), all of which simultaneously and paradoxically attest to both the state of a dying world and the poet's undying love for Elsa, who is the raison d'être of all his writing after 1939. In "Nuit de Mai" (translated as "Night in May," 1945), in *Les Yeux d'Elsa*, Aragon reflects on the conjunction of war and night as the coincidence or interpenetration of beings, reducing ontology to an interplay of phonemes and syntax:

Les vivants et les morts se ressemblent s'ils tremblent
Les vivants sont des morts qui dorment dans leurs lits
Cette nuit les vivants sont désensevelis
Et les morts réveillés tremblent et leur ressemblent.

In Rolfe Humphries and Malcolm Cowley's translation in the 1945 anthology *Aragon, Poet of the French Resistance,* these lines are rendered as

The dead resemble the living if they tremble
Asleep in bed, the living are the dead
Tonight the dead men tremble and resemble
The living, who are dead men disinterred.

Between the dead and the living of war is Elsa, the irresistible beloved who is the animus for resisting war, as in a passage from the "Ouverture" (overture) of another poem in *Les Yeux d'Elsa,* "Cantique à Elsa" (Canticle to Elsa):

Je te touche et je vois ton corps et tu respires
Ce ne sont plus les jours de vivre séparés
C'est toi tu vas tu viens et je suis ton empire
   Pour le meilleur et pour le pire
Et jamais tu ne fus si lointaine à mon grés

(I touch you and I see your body and you breathe
These are no longer the days of living apart
It's you you go you come and I am your dominion
   For better, for worse
And never were you so distant in my opinion).

If John Donne had been a Dadaist, a Surrealist, a Communist, and a francophone, he might have expressed his "Valediction: Forbidding Mourning" (1633) in these tropes.

All these writings, along with his participation in the intellectual resistance, were part of his personal war effort. In the years immediately after the war, Aragon devoted himself to writing a variety of nonfictional works. These works fall into several categories: studies of French writers, such as the commentaries in the anthology *Avez-vous lu Victor Hugo?* (Have You Read Victor Hugo? 1952) and the monographs *Hugo, poète réaliste* (Hugo, Realist Poet, 1952) and *La Lumière de Stendhal* (The Light of Stendhal, 1954); works on French and German art, such as *L'Exemple de Courbet* (The Example of Courbet, 1952) and, with Jean Cocteau, *Entretiens sur le Musée de Dresde* (1957; translated as *Conversations on the Dresden Gallery,* 1982); and books on history and politics, such as *La Lumière et la paix* (The Light and the Peace, 1950) and *La Vraie Liberté de la culture, réduire notre train de mort pour accroître notre train de vie* (The True Freedom of Culture, to Reduce Our Way of

Aragon and Triolet in 1967 (photograph by Benichou)

Death to Increase Our Way of Life, 1952). He also collaborated with André Maurois on an historical study of
the United States and the Soviet Union, first published
as the four-volume *Histoire parallèle* (Parallel History,
1962) and republished as the five-volume *Les Deux
Géants: Histoire des Etats-Unis et de l'U.R.S.S., de 1917 à nos
jours* (The Two Giants: History of the United States
and the U.S.S.R. from 1917 to Our Times, 1962–1964).
Aragon's contributions in volumes two and three of
Histoire parallèle were translated by Patrick O'Brian in
1964 as *A History of the USSR from Lenin to Krushchev* and
were republished in French in 1972 as the three-volume
Histoire de l'U.R.S.S.: 1917 à 1960 (History of the
U.S.S.R.: 1917 to 1960).

   Aragon's postwar works did as much as Gaullist
politics to reshape a country disfigured by war. As were
the existentialists Jean-Paul Sartre, Simone de Beauvoir,
and Albert Camus, Aragon was a commanding intellect
of *la France réveillée* (France awakened). One his greatest
accomplishments at the time was to take on the editorship in 1953 of the journal *Les Lettres Françaises,* for

which he had served as a staff writer since 1949. He
continued to serve as editor until 1982. During the
1950s he also worked to strengthen literary alliances
between France and the Soviet Union, recording his
theories in the critical study *Littératures soviétiques* (Soviet
Literatures, 1955) and his introduction to the anthology
Introduction aux littératures soviétiques: Contes et nouvelles
(Introduction to Soviet Literatures: Tales and Short
Stories, 1956).

   He published several works on modern painters
and art—such as the two-volume *Henri Matisse: Roman*
(1971; translated as *Henri Matisse: A Novel,* 1972), a profile of the artist whom he had known since 1941; the
critical study *L'Essai Max Ernst* (Essay on Max Ernst,
1976), and *Ecrits sur l'art moderne* (Writings on Modern
Art, 1981)—and even made artists the focus of some of
his poetry, as in *Elegie à Pablo Neruda* (Elegy for Pablo
Neruda, 1966) and *Cantate à André Masson* (Canticle for
André Masson, 1979). Aragon's mature verse is no less
ragged than his earliest Dada poems, but here the edges
of language, image, and ideas seem to have been

formed with a pallet rather than by a tear in the canvas. He continued to offer his paeans to Elsa right up until the end—as it happened—her end, as in *Le Fou d'Elsa* (Elsa's Madman, 1963) and *Il ne m'est Paris que d'Elsa* (There Is Only Elsa's Paris to Me, 1964), both of which cast her in a series of at times cogent, at times rambling, historical and philosophical meditations. When Elsa Triolet died of a heart attack on 16 June 1970, Aragon lost the love of his life, and, in an almost Dadaesque touch, his career began to end.

His last novels, *La Mise à Mort* (The Execution, 1965), *Blanche, ou l'oubli* (Blanche, or Forgetting, 1967), and *Théâtre/Roman* (Theater/Novel, 1974), and his short-story collection *Le Mentir-vrai* (The Lie-Truth, 1980), are, historically speaking, within the *nouveau roman* tradition; and yet they are betrayed by a Surrealist spirit, informed as they are by the *Aragonesquerie* of the 1920s and 1930s, of which Aragon remarks in his *Pour expliquer ce que j'étais:* "Cette période de la vie parisienne a été traversée par cette bande sauvage, aggressive, animée d'un étrange mélange d'humour et de gravité sombre, dont on gardera le souvenir" (This period in Parisian life had been traversed by this wild bunch, aggressive, driven by a strange mixture of humor and of grave seriousness, of which one will guard the memory). The memory of this period, of Dada, Surrealism, Communism, and Elsa, all survive in Louis Aragon's late fiction, poetry, and essays, in his collected works, and in his posthumous publications and in the books written to acknowledge his centenary in 1997. Aragon died peacefully in his sleep during the night of 23 December or early morning of 24 December 1982, after two months of deteriorating health. His death marked *une mise à mort* (a putting to death), not only the "putting" to rest of one of the greatest modern French writers, his final deconstruction into literary categories, in particular Barthes's category of the "dead author," but also the end of a modern art still capable of shocking the audience, the end, in a word, of "Dadaragon."

Letters:

Louis Aragon, *Lettres à Denise,* edited by Pierre Daix (Paris: Maurice Nadeau, 1994);

Aragon, Jean Paulhan, and Elsa Triolet, *"Le Temps traversé": Correspondance 1920–1964,* edited and annotated by Bernard Leuilliot (Paris: Gallimard, 1994).

Interviews:

Francis Crémieux, *Entretiens avec Francis Crémieux* (Paris: Gallimard, 1964);

Dominique Arban, *Aragon parle avec Dominique Arban* (Paris: Seghers, 1968);

Jean Ristat, *Sur Henri Matisse: Entretiens avec Jean Ristat* (Paris: Stock, 1999).

Bibliography:

Crispin Geoghegan, *Louis Aragon: Essai de bibliographie,* 2 volumes (London: Grant & Cutler, 1979).

Biographies:

Pierre Daix, *Aragon, une vie à changer* (Paris: Seuil, 1975);

Daniel Wallard, *Aragon: Un portrait* (Paris: Editions Cercle d'Art, 1979).

References:

Maxwell Adereth, *Aragon: The Resistance Poems: (Le crève-coeur, Les yeux d'Elsa and La Diane française),* Critical Guides to French Texts, no. 43 (London: Grant & Cutler, 1985);

Adereth, *Commitment in Modern French Literature: A Brief Study of "Littérature Engagée" in the Works of Péguy, Aragon, and Sartre* (London: Gollancz, 1967); republished as *Commitment in Modern French Literature: Politics and Society in Péguy, Aragon, and Sartre* (New York: Schocken, 1968);

Adereth, *Elsa Triolet and Louis Aragon: An Introduction to Their Interwoven Lives and Works* (Lewiston, N.Y.: Edwin Mellen Press, 1994);

Anna Balakian, "The Post-Surrealism of Aragon and Eluard," *Yale French Studies,* 2 (1948): 93–102;

Olivier Barbarant, *Aragon: La Mémoire et l'excès* (Seyssel: Champ Valton, 1997);

Lucille F. Becker, *Louis Aragon* (New York: Twayne, 1971);

Becker and Alba della Fazia, "The Versification Techniques of Louis Aragon," *French Review,* 38 (May 1965): 734–743;

John H. Bennett, *Aragon, Londres et la France libre: Réception de l'œuvre en Grande-Bretagne, 1940–1946,* translated by Emile-Jean Dumay, preface by Michel Apel-Muller (Paris: Harmattan, 1998);

Jacqueline Bernard, *Aragon: Le Permanence du Surréalisme dans le cycle du Monde réel* (Paris: José Corti, 1984);

Marc Bertrand and Geneviève Torlay, *Louis Aragon et Marceline Desbordes-Valmore: Essai de prosodie comparée* (Paris: Publications M.B. et G.T., 1997);

Sophie Bibrowska, *Une Mise à mort: L'Itinéraire romanesque d'Aragon* (Paris: Les Lettres Nouvelles, 1972);

Hervé Bismuth and Suzanne Ravis, eds., *Au miroir de l'autre: Les Lieux de l'hétérogénéité dans "Le Fou d'Elsa"* (Aix-en-Provence: Publications de l'Université de Provence, 1997);

Willard Bohn, "Louis Aragon and the Critical Muse," *Romanic Review,* 89 (May 1998): 367–374;

Roger Bordier, "L'Inévitable rendez-vous: Aragon et Hugo," *Europe,* 69 (May 1991): 112–117;

Gavin Bowd and Jeremy Stubbs, eds., *Louis Aragon: Du surréalisme au réalisme socialiste, du Libertinage au Men-*

tir vrai, des Incipit à la postérité (Manchester, U.K.: AURA Publication, 1997);

H. K. Brugmans, "Aragon, résistant, conteur ou poète," *Erasme,* 1 (1946): 210–236;

Dominique Desanti, *Les Aragonautes: Les Cercles du poète disparu* (Paris: Calmann-Lévy, 1997);

Frédéric Ferney, *Aragon: La Seule Façon d'exister* (Paris: Grasset, 1997);

Roger Garaudy, *L'Itinéraire d'Aragon: Du surréalisme au monde réel,* Vocations, no. 10 (Paris: Gallimard, 1961);

André Gavillet, *La Littérature au défi: Aragon surréaliste* (Neuchâtel, Switzerland: La Baconnière, 1957);

Yvette Gindine, *Aragon prosateur surréaliste* (Geneva: Droz, 1966);

Nedim Gürsel, Le Mouvement perpétuel *d'Aragon: De la révolte dadaïste au "Monde réel"* (Paris: Harmattan, 1997);

Jacques Guyaux, "Aragon et son énigme," *Revue Générale,* 132 (August–September 1997): 87–91;

Charles Haroche, *L'Idée de l'amour dans* Le Fou d'Elsa *et l'œuvre d'Aragon* (Paris: Gallimard, 1966);

Mireille Hilsum, Carine Trévisan, and Maryse Vassevière, eds., *Lire Aragon* (Paris: Champion, 2000);

Pierre Hulin, *Elsa et Aragon: Souvenirs croisés* (Paris: Ramsay, 1997);

Alain Huraut, *Louis Aragon, prisonnier politique* (Paris: Ballard, 1970);

Hubert Juin, *Aragon* (Paris: Gallimard, 1960);

Angela Kimyongur, "Nouvelle occupation, nouvelle resistance: Aragon, Poetry and the Cold War," *French Cultural Studies,* 8 (February 1997): 93–102;

Raphaël Lafhail-Molino, *Paysages urbains dans "Les beaux quartiers" d'Aragon: Pour une théorie de la description dans le roman,* preface by Jean-Bernard Racine (Bern & New York: Peter Lang, 1997);

Jacques Lardoux, *Deux essais sur l'éternité poétique: Les anachronismes dans* Le fou d'Elsa *et* Les Anthologies de la poésie française de 1940 à 1960 (Paris: Prométhée, 1991);

Bernard Lecherbonnier, *Aragon,* Univers des lettres, no. 805 (Paris: Bordas, 1971);

Lecherbonnier, ed., *Critiques de notre temps et Aragon* (Paris: Garnier, 1976);

Lecherbonnier, *Le Cycle d'Elsa, Aragon: Analyse critique,* Le Profil d'une œuvre, no. 48 (Paris: Hatier, 1974);

Pierre de Lescure, *Aragon, romancier* (Paris: Gallimard, 1960);

Jacqueline Lévi-Valensi, *Aragon romancier: D'Anicet à Aurélien* (Paris: Société d'Edition d'Enseignement Supérieur, 1989);

Jack Lindsay, *Meetings with Poets: Memories of Dylan Thomas, Edith Sitwell, Louis Aragon, Paul Eluard, Tristan Tzara* (London: Muller, 1968; New York: Ungar, 1969);

Henri Mitterand, "Marques et masques du lecteur dans 'Les Cloches de Bale' de Louis Aragon," *Revue Canadienne de Littérature Comparée,* 19 (March–June 1992): 281–294;

Paul Morelle, *Un Nouveau Cadavre: Aragon* (Paris: La Table Ronde, 1984);

Alain Nicolas and Henriette Zoughebi, eds., *Aragon,* Le Mouvement perpétuel (Paris: Stock, 1997);

Nathalie Piégay-Gros, *L'Esthétique d'Aragon* (Paris: Société d'Edition d'Enseignement Supérieur, 1997);

Georges Raillard, *Aragon,* Classiques du XXe siécle, no. 67 (Paris: Editions Universitaires, 1964);

Ravis, ed., *Aurélien, ou, L'écriture indirecte* (Paris: Champion, 1988);

Léon Roudiez, "The Case of Louis Aragon and Surrealism," *French Review,* 26 (December 1952): 96–104;

Claude Roy, *Aragon: Une étude,* Poètes d'aujourd'hui, no. 2 (Paris: Seghers, 1945);

Valère Staraselski, *Aragon: La Liaison délibérée, faits et textes* (Paris: Harmattan, 1995);

Staraselski, *Aragon l'inclassable, essai littéraire: Lire Aragon à partir de* La Mise à Mort *et de* Théâtre/Roman (Paris: Harmattan, 1997);

Jean Sur, *Aragon: Le Réalisme de l'amour* (Paris: Centurion, 1966);

François Taillandier, *Aragon, 1897–1982: "Quel est celui qu'on prend pour moi"* (Paris: Fayard, 1997);

Carine Trévisar, *Aurélien d'Aragon: Un "nouveau mal du siècle"* (Paris: Diffusion Les Belles Lettres, 1996);

Maryse Vassevière, *Aragon romancier intertextuel, ou, Les pas de l'étranger* (Paris: Harmattan, 1998);

Jean-Marie Viprey, *Espaces d'Aurélien: Le réalisme poétique au risque du patriotisme,* Annales Littéraires de l'Université de Besançon, no. 538 (Paris: Diffusion Les Belles Lettres, 1994);

Marie-Noelle Wucher, "De l'influence d'une legende: Majnun Layla et 'Le Fou d'Elsa,'" *Europe,* 69 (May 1991): 91–96.

Papers:

The largest collection of Louis Aragon's early manuscripts and correspondence is in the Fonds Jacques Doucet at the Bibliothèque Sainte-Geneviève, Paris; most of his later manuscripts are at the Centre National de la Recherche Scientifique, Paris.

Antonin Artaud

(4 September 1896 – 4 March 1948)

Adrian Morfee
Université Lumière Lyon 2

BOOKS: *Tric Trac du ciel,* illustrated by Elie Lascaux (Paris: Galerie Simon, 1923);

L'Ombilic des Limbes (Paris: Editions de la Nouvelle Revue Française, 1925);

Le Pèse-Nerfs (Paris, 1925); enlarged as *Le Pèse-Nerfs, suivi des Fragments d'un Journal d'Enfer,* Collection Critique, no. 5 (Marseilles: Cahiers du Sud, 1927);

Correspondance avec Jacques Rivière (Paris: Editions de la Nouvelle Revue Française, 1927);

A la grande nuit, ou Le Bluff surréaliste (Paris: Antonin Artaud, 1927);

L'Art et la Mort (Paris: A l'Enseigne des Trois Magots/ Denoël, 1929);

Le Théâtre Alfred Jarry et l'Hostilité Publique, by Artaud and Roger Vitrac (Paris, 1930);

Le Moine de M. G. Lewis, raconté par Antonin Artaud (Paris: Denoël & Steele, 1931);

Héliogabale ou L'Anarchiste couronné, illustrated by André Derain (Paris: Denoël & Steele, 1934);

Les Nouvelles Révélations de l'Être, as Le Révélé (Paris: Denoël, 1937);

Le Théâtre et son double (Paris: Gallimard, 1938); translated by Mary Caroline Richards as *The Theater and Its Double* (New York: Grove, 1958);

Revolte contre la poésie (Paris, 1944);

D'un voyage au pays des Tarahumaras, Collection L'Age d'Or, no. 9 (Paris: Editions Fontaine, 1945); enlarged as *Les Tarahumaras* (Décines, Isère: L'Arbalète, 1955; revised edition, Paris: Gallimard, 1974); translated by Helen Weaver as *The Peyote Dance* (New York: Farrar, Straus & Giroux, 1976);

Lettres de Rodez (Paris: Editions G.L.M., 1946);

Xylophone contre la grande presse et son petit public, by Artaud and Henri Pichette (Paris: Impremerie Davy, 1946);

Artaud le Mômo (Paris: Bordas, 1947); translated by Clayton Eshleman and Norman Glass as *Artaud the Momo* (Santa Barbara, Cal.: Black Sparrow Press, 1976);

Van Gogh, le suicidé de la société (Paris: K Editeur, 1947); translated as "Van Gogh: The Man Suicided by Society," in *The Trembling Lamb: Artaud, Carl Solomon, Leroi Jones,* edited by John Fles (New York: Phoenix Book Shop, 1959);

Ci-gît, précédé de La Culture indienne (Paris: K Editeur, 1947);

Pour en finir avec le jugement de dieu, émission radiophonique enregistrée le 28 novembre 1947 (Paris: K Editeur, 1948); translated by Guy Wernham as *To Have Done with the Judgment of God: Words for Radio Dated Nov. 28, 1947* (San Francisco: Bern Porter, 1956);

Lettre contre la Cabbale: Adressé à Jacques Prevel (Paris: Haumont, 1949);

Supplément aux Lettres de Rodez, suivi de Coleridge le traitre (Paris: Editions G.L.M., 1949);

Vie et Mort de Satan le Feu, suivi de Textes Mexicains pour un Nouveau Mythe, preface by Serge Berna (Paris: Editions Arcanes, 1953); translated by Alastair Hamilton and Victor Corti as *The Death of Satan, and Other Mystical Writings* (London: Calder & Boyars, 1974);

Galapagos: Les Iles du bout du monde, illustrated by Max Ernst (Paris: Broder, 1955);

Œuvres complètes: Antonin Artaud, edited by Paule Thévenin (Paris: Gallimard, 1956–)–includes volume 1, *Préambule. Correspondance avec Jacques Rivière. L'Ombilic des limbes. Le Pèse-nerfs. L'Art et la mort. Textes et poèmes inédits* (1956); revised and enlarged, in two volumes, as *Préambule; Adresse au pape; Adresse au dalaï-lama; Correspondance avec Jacques Rivière; L'Ombilic des limbes; Le Pèse-nerfs; suivi des Fragments d'un journal d'enfer; L'Art et la mort; Premiers poèmes, 1913–1923; Premières proses; Tric trac du ciel; Bilboquet; Poèmes, 1924–1935* and *Textes surréalistes; Lettres* (1970; revised and enlarged, 1976; revised and enlarged, 1984); volume 2 (1961; revised and enlarged, 1980); volume 3, *Scenari. A propos du cinéma. Lettres. Interviews* (1961; revised and enlarged, 1978); volume 4, *Le Théâtre et son double, Le Théâtre de Séraphin, Les Cenci* (1964; revised and enlarged, 1978); volume 5, *Autour du "Théâtre et son double" et des "Cenci"* (1964; revised and enlarged, 1979); volume 6, *Le Moine de Lewis raconté par Antonin Artaud* (1966; revised and enlarged, 1982); volume 7, *Héliogabale ou l'Anarchiste couronné; Les Nouvelles révélations de l'être* (1967; revised and enlarged, 1982); volume 8, *De "Quelques problèmes d'actualité" aux "Messages révolutionnaires"; Lettres du Mexique* (1971; revised and enlarged, 1980); volume 9, *Les Tarahumaras; Lettres de Rodez* (1971; revised and enlarged, 1979); volume 10, *Lettres écrites de Rodez: 1943–1944* (1974); volume 11, *Lettres écrites de Rodez: 1945–1946* (1974); volume 12, *Artaud le Mômo; Ci-gît; précédé de La Culture indienne* (1974); volume 13, *Van Gogh, le suicidé de la société; Pour en finir avec le jugement de dieu; (suivi de) Le Théâtre de la cruauté; Lettres à propos de "Pour en finir avec le jugement de dieu"* (1974); volume 14, *Suppôts et suppliciations,* 2 parts (1978); volume 15, *Cahiers de Rodez: Février–avril 1945* (1981); volume 16, *Cahiers de Rodez: Mai–juin 1945* (1981); volume 17, *Cahiers de Rodez: Juillet–août 1945* (1982); volume 18, *Cahiers de Rodez: Septembre–novembre 1945* (1983); volume 19, *Cahiers de Rodez: Décembre 1945–janvier 1946* (1984); volume 20, *Cahiers de Rodez: Février–mars 1946* (1984); volume 21, *Cahiers de Rodez: Avril–25 mai 1946* (1985); volume 22, *Cahiers du retour à Paris: 26 mai–juillet 1946* (1986); volume 23, *Cahiers du retour à Paris: Août–septembre 1946* (1987); volume 24, *Cahiers du retour à Paris: Octobre–novembre 1946* (1988); volume 25, *Cahiers du retour à Paris: Décembre 1946–janvier 1947* (1990); volume 26, *Histoire vécue d'Artaud-Mômo: Tête-à-tête* (1994);

Autre chose que de l'enfant beau, illustrated by Pablo Picasso (Paris: Broder, 1957);

Voici un endroit (Alès: Editions P.A.B., 1958);

México, Spanish version, edited, with an introduction and notes, by Luis Cardoza y Aragón (Mexico City: Universidad Nacional Autónoma de México, 1962); enlarged French version published as *Messages Révolutionnaires* (Paris: Gallimard, 1979);

Antonin Artaud: 1896–1948, dessins, Cahiers de l'Abbaye Sainte-Croix, no. 37 (Sables d'Olonne, France: Musée de l'Abbaye Sainte-Croix, 1980);

Antonin Artaud: Dessins (Paris: Editions du Centre Georges-Pompidou, 1987);

L'Arve et l'aume; suivi de 24 lettres à Marc Barbezat (Décines Isère: L'Arbalète, 1989);

Antonin Artaud: Œuvres sur papier (Marseilles: Musées de Marseille / Paris: Réunion des Musées Nationaux, 1995).

Edition: *Van Gogh, le suicidé de la société,* deluxe illustrated edition (Paris: Gallimard, 1990).

Editions in English: *Antonin Artaud Anthology,* translated by Bernard Brechtman and others, edited by Jack Hirschman (San Francisco: City Lights Books, 1965);

Collected Works, 4 volumes, translated by Victor Corti (London: Calder & Boyars, 1968–1974)–volume 1 (1968) includes "Umbilical Limbo," "Nerve Scales," "Art and Death," and "Cup and Ball";

The Cenci, translated by Simon Watson-Taylor (London: Calder & Boyars, 1969; New York: Grove, 1970);

The Theater and Its Double: Essays, translated by Corti (London: Calder & Boyars, 1970);

To Have Done with the Judgment of God, translated by Clayton Eshleman and Norman Glass (Los Angeles: Black Sparrow Press, 1975);

Antonin Artaud: Selected Writings, translated by Helen Weaver, edited, with an introduction, by Susan Sontag (New York: Farrar, Straus & Giroux, 1976)–includes "Correspondence with Jacques Rivière," "Fragments of a Diary from Hell," and "Situation of the Flesh";

Antonin Artaud: Four Texts, translations by Eshleman and Glass (Los Angeles: Panjandrum Books, 1982)–comprises "To Georges Le Breton (Draft of a Letter)," "Artaud the Mômo," "To Have Done with the Judgment of God," and "The Theater of Cruelty and an Open Letter to the Reverend Father Laval";

Artaud on Theatre, translated and edited by Claude Schumacher (London: Methuen Drama, 1989; revised and enlarged, edited and translated by Schumacher and Brian Singleton, 2001);

Watchfiends and Rack Screams: Works from the Final Period, edited and translated by Eshleman and Bernard Bador (Boston: Exact Change, 1995).

PLAY PRODUCTIONS: *Ventre Brûlé ou La Mère Folle,* Paris, Théâtre Alfred Jarry, 1 June 1927;

Les Cenci, adaptation of Percy Bysshe Shelley's *The Cenci,* Paris, Théâtre de la Cruauté, May 1935.

PRODUCED SCRIPT: *La Coquille et le Clergyman,* motion picture, 1927.

SELECTED PERIODICAL PUBLICATIONS–
UNCOLLECTED: "Lettre (à Adamov) et Fragments," *L'Arche,* 16 (June 1946): 38–40;

"J'ai depuis trente ans une chose capitale à dire," *Combat* (1 November 1947): 2;

"La magre à la condition la même et magre à l'inconditionné," *84,* no. 1 (1947): 1–3;

"Les malades et les médecins," *Quatre Vents,* no. 8 (1947);

"Paris-Varsovie," *84,* nos. 3–4 (1948): 54–56; revised as "Je hais et abjecte en lâche," *84,* nos. 8–9 (1949): 278–328;

"Les pensées ne passent pas de l'une à l'autre . . . ," "Les êtres ne sortent pas dans le jour extérieur . . . ," "Le corps est le corps . . . ," "J'étais vivant . . . ," "L'endroit où l'on souffre . . . ," "Lettre à Paule Thévenin du 1er septembre 1947," "L'être a des états innombrables . . . ," "Je n'admets pas . . . ," "Il n'y a pas de plein . . . ," "Et si je parle de remise en cause du jugement dernier . . . ," "C'est moi / l'Homme . . . ," "Où vais-je à l'infini? . . . ," "En guise de / choix . . . ," "Il fait très froid . . . ," "Oui il y a encore . . . ," "Ce matin . . . ," "Il faudra que je retrouve . . . ," "Y-a temimazza," "Faites le mal . . . ," "Il n'est pas possible à la fin . . . ," "La question qui / compte . . . ," "J'arme mon bras droit . . . ," *84,* nos. 5–6 (1948);

"Le visage humain," *Mercure de France,* no. 1017 (May 1948): 98–102;

"Main d'ouvrier et Main de singe," "Lettres (à Maurice Saillet)," "Lettre (à Adrienne Monnier)," "Il fallait d'abord avoir envie de vivre," *K,* nos. 1–2 (June 1948): 3–5, 108–114, 115–117, 128–131;

"Aliéner l'acteur," "Le Théâtre et la science," *L'Arbalète,* no. 13 (Summer 1948): 7–14;

"C'est qu'un jour . . . ," "Je suis l'inerte . . . ," "L'erreur est dans le fait . . . ," *84,* nos. 10–11 (1949): 404–408;

"Je n'ai jamais rien étudié . . . ," "Dépendre corps; l'amour unique," *84,* no. 16 (December 1950): 11–18, 20;

"L'éperon malicieux," "Le double cheval," *Botteghe Oscure,* no. 8 (1952): 25–30;

"Trois textes (écrits pour être lus à la galerie Pierre)," *Le Disque Vert,* no. 4 (November–December 1953): 37–49;

"Chiote à l'esprit," *Tel Quel,* no. 3 (Autumn 1960): 3–8;

"Ainsi donc la question," *Tel Quel,* no. 30 (Summer 1967): 12–22;

"Il y a dans la magie . . . ," *Tel Quel,* no. 35 (Autumn 1968): 90–95;

"L'amour est un arbre . . . ," *Tel Quel,* no. 39 (Autumn 1969);

"Notes pour une 'Lettre aux Balinais,'" *Tel Quel,* no. 46 (Summer 1971): 10–34;

"Dix ans que le langage est parti . . . ," *Luna-Park,* no. 5 (1979): 7–10;

"Moi, je vous dis . . . ," *Obsidiane,* no. 5 (1979): 8–10;

"La force du Mexique," *Nouvelle Revue Française,* no. 345 (August 1982): 3–7;

"Lorsque je tire sur un être . . . ," *TXT,* no. 28 (1991): 5–9.

When Antonin Artaud died of cancer in 1948 at the age of fifty-one, he was a marginal figure in the French artistic world. A minor motion-picture actor and founder of two short-lived avant-garde theater companies, Artaud was scarcely known as a writer other than to those familiar with the Surrealist movement. Since his death he has become one of the cultural legends of the twentieth century and is remembered for having changed the course of Western theater. His greatest significance, however, lies in the displacement effected by his poetic writing of commonly held ideas about literature. All his literary production, and especially his late writing, severely disrupts the limits of the modernist artistic and conceptual tradition.

The significance of Artaud's writings was long largely unrecognized, mostly because his name has been entangled with the clichés of literary madman and *poète maudit* (accursed poet). Ill-informed opinion still confines him to the role of last in a great lineage of failed, self-destructive geniuses. His violently blasphemous later writings were banned, and *Suppôts et suppliciations* (Henchmen and Torturings), his summative late work, went unpublished for thirty years, appearing only in 1978 as volume fourteen (two parts) of *Œuvres complètes: Antonin Artaud* (Complete Works: Antonin Artaud, 1956–). In the 1960s his notoriety spread beyond France with anglophone countercultural movements feting him as a drug user, internee, and genius schizophrenic who had seen with unparalleled vision through the straitjackets of rationality and decried man's imprisonment within socially constituted norms. At the same time he was notably championed by several important post-structuralist thinkers (including Jacques Derrida and Julia Kristeva), who applauded the challenges his work posed to the fundamental categories underpinning the orthodoxies of Western thought. Along with Georges Bataille and Friedrich Nietzsche he was cited as one of a select band whose writings were saturated in a radical and corrosive negativity that modernism could not contain. His work was said to necessitate a rethinking of the linguistic subject. And certainly all Artaud's work is a response to the idea that "language speaks us"–that human beings use a preexisting linguistic structure, one that serves as a repository of cultural meaning and thus determines the social world and individual identity. Discussion of Artaud's work has since been inseparable from its interrogation by post-structuralist theory.

Artaud is most widely known for his seminal collection of essays, *Le Théâtre et son double* (1938; translated as *The Theater and its Double,* 1958), which sets out a vision of a theatrical practice revelatory of primal universal forces–a "Théâtre de la cruauté" (Theatre of Cruelty), as he called it. Artaud's dramaturgical writings are generally recognized as among the most fertile and vigorous influences on twentieth-century Western theater, which he condemns for its reliance on the text and on conventions of plot and character. He is also remembered, though to a lesser extent, for a piece that originally appeared in *Nouvelle Revue Française* in 1924, *Correspondance avec Jacques Rivière* (1927; translated as "Correspondence with Jacques Rivière," 1968), one of the definitive modernist discussions of a favored topic, literature and silence.

But Artaud wrote many other texts in a variety of modes, including letters, notes, essays, prose, and prose poetry. His writing resists categorization into traditional genres and fuses modes; the most prominent forms are the open-letter-essay-poem of Artaud's early years and the poetic-fantastic-metaphysical-diatribe of his later years, both highly rhetoricized. Artaud frequently incorporated letters into his works, destabilizing the relationship of art to life. The most striking thing about his writing is its difficulty. It is violent, imprecatory, and short-winded. His poetic texts are typically only a page or so long. His writing is so unusually fragmented that it is generally artificial to differentiate texts intended for publication from jottings originally meant only for his own reading.

Artaud in Marseilles, 1918

There are three phases to Artaud's literary trajectory. The first phase, during which his texts focus on an existential and expressive void, opens on the strong note of *Correspondance avec Jacques Rivière* and runs to *L'Art et la Mort* (1929; translated as "Art and Death," 1968), his final Surrealist collection. The second phase, in which his poetics are transferred to other modes, runs until 1937 and includes his theatrical and cinematic writings, and texts inscribed within ancient, primitive, and esoteric culture–*Héliogabale ou L'Anarchiste couronné* (Helogabalus, or The Crowned Anarchist, 1934), *D'un voyage au pays des Tarahumaras* (1945; translated as *The Peyote Dance,* 1976), and *Les Nouvelles Révélations de l'Être* (New Revelations of Being, 1937), respectively. Here his sense of void generates an increasingly desperate and metaphysical slant. In 1937 Artaud was committed to a mental asylum; he was released in 1946. With his transfer to Rodez asylum in 1943 he returned gradually to writing. The third phase, only fully underway in 1945, includes the Rodez writings and the crescendo of texts of the final years of his life back in Paris, most notably *Artaud le Mômo* (1947; translated as *Artaud the Momo,* 1976), *Pour en finir avec le jugement de dieu, émission radiophonique enregistrée le 28 novembre 1947* (1948; translated as *To Have Done with the Judgment of God: Words for Radio Dated Nov. 28, 1947,* 1956), and *Suppôts et suppliciations.* With the conflagration of these final-phase texts there is a change in mood and register. They are of a different order of conceptual and linguistic extravagance. While his early writing is challenging, his late masterpieces operate in the penumbra of delirium.

Throughout his career Artaud's energies were channeled in the direction of what Camille Dumoulié, a leading Artaud critic, refers to in his 1996 monograph as "automythography." That is not to say Artaud's work is autobiographical. His texts are concerned with a self-writing; however, it is of the first importance to appreciate that his efforts are directed not toward the successful narration of an inner and outer life but toward writing an imagined and more authentic form of self. Initially, this dream of a pure and wholly undetermined self was conducted by way of the aspiration for an all-saying language. By the end of his life Artaud added to this aspiration the idea of an entirely new form of bodily existence and a radically different metaphysical and ontological order. As becomes clear to the reader of the late writings, Artaud's texts are an ongoing recasting of a life story in epic terms, in which the writing is to function not as a representation of what is, as a retelling of Artaud's self, but instead as a magically creative performance eliciting a reconstituted self and universe, which Artaud describes as perpetually on the point of emergence. Artaud's writing is thus situated in a domain particular to him, an interzone between the theorizing of a speculative conceptual system and the writing of a *univers imaginaire* (imaginary universe). Rightly renowned for its extraordinary difficulty, the fantasist late writing, which enthusiastically details God's possession of Artaud's digestive and sexual organs, has been dismissed as rant wallowing in an infantile defiling of the sacred with the abject. But attention given since the 1990s to its signifying processes reveals a trenchant, muscular writing crafting a mythic world; this automythographic space is convulsed as Artaud dismantles and reconstructs its constitutent myths. But this very process of structuration and dissolution is part of Artaud's carnavalesque rewritings of key identity notions and in fact contributes much to its real and surprising aesthetic power.

Antoine Marie Joseph Artaud was born in Marseilles on 4 September 1896 at 15 rue Jardin des Plantes (he later claimed, for abstruse numerological reasons, that it was number 4). His mother, Euphrasie Nalpas, came from the Turkish port of Smyrna (now Izmir), and his father, Antoine-Roi Artaud, a wealthy shipping agent, was frequently absent. The extent of Artaud's identification with the feminine is apparent in the androgynous redistributed anatomies of his late texts and drawings, and in the claims of his final writing to be a matrix that gives birth to a new Artaud. More than one commentator has noted the pronounced Oedipal dimension to Artaud's relations with his mother, whose maiden name he temporarily adopted during his prolonged period of mental instability. His two grandmothers, who were sisters, were strongly present in his childhood and are steady figures in an otherwise fluctuating group that figures prominently in his late productions, his "filles de cœur à naître" (daughters of the heart to be born). Incest and transgressive genealogies are integral to Artaud's texts.

Of the givens of his *état civil* (family background), it is Artaud's name that plays the most important role in his late poetry. The influence of the names Marie and Joseph may be found in the Christic posturing of the poetry, in his claim to be the archetypal victim of the Christian ideological order, and in his parallel counterclaim to be androgynous and the progenitor of a new spiritual elite of "filles de cœur." More generally, his writing may be interpreted as an attempt to accede to the status of self-naming (auto-nomy). The adopted name "Antonin" is doubly diminutive: it is a derivative of "Antoine," and it distinguishes him from his father, Antoine-Roi (a name of great Oedipal resonance). The great drive in his late writing to assume the name Antonin Artaud without thereby losing his autonomy is part of a larger campaign to escape from the linguistic and biological orders. His best-known late work, *Pour en finir avec le jugement de dieu,* collected in volume thirteen of the *Œuvres complètes* (1974), closes on a postscript that asks "Qui suis-je / D'où viens-je / Je suis Antonin Artaud / et que je le dise / comme je sais le dire / immédiatement / vous verrez / mon corps actuel / voler en éclats / et se ramasser / sous dix milles aspects / notoires" (Who am I? / Where do I come from? / I am Antonin Artaud / and let me say this / as I know how to say it / immediately / you will see / my present body / burst into fragments / and remake itself / in ten thousand manifest aspects). After his release from Rodez he felt able to name himself Artaud le Mômo (Marseilles slang for idiot, derived from Momos, the Greek God of raillery): Artaud the self-named idiot-god of a parodic order.

But the intellectual sophistries and sophistication of Artaud's later writing and its challenges to Western thought are worlds apart from his staid upbringing. His was a traditional French Catholic bourgeois childhood, overshadowed by suffering and death, two keynotes of his work. At the age of four he contracted meningitis and subsequently suffered from neuralgia and stammering. He was one of only three to survive out of nine infants, and when he was seven was profoundly affected by the death of a seven-month-old baby sister,

Germaine; in his late poetry he claims her as his spiritual offspring and her name becomes associated with ideas of existential and metaphysical regeneration.

Artaud's school career was unexceptional. He began writing derivative verse at the age of fourteen (using the decadent pseudonym Louis des Attides), but at the age of seventeen, suffering from neurasthenia (depression), he destroyed his writings and withdrew from the *baccalauréat* (school-leaving exam). In 1915 he was sent to a sanatorium outside Marseilles. This visit was the first of a series of private "rest cures." Some biographers see these as having less to do with mental disorders than with quieting the troublesome son of a good family. Apart from a brief interruption in 1916 when Artaud was conscripted into the army–he was discharged after two months, allegedly for sleepwalking–he spent most of the next five years in sanatoriums, in what was the most stable period of his adult life. He spent his time drawing and reading (particularly the works of Arthur Rimbaud, Charles Baudelaire, and Edgar Allan Poe). In 1919 he was prescribed laudanum, precipitating a lifelong addiction to opiates and other drugs. He later claimed–in, for example, "Lettre a Monsieur le Législateur de la loi sur les stupéfiants," published in 1925 in *L'Ombilic des Limbes* (translated as "Umbilical Limbo," 1968)–that society had no right to persecute "non-voluptuous" drug users, for only the individual could gauge his own pain and weigh this discomfort against that of narcotic dependency. Artaud made repeated, brutal attempts at unsupervised detoxification. These early stays in sanatoriums foreshadow the nine-year internment of 1937–1946, and his final two years spent under partial supervision in a convalescence clinic. All in all more than half (sixteen years) of Artaud's adult life was spent in some type of medical institution.

In 1920 the family arranged for the twenty-three-year-old Artaud to go to Paris to attempt an artistic, literary, and theatrical career. He was referred to a leading psychotherapist, Dr. Toulouse, who asked him to edit and write reviews for his artistic and scientific journal, *Demain.* Initially Artaud lodged with the Toulouse family, but he soon began an itinerant life, moving between hotel rooms and friends, sometimes with nowhere to stay. This mode of existence continued until his committal in 1937.

The beginnings to Artaud's writing career were slow and in no way suggested the arrival of a revolutionary figure on the literary scene. He published undistinguished symbolist-inspired poems, and rather better essays, in half a dozen reviews. His first collection of poetry, *Tric trac du ciel* (Backgammon of Heaven), appeared in 1923. The poems are in rhyming stanzas, and Artaud excluded this volume from his plan for his

ANTONIN ARTAUD

Tric Trac du Ciel

ILLUSTRÉ DE GRAVURES SUR BOIS

PAR

ELIE LASCAUX

GALERIE SIMON
29ᵐᵉ Rue d'Astorg (vᴵᴵᴵᵉ)
Près Saint Augustin
PARIS

Title page for Artaud's first collection of poetry, published in 1923 (University of Iowa Library, Iowa City)

Œuvres complètes, though it was in fact included in the second edition of volume one (1970; revised and enlarged, 1976; revised and enlarged again, 1984) In 1923 he also produced *Bilboquet* (translated as "Cup and Ball," 1968), a slim review in pamphlet form that appeared twice and was financed and wholly written by himself; these texts were also collected in the 1970 edition of volume one of his *Œuvres Complètes.* They stand midway between the traditional rhyming stanzas of the earlier poems and the self-analytic poetic fragments developed to the fullness of their power during his alliance with Surrealism.

Over these early years of the 1920s Artaud concentrated his energies on acting. His cousin Louis Nalpas, a successful motion-picture producer, had advised him to acquire stage experience before trying a movie career. For four years Artaud performed with influential adventurous theater companies, first with Lugné-Poë's

Théâtre de l'Œuvre and then with Charles Dullin's L'Atelier, for which he also designed costumes and scenery. His roles were frequently minor, but he attracted attention, and displeasure, by his idiosyncratic gestural style of acting: with L'Atelier, for example, Artaud played Charlemagne and in rehearsals insisted on crawling into the throne room. In the course of his work with L'Atelier, Artaud met a striking Romanian actress called Génica Athanasiou. Artaud himself was fiercely handsome, with strong prominent cheekbones, deep-set dark eyes, luxuriant swept-back hair, and, reputedly, lips stained purple by laudanum. A passionate sexual liaison developed, although Athanasiou was bewildered by Artaud's letters, which analyzed his nervous condition, suffering, and dependency on drugs. She broke off the liaison after six years in 1927. Artaud continued to write to her until 1940, and he tried to locate her after his release from Rodez. His *Lettres à Génica Athanasiou* were published posthumously, in 1969. Artaud is not known to have had any other major sexual relationship.

Over this period André Breton's Surrealist movement was superseding Dadaism. Artaud joined the circle of the painter André Masson and through this connection began attending Breton's gatherings in 1924. In a letter to Madame Toulouse written in October of that year, collected in the supplement to the revised edition of volume one of *Œuvres complètes,* Artaud explains that whereas for others Surrealism was a willed, aestheticized vision, for him it was "le système du monde et de la pensée que je me suis faite depuis toujours"(the worldview and way of thinking I devised for myself from the beginning). He rapidly became a leading figure in Breton's movement, and in 1925 he was nominated director of the Bureau de recherches surréalistes. This prominent role allowed him to introduce his own urgent concerns into the movement. Stephen Barber, in his 1993 biography of Artaud, suggests that his expulsion from the Surrealist movement in 1926 (at the same time as Phillipe Soupault, the co-pioneer of automatic writing) was in large part a result of Breton's disquiet at the guiding force Artaud had become.

Artaud's fiercely provocative, polemical, and iconoclastic writing cut against the rarefied complacency of early Surrealist literary activity. Whereas, prior to its politicization in the late 1920s, the emphasis in Surrealist writing was on a creative liberation from rational orthodoxy and a joyous release of energies, Artaud's writing was one of violent socioreligious invective and channeled hatred against everything he saw as a barrier to freedom. The third edition of the standard-bearing review *La Révolution Surréaliste* (The Surrealist Revolution, 1925), edited by Artaud, includes open letters of virulent insult to the Pope, the rectors of European universities, and the head doctors of asylums (the last two written by Michel Leiris and Robert Desnos respectively, but closely overseen by Artaud). There are two further open letters, to the Dalai Lama and the "Ecoles du Bouddha" (Schools of Buddha), awash with a neophytic admiration for Eastern culture. In versions rewritten in 1946 to head his projected *Œuvres complètes* the invective is as intense as in the early letters against the Western instruments of state; by the end of Artaud's career, culturally specific anger had become generalized existential wrath. These revised versions of the letters were included in the 1970 edition of volume one of the *Œuvres complètes.*

Artaud's greatest discontent was with discursive structures. His first-phase writings, including *Correspondance avec Jacques Rivière; L'Ombilic des Limbes; Le Pèse-Nerfs* (1925; translated as "Nerve Scales," 1968); and *Fragments d'un Journal d'Enfer* (1926; translated as "Fragments of a Diary from Hell," 1976), are powerful accounts of the silences, misdirections, and stallings of linguistic consciousness. Artaud's ideas overlapped extensively with those of fellow poets concurrently elaborating Surrealist philosophies of language: all shared the belief that language is desiccated of suppleness, exactitude, and vital dynamism by rational modes of thought; if it could circumvent these modes, they argued, poetry would acquire so radical and magical a creative potential that it might change reality (an idea Artaud later pushed to unusual extremes). But Artaud's writing diverged sharply from that of canonical Surrealist practitioners in its quickened sense of imminent existential dissolution and the imaginative, self-analytical theorizings this condition provoked. Whereas the poetry of Breton and Louis Aragon celebrates the split within the linguistic subject (the possibility of being aware of one's own consciousness) as introducing a rejuvenating strangeness into experience, Artaud's texts repeatedly rework his sense of linguistic breakdown and self-alienation.

Correspondance avec Jacques Rivière, an exchange of letters slightly predating his involvement with Breton's movement, explores Artaud's acute sense of derealization within discourse. Rivière, the editor of the vanguard *Nouvelle Revue Française,* had turned down some poetry by Artaud. A brief correspondence ensued, and Artaud's five self-analytic letters neglect all questions of poetic practice to reenact the passion of thought endeavoring to think itself. He suggests that an authentic articulation of thought remains tantalizingly beyond his grasp, yet he insists on the value of his writing as testimony to an "effondrement central de l'âme, à une espèce d'érosion, essentielle à la fois et fugace de la pensée" (a central collapse of the soul, to a sort of essential yet fleeting erosion of thought). While such a linguistic and existential vacuum is difficult to discern in his insipid verse offerings, Artaud's exposition of intellectual and linguistic crisis is of a dazzling brilliance and stands as a defining event in the writing of negativity.

Correspondance avec Jacques Rivière presents Artaud's sense of the disjuncture between language and reality as both exemplary of and exceeding a generalized human condition of alienation within discourse. Practitioners of modern literature such as Tristan Tzara or Breton abdicate to language through aesthetic choice; Artaud does so out of necessity, for "Cette inapplication à l'objet qui caractérise la littérature est chez moi une inapplication à la vie. Je puis dire, moi, vraiment, que je ne suis pas au monde, et ce n'est pas une simple attitude d'esprit" (This failure to attend to the object which characterizes literature is in my case a failure to attend to life. I can truly say that I am not in the world, and this is no mere mental stance). He is dispossessed of his thought by an essential flaw in the processes of reflexive, verbalized consciousness, "quelque chose qui détruit ma pensée . . . un quelque chose de furtif qui m'enlève les mots *que j'ai trouvés*" (something which destroys my thought . . . a furtive something which robs me of the words *which I have found*). For Artaud, literature is thus not an aesthetic issue but an ontological and existential one. The authorship and proprietorship of utterance is threatened by the very processes in which it originates. So when Artaud poses the question of the literary existence of his thought, and whether he should content himself with his literary scraps— "raclures de l'âme" (scrapings of the soul) and "déchets de moi-même" (detritus of myself), as he puts it in *Le Pèse-Nerfs*—he is asking whether he should accept existence and write with the flawed grain of subjecthood or whether he should pour his energies into writing against fundamental existential givens and against language. He opts, famously, for writing against.

This discovery that language is necessarily alienating and self-presence impossible in linguistic consciousness—that it speaks him as much as he speaks it—set Artaud's intellectual trajectory. It deflected his energies away from the sustained production of literary texts to a fragmented speculation on a linguistic and existential crisis perceived as the primordial fact of the human condition. *L'Ombilic des Limbes* and *Le Pèse-Nerfs,* Artaud's first significant poetic collections, worry away at this question of language and being. Published within a week of one another, these twin works coincide with Artaud's burst of writing for *La Révolution Surréaliste*. These much-neglected texts, which were collected with other works as "Textes Surréalistes" (Surrealist Texts) in the supplement to volume one of *Œuvres complètes,* are crucial to a proper understanding of Artaud. Their fragmentary

prose texts are jagged shards of artfully frustrated writing barely sustained beyond the status of literary debris.

L'Ombilic des Limbes opens with a brief manifesto declaring the ideal inseparability of text and self and railing against the violence done to the experiential world in its passage into consciousness. This opening sets the tone, and there follow four prose analyses of bodily pain and hiatuses in consciousness (these texts are derived from Artaud's experience of narcotic dependency, but this origin is incidental to their presentation of suffering as a metaphysical phenomenon), three brief verse texts, three polemical open letters (two relating to narcotics), and a Surrealist one-act play of apocalyptic violence and sexuality. *Le Pèse-Nerfs* is composed of eight pairs of texts, a first of one or two paragraphs and a second of a few sentences, and two more-sustained pieces of two and three pages, including the well-known antiliterary manifesto "Toute l'écriture est de la cochonnerie" (All Writing Is Pigshit). Self-analytic studies of pain, of his sense of the insubstantiality of consciousness, and of ontological thinness are counterbalanced by oracular texts invoking a state of plenitude and intense yet fleeting mental pleasure. The collection closes with three letters to Athanasiou, venting Artaud's exasperation at the impossibility of communication. In a second edition of 1927, *Le Pèse-Nerfs* was supplemented by *Fragments d'un Journal d'Enfer,* a bleak homage to Rimbaud composed of texts of greater poetic condensation that directly address the reader with commentary on the failures of consciousness and language.

Artaud's corrosive early writing denies reflexive consciousness its traditional ontological preeminence, promoting in its place his sense of painful fleshly existence. Thus, *Fragments d'un Journal d'Enfer,* however bleak an exposé of the dispersal of the subject, affirms the possibility of a new, bodily-rooted consciousness that would allow for a recuperation of the self and a new order of truth. Similarly, Artaud presents his acute awareness of alienation within language as potentially generative of greater existential authenticity. Together the two lead to the idea of an "esprit dans la chair" (mind in the flesh), as Artaud put it in "Position de la Chair" (translated as "Situation of the Flesh," 1976), a piece first published in *Nouvelle Revue Française* (December 1925) and collected in *Œuvres complètes* as part of "Textes Surréalistes." In the "Textes Surréalistes" Artaud writes repeatedly of a form of rudimentary awareness of the functioning, sentient body-in-the-world, an awareness occurring at a level prior to linguistic self-consciousness and in which the subject would be wholly self-present. However much Artaud's first phase of writing might be concerned with an existential and ontological void and denaturation of experience by discourse, this awareness is revelatory of the loss of an orig-

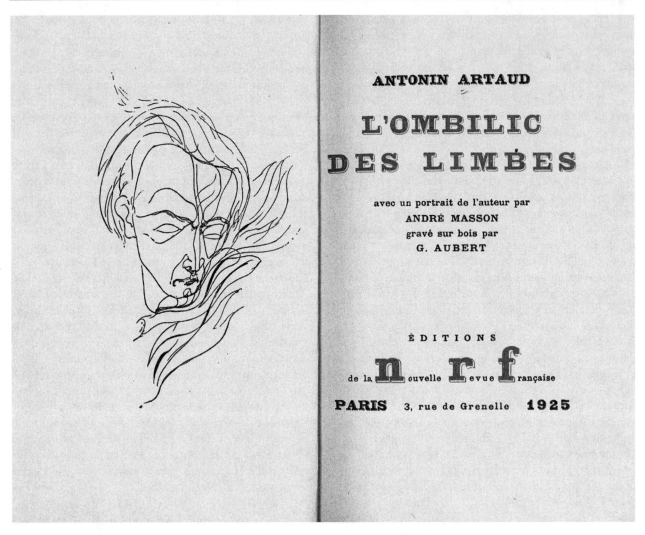

*Frontispiece by André Masson and title page for Artaud's second book, which includes
prose and poetry (Trinity College Library, Hartford, Connecticut)*

inary, prediscursive self-presence. The idea of a
homeopathic inner archaeology of suffering and dissolution, offering a way out of a flawed creation, is common
to all his subsequent writing.

Artaud's early texts are clearly already situated on
the limits of literature. But however direct and apparently guileless a voice these texts articulate they are
sophisticated literary constructs. The reiterated claim to
write beyond the boundaries of literature and against
the limits of language is a rhetoric of antirhetoric. Pre-
tending to reveal Artaud's naked being uncloaked by literary artifice, it actually enacts his self-analyses. Failures
and frustrations are things of which they speak, not
qualities of the texts themselves. Fragmentation is managed. Artaud's texts are the space for a frenzied
mise-en-scène of a rhetoric of failure and suffering, for a
metaphysical performance and not a simple presentation
of experience.

Artaud was expelled from the Surrealist group in
November 1926. The Surrealists could not approve of
his acting in commercial movies (Artaud's main yet
meager source of income) and had hampered his plans
for a Théâtre Alfred Jarry (named after the French
avant-garde writer whose cycle of *Ubu* plays subvert
realistic theater and traditional forms of sense). Artaud,
together with the poet Roger Vitrac (already expelled
by the Surrealists in 1924) and the essayist Raymond
Aron, had envisioned an existentially charged theatrical
activity in which dreamscapes and oneiric thought
modes would be realized on stage. This vision was a
direct transposition of Surrealist ideas to the theater,
but for Breton's movement, now embarking on its alliance with communism, all theater was capitalist. These
frictions culminated in *Au grand jour* (In the Light of
Day, 1927), a pamphlet by Breton, Aragon, Paul Eluard, Benjamin Péret, and Pierre Unik proclaiming the

adherence of the movement to the French Communist Party and denouncing Artaud for his so-called counterrevolutionary obsession with negativity and his supposedly imminent conversion to Catholicism. Artaud's acrimonious retort, privately printed as *A la grande nuit, ou Le Bluff surréaliste* (In the Dark of Night, or the Surrealist Bluff, 1927) and collected with "Textes Surréalistes" in the supplement to the revised volume one of the *Œuvres complètes,* while arguing strongly for the merits of Surrealist textual practice, condemns the movement for contenting itself with being a merely literary experiment when sufficient daring would have made it a regenerative vision of reality.

At stake is a different conception of the true Surrealist revolution. For Breton and his followers, artistic revolution was a prelude to sociopolitical revolution. For Artaud revolution was fundamentally spiritual, and sociopolitical change was wholly irrelevant, for it left the individual's constitution as a culturally constituted, Judeo-Christian, post-Enlightenment humanist subject—as Western man—untouched. All Artaud's writing is informed by the idea of what he calls in *A la grande nuit, ou Le Bluff surréaliste* an "incendie à la base de toute réalité" (a conflagration at the base of all reality) that would "désaxer le fondement actuel des choses" (unbalance the fundamental state of things). Revolution, to be worthy of the name, had to be a quasi-epiphanic inner experience of a radical mental and existential shift: "Que chaque homme ne veuille rien considérer au delà de sa sensibilité profonde, de son moi intime, voilà pour moi le point de vue de la Révolution intégrale" (For me the stance of the integral Revolution is that each individual should consider nothing outside his deep sensibility, his intimate self). As in *Correspondance avec Jacques Rivière,* the arena of true artistic and intellectual revolutionary endeavor is ontological.

Artaud's dismissal from the Surrealist movement coincided with the eclipse of his poetic energies. A third slim volume of poetic prose writings, *L'Art et la Mort,* appeared in 1929. A post hoc collection of texts written during his adherence, it is less powerful and bold in its ideas than the earlier collections and follows more closely Surrealist practice in its tone of fractured lyricism. But the period from 1927 to 1931 was one of fervent experimentation for Artaud, who attempted to translate the principles developed during his alliance with Surrealism to theater and cinema. Although now generally seen as a secondary part of his career, Artaud's period of cinematic activity ran from 1924 to 1935. He worked as actor, critic, and scriptwriter, and he sought to produce motion-picture sets and to direct. Despite his fierce attachment to the cinematic avantgarde, financial imperatives led him to act in all sorts of movies, increasingly of dubious quality, in secondary

and frequently minor parts. He is remembered for his exaggeratedly gestural acting, best displayed in his roles as Marat in Abel Gance's *Napoléon* (1927) and as the monk Jean Massieu in Carl Theodor Dreyer's *La Passion de Jeanne d'Arc* (1928; released in the United States as *The Passion of Joan of Arc,* 1928). Artaud's significant contribution to cinema is his scenario for *La Coquille et le Clergyman* (The Seashell and the Clergyman, 1927), one of the key pieces of Surrealist cinema (Artaud wrote more than a dozen scenarios, but only this one was filmed). The director, Germaine Dulac, minimized the involvement of Artaud, who had wanted to codirect and act. Despite Artaud's dissatisfaction with the motion picture (he enlisted the Surrealists to disrupt the premiere), by 1932 he was claiming that such definitive Surrealist works as Luis Buñuel and Salvador Dali's *Un Chien Andalou* (An Andalusian Dog, 1928) and Jean Cocteau's *Le Sang d'un Poète* (The Blood of a Poet, 1932) had borrowed heavily from the hallucinatory and displacement techniques used in *La Coquille et le Clergyman.*

Although nowhere fully elaborated into a theory of cinema, Artaud's ideas are clearly inscribed within his search for a Surrealist poetic able to rewrite in renewed epic terms the modern condition of man. His letters and fragmentary scenarios evoke an art form of isolated, jarring elements somehow capable of acting directly on the bodies of those attending the performance (his late poetry has an identical aspiration). His scenarios work the brute stuff of psychic drives and mythic thought-modes—eroticism, cruelty, perversity, and violence. But unlike other Surrealist cinema, Artaud's scenarios seek not to convey dreamscapes but to expose the modalities of psychic drives, enacting "la vérité sombre de l'esprit" (the dark truth of the mind), as he puts it in "Cinéma et Realité" (translated as "Cinema and Reality," 1976), a piece originally published in *Nouvelle Revue Française* in 1927 and collected in volume three (1961; revised and enlarged, 1978) of the *Œuvres complètes.* Artaud writes in this piece of cinema as the only truly poetic and revolutionary art form, alone capable of expressing the deep grammar of the mind. For Artaud, motion pictures might transpose "la sensation physique de la vie pure . . . les convulsions et les sursauts d'une réalité qui semble se détruire elle-même avec une ironie où l'on entend crier les extrémités de l'esprit" (the physical sensation of pure life . . . the convulsions and the starts of a reality which seems to destroy itself with an irony in which you hear the extremities of the mind screaming).

Artaud sought to disarticulate cinematic language to the point where it shed intellectually recognizable syntax. Hermetic image sequences would operate as a "langage inorganique qui émeut l'esprit par osmose"

Cover for the 1925 collection that includes Artaud's antiliterary manifesto "Toute l'écriture est de la cochonnerie" (from Obliques, *no. 10–11[1976])*

(an inorganic language operating on the mind by osmosis), with the interplay of disarticulated images generating "une synthèse objective plus pénétrante que n'importe quelle abstraction" (an objective synthesis of greater penetration than any abstraction). In "Cinéma et réalité" he even speaks of an antirepresentational language of archaic forcefulness that would "faire oublier l'essence même du langage" (make us forget the very essence of language). Artaud's opposition to spoken cinema is thus invincible. But this nonlinguistic language of naked, primal images is ultimately tainted in the same way as the language of text and speech. All languages proceed by the dissection of a continuum, and by 1932 Artaud realized that cinema could not convey the flows of thought and its desire-driven grammar, only halt flux according to an altered syntax. As he writes in a piece published in a 1933 issue of *Les Cahiers Jaunes* and collected in volume three of the *Œuvres complètes*, "La Viellesse précoce du Cinéma" (translated as "The Premature Old Age of the Cinema," 1976), even

filmic languages offer "une prise de possession fragmentaire. . . . stratifiée et glacée . . . un monde de vibrations clos" (a stratified, frozen and fragmentary laying hold. . . . a world of circumscribed vibrations) unable to "restitue les Mythes de l'homme et de la vie" (reinstate the Myths of man and life).

Concurrent with these cinematic projects were Artaud's projects for the Théâtre Alfred Jarry, relaunched in 1927 (after abortive attempts in 1925 and 1926). Here, too, he sought to put the basic thought-modes and framework of existence on stage. The company suffered from financial difficulties, no rehearsals, increasingly stormy relations between its codirectors, and the uniform incomprehension of critics and the public. After four programs—the first consisting of three pieces by the three codirectors (Artaud had hoped for a collaborative manifesto-play), including Artaud's musical comedy sketch, *Ventre Brûlé ou La Mère Folle* (Burnt Belly, or, The Insane Mother), the second program comprising the screening of a movie by Vsevolod Pudovkin that had been banned by the French government and the deliberately derisive performance of part of a Paul Claudel play, the third a production of a play by the Swedish dramatist August Strindberg, and the last of a play by Vitrac—the company collapsed in recriminations in 1929. Its performances were marked by disruptions by Breton and his followers, which Artaud addressed in the pamphlet—co-authored with Vitrac—*Le Théâtre Alfred Jarry et l'Hostilité Publique* (The Alfred Jarry Theater and Public Hostility, 1930), first published in *Nouvelle Revue française* in 1926 and collected in volume two (1961; revised and enlarged, 1980) of the *Œuvres complètes*. Yet, through its destructive humor and emphasis on provocative, experimental performance, the Théâtre Alfred Jarry amounted to a Dada-Surrealist theater of the purest tradition. It was a theater of poets, and, although not explicitly theorized, the moving spirit was the annihilation of a Western dramaturgy of illusion in favor of a theater described by Artaud in his pamphlet as effecting "la formation d'une réalité, l'irruption inédite d'un monde . . . ce monde tangent au réel" (the formation of a reality, the original bursting forth of a world . . . this world which is tangential to the real). It sought to give the performance space over to the pure brutality of dream and hallucination. There were no sets, and Artaud planned to use loudspeakers during performance intervals, he writes in *Le Théâtre Alfred Jarry et l'Hostilité Publique,* to intensify the atmosphere "jusqu'à l'obsession" (to the point of obsession). Like his mental cinema, the theater as conceived by Artaud was to operate directly on each audience member's body and to reveal the primal metaphysical underpinnings of existence. For instance, in a piece collected in volume two of the *Œuvres complètes,* "La Pierre Philosophale" (The Philosopher's Stone), an actor on stage silently mouths the words spoken offstage, revealing the actor's body as a "double" of a real presence existing beyond it.

But the Théâtre Alfred Jarry was a failure. Approaching thirty-five, Artaud was nearly destitute and increasingly struggling with his drug addiction. He was isolated from any artistic groups, had abandoned poetry, and his attempts to produce a theater and cinema of poetic archetype had met with incomprehension. In a state of acute nervous depression Artaud began to study ancient civilizations and esoteric systems and accepted a commission for a free translation of Matthew Gregory Lewis's English Gothic novel *The Monk* (1796). While following closely Léon de Wailly's 1840 literal translation into French, Artaud's *Le Moine* (1931) accentuates the violent dichotomy of good and evil structuring the novel to the point of axiological dissolution, although as he explained to Jean Paulhan in a letter of 13 January 1931, he still had to restrain his "mouvement personnel qui m'aurait induit à introduire dans toutes ces histoires une anarchie intellectuelle qui les auraient rendues imperméables au Grand Public" (natural inclination that would have induced me to inject into all these stories an intellectual anarchy that would have rendered them impenetrable to the General Public). Artaud was in part ashamed at this derivative production, implicitly admitting it in a letter of late November 1930 to be "très inférieur à mes autres œuvres" (far inferior to my other works). He nevertheless included it in the list he drew up for his *Œuvres complètes,* considering it to be his work, neither a translation nor an adaptation, as he explained in his preface, but "une sorte de 'copie' en français du texte original" (a sort of "copy" in French of the original text). In a letter dated 21 March 1931, written to Paulhan shortly after the publication of *Le Moine,* Artaud insists that the work is significant since "c'est la première fois que je fais d'une traite un gros livre destiné au grand public" (it is the first time I write straight off a big book for the general public). It is true that the comparatively traditional *Le Moine* is something of an oddity in Artaud's body of work. His other novel, *Héliogabale,* is more intellectually adventurous and complex, and his later works supposedly written for a general public, *Van Gogh, le suicidé de la société* (1947; translated as "Van Gogh, the Man Suicided by Society," 1959) and *Pour en finir avec le jugement de dieu,* remain highly abstruse. *Le Moine* simply lacks the generic, stylistic, and intellectual originality of his better writings.

In August 1931 Artaud saw a performance of Balinese dance theater, which evokes supernatural and metaphysical forces through gestural performance. He saw in this performative mode a move away from the representation inherent to textual theater toward an orchestrated spontaneity, and he grafted this idea of nonrepresentationality onto his earlier theatrical and filmic principles. The result was the series of articles that became *Le Théâtre et son double.* Initially Artaud hoped to receive the backing of the prestigious *Nouvelle Revue Française,* but an overhasty press announcement scuttled this arrangement. Nevertheless, through the support of its editor, Jean Paulhan (one of his staunchest friends), Artaud published several articles in *Nouvelle Revue Française* and gave public readings of his tracts at the Sorbonne. In 1936 he started organizing his material for collection, supplementing it with further texts and open letters. *Le Théâtre et son double* appeared in 1938, when Artaud had already been confined to an asylum for a year.

Artaud offers no program of practical precepts for his Theatre of Cruelty but an inspired, unclear vision. It is in fact an impossible vision, seeking to jump clear outside the logic of representation and signifying processes. The stage is conceived as a space of metaphysical immediacy where the unsayable nature of things is realized in virtual form. At the heart of this vision is the idea of a nonrepresentational language of physical and spatial configuration. By means of a controlled anarchy and dissonance Artaudian theater is to decompose traditional signifying patterns, and by the rigorous deployment of multiple planes of sound, light, materiality, and movement, to generate a new world of signs hewn out of the very stuff of life. The Theatre of Cruelty is thus wholly removed from the realm of narrative and psychology. It is, as were the Eleusinian mysteries of ancient Greece, positioned at an intersection of myth, metaphysics, and magic.

In the dozen essays, open letters, and manifestos of *Le Théâtre et son double,* Artaud develops his ideas through extended metaphors. As in all of his 1930s writings, he employs a range of esoteric and mythic lexicons as discursive frameworks for exploring his sense of alienation from reality. The opening essay, "Le théâtre et la peste" ("The Theater and the Plague"), deploys plague imagery both to evoke the violence and viscerality of Artaudian performance and also to suggest the devastating conceptual transformations a Theatre of Cruelty would unleash, resulting (on a virtual level), like the plague, in either the death or fortification of Western man. A secondary automythographic line of reading identifies Artaud with both poetry and plague: he becomes the scapegoat of Western culture, effecting its magical recovery of true meaning at the cost of his own existence. Taking its lesson from the "poésie dans l'espace" (spatialized poetry) of Lucas van Leyden's painting *Lot and His Daughters* (circa 1520),

ANTONIN ARTAUD

L'Art et la Mort

A l'Enseigne des Trois Magots
Robert DENOEL, Editeur
60, Avenue La Bourdonnais
PARIS

Frontispiece and title page for the 1929 collection that includes Artaud's most markedly Surrealist poetry
(Sterling Memorial Library, Yale University)

"La mise en scène et la métaphysique" (translated as "*Mise en scène* and Metaphysics") calls for a theater that would replace spoken language with a "langage physique . . . matériel et solide" (physical . . . material, solid language). "Le Théâtre alchimique" ("The Alchemical Theater") develops this idea of a regeneration of language, suggesting that as the alchemist seeks to dissolve base matter to reconstitute it as gold, so true theater seeks the purification of base human language.

Behind these explicit images and narratives is a structuring Gnostic sensibility. The Gnostic heresy tells how the world is the work of an evil Demiurge, with the true ontological principle remaining unrevealed in a fundamentally vitiated creation. Cruelty, Artaud's key notion, does not refer to "sadisme" (sadism) and "sang" (blood) but to the far larger idea of implacable necessities eternally operating at all levels of a reality of conflicting, primordial cosmic forces. Human existence is literally cruelty incarnate, fundamentally marked by

self-division. *Le Théâtre et son double* responds by prescribing a dramatic orgy of self-alienation. A Theatre of Cruelty would vicariously live out the warring principles of the ontological order of cruelty, thus reuniting them in an apocalyptic dissolution of being. The function of theater is to be a virtual, apocalyptic enactment of the dynamics of metaphysical rupture.

Given Artaud's emphasis on a physical language spontaneously enacting anarchic forces, the Theatre of Cruelty cannot be textual, and "En finir avec les chefs-d'œuvres" (translated as "An End to Masterpieces") rejects the entire language-based Western dramatic tradition. More radically, "Lettres sur le langage" ("Letters on Language") evokes a "Parole d'avant les mots" (Speech prior to words). This speech is not an ineffable original language but a signifying process in which poetry, no longer confined to words, is realized in the flesh of the performer (thus reworking Artaud's idea of an "esprit dans la chair"). In the famous image of his preface the actor's body is to become a dynamic hieroglyph burning with metaphysical forces. Human existence is no longer represented on stage: instead its prime metaphysical energies would be made real and organized in bodies and space. Such ideas assault the primacy of language, a cornerstone of the Western tradition. Derrida, in "Le Théâtre de la cruauté et la clôture de la représentation" (The Theater of Cruelty and the Closure of Representation), an essay included in his *L'Ecriture et la différence* (Writing and Difference, 1967), identified this desired shift away from representation toward generative performance as the most subversive aspect of Artaud's theories. In this context it is worth remembering that the French critic Maurice Blanchot, in an article collected in his 1969 book *L'Entretien infini* (The Infinite Conversation), suggested Artaud's theories of a Theatre of Cruelty were primarily an exposition of a larger *ars poetica*. This desire to exceed representation reappears in his late poetry, which claims to dissolve the order of reality and re-create the body of the poet from the primal flux of words.

While working on *Le Théâtre et son double,* Artaud wrote *Héliogabale ou l'Anarchiste couronné,* collected in volume seven (1967; revised and enlarged, 1982) of the *Œuvres complètes.* This fiction retells the story of the anarchic, violent reign of Caesar Marcus Aurelius Antoninus Augustus–known as Heliogabalus or Elogabalus–the third-century A.D. Roman emperor and priest of the sun god Baal, in a discursive framework drawn from alchemy and ancient solar religions. Despite extensive historical and mythological research, Artaud's account is primarily a poetic projection of the view that had so heavily marked *Le Théâtre et son double,* of existence as a metaphysical drama. Key moments in Héliogabale's career, particularly his coronation and death, are excessively dramatized, and some critics see *Héliogabale* as the best approximation (certainly during this period) of the ideals of Artaud's Theatre of Cruelty.

Artaud's text delights in detailing the sexual and social anarchy unleashed by Héliogabale. He disguises himself as a woman and lends his orifices to sexual penetration; dignitaries are appointed for the size of their members; and for his triumphal arrival in Rome, Héliogabale walks backward, his buttocks exposed, being symbolically sodomized by the city. Artaud departs from historical sources, however, in interpreting such transgressions as obeying a larger ordering ideal. The prose of *Héliogabale* is remarkable for its incantatory cadence, hypnotic litanies, and complex rhythmic patterning. The deep respiration of this formalized prose is what enables the text to integrate great fluxes of transgressive disorder and to present Héliogabale's activity as a "désordre qui n'est que l'appari-

tion d'une idée métaphysique et supérieure de l'ordre" (disorder which is only the apparition of a superior, metaphysical idea of order). Héliogabale operates on a virtual level, directing a carnival that would reunify the warring principles of Male and Female. The torrential flows of blood, sperm, and feces circulating at Héliogabale's birth and brutal death illustrate how he issues from, embodies, and returns to an anarchic unity transcending life. He is both masculine and feminine, anarchist and emperor, and more importantly both victim and celebrant of a dramatized ritual of dissolution, transgression, and dispersal. As such, some see *Héliogabale* as a prophetic announcement of the course Artaud was to follow.

Héliogabale extends a process at work in Artaud's 1920s writings, in which he had developed parallels and fusions between his writing self and historical figures such as Abelard and Uccello. In a letter of 20 August 1934 to Paulhan, collected in volume seven of *Œuvres complètes,* Artaud explicitly identified himself with the title character of *Héliogabale,* described in that work as a "mythomane dans le sens littéral . . . il voit les mythes qui sont, et . . . il les applique" (mythomaniac in the literal sense of the term . . . he sees the myths that exist and . . . he applies them). More significantly, the oralization of Artaud's prose, which dominates his later writing, is a technique of incorporating and identifying with his text and his textual alter ego. Increasingly Artaud sought to embody his metaphysics in textual alter egos, and *Héliogabale* projects this concern with self-writing onto a larger and more complex plane.

In 1935 Artaud staged the only production of his Theatre of Cruelty. He adapted Percy Bysshe Shelley's tragedy *The Cenci* (1819), a tale of a sixteenth-century Italian count (played by Artaud in his version) who rapes his daughter before being gruesomely murdered by his servants; in Artaud's version the daughter is tortured and executed for her part in the murder. Artaud sought to depersonalize the tale, making the characters forces of violence incarnate. Incest in particular (already present in *Héliogabale* and in the inspirational painting *Lot and His Daughters*) was an anarchic metaphysical force for Artaud, annihilating the differential systems that constitute human culture and returning it to a primary state of chaos. Nevertheless, he lamented that as a textual play *Les Cenci* was far removed from his projected theater of metaphysically-laden gesture; in a commentary on the play, collected in volume five (1964; revised and enlarged, 1979) of the *Œuvres complètes,* Artaud describes the difference as that between a tempest and its recorded sound. Furthermore, financial imperatives obliged Artaud to distribute parts to wealthy amateurs. Despite his efforts, the production closed amid hostile reviews after seventeen perfor-

Artaud (center) in a scene from his 1935 adaptation of Percy Bysshe Shelley's The Cenci *(photograph Lipnitzki-Roger-Viollet)*

mances. This performance was Artaud's last involvement with a theatrical production.

Resolved against all further collaborative ventures, Artaud came to conceive of his bodily self as the site for his Theatre of Cruelty. In 1936 he left France for Mexico; before leaving Paris he wrote Paulhan in a 19 July 1935 letter–collected in volume eight (1971; revised and enlarged, 1980) of the *Œuvres complètes*–that he hoped that in Mexico "le théâtre que j'imagine, que je contiens peut-être, s'exprime directement" (the theater that I imagine, and perhaps carry within me, is directly expressed). This trip was the first of three that Artaud made in 1936 and 1937. Artaud had been preoccupied with esoteric and primitive modes of knowledge since his rupture with the Surrealists (who shared this enthusiasm). An obsessive interest in apocalyptic prophecy now rapidly distanced his from any shared view of reality. In Mexico he hoped to discover a society alive to pre-Conquest myths, and his presence was to inflame these revolutionary forces. This hope was disappointed, but he gave a series of public lectures later collected in a Spanish version as *México* (1962) and subsequently published in French as *Messages révolution-*

naires (Revolutionary Messages), first in 1971 as part of volume eight of the *Œuvres complètes* and then separately in 1979. While varying widely in content, his lectures enjoined the overthrow of European values, identified with a stifling humanism and rationalism, and a return to a culture of magical primitivism. The original French manuscripts were lost, and these texts only exist as translations back from Spanish, which lack the verve of Artaud's best writing.

Artaud's second purpose was to visit the Tarahumara, a North Mexican Indian tribe whose culture he saw as exemplary of the organic primitivism necessary for a return to the metaphysical sources of existence. His writings about his visit, originally published as *D'un voyage au pays des Tarahumaras* and later enlarged with the shorter title *Les Tarahumaras,* tell the story of a frustrated odyssey in a landscape alive with forces. Written mostly in 1937, first published in 1945 and enlarged in 1955, this work was collected in volume nine (1971; revised and enlarged, 1979) of the *Œuvres complètes*. Artaud presents Tarahumara culture as a perpetual reading and writing of a metaphysical dialogue with nature. They treat the landscape and their movement as inscriptions, answering the semiotic forms of their environment with engraved signs. The opposition of cosmic forces, already disclosed in the landscape, is heightened by the "arbres brûlés volontairement en forme de croix, ou en forme d'êtres, et souvent ces êtres sont doublés et ils se font face, comme pour manifester la dualité essentielle des choses" (trees deliberately burnt into the form of crosses or the form of beings, and often these beings are doubled and face to face, as though to portray the essential duality of things). The landscape enacts "une histoire d'enfantement dans la guerre, une histoire de genèse et de chaos" (a story of childbearing in war, a story of genesis and chaos). Artaud depicts the Sierra Tarahumara as the concrete manifestation of a Theatre of Cruelty.

Until the end of his life, Artaud reworked his Tarahumara texts in the light of his fluctuating religious and metaphysical dispositions. The earlier texts interpret the Mexican rites as part of a universal esotericism (linking Atlantis to the Holy Grail to the Rosicrucians to the Bible). Those written in the early 1940s develop a mystical Christian interpretation. A text written just before Artaud's death describes the Tarahumara rite as an act of provocation against a perverse God and homeopathic passage through abjection, resulting in the emergence of scarred yet autonomous man. The most important text is "Le rite du peyotl chez les tarahumaras" (The Peyote Ritual of the Tarahumaras), which describes rituals involving the ingestion of a powerful hallucinogenic, peyote. Artaud expected this peyote rite to amount to a rebirth (others of his generation, such as Aldous Huxley and Henri Michaux, wrote of the existential qualities of hallucinogens). He describes how the dancers' feet trace the letters *S, U,* and *J* (the first three letters of the French word for *subject*) suggesting imminent self-presence. But the inscriptions end on the letters *J* and what Artaud calls a sad *E* (the two letters of the French for *I*). As in the 1920s texts, he is caught within the linguistically constituted self.

On his return to France, Artaud traveled to Brussels to give a public lecture and to meet the family of Cecile Schramme, to whom he had improbably become engaged. He had met her in 1935 in a detoxification clinic, and after his return from Mexico a volatile affair had developed. His lecture, like previous public performances of his Theatre of Cruelty articles and a famous final performance at the Vieux-Colombier in 1947, became a confrontation with his audience. Each time Artaud used his text as a starting point for an improvised performance of the subject in hand. The marriage was called off, and Artaud returned to Paris where, over the summer months, he was effectively reduced to mendicancy.

After the failure of the controlled self-dissolution in the rites of the Theatre of Cruelty and of the Tarahumara Indians, the tempo of Artaud's work quickened. In a state of eerie lucidity engendered by the advanced disintegration of his sense of reality Artaud wrote *Les Nouvelles Révélations de l'Être,* a short, fragmented oracular text of anguished self-interrogation. First published in 1937, the work was collected in volume seven of the *Œuvres complètes.* Explicitly it is an apocalyptic reading of the Tarot cards, announcing a fiery destruction of the world in which Male will triumph over Female, overseen by a king who is mistaken by all for a madman. Through this vision Artaud announces a cognitive epiphany coinciding with the paroxysmal destruction of self and world. The text does not bear Artaud's name but is signed "Le Revelé" (The Revealed), thus implicitly claiming that in revealing "Being," the author has become "Being." But such a claim can only be made at the price of losing any separate, nameable identity. (Artaud was concerned during this period that the Tarahumara texts, likewise, should appear anonymously, although in fact only the article that appeared in *Nouvelle Revue Française* in 1937 was unsigned). And despite the hammering, visionary refrain—"Qu'est-ce que cela veut dire? / Cela veut dire que. . . ." (What does that mean / That means that. . . .)—which punctuates nearly every page of the text, the closing words of the preface belie this forced note of epistemological triumphalism: "Je ne suis pas mort" (I am not dead), the text records in a diminuendo, "mais je suis séparé" (but I am separated).

In August 1937—in a state of severe confusion—Artaud departed for Ireland on a mission to return to the Irish people what he maintained to the end of his life was St. Patrick's cane (actually an unusually carved cane given to him by a friend). The precise events of the trip are unclear; however, it is clear that Artaud had increasingly been seeing himself as a Christic prince of the Apocalypse and sacrificial scapegoat. In a postcard sent from Ireland to Anne Manson, later published in volume seven of the *Œuvres complètes,* he pushed the parallel to the point of demanding that she publicly betray him (in the famous Deux Magots literary café) and reveal his true identity. In September Artaud was expelled from Ireland. In the boat back he had to be forcibly restrained, and on his arrival in Le Havre he was placed in a straitjacket and taken to the asylum there, before being moved to Sotteville-lès-Rouen. At his mother's request he was moved to Sainte-Anne, a Parisian asylum, in 1938 and thence to Ville-Evrard. In wartime France asylum conditions were extremely severe, and Artaud, untreated and undernourished, was physically transformed into the emaciated, toothless figure known from photographs of the late 1940s.

The psychiatric hospital at Rodez, where Artaud was confined during the 1940s

In 1943 his friends and family had Artaud transferred to the asylum of Rodez in Vichy French. Conditions were far better. He was treated by doctors who were aware of his work, but they administered three courses of unanesthetized electroshock therapy (inducing fifty-one comas), against which Artaud vociferates so violently in his writings that the polemic over his treatment still continues. On arriving at Rodez, Artaud had written nothing, with the exception of a handful of letters, for six years. During this period he had undergone a profound religious conversion and decided to call himself Nalpas (his mother's maiden name). Within months after his arrival at Rodez he had reverted to calling himself Artaud and had begun to write. From this point on in his writing he repeatedly reworks the great narratives of Western religious and philosophical thought. These rewritings of conceptuo-mythic narratives generate a rapidly mutating imaginary textual universe. If they resist schematic summary, this resistance is less because of their extravagance than because the functioning of any one narrative segment depends partially on reworkings performed elsewhere on other segments. The only way for a reader to enter into the late Artaudian textual system is to proceed patiently through the details.

At first Artaud only wrote letters to a few intimates detailing the idiosyncrasies of an apocalyptic mysticism coinciding extensively with gnostic thought. These letters set out a vision, derived from his 1930s writings, of his bodily existence as a battleground of warring cosmic principles. At times he figures as a body-sieve, a demonic sexual carcass awash with abject fluids, at others as a pure angelic body of energy. In particular he insists his daily movements are surrounded by occult forces unleashed by sexual rites of hostile "envoûteurs" (bewitchers), and that human reproduction occurs asexually. Whereas the post–1945 texts (written after his relinquishment of Christianity) are, despite their difficulty, clearly an exciting aesthetic and intellectual challenge, these letters of 1943–1944 seem fuzzy-headed and monotonous, the dull and deluded outpourings of a fanatical heretic. The writing is of disappointingly inferior caliber, veering toward a tired pastiche of evangelic and mystic tropes. But these earlier Rodez writings set out many elements of the mythic narratives of the final creative phase: the well-known notion of the "corps sans organes" (body without organs), for example, that will resist divine interference, issues from theological ideas expounded during this period.

In late 1943 Artaud had produced five short translations, including part of Lewis Carroll's "Jabberwocky" (1855). These works were published as "Cinq adaptations de textes anglais" (Five Adaptations of English Texts) in volume nine of *Œuvres complètes*. Artaud's "Jabberwocky" dissolves the original so fully that the French philosopher Gilles Deleuze, in his influential *Logique du sens* (The Logic of Meaning, 1969), presented it as exemplarily schizophrenic language. For example, in his rendering of "Did gyre and gimble in the wabe" Artaud adds a line that has no correlate in the English and that threatens the text with linguistic anarchy: "Allaient en gilroyant et en brimbulkdriquant / Jusque-là où la rourghe est a rouarghe a rangmbde et rangmbde a rouarghambde." A major concern of Artaud's, however, was to challenge normal patterns of discourse. This drive toward discursive autonomy is central to the first unguided literary fragments written at Rodez. His letters of 1943–1944 had portrayed God as the origin of meaning and the poet, though at the top of the epistemic hierarchy of human expression, as the mere scribe or double of a Divine Word. In a few opaque fragments known as "Révolte contre la poésie" (Revolt against poetry), collected as part of "Trois textes écrits en 1944 a Rodez" (Three Texts Written in 1944 at Rodez) in volume nine of the *Œuvres complètes,* the alienating incapabilities of language are now attributed to "le Verbe" (the Word). God is thus found at the very center of language and the (linguistically constituted) subject: "Le poète qui écrit s'adresse au Verbe et le Verbe a ses lois. Il est dans l'inconscient du poète de croire automatiquement à ces lois. Il se croit libre et il ne l'est pas" (The poet who writes appeals to the Word and the Word has its laws. It is in the poet's unconscious to believe automatically in these laws. He believes himself to be free but he is not).

These fragments are the unlikely beginning of Artaud's celebrated flamboyant anti-God narratives. If God is present in language it follows that true poetry be an anti-Logos, written against the inaugural Divine Word and the habitual patterning of language. And yet, Artaud's theorizings imitate the original Word, for they are to become true by the fact of their formulation. Such self-validation marks all of Artaud's late writings. Equally, the tendency to indict conceptual systems for harboring alienating forces and yet reenact their structures is characteristic of Artaud's late writing, which depends symbiotically on the discursive systems it excoriates.

By 1945 the tensions in Artaud's Gnostic worldview had become uncontainable. The resultant violent disillusionment with religious thought modes provoked a creative outpouring. He produced heavily scoured, disturbing drawings of dissected, perforated bodies as well as a torrent of writing that took to the fullness of their power the ideas and strategies of his gnostically influenced productions. In the three years to his death Artaud wrote more than twice as much as he had in the preceding twenty-five, filling more than four thousand pages of exercise books with notes and producing six collections unlike anything else in modern letters.

Artaud's writings in his *cahiers* (notebooks) are an integral and major part of his late work. Volumes fifteen through twenty-five (1981–1990) of the *Œuvres complètes* comprise 232 of these *cahiers,* corresponding to the period from 1945 to January 1947. An additional volume (twenty-six) includes notes for a lecture Artaud gave in January 1947 at the Théâtre du Vieux-Colombier. The contents of these volumes are fragmented, discontinuous, unstructured shards of diatribe. Surrealist-inspired slippage, erasure, overwriting, and a battery of sophisticated wordplays and word-ploys are used to subvert the received conceptual order and the entire ethic of Western thought by what he calls in *Suppôts et suppliciations* a "humour absolu concret mais de l'humour" (absolute concrete humor but still humor). But playfulness shades alarmingly toward unreadability. Artaud's writing repeatedly and insistently enacts violent sexual dramas between members of the divine family and himself that are inscrutable to an outside reader-spectator. Acts of vampirism, rape, incest, defecation, and demonic possession of the sexual organs figure prominently. Phantasmagoric choreographies of maimed bodily parts recur in which Artaud's skeleton and organism are repeatedly broken down and reconstituted. More radically (and following from "Révolte contre la poésie") the goal of Artaud's post–1945 writing is to create an autonomous and especially God-free self through a textual practice purged of all traces of the alienating thought structures of Western ontology and theology. Artaud's writing has therefore passed beyond the idea of text as medium of self-representation to text as means of self-dissolution and self-creation. The private space of the *cahiers* is where Artaud gives freest reign to this phantasmagoric self-generating writing. The notebook texts equally claim to generate his "filles de cœur à naître," a fluctuating mythical group with which the textual father maintains violent, erotically charged relationships. Independently of any problematic content, such a radical repositioning and transformation of writing compromises its intelligibility. While all Artaud's best writing challenges the limits of literature, many critics believe the notebooks to exceed those limits.

In late 1945 Artaud wrote a series of letters to Henri Parisot, the publisher of his Tarahumara texts. These five texts, published as *Lettres de Rodez* (Letters from Rodez–not to be confused with Artaud's corre-

Artaud and his doctor at Rodez, Gaston Ferdière

spondence collected in volumes ten and eleven of the *Œuvres complètes* as "Lettres écrites de Rodez"), turn around questions of automythography and socially consecrated "envoûtement" (bewitchment). They reformulate the story of Artaud's life as a series of aggressions, starting with an imagined attack by a pimp in Marseilles in 1917 and culminating in mass acts of sexual black magic directed against the confined Artaud from the streets of Paris. He writes with particular violence against his internment and electroshock treatment. The terms used prefigure his idea of a "suicidé de la société" (societal suicide victim), an artist who is the victim of violent repression for the threat that his works pose to the social order. This idea is developed in a later open letter written at Rodez and included in *Suppots et suppliciations,* on the Comte de Lautréamont (pseudonymn of Isidore Lucien Ducasse), the pre-Surrealist prose poet. It is taken to its heights in the final collections, where Artaud identifies with Gerard de Nerval, the French Romantic poet and story writer, with Edgar Allan Poe, the American poet of the macabre, and with Vincent Van Gogh, the archetypal "suicidé de la société." In *Lettres de Rodez* Artaud claims that the reason behind the attempts to circumscribe his activity is because his writing reveals the true nature of reality, and in particular the fecality of existence.

What is truly remarkable about Artaud's late textual performances, including the *Lettres de Rodez,* is not the extravagant ideas but the thrusting linguistic forcefulness these ideas inspire. It is possible to trace the intercrossings of his *mythemes* (myth units), but the fullest explications still fail to dispel the dominant impression, which is not of abstruse metaphoricity but of a writing given over to unchecked *jouissance* (intense yet fleeting gratification) in its own antisensical linguistic performances. An uncharitable view might consider taboo-flouting rant as Artaud's habitual mode of discourse. A celebrated sentence from *Lettres de Rodez,* on fecal poetry, conveys the feel of late Artaudian textuality:

Ce siècle ne comprend plus la poésie fécale, l'intestine malheur de celle, Madame Morte, qui depuis le siècle des siècles sonde sa colonne de mort, sa colonne anale de morte, dans l'excrément d'une survie abolie, cadavre aussi de ses mois abolis, et qui pour le crime de n'avoir pu être, de jamais n'avoir pu être un être, a dû tomber pour se sonder mieux être, dans ce gouffre de la matière immonde et d'ailleurs si gentiment immonde où le cadavre de Madame Morte, de madame utérine fécale, madame anus, géhenne d'excrément par géhenne, dans l'opium de son excrément, fomente fama, le destin fécal de son âme, dans l'utérus de son propre foyer.

(This century no longer understands fecal poetry, the intestinal misfortune of her, Madame Death, who from the century of centuries plumbs her column of death, her anal column of death, in the excrement of an abolished afterlife, corpse likewise of her abolished selves, and who for the crime of not having been able to be, of never having been able to be a being, had to fall, the better to plumb her being, into this chasm of unspeakable and furthermore in the nicest possible way unspeakable matter where the corpse of Madame Death, of madame uterine fecal, madame anus, Gehenna of excrement by Gehenna, in the opium of her excrement, foments fama, the fecal destiny of her soul, in the uterus of her own heart).

The densely interwoven phonic patterning and reprises are integral to the signifying processes of such slippery, multilayered poetic prose. Whereas rant is predicated on semantic fixity, Artaud's riotously exuberant late writing works hard on the linguistic medium to endow it with maximal fluidity.

A related striking feature of all Artaud's late writing is the incorporation of extended passages of linguistic debris. The first significant instance is in *Lettres de Rodez,* where he claims to have written an entire lost work, "Letura d'Eprahi Falli Tetar Fendi Photia o Fotre Indi," in such a language, giving as an example "ratara ratara ratara / atara tatara rana / otara otara katara / otara ratara kana." This legend of a lost work follows the logic that Artaud uses in his lineage of artistic brethren. Both are a way of inventing for himself a poetic as opposed to biological origin. He claimed his invented syllables, derived from the French, Greek, and Italian to which he was exposed when a child, were part of a universal tongue that operated directly on the psyche. These glossolalia have been shown to yield meanings when subjected to close philological study; however, within the overall scheme of Artaud's writing their greater importance lies in their being essentially performative, with implicit claims to emulate the "Divine Word" and act magically on reality.

In May 1946, following a few trial sorties, Artaud was released. His doctor felt him to be deranged but stable. He had spent eight years and eight months of internment, a period that Artaud, increasingly working with his idea of poetic practice as self-generation, interpreted as a gestation culminating in his self-birth as "Artaud le Mômo." Two conditions of Artaud's release were that his financial security be assured and that he reside in a nursing home. Many paintings and manuscripts were donated (by such writers and artists as

Jean-Paul Sartre, Simone de Beauvoir, Bataille, Pablo Picasso, Georges Braque, and Alberto Giacometti) and auctioned shortly after his release. The proceeds were handsome, although Artaud was not given direct control of the money. A young medical student named Paule Thévenin was asked to find Artaud a clinic, and she found a place at Ivry-sur-Seine, in the Parisian suburbs. She became Artaud's secretary, friend, and literary executor.

Subsequent to the *Lettres de Rodez* Artaud thought more than ever of the text as an abject double of the poet. In his final works he therefore sought to maximize the orality of his writing, orality involving a shift from text as representation (as double, to his mind) to text as performance (as self-present meaning). At Ivry he famously dictated his works while pounding a wooden block sliced from a tree trunk with a hammer (which he did with such violence that various secretaries who had come to take dictation were apparently terrorized, and the blocks rapidly destroyed). According to various memoirs he also practiced screaming, accompanying his cries with knife blows on surrounding furniture. (Screams came to represent the most authentic form of expression for Artaud, and those recorded for *Pour en finir avec le jugement de dieu* eerily evoke an alternative discursive order.) His texts claim to be empowered with just this kind of direct violence and to wield language as a physical weapon, as he writes in *Suppôts et suppliciations:* "Les mots que nous employons on me les a passés et je les / emploie, mais pas pour me faire comprendre . . . / alors pourquoi? / C'est que justement *je ne les emploie pas,* / en réalité je ne fais pas autre chose que de me taire/ et de cogner" (They have given me the words that we use and I use them, but not to make myself understood . . . / so why? / The truth is *I do not use them,* / in reality I do nothing other than keep quiet / and hit out). In the final collections, language usage is no longer an ideational act for Artaud: it is as physically real and destructive as his blows pulverizing blocks of wood as he declaims his poems.

In *Artaud le Mômo, Ci-gît* (Here Lies, 1947), *Pour en finir avec le jugement de dieu,* and *Suppôts et suppliciations,* all written after his release, the self-mythologization commenced in the Rodez texts is carried to new levels. These collections interpret Artaud's life history in the light of an originary act of divine aggression that determines the structures of existence. They enact the mutating narratives of two overarching metaphysical myths. On the one hand, an epic conflict opposes Artaud and "god" (deprived, by Artaud, of his capital letter), who, with his henchmen, takes possession of Artaud's body. Further, the negative theology has permeated Artaud's entire worldview, leading him to denounce all inherited

Artaud in his room at the nursing home in Ivry-sur-Seine, where he stayed after his release from the mental hospital in May 1946 (Denise Colomb)

discursive structures. Artaud decides that the reason he has never been able to write the self is because god and divinely infected discourse prevent self-identity by an act of ontological parasitism. And so, on the other hand, a parallel epic narrative announces the explosive future appearance of a transformed body (his image of a "corps sans organes") that would eject god and act as the locus of pure self-identity. "Artaud" has become a mythologized textual figure, defined by his resistance to a libidinous, fecal, vampiric, thieving god. As part of this extravagant automythographizing Artaud subjects his name to extensive onomastic play ("Totaud," "tarto," "outo," "arto," and so on). Concurrently his writing proclaims its power to overthrow the biological and ontological order of the Père-Mère (Father-Mother) and to write a new bodily self. Artaud's poetic word is thus to effect a new Genesis and to generate a new existential order.

Artaud most fully works out these epic narratives in the two-volume *Suppôts et suppliciations*. Shortly before leaving Rodez he had started to plan a work paralleling the power of his body and writing to that of a dormant Mexican volcano, under the title *Pour le Pauvre Popocatepel la charité esse vé pé*. He expanded this work into the inflammatory *Suppôts et suppliciations*. By far the longest of Artaud's works, it is composed of

"Fragmentations," thirty-three nonsensical fragments and eight brief prose texts drawn from the *cahiers,* thirty-five letters written from Rodez, and "Interjections," seventy-five pieces of highly vocalized prose poetry dictated in late 1946 and early 1947. Its explicit aim is to act as an overstructure for Artaud's life story, yet he playfully describes it in a notebook entry dated 31 January 1947 as a "livre emmerdant absolument impossible à lire"(shitty absolutely impossible to read book). Although modern readers might find the blasphemy of *Suppots et suppliciations* more puzzling than shocking, Louis Broder, who had initially agreed to publish the work, underwent a religious crisis upon reading the manuscript and refused to print it.

The "Interjections" include some of Artaud's most powerful late writing, inspired by denouncing a divine presence living his life in his place: "Au-dessus de la psychologie d'Antonin Artaud il y a la psychologie d'un autre / qui vit, boit, mange, dort, pense et rêve dans mon corps" (Above the psychology of Antonin Artaud there is the psychology of an other / who lives, drinks, eats, sleeps, thinks and dreams in my body). "Je n'admets pas . . ." (I Don't Admit . . .), an uncollected text of the same period, published in *84* (1948), adapts the Gnostic idea of a catastrophic origin, telling how Artaud lost his bodily place at birth. The drama of

Artaud's birth is "celle de ce corps / qui *poursuivait* (et ne suivait pas) le mien / et qui pour passer premier et naître / se projeta à travers mon corps / et / naquit / par l'éventration de mon corps / dont il garda un morceau sur lui / afin / de se faire passer / pour moi-même" (that of this body / that pursued [and did not follow] mine / and which to pass first and be born / projected itself through my body / and / was born / by the disembowelment of my body, / of which it kept a piece on itself / in order / to pass itself off / as myself). Most frequently in "Interjections" Artaud's god appears not just a thieving other but a libidinous vampire reveling in a brutish, crapulent sexual possession of Artaud's body: "dieu a dit: / Et moi je suis une bonne bête en face de tout ce corps / d'Antonin Artaud, / et non de l'homme: / Antonin Artaud / qui n'en occupe qu'une petite partie, et qui s'en ira / et je trouverai bien . . . le moyen de resurgir à la place de son cœur, et d'en éliminer l'homme en humant . . . après avoir bité, glotté, / luthé, limé" (god said: And I am a dumb animal in front of all this body / of Antonin Artaud, / and not of the man: / Antonin Artaud / who occupies only a little part of it, and who shall go away / and I will certainly find . . . the way to reappear in his heart's place, and to eliminate the man by sniffing him up . . . after having dicked [or duped], tongued, / struggled, and ground). This divine possession is imitated by unspecified hordes who gleefully displace Artaud and tell of his dispossession through his pen: "Que fais-tu là, Antonin Artaud? / Oui, que fais-tu là? Tu nous gênes. / Et à la fin sors de ton corps, c'est à nous à tenir ta place . . . " (What are you doing there, Antonin Artaud? / Yes, what are you doing there? You're in our way. / And in the end get out of your body, it's for us to have your place . . .).

Many "Interjections" weave these narrative strands together. An ejaculatory, insurgent, oralized poetry of resounding affirmatory power details how god exists vicariously through cavorting with his henchmen in Artaud's lower bodily organs: "[dieu] ne vit, que d'être / boulotté au milieu d'Artaud, masturbé au milieu d'Artaud, rappelé en esprit dans Artaud, / par la pensée abdominale et le coït, / drainé le long de la colonne œsophagique d'Artaud, / ravivé par l'orgasme et l'expulsion excrémentielle anale des aliments d'Artaud / rendu présent par l'acte de pulation à deux appelé la co-pulation, / non d'Artaud, / mais d'un et de l'autre, / du microbe un et de l'autre / au milieu du sexe d'Artaud" ([god] only lives by being / eaten in the middle of Artaud, masturbated in the middle of Artaud, spiritually recalled in Artaud, / by abdominal thought and coitus, / siphoned along the oesophageal column of Artaud, / reanimated by orgasm and the excremental expulsion of Artaud's foods, / made present by the double act of pulation called co-pulation, / not of Artaud, /

but of one and of the other, / of microbe number one and of the other, / in the middle of Artaud's sex). This "hideuse histoire du Démiurge" (hideous story of the Demiurge), as Artaud calls it in "Je n'admets pas . . . ," affords him the ideal topic to be as indecorous as possible when, for example, he claims that god inhabits his rectum, or that his "suppôts" (henchmen) feed off his hemorrhoidal discharges. The flitting between a high conceptualizing mode and abject profanity challenges the ethos of Western thinking. Yet, despite the rhetoric of abject sexuality and fecality, the final texts obey an unnerving coherence of thrust. Such texts work in an interzone between the theorizing of a conceptual system and the writing of a *univers imaginaire*.

Artaud's late writing is famous for its vilifying descriptions of the human body, described in *Suppôts et suppliciations* as a "viandasse de carne grayasse [*sic*]" (rubbishy meat of greashy flesh), equivalent to the descriptions in *Artaud le Mômo* "la barbaque / bien crottée et mirée / dans le cu d'une poule / morte et désirée" (the stinking meat, / thoroughly shat and gazed upon, / in the ass of a hooker / dead and desired), reduced to holes and tumescences, "Cette langue entre quatre gencives, / cette viande entre deux genoux, / ce morceau de trou" (This tongue between four gums, / this meat between two knees, / this piece of hole). These descriptions are shock writing of the first order, writing the sexual, digestory, death-bound body back into literary discourse. But this orifice-ridden, libidinous lump of putrid flesh awash with abject fluids is the defiling god-given and parent-given biological anatomy. Artaud's attempt to write an ending to this story of ontological vampirism leads him to imagine a new body, a hardened, desiccated, and organless block immune to the sexual and vampiric incursions of God and Other.

Artaud's image of the "corps sans organes"–like his anti-God narratives–takes on a life of its own. It is stripped down to its bones, as he writes in the *cahier* entry published in volume sixteen (1981) of the *Œuvres complètes* under the title "La Recherche du Nouveau Simple" (Search for a New Simple Being): "je suis . . . un cliquetis d'os particuliers sans viande" (I am . . . a rattling of specific bones without meat). In the closing "Interjections" the last vestiges of the corporeal are lost as the body becomes a wooden structure with ever-fewer chinks: "je suis un morceau de bois . . . reprenant les morceaux du corps tombé pour les reclouer l'un sur l'autre toujours plus étroitement et de plus près" (I am a piece of wood . . . picking up the pieces of fallen body to nail them back on again on one another ever more tightly and closely). By the final texts the new bodily self is pure energy: "Je suis un bloc de feu plus dur et plus dense que tout corps et qui ramènera les choses au crible de sa densité" (I am a block of fire harder and denser than any body and will return things to the perforations of their density). Artaud's new body becomes a massive, incandescent new space of will and energy that engulfs his textual world.

The most adventurous of Artaud's final poems were written alongside *Suppôts et suppliciations* in autumn 1946 and collected under the title *Artaud le Mômo* (though not part of this collection, *Ci-gît* is part of the same creative upsurge). These slender texts represent a peak of linguistic experimentation. Artaud creates densely interwoven, mesmeric sound-textures that combine standard words with a language halfway between neologism and glossolalia: "C'est la toile d'araignée pentrale, / la poile onoure / d'ou-ou la voile, / la plaque anale d'anavou" (It's the penetral spider web, / the female onour hair, / from whe-whence the female veil, / the anal patch of anayou"). Phonic patterning privileges the performative dimension, while the asignificatory elements prevent the text from being referred back to any originary meaning that could "double" the performance and enmesh it in a representational textuality.

The ambition of Artaud's ideas exceeds even his linguistic inventiveness, as his narrativized theorizings on body-theft and self-closing swell in these few texts to a fullness of amplitude surpassing the voluminous *Suppôts et suppliciations*. In *Artaud le Mômo* the new body bursts forth in its irrepressible linguistic autonomy:

Non la membrane de la voûte,
non le membre omis de ce foutre,
d'une déprédation issu,

mais une carne,
hors membrane,
hors de là où c'est dur ou mou.

Ja passé par le dur et mou,
étendue cette carne en paume,
tirée, tendue comme une paume
        de main
exsangue de se tenir raide.

(Not the membrane of the vault,
not the member omitted from this sperm,
issued from a depredation,

but a meat,
outside membranes,
outside where it is hard or soft.

Oiz been through the hard and soft,
stretched out this meat palm flat,
stretched, tightened like a palm
        of a hand,
bloodless from stretching itself rigid).

Artaud lives up to his new self-given name as Artaud the idiot-god and rails mockingly against all genealogies: "ni de mère, ni / de père inné, / n'étant pas / la viande minette / qu'on copule / à patron-minet" (neither mother nor / father innate, / not being / the pussy meat / they copulate / at boss-puss [or at the crack of dawn]). This reviling does not just overturn his biological genealogy; parents and god blur into one, for "qui est donc Patron-Minet? / C'est dieu" (who then is Boss-Puss? / It's god). The textual Artaud transcends distinctions, being male and female, creator and progeny: "Moi, Antonin Artaud, je suis mon fils, mon père, ma mère, / et moi" (I, Antonin Artaud, I am my son, my father, my mother, / and myself), enclosing the new "Antonin Artaud" in a loop of self-identity between "Moi" and "moi." Textual style and bodily realities fuse. "Le style c'est l'homme," Artaud notes in a Rodez *cahier,* collected in volume twenty-one (1985) of the *Œuvres complètes,* "et c'est son corps" (The style is the man, / and it is his body).

In the final year of his life Artaud was concerned with reaching the widest possible audience and wrote two comparatively more accessible works. Part essay, part poem, part open letter, *Van Gogh, le suicidé de la société,* for which Artaud received his only literary prize (the modest Prix Sainte-Beuve), was written in early 1947. He wrote it after visiting an exhibition of the paintings of the Dutch artist Van Gogh and in response to a newspaper article offering a psychiatric diagnosis of the painter resembling that which Artaud's doctors had offered of his own mental condition. Artaud tells how Van Gogh, Nerval, Baudelaire, and Poe were covertly murdered by a collective social will. His imprecatory poem is a counterattack on society. It sets out Artaud's idea of the "aliéné authentique" (authentic madman) who is "un homme qui a préféré devenir fou, dans le sens ou socialement on l'entend, que de forfaire à une certaine idée supérieure de l'honneur humain" (a man who preferred to become mad, in the social meaning of the term, than to be false to a certain superior idea of human honor). It is in this spirit that the text opens with an extraordinary sentence of gleeful "absolute, concrete humor": "On peut parler de la bonne santé mentale de Van Gogh qui, dans toute sa vie, ne s'est fait cuire qu'une main et n'a pas fait plus, pour le reste, que de se trancher une fois l'oreille gauche, / dans un monde où on mange chaque jour du vagin cuit à la sauce verte ou du sexe du nouveau-né flagellé et mis en rage, / tel que cueilli à sa sortie du sexe maternel. / Et ceci n'est pas un image" (One may talk of Van Gogh's sound mental health, who, in all his life, only cooked himself one hand and did no more, as for the rest, than once to cut off his left ear, / in a world where every day people eat vagina cooked in green sauce or flagellated,

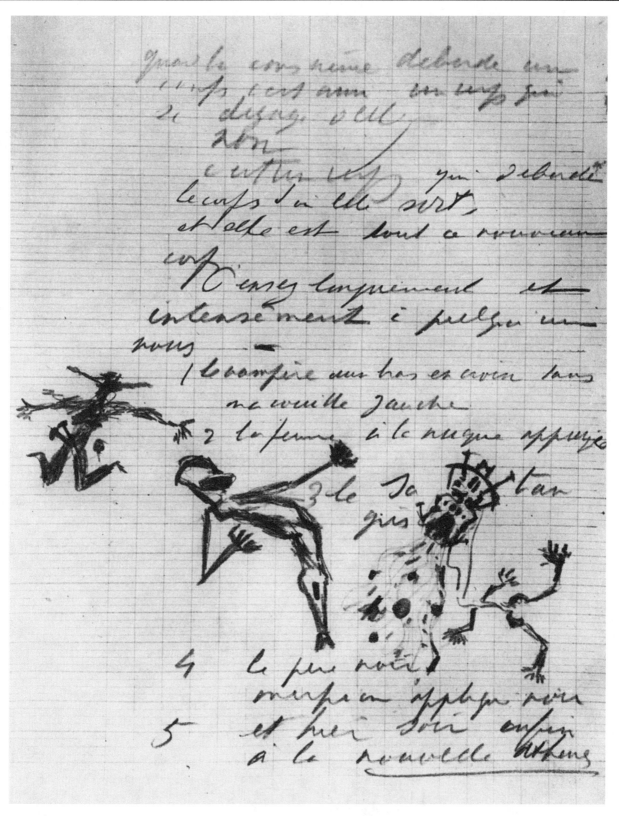

Page written during December 1946 in the notebook Artaud kept at Ivry-sur-Seine (from Paule Thévenin and Jacques Derrida,
Antonin Artaud: Dessins et portraits, *1986)*

enraged newly-born genitals, / as picked on emerging from the maternal sex. And this is not an image). As part of this inversion of the hierarchy of sanity, Artaud's text fulminates bitterly against his psychiatrists, indicting them of hypocritical erotomania, thus interweaving the two life stories of Van Gogh and Artaud.

Van Gogh, le suicidé de la société is not just an arena for imprecation and anger. Artaud displays great verve in his envisioning of Van Gogh's paintings. His writing shifts powerfully and smoothly between astonishingly rapid and sure evocations of Van Gogh's work and imagery fusing Van Gogh's vision and his own vision of the human body: "Le corps sous la peau est une usine surchauffée, / et, dehors / le malade brille, / il luit, / de tous ses pores / éclatés. / Ainsi un paysage / de Van Gogh / à midi." (The body beneath the skin is an overheated factory, / and outside / the sick man blazes / he glows / with all his pores / burst open. / Like a landscape / by Van Gogh / at noon). The paintings are described in terms of an apocalypse revealing the natural world in its true colors. By the "coups de massue" (club blows) of his brush strokes Van Gogh effected a quasi-alchemical transformation of the "sordide simplicité" (sordid simplicity) of things. A "mouvement de régression violente" (violent regressive movement) leads to "la porte occulte . . . d'un énigmatique et sinistre au-délà" (the open door . . . onto an enigmatic and sinister beyond). Associating his approach to that of Van Gogh, Artaud compares two different modes of investing reality with value: the traditional Western mode of elevation, and a truer mode of descending so far into physical objects that their metaphysical dimension is intuited. "Gaugin pensait que l'artiste doit chercher le symbole, . . . agrandir les choses de la vie jusqu'au mythe, / alors que Van Gogh pensait qu'il faut savoir déduire le mythe des choses les plus terre-à-terre de la vie. / En quoi je pense, moi, qu'il avait foutrement raison" (Gaugin thought that the artist should seek the symbol, . . . aggrandize the things of life to the point of myth, / whereas Van Gogh thought that you have to know how to deduce myth from the most down-to-earth things. / Wherein I personally think he was fucking right). The "corps sans organes," which appears in the sister work *Pour en finir avec le jugement de dieu,* is just such an instance of earthy myth, brute metaphysics, and violently anti-intellectual language.

Through Thévenin, Artaud was asked to write and read material for a radio broadcast. This request resulted in his best-known late text, *Pour en finir avec le jugement de dieu,* written in October and November 1947, which Artaud recorded but which was banned just before its planned broadcast in February 1948 as too blasphemous. It is part of the same creative phase as *Van Gogh, le suicidé de la société* and presents the *mythemes* of Artaud's final collections for a wider audience. The most accessible of his late works, it is composed of five short poetic texts (a sixth, "Le Théâtre de cruauté," was excluded from the projected radio broadcast because of time constraints). The opening, mischievous text mocks the politico-moral soul-searching and trauma of the postwar world, by recounting the fiction of a United States fabricating cannon fodder through a clandestine program of mass artificial insemination. This culturally sterile West is implicitly compared to the Tarahumara culture of spatial inscription in a second text that describes the peyote dance as a virtual redrawing of the human body. The remaining texts retell God's possession of the human body and the bankruptcy of ideational processes, before a conclusion insists on the superiority of Artaud's metaphysics of folly and its emblematic "corps sans organes."

The major concern of *Pour en finir avec le jugement de dieu* is the superiority of Artaud's metaphysical mythologizing to rationalistic thought. He parodies syllogistic thinking, for example, when, having defined existence as fecal, he asks, "Dieu est-il un être? / S'il en est un c'est de la merde. / S'il n'en est pas un / il n'est pas. / Or il n'est pas" (Is God a being? / If he is one it's shit / If he isn't one / he is not. / Thus he is not). And a celebrated passage rails against what Artaud sees as the deep meaninglessness of abstract terms:

Et qu'est-ce que l'infini?

Au juste nous ne le savons pas!

C'est un mot
dont nous nous servons
pour indiquer
l'ouverture
de notre conscience
vers la possibilité
démesurée,
inlassable et démesurée.

Et qu'est-ce que au juste que la conscience?

Au juste nous ne le savons pas.

C'est le néant.

Un néant
dont nous nous servons
pour indiquer
quand nous ne savons pas quelque chose
de quel côté

nous ne le savons
et nous disons
alors
conscience,
du côté de la conscience,
mais il y a cent mille autres côtés.

(And what is the infinite?

We do not know exactly!

It is a word
which we use
to indicate
the opening
of our consciousness
towards possibilities
inordinate
indefatigable and inordinate.

And what exactly is consciousness?

We do not know exactly.

It is nothingness.

A nothingness
which we use
to indicate
when we do not know something
towards which side
we do not know
and we say
then
consciousness
on the side of consciousness
but there are a hundred thousand other sides).

As this passage makes clear, for Artaud the fact that meaning is caught in a perpetual round of deferral is catastrophic. His is the crisis of modern consciousness, and for all his actuality he must be seen as an iconoclast working at the death of a phase of intellectual history, not as the herald of postmodern thought modes.

Artaud's late writing seeks to escape the prison house of the sayable and accede to what he calls, in *Suppôts et suppliciations,* the "ordre de non-détermination totale, / irrévocable / et absolue" (order of total non-determination, / irrevocable / and absolute). Existing free from all determination, however, leads to being undefined to the point of being nothing. The conceptual and linguistic game of a new bodily self is by definition irrepresentable, as Artaud writes in a June 1946 *cahier* collected in volume twenty-two of the *Œuves complètes:* "Je suis un être *indéfinissable* dans un état, étatifier, c'est me détruire" (I am a being *undefinable* in any state, statifying amounts to destroying

me). He writes of his textual universe as having left language and existence far behind. Ideation is banished. Only physical bodies exist. Artaud loudly affirms how simple his textual world is, but at the same time it attains such convoluted abstractions that it shades toward the incomprehensible. Artaud's textual journey ends in the outer reaches of language and the conceivable, amid the detritus of the mother tongue that, as he wrote of the body, he compacted ever tighter together.

Antonin Artaud died of a tardily diagnosed cancer of the rectum on 4 March 1948. In the last weeks of his life he had been claiming he had nothing further to write. Two days before his death he had drawn up a testament for Thévenin to be his literary executor. Despite a high level of chloral in his blood (which he had been taking in the final stages of his illness) there is no evidence for the popular misconception that he purposely committed suicide. He is buried in Marseilles.

Since the 1990s Artaud's tortured drawings of dismembered bodies, dating from the end of his life, have figured in major exhibitions of outsider art in Paris and New York. His name is bandied as evidence of progressive cultural and intellectual credentials, but the Artaud legends, all emphasizing his liminality, have overshadowed his works and prevented its being read, or read with sufficient attention. The standard Gallimard edition of his *Œuvres complètes*–expansion of which was suspended upon the death of Artaud's literary executor, Thévenin, in 1993–runs to twenty-six volumes and includes the quasi-totality of his texts and the larger part of his notebooks. With the majority of his texts now in the public domain a balanced appraisal of his work has begun. Attentive global readings present a vision of Artaud which goes beyond seeing him as a "case" to appreciating his significance as a leading figure of twentieth-century European letters and a wordsmith of the first order.

Letters:

"Lettres (à Maurice Bataille d'octobre 1947)," *France-Asie,* no. 30 (September 1948): 1049–1058;

Lettres d'Antonin Artaud à Jean-Louis Barrault, edited, with a preface, by Paul Arnold and notes by André Frank (Paris: Bordas, 1952);

"Lettre (à Pierre Loeb du 23 avril 1947)," *Les Lettres nouvelles,* no. 6 (April 1958): 481–486;

"Lettre (à Albert Camus)," *Nouvelle Revue Française,* no. 89 (May 1960): 1012–1020;

"Lettre (à Roger Karl du 1er mars 1939)," *Lettre ouverte,* no. 2 (March 1961): 59–60;

"Onze lettres à Anaïs Nin," *Tel Quel,* no. 20 (Winter 1964): 3–11;

"Lettres inédites (de 1930 à 1933)," *Opus International,* no. 3 (1967): 62–69;

Lettres à Génica Athanasiou: Précédées de deux poèmes à elle dédiés (Paris: Gallimard, 1969);

"La dernière lettre de Rodez," *Magazine littéraire,* no. 95 (December 1974): 51;

Lettres à Anie Besnard, edited by Françoise Buisson (Paris: Le Nouveau Commerce, 1977);

Nouveaux écrits de Rodez: Lettres au docteur Ferdière, 1943–1946, et autres textes inédits, suivis de six lettres à Marie Dubuc, 1935–1937, preface by Gaston Ferdière, présentation et notes by Pierre Chaleix (Paris: Gallimard, 1977);

"Lettres à Janine," *Nouvelle Revue Française,* nos. 316–317 (May–June 1979): 177–191, 167–179;

"Lettres (à Pierre Bordas)," *Nouvelle Revue Française,* no. 364 (May 1983): 170–188;

"Lettres (à A. Adamov et J. Lemarchand)," *Nouvelle Revue Française,* no. 413 (June 1987): 112–119.

Bibliography:
Claude-Jean Rameil, "Bibliographie," *Obliques,* nos. 10–11 (1976): 257–283.

Biographies:
Otto Hahn, *Portrait d'Antonin Artaud* (Paris: Le Soleil Noir, 1968);

Jacques Prevel, *En compagnie d'Antonin Artaud,* edited by Bernard Noël (Paris: Flammarion, 1974);

Thomas Maeder, *Antonin Artaud* (Paris: Plon, 1978);

Stephen Barber, *Antonin Artaud: Blows and Bombs* (London: Faber & Faber, 1993);

André Roumieux, *Artaud et l'asile,* 2 volumes (Paris: Séguier, 1996).

References:
Leo Bersani, "Artaud, defecation and birth," in his *A Future for Astyanax: Character and Desire in Literature* (Boston: Little, Brown, 1976), pp. 259–272;

Maurice Blanchot, "La Cruelle raison poétique," in his *L'Entretien infini* (Paris: Gallimard, 1969), pp. 432–438;

Blanchot, "Recherches: Artaud," *Nouvelle Revue Française,* 8 (1956): 873–881;

Cahiers de la Compagnie Renaud-Barrault, special Artaud issue, 22–23 (1958);

Mary Ann Caws, *The Inner Theatre of Recent French Poetry: Cendrars, Tzara, Péret, Artaud, Bonnefoy* (Princeton: Princeton University Press, 1972);

Georges Charbonnier, *Essai sur Antonin Artaud* (Paris: Seghers, 1959);

Julia F. Costich, *Antonin Artaud,* Twayne's World Authors Series, no. 492 (Boston: Twayne, 1978);

Gilles Deleuze, "Le Schizophrène et le mot," in his *Logique du sens* (Paris: Editions de Minuit, 1969), pp. 101–114;

Jacques Derrida and Paule Thévenin, *Antonin Artaud: Dessins et portraits* (Paris: Gallimard, 1986); translated, with a preface, by Caws as *The Secret Art of Antonin Artaud* (Cambridge, Mass.: MIT Press, 1998);

Derrida, "La Parole soufflée," "Le Théâtre de la cruauté et la clôture de la représentation," in his *L'Ecriture et la différence* (Paris: Seuil, 1967), pp. 253–292, 341–368;

Camille Dumoulié, *Antonin Artaud,* Les Contemporains, no. 19 (Paris: Seuil, 1996);

Dumoulié, *Nietzsche et Artaud: Pour une éthique de la cruauté* (Paris: Presses Universitaires de France, 1992);

Dumoulié, ed., *Les Théâtres de la cruauté: Hommage à Antonin Artaud* (Paris: Desjonquères, 2000);

Gérard Durozoi, *Artaud, l'aliénation et la folie* (Paris: Larousse, 1972);

Europe, special Artaud issue, nos. 667–668 (1984);

Katell Floc'h, *Antonin Artaud et la conquête du corps* (Paris: Découvrir, 1995);

Jacques Garelli, *Artaud et la question du lieu* (Paris: J. Corti, 1982);

Rodolphe Gasché, "Self-Engendering as a Verbal Body," *Modern Language Notes,* 93 (1978): 677–694;

Xavière Gauthier and others, *Artaud: Communications et Interventions du colloque Cérisy, juin-juillet 1972,* edited by Philippe Sollers (Paris: Union Générale d'Editions, 1973);

Jane Goodall, *Artaud and the Gnostic Drama* (Oxford: Clarendon Press, 1994);

Henri Gouhier, *Antonin Artaud et l'essence du théâtre* (Paris: Vrin, 1974);

Evelyne Grossman, *Artaud/Joyce: Le Corps et le texte* (Paris: Nathan, 1996);

Simon Harel, *Vies et morts d'Antonin Artaud: Le Séjour à Rodez* (Longueuil, Quebec: Editions Le Préambule, 1990);

Jean Hort, *Antonin Artaud: Le suicidé de la société* (Geneva: Editions Connaître, 1960);

Carol Jacob, "The Assimilating Harmony: A Reading of Antonin Artaud's *Héliogabale,*" *Sub-Stance,* no. 17 (1977): 115–138;

Laurent Jenny, *La Terreur et les signes: Poétiques de rupture* (Paris: Gallimard, 1982), pp. 209–267;

Vincent Kaufmann, *Post Scripts: The Writer's Workshop,* translated by Deborah Triesman (Cambridge,

Mass.: Harvard University Press, 1994), pp. 96–106, 141–146;

David Kelley, "Antonin Artaud: 'Madness' and Self-Expression," in *Modernism and the European Unconscious,* edited by Peter Collier and Judy Davies (Cambridge: Polity Press, 1990), pp. 230–245;

Bettina L. Knapp, "Mexico: The Myth of *Renovatio,"* *Sub-Stance,* no. 50 (1986): 61–68;

Florence de Mèredieu, *Antonin Artaud: Les Couilles de l'Ange* (Paris: Blusson, 1992);

Obliques, special Artaud issue, nos. 10–11 (1976);

Michel Pierssens, *Savoirs à l'œuvre: Essais d'epistémocritique* (Lille: Presses Universitaires de Lille, 1990), pp. 109–119;

Gene A. Plunka, ed., *Antonin Artaud and the Modern Theater* (Rutherford, N.J.: Fairleigh Dickinson University Press / London & Cranbury, N.J.: Associated University Presses, 1994);

Jean-Michel Rey, *La Naissance de la poésie: Antonin Artaud* (Paris: Editions Métailié, 1991);

Guy Scarpetta, "Artaud écrit ou La canne de Saint Patrick," *Tel Quel,* no. 81 (1979) 66–85;

Eric Sellin, *The Dramatic Concepts of Antonin Artaud* (Chicago & London: University of Chicago Press, 1968);

Roger Shattuck, "Artaud Possessed," in his *The Innocent Eye* (Toronto: Collins, 1984), pp. 169–186;

Brian Singleton, *Artaud: Le Théâtre et son Double,* Critical Guides to French Texts, no. 118 (London: Grant & Cutler, 1998);

Philippe Sollers, "La Pensée émet des signes," in his *L'Ecriture et l'expérience des limites* (Paris: Gallimard, 1971), pp. 88–104;

Susan Sontag, "Approaching Artaud," in *Antonin Artaud: Selected Writings,* translated by Helen Weaver (New York: Farrar, Straus & Giroux, 1976), pp. xvii–lix;

Jean-Luc Steinmetz, "Hapax," in his *Signets: Essais critiques sur la poésie du XVIIIe au XXe siècle* (Paris: J. Corti, 1995), pp. 275–288;

John C. Stout, *Antonin Artaud's Alternate Genealogies: Self-Portraits and Family Romances* (Waterloo, Ontario: Wilfrid Laurier University Press, 1996);

Thévenin, *Antonin Artaud, ce désespéré qui vous parle* (Paris: Seuil, 1993);

Thévenin, "L'Automatisme en question," in *Folie et psychanalyse dans l'expérience surréaliste,* edited by Fabienne Hulak (Nice: Z'Editions, 1992), pp. 35–73;

La Tour de Feu, special Artaud issue, nos. 63–64 (1959);

Alain Virmaux and Odette Virmaux, *Antonin Artaud: Qui êtes-vous?* (Lyon: La Manufacture, 1989);

Virmaux and Virmaux, *Artaud, un bilan critique* (Paris: Belfond, 1979);

Kenneth White, *Le Monde d'Antonin Artaud,* Le Regard Littéraire, no. 29 (Brussels: Editions Complexe, 1989).

Yves Bonnefoy

(24 June 1923 –   )

J. M. Reibetanz
University of Toronto

BOOKS: *Traité du pianiste* (Paris: La Révolution la nuit, 1946); republished as *Traité du pianiste: Yves Bonnefoy,* bilingual edition, with English translation by Anthony Rudolf and afterword by Bonnefoy (Birmingham, U.K.: Delos Press, 1993);

Du Mouvement et de l'immobilité de Douve (Paris: Mercure de France, 1953); enlarged as *Du Mouvement et de l'immobilité de Douve, suivi de Hier régnant désert et accompagné d'Anti-Platon et de deux essais,* Collection Poésie, no. 52 (Paris: Gallimard, 1960); translated by Galway Kinnell as *On the Motion and Immobility of Douve,* bilingual edition (Athens: Ohio University Press, 1968; Newcastle upon Tyne, U.K.: Bloodaxe, 1992);

Peintures murales de la France gothique, photographs by Pierre Devinoy (Paris: Paul Hartmann, 1954);

Hier régnant désert (Paris: Mercure de France, 1958); translated by Anthony Rudolf in *Yesterday's Wilderness Kingdom/Hier régnant désert,* bilingual edition, foreword by John E. Jackson (London: MPT Books, 2000);

Pierre écrite, illustrated by Raoul Ubac (Paris: Maeght, 1958; enlarged edition, Paris: Mercure de France, 1965); translated by Susanna Lang in *Pierre écrite/ Words in Stone,* bilingual edition (Amherst: University of Massachusetts Press, 1976);

L'Improbable (Paris: Mercure de France, 1959); revised and enlarged as *L'Improbable; suivi de, Un reve fait à Mantoue* (Paris: Mercure de France, 1980); enlarged edition republished as *L'Improbable: Et autres essais; suivi de Un rêve fait à Mantoue,* Collection Folio/Essais, no. 203 (Paris: Gallimard, 1992);

Rimbaud par lui-même, Ecrivains de toujours, no. 54 (Paris: Seuil, 1961); republished as *Rimbaud* (Paris: Seuil, 1961); translated by Paul Schmidt as *Rimbaud* (New York: Harper & Row, 1973);

La Seconde simplicité (Paris: Mercure de France, 1961);

Anti-platon, etchings by Joan Miró (Paris: Maeght, 1962);

La Religion de Chagall, Derrière le miroir, no. 132 (Paris: Maeght, 1962);

Yves Bonnefoy (photograph © Mathilde Bonnefoy)

Miró, Italian version (Milan: Silvana Editoriale d'Arte, 1964; republished in French, Paris: La Bibliothèque des Arts, 1964); Italian version translated by Judith Landry as *Miró* (London: Faber & Faber, 1967; New York: Viking, 1967);

La Poésie Française et le principe d'identité, engravings by Raoul Ubac (Paris: Maeght, 1967);

Un Rêve fait à Mantoue (Paris: Mercure de France, 1967);

Rome 1630: L'Horizon due premier baroque (Paris: Flammarion, 1970); revised and enlarged as *Rome, 1630: L'Horizon du premier baroque; suivi de, Un des siècles du culte des images* (Paris: Flammarion, 1994);

L'Arrière-pays (Geneva: Skira, 1972; Geneva: Skira / Paris: Flammarion, 1982);

Une peinture métaphysique: Denise Estéban (Paris: Fequet & Baudier, 1973);

L'Ordalie, engravings by Claude Garache (Paris: Maeght, 1974);

Dans le leurre du seuil (Paris: Mercure de France, 1975);

Garache, by Bonnefoy and Jacques Thuillier, Derrière le miroir, no. 213 (Paris: Maeght, 1975);

Le Nuage rouge (Paris: Mercure de France, 1977);

Rue Traversière (Paris: Mercure de France, 1977); enlarged as *Rue Traversière; et autres Récits en rêve,* afterword by Jackson, Collection Poésie, no. 262 (Paris: Gallimard, 1992);

Collège de France: Chaire d'études comparées de la fonction poétique: Leçon inaugurale faite le vendredi 4 décembre 1981 (Paris: Collège de France, 1981); republished as *La Présence et l'image: Leçon inaugurale de la chaire d'études comparées de la fonction poétique au Collège de France, 1981* (Paris: Mercure de France, 1983);

La Poésie et l'Université, edited by Jean Roudaut, Discours universitaires, new series no. 36 (Fribourg, Switzerland: Editions Universitaires Fribourg Suisse, 1984);

Ce qui fut sans lumière (Paris: Mercure de France, 1987); translated by John T. Naughton as *In the Shadow's Light,* bilingual edition (Chicago & London: University of Chicago Press, 1991)–translation includes an interview with Bonnefoy, pp. 159–179; French edition enlarged as *Ce qui fut sans lumière; suivi de Début et fin de la neige et de Là où retombe la flèche* (Paris: Gallimard, 1995);

Récits en rêve (Paris: Mercure de France, 1987);

The Grapes of Zeuxis: And Other Fables/Les Raisons de Zeuxis et d'autres fables, bilingual edition, English translation by Richard Stamelman, with etchings by George Nama (Montauk, N.Y.: Monument Press, 1987);

Là où retombe la flèche (Paris: Mercure de France, 1988);

Une autre époque de l'écriture (Paris: Mercure de France, 1988);

La Vérité de parole (Paris: Mercure de France, 1988); enlarged as *La Vérité de parole et autre essais,* Collection Folio/Essais, no. 272 (Paris: Gallimard, 1992);

Début et fin de la neige, illustrated by Geneviève Asse (Geneva: Jacques T. Quentin, 1989); enlarged as *Début et fin de la neige; suivi de Là où retombe la flèche* (Paris: Mercure de France, 1991);

Sur un sculpteur et des peintres (Paris: Plon, 1989);

Once More the Grapes of Zeuxis/Encore les Raisins de Zeuxis, bilingual edition, English translation by Stamelman, etchings by Nama (Montauk, N.Y.: Monument Press, 1990);

Alberto Giacometti: Biographie d'une œuvre (Paris: Flammarion, 1991); translated by Jean Stewart as *Alberto Giacometti: A Biography of His Work* (Paris: Flammarion, 1991); translation republished as *Giacometti* (Paris: Flammarion / London: Thames & Hudson, 2001);

Alechinsky, les traversées, afterword by François Bellec (Saint-Clément-la-Rivière: Fata Morgana, 1992);

La Vie errante, illustrated by Miklos Bokor (Paris: Maeght, 1992); enlarged as *La Vie errante; suivi de Une autre époque de l'écriture* (Paris: Mercure de France, 1993)–includes *Les Raisons de Zeuxis* and *Encore les Raisins de Zeuxis;* enlarged again as *La Vie errante; suivi de Une autre époque de l'écriture; et de Remarques sur le dessin,* Collection Poésie, no. 313 (Paris: Gallimard, 1997);

Delacroix & Hamlet, by Bonnefoy and Arlette Sérullaz (Paris: Réunion des Musées Nationaux/Seuil, 1993);

Remarques sur le dessin (Paris: Mercure de France, 1993);

Palézieux, by Bonnefoy and Florian Rodari (Geneva: Skira, 1994);

La Petite phrase et la longue phrase, Collection Essais, no. 50 (Paris: La Tilv, 1994);

Dessin, couleur et lumière (Paris: Mercure de France, 1995);

La Journée d'Alexandre Hollan (Cognac: Le Temps Qu'il Fait / Paris: Galerie Vieille-du-Temple / Geneva: Galerie Foëx, 1995);

Alberto Giacometti (Paris: Assouline, 1998);

Théâtre et poésie: Shakespeare et Yeats (Paris: Mercure de France, 1998);

Lieux et destins de l'image: Un cours de poétique au Collège de France, 1981–1993 (Paris: Seuil, 1999);

Baudelaire: La Tentation de l'oubli (Paris: Bibliothèque Nationale de France, 2000);

Keats et Leopardi: Quelques traductions nouvelles (Paris: Mercure de France, 2000);

La Communauté des traducteurs (Strasbourg: Presses Universitaires de Strasbourg, 2000);

L'Enseignement et l'exemple de Leopardi (Bordeaux: William Blake & Co, 2001);

André Breton à l'avant de soi (Tours: Farrago, 2001);

Les Planches courbes (Paris: Mercure de France, 2001);

Le Cœur-espace (Tours: Farrago, 2001).

Collection: *Poèmes: Yves Bonnefoy* (Paris: Mercure de France, 1978; republished, with a preface by Jean Starobinski, Collection Poésie, no. 158, Paris: Gallimard, 1982)–comprises *Du Mouvement et de l'immobilité de Douve, Hier régnant désert, Pierre écrite,* and *Dans le leurre du seuil.*

Editions in English: *Selected Poems,* translated by Anthony Rudolf (London: Cape, 1968);

Poems 1959–1975: Yves Bonnefoy, translated by Richard Pevear (New York: Random House, 1985)–comprises translations of poems from *Pierre écrite* and *Dans le leurre du seuil;*

Things Dying Things Newborn: Selected Poems, translated by Rudolf (London: Menard, 1985);

The Act and the Place of Poetry: Selected Essays, edited, with an introduction, by John T. Naughton, translated by

Naughton and others (Chicago & London: University of Chicago Press, 1989);

Early Poems, 1947–1959: Yves Bonnefoy, translated by Galway Kinnell and Pevear (Athens: Ohio University Press, 1990);

The Lure and the Truth of Painting: Selected Essays on Art, edited, with an introduction and afterword, by Richard Stamelman, translated by Stamelman and others, preface by Bonnefoy (Chicago & London: University of Chicago Press, 1995);

New and Selected Poems: Yves Bonnefoy, edited by Naughton and Rudolf, translated by Naughton and others (Chicago & London: University of Chicago Press, 1995).

OTHER: *La Quête du Saint Graal,* edited by Bonnefoy and Albert Béguin, Astrée, no. 14 (Paris: Le Club du Meilleur Livre, 1958);

Georges Duthuit, *Représentation et présence: Premiers écrits et travaux, 1923–1952,* introduction by Bonnefoy, Idées et recherches, no. 2 (Paris: Flammarion, 1974);

Stéphane Mallarmé, *Igitur, Divagations, Un coup de dés,* edited by Bonnefoy, Collection Poésie, no. 113 (Paris: Gallimard, 1976);

Andrea Mantegna, *Tout l'œuvre peint de Mantegna,* documentation by Niny Garavaglia, translated by Simone Darses, introduction by Bonnefoy (Paris: Flammarion, 1978);

Haïku, edited and translated by Roger Munier, preface by Bonnefoy, Documents spirituels, no. 15 (Paris: Fayard, 1978);

Dictionnaire des mythologies et des religions des sociétés traditionnelles et du monde antique, 2 volumes, compiled by Bonnefoy (Paris: Flammarion, 1981); translated by Gerald Honigsblum and others as *Mythologies,* 2 volumes, edited by Wendy Doniger (Chicago: University of Chicago Press, 1991);

Jacques Hartmann, peintures et dessins, preface by Bonnefoy, Collection Berggruen, no. 73 (Paris: Berggruen & Cie, 1982);

Marceline Desbordes-Valmore, *Poésies: Marceline Desbordes-Valmore,* edited, with an introduction, by Bonnefoy, Collection Poésie, no. 178 (Paris: Gallimard, 1983);

Pierre-Albert Jourdan, *Les Sandales de paille,* edited by Yves Leclair, preface by Bonnefoy (Paris: Mercure de France, 1987);

Giórgos Séféris, *Poèmes: 1933–1955,* translated by Jacques Lacarrière and Egérie Mavraki, preface by Bonnefoy, afterword by Gaëtan Picon (Paris: Mercure de France, 1988);

Vérité poétique et vérité scientifique: Offert à Gilbert Gadoffre à l'occasion du quarantième anniversaire de l'Institut collégial européen par ses collègues du séminaire interdisciplinaire du

Collège de France et par ses amis européens, américains et asiatiques, edited by Bonnefoy, André Lichnérowicz, and Marcel Paul Schützenberger (Paris: Presses Universitaires de France, 1989);

Alain Morin, *Pour quel temps inconnu?* preface by Bonnefoy (Mortemart: Rougerie, 1990);

Lorne Campbell, *Portraits de la Renaissance: La Peinture des portraits en Europe aux XIVᵉ, XVᵉ et XVIᵉ siècles,* translated by Dominique Le Bourg, preface by Bonnefoy (Paris: Hazan, 1991);

Thomas M. Greene, *Poésie et magie,* preface by Bonnefoy (Paris: Juilliard, 1991);

Michel Jourdan, *Journal du réel gravé sur un bâton,* preface by Bonnefoy (Paris: Critérion, 1991);

Maria Luisa Spaziani, *Jardin d'été, palais d'hiver: Choix de poèmes, 1954–1992,* translated by Patrice Dyerval Angelini, introduction by Bonnefoy (Paris: Mercure de France, 1994);

Jouve poète, romancier, critique: Colloque de la Fondation Hugot du Collège de France, edited by Bonnefoy and Odile Bombarde, Collection Pleine marge, no. 6 (Paris: Lachenal & Ritter, 1995);

Mallarmé, *Correspondance complète, 1862–1871; suivi de Lettres sur la poésie, 1872–1898: Avec des lettres inédites,* edited by Bertrand Marchal, preface by Bonnefoy (Paris: Gallimard, 1995);

Patrice Hugues, *Tissu et travail de civilisation,* preface by Bonnefoy (Rouen: Médianes, 1996);

Mallarmé, *Vers de circonstance: Avec des inédits,* edited by Marchal, preface by Bonnefoy, Collection Poésie, no. 296 (Paris: Gallimard, 1996);

Picon, *1863, naissance de la peinture moderne,* preface by Bonnefoy, afterword by Alain Bonfand, Folio Essais, no. 295 (Paris: Gallimard, 1996);

Poésie et rhétorique: La Conscience de soi de la poésie: Colloque de la Fondation Hugot du Collège de France, edited by Bonnefoy and Odile Bombarde (Paris: Lachenal & Ritter, 1997);

Pierre-Jean Rémy, *Retour d'Hélène,* preface by Bonnefoy (Paris: Gallimard, 1997);

Charles Baudelaire, *Les Fleurs du Mal,* edited by John E. Jackson, preface by Bonnefoy (Paris: Le Livre de Poche Classique, 1999);

Roberto Mussapi, *Le Voyage de midi; suivi de Voix du fond de la nuit,* translated by Jean-Yves Masson, preface by Bonnefoy (Paris: Gallimard, 1999).

TRANSLATIONS: William Shakespeare, *Henry IV (I); Jules César; Hamlet; Le Conte d'hiver; Vénus et Adonis; Le Viol de Lucrèce,* 6 volumes (Paris: Club Français du Livre, 1957–1960);

Shakespeare, *Le Roi Lear* (Paris: Mercure de France, 1965);

Shakespeare, *Roméo et Juliette* (Paris: Mercure de France, 1968);

Shakespeare, *Hamlet; Le Roi Lear,* Collection Folio (Paris: Gallimard, 1978);

Shakespeare, *Macbeth* (Paris: Mercure de France, 1983);

William Butler Yeats, *Quarante-cinq poèmes de W. B. Yeats* (Paris: Hermann, 1989);

Shakespeare, *Les Poèmes de Shakespeare* (Paris: Mercure de France, 1993);

John Donne, *Trois des derniers poèmes* (Losne: T. Bouchard / Bédée: Folle Avoine, 1994);

Shakespeare, *Le Conte d'hiver* (Paris: Mercure de France, 1994);

Shakespeare, *XXIV Sonnets de Shakespeare* (Paris: Les Bibliophiles de France, 1994);

Shakespeare, *Jules César* (Paris: Mercure de France, 1995);

Shakespeare, *La Tempête* (Paris: Gallimard, 1998);

Shakespeare, *Antoine et Cléopâtre,* bilingual edition, French translation, with an introduction and notes, by Bonnefoy, edited by Gisèle Venet (Paris: Gallimard, 1999).

Poet, translator, and respected critic of both literature and art, Yves Bonnefoy is widely acknowledged as the most significant and influential figure in contemporary French poetry. He has held visiting professorships at Yale, Princeton, Williams, Brandeis, Wesleyan, and the University of California. In 1981 he was elected to the chair previously held by Roland Barthes at the Collège de France in Paris, and since 1993 he has served as Professor of Comparative Poetics. Bonnefoy was awarded the Prix Montaigne in 1978, the Prix Goncourt in 1987, and the Grand Prix Nationale de Poèsie in 1993; in 1992 he was the subject of a comprehensive exhibition of manuscripts, first editions, and pictures at the Bibliothèque Nationale. Since 1953 he has produced six major collections of poetry that are notable for the intensity of their vision and the consistency of their voice, a body of work resembling in these respects the writings of the modern English poet he has most deeply admired and brilliantly translated, William Butler Yeats.

Bonnefoy was born in Tours on 24 June 1923, the son of Marius Elie Bonnefoy, a railroad worker, and Hélène Maury Bonnefoy, a teacher. He had an older sister, Suzanne, born in 1914. Bonnefoy spent his childhood summers at his grandfather's house in Toirac, near the Lot River. This summer landscape, he is quoted as saying, in the preface to *New and Selected Poems: Yves Bonnefoy* (1995), "formed me in my deepest choices, with its vast, deserted plateaus and gray stone," providing images and themes that his poetry has probed ever more deeply over the years. His early life was also profoundly influenced by the loss of his father, who died when Bonnefoy was thir-

teen. As, in similar circumstances, did Arthur Rimbaud, whose poetry he cherished, Bonnefoy reacted to this loss by immersing himself in his studies. He graduated with honors from the Lycée Descartes in 1941 and then studied mathematics, science, and philosophy at the Université de Poitiers and the Sorbonne. A more lasting and more poetically resonant impact of his father's loss may be found in the sense of desolation that pervades his early work, relieved, however, by moments of clarity and illumination redolent of his idyllic childhood summers.

Arriving in occupied Paris in 1944 to study at the Sorbonne, Bonnefoy began to write poetry under the influence of such Surrealists as André Breton and Victor Brauner. Although he later described himself, in a 1976 interview with John E. Jackson republished in *The Act and the Place of Poetry: Selected Essays* (1989), as "a rather marginal member of the group," its uncompromising dedication to poetry precipitated a definitive change in his primary intellectual focus, from mathematics and philosophy to literature. With the encouragement of Jean Wahl, Bonnefoy put aside his philosophy thesis and worked for three years at the Centre national de la recherche scientifique (National Center for Scientific Research) studying English literary creativity, reading such literary theorists as I. A. Richards and R. P. Blackmur and writing his own poetry. His first major collection, *Du Mouvement et de l'immobilité de Douve* (translated as *On the Motion and Immobility of Douve,* 1968), was published in 1953 to immediate acclaim. In this collection, Douve (a mysterious muse figure, a dead woman whose remoteness and physical decomposition are suggested by the French word *douve,* meaning both "moat" and "ditch") serves as the focal point for a sequence of probing and at times harrowing meditations on the poet's capacity to reach and to express the light at the center of being, the ultimate reality—consistently referred to as *présence* (presence) in Bonnefoy's writings—behind and beyond the facade of received ideas. This task became the central quest of Bonnefoy's career. The terms in which he expresses it in "Aux Arbres" (To the Trees) epitomize the approach of *Du Mouvement et de l'immobilité de Douve* and of his later collections:

Que saisir sinon qui s'échappe,
Que voir sinon qui s'obscurcit,
Que désirer sinon que meurt,
Sinon qui parle et se déchire?

(What to seize but what escapes,
What to see but what darkens,
What to desire but what dies,
But what speaks and tears itself apart?)
(translation by J. M. Reibetanz)

By the mere fact of being questions, these lines convey Bonnefoy's skepticism about conventional objects of repre-

Bonnefoy in the early 1950s

sentation and means of consolation: poetry cannot be built on a sure foundation of affirmatives in a world that acknowledges no self-evident universals, a world perpetually unmade by death. Yet, the form of these questions opens a door beyond their darkness. They are oxymorons, and as Bonnefoy stated explicitly in a 1989 interview with John T. Naughton—included in *In the Shadow's Light,* the 1991 translation of *Ce qui fut sans lumière* (What Was Without Light, 1987)—the oxymoron is the primary resource of poetry because it is "one of the ways of remembering what is beyond language"; in fact, "the fusion of opposites is the star that guides poetry." By questioning

and circumventing the logic of everyday discourse—a language of abstract concepts that surrounds one with a veil of illusory permanence—the oxymoron gives the reader a momentary, intuitive glimpse of ultimate reality, the essential Being or *présence* that exists beyond human consciousness of death and before the *langue* (language) that has separated humanity from *présence*. The oxymoron thus manifests the essential task of poetry to look straight through negation and, abandoning logic for intuition, provide an experience of the ultimate unity of being. This poetics involves a special usage of the linguist Ferdinand de Saussure's dichotomy of *langue/parole* (language/speech):

YVES BONNEFOY

DU MOUVEMENT
ET DE L'IMMOBILITÉ
DE DOUVE

PARIS
MERCURE DE FRANCE
MCMLXVII

*Cover for the 1967 edition of Bonnefoy's first major collection of poetry
(Ralph Brown Draughon Library, Auburn University)*

here *langue* denotes a formal system that attempts to deny or mask mortality, while *parole* (the "qui parle" from "Aux Arbres," the domain of poetry) acknowledges mortality and finds the only universality in it. The explication of this poetics and the exploration of its consequences has become the lifelong undertaking of Bonnefoy's writings. In *Du Mouvement et de l'immobilité de Douve* the death and decomposition of Douve convey, therefore, not only the inescapable mortality of the body, sometimes in shockingly frank terms, but also the lifelessness of a conventional mimesis that attempts to reify descriptive images: "rejetés ces draps de verdure et de boue / Il ne reste qu'un feu du royaume de mort" (should you throw back these sheets of greenness and mud, nothing remains but a fire in the kingdom of death). The poems of *Du Mouvement et de l'immobilité de Douve* throw back those sheets, probing what "Une Autre Voix" (Another Voice) refers to as the "minuit dans l'etre" (midnight within being), and affirming as does "Aux Arbres" that "Sera lumière encore n'étant rien" (She will be light once more being nothing).

This confidence appears severely shaken in Bonnefoy's 1958 collection, *Hier régnant désert* (translated as *Yesterday's Wilderness Kingdom,* 2000), in which he rigorously pursues the disturbing personal implications of the art of his previous work. In an interview with Shusha Guppy published in *Paris Review* (Summer 1994), Bonnefoy explained how the writing of a book entails for him a highly intuitive revision of what has come before it: "I will not start writing again except when I notice that the last book is no longer sufficient to express or order my relationship with the world." Increasingly, it seems, Bonnefoy found himself troubled by the remoteness from the world of lived experience that the affirmations of his first book entailed: he worried that, in seeking to escape the closed systems of conventional language, he had produced a closed system of his own. Brimming with discontent at formal symmetries, *Hier régnant désert* conducts a poetic purge by centering on the theme of trial by ordeal and by focusing on such unflowering images as the iron bridge, the mortal face, stony rubble, and a harbor of black clay. The poem "L'Imperfection Est la Cime" (Imperfection is the Summit) spells out the governing aesthetic of the book explicitly: "Il y avait qu'il fallait détruire et détruire et détruire, / Il y avait que le salut n'est qu'à ce prix" (So it was that one must destroy and destroy and destroy, / So it was that salvation is only at this price [translation by Reibetanz]). In a move that proves especially fruitful in Bonnefoy's later works, the closure of *Hier régnant désert* manifests this destructive impulse by breaking down into prose-poetry in "Dévotion" (Devotion), a sequence that affirms devotion to concrete objects in the real world by calling them up as sentence fragments. The restless dissatisfaction evident here has even spilled over into later versions of *Hier régnant désert,* subjected to constant revision and reordering by the author when the poems were republished in later collections.

Bonnefoy's 1965 collection, *Pierre écrite* (translated as *Words in Stone,* 1976), stands in welcome contrast to such spiritual and formal upheaval. The world of simple, concrete objects that had been appealed to in "Dévotion" presides over *Pierre écrite* as a tutelary spirit, informing the book with sureness and generating a sense of contentment. The barren landscape of *Hier régnant désert* is replaced by images of water, trees, and gardens, and the garden image holds particular promise–as the opening poem, "L'été de nuit" (The Summer of Night), makes clear: "Nous sommes entrés dans le jardin, dont l'ange / A refermé les portes sans retour" (We have come into the garden whose gates the angel has shut irreversibly [translation by Reibetanz]). Readers of T. S. Eliot will recognize this experience as analogous to the rose garden of *Burnt Norton* (1936), and the import is the same: this garden takes the reader fleetingly back to the prelapsarian garden of ultimate reality or *présence.* The difference is that for

Bonnefoy, the sense of presence is achieved by embracing the real object in its temporality, rather than by leaving it behind. As Bonnefoy wrote in an essay published in *Preuves* (June 1959), "Shakespeare et le poète français" (translated as "Shakespeare and the French Poet" in *The Act and the Place of Poetry*), "the Thing, the real object, in its separation from ourselves, its infinite otherness . . . can give us an instantaneous glimpse of essential being and thus be our salvation." Standing behind the assurances of *Pierre écrite* are two important events in Bonnefoy's life: his meeting in 1965 with the American painter Lucy Vines, and the couple's discovery and restoration of an abandoned monastic farmhouse at Valsaintes, in Provence. Vines seems to be the source of the "other" addressed in *Pierre écrite,* a being whose strong physical presence contrasts with the disembodied, metaphoric objects of address in Bonnefoy's earlier poetry; and the house and country around Valsaintes solidly ground the natural images in the book. Yet, thanks to the strong urge toward transcendence that typifies Bonnefoy's poetics (he chooses the word "salvation" quite deliberately in "Shakespeare and the French Poet") and to the poet's earlier immersion in the nondescriptive poetics of Surrealism, this concreteness does not maroon the poetry in the material world. The first two stanzas of "La Chambre" (The Room) exemplify the radiance that imbues the images in the book:

> Le miroir et le fleuve en crue, ce matin
> S'appelaient à travers la chambre, deux lumières
> Se trouvent et s'unissent dans l'obscur
> Des meubles de la chambre descellée.
> Et nous étions deux pays de sommeil
> Communiquant par leurs marches de pierre
> Où se perdait l'eau non trouble d'un rêve
> Toujours se reformant, toujours brisé.
>
> (The mirror and the stream in flood, this morning
> Called to each other across the room, two lights
> Find each other and join in the dark
> Of the furniture of the unsealed room.
> And we were two countries of sleep
> Communicating through their stone walks
> Where water untroubled by a dream lost itself,
> Forever reforming itself, forever broken).
> (translation by Reibetanz)

This use of metaphor is not grotesque or bizarre, as are the extreme images of Surrealism, but neither is it merely an alternative way of expressing a literal observation. The poem uses metaphor neither to disarrange nor to describe, but to create embodiments of coherent suggestiveness. It points the reader to solid images–the mirror, the stream, the stone walks–that resonate, fleetingly, with a sense of transcendent oneness: "from within, the infinite that we thought was lost, the plenitude that saves–the moment

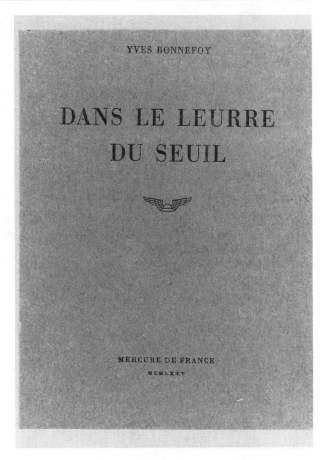

Cover for Bonnefoy's second collection of poems inspired by his house in Valseintes and the surrounding countryside (William T. Young Library, University of Kentucky)

replacing the eternal," as Bonnefoy put it in his 1976 interview with Jackson.

In 1966 Bonnefoy cofounded the review *L'Ephéme,* with Gaëtan Picon, André du Bouchet, and others; he co-edited the review until it ceased publication in 1972. In 1968 Bonnefoy and Lucy Vines married; the couple have a daughter, Mathilde. Bonnefoy was an associate professor at the Centre Universitaire de Vincennes from 1969 to 1970, and then held the same position at the Université de Nice from 1973 to 1976 and the Université d'Aix-en-Provence from 1979 to 1981, before becoming a full professor at the Collège de France in 1981.

Although some ten years separate the enlarged version of *Pierre écrite* from Bonnefoy's next major work of poetry, *Dans le leurre du seuil* (In the Lure of the Threshold, 1975), the two works partake of the same affirmative vision and are rooted in the same images associated with the house at Valsaintes. Indeed, a passage from the section titled "La Terre" (The Earth) seems to gesture back to the earlier work and to acknowledge points of connection: "Oui, toutes choses simples / Rétablies / Ici et là, sur leurs / Piliers de feu" (Yes, all simple things / Restored / Here and there, on their / Pillars of fire). But the simple things and the pillars are part of a much more ambitious structure in *Dans le leurre du seuil,* Bonnefoy's longest and most intricately unified work. Rather than a collection or sequence of allied poems, *Dans le leurre du seuil* is a long poem in seven sections–following a single movement of consciousness through a cycle of self-doubt, revision, regeneration, and affirmation. Here, the source of affirmation is the recurrent image of a child in an almond tree–the tree rooted in solid earth, the child elevated by it to a position where his unspoiled vision can take in distances. As Bonnefoy described this figure in his interview with Naughton, "the one who has the absolute in his eyes both looks into our dream and sees higher and farther." As a result of this heightened and broadened perception "Ici fleurit le rien" (Here nothingness flowers), and the flowering carries the last three sections of the book into a powerful, Whitmanesque embrace of the felt particulars of existence, newly shimmering with meaning. Strong reiterative cadences summon up clouds, summer, night, the child, and even death itself, greeting them all with a repeated "yes" of affirmation. Unlike Walt Whitman, however, who folds the particulars of the world into the self, Bonnefoy enters into the "infinite otherness" of their realities.

This process of crisis and recovery is repeated in Bonnefoy's 1987 collection *Ce qui fut sans lumière,* a book haunted by the poet's having to abandon the house at Valsaintes because it became too arduous to maintain. This move is a painful relinquishment, emblematic and anticipatory (as the work constantly reminds the reader) of the relinquishment of life itself, but it occasions some of Bonnefoy's finest poetry. At its heart are the words that Bonnefoy gives to the genius loci, the voice that rises up to tell him: "je t'aurai donné, en la reprenant, / Une terre natale, et il n'est rien d'autre" (I will have given you, in taking it back, / A native earth, and there is nothing else [translations by Reibetanz]). The giving and the taking, the "is" and the "nothing," spiral like a Möbius strip through the poems, insinuating that identity of opposites that Bonnefoy has associated with the device of oxymoron and with the spirit of *présence.* The poetry realizes both the bleakest and the most radiant implications of the dichotomy: on the one hand, Bonnefoy sees in "Le Puits, Les Ronces" ("The Well, the Brambles") that "les ronces / Qui griffent nos visages . . . ne sont / Que le rien qui griffe le rien dans la lumière" (the brambles / That scratch our faces . . . are nothing but the nothingness which scratches the nothingness in the light), and so the night sky emerges from "Le Haut du monde" (The Top of the World) as a "coffre qui étincelle mais plein de cendres" (chest which glitters but full of ashes); on the other hand, the abandoned house and its paths emerge as fleeting repositories of light–and so, in "Psyché devant le château d'Amor" (Psyche before the Castle of Love), the

stars glitter "parmi les pierres" (among the stones), and in "La Barque aux deux sommeils" (The Boat of Two Dreams), the poet further asserts the propinquity of opposites: "Dans la vie comme dans les images / C'est vrai que la valeur la plus claire avoisine / L'ombre noire" (In life as in images, / It's true that the brightest luster is near / The black shade). The book moves toward the more affirmative of these poles with the help of two sources of recognition–the art of the painter, and the experience of love. Bonnefoy has frequently acknowledged both of these sources as vehicles of *présence* in his other writings. In the interview with Naughton he observed that painting matters to poetry because it feeds the poet's desire to be in the world itself, rather than merely enmeshed in words: "Painters can perceive directly . . . the pure sensory quality that is denied to language, that is beyond the word in things." Writing on *King Lear,* in a preface to his 1978 translation of that play and *Hamlet,* translated as "Readiness, Ripeness: *Hamlet, King Lear*" in *The Act and the Place of Poetry,* Bonnefoy notes that Edgar's capacity for love makes him an "agent of redemption," as the "solidarity that brings things together and provides comfort" provides the occasion "for opening oneself to a conception of Presence." In *Ce qui fut sans lumière* the primary tribute to the painter's art occurs in the brilliant long lyric "Dedham, vu de Langham" (Dedham, Seen from Langham), a celebration of the power of English painter John Constable to capture "des choses claires" (bright things) by knowing how to "mêler à ta couleur / Une sorte de sable qui du ciel / Accueille l'étincellement dans la matière" (mix in your color / A kind of sand which, from the sky / Receives what glitters in matter). This process involves a recognition of the sand of mortality as the human source of ultimate light, just as in "Passant auprès du feu" (Passing near the Fire) the light of love between perishing mortals can manifest "Temps si riche de soi qu'il a cessé d'être" (Time so rich in itself that it has ceased to be).

If, as Bonnefoy asserts, each of his books has entailed a clarification of its predecessor, so each one has included formal and thematic seeds of what is to come. In *Ce qui fut sans lumière* the most prophetic formal development is the prose-poem, first tried by Bonnefoy in *Hier régnant désert* but more richly mined here in the sequence "Par où la terre finit" (Over Where the Earth Ends), characterized by a fine congruency between style and theme; through the abrupt, random cadences of prose, Bonnefoy takes the reader to where the earth ends "comme un bord abrupt de falaise" (like a sheer edge of cliff)–emphasizing once again the importance of the unpremeditated in art. The prose-poem has been an increasingly dominant form in Bonnefoy's art since *Ce qui fut sans lumière,* appearing in both *Là où retombe la flèche* (There Where the Arrow Falls)– a sequence first published separately in 1988 and repub-

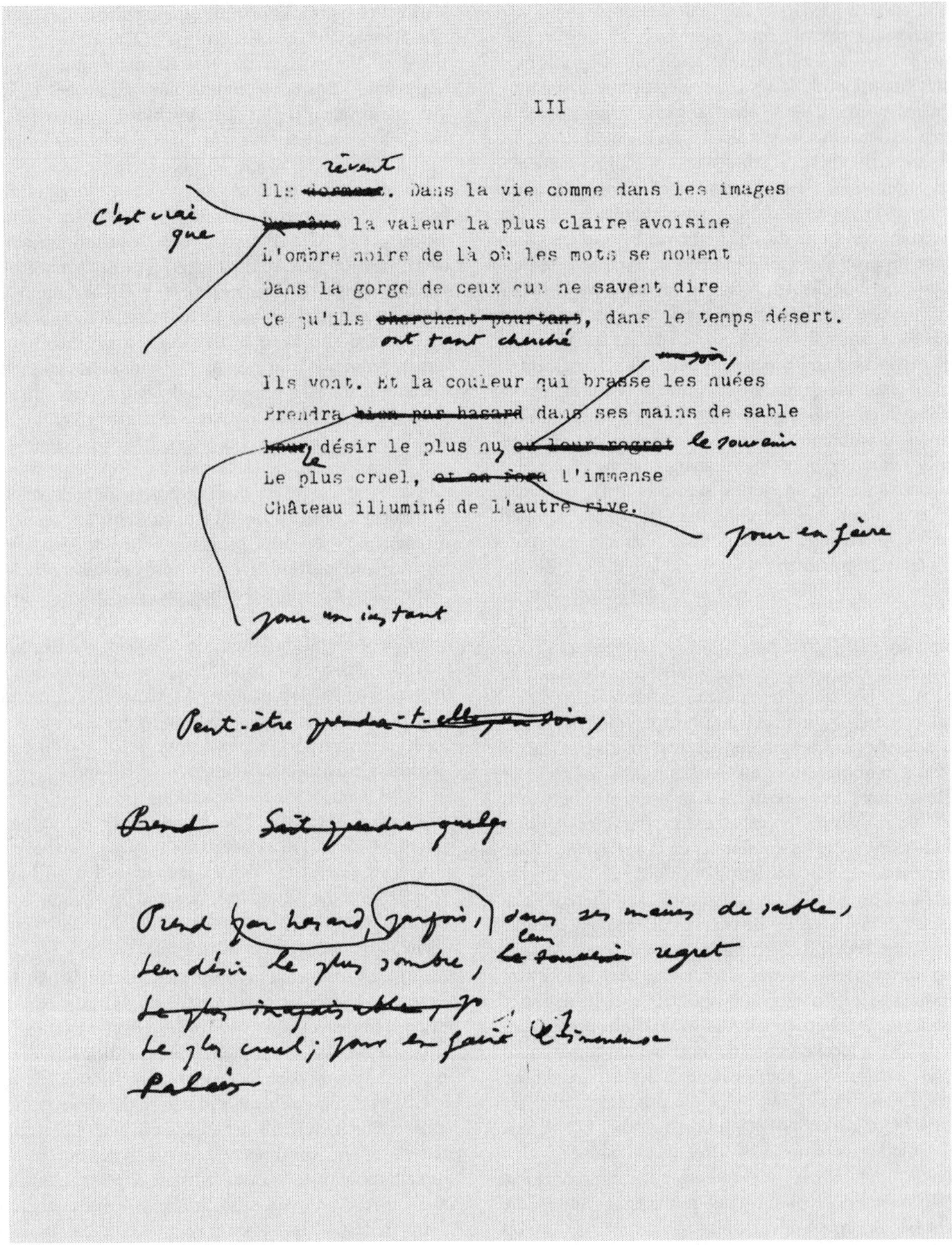

III

rêvent

C'est vrai que

Ils ~~dorment~~. Dans la vie comme dans les images
~~Prendre~~ la valeur la plus claire avoisine
L'ombre noire de là où les mots se nouent
Dans la gorge de ceux qui ne savent dire
Ce qu'ils ~~cherchent pourtant~~, dans le temps désert.
ont tant cherché

un soir,

Ils vont. Et la couleur qui brasse les nuées
Prendra ~~bien par hasard~~ dans ses mains de sable
~~leur~~ désir le plus nu ~~ou leur regret~~ *le souvenir*
le
Le plus cruel, ~~et en fera~~ l'immense
Château illuminé de l'autre ~~rive~~.

pour en faire

pour un instant

Peut-être prendra-t-elle un soir,

Prend   Sait prendre quelq

Prend par hasard, (parfois,) dans ses mains de sable,
leur
Leur désir le plus sombre, le souvenir regret
Le plus inoubliable, je
Le plus cruel; pour en faire l'immense
Palais

Page from the typescript for the title poem in Bonnefoy's 1987 collection Ce qui fut sans lumière *(from* Paris Review, *Summer 1994)*

YVES BONNEFOY

DÉBUT ET FIN
DE LA NEIGE

suivi de

LÀ OÙ RETOMBE LA FLÈCHE

MERCVRE DE FRANCE
M C M X C I

Title page for the 1991 book that includes Bonnefoy's 1988 prose-poem cycle and his 1989 collection of poems about transformations (Ralph Brown Draughon Library, Auburn University)

lished in 1991 in a volume with *Début et fin de la neige* (Beginning and End of the Snow, 1989)—and *La Vie errante* (The Wandering Life, 1992). The prose-poem, even more than does free verse, frees Bonnefoy from the artful restrictions of poetry, and it may be thought of as a fitting destination for a creative temperament that has from the beginning striven to transcend the limitations of conventional forms of representation. The thematic, rather than formal, element of *Ce qui fut sans lumière* that most closely anticipates his later achievements is the identification of light with snow in "La Neige" (The Snow). In his *Paris Review* interview Bonnefoy stated that "snow is a form of light," and this recognition animates his 1991 collection, *Début et fin de la neige; suivi de Là où retombe la flèche.* Here the reader finds a series of poems of transformation, the earth

transformed by what is instantaneous and weightless; as "La Grande Neige" (The Heavy Snow) puts it, "Un peu de vent / Ecrit du bout du pied un mot hors du monde" (A bit of wind / Writes with the tip of its foot a word beyond the world). Fleeting, white, luminous, and individuated with a complexity beyond that of any human *langue,* the snow embodies the kind of writing that Bonnefoy has sought throughout his life; and these poems celebrate such writing with typical deftness and variety, ranging from haiku-like apperceptions and invocations to more personal narratives. Having at last discovered and realized the potential of this most translucent of images, in his poetry Bonnefoy radiates a deeply earned confidence in the capacity of art to remind the individual of *présence:* in "Les Flambeaux" (The Torches) he even conjectures, with a witty bilingual neologism or pun, that "un autre mot encore, à inventer, / Rédimerait le monde" (still another word, to be invented / Might redeem [or resay to me] the world). Yet, grounding the confidence and reminding the reader that this poet is the same one who proclaimed in *Hier régnant désert* that imperfection was the summit of art, the final image of *Début et fin de la neige* conveys once more—and most resonantly—Yves Bonnefoy's abiding conviction that the source of all beauty and presence is mortal: "La neige piétinée est la seul rose" (Trampled snow is the only rose).

Interviews:

Entretiens sur la poésie: Yves Bonnefoy (Neuchâtel, Switzerland: A La Baconnière / Paris & Lausanne, Switzerland: Payot, 1981); enlarged as *Entretiens sur la poésie: 1972–1990: Yves Bonnefoy* (Paris: Mercure de France, 1990);

Shusha Guppy, "Yves Bonnefoy: The Art of Poetry LXIX," *Paris Review,* 131 (Summer 1994): 108–133.

References:

Mary Ann Caws, *Yves Bonnefoy* (Boston: Twayne, 1984);

John E. Jackson, *Yves Bonnefoy,* Poètes d'aujourd'hui, no. 229 (Paris: Seghers, 1976);

Florence de Lussy, comp., *Yves Bonnefoy: Exposition: Bibliothèque nationale, Paris, 9 octobre–30 novembre 1992,* introduction by Emmanuel Le Roy Ladurie, preface by Jean Starobinski (Paris: Bibliothèque Nationale/Mercure de France, 1992);

John T. Naughton, *The Poetics of Yves Bonnefoy* (Chicago & London: University of Chicago Press, 1984);

Richard Stamelman, *Lost Beyond Telling: Representations of Death and Absence in Modern French Poetry* (Ithaca, N.Y. & London: Cornell University Press, 1990).

André Breton

(19 February 1896 – 28 September 1966)

Margaret M. Bolovan

See also the Breton entry in *DLB 65: French Novelists, 1900–1930*.

BOOKS: *Mont de Piété* (Paris: Au Sans Pareil, 1919);

Les Champs magnétiques, by Breton and Philippe Soupault (Paris: Au Sans Pareil, 1920); enlarged as *Les Champs magnétiques, suivi de Vous m'oublierez et de S'il vous plaît,* foreword by Alain Jouffroy (Paris: Gallimard, 1967); *Les Champs magnétiques* translated by David Gascoyne as *The Magnetic Fields* (London: Atlas, 1985);

Clair de terre (Paris: Collection de Littérature, 1923); translated by Bill Zavatsky and Zack Rogow as *Earthlight* (Los Angeles: Sun & Moon Press, 1993);

Les Pas perdus, Les Documents bleus, no. 6 (Paris: Editions de la Nouvelle Revue Française, 1924; revised and corrected edition, Paris: Gallimard, 1969); translated by Mark Polizzotti as *The Lost Steps* (Lincoln: University of Nebraska Press, 1996);

Manifeste du surréalisme; Poisson soluble (Paris: Editions du Sagittaire, 1924); republished with new preface and "Lettre aux voyantes" (Paris: Editions Kra, 1929);

Légitime Défense (Paris: Editions Surréalistes, 1926);

Introduction au discours sur le peu de réalité (Paris: Gallimard, 1927);

Le Surréalisme et la peinture: Avec soixante-dix-sept photogravures d'après Max Ernst, Giorgio de Chirico, Joan Miró, Georges Bracque, Jean Arp, Francis Picabia, Pablo Picasso, Man Ray, André Masson, Yves Tanguy (Paris: Gallimard, 1928); enlarged as *Le Surréalisme et la peinture, suivi de Genèse et perspectives artistiques du surréalisme et de Fragments inédits* (New York: Brentano's, 1945); revised, corrected, and further enlarged as *Le Surréalisme et la peinture* (Paris: Gallimard, 1965); translated by Simon Watson Taylor as *Surrealism and Painting* (New York: Harper & Row, 1972; London: Macdonald, 1972);

Nadja (Paris: Gallimard/Editions de la Nouvelle Revue Française, 1928); translated by Richard Howard (New York: Grove / London: Evergreen, 1960); French edition revised (Paris: Gallimard, 1963);

Ralentir travaux, by Breton, René Char, and Paul Eluard (Paris: Editions Surréalistes, 1930); translated by Keith Waldrop as *Ralentir Travaux/Slow Under Construction* (Cambridge, Mass.: Exact Change, 1990);

Second Manifeste du surréalisme (Paris: Editions Kra, 1930);

L'Immaculée Conception, by Breton and Eluard (Paris: Editions Surréalistes, 1930); translated by Jon Graham as *The Immaculate Conception* (London: Atlas, 1990);

L'Union libre, anonymous (N. p., 1931);

Le Revolver à cheveux blancs (Paris: Editions des Cahiers libres, 1932);

Les Vases communicants (Paris: Editions des Cahiers libres, 1932; enlarged edition, Paris: Gallimard, 1955); translated by Mary Ann Caws and Geoffrey T. Harris as *Communicating Vessels* (Lincoln: University of Nebraska Press, 1990);

Misère de la poésie: "L'Affaire Aragon" devant l'opinion publique (Paris: Editions Surréalistes, 1932);

Qu'est-ce que le surréalisme? (Brussels: René Henriquez, 1934); translated by Gascoyne as *What Is Surrealism?* (London: Faber & Faber, 1936);

Point du jour (Paris: Editions de la Nouvelle Revue Française, 1934; revised and corrected edition, Paris: Gallimard, 1970); translated by Polizzotti and Caws as *Break of Day* (Lincoln: University of Nebraska Press, 1999);

L'Air de l'eau (Paris: Editions Cahiers d'Art, 1934);

Du temps que les surréalistes avaient raison (Paris: Editions Surréalistes, 1935);

Position politique du surréalisme (Paris: Editions du Sagittaire, 1935);

Au lavoir noir: Avec une fenêtre de Marcel Duchamp (Paris: Editions G.L.M., 1936);

André Breton

Notes sur la poésie, by Breton and Eluard (Paris: Editions G.L.M., 1936);

Le Château étoilé (Paris: Editions du Minotaure, 1937);

L'Amour fou, Collection Métamorphoses, no. 3 (Paris: Gallimard, 1937); translated by Caws as *Mad Love* (Lincoln: University of Nebraska Press, 1987);

Fata Morgana, illustrated by Wilfredo Lam (suppressed edition, Marseilles: Editions du Sagittaire, 1941; Buenos Aires: Sur/Editions des Lettres Françaises, 1942); translated by Clark Mills (Chicago: Black Swan Press, 1969);

Arcane 17 (limited edition, New York: Brentano's, 1944; trade edition, 1945); revised as *Arcane 17, enté d'Ajours* (Paris: Editions du Sagittaire, 1947);

Situation du surréalisme entre les deux guerres (Paris & Algiers: Editions de la Revue *Fontaine,* 1945);

Young Cherry Trees Secured Against Hares/Jeunes Cérisiers garantis contre les lièvres, bilingual edition, English translations by Edouard Roditi (New York: View Editions, 1946);

Les Manifestes du surréalisme, suivis de Prolégomènes à un troisième manifeste du surréalisme ou non (Paris: Editions du Sagittaire, 1946); enlarged as *Les Manifestes du surréalisme, suivis de Prolégomènes à un troisième manifeste du surréalisme ou non; Du Surréalisme en ses œuvres vives; et d'Ephémérides surréalistes* (Paris: Editions du Sagittaire, 1955);

Yves Tanguy, bilingual edition, English translation by Bravig Imbs (New York: Pierre Matisse Editions, 1946);

Ode à Charles Fourier (Paris: Editions de la Revue *Fontaine,* 1947); translated by Kenneth White as *Ode to Charles Fourier* (London: Cape Goliard, 1969; London: Cape Goliard / New York: Grossman, 1970);

Martinique, charmeuse de serpents, by Breton and André Masson (Paris: Editions du Sagittaire, 1948; new edition, Paris: Jean-Jacques Pauvert, 1972);

La Lampe dans l'horloge (Paris: Robert Marin, 1948);

Poèmes (Paris: Gallimard, 1948);

Flagrant Délit: Rimbaud devant la conjuration de l'imposture et du truquage (Paris: Editions Thésée, 1949);

La Clé des champs (Paris: Editions du Sagittaire, 1953); translated by Michel Parmentier and Jacqueline d'Amboise as *Free Rein* (Lincoln: University of Nebraska Press, 1995);

Adieu ne plaise (Alès: Editions P.A.B., 1954);

L'Art magique, by Breton and Gérard Legrand (Paris: Club Français du Livre, 1957);

Antonin Artaud, ou, La Santé des poètes, by Breton and others (Paris: La Tour de Feu, 1959);

Constellations, with 22 illustrations by Joan Miró (New York: Pierre Matisse, 1959); translated by Paul Hammond as *Constellations of Miró, Breton* (San Francisco: City Lights Books, 2000);

Le La, with a lithograph by Jean Benoît (Alès: Editions P.A.B., 1961);

L'Affaire Rimbaud, by Breton, Antoine Adam, and René Etiemble (Paris: Pauvert, 1962);

Le Groupe, la rupture, by Breton and others (Paris: Seuil, 1970);

Perspective cavalière, edited by Marguerite Bonnet (Paris: Gallimard, 1970);

L'Un dans l'autre (Paris: Losfeld, 1970).

Editions and Collections: *Poésie et autre,* edited by Gérard Legrand (Paris: Club du Meilleur Livre, 1960);

Ode à Charles Fourier, edited, with an introduction, by Jean Gaulmier (Paris: Klincksieck, 1961; republished, Fonterfroide, France: Editions Fata Morgana, 1994);

Manifestes du surréalisme (Paris: Pauvert, 1962)—comprises *Manifeste du surréalisme; Second manifeste du surréalisme; Prolégomènes à un troisième manifeste du surréalisme ou non;* extracts from *Position politique du surréalisme; Poisson soluble; Lettre aux voyantes;* and *Du Surréalisme en ses oeuvres vives;* abridged edition, Collection Idées, no. 23 (Paris: Gallimard, 1963); 1962 edition translated by Richard Seaver and Helen R. Lane as *Manifestoes of Surrealism* (Ann Arbor: University of Michigan Press, 1969);

Arcane 17 enté d'Ajours: Suivi de André Breton ou la transparence, critical essay by Michel Beaujour (Paris: Union Générale d'Editions, 1965);

Signe ascendant: Suivi de Fata Morgana, Les Etats Généraux, Des épingles tremblantes, Xénophiles, Ode à Charles Fourier, Constellations, Le La, Collection Poésie, no. 37 (Paris: Gallimard, 1968; revised edition, Collection Poésie, no. 330, Paris: Gallimard, 1999);

Œuvres complètes: André Breton, 3 volumes, edited by Marguerite Bonnet, Bibliothèque de la Pléiade, nos. 346, 392, and 459 (Paris: Gallimard, 1988–1999);

L'Immaculée conception, edited by Bonnet and Etienne-Alain Hubert (Paris: José Corti, 1991);

Ode à Charles Fourier, commentary by Gaulmier (Fonterfroide, France: Editions Fata Morgana, 1994).

Editions in English: "Prolegomena to a Third Manifesto of Surrealism or Else," *VVV,* 1 (June 1942): 18–26;

If You Please, by Breton and Philippe Soupault, translated by George E. Wellwarth, in *Modern French Theater: An Anthology of Plays,* edited by Michael Benedikt and Wellwarth (New York: Dutton, 1964), pp. 147–173;

Selected Poems: André Breton, translated by Kenneth White (London: Cape, 1969);

What Is Surrealism? Selected Writings of André Breton, edited and introduced by Franklin Rosemont (London: Pluto Press, 1978; New York: Monad, 1978);

Poems of André Breton: A Bilingual Anthology, translated and edited by Jean-Pierre Cauvin and Mary Ann Caws (Austin: University of Texas Press, 1982);

Arcanum 17: With Apertures Grafted to the End, translated by Zack Rogow, introduction by Anna Balakian (Los Angeles: Sun & Moon Press, 1994);

Selections: The Automatic Message, The Magnetic Fields, The Immaculate Conception, translated by David Gascoyne, Anthony Melville, and Jon Graham (London: Atlas, 1997);

My Heart Through Which Her Heart Has Passed: Poems of Love and Desperation, 1926–1931, translated by Mark Polizzotti (Paris & London: Alyscamps, 1998).

SELECTED BROADSIDES: *Pour un art révolutionnaire indépendant,* broadside, by Breton and Leon Trotsky (Mexico, 1938);

Pleine marge, illustrated by Kurt Seligmann (New York: Nierendorf Gallery, 1943; clandestine edition, Paris: Editions de la Main à Plume, 1943);

Au regard des divinités (Paris: Editions Messages, 1949).

OTHER: "Violette Nozières," in *Violette Nozières* (Brussels: Editions Nicolas Flamel, 1933), pp. 7–14;

Anthologie de l'humour noir, compiled and edited by Breton (Paris: Editions du Sagittaire, 1940); enlarged edition (Paris: Editions du Sagittaire, 1950); revised edition (Paris: Jean-Jacques Pauvert, 1966); translated by Mark Polizzotti as *Anthology of Black Humor* (San Francisco: City Lights Books, 1997);

First Papers of Surrealism: Hanging by André Breton, his Twine Marcel Duchamp, edited by Breton and Marcel Duchamp (New York: New York City Coordinating Council of French Relief Societies, 1942).

André Breton is widely known as the founder and prominent figure of the Surrealist movement in France. His manifestos and essays, including the extended novelistic essay *Nadja* (1928; translated, 1960), articulate the literary and philosophical stance of the Surrealists. His earliest writings, however, are poems, and poetic expression holds a pivotal place in conceptions of the Surreal. Breton and his colleagues often cited the statement of the Comte de Lautréamont (pseudonym of Isidore Lucien Ducasse) that poetry must be made by all, and to this remark Breton added that it must also be heard by all. Indeed, throughout his life Breton attempted to embody his aesthetic notions in the poems he wrote.

Breton was born at Tinchebray (Orne) on 19 February 1896 to Louis Breton and Marguerite Breton. His family moved to the industrial suburb of Paris when he was four years old. He was first sent to school at Maison Sainte-Elisabeth, which was run by an order of nuns; then, in 1902, he was transferred to the secular Pantin school. He attended Collège Chaptal in Paris from 1906 to 1912, and during this time Breton published his first poems, "Le Rêve" (The Dream, September 1911) and "Eden" (April 1912), in the student literary magazine, *Vers l'Idéal* (Toward the Ideal), under the pseudonym of René Dobrant (an anagram).

"Le Rêve," comprised of four quatrains of alexandrines, exhibits the interest in dreams that recurs in Breton's poetry and manifestos throughout his life. The poem is especially effective at conveying fanciful ethereal visions:

Est-ce toi, triste Nuit, quand tu descends sur terre,
Qui jettes de ton char ce beau sable doré
Sur la pensée errante et toujours solitaire,
En secouant dans l'air ton manteau déchiré?

(Is it you, sad Night, when you descend on earth,
Who throws from your chariot this beautiful golden sand
On the wandering and ever solitary thought,
While shaking in the air your torn coat?).

The vagueness, the interplay of light and dark, and the dream-like notion all foreshadow Breton's later poetic writings.

In "Eden" Breton displays developing skill as a poet, as evidenced by his effective use of rhyming couplets of alternating octosyllabic and trisyllabic lines, pauses, and suspense, to convey the theme of the privileged moment of the dawn:

Ce serait un jardin d'amour
Où le jour
Point, dans l'aube couleur d'opale
Ou plus pâle . . .

(It would be a garden of love
Where day
Breaks, in the dawn color of opal
Or more pale . . .).

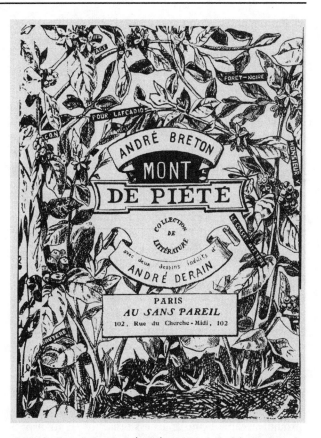

Cover for Breton's first book (1919), which includes "Age," a poem he sent to Paul Valéry three years earlier (from André Breton, Poésie et autre, *edited by Gérard Legrand, 1960)*

Both poems reveal the influences of several predecessors, particularly the French Symbolists. Breton acknowledged his indebtedness to, and expressed his opinion of many poets who influenced his style in his correspondence with his friend Théodore Fraenkel. Throughout the summer of 1913 they exchanged letters that included often lengthy critiques of the major authors of the day. Breton's highest praise was reserved for the work of Stéphane Mallarmé. In a letter to Fraenkel dated 22 June 1914, Breton asserted: "Mallarmé règne: de ma part, nulle idolatrie, mais comme une dévotion au Dieu manifesté" (Mallarmé reigns: this is not idolatry on my part, but simply devotion to God made manifest). The influence that Mallarmé's writing had on Breton's early poetry in terms of both style and theme is substantial.

At the age of seventeen Breton began premedical studies at the Faculté de Médecine in Paris. In choosing this course of study, he was probably more motivated in ensuring continued financial support from his parents rather than by an interest in a medical career. In 1914 he wrote several poems for the neosymbolist journal *La Phalange* (Phalanx). These poems utilized a syntax and obscurity that owed much to the writings of

Mallarmé, and one of the poems, "Rieuse" (Laughing), was dedicated to another Mallarméan disciple, Paul Valéry. Breton initiated a correspondence with Valéry, during the course of which he shared several of his poems, and the two became acquaintances.

Breton's medical studies were neglected as he devoted more of his time to writing. Following the outbreak of World War I in 1914, he was called to service and, because of his studies, became a medical assistant in army psychiatric centers from 1915 to 1919. Breton had learned from Valéry the importance of closely examining his subject, and the result of this influence is clearly exhibited in the poem appropriately titled "Sujet" (Subject, 1916), a prose monologue directly based on Breton's observation of a particular medical case at Saint-Dizier. "Sujet" reads like a personal narrative from the patient's perspective. The subject calmly states: "J'ai enjambé, c'est vrai, des cadavres. On en pourvoit les salles de dissection. Encore un bon nombre d'entre eux pouvaient-ils être en cire" (True, I have stepped over corpses. They stock the dissection rooms with them. A good number more might have been made of wax). Rather than the lyrical, Breton here strives for descriptive accuracy inspired by his psychiatric readings and experiences and in so doing re-creates through stream-of-consciousness prose the thought process of a patient.

In 1916 Breton sent a letter to Valéry that included a poem titled simply "Poème," later published in *Mont de piété* (Mount of Piety, 1919) under the title "Age." The poem was significant to Breton as a celebration of maturity: "Aube, adieu! Je sors du bois hanté; j'affronte les routes" (Dawn, farewell! I emerge from the haunted forest; I'm braving the roads). Breton did not just feel that he had come of age, he was also suggesting that he was ready to strike out on his own, that he would no longer be dependent on his predecessors for style and form. To an extent the influence of the French Symbolists continued to shape his poetics, but with "Age" he embarked on his own path.

The roads that Breton chose led him more and more toward poetry. In 1917 he formed an intellectual roundtable called the Sophist's Club, the members of which would read the so-called *poètes maudits* (accursed poets) aloud. Breton expressed admiration for J. K. Huysmans, Gustave Moreau, and the Symbolists, especially Mallarmé and Arthur Rimbaud; however, "Age" is indicative of a change in influences. This transformation was in part a result of his experiences with the psychological problems of soldiers during wartime.

His interest in psychiatric states, coupled with exposure to new literary forms, moved Breton to reject what he saw as literary and artistic pretension. The "modernity" of another new acquaintance, Guillaume Apollinaire, inspired him. Breton corresponded with Apollinaire while he was in the army and, upon his return to Paris, began to visit with him regularly. Apollinaire introduced him to the review *Dada,* as well as to adherents of this new nihilistic movement, which came to exert a great influence upon him; however, perhaps the single greatest influence for Breton in these early years was Jacques-Pierre Vaché, whom he had met in Nantes in February of 1916, when both were in the army. Vaché, the son of a career officer, was born into a prominent family from Brittany. He held a strong contempt for literature and was full of ridicule for it. Breton later remarked in *Les Pas perdus* (1924; translated as *The Lost Steps,* 1996): "Sans lui j'aurais peut-être été un poète" (But for him I would have been a poet).

Immediately after his meeting with Vaché, Breton told Valéry that he was "délivré de l'obsession poétique" (freed from his obsession with poetry) and that he was now seeking in the cinema and in the pages of the newspapers the aesthetic pleasure he claimed no longer to find in printed verse. Much of what is known about Vaché comes from Breton's writing, which conveys an attitude toward poetry and life that seems to anticipate the Dadaesque acceptance of nothing. At the same time, Vaché displayed a form of black humor that he called *umour.* Breton regarded this black humor as a manifestation of the same *esprit nouveau* (new spirit) that he had previously glimpsed in the writings of Rimbaud and Apollinaire. Until Vaché's death on 7 January 1919, reportedly from an overdose of opium, the two engaged in creating "poetic moments," pasting together a collage of unrelated fleeting sequences by moving from café to café or even from theater to theater, seeing only bits and pieces and often disturbing other patrons. Breton referred to himself and Vaché as "gais terroristes" (joyful terrorists).

Together with Philippe Soupault and Louis Aragon, with whom he was already acquainted, Breton founded the magazine *Littérature,* which appeared for the first time in March 1919. In the first four issues of the magazine they serialized the *Poésies* of Lautréamont, transcribed by Breton from the only known copy, held by the Bibliothèque Nationale de France, the French national library. These texts were quite influential on Surrealist thought, especially in terms of Lautréamont's unexpected juxtapositions of the finite world with the infinite.

Although he had divested himself from the title of "pohète" (po-wet), as Vaché had sarcastically referred to him, Breton did continue to write poetry. The collection *Mont de Piété,* published in June of 1919, exhibits the full range of poetic influences of Breton's early years. In the "Mallarméan" poems he sought to unite rhythm and sound in "le hasard demeuré aux termes" (the chance that resides in terms). The "Corset Mystère" (Corset Mystery) followed the route blazed by Apollinaire, in which the poetic act becomes a quest for the marvelous. At times this quest bordered on obsession. "Forêt-noire" (Black Forest), a poem only thirty words long, took Breton six months to compose. Although *Mont de Piété* did not receive much attention, Aragon asserted in the October 1919 issue of *Littérature* that Breton was a writer ahead of his time.

In 1919 Breton also began to pay special attention to the phrases that would run through his head just before he fell asleep. These phrases seemed to him quite poetic in their striking imagery and syntax. So he undertook with Soupault to reproduce, by the deliberate exclusion of all extraneous thoughts and ideas, the state in which the proximity of sleep released new and exciting poetic elements. They carried out intense writing sessions. During one eight-day period of self-hypnotic trance, the two poets wrote a series of hallucinatory prose poems, first published in *Littérature* and collected in 1920 as *Les Champs magnétiques* (translated as *The Magnetic Fields,* 1985). They sought to become receptive to subliminal messages and inner voices by entering into this trance state. This approach to automatic writing, with the poet serving as a passive scribe of the unconscious, was integral to the emergence of Surrealism.

The early 1920s were pivotal years for Breton. He married Simone Kahn in 1921. A matrix of influences guided Breton toward what became Surrealism. In his studies and his work Breton encountered the ideas of contemporary psychologists, who had begun experimenting with automatic writing, hypnosis, and dream analysis as means of tapping the unconscious mind. Breton read this research and sought to apply these techniques to the realm of the arts. Sigmund Freud's theories of the unconscious were of particular interest to him. He even secured an interview with Freud after having utilized his methods of psychoanalysis while recording monologues of patients in 1921.

But while Freud examined the unconscious for the roots of psychological illness, Breton wanted to reconcile the unconscious with the conscious mind to form a higher synthesis. He later wrote of this process in *Manifeste du surréalisme* (Manifesto of Surrealism, 1924): "Je crois à la résolution future de ces deux états, en apparence si contradictoires, que sont le rêve et la réalité, en une sorte de réalité absolue, de *surréalité*" (I believe that in the future these two so apparently contradictory states of dream and reality will be resolved into a sort of absolute reality, of surreality). Breton and his colleagues, including Aragon, Soupault, Paul Eluard, Robert Desnos, and René Crevel, experimented daily with writing "textes automatiques" (automatic texts), recounting dreams

Breton attending Francis Picabia's reading of his Manifeste cannibale dada *at the Théâtre de la Maison de l'Œuvre, 27 March 1920*

while in hypnotic trances, deliberately inducing hallucinations, and holding séances.

During this time, through Valéry's intercession, Gaston Gallimard hired Breton, who was often short on money, as an assistant at his publishing firm. Breton earned *f*400 per month for various administrative tasks, including handling correspondence and sending copies of *La Nouvelle Revue Française* (which was often derided in *Littérature*) to subscribers. He also helped Marcel Proust correct proofs of *Le Cote de Guermantes* (The Guermantes Way, 1920), soon to be published by Gallimard. Although Breton did not especially sympathize with Proust's style, he came to appreciate certain "poetic treasures" in Proust's work. As a proofreader, however, Breton was not a perfectionist, and after *Cote de Guermantes* was published, Proust had to create an errata list of more than two hundred corrections.

Breton had encountered the writing of the Romanian-born author Tristan Tzara in journals at Apollinaire's apartment and became enraptured with the Dadaist adventure, especially after Tzara arrived in Paris in 1920. The Dadaists, a group of writers and artists in Zurich whose activities were presented in the review *Dada,* called for a complete rejection of logic. To the Dadaists, logical thought was culpable for leading mankind into World War I and, therefore, needed to be overcome. The Dadaists engaged in artistic creation, utilizing random factors and imitating "primitive" art. The movement reflected a revolt against the moral values associated with western European culture in an effort to liberate man from the constrictiveness of civilization.

Breton had participated in Dadaist activities in Paris as early as 1919 and for a short time was one of the staunchest supporters of the movement. When Tzara arrived in Paris, he was greeted with great enthusiasm by Breton, among others. In 1921, however, Breton organized a Congress for the Determination of the Modern Spirit in an attempt to give a constructive basis to Dada manifestations. The more "orthodox" Dadaists opposed such an idea, and the friction that had been latent among certain members of differing tendencies came to the surface. In 1922 Breton argued that the basic insights of Dadaism were correct but that the movement offered no positive alternatives. Gradually, he reached the conclusion that Dadaist practice limited its ambition to a destructive program. Dada, in his opinion, was ceasing to progress, and Breton and his friends soon broke from Tzara. In contrast to the negativism of Dada, Breton called for an artistic search beyond logic to a state of "surréalité" (surreality), the objective of which was "*la plus grande liberté* d'esprit" (the total liberation of the mind).

Breton's primary criticism of the Dada movement was that it was used by some as a way out, a way that led neither to adventure nor revolution but rather to armchair philosophizing and café discussion. Such a strictly rhetorical revolution had no consequences in the world. In "Lâchez tout" (Leave Everything) Breton therefore admonishes his colleagues to:

> Lâchez tout.
> Lâchez Dada.
> Lâchez votre femme, lâchez votre maîtresse.
> Lâchez vos espérances et vos craintes.
> Semez vos enfants au coin d'un bois.
> Lâchez la proie pour l'ombre.
> Lâchez au besoin d'une vie aisée, ce qu'on vous donne pour
>   une situation d'avenir.
> Partez sur les routes.

> (Leave everything.
> Leave Dada.
> Leave your wife, leave your mistress.
> Leave your hopes and your fears.
> Sow your children in the corner of a forest.

> Leave the prey for the shadow.
> Leave, if need be, an easy life and all you are given
>   for a possible situation in the future.
> Set out on the highways).

Breton soon detached himself from Dadaism, and he was followed by many of his peers.

Indeed, in the spring of 1923 a discouraged Breton contemplated ceasing to write altogether. In an interview granted to Roger Vitrac for *Le Journal du peuple* in April, Breton affirmed his decision to stop writing. However, he soon decided instead on a revival of automatic poetry, which resulted in an increased importance being placed on various experiments in writing. The publication on 15 November 1923, in a limited edition of 240 copies, of the collection *Clair de terre* (translated as *Earthlight,* 1993) signaled that Breton's poetic voice was indeed alive and well.

The collection, which includes an etching by Pablo Picasso, comprises poems from his Dada period (1920–1921), as well as four of his *récits de rêves* (dream narratives). In a letter to Jacques Doucet composed in Lorient on 22 August 1923, Breton wrote: "Quelques-uns des poèmes qui entrent dans ce recueil (une vingtaine sont de ce dernier mois) comptent peut-être pour moi un peu plus que tout ce que j'ai écrit jusqu'ici. J'en suis même content, ce qui est rare" (Some of these poems in the collection [around twenty are from this past month] count for me perhaps a bit more than everything I have written until now. I am even happy about them, which is rare).

Several of the poems in the collection had already been printed in *Littérature.* Others were written during Breton's stay in Lorient in the summer of 1923. Among the latter is the poem "A Rrose Sélavy" (To Rrose Sélavy), which in earlier versions had been titled "A Marcel Duchamp." Rrose Sélavy was the name taken by Duchamp for his feminine alter ego (a play on "eros c'est la vie" [Eros is life]). Interestingly, the name Rrose Sélavy was also adopted by Desnos, who claimed to be linking with Duchamp telepathically as he composed stream-of-consciousness poetry. As the last poem in the collection, "A Rrose Sélavy" is highly significant. In the two-line poem Breton writes: "J'ai quitté mes effets, / mes beaux effets de neige!" (I've given up my effects, / my beautiful snow effects!). Duchamp, then living in New York, had ceased his artistic activities, just as Breton had announced he would. However, the poem by its very existence makes clear that Breton had reversed his decision to cease writing.

Clair de terre was warmly received by Breton's colleagues. Aragon in the *Paris-Journal* (11 January 1924), Eluard in *Intentions* (January 1924), Soupault in *La Revue européenne* (April 1924), and Francis Gérard in *Phi-*

Page from the manuscript for Breton's contribution to Les Champs magnétiques *(1920),*
a book he wrote with Philippe Soupault (Bibliothèque Nationale, Paris)

losophies (15 May 1924) all wrote glowing reviews. For example, Gérard asserted that "André Breton donne à la poésie le charme des fables incroyables, des mystères les plus séduisants, les plus redoutables . . . l'Univers marque pour toujours son passage" (André Breton invests poetry with the charm of incredible fables, of the most seductive, formidable mysteries . . . the Universe will forever note his passage). André Fontainas was the most hostile of Breton's few detractors. In the 15 July 1924 issue of the *Mercure de France* Fontainas attacked the collection, referring to it as *"Clair de lune"* (Moonlight), to which attack Breton wrote a scathing reply published in the 1 September 1924 issue of the same journal.

For the next few years, Breton and his colleagues turned back to automatic writing and stream-of-consciousness recitals of dreams, which were as influenced by Freud and Karl Marx as by Dada and their other poetic predecessors. In an article titled "Les Mots sans rides" (Words Without Wrinkles), published in *Littérature* (7 December 1922) and collected in *Les Pas perdus,* Breton spoke out for innovation in poetic language and cited the verbal effects and wordplay of Desnos and Duchamp. The early 1920s was considered by many to be a renaissance for French poetry. Desnos was at work on "Rrose Sélavy" (1930), "L'Aumonyme" (1923), and "Langage cuit" (Cooked Language, 1923), Vitrac was preparing *Peau-Asie,* and Eluard was engaged in composing his *Exemples* (Examples, 1921).

Breton had become the sole editor of the journal *Littérature* in 1922. However, despite the marketing of the journal by Gallimard, *Littérature* had a dwindling readership and only published two more issues, both of which reflected Breton's own return to verse. In June of 1924, the journal ceased publication altogether.

Breton articulated and confirmed the positions of the Surrealist movement in his first *Manifeste du surréalisme,* published that same year. Logic is rejected, and in its place is offered the pursuit of a total liberation of thought, where dreams and imagination are revealed through casting off the restrictions imposed by the rational world. Automatic writing is presented as a means of reaching a totally liberated realm: surreality. From its inception, Surrealism was attacked by critics as unstable. However, *Manifeste du surréalisme* motivated several former Dadaists and new allies to rally around Breton. Among the first writers and artists to associate themselves with Surrealism were Aragon, Antonin Artaud, Eluard, Max Ernst, Pierre Naville, Soupault, and Vitrac.

Breton asserted that logic limits the potential of mankind, and he therefore sought the discovery of something more powerful, something that lay below the surface of the real. He was soon setting the guiding principles of the group for whom he defined Surrealism as

Automatisme psychique pur par lequel on se propose d'exprimer, soit verbalement, soit par écrit, soit de toute autre manière le fonctionnement réel de la pensée. Dictée de la pensée, en l'absence de toute contrôle exercé par la raison, en dehors de toute préoccupation esthétique ou morale.

(Pure psychic automatism by which one proposes to express verbally, in writing, or in any other manner, the actual functioning of thought. Dictation of thought, in the absence of any control exercised by reason, and exempt from any aesthetic or moral concern).

At the same time, the experiments in dream narration and automatic writing had reached a point where they often became self-destructive. A story is told of a group of Surrealists, including Crevel, attempting to hang themselves from the chandeliers after a hypnotic sleep session. Under Breton's guidance, the group abandoned some of these practices, turning instead to the more creative impulses of modern psychology, the occult, and the primitive.

In *Légitime Défense* (Legitimate Defense, 1926) Breton declared in the name of the Surrealists that revolt alone was creative. The following year the antirational emphasis of *Manifeste du surréalisme* was confirmed by his *Introduction au discours sur le peu de réalité* (Introduction to Discourse on the Lack of Reality). Meanwhile, Breton was confronting the problem of applying Surrealist principles to the practice and evaluation of painting in a series of articles written for the magazine *La Révolution surréaliste,* which replaced *Littérature* and of which he was the editor from 1925 to 1929. These articles were collected in a volume titled *Le Surréalisme et la peinture* (translated as *Surrealism and Painting,* 1972), published in February of 1928.

Among Breton's most successful works is *Nadja,* one of the few novels written by a Surrealist, which was published in May of the same year. The book chronicles encounters between the author and a woman. *Nadja* is an ostensibly faithful but fictionalized diary of their unsuccessful love affair. More significantly, it is the account of the Surrealist revelations gleaned from his association with her. The avowed intent of the narrative is to capture the tone of a medical report, but it culminates in images of "beauté convulsive" (convulsive beauty). She is the object of his desire, his guide, and the manifestation of creative freedom, even of the Surreal itself. Nadja, as portrayed by Breton, incarnates the spirit of Surrealism.

Nadja lives a spontaneous, poetic life permeated with startling coincidences and chance encounters.

Although their relationship lasted for only one week before Nadja was committed to a mental institution, Breton asserts that he learned from her the importance of creative freedom: "libre de tout lien terrestre, tant elle tient peu, mais merveilleusement, à la vie" (free from all earthly bonds, so little does she belong, but marvelously, to life).

In *Nadja,* Breton recounts the repeated inexplicable coincidences he has witnessed. Nadja embodies the union of opposites and the linking of the dream world with that of reality. The Surrealists were already exploring what they called "daily magic," and Breton's Nadja radiates a sense of the marvelous. For Breton, this "créature inspirante" (inspiring creature) was proof that the Surreal is not apart from reality, but rather contained within it.

The first sentence of *Nadja* is "Qui suis-je?"—meaning both "Who am I?" and "Whom am I following?"—an indication that though Nadja is the object of the narrative, this journey is an internal one. Nadja was committed to an asylum at the end of their brief liaison, leaving Breton with both feelings of guilt and a fascination with the freedom that madness grants the imagination.

Second Manifeste du surréalisme (Second Manifesto of Surrealism, 1930) links Surrealism to political action and communism. From 1929 to 1935 the Surrealists were closely aligned with the French Communist Party. Breton's adherence to the Communist Party marked the beginning of his engagement in political action. He declared in "Discours au Congrès des écrivains" (Discourse to the Writers' Congress), a speech made in Paris on June 1935, recorded in *Position politique du surréalisme* (Political Position of Surrealism, 1935): "'Transformer le monde,' a dit Marx; 'changer la vie,' a dit Rimbaud: ces deux mots d'ordre pour nous n'en font qu'un" ("Transform the world," said Marx; "change life," said Rimbaud: these two goals make only one for us). Although Breton felt some sympathy with the aspirations of the communists, he was actually influenced by many other sources, of which poetic inspiration took precedence, as he writes in *Second Manifeste du surréalisme:* "Inutile de s'embarrasser à ce propos de subtilités, on sait assez ce qu'est l'inspiration. Il n'y a pas à s'y méprendre, c'est elle qui a pourvu aux besoins suprêmes d'expression en tout temps en tous lieux" (Useless to get caught up in this talk of subtleties, we are well aware what inspiration is. There is no mistaking it, it has provided for the great needs of expression every time everywhere). The declaration "Les mots font l'amour" (Words make love) is not merely a provocative flourish but a key to Breton's attitude toward language. The dreams analyzed near the start of *Les Vases commu-*

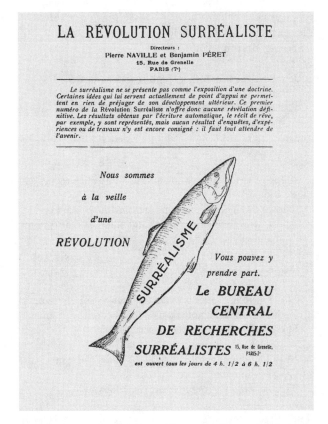

Cover for the December 1924 issue of the magazine Breton edited during the early 1920s (from Paul Eluard, Le Poète et son ombre, *1963)*

nicants (1932; translated as *Communicating Vessels,* 1990)—which is dedicated to Freud—are prosaic in style, but though they lend themselves to scientific scrutiny, they are steeped in the imaginary.

In 1930 Breton left Paris for a visit to Avignon, where he was joined by René Char and Eluard. The three men wrote poetry: at a café, while walking along the road, or driving in a car. Thirty short texts, ranging from three to twenty-five lines each, were written during the five-day visit from 25 March to 30 March. The title of the collection that resulted was suggested by chance during a car ride along the Durance River, when they saw a sign warning of road repairs ahead: *Ralentir travaux* (1930; translated as *Slow Under Construction,* 1990).

The poems are wonderfully representative of Surrealism in their impromptu composition and in their collaborative nature. Love is a prevalent theme throughout the collection, but it is not portrayed in an especially positive way; in fact, more reference is made to the impossiblity of love—both Breton and Eluard worked on *Ralentir travaux* after having recently ended serious love affairs. The authors would often take turns writing a single poem. Both the inconstancy of love and the seamless collaboration of these poets is evident in "Je m'écoute encore parler" (I Listen to Myself Still Talking). Breton wrote:

Je serre dans mes bras les femmes qui ne veulent être qu'à
    un autre
Celles qui dans l'amour entendent le vent passer sur les
    peupliers
Celles qui dans la haine sont plus élancées que les mantes
    religieuses

(I hold in my arms women who want only to be with
    another
Those who in love hear wind crossing the poplars
Those who in hate are taller and slimmer than praying
    mantises).

To which Eluard added:

Et j'ai serré dans mes bras des apparitions sous le signe
De la cendre et d'amours plus nouveaux que le premier
Qui m'a fermé les yeux l'espoir la jalousie

(And I held in my arms apparitions under the sign
Of ashes and loves newer than the first
That closed my eyes my hope my jealousy).

The three poets are successful in retaining a strange unity of tone and theme in these poems. The collection received extensive favorable commentary.

By 1930 the Surrealists had connected their poetic liberation to a more general search for revolution, and they had joined the French Communist Party en masse. Automatic writing gave way to political action. From 1930 to 1933 Breton served as editor of *Le Surréalisme au Service de la Révolution* (Surrealism at the Service of the Revolution). Throughout the 1930s the Surrealist group conducted research, published books and magazines, and organized art exhibitions, theatrical performances, and poetry readings. Breton and Eluard collaborated on a second text, *Notes sur la poésie* (Notes on Poetry, 1936), supposedly written in a fortnight during their free time.

One of the best-known Surrealist works, *L'Immaculée Conception* (1930; translated as *The Immaculate Conception,* 1990) is another collaboration between Breton and Eluard. The work lies midway between poetry and manifesto. On one level, the book is a series of texts describing the various creative impulses of mankind. The first section of *L'Immaculée Conception,* "L'Homme" (Man), includes examples of automatic writing. A chapter of the third section called "L'Amour" (Love) is a rewriting of the *Kama Sutra* (the fifth-century Sanskrit erotic manual) that replaces the standard variations with thirty-two new sexual positions. The final section, "Le Jugement originel" (The Original Judgment), is a Surrealist credo of short maxims. Together they convey

an antimoralistic stance, rejecting the predictable in favor of revolt.

However, the second section of the book, "Les Possessions," has received the most attention. Breton's interest in insanity, stemming from his experiences during World War I, had been reinforced by his encounter with Nadja. In the narrative of this section, Breton and Eluard attempt to reconstruct the discourse of psychotic states. Breton resisted what he viewed as the misguided presumption that the language of reason could elucidate poetry. Instead, he asserted that the poetic discourse defies explanation. In fact, poetry is for Breton an exploratory venture. His experiences convinced him that any boundary between the language of insanity and that of poetry was elusive at best. The conception of artistic delirium was not a new one. The German philosopher Georg Wilhelm Friedrich Hegel had certainly suggested as much in his *Phänomenologie des Geistes* (Phenomenology of the Mind, 1807), and the Spanish artist Salvador Dalí was actively expressing the psychotic in his paintings and prints. Still, publishers considered *L'Immaculée Conception* too disorienting and bizarre and insisted on an advance of ƒ25,000 before they would print the book.

In the face of the distrust of the French Communists and the ill will of several of his former colleagues, including Aragon, Breton decided to quit the Surrealist movement. He went so far as to write a letter of resignation on 15 January 1931. However, the other Surrealists urged him to reconsider, and the resignation was retracted. Several changes did occur in the activities of the group. First, the Surrealists stopped gathering exclusively at Breton's place in Place Blanche, shifting instead to Tzara's more neutral domicile. Moreover, Breton strove to bridge the gap between diehard Communists such as Aragon, Jacques Sadoul, and Pierre Unik and those more interested in poetic concerns. As a compromise, more focus was given to anticlericalism, an issue most members could agree on.

During this period Breton suffered constantly from poverty. On 30 March, his divorce from Kahn was granted, and she left with many of their possessions, including half of their art collection. More emotionally devastating for Breton, however, was the termination of his three-year love affair with Suzanne Muzard. The increased output of poetry at this time is often attributed to the ending of the affair. Again, failed love appears constantly as a theme in the poetry written at this time. In "Après le grand tamanoir" (After the Great Anteater), collected in *Le Revolver à cheveux blancs* (The White-Haired Revolver, 1932), he writes of the nameless woman "Qui brise en mille éclats le bijou du jour" (Who smashes the jewel of the day into a thousand shards).

At times Breton would write poem after poem for hours on end. In one instance, he wrote a series of "genre poems," with titles such as "Poème prophétique" (Prophetic Poem), "Poème scatologique" (Scatological Poem), "Poème avec vocabulaire" (Poem with Vocabulary), and "Poème fin du monde" (End-of-the-World Poem) in a single sitting. These writings tend to contain stark expressions of bitterness and sorrow. One titled "Poème exhibitionniste" (Exhibitionistic Poem) speaks of

> les épines du hérisson de mon nom
> Quand on le prononce à la cantonade
> Dans un murmure comme si l'on m'aimait encore
> Comme si l'on m'avait jamais aimé
>
> (the porcupine quills of my name
> When it is spoken in the round
> In a murmur as if I were still loved
> As if I had ever been loved).

Many of these genre poems remained unpublished during Breton's lifetime.

L'Union libre (Free Union), arguably Breton's most famous poem, was published anonymously in 1931. The poem was originally printed as a pamphlet in a limited edition of only seventy-five copies. He had composed the poem while on vacation in Lyons-la-Forêt, and it was most likely inspired by Muzard. A long litany of his lover's physical features are recounted in the manner of the Renaissance *blason* (blazon). *L'Union libre* seems both to conjure up Muzard's erotic reality for one final time and also to etch her body, inch by inch, in Breton's memory forever:

> Ma femme à la chevelure de feu de bois
> Aux pensées d'éclairs de chaleur
> A la taille de sablier. . .
> Ma femme aux fesses de grès et d'amiante
> Ma femme aux fesses de dos de cygne
> Ma femme aux fesses de printemps
> Au sexe de glaïeul
> Ma femme au sexe de placer et d'ornithorynque
>
> (My woman whose hair is a brush fire
> Whose thoughts are summer lightning
> Whose waist is an hourglass . . .
> My woman whose buttocks are sandstone and asbestos
> Whose buttocks are the back of a swan and the spring
> My woman with the sex of an iris
> A mine and a platypus).

The passages are rich with imagery, the moods constantly shifting. The poem is written partly in opposition to the institution of marriage, offering an alternative conception of love. The succession of freely associated images exists not in the realm of the

Breton's lover Suzanne Muzard, circa 1928

logical and rational but rather the realm of circumstantial magic.

The title itself takes on several related connotations. The "free union," given the litany of female body parts, undoubtedly evokes images of love without moral taboos or restrictions, but it also refers to the free flow of linked ideas invoking automatism. Throughout the poem such verses as "Ma femme aux mollets de moelle de sureau" (My woman with calves of elder pith) and "Ma femme aux cils de bâtons d'écriture d'enfant" (My woman with eyelashes of straight lines in the handwriting of a child) create relationships of sound and meaning that exist outside of rational thought. Sound associations similar to those practiced by Raymond Roussel articulate surreal desires and meanings. At the same time, the convulsive beauty conveyed by the poet actually causes desire to seek out the object of its realization.

The following spring Breton finally acknowledged authorship by including *L'Union libre* in a collection of poems titled *Le Revolver à cheveux blancs* published by the newly founded Editions des Cahiers Libres. The same publisher printed two other volumes of Surrealist poetry simultaneously: *La Vie immédiate* (Immediate Life) by Eluard, to whom *Le Revolver à cheveux blancs* is dedicated, and Tzara's *Où boivent les loups* (Where the Wolves Drink). All three books bear the same line: "Le sujet de ce livre est un être mobile" (The subject of this book is a mobile being).

Le Revolver à cheveux blancs was an ambitious collection that includes most of Breton's verse written since *Clair de terre* as well as several poems from his earlier collections. The first half of *Le Revolver à cheveux blancs* constitutes an anthology of previously published poems, including about half of the long poems of *Clair de terre*. Only seventeen out of fifty-five poems in the collection were entirely new.

For about ten years Breton had written primarily manifestos, while such other Surrealists as Eluard, Desnos, and Aragon wrote poetry. With *Le Revolver à cheveux blancs,* Breton showed that he was still engaged as a poet. Breton prefaced this collection with the statement: "Imagination n'est pas don mais par excellence objet de conquête" (Imagination is not a gift but an object of conquest par excellence). Except for the opening text, "Il y aura une fois" (Once Upon a Time There Will Be), which is presented separately as a preface, the other poems are grouped in three dated parts: six poems for the period 1915–1919; twenty-one for the period 1919–1924; and twenty-seven for the period 1924–1932.

The edition of *Le Revolver à cheveux blancs* consisted of 1,010 copies, 10 of which included an etching by Dalí. The book is dedicated to Eluard: "à un ami UNIQUE: et à l'admirable construction de rêve, de liberté, de poésie, d'amour / et de jeunesse éternelle / à laquelle est attaché son nom" (to a UNIQUE friend: and to the admirable construction of dream, liberty, poetry, love / and eternal youth / with which his name is associated). The title of the work comes from a text in *Poisson soluble II* (Soluble Fish II), written eight years earlier (1924), which ends with

Heureusement la palme ramenait enfin toute la scène à ses justes limites par un ralenti savant et permettait l'entrée en grande pompe du revolver à cheveux blancs, sérieux comme pas un, qui balayait à temps cette scène grotesque du revers de la justification totale et du printemps cavalier.

(Fortunately the palm finally restored the entire scene to its very limits with a skillful slow motion and allowed for the entrance with great pomp of the white-haired revolver, serious like no other, which swept away in time this grotesque scene from the reverse of total justification and from the cavalier spring).

The title of *Le Revolver à cheveux blancs* evokes several connotations that are not mutually exclusive. There is the image of the still-smoking gun after an attempt at suicide, as well as an analogous sexual metaphor.

"Il y aura une fois" calls upon poets not to limit the powers of the imagination. The text proceeds in three movements: a theoretical opening, the description of an imaginary dwelling place, and after the points of suspension a conclusion that leads the reader back to the title. Following the structure of a traditional *conte*, the narrative describes an immense dwelling in which are several beautiful young women. But in this dystopic setting, which recalls the writings of the Marquis de Sade, it is "formellement interdit, sous peine d'expulsion immédiate et définitive . . . d'accomplir, dans les limites de l'encerclement par le mur du parc, l'acte de l'amour" (strictly forbidden, on pain of immediate and permanent expulsion . . . to perform, within the walls encircling the grounds, the act of love).

In *Le Revolver à cheveux blancs* Breton defines the imaginary as "ce qui tend à devenir réel" (what tends to become real), which is tied to the constant flux and transitory nature of the world presented in his poetry. Each of the poems in *Le Revolver à cheveux blancs* represents a descent "à l'intérieur de ma pensée" (into the interior of my thought). Thought, here, is of course not reasoned observation. Rather, the poet becomes an explorer who discovers that the bars he thought were keeping him from getting out are actually internal. He finds a way to force them apart, escaping inward. In fact he asserts: "Je tiens le fil" (I hold the thread). Here the poet identifies himself with the hero and the alchemist, providing a *fil conducteur* (guiding thread) between apparently disconnected elements—so that a woman passes "dans un bruit de fleurs" (with the sound of flowers), and voices have "la couleur du sable sur des rivages tendres et dangereux" (the color of sand on tender and dangerous shores). Throughout are revelations for which there are no substitutes in the world of everyday reality, revelations to make the windows fly open. Furthermore, one of the dominant themes of the collection is the idea of transparency or penetrating appearances. In "La Forêt dans la hache" (The Forest in the Axe) he writes: "Je n'ai plus qu'un corps transparent à l'intérieur duquel des colombes transparentes se jettent sur un poignard transparent tenu par une main transparente" (I have only a transparent body within which transparent doves hurl themselves upon a transparent dagger held by a transparent hand).

The narratives of the poems are filled with automatic discourse and distinct connections to the dreamworld. "Vigilance" creates a circular oneiric realm in which the poet sets fire to his own dreaming body which in turn dreams that he is setting fire to his body as he dreams. "Rideau rideau" (Curtain Curtain) is a brief poetic autobiography, in which Breton serves as both the actor onstage and the spectator. His life is revisited on multiple stages before him. So he watches himself perform, sometimes contemptuously, sometimes despairing. Breton the spectator relives the scenes from his life as hero, villain, and victim within his own theater. Still, the interlacing of selves is not the only use of the *fil conducteur*. In "Sur la route qui monte et qui descend" (On the Road that Goes Up and Down), for example, the same words and alliterations—notably of *f*: *feuillage* (foliage), *flamme* (flame), *filet* (trickle), *feuille* (leaf), *feu* (fire)—recur again and again, weaving a sonorous web to reinforce the intertwining of imagery.

That spring, even as they were bringing out their new volumes of poetry, Breton and Eluard set to work editing *Petite Anthologie poétique du surréalisme* (Little Anthology of Surrealist Verse). Two years were spent gathering a representative sampling of the poetic output of the movement. The Surrealists also returned to games, such as crossword puzzles with curious clues. Another trend that gained in popularity around 1931 was the appearance of "Surrealist objects." These objects were at times fabricated, at other times embellished, or even simply found. Taken out of their habitual context, they are meant to provoke an unaccustomed response in the viewer.

In the 1932 book *Les Vases communicants* Breton seeks to demonstrate that the dreamworld and the real world are one and the same. The entire collection is concerned with the "communicating vessels" of dreaming and waking experiences, coupled with a search for liberation. Surrealism makes that connection between the often dissociated worlds of waking and dreaming explicit in its poetry, drawing attention to the constant interchange between internal and external worlds. In the interpenetration of dream and reality highlighted in *Les Vases communicants,* Breton reveals his increasing awareness of the social and moral consequences inherent in the principle of integral freedom. He attempts to move from interpreting the world to transforming it.

In August of 1934 Breton married Jacqueline Lamba, a twenty-four-year-old artist whom he celebrated in his next volume of poetry, *L'Air de l'eau* (The Air of Water, 1934). The collection explores the "infiltrations merveilleuses" (marvelous infiltrations) that release wonder in the poet. These infiltrations are granted through the creative play of analogies when "les barreaux du spectacle sont merveilleusement tordus" (the bars of the spectacle are marvelously

Title page for Breton's 1937 book, in which he argued that poetry should startle readers into discovering things about themselves (Thomas Cooper Library, University of South Carolina)

twisted), and the facade of the real crumbles to uncover the surreal.

If there is an overriding theme connecting the various poems of *L'Air de l'eau,* it is that each one can be interpreted as an intertwining thread connecting previously disconnected ideas, like air and water that blend together in the iridescence or the movement. Together, the poems reinforce one other in their contrasts, their tensions, their associations, and their conclusions, each ending with a union.

The transparency of self that appears in *Le Revolver à cheveux blancs* reemerges in this volume in "Je rêve je te vois . . ." (I dream I see you . . .), allowing Breton to merge with the image of his beloved:

Je rêve je te vois superposé indéfiniment à toi-même
Tu es assise sur le haut tabouret de corail
Devant ton miroir toujours à son premier quartier

(I dream I see you superimposed indefinitely upon your-
self
You are seated on the high stool of coral
Before your mirror always in its first quarter).

In the incantation to the couple, a unity is created
through the use of *je* (I), *tu* (you), and *nous* (we), each of
which is superimposed or reflected in the others. Reflection and automatism are united. The other is generally
evoked through the body of the woman, who is always
naked and under the gaze of the poet. Breton looks at
the "plus tendres plis de son corps" (most tender folds
of her body). The sensual imagery at times becomes
exuberant, even brutal, and is evoked primarily
through natural and animal imagery: the amorous combat of the great turtles, the exultant flight of the eagle,
the fall of golden leaves.

Breton restated the theoretical positions of Surrealism in *Qu'est-ce que le surréalisme?* (1934; translated
as *What Is Surrealism?* 1936) and conveyed the sense
of public responsibility in *Position politique du surréalisme* (Political Position of Surrealism, 1935), both of
which works are comprised of lectures. The same
sense of responsibility that had appeared in Surrealist
poetry and manifestos had also led them to ally
themselves for a time with the Communists, seeking
conciliation between the two revolutionary movements. Breton had asserted that in order to attain full
liberty, they would have to do combat on the political plane. In the early 1930s, several of the Surrealists were active in the French Communist Party but
for others, such as Breton, the alliance that existed
was always uneasy. For many Surrealists, one of the
primary revolutionary tenets was free thought. Once
the Soviet dictator Joseph Stalin began his bloody
purges, there was little possibility of Breton continuing to seek unity with the Communists. Breton was
in fact one of the founders of the Commission of
Inquiry into the Moscow Trials in 1936.

The split between the Surrealists and the Communists was exacerbated by differing conceptions of
poetry. Aragon had written a poem "Le Front rouge,"
which was criticized publically both for its political
overtones and its poetic attributes. Breton came to the
defense of the poem as poetry, downplaying its political
significance in *Misère de la poésie: "L'Affaire Aragon" devant
l'opinion publique* (Misery of Poetry, 1932). Aragon, perhaps under pressure from French and Soviet Communists, renounced Breton's defense of him and in 1935
publically broke with the Surrealists. The argument had
serious repercussions and opened a debate by critics
around the world over the relationship between politics
and poetry. The French Communist Party had never
had great faith in the Surrealists, whose alliance they

believed to be more of a poetic pose than a practical
commitment. After 1935 the Surrealists broke with the
Communists. They did, however, retain strong Marxist
inclinations and fervent admiration for Leon Trotsky.
In fact, Breton later joined Trotsky in Mexico in 1938
and with him wrote a manifesto titled *Pour un art révolutionnaire indépendant* (For an Independent Revolutionary
Art, 1938). Breton's acquaintance with Trotsky reaf-
firmed his staunch opposition to Stalinism and further
inspired the campaign he later led against socialist realism in 1951.

Although he remained a political leftist for the
remainder of his life, Breton refused to support the
Soviet Union. The Surrealists and Communists at times
took similar positions, but there remained a good deal
of animosity between them. At the time of the May
1968 student and worker uprising in France, the Surrealists even spoke out against the "nonrevolutionary"
attitude of the French Communist Party.

In *L'Amour fou* (1937; translated as *Mad Love*,
1987) Breton, echoing Apollinaire's maxim, writes: "La
surprise doit être recherchée pour elle-même, incondi-
tionnellement" (Surprise must be sought for itself,
unconditionally). The significance of this statement is
found in the Surrealists' understanding of the ability of
language to surprise the poet himself before it surprises
his readers. Breton is referring to the verbal *trouvaille*
(find), which has the effect of bringing to the poet's
attention, with the shock of surprise, elements of his
own thought and feeling previously imprisoned within
the unconscious.

The demands of love are to be met within the
social framework by abandoning logical paths. Breton
had ended *Nadja* with a sentence that he later repeated
in an essay on Ernst in 1942: "La beauté sera CONVUL-
SIVE ou ne sera pas" (Beauty will be CONVULSIVE or will
not exist). The presence of convulsive love is guaranteed,
Breton claims, by what he calls "magique-circonstancielle"
(circumstantial magic). *L'Amour fou* demonstrates that
desire is the key to convulsive love. Desire is seen to
have ways of seeking out and taking possession of an
object. Looking back at his own life, Breton suggests
that "Tournesol" (Sunflower), which he wrote in 1923,
forecast events that did not take place until 1934, which
culminated in his marriage with Lamba. He also speaks
of visiting the flea market with Alberto Giacometti and
of finding a mask and wooden spoon. Then he explains
how the mask appeared to "prendre une place" (take its
place) in Giacometti's personal search (inspiring the finishing touches on a sculpture, which had been eluding
him) and how the spoon answered some unconscious
needs of his own.

Chance now seemed to be embodied in *objets
trouvés* (found objects), as Breton concluded that *la trou-*

Mexican artist Diego Rivera, exiled Russian Communist Leon Trotsky, and Breton
in Mexico, 1938 (photograph by Manuel Alvarez Bravo)

vaille (the find) exercises a remarkable magnetism because it is capable of revealing in an individual desires of which he or she has remained ignorant. In a footnote in *L'Amour fou,* the *trouvaille* is revealed to have the same function as the dream, "en ce sens qu'elle libère l'individu de scrupules affectifs paralysants, le réconforte et lui fait comprendre que l'obstacle qu'il pouvait croire insurmontable est franchi" (in that it liberates the individual from paralyzing affective scruples, comforts him and allows him to understand that the obstacle which he might have believed insurmountable has been passed). The *trouvaille* relates to the individual's inner needs. Love is the supreme form of desire, capable of the kind of transformation that sheds light on the real. Breton even suggests that rewards are obtainable if one is willing to accept all that chance may place in one's path: "Indépendamment de ce qui arrive, n'arrive pas, c'est l'attente qui est magnifique" (Beyond what happens or does not happen, it is waiting which is magnificent).

In 1939 Breton was recalled to military service as the medical director of the Ecole de Pilotage, the flight school at Poitiers. After the collapse of the French army in 1940, he was demobilized. With the advent of World War II and the Nazi invasion of France, the Surrealist group broke up. Breton fled with his family to Marseilles, in the southern part of Vichy France.

Breton's longest and most ambitious poem from this period is an epic work called *Fata Morgana,* a poem of action, but action that is purely imaginary. The voyage is in every way more marvelous. In a rebellion against the generally accepted limits of imagination and of life, the poet is "Quitte enfin de ses limites" (Finally free of [his] limits).

Originally dedicated to his wife, Jacqueline Breton, this exceptionally long poem was written in December 1940 at the Air-Bel villa (63 avenue Jean Lombard in Marseilles) during the period when Breton was host of the Comité Américain de Secours aux Intellectuels. The poem first appeared in print in an English translation by Clark Mills in the American review *New Directions in Prose and Poetry* in 1941 (the translation was republished in book form in 1969). Scheduled for publication on 10 March 1941, the original edition was suppressed and the French text was not publically available until 1942, when it was published in Buenos Aires by Editions des Lettres Françaises.

The title *Fata Morgana* refers to an Italian legend about a mirage sometimes seen in the Strait of Messina (between Italy and Sicily), named after the fairy enchantress Morgan Le Fay of the Arthurian Romances. Apollinaire, notably in *L'Enchanteur pourrissant,* had already reused this legend. Like Morgan herself, the *Fata Morgana* consists of a succession of illusions and digressions in which automatism plays a great role. As in other poems by Breton, the "je," "tu," and "nous" are intertwined. But the primary theme is the birth of a new day, reflecting Breton's efforts to resist the surrounding realities of war and defeat by reaching beyond them, toward a universe governed by marvels. *Fata Morgana* is a reaffirmation of life in the face of this "pièce sans entractes" (play without intermissions), and of Breton's love for his wife. The alternating between a stream of desire and references to Breton's actual circumstances gives the reader of *Fata Morgana* the feeling of constantly drifting in and out of consciousness.

Fata Morgana illustrates the importance Breton accords to the interior voyage and to the spectacle of the marvelous. It is just as clearly the poem of Surrealist hope:

> Ce matin la fille de la montagne tient sur ses
>   genoux un accordéon de chauves-souris blancs
> Un jour un nouveau jour ...

> (This morning the mountain girl holds on her knees
>   an accordion of white bats
> One day a new day ...)

The motif "un nouveau jour" is repeated, each time rearticulated so that love and life are always seen as if for the first time.

As one might expect, all the poems, games, and activities could keep reality at bay only imperfectly, and life at Air-Bel, despite its diversions, entailed many hardships and frustrations. The villa went unheated through the freezing winter nights. Food was at times scarce. Perhaps worst of all for Breton was the feeling that he should be doing more to resist the events occurring in France:

> Ce qui *se passe*
> Est de toute importance pour nous peut-être faudrait-il
>   revenir
> Avoir le courage de sonner
> Qui dit qu'on ne nous accueillerait pas à bras ouverts
> Mais rien n'est vérifié tous ont peur nous-mêmes
> Avons presque aussi peur

> (What *happens*
>   Is of the utmost importance to us perhaps we should
> return
> Have the courage to ring
> Who says we would not be welcomed with open arms
> But nothing is sure all are afraid we ourselves
> Are almost afraid as well).

That fear would prevent Breton from fighting for freedom is a possibility he himself envisioned. Yet, when interviewed in New York City in 1941 by Charles-Henri Ford for the magazine *View*, Breton avowed his commitment to resisting tyranny. In this interview, collected in *Entretiens 1913–1952* (1952; translated as *Conversations: The Autobiography of Surrealism,* 1993), he declared that he wanted to affirm here his "position de résistance plus intransigeante que jamais aux entreprises masochistes qui tendent en France, à restreindre la liberté poétique ou à l'immoler sur le même autel que les autres" (position of resistance, which is more intransigent than ever, to the masochistic enterprises in France that tended to restrict poetic freedom or to immolate it on the same altar as other freedoms).

To confront the racist ideology of Marshal Philippe Pétain's government, Breton decided to have his book illustrated by Wilfredo Lam, who was of mixed race. As a result of Breton's defiance and Lam's participation, the Vichy government denied permission to publish *Fata Morgana*. Breton succeeded in having printed only five personal copies of the poem, which included the Lam illustrations, hand colored by the artist. His other major work during this time, *Anthologie de l'humour noir* (1940; translated as *Anthology of Black Humor,* 1997), was also banned.

The perilousness of Breton's situation became obvious when Pétain planned a state visit to Marseilles on 4 December 1940. The day before Pétain's visit, several plainclothes policemen arrived at the Air-Bel villa, interrogated Breton, and searched the premises. They implied in both words and actions that Breton was under suspicion as a possible terrorist.

Breton's flight from France has caused a good deal of controversy. Despite his calls to action, Breton left the country, while other Surrealists remained in France to fight and even die for their beliefs. For some, Breton's actions brought dishonor to him and his movement. Georges Hugnet expressed a typical sentiment when he later wrote that Breton had "dishonored Surrealism." However, with a wife and young daughter, Aube (born 1935), in his care, Breton saw little advantage in staying in an increasingly hostile France, awaiting almost certain arrest and deportation.

Leaving France in 1941 Breton took his family first to the French colony of Martinique; from there they traveled to New York City to join other exiled

Surrealists. In fact, the Surrealist group reformed in New York with new members who were living in exile. They held meetings and began publishing the magazine *VVV*, which Breton founded with David Hare. For a while Breton even broadcast for the Voice of America.

Breton's period of residence in the United States was marked by two important statements on Surrealism: a lecture delivered at Yale University on 10 December 1942, published in 1945 as *Situation du surréalisme entre les deux guerres* (Situation of Surrealism Between the Two Wars), and *Prolégomènes à un troisième manifeste du surréalisme ou non* (Prolegomena to a Third Manifesto of Surrealism or Else), published in *VVV* in 1942 and republished in *Les Manifestes du surréalisme, suivis de Prolégomènes à un troisième manifeste du surréalisme ou non* (1946). In these statements Breton publically confirmed the revolutionary entrenchment of Surrealism.

During his exile Breton took several trips to the American Southwest, visiting Arizona and New Mexico in search of pre-Colombian relics and conducting research into Native American arts and customs. He also traveled to the Canary Islands and to Canada. The texts he wrote during this time were mystical, in the vein of his *Fata Morgana*.

Despite all of these activities, Breton found his American period rather unpleasant. He and his wife had little money, and their poverty was exacerbated by Breton's refusal to learn English. He justified this refusal as an unwillingness to "tarnish" his command of French, but perhaps there was also a fear of not being able to master a new language. Regardless, his lack of English cost him a teaching position at the recently founded New School for Social Research. The language barrier also prevented the ideas of the Surrealist movement from taking root in the United States. Few of Breton's theoretical writings existed in English, and though some Surrealist artists were beginning to be noticed, Surrealist poetry remained largely unknown on the American scene for another decade.

Breton was not entirely wanting for friendships in New York, however. He had gathered many of the French exiles around him, and he had also made several interesting new contacts in the United States. André, Jacqueline, and Aube Breton resided in a home in Hampton Bays, Long Island. While there, he began working on a new epic poem titled "Les Etats généraux" (The States General), after the eighteenth-century governing body that had helped spark the French Revolution.

"Les Etats généraux," generally considered to be Breton's most significant poem from the New York years, conveys an emotional and spiritual darkness but with glimmers cast by the names of past rebels who defied human oppression. The poem provides a win-

Breton and his wife, Jacqueline, in 1940

dow on elements of Breton's life in New York, including glimpses of the Long Island countryside and the electrical brownouts that were frequent on the home front. In the course of writing this poem, he separated from his wife, and his sadness at this loss is reflected in the verse: "Elle n'accepte le joug lui ne lise sa perte" (She does not accept the yoke he cannot read his loss). On 30 July 1945, he divorced Jacqueline Breton in Reno, Nevada. Some accounts maintain that he married Elisa Bindhoff the same day, but by other accounts he married her on 20 August 1945.

Breton had discovered in a horticultural catalogue an odd phrase that struck his fancy, "Young Cherry Trees Secured Against Hares." He had been searching for a title for a small anthology of his verse; the collection, *Young Cherry Trees Secured Against Hares/ Jeunes Cérisiers garantis contre les lièvres,* was published in a bilingual edition in 1946. For the book, Breton selected verse from *Clair de terre, Le Revolver à cheveux blancs,* and *L'Air de l'eau,* as well as *L'Union libre* (here translated as

Breton and his daughter, Aube, in Marseilles, 1940

during the Occupation, and that included Resistance verse by former Surrealists Aragon, Eluard, and Hugnet. Péret's pamphlet attacked those poets who had renounced poetry, turning instead to politics, religion, and money. "All told," he writes, "the honor of these 'poets' consists of ceasing to be poets in order to become advertising agents." Many French poets, particularly those who had remained in France to resist the German occupation, were outraged by the pamphlet, and there was animus against Péret as well as against Breton, his supporter.

With a few exceptions, Breton's poetic voice was quiet during the New York years. He did republish the manifestos in 1946 and an essay titled *Arcane 17* in 1947. *Arcane 17*, written in the Gaspé Peninsula of Québec, is an ode to love and to the mysteries of the alchemical and the arcane. But it also displays Breton's concern for pressing personal problems and continued Surrealist themes that run through the essays written during the 1920s and 1930s.

After World War II Breton returned to Paris to resurrect the Surrealist group, though many of the original members were now living overseas. Breton was attacked by Tzara and others for having chosen exile over resistance. By this time, however, Surrealism was a major influence in the international art world. Individual Surrealists, such as Dalí, Ernst, and René Magritte, had achieved recognition for their work, while the group's theoretical ideas, primarily composed by Breton, were becoming known worldwide. His creative writings were also circulating, though most of his work during the years following his return to France was as an art critic.

Back in Paris he organized two international expositions of Surrealism, in 1947 and 1965, and published his *Ode à Charles Fourier* (1947; translated as *Ode to Charles Fourier*, 1969); a collected edition of his poetry, *Poèmes* (1948); and essays on art: *Le Surréalisme et la peinture* (1946) and a book compiled with the assistance of Gérard Legrand, *L'Art magique* (The Magic Art, 1957). In terms of poetry, the most significant work in the postwar period was *Ode à Charles Fourier*, a poem that extols the "sens de la fête" (sense of the feast).

Breton had become interested in Fourier's theories during his time in New York. His thoughts on Fourier's social prescriptions merged with his observations of Nevada life, his awe at the sprawling landscape, and his appreciation of the Native American ethos, to produce a vast poetic treatise, freer in form than anything he had yet written. In the course of the poem, Breton presents the abstract of Fourier's theses, along with bits of his own travels thrown in like scrapbook captions: "Fourier je te salue du Grand Canon du Colorado" (Fourier I salute you from the Grand Canyon from

"Freedom of Love"), excerpts from *Fata Morgana,* and some of his most recent poems.

Breton's fears were compounded in January 1945 during a visit from Jean-Paul Sartre. Breton later remarked: "Sartre insistait particulièrement sur la 'terreur' que les staliniens faisaient régner dans les lettres" (Sartre particularly stressed the "terror" that the Stalinists waged over the literary world). Another worrisome development from Breton's viewpoint was the rise in France of "Resistance poetry" or "occasional verse." Poetry of this sort, linked in such a way to the external world so that it often becomes a vehicle for propaganda, was a primary target of the Surrealists.

Breton was thus thrilled by the publication in Mexico of Péret's *Le Déshonneur des poètes* (The Dishonor of Poets, 1945). The text was a rebuttal to a widely read anthology called *L'Honneur des poètes* (The Honor of Poets), which had circulated clandestinely in France

Colorado). Breton made the nineteenth-century socialist and reformer his last great intellectual guide, supplanting even Trotsky. Fourier was the theorist of the "phalanstère" (phalanstery), a commune-like society whose literary antecedents went back to Thomas More's Utopia and François Rabelais's Abbey of Thélème and whose practical applications included the short-lived Brook Farm experiment in the 1840s. In Fourier's view, the ideal society was an association based on harmonious labor and a minutely regulated code of desire rather than commerce and civic or marital convention.

This one poem includes references to almost all of the main Surrealist attitudes. Breton utilizes the poem to attack what Fourier viewed as the menaces of social institutions, such as nations, wars, and religions, each of which might dull the instinct to explore the new:

> *Indigence fourberie oppression carnage* ce sont toujours
>   les mêmes maux dont tu as marqué la civilisation au
>   fer rouge
> Fourier on s'est moqué mais il faudra bien qu'on tâte
>   un jour bon gré mal gré de ton remède
>
> (*Poverty swindling oppression slaughter* are the same ills for
>   which you
>   branded civilization
> Fourier they've scoffed but one day they'll have to try
>   your remedy whether they like it or not).

What Fourier had offered as an alternative included an insistence on ritual and the value of the world of sleep.

Ode à Charles Fourier was Breton's last major poetic work and was distinctive in terms of form and content. Like much of Breton's writing, the ode took its point of departure in automatism, but its unity and direction is to be found in Fourier's work. Breton was particularly drawn to Fourier's belief in the lost paradise of an erotic civilization, where one could love, as he put it in "Le marquis de Sade . . . " in *L'Air de l'eau,* "Comme le premier homme aima la première femme / En toute liberté" (The way the first man loved the first woman / In total freedom). However, *Ode à Charles Fourier* was Breton's only philosophical poem, and it addresses the inner demands of the poet to seek the key to the mental prison that might allow an individual to attain the liberation of self.

Breton's anthology titled *Poèmes* was published by Gallimard at the end of 1948. The collection includes poems spanning Breton's career, some from earlier collections, others previously uncollected. Only a few postwar works are present. One of these poems, "Sur la route de San Romano" (On the Road to San Romano), which had appeared in 1948 in the journal *Néon,* is his last piece of published verse. The poem commences:

Breton at work, 1960

> La poésie se fait dans un lit comme l'amour
> Ses draps défaits sont l'aurore des choses
> La poésie se fait dans les bois
>
> (Poetry is made in bed like love
> Its unmade sheets are the dawn of things
> Poetry is made in a forest).

Art, Breton always insisted, cannot be used, it must be free; and here Breton quotes the young Marx on the necessary liberty of the pen. Freedom of the mind is, from the Surrealist point of view, even more important than freedom from hunger. It is only by reaching the level where opposites are reconciled that the poet can gain freedom, as Breton writes in *Second manifeste du surréalisme:*

> Tout porte à croire qu'il existe un certain point de l'esprit d'où la vie et la mort, le réel et l'imaginaire, le passé et le futur, le communicable et l'incommunicable,

le haut et le bas cessent d'être perçus contradictoire-
ment.

(Everything leads us to believe that there is a certain
state of mind from which life and death, the real and
the imaginary, the past and the future, the communica-
ble and the incommunicable, the high and the low are
no longer perceived as contradictory).

Furthermore, poetry and art must bear juxtaposition
with the greatest human suffering if they are to be
worth anything at all. For Breton it is essential that people be in permanent revolt against limits of all kinds;
and thus the Surrealists have never ceased to speak out
for various causes.

André Breton died of a heart attack on 28 September 1966. But his poetry continued to influence the
artistic and political stances of French writers. He also
had a major impact on Latin American and Negritude
writers. The mixture of deep personal poetic voice with
the compulsion for liberation has appealed to poets
from around the globe.

Interview:

Entretiens 1913–1952, Collection Le Point du jour
(Paris: Gallimard, 1952); translated by Mark
Polizzotti as *Conversations: The Autobiography of Sur-
realism* (New York: Paragon House, 1993).

Bibliographies:

Michael Sheringham, *André Breton: A Bibliography* (London: Grant & Cutler, 1972);

Marguerite Bonnet and Jacqueline Chenieux-Gendron,
*Revues surréalistes françaises autour d'André Breton,
1948–1972* (Millwood, N.Y.: Kraus International
Publications, 1982);

Rudolf E. Kuenzli, "André Breton: A Selective Bibliography, 1971–1988," *Dada/Surrealism,* 17 (1988):
129–145;

Elza Adamowicz, *André Breton: A Bibliography (1972–
1989)* (London: Grant & Cutler, 1992).

Biographies:

J. H. Matthews, *André Breton: Sketch for an Early Portrait*
(Amsterdam & Philadelphia: John Benjamins,
1986);

Henri Béhar, *André Breton: Le Grand indésirable,* edited by
Claude Glayman (Paris: Calmann-Lévy, 1990);

Mark Polizzotti, *Revolution of the Mind: The Life of André
Breton* (New York: Farrar, Straus & Giroux, 1995;
London: Bloomsbury, 1995).

References:

Keith Aspley, *André Breton the Poet* (Glasgow: University
of Glasgow French and German Publications,
1989);

Anna Balakian, *André Breton: Magus of Surrealism* (New
York: Oxford University Press, 1971);

Balakian and Rudolf E. Kuenzli, eds., *André Breton
Today* (New York: Willis, Locker & Owens,
1989);

Michel Beaujour, "La Poétique de l'automatisme chez
André Breton," *Poétique,* 25 (1976): 116–123;

Jean-Louis Bédouin, *André Breton: Une étude,* Poètes
d'aujourd'hui, no. 18 (Paris: Seghers, 1950);

Mathieu Bénézet, *André Breton, rêveur définitif: Essai de lire*
(Monaco: Editions du Rocher, 1996);

Jean-Claude Blachère, *Les Totems d'André Breton: Surréalisme et primitivisme littéraire* (Paris: L'Harmattan,
1996);

Willard Bohn, "Where Dream Becomes Reality,"
L'Esprit créateur, 36 (Winter 1996): 43–51;

Marguerite Bonnet, *André Breton: Naissance de l'aventure
surréaliste* (Paris: José Corti, 1975);

Clifford Browder, *André Breton: Arbiter of Surrealism*
(Geneva: Droz, 1967);

Michel Carrouges, *André Breton et les données fondamentales
du surréalisme* (Paris: Gallimard, 1950); translated
by Maura Prendergast as *André Breton and the Basic
Concepts of Surrealism* (University: University of
Alabama Press, 1974);

Mary Ann Caws, *André Breton,* revised edition (New
York: Twayne / London: Prentice Hall, 1996);

Caws, "Linkings and Reflections: André Breton and
His *Communicating Vessels*," *Dada/Surrealism,* 17
(1988): 91–100;

Caws, *Surrealism and the Literary Imagination: A Study of
Breton and Bachelard* (The Hague: Mouton, 1966);

Albert Chesneau, "André Breton et l'expérimentation
poétique," *French Review,* 42 (1969): 371–379;

Victor Crastre, *André Breton* (N.p., Arcanes, 1952);

Richard Danier, *L'Hermétisme alchimique chez André Breton:
Interprétation de la symbolique de trois œuvres du poète,*
preface by Patrick Rivière (Villeselve, France:
Ramuel, 1997);

Jean Decottignies, *L'Invention de la poésie: Breton, Aragon,
Duchamp* (Lille: Presses Universitaires de Lille,
1994);

Charles Dedeyan, "André Breton et Arthur Rimbaud,"
Studi di Letteratura Francese, 20 (1994): 39–46;

Gérard Durozoi and Bernard Lecherbonnier, *André Breton: L'Ecriture surréaliste* (Paris: Larousse, 1974);

Marc Eigeldinger, ed., *André Breton: Essais et témoignages*
(Neuchâtel, Switzerland: Baconnière, 1950);

Julien Gracq, *André Breton: Quelques aspects de l'écrivain*
(Paris: José Corti, 1948);

Philippe Jaccottet, "Un Discours a crête de flamme," *Nouvelle Revue Française,* 15 (April 1967): 800–806;

Christine Martineau-Geniez, "Autour des images et de l'érotique surréalistes: *L'Union libre,*" *Annales de la Faculté de Nice,* 8, no. 2 (1969): 171–186;

J. H. Matthews, "André Breton and Joan Miró: *Constellations,*" *Symposium,* 34 (Winter 1980–1881): 353–376;

Claude Mauriac, *André Breton: Essai* (Paris: Flore, 1949);

François Migeot, *A la fenêtre noire des poètes: Lectures bretoniennes,* preface by Gérard Bonnet (Paris: Les Belles-Lettres, 1996);

Michel Murat, Marie-Claire Dumas, and Jean-Michel Gautier, *André Breton: Cahier* (Paris: L'Herne, 1998);

José Pierre, "André Breton et le 'poème objet,'" in *L'Objet au défi,* edited by Jacqueline Chenieux-Gendron and Dumas (Paris: Presses Universitaires de France, 1987), pp. 131–142;

Paule Plouvier, *Poétique de l'amour chez André Breton* (Paris: José Corti, 1983);

Plouvier, Renée Ventresque, and Jean-Claude Blachère, eds., *Trois poètes face à la crise de l'histoire: André Breton, Saint-John Perse, René Char: Actes du colloque de Montpellier III (22–23 mars 1996)* (Paris: L'Harmattan, 1997);

Marc Saporta and Henri Béhar, eds., *André Breton, ou, Le Surréalisme, même* (Lausanne, Switzerland: L'Age d'homme, 1988);

Michael Sheringham, "From the Labyrinth of Language to the Language of the Senses: The Poetry of André Breton," in *Sensibility and Creation: Studies in Twentieth-Century French Poetry,* edited by Roger Cardinal (London: Croom Helm / New York: Barnes & Noble, 1977), pp. 72–102;

Philippe Soupault, *Le Vrai André Breton* (Liège: Editions Dynamo, 1966);

Richard Stamelman, "André Breton and the Poetry of Intimate Presence," *Dada/Surrealism,* 5 (1975): 58–65;

André Vielwahr, *S'affranchir des contradictions: André Breton de 1925 à 1930* (Paris: L'Harmattan, 1998);

Vielwahr, *Sous le signe de contradictions: André Breton de 1913 à 1924* (Paris: Nizet, 1980);

Alain Virmaux and Odette Virmaux, *André Breton* (Lyon: La Manufacture, 1987);

Virmaux and Virmaux, *André Breton: Le Pôle magnétique: Essai* (Paris: Olbia, 1998).

Papers:
The majority of André Breton's papers are held by the Fondation Doucet, Paris; they will not be made available to the public until 2016, the fiftieth anniversary of his death.

Blaise Cendrars

(1 September 1887 – 21 January 1961)

David Rampton
University of Ottawa

BOOKS: *Les Pâques* (Paris: Editions des Hommes Nouveaux, 1912); republished as *Les Pâques à New-York,* illustrated by Frans Masereel (Paris: Editions René Kieffer, 1926);

La Prose du Transsibérien et de la Petite Jehanne de France, gouache by Sonia Delaunay (Paris: Editions des Hommes Nouveaux, 1913); translated by Anselm Hollo as "The Trans-Siberian Express," in *Evergreen Review Reader, 1957–1967: A Ten-Year Anthology,* edited by Barney Rosset (New York: Grove, 1968), pp. 621–630;

Séquences (Paris: Editions des Hommes Nouveaux, 1913);

La Guerre au Luxembourg (Paris: Niestlé, 1916);

Profond Aujourd'hui, illustrated by Angel Zárraga (Paris: A La Belle Edition, 1917); translated by Harold Loeb as "Profound Today," *Broom,* 1 (January 1922): 265–267;

Le Panama; ou, Les Aventures de mes sept oncles (Paris: Editions de la Sirène, 1918); translated by John Dos Passos as *Panama: or, The Adventures of My Seven Uncles,* illustrated by Dos Passos (New York & London: Harper, 1931);

J'ai tué, illustrated by Fernand Léger (Paris: A La Belle Edition, 1918);

Dix-neuf poèmes élastiques, Collection de littérature, no. 4 (Paris: Au Sans Pareil, 1919);

La Fin du monde filmée par l'Ange N.-D., illustrated by Léger (Paris: Editions de la Sirène, 1919);

Anthologie nègre (Paris: Editions de la Sirène, 1921); translated by Margery Bianco as *The African Saga,* introduction by Arthur B. Spingarn (New York: Payson & Clarke, 1927);

Kodak (Documentaires) (Paris: Stock, Dellamain & Boutelleau, 1924);

Le Formose, part 1 of *Feuilles de Route* (Paris: Au Sans Pareil, 1924);

L'Or: La Merveilleuse histoire du Genéral Johann August Suter (Paris: Grasset, 1925); translated by Henry Longan Stuart as *Sutter's Gold* (New York & London: Harper, 1926; London: Heinemann, 1927);

Blaise Cendrars in 1930

Moravagine: Roman (Paris: Grasset, 1926); revised and enlarged as *Moravagine, roman; suivi de Pro domo: Comment j'ai écrit "Moravagine"* (Paris: Grasset, 1956); translated by Alan Brown as *Moravagine: A Novel* (London: Owen, 1968; Garden City, N.Y.: Doubleday, 1970);

L'ABC du cinéma (Paris: Les Ecrivains Réunis, 1926);

L'Eubage aux antipodes de l'unité, illustrated by Joseph Hecht (Paris: Au Sans Pareil, 1926); translated by Matthew Josephson as "At the Antipodes of Unity," *Broom,* 3 (October 1922): 182–193;

94

Eloge de la vie dangereuse, Tout autour d'aujourd'hui, no. 2 (Paris: Les Ecrivains Réunis, 1926);

Petits contes nègres pour les enfants des blancs (Paris: Editions des Portiques, 1928); translated by Bianco as *Little Black Stories for Little White Children* (New York: Payson & Clarke, 1929); translation republished as *Little Black Stories* (New York: Brewer & Warren, 1931);

Le Plan de l'Aiguille (Paris: Au Sans Pareil, 1929); translated by John Rodker as *Antarctic Fugue* (London: Pushkin, 1948; New York: Anglobooks, 1948); revised and enlarged as *Dan Yack: Roman* (Paris: Editions de la Tour, 1946); translated by Nina Rootes as *Dan Yack* (London: Owen, 1987; New York: Kesend, 1987);

Les Confessions de Dan Yack (Paris: Au Sans Pareil, 1929); translated by Rootes as *Confessions of Dan Yack* (London: Owen, 1990);

Une nuit dans la forêt: Premier fragment d'une autobiographie (Lausanne, Switzerland: Editions du Verseau, 1929); translated by Margaret Kidder Ewing as *A Night in the Forest: First Fragment of an Autobiography* (Columbia: University of Missouri Press, 1985);

Rhum: L'Aventure de Jean Galmot (Paris: Grasset, 1930); republished as *La Vie secrète de Jean Galmot* (Paris: Editions de France, 1934);

Comment les Blancs sont d'anciens Noirs, illustrated by Alfred Latour (Paris: Au Sans Pareil, 1930);

Aujourd'hui (Paris: Grasset, 1931);

Vol à voile, Les Cahiers romands, second series no. 6 (Lausanne, Switzerland: Payot, 1932);

Panorama de la pègre (Grenoble: Arthaud, 1935);

Hollywood, la Mecque du cinéma, illustrated by Jean Guérin (Paris: Grasset, 1937); translated, with an introduction, by Garrett White as *Hollywood: Mecca of the Movies* (Berkeley & London: University of California Press, 1994);

Histoires vraies (Paris: Grasset, 1938);

La Vie dangereuse (Paris: Grasset, 1938);

D'Oultremer à indigo (Paris: Grasset, 1940);

Chez l'armée anglaise (Paris: Corréa, 1940);

Poésies complètes de Blaise Cendrars, introduction by Jacques-Henri Lévesque (Paris: Denoël, 1944); translated by Ron Padgett as *Complete Poems: Blaise Cendrars,* introduction and notes by Jay Bochner (Berkeley & Los Angeles: University of California Press, 1992);

L'Homme foudroyé (Paris: Denoël, 1945); translated by Rootes as *The Astonished Man: A Novel* (London: Owen, 1970);

La Main coupée (Paris: Denoël, 1946); abridged and translated by Rootes as *Lice* (London: Owen, 1973);

Le Vieux-Port, lithographs by René Bouveret (Paris & Marseilles: Vigneau, 1946);

Bourlinguer (Paris: Denoël, 1948); abridged and translated by Rootes as *Planus* (London: Owen, 1972);

Le Lotissement du ciel (Paris: Denoël, 1949); translated by Rootes as *Sky: Memoirs,* introduction by Marjorie Perloff (New York: Paragon House, 1992);

Noël aux quatre coins du monde (Paris: Robert Cayla, 1953); translated by Bertrand Mathieu as *Christmas at the Four Corners of the Earth,* illustrated by Denzil Walker (Brockport, N.Y.: BOA Editions, 1994);

Emmène-moi au bout du monde! (Paris: Denoël, 1956); translated by Brown as *To the End of the World* (New York: Grove, 1966; London: Owen, 1967);

Trop c'est trop (Paris: Denoël, 1957);

Du monde entier au coeur du monde (Paris: Denoël, 1957);

Films sans images (Paris: Denoël, 1959);

Saint Joseph de Cupertino: Le Nouveau patron de l'aviation le vol arriere (Paris: Le Club du Livre Chretien, 1960);

Œuvres Complètes: Blaise Cendrars, 8 volumes (Paris: Denoël, 1960–1964);

Blaise Cendrars: Œuvres Complètes, 16 volumes, edited by Nino Franck and others (Paris: Club Français du Livre, 1968–1971)–includes volume 16, *Inédits Secrets,* edited by Miriam Cendrars (1969);

Jéroboam et La Sirène, preface by Hughes Richard (La Chaux de Cossonay, Switzerland: F.A. Parisot, 1979; Saint-Imier: Canevas, 1992);

Aujourd'hui 1917–1929 suivi de Essais et Réflexions 1910–1916, edited by Miriam Cendrars (Paris: Denoël, 1987).

Editions and Collections: *Du monde entier* (Paris: Editions de la Nouvelle Revue Française, 1919)–comprises *Les Pâques à New-York, Prose du Transsibérien et de la Petite Jeanne de France,* and *Le Panama; ou, Les Aventures de mes sept oncles;*

A L'Aventure: Textes choisis (Paris: Denoël, 1958); also published as *L'Aventure* (Paris: Club des Jeunes Amis du Livre, 1958);

Dix neuf poèmes élastiques de Blaise Cendrars: Edition critique et commentée, edited by Jean-Pierre Goldenstein (Paris: Méridiens Klincksieck, 1986);

L'Eubage: Aux antipodes de l'unité, edited by Jean-Carlo Flückiger, Cahiers Blaise Cendrars, no. 2 (Paris: H. Champion / Geneva: Editions Slatkine, 1995).

Editions and Collections in English: *Selected Writings of Blaise Cendrars,* edited, with a critical introduction, by Walter Albert, preface by Henry Miller (New York: New Directions, 1966);

Complete Postcards from the Americas: Poems of Road and Sea, bilingual edition, translated by Monique Chefdor (Berkeley, Los Angeles & London: University of

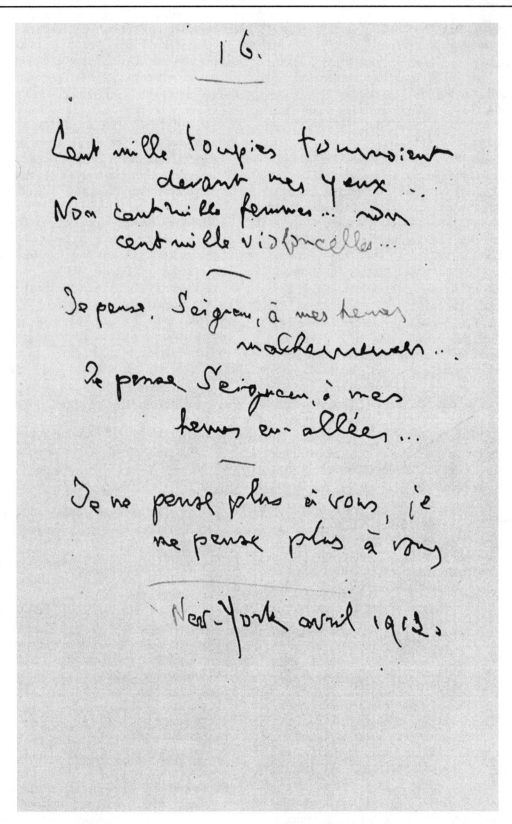

Page from the manuscript for Cendrars's revised version (1919) of Les Pâques à New-York, *a long poem first published in 1912 (from Albert T'Serstevens,* L'Homme que fut Blaise Cendrars: Souvenirs, *1972)*

California Press, 1976)—comprises translations of *Le Formose* and *Kodak (Documentaires);*

Selected Poems: Blaise Cendrars, translated by Peter Hoida, introduction by Mary Ann Caws (Harmondsworth, U.K. & New York: Penguin, 1979);

Gold: The Marvellous History of General John Augustus Sutter, translated by Nina Rootes (London & Boston: Owen, 1982); republished as *Gold: Being the Marvellous History of General John Augustus Sutter* (New York: Kesend, 1984);

Shadow, translated and illustrated by Marcia Brown (New York: Scribners, 1982);

Modernities and Other Writings by Blaise Cendrars, translated by Esther Allen and Chefdor, edited, with an introduction, by Chefdor (Lincoln & London: University of Nebraska Press, 1992).

PLAY PRODUCTION: *La Création du Monde,* by Cendrars and Fernand Léger, Paris, Théatre des Champs Elysées, 25 October 1923.

OTHER: Hans Bringolf, *Feu le lieutenant Bringolf,* translated and edited by Cendrars, Collection Les Têtes brûlées, no. 1 (Paris: Au Sans Pareil, 1930); translated by Warre B. Wells as *I Have No Regrets: The Strange Life of a Diplomat-Vagrant, Being the Memoirs of Lieutenant Bringolf* (London: Jarrolds, 1931; New York: Dutton, 1932);

Fred D. Pasley, *Al Capone le Balafré, tsar des bandits de Chicago,* translated, with a preface, by Cendrars, Collection Les Têtes brûlées, no. 2 (Paris: Au Sans Pareil, 1930);

Al Jennings, *Hors la loi ! . . . La vie d'un Outlaw américain racontée par lui-même,* translated, with an introduction, by Cendrars (Paris: Grasset, 1936);

José Maria Ferreira Borges de Castro, *Forêt vierge,* translated, with an introduction, by Cendrars (Paris: Grasset, 1938);

Robert Doisneau, *La Banlieue de Paris,* introduction by Cendrars (Paris: Seghers / Lausanne, Switzerland: Guilde du Livre, 1949); translated by Anne Marie Callimach as *Robert Doisneau's Paris: 148 Photographs* (New York: Simon & Schuster, 1956);

Jean Manzon, *Le Brésil,* introduction by Cendrars (Monaco: Les Documents d'Art, 1952).

Blaise Cendrars is in every way an extraordinary figure. His life was full of fascinating adventures, yet he invented a series of myths about himself to make it seem even more fascinating. He revolutionized twentieth-century French poetry—"La poèsie date d'aujord'hui" (Poetry dates from today), from *Le Panama; ou, Les Aventures de mes sept oncles* (1918; translated as *Panama: or, The Adventures of My Seven*

Uncles, 1931) is one of his most oft-quoted remarks—but actually worked as a poet for just over a decade, going on to spend the rest of his career writing in prose and experimenting with other art forms. He consistently flouted public taste but was intent on being a celebrity. He was a strident supporter of the working class who fought for the capitalists in World War I. He was a dreamer who, all the while insisting that the truth was imaginary, constantly worked at conflating the language of his verse with the world of things. Although he worked with some of the most-famous creative minds of the twentieth century, he was a loner who resolutely refused membership in any group. He said that the poet was the conscience of the race but also insisted that writing was a vice and that he was not a writer at all but a simple libertine. He published on average almost a book a year during a long, astonishingly productive, and variegated career but died in poverty and critical neglect.

Frédéric Louis Sauser was born on 1 September 1887 in La Chaux-de-Fonds, Switzerland, the son of Georges Frédéric Sauser, a merchant, and Marie-Louise Dorner. As a boy he moved about a great deal with his family: Egypt, Naples (where he attended an elementary school), Germany, perhaps England and Paris as well. From 1904 to 1907 he worked for H. A. Leuba, a watchmaker in St. Petersburg who traveled extensively in Russia and the Far East. Sauser stayed for long periods in St. Petersburg and Moscow, saw the beginnings of the Russian Revolution firsthand, and met a St. Petersburg girl named Hélène, whose tragic death in a fire in 1907, soon after his return to Switzerland, haunted him for the rest of his life. He worked at a variety of jobs in Germany, France, and Belgium, and did some desultory work at the university of Bern, where he studied medicine in 1909. In Bern he met and fell in love with Féla Poznanska, a Polish student, and the two moved to Paris, where they lived from 1910 to 1911. Poznanska left to work in New York in March of 1911 and in December of 1911 sent him a ticket to join her. Six months later he returned to Paris without Poznanska but with a new name, Blaise Cendrars, chosen for all its smouldering-phoenix suggestiveness—with its echoes of *les braises* (the glowing embers) and *cendre* (ashes or cinders)—and a new project as an avant-garde poet.

In 1912 he published his first important poem, *Les Pâques* (Easter), better known as *Les Pâques à New-York* (Easter in New York), the title it was given in the 1919 collection *Du monde entier* (Of the Whole World) and under which it was republished separately in 1926. This long poem is a plea addressed to the Christian God, doubling as a reflection on the difference between contemporary religion and its

Cendrars in 1914, shortly after enlisting in the French Foreign Legion

that God remains absent to the poet of the contemporary world in a city like New York.

The verse in which this penetrating vision is conjured up figures among the most lyrical and evocative ever published in French, and to read it is to understand something of what it must have been like to live at the dawn of a new era in modern literature. The hauntingly disjunctive cadences of the unmetered rhyming couplets make a splendid formal link with Cendrars's subject matter and with his great forebears, even as they set the stage for the great experiment in twentieth-century verse that he produced the following year.

The years 1912–1914 were an intensely creative period for Cendrars, and he spent them in a city in artistic ferment. For it was precisely at this time that all sorts of important artists—including Cendrars's closest friends, Guillaume Apollinaire, Marc Chagall, Roger and Sonia Delaunay, Fernand Saint-Léger (who wrote under the name of Saint-John Perse), Jacques Lipschitz, Amedeo Modigliani, Chaim Soutine—were making the French capital the center of modern art. In the summer of 1913, on a two-meter-tall silk-screen abstract painting created by Sonia Delaunay (now in the Hermitage in St. Petersburg), Cendrars created his next masterpiece, *La Prose du Transsibérien et de la Petite Jehanne de France* (The Prose of the Trans-Siberian and of Little Jeanne of France), which was translated as "The Trans-Siberian Express" in the *Evergreen Review* in 1964 (collected 1968). Printed on a single nearly seven-foot sheet of paper, then folded once across and pleated accordion-style, the parallel columns of text by Cendrars and painting by Delaunay is the quintessential example of modernist French poetry and one of the most evocative. Because the poem was meant to be seen with Delaunay's painting, with all its bright colors and abstract glory, and because Cendrars uses fonts, justification, and juxtapositions in strikingly original ways, a simple account of the verbal content of the poem will perforce constitute a somewhat limited encounter with it.

La Prose du Transsibérien et de la Petite Jehanne de France begins with a young man's evocation of a railway journey: adventure had become Cendrars's great subject. "En ce temps-là j'étais en mon adolescence" (At that time I was in my adolescence) is the phrase that sets the stage for the wistful egocentricity that informs the entire poem. In the first lines the reader hears the voice of the figure that came to dominate modern literature: the quintessential solitary—in a city crowd, on the road—determined to forge for himself a new aesthetic sensibility, equating the political upheavals of his time with those in his own life,

manifestations in the past. It begins with an evocation of the God of old books, old churches, old modes of worship. The speaker confesses to not knowing this God in his youth, but asserts, with an urgency that does not really convince, that this night God is at his side. His walk in the darkness mimics Christ's Passion, a grim march toward crucifixion, and he compares the destitute throngs he sees with the ones that made the journey with Christ 1,900 years ago. The scene inspires him to ask the Lord's pity for prostitutes, for the homeless, for the dispossessed generally. Yet, in the end it is the contrast between the beautiful religious services of the past and the empty, monotonous recitations of the present that most strikes this observer. The spiritual emptiness of the contemporary city depresses him and he is "triste . . . d'être si triste" (sad . . . to feel so sad). The city of modernist poetry, an endless crowd of people lost in a nightmare of darkness and loneliness, reasserts itself in the end. There is no sign of a resurrection, and the poem concludes with the reiteration

Cover, designed by Raoul Dufy, for the 1918 poem in which Cendrars wrote a fictionalized account of his childhood (Bibliothèque Nationale Suisse, Berne)

articulating his exultation and despair in retrospect, exploring the fragmentary, evanescent existence of the world of things and memories. The movement of the wheels of the train provides the driving rhythm that gives the poem its life. When he arrives in Russia, the poet's heart burns "comme la Place Rouge de Moscou" (like Red Square in Moscow), and he feels within himself the desire to eat, drink, experience, and destroy everything: "Je pressentais la venue du grand Christ rouge de la révolution russe" (I foresaw the coming of the great red Christ of the Russian Revolution). The life of a whole continent, Europe as seen from this train as it makes its way east, he compares to his own poor life. Yet, in the end his is a triumphant story of failure: he insists on the fact that his inexperience as a poet prevented him from going all the way, from experiencing and articulating these things properly.

The speaker's thoughts then turn to Jeanne or Jehanne, his mistress, the girl who accompanies him on his journey. She is a young prostitute: blonde, beautiful, and at the same time someone incorporeal, a faded flower who "n'a pas de corps—elle est trop pauvre" (doesn't have a body—she is too poor). Her plaintive refrain—"Dis, Blaise, sommes-nous bien loin de Montmartre?" (Tell me, Blaise, are we really far from Montmartre?)—punctuates the poem, making it his attempt to explain to her, to explain to himself, just where they are going and what they are doing. Memories of childhood lead the speaker to see himself as a permanent wanderer, dreaming of ever-more distant destinations while the world shrinks around him. The surreal images that seem to be rushing by them confirm his sense of isolation. This sense of isolation, in turn, leads him to think about the power of the forces allied against the individual in the modern world and his limited defenses.

Some fairly stereotyped visions of escapes to exotic haunts are followed by a renewed emphasis on the sounds of the train and on the nature of language itself: "Tric-trac / Billard / Caramboles / Paraboles" (Backgammon / Billiards / Cannons [in billiards] / Parabolas [and parables]). In these lines the words, selected in part for their sound effects, lead the poet to his conclusion, namely that the railway is a "nouvelle géométrie" (new geometry), related to the

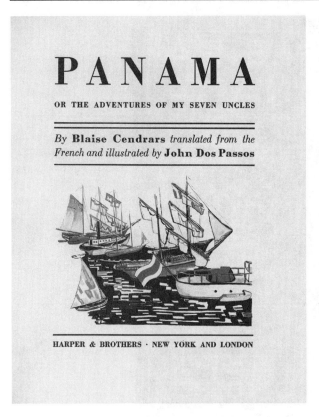

PANAMA

OR THE ADVENTURES OF MY SEVEN UNCLES

By **Blaise Cendrars** *translated from the French and illustrated by* **John Dos Passos**

HARPER & BROTHERS · NEW YORK AND LONDON

Cover for John Dos Passos's 1931 translation of Cendrars's poetry
(Collection of Richard Layman)

forces that have exploded the old forms and created a new set of mores: these forces include the soldiers who killed Archimedes as well as the technological ones that have so marked the modern age. The task of the writer in such an age is to reproduce all of this dynamic change in his work. The leaps of memory that constitute this poem will provide the only possible form for this new content. Read symbolically, the world is a scattered collection of a violent beauty of which the poet takes possession.

As is so often the case in Cendrars's poetry, the conclusion depicts a literal or symbolic return to Paris. The last section is an apostrophe to the city of light that gradually transposes into an evocation of a series of women whom the poet fondly remembers. What is so striking about the ending is the lack of exultation, the absence of any suggestion that the poem moves toward a moment in which the significance of what has gone before is now revealed. The journeys do not "mean" anything. The whole poem is dedicated to Jehanne de France, but the poet ends by announcing that now "J'irai au *Lapin agile* me ressouvenir de ma jeunesse perdue" (I will go to the *Lapin agile* [a bar] to re-remember my lost youth) and then "je renterai seul" (I will go home alone).

Just as in *Les Pâques à New-York,* in which Cendrars partly eliminates punctuation to make his verse less static, so in *La Prose du Transsibérien et de la Petite Jehanne de France* he works at creating a form that mimics the chaotic spontaneity of life in the early twentieth century. But in this poem objects described in the most realistic fashion serve at the same time as surrealistic symbols. The wheels of the train, for example, come to represent all the things associated with force, rhythm, journeys, and exploration in every sense. This technique marks a link between Cendrars and the Surrealists who came after and represents one of his permanent contributions to the reanimation of poetry in his time.

The third and longest poem for which Cendrars is famous, *Le Panama; ou, Les Aventures de mes sept oncles,* was written in the same fertile period, 1913–1914, though it was not published until 1918. It is another plaintive evocation of time past, another exploration of the contrast between the dreamy world of books and its real-life counterpart, another solipsistic encounter with the shock of the new, another intriguing combination of crude power and subtle effects.

In an opening section, readers are introduced to what amounts to three different worlds: the first turns around the figure of his mother, the poet as a child at home, and his books and the reveries induced by them; the second, around the straitened circumstances created by the father's loss of his fortune when the French Panama Canal project went bankrupt in 1889; and the third is the one indicated in the title, the exotic "other world" evoked in the letters that arrive from his uncles recounting their adventures. The threat posed by real-life events in the second world to the very existence of the speaker's imagined worlds prompts him to become a poet and re-create all three. In short, the poem confirms the extent to which Cendrars, whose great theme is always the journey, travel, and adventure, was inspired by staying home reading books.

The seven uncles are all adventurers of various stripes: one does time in prison for holding up a stagecoach, becomes a hunter in California, joins the Alaskan gold rush, marries the best baker in the district, and ultimately dies mysteriously, his head smashed in by a rifle; another is a Buddhist who buys dynamite in Tahiti to mount terrorist attacks against the English in Bombay; a third is a renowned chef who has worked in all the important cities of the world and has had many dishes named after him; and so on. Their careers provide the poet with a great swatch of international color, but his real subject lies elsewhere, namely in the growth of his imaginative talents as a poet. The first words of the poem are "Des livres" (Some books), and *Le Panama* is, in an important sense, a hymn to the incantatory power of literature itself. Books that tell the story of the Panama Canal or of the 1889 financial crash are dismissed as irrelevant because they are merely objective, historical accounts; rather, it is the stories told in his children's books, the exotic images of whales, walruses, and rattlesnakes that he encountered there, that made him grow up the way he did, evoked places in ways that incited him to make his own explorations, and made him capable of deciphering his uncles' letters when they did arrive. At one point in the poem he incorporates a long chamber-of-commerce piece extolling (in English) the virtues of Denver, Colorado, into his poem, which shows how keen he is to break down traditional notions of poetic form, an example of his avant-gardism.

The Cendrarses had their first son, Odilon, in April 1914; they married in September of the same year, just before Blaise left to work in the front in World War I as a member of the French Foreign Legion. The following year his regiment suffered horrendous losses in the trench warfare in northern France. In September 1915 Cendrars lost his right arm in the assault of the Navarin Farm in Champagne. The writer had to learn to write with his new "main amie" (friendly hand) and to deal with the psychological effects of his amputation. In April of 1916 his second son, Rémy, was born, but by then Cendrars had already begun to drift away from his wife, attracted to a girl named Gabrielle, a model for Modigliani, for whom he abandoned his marriage. The following autumn he met Raymone Duchâteau, a young actress, who bore Cendrars a daughter, Miriam, in 1919. Most of the poems in his next book, *Dix-neuf poèmes élastiques* (Nineteen Elastic Poems, 1919), were written before the war. An intriguing mix, they cover a wide range of topics: there is a moving confessional poem, "On a beau ne pas parler de soi-même" (It's all very well not to want to talk about oneself); a detailed account of the iconography of the Eiffel Tower—"Tu es tout / Tour / Dieu antique / Bête moderne / Spectre solaire / sujet de mon poème" (You are everything / Tower / Ancient God / Modern beast / Solar specter / Subject of my poem); "Portrait," a depiction of his friend Chagall at work in his atelier; "Sur la Robe Elle a une Corps" (On the Dress She Had a Body), a hymn to the female body beneath a dress; "Dernière Heure" (Last Hour), a more-or-less-exact transcription of a newspaper account of a murderous prison break in Oklahoma (an early "found" poem); and "Natures Mortes" (Still Lifes), a series of images conveyed

Cendrars at work on his quasi-autobiographical Le Lotissement du ciel, *published in 1949 (photograph by Robert Doisneau)*

with a minium of verbs, which sit in imagistic immobility upon the page.

Cendrars's last two volumes of poetry, *Kodak (Documentaires)* (Kodak [Documentary]) and *Le Formose* (Formosa), part 1 of *Feuilles de Route* (Travel Notes), both appeared in 1924. These volumes were translated by Monique Chefdor in *Complete Postcards from the Americas: Poems of Road and Sea* (1976). Additional "feuilles" were published in various journals throughout the 1920s, but all of them are dated 1924, so Cendrars is believed to have stopped writing poetry at this point. The verse is always interesting, often stunningly vivid, but there is a marked loss of evocative power. As Jay Bochner, one of the most perceptive Cendrars scholars, points out in his introduction to *Complete Poems: Blaise Cendrars* (1992), Ron Padgett's translation of *Poésies complètes de Blaise Cendrars* (1944), these volumes represent an idiosyncratic sort of travelogue: "The poems are made almost entirely of description, quite eventless, like snapshots in a family album. We flip the pages but make few profound links. Each poem is largely mute, showing without saying much, while just below these surfaces of heat, rain, and mud, of cool bungalows, unfamiliar birds, trees, flowers and fish, lies an odd sort of secret quotidian." *Kodak (Documentaires)* is Cendrars's creation in a somewhat specialized sense, in that he lifted it practically entire from *Le Mystérieux docteur Cornélius* (The Mysterious Doctor Cornelius, 1918), a contemporary popular romance by Gustave Le Rouge, in order to show, as he admitted some twenty years later in *L'Homme foudroyé* (1945; translated as *The Astonished Man,* 1970), that the minute particulars Le Rouge had thought of as mere background actually constituted the real creative essence of the work, an essence obscured by the moralized narrative through which Cendrars was perceptive enough to see.

By the mid 1920s Cendrars was ready to turn to prose (including some remarkable prose poems), cinema, and other modes of communication. Dreaming of reaching out to the largest possible audience, he envied the poet Vladimir Mayakovsky, who worked as a Bolshevik propagandist and could gain direct access to the masses through public readings in barracks and factories. Yet, his attempts to make a link with a large public was a mixed success. He helped with the production of several motion pictures, worked for various literary magazines, and wrote scenarios for opera and ballet, one of which made it to the Paris stage in 1923: *La Création du Monde* (The Creation of the World). Between 1924 and 1930 he went to Brazil half a dozen times and wrote some of his most important novels: *L'Or: La Merveilleuse histoire du Genéral Johann August Suter* (Gold: The Marvelous History of General Johann August Sutter, 1925; translated as *Sutter's Gold,* 1926), based on the life of the man on whose California property gold was discovered in 1849; *Moravagine* (1926; translated, 1968), the title character of which is an insane serial killer; and a novel featuring the fictional explorer Dan Yack, first published in two volumes as *Le Plan de l'Aiguille* (The Plan of the Needle, 1929; translated as *Antarctic Fugue,* 1948) and *Les Confessions de Dan Yack* (1929; translated as *Confessions of Dan Yack,* 1990), then republished in one volume as *Dan Yack* (1946; translated, 1987). In the 1930s he concentrated on reportage and various other projects with avant-garde journals.

In 1939 he became a war correspondent but when France surrendered in 1940 he retired to the South of France, where he helped the French Resistance. After writing nothing during these years, in 1943 he began the huge autobiographical saga in four volumes that constitutes the last important part of his prose legacy: *L'Homme foudroyé, La Main coupée* (The Severed Hand, 1946; translated as *Lice,* 1973), *Bourlinguer* (To Get Around a Lot, 1948; abridged

and translated as *Planus,* 1972), and *Le Lotissement du ciel* (The Housing Estate of the Sky, 1949; translated as *Sky: Memoirs,* 1992). In 1949 he married his lover, Duchâteau (Féla Cendrars had died during the war) and settled in Paris. The French government made him a commander of the Légion d'Honneur in 1958, and he was awarded the Grand Prix Littéraire de Paris just weeks before he died on 21 January 1961. The last volumes of an excellent eight-volume hardcover edition of his works were published posthumously by Editions Denoël.

Blaise Cendrars always said that the most characteristic trait of a genius was the need to create his own legend. In his poetry the reader will find an important part of that creation: the exaltation of the journey, particularly at the moment of departure, the impressions sent back en route, the foregrounding of the means—writing, verse—by which its inner counterpart, the internal journey, takes place, and the return to the point of departure. The great adventure, the great roaming back and forth in what he calls in *Le Panama* "la cage des méridiens" (the cage of the meridians) was nothing less than Cendrars's attempt to abolish the barriers between life and art. An essential contribution to twentieth-century verse, his great poems are now recognized as an articulate and moving account of that attempt.

Letters:

"J'écris. Écrivez-moi." Correspondance, 1924–1959: Blaise Cendrars–Jacques-Henry Lévesque, edited by Monique Chefdor, volume 9 of *Œuvres complètes: Blaise Cendrars* (Paris: Denoël, 1993);

Correspondance 1934–1979: 45 ans d'amitié Blaise Cendrars, Henry Miller, edited by Miriam Cendrars, introduction by Frédéric-Jacques Temple and notes by Jay Bochner (Paris: Denoël, 1995).

Interviews:

Blaise Cendrars vous parle, edited by Michel Manoll (Paris: Denoël, 1952);

Entretien de Fernand Léger avec Blaise Cendrars et Louis Carré sur le paysage dans l'œuvre de Léger (Paris: Louis Carré, 1956);

Dites-nous, Monsieur Blaise Cendrars: Réponses aux enquêtes littéraires de 1919 à 1957, edited by Hughes Richard (Lausanne, Switzerland: Editions Rencontres, 1969).

Bibliographies:

Jacques-Henri Lévesque, "Bibliographie des œuvres de Blaise Cendrars," in *Blaise Cendrars: Une etude,* by Louis Parrot, second edition, Poetes d'aujourd'hui, no. 11 (Paris: Seghers, 1953), pp. 219–234;

Hughes Richard, "Etude bibliographique," in volume 8 of *Œuvres Complètes: Blaise Cendrars* (Paris: Denoël, 1964);

Annual updates in *Feuilles de routes: Blaise Cendrars International Society Bulletin,* edited by Jacqueline Bernard (1979–);

Annual updates in *Continent Cendrars: Bulletin annuel du Centre d'études Blaise Cendrars de l'Université de Berne* (1986–).

Biographies:

Jean Buhler, *Blaise Cendrars: Homme libre, poète au cœur du monde,* Célébrités suisses, no. 2 (Bienne, Switzerland: Editions du Panorama / Paris: Edition Fischbacher, 1960);

Hughes Richard, *"Sauser avant Cendrars,"* Revue Neuchateloise, 23 (Winter 1979–1980);

Miriam Cendrars, *Blaise Cendrars* (Paris: Balland, 1984).

References:

Jacqueline Bernard, ed., *Le Texte cendrarsien: Colloque organisé par le Centre de recherche en didactique du texte et du livre, Université Stendahl–Grenoble, 20 et 21 novembre 1987* (Grenoble: Centre de Création Littéraire, 1988);

Jay Bochner, *Blaise Cendrars: Discovery and Re-creation* (Toronto, Buffalo & London: University of Toronto Press, 1978);

Yvette Bozon-Scalzitti, *Blaise Cendrars ou La Passion de l'Ecriture* (Lausanne, Switzerland: L'Age d'Homme, 1977);

Bozon-Scalzitti, *Blaise Cendrars et le Symbolisme: De "Moganni Nameh" au "Transsibérien,"* Archives des Lettres Modernes, no. 137 (Paris: Lettres Modernes, 1972);

Monique Chefdor, *Blaise Cendrars* (Boston: Twayne, 1980);

Chefdor, ed., *La Fable du lieu: Etudes sur Blaise Cendrars* (Paris: H. Champion / Geneva: Editions Slatkine, 1999);

Alexandre Eulalio, ed., *A Aventura Brasileira de Blaise Cendrars: Ensaio, cronologia, filme, depoimentos, antologia* (São Paulo: Edições Quíron, 1978);

Jean-Carlo Flückiger and Claude Leroy, eds., *Cendrars, le bourlingueur des deux rives* (Paris: Armand Colin, 1995);

Maria Teresa de Freitas and Leroy, eds., *Brésil: L'Utopialand de Blaise Cendrars* (Paris & Montréal: L'Harmattan, 1998);

Amanda Leamon, *Shades of Sexuality: Colors and Sexual Identity in the Novels of Blaise Cendrars* (Amsterdam & Atlanta: Rodopi, 1997);

Leroy, ed., *Blaise Cendrars et la Guerre* (Paris: Armand Colin, 1995);

Leroy, ed., *Blaise Cendrars 20 ans après: Colloque de Nanterre, 12 et 13 juin 1981* (Paris: Klincksieck, 1983);

Leroy, ed., *Cendrars et "Le Lotissement du ciel"* (Paris: Armand Colin, 1995);

Leroy, *La Main de Cendrars,* preface by Miriam Cendrars (Villeneuve d'Ascq: Presses Universitaires du Septentrion, 1996);

Leroy, *"L'Or" de Blaise Cendrars* (Paris: Gallimard, 1991);

Henry Miller, *Blaise Cendrars* (Paris: Denoël, 1951);

Michèle Touret, ed., *Cendrars au pays de Jean Galmot: Roman et reportage* (Rennes: Presses Universitaires de Rennes, 1998);

Albert T'Serstevens, *L'Homme que fut Blaise Cendrars: Souvenirs* (Paris: Denoël, 1972).

Papers:

Collections of Blaise Cendrars's papers are located in the Fonds Blaise Cendrars, Archives Littérraires Suisses, Bibliothèque Nationale Suisse, Bern, Switzerland; and the Centre d'Etudes Blaise Cendrars, University of Bern.

René Char

(14 June 1907 – 19 February 1988)

Van Kelly
University of Kansas

SELECTED BOOKS: *Les Cloches sur le cœur,* as René-Emile Char (Paris: Le Rouge et le Noir, 1928);

Arsenal (Nîmes: Méridiens, 1929; revised edition, Nîmes: De la Main à la Main, 1930);

Le Tombeau des secrets (Nîmes: Imprimerie Larguier, 1930);

Ralentir travaux, by Char, André Breton, and Paul Eluard (Paris: Editions Surréalistes, 1930); translated by Keith Waldrop as *Ralentir travaux/Slow Under Construction* (Cambridge, Mass.: Exact Change, 1990);

Artine (Paris: Editions Surréalistes, 1930); enlarged as *Artine et Autres poèmes* (Paris: Tchou, 1967);

L'Action de la justice est éteinte (Paris: Editions Surréalistes, 1931);

Le Marteau sans maître (Paris: Editions Surréalistes, 1934); revised and enlarged as *Le Marteau sans maître: Suivi de, Moulin premier, 1927–1935* (Paris: José Corti, 1945);

Dépendance de l'adieu, with a drawing by Pablo Picasso, Repères, no. 14 (Paris: Editions G.L.M., 1936);

Moulin premier (Paris: Editions G.L.M., 1936);

Placard pour un chemin des écoliers, illustrated by Valentine Hugo (Paris: Editions G.L.M., 1937);

Dehors la nuit est gouvernée (Paris: Editions G.L.M., 1938); revised and enlarged as *Dehors la nuit est gouvernée, précédé de Placard pour un chemin des écoliers* (Paris: Editions G.L.M., 1949);

Le Visage nuptial (Paris: Imprimerie Beresniak, 1938);

Seuls demeurent (Paris: Gallimard, 1945);

Feuillets d'Hypnos (Paris: Gallimard, 1946); translated by Cid Corman as *Leaves of Hypnos* (New York: Grossman, 1973);

Premières alluvions, Collection L'âge d'or, no. 27 (Paris: Editions de la revue Fontaine, 1946);

Le Poème pulvérisé (Paris: Editions de la revue Fontaine, 1947);

Fureur et mystère (Paris: Gallimard, 1948; revised, 1962);

Fête des arbres et du chasseur, with a lithograph by Joan Miró (Paris: Editions G.L.M., 1948);

René Char in 1980 (photograph by Willy Ronis/Rapho)

Le Soleil des eaux, illustrated by Georges Braque (Paris: Henri Matarasso, 1949; enlarged edition, Paris: Gallimard, 1951);

Claire: Théâtre de verdure (Paris: Gallimard, 1949);

Les Matinaux (Paris: Gallimard, 1950; revised, 1964); translated by Michael Worton in *The Dawn Breakers/Les Matinaux,* bilingual edition, edited by Worton (Newcastle upon Tyne: Bloodaxe, 1992);

Art bref, suivi de Premières alluvions (Paris: Editions G.L.M., 1950);

Quatre fascinants: La Minutieuse, frontispiece by Pierre Charbonnier (Paris: Imp. de A. Tournon, 1951);

A une sérénité crispée, illustrated by Louis Fernandez (Paris: Gallimard, 1951); translated by Bradford Cook in "A une sérénité crispée / To a Tensed Serenity," bilingual edition, *Botteghe Oscure,* 22 (1958): 74–113;

Poèmes, illustrated by Nicolas de Staël (Paris, 1951);

La Paroi et la prairie (Paris: Editions G.L.M., 1952);

Lettera amorosa (Paris: Gallimard, 1953; illustrated edition, with lithographs by Braque, Geneva: Edwin Engelberts, 1963);

Arrière-histoire du Poème pulvérisé, illustrated by Nicolas de Staël (Paris: Jean Hugues, 1953);

Choix de poemes, introduction by Jean Pénard (Mendoza, Argentina: Brigadas Liricas, 1953);

Le Rempart de brindilles, etchings by Wifredo Lam, Ecrits et gravures, no. 1 (Paris: Louis Broder, 1953);

Rengaines d'Odin le Roc: Vagabond luni-solaire, with two gouaches by Pierre-André Benoit (Alès: Editions P.A.B., 1954);

A la santé du serpent, illustrated by Miró (Paris: Editions G.L.M., 1954);

Le Deuil des Névons, with an etching by Fernandez (Brussels: Le Cormier, 1954);

Recherche de la base et du sommet, suivi de Pauvreté et privilège (Paris: Gallimard, 1955; revised and enlarged, 1965; revised and enlarged, 1971);

Poèmes des deux années, 1953–1954 (Paris: Editions G.L.M., 1955);

La Fauvette des roseaux, illustrated by Jean Hugo (Alès: Editions P.A.B., 1955);

Chanson des étages, engraving by Jean Hugo (Alès: Editions P.A.B., 1955);

A Braque, by Char and Benoit (Alès: Editions P.A.B., 1955);

La Bibliothèque est en feu (Paris: Louis Broder, 1956); enlarged as *La Bibliothèque est en feu et autres poèmes* (Paris: Editions G.L.M., 1957);

En trente-trois morceaux, with an engraving by Char (Paris: Editions G.L.M., 1956);

Pour nous, Rimbaud– (Paris: Editions G.L.M., 1956);

Jeanne qu'on brûla verte, illustration by Braque (Alès: Editions P.A.B., 1956);

L'Abominable Homme des neiges (Cairo: Librairie L.D.F., 1956);

De moment en moment, two engravings by Miró, La Carotide, no. 5 (Alès: Editions P.A.B., 1957);

Les Compagnons dans le jardin, engravings by Zao Wou-ki, Miroir du poète, no. 2 (Paris: Louis Broder, 1957);

L'Une et l'autre, illustrated by Char (Alès: Editions P.A.B., 1957);

Elisabeth petite fille, illustrated by Char (Alès: Editions P.A.B., 1958);

Le Dernier couac (Paris: Editions G.L.M., 1958);

L'Escalier de Flore, with two engravings by Picasso (Alès: Editions P.A.B., 1958);

Sur la poésie (Paris: Editions G.L.M., 1958; enlarged, 1967; enlarged again, 1974);

Cinq poésies en hommage à Georges Braque, with a lithograph by Braque (Geneva: Edwin Engelberts, 1958);

La Faux relevée, illustrated by Char (Alès: Editions P.A.B., 1959);

Eros suspendu, with two engravings by Char (Alès: Editions P.A.B., 1960);

Anthologie, Collection Voix de la terre, new series no. 4 (Paris: Editions G.L.M., 1960); enlarged as *Poèmes de René Char* (Paris: Editions G.L.M., 1969);

Pourquoi la journée vole, engraving by Picasso (Alès: Editions P.A.B., 1960);

Le Rebanqué, with photographs by Benoit (Alès: Editions P.A.B., 1960);

Les Dentelles de Montmirail, illustrated by Benoit (Alès: Editions P.A.B., 1960);

L'Allégresse, engraving by Madeleine Grenier (Alès: Editions P.A.B., 1960);

La Montée de la nuit (Alès: Editions P.A.B., 1961; republished, illustrated by Jesse Reichek, 1961);

L'Issue (Alès: Editions P.A.B., 1961; republished, with an engraving by Char, 1961);

La Parole en archipel (Paris: Gallimard, 1962);

Flux de l'aimant, illustrated with engravings by Miró (Paris: Maeght, 1964); republished, with one engraving by Miró (Veilhes: Gaston Puel, 1965);

Commune présence, preface by Georges Blin (Paris: Gallimard, 1964; revised and enlarged, 1978);

La Provence point oméga (Paris: Imprimerie Union, 1965);

Retour amont, illustrated by Alberto Giacometti (Paris: Editions G.L.M., 1965);

Les Transparents, illustrated by Picasso (Alès: Editions P.A.B., 1967);

Trois coups sous les arbres: Théâtre saisonnier (Paris: Gallimard, 1967);

Dans la pluie giboyeuse (Paris: Gallimard, 1968);

Le Chien decoeur, with a lithography by Miró (Paris: Editions G.L.M., 1969);

L'Effroi la joie, illustrated by Braque (Saint-Paul-de-Vence: Au Vent d'Arles, 1969);

Le Nu perdu (Paris: Gallimard, 1971); enlarged as *Le Nu perdu et autres poèmes, 1964–1975* (Paris: Gallimard, 1978);

La Nuit talismanique, illustrated by Char (Geneva: Skira, 1972);

Aromates chasseurs (Paris: Gallimard, 1975);

Contre une maison sèche, engravings by Lam (Paris: Jean Hugues, 1975);

Faire du chemin avec . . . (Paris: Imprimerie Union, 1976);

Chants de la Balandrane (Paris: Gallimard, 1977);

Fenêtres dormantes et porte sur le toit (Paris: Gallimard, 1979);

René Char: Œuvres complètes, edited, with an introduction, by Jean Roudaut, Bibliothèque de la Pléiade, no. 308 (Paris: Gallimard, 1983; enlarged, 1995);

Les Voisinages de Van Gogh (Paris: Gallimard, 1985);

Eloge d'une Soupçonnée (Paris: Gallimard, 1988);

Dans l'atelier du poète: René Char, edited by Marie-Claude Char, Collection Quarto (Paris: Gallimard, 1996).

Collections: *Poèmes et prose choisis* (Paris: Gallimard, 1957);

L'Inclémence lointaine, illustrated by Vieira da Silva (Paris: P. Berès, 1961);

Le Monde de l'art n'est pas le monde du pardon, preface by Jacques Dupin (Paris: Maeght, 1974);

Le Marteau sans maître, engravings by Joan Miró (Paris: Au Vent d'Arles, 1976).

Editions in English: *Poems: René Char,* translated by Denis Devlin and Jackson Mathews (Rome: Botteghe Oscure, 1952);

Hypnos Waking: Poems and Prose by René Char, translated and edited by Mathews with the collaboration of William Carlos Williams, W. S. Merwin, and others (New York: Random House, 1956);

Poems of René Char, translated and edited by Mary Ann Caws and Jonathan Griffin (Princeton: Princeton University Press, 1976);

No Siege is Absolute, translated and edited by Franz Wright (Providence, R.I.: Lost Roads, 1984);

Selected Poems of René Char, translated and edited by Caws and Tina Jolas (New York: New Directions, 1992);

"Translations from René Char," translated by John Thompson, in his *Collected Poems and Translations* (Fredericton, Canada: Goose Lane, 1995), pp. 167–220.

PLAY PRODUCTIONS: *La Conjuration,* Paris, Théâtre des Champs-Elysées, May 1947;

Claire, Lyon, Théâtre de la Comédie, 1952;

L'Homme qui marchait dans un rayon de soleil, translated by Roger Shattuck as "The Man Who Walked in a Ray of Sunshine," Cambridge, Mass., The Poet's Theater, 1954;

Le Soleil des eaux, Paris, Studio des Champs-Elysées, 1968.

PRODUCED SCRIPTS: *Le Soleil des eaux,* radio, Radiodiffusion française, April 1948;

Sur les Hauteurs, motion picture, SPEDIC Films, 1949;

Claire, radio, Radiodiffusion française, May 1951.

OTHER: René, Jean, Georges, and Claude Roux, *Les Quatre Frères Roux: Quand le Soir menace,* preface by Char (Paris: Editions G.L.M., 1939);

Roger Bernard, *Ma faim noire déjà,* preface and afterword by Char (Paris: Editions des Cahiers d'Art, 1945);

Héraclite d'Ephèse, translated by Yves Battistini, preface by Char (Paris: Editions des Cahiers d'Art, 1948);

Jacques Dupin, *Cendrier du voyage,* preface by Char (Paris: Editions G.L.M., 1950);

Arthur Rimbaud, *Oeuvres,* edited, with a preface, by Char, Poésie, no. 15 (Paris: Club Français du livre, 1957);

Exposition Picasso, 1970–1972, 201 Peintures, du 23 mai au 23 septembre 1973, preface by Char (Avignon: Musée du Palais des papes, 1973); republished as *Picasso sous les vents étésiens* (Paris: Editions G.L.M., 1973);

La Planche de vivre, translated by Char and Tina Jolas (Paris: Gallimard, 1981).

The poetry of René Char emphasizes struggle and strife, rejects compromise both formally and ethically, and puts desire at the center of the poet's inspiration. Other elements are strongly associated with his works: abundant use of landscape (especially that of Provence), the aphorism as a poetic vehicle for expressing his ethics, an idyllic register that softens his view of the life struggle, and a metapoetic vein whereby his poems comment on their own internal laws and significance. His voice was as influential and dominant after World War II as that of Saint-John Perse or Francis Ponge.

René-Emile Char was born in the French town of L'Isle-sur-la-Sorgue, in the department of the Vaucluse, on 14 June 1907. His poetry does celebrate sites such as Autun, Lascaux, and Alsace that lie outside his native region, and occasionally they become major symbols of creativity, love, or war, but the hill country of southeastern France dominates his poetic topography. Char is by no means a regional poet, however: he uses his native locale to stage universal struggles of good versus injustice, where the individual resists a repressive, conformist society. One of his major symbols, Mont Ventoux, is linked directly to Petrarch, and his evocations of the southern countryside seek the universal behind the particular.

René was the youngest of four children born to Joseph Emile Char, businessman and town mayor, and his second wife, Marie-Thérèse Rouget Char. Emile

Char in Céreste, 1943, when he was a captain in the French Resistance (photograph by Roger-Viollet)

Char's first marriage had been to Marie-Thérèse's older sister, Julia, who died of tuberculosis after barely a year of marriage. René Char plays on this endogamy in poems such as "Jacquemard et Julia," in the collection *Fureur et mystère* (Furor and Mystery, 1948), where the first marriage stands in idyllic counterpoint to the poet's own tense relationship with his mother. His maternal grandfather had been a miller in L'Isle-sur-la-Sorgue. His paternal grandfather was an abandoned child whose passage through the *Assistance publique* (orphanage) is reflected in the picturesque patronymic that the authorities bestowed upon him: Magne Char, later abbreviated to Char. The grandfather was placed on a farm as a shepherd around Mont Ventoux, but he fled his harsh employers and migrated to L'Isle-sur-la-Sorgue where jobs were available in the plaster industry, the mainstay of the local economy, along with fishing in the river Sorgue and agriculture. During René

Char's childhood, his family lived in the Névons, a large house surrounded by a park on the edge of town.

Char's father died on 15 January 1918. This event had a profound effect on the boy, who was not yet eleven, and many poems, such as "Jouvence des Névons" (Youth at the Névons), from *Les Matinaux* (1950; translated as *The Dawn Breakers,* 1992), bear witness to Char's subsequent sense of dispossession and metaphysical solitude. Such feelings characterize a significant portion of his poetry, though they temper rather than dominate his basic optimism. As the critic Christine Dupouy notes in her 1987 monograph on Char, the family house and the extensive park surrounding it galvanized Char's poetic and psychological energies: the property symbolized the beauty of nature in his father's former realm, and by contrast underscored the poet's rebellion against maternal authority. Shortly after his father's death, Char became an intern

Manuscript for "Envoutement à la Renardière," a poem included in the 1948 collection Fureur et mystère
(*from Pierre Berger,* René Char: Une Essai, *1951*)

at the lycée of Avignon. Prior to this time, he had been a pupil at the grammar school of L'Isle-sur-la-Sorgue. Char never completed the *baccalauréat,* a prestigious diploma that crowns secondary studies in France. Instead, in 1925 he enrolled in a business school at Marseilles and in 1926 took a job in Cavaillon, a few kilometers south of L'Isle-sur-la-Sorgue. From 1927 to 1928 he did his military service in an artillery unit at Nîmes and published his first book of verse, *Les Cloches sur le cœur* (Bells on the Heart, 1928), most copies of which he later destroyed. This work is the only book published under his given name of René-Emile Char.

In 1929 he co-edited a literary review, *Méridiens,* with future French movie star and director André Cayatte, but Char abandoned this endeavor after three issues, announcing that he would join the Surrealists in Paris. Headed by André Breton, Paul Eluard, and Louis Aragon, Surrealism had replaced Dadaism in the vanguard of the Paris literary scene shortly after the end of World War I. Char's move to Paris was occasioned in part by his second book of poetry, *Arsenal,* first published in August 1929, a copy of which he had sent to Eluard, who was impressed enough to pay Char a visit in L'Isle-sur-la-Sorgue that fall. Char moved to Paris at the end of November 1929, though he did not abandon his native region, as is shown by the book *Ralentir travaux* (translated as *Slow Under Construction,* 1990), which Char, Eluard, and Breton wrote collectively and which was published in April 1930. The poems were improvised during a trip the three poets made by car around the Vaucluse in March of that year. Along with automatic writings such as Breton and Philippe Soupault's *Les Champs magnétiques* (1920; translated as *The Magnetic Fields,* 1985) and simulations of alienated discourse such as Breton and Eluard's *L'Immaculée Conception* (1930; translated as *The Immaculate Conception,* 1990), *Ralentir travaux* is a landmark of Surrealism and, as an experiment in collective writing, constituted a frontal attack on the French literary establishment and its cult of the author. *Ralentir travaux* is directly related to the cultural subversion that Breton set as a goal for the movement in his first and second *Manifeste du surréalisme* (1924, 1930; translated as *Manifestoes of Surrealism,* 1969). Char's third collection of poetry, *Le Tombeau des secrets* (Tomb of Secrets, 1930), published at his own expense, adopts a broad idea of what constitutes poetry: the collection consists of poems interspersed with photographs, mostly of family, acquaintances, and places in L'Isle-sur-la-Sorgue. The use of photography is reminiscent of Breton's *Nadja* (1928; translated 1960), though Char, unlike Breton, does not seem to offer his photographs as a systematic replacement for passages of literary description. From late 1929 through much of 1934, Char was part of the Surrealist movement. He pub-

lished poems in the Surrealist reviews *La Révolution surréaliste* (The Surrealist Revolution) and *Le Surréalisme au service de la révolution* (Surrealism in the Service of the Revolution). He also participated in Surrealist political protests, such as the one directed against the 1931 Colonial Exposition in Paris. As did the other Surrealists, Char made a cult figure of the Marquis de Sade, though in his case it was as much a result of acquaintances in L'Isle-sur-la-Sorgue as it was because of avant-garde adulation. Char was friends with the Roze sisters, descendants of one of de Sade's notaries for his domains in Provence, and they allowed him to consult correspondence in their ancestor's archives. In 1931 he also signed the Surrealist tract supporting Luis Buñuel's motion picture *L'Age d'or* (The Golden Age), which ends with an allusion to de Sade, whom Char considered an exemplary rebel against society and religion. Following in the footsteps of Breton, whose female figure Nadja represents alienation and inspiration, Char created his own avatar of the Surrealist dream woman, Artine, who presided over his loves, dreams, and poetry. On 25 October 1932 Char married Georgette Goldstein, whose family lived in Saumane, a hilltop village a few kilometers north of L'Isle-sur-la-Sorgue. Saumane, coincidentally, is also the site of a château belonging to the de Sade family.

Many of Char's poems from 1927 to 1934, including those that had previously appeared in *L'Action de la justice est éteinte* (The Case is Closed, 1931), were soon published under a title alluding to alchemy, *Le Marteau sans maître* (The Hammer without a Master, 1934). Several traits in this collection eventually carried over into his post–World War II poetry and became touchstones of his art. The strong ethical orientation of his writing, one of its enduring characteristics, resonates forcefully in *Le Marteau sans maître.* The collection depicts a dangerous, hostile world–humanity is "criblé de lésions" (perforated with lesions), as Char says in "Sommaire" (Summary)–that nevertheless fails to dampen the poet's basic faith in life: in "Les rapports entre parasites" (Relations between Parasites), he asserts his own vocation for building "une postérité sans amertume" (a future without bitterness). As did other Surrealists, Char espoused the idea that contraries structure everyday life and form the antithetical basis for all worthwhile poetic images, yet his poetry emphasizes fruitful transformation, as in "Crésus": "L'indiscernable blé des cratères / Croît en se consumant" (The invisible wheat of craters / Grows, consuming itself). In a similar vein, the critic Mary Ann Caws has shown how images of alchemical metamorphosis pervade Char's poetry, in which destruction or calcination leads to the creation of higher values in the crucible of language. The heavy emphasis on conflict also laid the

Char and Albert Camus, his editor at Gallimard, September 1949

Teller; an allusion to one of de Sade's novels), in which the speaker praises his beloved for ". . . Ses lèvres de fleuve / Sa jouissance grandiose / Tout ce qui se détache convulsivement de l'unité du monde . . ." (. . . Her riverlike lips / Her immense pleasure / Everything that is seized convulsively out of the world's unity . . .).

During the early 1930s Char established ties with many avant-garde painters, some of whom were Surrealists, others not. The first thirty copies of Char's *Artine* (1930) included an engraving by Salvador Dalí. Select copies of *Le Marteau sans maître* were bound with a *pointe sèche* (drypoint) print designed by Vassily Kandinsky. Writers commonly enhanced the notoriety of their books by asking well-known artists to illustrate them, but Char turned such creative collaboration into his own salient trait, especially after World War II, writing encomiastic, sympathetic interpretations of the work of such friends as Pablo Picasso, Georges Braque, Joan Miró, and Alberto Giacometti. Between 1930 and 1940 Char established the foundations for his highly poetic writings on art, though it bloomed fully only after 1945. Highly significant in this respect was a 1934 exhibit that he saw in Paris, which included works of the seventeenth-century French painter Georges de La Tour with his baroque contrasts of night and candlelight on the human face. The painter became a part of Char's imagination, occasioning such poems as "Madeleine à la veilleuse" (Magdalen by Lamplight) in *Fureur et mystère*. During the German occupation of France in World War II, Char drew inspiration from a reproduction of de La Tour's painting *Le Prisonnier* (The Prisoner, 1644 [?]), which he kept nearby.

Char continued to sign political tracts sponsored or supported by the Surrealists, including the late 1934 protest against Trotsky's expulsion from France, but his break with the movement (and especially with Breton) was not long in coming. The political atmosphere in Europe was quickly deteriorating. Adolf Hitler became German chancellor in January 1933, and Austrian chancellor Engelbert Dollfuss was assassinated by Nazi sympathizers in July 1934. Char briefly visited Berlin in January 1933 to help friends prepare a hasty departure. The Surrealists were marginalized within the French political Left, and this tension broke into open conflict between the Surrealists and the Communist Party in 1935. Char's friend, René Crevel, caught between his Communist and Surrealist allegiances, committed suicide, perhaps because of the irreconcilable differences between Breton and Communist representatives. Char, on one of his rare trips outside France, visited Crevel and Eluard at a sanatorium in Davos, Switzerland, in the winter of 1935, shortly before Crevel's suicide in June of that year.

ground for his enthusiastic reception in the late 1930s of the French translations of Friedrich Nietzsche, especially Geneviève Bianquis's renditions of the German philosopher's early works on the origins of tragedy and philosophy, in which Apollo and Dionysos, unity and orgiastic expenditure, vie.

Other traits that appear insistently in *Le Marteau sans maître,* such as the marked use of allegory, are recognizable features of Char's later work. Bourgeois oppression is represented as "la loi corruptrice du Borgne" (corrupting One-Eyed law), but Char also deployed symbols of opposition, resistance, and justice, such as the "Equarisseur" (Stone-Cutter) who battles the dictates of conformity and subservience. The repertory of these allegorical figures grew larger and larger the more Char wrote. The characters depicted in the poems collectively titled *Les Transparents* (The Transparent Ones), included in the postwar collection *Les Matinaux,* are perhaps the best known of Char's later allegorical figures, and poetry itself becomes the "Soupçonnée" (Suspected One) in his last collection, *Eloge d'une Soupçonnée* (Praise for a Suspected One, 1988). Finally, the depiction of desire, which remained paramount throughout Char's writing career, assumes both paroxystic and cosmic dimensions in *Le Marteau sans maître,* as illustrated by an image from the poem "L'Historienne" (The Story

Although Char broke his ties with Surrealism, he remained friends with Eluard. In the spring of 1935 he moved back to L'Isle-sur-la-Sorgue and attempted to take over and run his father's former plaster works (La Société anonyme des Platrières de Vaucluse) in which his family still held shares. The maneuvers of Char and his business allies succeeded, and he became chief administrator in 1936. However, he then suffered a bout of septicemia, which lasted more than two months and nearly killed him. The slowness of his recovery forced him to resign his position in May 1937. Char spent part of his convalescence in the hill country east of the town of Apt, between the Lower Alps and the Luberon mountains, in a village called Céreste. This sojourn was important, since it was in Céreste that Char created a resistance unit in World War II.

Moulin premier (First Mill), published in December of 1936 by Editions G.L.M., the small press run by poet and typographer Guy Lévis-Mano, marked Char's public, aesthetic declaration of independence from Surrealism, as Virginia A. La Charité and Jean-Claude Mathieu have shown (though, as critics have also argued, significant portions of *Moulin premier* also satirize the nineteenth- century poet Victor Hugo, one of the bêtes noires of the Surrealists). The title of the collection of poetic aphorisms evokes the artistic fabrication of paper that once typified the Vaucluse region. The 1945 José Corti edition of *Le Marteau sans maître* includes *Moulin premier,* and the Gallimard edition of Char's *Œuvres complètes* (Complete Works, 1983; enlarged, 1995) also groups *Moulin premier* with *Le Marteau sans maître,* but *Moulin premier* was not part of the original, or Surrealist, edition, of *Le Marteau sans maître* as published in 1934.

Moulin premier, on the surface, avails itself of the alchemical idiom that typified Char's Surrealist profile as what he calls "porteur d'alluvions en flamme" (bearer of flaming alluvia) and as polemicist against a society that does not recognize individual freedom: "La bêtise aime à gouverner. Lui arracher ses chances" (Stupidity likes to rule. Snatch away its chances). Other, non-Surrealist, notes surface, however, and they include traits now recognized as part of Char's style but that were only latent in *Le Marteau sans maître.* Char's poetic diction in *Moulin premier* accentuates landscape: "Terre, devenir de mon abîme . . ." (Earth, the future of my abyss . . .). He now rejects the communal life crucial to avant-garde movements such as Surrealism, declaring: "Nombre d'autres touchent, esclaves, leur ration de fouet" (Many others, slaves, get their ration of the whip). The style of *Moulin premier* abounds in aphorisms: "La pensée de la mort en nous contraignant à mesurer notre vitesse nous facilite et adoucit nos mutations" (The thought of death eases and softens our metamorphoses by forcing us to measure our speed). A

new, unmistakable distaste for the blend of art and politics that Breton sought in his second *Manifeste du surréalisme* and in his *Les Vases commmunicants* (1932; translated as *Communicating Vessels,* 1990) clearly separates Char from his erstwhile companions, as he declares in *Moulin premier:* "Le poète devance l'homme d'action, puis le rencontrant, lui déclare la guerre" (The poet surpasses the man of action, and when he encounters him, he declares war). Separation and solitude replace group activity as focal points of Char's aesthetics. *Moulin premier* ends a chapter in Char's career that *Ralentir travaux,* an exercise in collective writing, had begun in 1930. Henceforth, Char was a free agent.

Although Char's name no longer appeared on the political tracts that typify Surrealism (and the Left in general) during this period, his works did not become suddenly apolitical, as can be seen in his collection *Placard pour un chemin des écoliers* (Posted on the Wandering Schoolchild's Path, 1937), which was dedicated to children killed in the Spanish Civil War. The collection is best understood in relation to Char's friends, Picasso and Miró, who at the time pursued their artistic development—as Picasso did in his *Guernica* (1937)—while not remaining aloof from the political storms of the 1930s. Char, Picasso, and Miró were antifascists, but it would be an exaggeration to compare them to such contemporary militants as the Communist Paul Nizan, the Surrealist-turned-Communist Aragon, or even the renowned pacifist intellectual Alain (pseudonym of Emile-Auguste Chartier). The historical tensions of the interwar period resonate throughout *Placard pour un chemin des écoliers,* but the commitment Char expresses resembles personal liberation more than political militancy, as the reader senses in the "révolte valide" (legitimate revolt) that soothes the child in "Les oursins de Pegomas" (Sea Urchins of Pegomas), or the "resistance" that the two lovers seek in "Les vivres du retour" (Supplies for the Return). Char depicts a world imperiled, but the register is eschatological rather than political.

Char's last major collection to appear before the outbreak of World War II, *Dehors la nuit est gouvernée* (Outside the Night is Governed), was published by Editions G. L. M. in May 1938, just after Hitler's takeover of Austria. The title deftly combined Char's long-standing interest in constellations with the dark, foreboding times of European dictatorships and impending war; however, the collection is not overtly political. A metaphysical voice instead echoes the rumor of war, as in "Tous compagnons de lit" (All in the Same Bed): "Nous ne nous avouons pas vaincu quand dans l'homme debout le mal surnage et le bien coule à pic" (We do not admit we are defeated when, within upright man, evil swims to the surface and goodness sinks keel high). The last poem of *Dehors la nuit est gouvernée,* "Validité,"

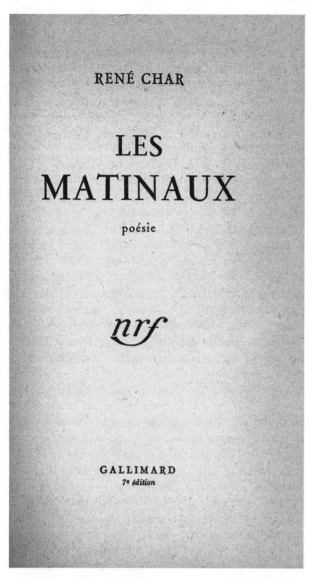

RENÉ CHAR

LES
MATINAUX

poésie

nrf

GALLIMARD
7ᵉ édition

Title page for the 1964 revised edition of Char's 1950 poetry collection (John C. Hodges Library, University of Tennessee, Knoxville)

depicts the onset of night, but Char insists on the cyclical rebirth of hope: "Demain ne tardera pas sur la voie" (Tomorrow will hasten along the rails). In the preface that Char wrote after the war for the revised and enlarged edition (1949) of *Dehors la nuit est gouvernée* and *Placard pour un chemin des écoliers,* he describes the years preceding World War II as "une marche forcée dans l'indicible, avec, pour tout viatique, les provisions hasardeuses du langage et la manne de l'observation et des pressentiments" (a forced march into the unspeakable, supplied only with the slim provisions of language and with the manna of observation and forebodings). Char's language, before and after the war, translated politics, ideology, and history into a metaphysical vein of expression.

At the end of December 1938 Char published the brief volume *Le Visage nuptial* (Nuptial Countenance), which was later included in his postwar collection *Fureur et mystère.* By the time of the Munich crisis in 1938 Char had acquired the important elements of personal voice and original diction that propelled him to fame after World War II. It is not a coincidence that in that same year Char's poems "Une Italienne de Corot" (Italian Girl by Corot) and "Courbet: Les casseurs de cailloux" (Courbet: The Stone Breakers), included in the collection *Dehors la nuit est gouvernée,* appeared in Christian Zervos's influential *Cahiers d'art,* an art review that championed the work of such avant-garde artists as Braque and Picasso. These two poems expressed Char's growing interest in landscape and in the relationship of poetry to painting. The nineteenth-century painters Camille Corot and Gustave Courbet belong to a realist tradition at some distance from the dream cities and deformed landscapes of such Surrealist painters as Yves Tanguy and Dalí, to which Char's *Le Marteau sans maître* of 1934 has striking affinities. "Une Italienne de Corot" and "Courbet: Les casseurs de cailloux," with their imaginative verbal descriptions of the paintings, anticipate the style of *Fureur et mystère,* in which subtle countrysides hover between realism and abstract fantasy.

Once World War II began, Char's life took a turn toward political and military commitment, and poetry was placed in temporary abeyance. Of the French writers who after the war publicly asserted their connections with the French Resistance, few, if any, measure up to Char's degree of commitment and risk. He was mobilized in September 1939, and poems in the section of *Fureur et mystère* titled "Avant-monde" (Prior World) and elsewhere bear witness to Char's passage through the so-called Phony War, when he served in the 173rd Régiment d'Artillerie Lourde, a heavy-artillery regiment, stationed first in Alsace and later in the departments of Meurthe-et-Moselle and the Lower Rhine. "Donnerbach Mühle" dramatically contrasts reminiscences from the past with the threat of a German invasion across the Maginot Line. During the prolonged inaction between the French declaration of war (3 September 1939) and the actual start of battle on the French frontiers (10 May 1940), Char and his comrades often hiked to the village of Donnerbach Mühle in the forest of Petite-Pierre near Strasbourg, as he relates in *Arrière-histoire du Poème pulvérisé* (Background for The Pulverized Poem, 1953), a gloss on the collection *Le Poème pulvérisé* (The Pulverized Poem, 1947), where "Donnerbach Mühle" first appeared. In spring 1940 Char was nominated to attend officers' training school, but the Germans invaded before he could report for duty.

Once fighting broke out, Char's unit was thrown back and had to make a fighting retreat toward the southwest into the regions of the Lot-et-Garonne and the Gers. The French government surrendered and signed an armistice with Germany on 22 June 1940, dividing the country roughly in half, with the north under German occupation and the south nominally self-ruling, administered mostly by French Vichy authorities under the government of Philippe Pétain, though effectively under German control. On 26 July 1940 Char, who held the rank of *maréchal-des-logis* (sergeant), was demobilized. After some hesitation, he returned in September to L'Isle-sur-la-Sorgue instead of occupied Paris, but there he fell under suspicion by the Vichy authorities, undoubtedly because of his antifascist sympathies but also because of his former links to Surrealism with its many political protests and tracts for left-wing (and often Communist) causes. On 20 December 1940 police searched Char's living quarters in L'Isle-sur-la-Sorgue. Char, tipped off that he was on the verge of arrest, went underground. Few French resistance fighters actually heard Charles de Gaulle's famous British Broadcasting Corporation (BBC) broadcast of 18 June 1940 calling on France to continue the fight rather than accept a dishonorable armistice dictated by the Germans. Char's move into dissidence and secrecy within the first six months of the German occupation puts him in the vanguard of the French Resistance.

Char took refuge in Céreste, which was in the Italian zone of occupation until Benito Mussolini's fall in 1942. Char organized a small group of resisters, and the French Armée Secrète (Secret Army) named him head of a military sector around the Durance river. De Gaulle had just begun to form links with the mainland Resistance, especially in southern France. The situation changed dramatically with the Allied invasion of North Africa, 8–11 November 1942, which provoked the German Wehrmacht to invade the south. This German invasion was a turning point for the French Resistance: the Germans were now omnipresent, and the cycle of resistance and reprisals escalated. The famous resister Jean Moulin, before the Gestapo tortured him to death in 1943, managed to unify the disparate elements of the mainland resistance and to win its broad (if conditional) support for de Gaulle. De Gaulle's Comité français de libération nationale (CFLN; French Committee for National Liberation), based in London, soon became the Gouvernement provisoire de la République française (GPRF; Provisional Government of the French Republic), with its primary center in Algiers. De Gaulle's organization had merged various military and paramilitary forces into the Forces françaises combattantes (FFC; French Combat Forces), which Char

joined in September 1943 with the rank of captain. The FFC included not only the regular French army divisions fighting under de Gaulle's overall command in Africa, Italy, and elsewhere, but also the French mainland resistance, whose combat units were officially called the Forces françaises de l'intérieur (FFI; French Interior Forces). It is important to remember, however, that the rivalry and power struggles between Gaullists and non-Gaullists within the internal, mainland resistance (especially its left-wing members) remained keen throughout the war. After the war, Char was hostile to de Gaulle, because, in his opinion, de Gaulle had reasserted traditional French conservative interests at the Liberation and thereby betrayed the faith the resistance had placed in him.

In anticipation of the Allied invasion of the Continent, de Gaulle's military intelligence and action apparatus in London and Algiers had organized a relatively efficient system for supplying the mainland French resistance with arms and money. When Char joined the FFC, he was named sector head in a portion of the lower Alps that stretched in a southerly direction roughly from Mont Ventoux to the towns of Apt, Forcalquier, and Valensole. Char organized the reception and clandestine stocking of arms from Allied parachute drops, and he oversaw the landings of Lysander airplanes during periods of full moon on the isolated plateaus of the region. These flights brought in Gaullist personnel, along with cash to fund the maquis (as the guerrilla fighters were called, after the thick scrubby underbrush and forested areas where the resistance fighters lived in hiding). Sector leaders, such as Char, had abandoned all pretense of a civilian life. During a military operation in April 1944, Char was seriously hurt as a result of a fall of several meters. After his recovery, he was ordered to Algiers to help prepare the Allied invasion of Provence. He was evacuated by plane to Corsica, and from there to Algeria, where he served under another early resister, General Gabriel Cochet. After the Allied landings in Provence, which took place on 15 August 1944, Char rejoined his maquis unit in Avignon and stayed with them until he was demobilized in September 1945, soon after the end of the war in Europe. Char rejoined his wife in Paris. During his stay in Algeria, he had resumed publishing, mostly in reviews connected to the resistance such as Max-Pol Fouchet's *Fontaine,* where selections from Char's *Feuillets d'Hypnos* (translated as *Leaves of Hypnos,* 1973) appeared in 1945, a year before the work was published in book form.

Although Char was one of the few French writers who did not publish during the occupation, he had not quit writing. *Feuillets d'Hypnos,* a poetic journal of the war, was composed in rare moments of respite from

RENÉ CHAR

Lettera amorosa .

COLLECTION
ESPOIR

nrf

DIRIGÉE PAR
ALBERT CAMUS

Gallimard

Title page for Char's 1953 poetry collection (Perkins Library, Duke University)

vasses. Il ne m'intéresse pas" (A man without faults is a mountain without crevasses. He does not interest me). Char uses the aphorism encomiastically to celebrate his companions in the resistance or lament their deaths, as in numbers 22 and 138: "AUX PRUDENTS: Il neige sur le maquis et c'est contre nous chasse perpétuelle" (WARNING TO THE WISE: it is snowing on the maquis and it is open season against us) and "Horrible journée! J'ai assisté, distant de quelque cent mètres, à l'exécution de B" (Horrible day! I witnessed, at a distance of some 100 meters, the execution of B[ernard]). The pseudonyms, or *pseudos,* that resistance leaders used to escape detection, become heroic epithets in *Feuillets d'Hypnos.* Char is Alexandre, just as Moulin was known as Rex. Poetry is never far away from war. In *Feuillets d'Hypnos* number 56 Char describes the poem as "ascension furieuse" (furious ascension), and in that sense the resistance was a wartime substitute for writing, since as a military leader Char was forced to put his literary talents into hibernation (hence the allusion in the title to the Greek god of sleep, Hypnos).

Feuillets d'Hypnos, however, was not Char's first major postwar publication. A revised and enlarged edition of *Le Marteau sans maître,* from Char's Surrealist days, was published by Librarie José Corti in August 1945. More importantly, in February of that year the book *Seuls demeurent* (They Alone Remain) appeared, and it marked Char's entry into the ranks of authors published by the prestigious French publisher Editions Gallimard. *Feuillets d'Hypnos* appeared a year later in the Gallimard series Collection Espoir, edited by Albert Camus, who had worked for the resistance newspaper *Combat.* Camus and Char soon built a close friendship; indeed, Char's social and intellectual circle grew rapidly following the war. Braque, a new acquaintance, designed the stage curtain and costumes for Char's ballet *La Conjuration* (The Plot), produced in 1947 at the Théâtre des Champs-Elysées. Char's association with Wifredo Lam, whose paintings combined tropical imagery from his native Cuba with abstract and fantastic images, dates from the same year.

Even more momentous was the publication of the collection of poetry *Fureur et mystère* by Gallimard in 1948. It incorporated *Seuls demeurent, Feuillets d'Hypnos,* and *Le Poème pulvérisé* into a larger, allegorical scheme reflecting Char's passage through the late 1930s, the resistance, and the Liberation. The prewar sense of impending disaster is reflected in such poems as "Bouge de l'historien" (The Historian's Hovel): "La pyramide des martyrs obsède la terre" (The pyramid of martyrs obsesses the earth). The aphorisms of *Feuillets d'Hypnos* and the war poems from the section of *Fureur et mystère* titled *Loyaux adversaires* (Loyal Adversaries) echo the struggles of the underground resisters to whom Char

1941 to 1944. When this work appeared in its entirety in 1946, it staked Char's claim as an authentic resistance poet who had risked his life against Nazi and Vichy oppression. Although Char focused *Feuillets d'Hypnos* on his experience of the resistance, the book nevertheless has profound formal and aesthetic links to his prewar poetry. From *Moulin premier* onward, Char had spent much creative energy developing his own version of the short, aphoristic writing that typified so much French literary production since the seventeenth century (including Blaise Pascal; François VI, duc de La Rochefoucauld; Jean de La Bruyère; Sébastien-Roch Nicolas Chamfort; and Luc de Clapiers, Marquis de Vauvenargues). *Feuillets d'Hypnos* relies heavily on striking, provocative adages, as in aphorism number 32: "Un homme sans défauts est une montagne sans cre-

joined his fate from 1940 to 1944. The closing sections, *Le Poème pulvérisé* and "La Fontaine narrative" (The Narrative Fountain), suggest that wartime destruction has been superseded at the Liberation by a return to creativity and love, as in the masterful poem "La Sorgue. Chanson pour Yvonne" (River Sorgue: Song for Yvonne): "Rivière au cœur jamais détruit dans ce monde fou de prison / Garde-nous violent et ami des abeilles de l'horizon" (River with a heart intact despite this world enamored of prison / Preserve our sting and keep us friendly with horizon's bees).

Poems that adopt the harsh, corrosive, "alchemical" style of the prewar *Le Marteau sans maître* still appear, but in counterpoint there are softer love poems such as "Evadné" (a title alluding to the French words for birth and escape). "Evadné," as does the prewar "Le Visage nuptial" (also included in *Fureur et mystère*), depicts two lovers momentarily and happily secluded in a sensual landscape: "La campagne mangeait la couleur de ta jupe odorante . . ." (The countryside devoured the color of your scented skirt . . .). Love and desire intervene strongly, too, in the aphoristic *ars poetica* (commentary on the art of poetry) titled "Partage formel" (Formal Divide), which includes Char's celebrated definition of the poem as an attempt to espouse protean desire and depict it from the inside, affectively: "Le poème est l'amour réalisé du désir demeuré désir," which might be loosely paraphrased as "The poem realizes the yearning to express what, in desire, escapes expression," although the rich connotations and strong tensions of this aphorism elude any brief translation. Many poems of *Fureur et mystère* adopt a lighter vein that eschews tragedy and seeks resolution, but nowhere is the collection entirely free from the battle of contraries that Char's title, with its furor and mystery, implies.

Fureur et mystère, despite Char's ostensible and frequent disclaimers of political commitment and intent, celebrated the resistance with such force that it inevitably struck political chords in its readers. Postwar France tried to forget the past and the extent of its collaboration with the German occupiers through a celebration of such individuals as Char, who had not compromised national honor. If any poet captured the intensity, the local color, and the moral tone of the French resistance, it was Char. In contrast to Aragon and Eluard's circumstantial and propagandistic resistance poetry, *Fureur et mystère* had the advantage of embracing, in a formally innovative way, the entire period from the antifascist struggle of the 1930s through the Liberation. After the war Char, unlike most French intellectuals, kept his distance from the Communist Party despite his praise for French Communist resistance fighters in World War II. He was an early and harsh critic of Soviet internal repression and maintained an antitotalitarian line simi-

lar to the one espoused by Camus in *L'Homme révolté* (Rebellious Man, 1951).

In April 1949, in the wake of *Fureur et mystère,* Char's play *Le Soleil des eaux* (Sun in Waters), a poetic drama about the cultural and ecological threat that modern industrial society posed for local Vaucluse traditions, was produced by French radio, with music by the composer Pierre Boulez. It was published that same year, as was another play, *Claire: Théâtre de verdure,* (Claire: Theater Among the Leaves), which is an allegorical fantasy set, as is *Le Soleil des eaux,* at riverside. Wartime denunciations, the maquis, love, and the clash of social classes swirl around the multiple, quasi-mythical protagonist, Claire, a river nymph born of the "violentes amours de la nuée et du glacier" (violent loves of the cloud and the glacier). Also in 1949 René and Georgette Char were divorced, though they remained on good terms thereafter.

Char's next large collection, *Les Matinaux,* published the following year, confirmed his position among the elite of postwar French poets. Whereas *Fureur et mystère* was filled with vivid contrasts between combat and love, resistance and landscape, *Les Matinaux* depicts the return to peace. Many of the poems convey delight that Hypnos, the poet, can now awaken from the throes of war and history. The seventeen character portraits titled *Les Transparents* (first published in 1949 in the review *Mercure de France*) reconfirm, as did the plays *Le Soleil des eaux* and *Claire,* Char's attachment to the Vaucluse. The *transparents* were colorful, itinerant characters from the region: the character Laurent de Venasque, alias the count of Sault (a town in the lower Alps) and based on the real-life Pierre de Vaucluse, performed his mime in the streets of L'Isle-sur-la-Sorgue. Char transforms local color into universal myth, and such characters as "Odin le Roc" and "Joseph Puissantseigneur" (Joseph Stronglord, Char's self-portrait) infuse *Les Matinaux* with a magic realism that contrasts with the sulfurous alchemical imagery of his prewar *Le Marteau sans maître* or the epic tendencies of *Fureur et mystère.* The notes of bucolic fantasy in *Les Matinaux* are, however, counterbalanced by several poems that assert personal nonconformism and revolt, such as "Le Permissionnaire" (Soldier on Leave) and "L'Adolescent souffleté" (The Adolescent Slapped).

Les Matinaux illustrates Char's turn away from the war toward personal reconstruction. The poem "Les Inventeurs" reproduces a contrast familiar to Char from his own childhood. Much like his paternal grandfather, who came down from the pastures of Mont Ventoux to L'Isle-sur-la-Sorgue, the rustic forest people in the poem come down into the town, warning the inhabitants of impending danger from beyond. A communion is struck between the hill dwellers, who accept

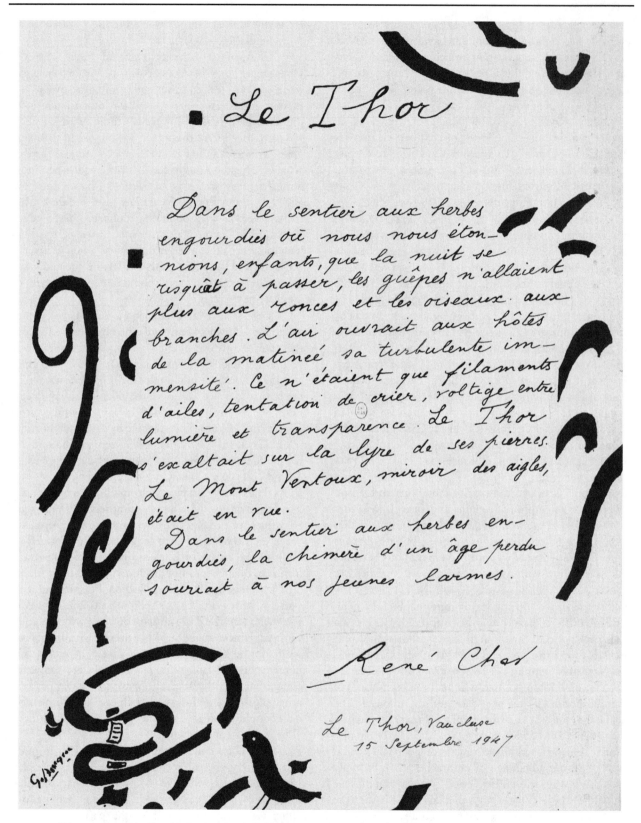

Fair copy of a poem collected in Recherche de la base et du sommet *(1955), with marginal decorations by Georges Braque*
(Bibliothèque Nationale, Paris)

their savage environment but remain wary of hostile outside forces, and the city dwellers, who have the equanimity of a civilization that has conquered past invasions and is confident it will meet future challenges. *Les Matinaux* closes with a series of poetic maxims, titled "Rougeur des Matinaux" (Reddening of the Dawn Breakers), which uses once more the themes of landscape and nature. "Rougeur des Matinaux" includes the often-quoted synopsis of Char's poetry of contraries: "Enfin, si tu détruis, que ce soit avec des outils nuptiaux" (Lastly, if you destroy, do it with nuptial means). *Les Matinaux* complements the tensions and commitment of *Fureur et mystère* by reestablishing the bucolic, acculturated values of creativity and relaxed contemplation, values that most French had perforce abandoned during World War II.

The period 1950–1962, extending from the publication of *Les Matinaux* to the appearance of Char's next major omnibus collection, *La Parole en archipel* (The Word as Archipelago), was extremely productive for Char, although most of his poetry appeared incrementally and was published by small presses, frequently with illustrations by such artists as Braque, Miró, Nicolas de Staël, and Maria Elena Vieira da Silva. Three such important, smaller books add to an understanding of Char's poetry of landscape, love, vivid images, and aphoristic concision: *La Paroi et la prairie* (The Inner Wall and the Prairie, 1952), *Lettera amorosa* (Love Letter, 1953), and *La Bibliothèque est en feu* (The Library is Burning, 1956).

In the past Char had frequently associated violent conflict with the origins of poetry, and this eschatological tendency informs the poems in *La Paroi et la prairie* that depict the cave art of Lascaux, such as "Homme-oiseau mort et bison mourant" (Bird-Man Dead Next to Dying Bison). During prehistory, inside the protection of the cave, the prototype of all artists made beautiful murals to depict the violence of the outer world. The close proximity of two extremes, art and death, no doubt appealed to Char. By contrast, the tone of *Lettera amorosa* is playful, as in its closing poem, "Sur le franc-bord" (On the Path's Edge): ". . . Iris plural, iris d'Eros, iris de *Lettera amorosa*" (. . . Plural iris, Eros's iris, the iris of *Love Letter*). In another vein, memories of the war were still omnipresent in Char's poetry. Especially notable in this regard is *La Bibliothèque est en feu*, the title of which directly evokes the resistance. Code phrases were broadcast over the BBC to the French Resistance, warning them of imminent parachute drops or instructing them to undertake such actions as the destruction of enemy rail shipments. The sentence "the library is burning" was one such transmission, a message for Char's maquis unit.

Whereas the Lascaux poems of *La Paroi et la prairie* praised the nameless prehistoric cave artists of the Dor-

dogne region, the lithography of the painter Staël, whom Char first met in 1951, adorns *Arrière-histoire du Poème pulvérisé*, published two years later, one of the few explicit glosses that he gave of his own poetry, in this case of a book that became a section of *Fureur et mystère*. As had Camus, Staël became enchanted with the Luberon region near L'Isle-sur-la-Sorgue. Char merged Staël's life and art into several poems, including "Vermillon" (Vermilion) in *La Parole en archipel* and "Libera II" in *Fenêtres dormantes et porte sur le toit* (Sleeping Windows and Door on the Roof, 1979). In 1952 Char and Staël collaborated on a ballet, *L'Abominable des neiges* (The Abominable Snowman), that was never produced but was published in the *Nouvelle Revue Française* in 1953 and later as a small book.

The first of several editions of *Recherche de la base et du sommet* (Search for the Base and the Summit) was published by Gallimard in 1955. The book was intended to be the repository for Char's texts on the war, on the arts, and on other philosophers, writers, and artists. Its first version, which included texts previously published in *Art bref* (Brief Art, 1950), was titled *Recherche de la base et du sommet, suivi de Pauvreté et privilège*. The first section, *Recherche de la base et du sommet*, consisted of Char's texts on the war and the maquis. The second, *Pauvreté et privilège* (Poverty and Privilege), incorporated his texts on other writers and artists. In later editions Char modified the subtitles and contents of these sections, and he added new sections of text. The final arrangement, as set out in the 1971 edition, reserves *Pauvreté et privilège* mostly for his war writings and uses two separate sections to cover, respectively, artists, "Alliés substantiels" (Essential Allies), and other writers, "Grands astreignants, ou, La Conversation souveraine" (Great Compellers, or, The Sovereign Conversation). Two long poems were added, respectively in the 1965 and 1971 editions, as the fourth and fifth sections: a revised version of a poem first published separately in 1951, *A une sérénité crispée* (translated as "To a Tense Serenity," 1958), and *L'Age cassant* (Ungrateful Age; first published separately in 1965).

In the final version of the book, *Pauvreté et privilège* includes a miscellany of texts on the Resistance but also comprises other items, such as "La lettre hors commerce" (Private Letter) that Char addressed to Breton in 1947, in which he refused to associate himself with the postwar reprise of official Surrealist activities. *Alliés substantiels* is devoted to painters and sculptors whose work Char admired. Of particular length and importance are "En vue de Georges Braque" (With respect to Georges Braque) and Char's piece on Miró, *Flux de l'aimant* (Magnetic Flow, 1964), though other artists, including Giacometti, Count Balthazar Klossowski de Rola (known as Balthus), Victor Brauner, and the lyri-

Char and Pablo Picasso in 1965 (from Eric Marty, René Char, *1990)*

cal abstractionist Vieira da Silva, receive homage, too. In Char's depiction of Miró's style, the reader can also hear a description of the explosive, fragmented nature of his own poetry: "A la manière de la ligne, à la manière de la couleur, la forme de Miró n'est que surgissement, rafale qui reflue pour rejaillir" (Like line, like color, Miró's form is entirely an uprising, a gust of wind that recoils in order to leap forward again). Char's art writing complements the impulse of his poetry.

The third section, *Grands astreignants, ou La Conversation souveraine,* concerns writers who challenged and invigorated the poet. Heraclitus is praised alongside such moderns as Eluard, Antonin Artaud, Camus, and Crevel. Pieces on Arthur Rimbaud, crucial for Char's conception of poetry, eventually found their way into this section of *Recherche de la base et du sommet.* Char edited and prefaced Rimbaud's *Oeuvres,* published in 1957 by Le Club Français du Livre. His preface was separately published, in an edition of seventy-five copies, as *Pour nous, Rimbaud–* (For Us, Rimbaud, 1956), and it also appears as the essay "Arthur Rimbaud" in *Recherche de la base et du sommet.* At the time the essay was originally published, it occasioned a polemical exchange with René Etiemble, a professor of comparative literature whose academic study *Le Mythe de Rimbaud* (The

Rimbaud Myth, 1952) would undoubtedly have resulted in a brawl with the prewar Surrealists, similar to the sack of the crassly commercial Maldoror bar in 1930 when Char received a knife wound defending the good name of the Comte de Lautréamont (pseudonym of Isidore Lucien Ducasse), the nineteenth-century author of *Les Chants de Maldoror* (Songs of Maldoror, 1869). The confrontation between Etiemble and Char, however, was limited to insults (scholarly and unscholarly), some of which appear in Char's *Le Dernier couac* (The Last Bad Note, 1958). In "Arthur Rimbaud" Char depicts the precocious nineteenth-century writer as someone who lived life without regret, rejecting Western culture when he quit its highest endeavor, poetry: "Cette espérance de retour est la pire perversion de la culture occidentale, sa plus folle aberration . . . Rimbaud avait éprouvé et repoussé cette tentation . . ." (This hope for a return [to past traditions] is the worst perversion of Western culture, its maddest aberration . . . Rimbaud felt that temptation and rejected it . . .).

The fourth section of *Recherche de la base et du sommet* is a revised version of the poetic sequence *A une sérénité crispée,* originally published separately in 1951. Char seems to have added *A une sérénité crispée* to *Recherche de la base et du sommet* in order to underscore the mixture or diversity of this heterogeneous book in which autobiography, history, elegies, praise, and writings on art, and poetry mingle: "Tant de mots sont synonymes d'adieu, tant de visages n'ont pas d'équivalent" (So many words are like good-byes, so many faces have no equivalent). This poem constructs the overall frame, or lesson, that justifies the preceding three sections of *Recherche de la base et du sommet,* devoted respectively to historical commemoration, praise for allies, and evaluation of influences. If people on the outside imitated the goodwill of the maquis fighters, artists, and writers whom Char celebrated within his inner circle, then justice and things of beauty would perhaps survive in the modern world. The prose poem *L'Age cassant,* the fifth and final section of this compendium, echoes the themes of *A une sérénité crispée* but adds its own distinct note, insisting on the elegiac finality of much of *Recherche de la base et du sommet.* By commemorating friends, artists, and writers, Char confronts his own mortality: "Sois consolé. En mourant, tu rends tout ce qui t'a été prêté, ton amour, tes amis" (Be consoled. In dying, you pay back all that was loaned to you, your love, your friends). *Recherche de la base et du sommet* is multifaceted, but the rich unity of its final version transcends circumstantial praise.

In contrast to the celebratory, commemorative nature of *Recherche de la base et du sommet,* the cutting of one of Char's major emotional ties to his past also occurred in 1955. His childhood home in L'Isle-sur-la-Sorgue, the Névons, was sold. His mother had died in 1951, and he and one of his sisters, Julia, had not managed to raise the money necessary to prevent the sale of the estate by their other siblings. In a poem contemporaneous with the event, "Deuil des Névons" (Mourning for the Névons), included in *La Parole en archipel,* the poet conveyed his feeling of cosmic homelessness. Personal setbacks notwithstanding, his public visibility widened considerably throughout this middle period of his career. In 1955 Boulez created another sequence of works based on Char's poetry, this time on the prewar *Le Marteau sans maître.* In 1957 Boulez also put *Le Visage nuptial* to music, for a production by Radio-Cologne. That same year Char published an anthology of his verse, *Poèmes et proses choisis* (Selected Poems and Prose), which partially anticipated what he considered the definitive anthology of his poetry, *Commune présence* (Common Presence, 1964; revised and enlarged, 1978).

As was the case with *Fureur et mystère,* the collection *La Parole en archipel,* which Gallimard published in 1962, reconfigured several previous brief collections into a grander scheme. Among the works that entered into the compendium were *La Paroi et la prairie, Lettera amorosa, Poèmes des deux années, 1953–1954* (Poems of the Two Years, 1953–1954, 1955), *La Bibliothèque est en feu et autres poèmes* (1957), and *L'Inclémence lointaine* (Distant Clemency, 1961). *La Parole en archipel* has as its central symbol a volcanic explosion symbolizing poetry's violent power of dissemination, an image that the critic Georges Poulet has explored in depth. Char accepts the lack of a grand narrative or design ordering nature's parts into a whole. In "Dans la marche" (In the March) he discerns even in the eyes of friends and lovers the reflections of imminent dissolution and death, "Ces incessantes et phosphorescentes traînées de la mort sur soi que nous lisons dans les yeux de ceux qui nous aiment, sans désirer les leur dissumuler" (Those unceasing phosphorescent tracks of one's death that we read in the eyes of those who love us, without wishing to hide the marks from them). In "L'éternité à Lourmarin" (An Eternity at Lourmarin), eulogizing Camus, who died in an automobile accident in 1960, Char portrays poetry as the act of interrogating ceaselessly "tout le poids de l'énigme" (all the weight of the enigma) of mortality.

Despite elegiac and tragic notes, many poems in *La Parole en archipel* depict vibrant participation and moments of epiphany, as in "L'Allégresse" (Exultation): "Les nuages sont dans les rivières, les torrents parcourent le ciel" (Clouds are in the rivers, torrents stream across the sky), a line that illustrates Char's tendency to represent special moments through a verbal landscape. Other poems describe the towering yet delicate geological outcroppings near Mont Ventoux, the Dentelles du Montmirail (Lace of Montmirail), as symbols of an exalted life struggle: "La réalité ne peut être franchie que soulevée" (Reality cannot be traversed unless it is upraised). As in *Fureur et mystère* and *Les Matinaux,* in the collection *La Parole en archipel* Char addresses the rich parallel between outer nature and inner thoughts.

It was several years before Char published another major work. As with the decade that elapsed between *Les Matinaux* and *La Parole en archipel,* the period from 1962 to 1971 was marked by several smaller publications, many of which were eventually incorporated under the title *Le Nu perdu* (Nakedness Lost, 1971): *Retour amont* (Return Upland, 1965), *Dans la pluie giboyeuse* (In the Game-Filled Rain, 1968), *Le Chien de cœur* (Dog of a Heart, 1969), and *L'Effroi la joie* (The Fright the Joy, 1969). Char did not neglect his earlier works during this period. The play *Le Soleil des eaux* was produced on stage in 1967 at the Studio des Champs-Elysées and then was reworked for television in 1968. In 1967 all Char's theatrical works were republished by Gallimard under the title *Trois coups sous les arbres: Théâtre saisonnier* (Three Taps Underneath the Trees: Seasonal Theatre).

RENÉ CHAR

Le nu perdu

nrf

GALLIMARD

Title page for the 1971 book in which Char collected most of the poetry he had written since 1962 (Thomas Cooper Library, University of South Carolina)

The 1960s were busy years for Char. In 1965 he wrote a brief protest against the construction of nuclear missile silos on the plateau of Albion in the vicinity of Mont Ventoux. Titled *La Provence point oméga* (Provence Ground Zero), the pamphlet translated into political terms what many critics see as the ecological, natural base of his poetry. Mont Ventoux, "miroir des aigles" (eagles' mirror) in Char's poem "Le Thor" (collected in *Fureur et Mystère*), dominates the skyline over the towns and perched villages of the Drôme, the Luberon, the Vaucluse, and the lower Alps. These villages often figure by name in Char's poems: Céreste, Vaison-La-Romaine, Viens, Forcalquier, Buoux, and Sault, for example. Char's image of Mont Ventoux as eagle's perch or eyrie ties the mountain to Nietzschean concepts of self-supremacy, but this mythical dimension should not make the reader forget Char's real biographical associations with Mont Ventoux. His grandfather used to take him as a child to visit towns near the

mountain, such as Buis-les-Baronnies, whose echo the reader encounters in "Dansons aux Baronnies" (Let's Dance at the Baronnies) from *Le Nu perdu*. On a different note, in the 1960s Char deepened his relationship with the German philosopher Martin Heidegger, whom he had first met in 1955. In the summers of 1966, 1968, and 1969 Heidegger conducted philosophy seminars in the town of Le Thor, near L'Isle-sur-la-Sorgue. About this time Char began to experience serious health problems, particularly in May 1968. In a gesture that typifies the belief that poetry is a way of life as well as an aesthetic construct, Char turned a serious arterial problem in his inner ear into poetry, declaring in a poem included in *Le Nu perdu*, "Dans la nuit du 3 au 4 mai 1968 . . ." (During the Night of 3–4 May 1968 . . .), that "La foudre et le sang, je l'appris, sont un" (Lightning and blood, I discovered, are one).

Char continued to support small presses and artistic printers such as Pierre André Benoit, who, under the imprint Editions P.A.B., published several "minuscules"–miniature books that usually consist of one of Char's poems along with photographs of sites in the Luberon or reproductions of works by painters and artists whose style adapted well to small formats (such as Arpad Szenes and Jean Hugo). In the spring of 1971 the Maeght Foundation at Saint-Paul-de-Vence devoted a major exhibit to Char. The exhibit, which dealt extensively with Char's relationships with artists, also traveled to the Musée d'Art Moderne de la Ville de Paris (Museum of Modern Art in Paris). Recognition was coming his way, but age brought its hecatomb of losses. Yvonne Zervos, who figured in his poetry and was an important link with other artists, died in 1970, followed the same year by her husband, the editor of *Cahiers d'art,* in which Char had frequently published since 1937.

Le Nu perdu, in which Char assembled most of his poetry written since 1964, proved to be his last large compendium, though he continued to write and publish. His favorite motif, the tension between contraries, does not disappear, but the exaltation in his earlier poetry gives way to a greater pessimism and to a concomitant morality of dogged endurance, as in the poem "Le jugement d'octobre" (October Judgment). Two *gueuses* (wildflowers) that the speaker encounters in late fall, "joue contre joue . . . en leur détresse roidie" (cheek to cheek . . . stiffened in their distress), offer an image of resistance that soon becomes a formula of doom when they are compared to an unsheltered flame about to be extinguished by the cold wind. Hopeful moments do, however, punctuate the ambient pessimism. In "Le banc d'ocre" (The Ochre Embankment) the speaker reads his beloved's fortune and, taking her hand, places "l'infime ver luisant sur le tracé de vie" (the minuscule glowworm on the line of life), creating a lamp to stave off shadowy death. Poetry of place or site remains a fulcrum for Char but in a sullenly violent way, as in "Sept parcelles du Luberon" (Seven Parcels of the Luberon), in which Char's allusions to early modern persecutions of Protestant religious dissidents in the Luberon introduce a millenarian, eschatological tone. Buoux, the hilltop refuge of the Valdese "heretics," clearly serves as an allegory of poetry, itself besieged and imperiled by a modern, philistine society.

In other respects, *Le Nu perdu* shows continuity with Char's previous poetry: for example, the section *Contre une maison sèche* (Against a Dry House; separately published in 1975) is a sequence of semi-oracular aphorisms similar to "Partage formel" in *Fureur et mystère,* or *Les Compagnons dans le jardin* (Friends in the Garden), a poem published separately in May 1957 and included in the enlarged edition of *La Bibliothèque est en feu,* published in October of that year. In contrast to more somber parts of *Le Nu perdu,* the dialogic poetic sequence *Contre une maison sèche* depicts Char's ideal of full, quasi-magical participation in life, through an exploration of the roots of poetic imagination: "Une simplicité s'ébauche: le feu monte, la terre emprunte, la neige vole, la rixe éclate . . ." (A simplicity sketches itself: the fire goes up, the earth borrows, the snow flies, the fight breaks out . . .). This enthusiastic ascension or espousal leads to a rebirth of poetry: "Qui là, parmi les menthes, est parvenu à naître dont toute chose, demain, se prévaudra?" (Who there, among the mint, has finally been born so that everything tomorrow will cite it as precedent?).

Some of the poems in Char's next book of verse, *La Nuit talismanique* (Talismanic Night, 1972), were accompanied by small drawings and artworks that Char made during sleepless nights from 1955 to 1958. The collection revolves in part around Char's thoughts concerning dreams, as in "Dévalant la rocaille aux plantes écarlates" (Descending the Rocky Slope and its Scarlet Plants), the opening poem, where the conscious world and the dream world both foil human intentions and willpower: "Nous n'avons pas plus de pouvoir s'attardant sur les décisions de notre vie que nous n'en possédons sur nos rêves à travers notre sommeil" (We have no more power by lingering over the decisions in our life than we have over our dreams during sleep). Char's reflection on the meaning of poetry is given an interesting rendition in another poem, "Baudelaire mécontente Nietzsche" (Baudelaire Irritates Nietzsche). This poem would probably displease historians of philosophy, but it reflects Char's encomiastic view of intellectual history, as exemplified in *Recherche de la base et du sommet.* Baudelaire and Nietzsche are pitted against each other in a staged controversy over which one best repre-

sents modernity. Char arranges for the debate to end in a draw: Baudelaire best symbolizes human suffering and the sacrifices entailed by the pursuit of poetry, but Nietzsche conveys equally important values of exaltation and sovereignty. Reacting against the Christianity that haunted Baudelaire, however, Char also takes the opportunity to enunciate his own negative metaphysics: human beings are "fils de rien et promis à rien" (sons of nothing and promised to nothing), except to the degree that writing redeems them. The poem "Eclore en hiver" (Bloom in winter) also evokes the threat of mortality: "La nuit s'imposant, mon premier geste fut de détruire le calendrier noeud de vipères où chaque jour abordé sautait aux yeux" (Once night imposed its presence, my first gesture was to destroy the calendar, that viper's nest, where each new day jumped in my face). Char was sixty-five when *La Nuit talismanique* appeared in print.

From 1972 to 1983, when the first edition of his *Œuvres complètes* in the prestigious Gallimard collection Bibliothèque de la Pléiade was published, Char maintained a steady pace of work. In 1974 he published *Le Monde de l'art n'est pas le monde du pardon* (The World of Art Is Not the World of Pardon), a collection of texts originally published between 1929 and 1972, accompanied by original illustrations. This rare book, published in an edition of only one hundred copies, is arguably the best overview of Char's collaborative relationship with artists as diverse as Braque, Miró, Victor Brauner, Pierre Charbonnier, and Vieira da Silva. Several smaller books of poetry, which combined roughly equal *Le Nu perdu* in length, also diversify Char's writing during this period: *Aromates chasseurs* (Hunting Herbs, 1975), *Chants de la Balandrane* (Songs from Balandrane, 1977), and *Fenêtres dormantes et porte sur le toit,* published in 1979.

Aromates chasseurs is remarkable for its sequence of poems devoted to the constellation and mythical figure, Orion, who represents, as Char says in his poetic preface, a third, cosmic space between the solitary imagination and the world of concrete things. In an interview with the journalist France Huser for the periodical *Le Nouvel observateur* (1980), Char told how Jean-Pancrace Nouguier, one of the older local characters of L'Isle-sur-la-Sorgue during the poet's childhood, had befriended him and taught him the rudiments of stargazing, including how to identify Orion. One cannot overestimate the extent to which his childhood and adolescent memories of L'Isle-sur-la-Sorgue and some of its picturesque and humane characters, such as Nouguier or Louis Curel de la Sorgue, gave a positive, magical cast to much of Char's subsequent poetry. In *Aromates chasseurs* the poetic dialogue between Orion and other constellations encompasses a wide range of topics,

Char in his study at his country house, Les Buclats, near his childhood home of
L'Isle-sur-la-Sorgue (photograph by Serge Assier)

ranging from the magic realism of the opening poem, "Evadé d'archipel" (Escaped from an Archipelago), in which Orion leaves the night sky and comes to live with humankind, to texts of praise for the painters Nicolas Poussin and Staël, and finally a political critique of twentieth-century totalitarianism, in the poem "Lombes": ". . . nous avons frissonné à l'horizon de Saint-Just et de Lénine. Mais Staline est perpétuellement imminent. On conserve avec égards la mâchoire d'Hitler" (. . . the perspectives of Saint-Just and Lenin made us shiver with joy. But Stalin is always an imminent threat. Hitler's jawbone is still conserved and revered). The thrust of the collection transcends ethics, however, and rejoins Char's familiar metaphysical themes: "Nuls dieux à l'extérieur de nous, car ils sont le fruit de la seule de nos pensées qui ne conquiert pas la mort . . ." (No gods beyond us, since they are the fruit of our only thought that does not conquer death . . .).

In the collection *Chants de la Balandrane,* the poet uses a fanciful etymological excursion (similar to the one that ended *Lettera amorosa*) to explain the meaning of his title: the word *balandran* is a shepherd's cape, a

balandrin is a smuggler, and so forth. As in many of Char's poems, however, the enigmatic name *la Balandrane* is also a local site, "une ferme sur un plateau boisé où subsistent les ruines de nombreux puits abandonnés" (a farm on a wooded plateau where the ruins of numerous abandoned wells remain). Char was an avid hiker, and he often gave a peripatetic allure to his poems and collections through allusions to places such as Balandrane. "Pacage de la Genestrière" (Pasture: La Genestrière), the opening poem of *Chants de la Balandrane,* underscores that the collection is an itinerary of sorts, though the journey, as the long poem "Cruels assortiments" (Cruel Assortments) makes clear, is not bereft of strife and anguish: "L'existence ne nous appartient que pour un bref essai. Devant l'incendie dévorant, nous ne faisons que pointiller l'espace" (We try life only briefly. Faced with the raging fire, we only trace out a few points in space). Although Char tends to transform local color into images of the cosmos, the path is occasionally reversed, as in "Le réviseur" (Proofreader), in which the poet casts a critical glance from the cosmos, or safe haven of poetry, down toward the political ugliness of his century: ". . . face à la glace diffusante des lunes et des soleils, le monde quotidien de l'internement, de la filature, de la déportation, des supplices, et de la crémation devenait pyramidal . . ." (. . . in the faithful mirror of moons and suns, the daily world of prison, surveillance, deportation, tortures, and cremation was steadily growing into a pyramid . . .).

Char's subsequent book of poetry, *Fenêtres dormantes et porte sur le toit,* includes several intensely lyrical and elegiac poems, such as "L'écoute au carreau" (Listening at the Pane) and "Ibrim"; however, two longer poems combining the political and the poetic give the collection its primary, didactic frame: "Faire du chemin avec . . ." (Walk the Path With . . .) and "Tous partis!" (Everyone Has Left!). These works are loosely structured, but Char uses the digressions to weave his central message into the poems: the only antidote to the "utopies sanglantes du XXe siècle" (bloody utopias of the twentieth century) is the loving focus on the individual person that the artist and poet bring to their work. Political militants are "épris de l'humanité et non de l'homme" (enamored with humanity and not with the man), as Char indicates in "Faire du chemin avec. . . ." He asserts unequivocally in "Tous partis!" that poetry "domine l'absurde" (dominates absurdity), or resists the absurdity of the world. To underline this message, an encomiastic section of *Fenêtres dormantes et porte sur le toit,* titled "Un jour entier sans controverse" (An Entire Day Without Controversy), celebrates the alliance between poetry and the plastic arts in the work of such artists as Vieira de Silva, Joseph Sima, Zao Wou-ki, and Picasso. Indeed, the three collections *Aromates chasseurs, Chants de la Balandrane,* and *Fenêtres dormantes et porte sur le toit* urgently voice one leitmotiv: for Char, poetry and art are valid forms of intellectual resistance against the many oppressive and inhumane aspects of the modern age.

Two years after *Fenêtres dormantes et porte sur le toit* appeared, Gallimard published a book of translations by Char and Tina Jolas, *La Planche de vivre* (The Last Resource, 1981). Char did some of the translations from Italian and English, but more significantly, the volume symbolizes his interest in the Soviet dissident poets, especially Boris Pasternak, Marina Tsvetaeva, Ossip Mandelstam, and Anna Akhmatova. In 1980 the Bibliothèque Nationale in Paris held a special exhibit of Char's manuscripts illuminated by his artist friends. Lam, whose work had also figured in *Le Monde de l'art n'est pas le monde du pardon,* continued to illustrate Char's works, including in 1975 a special edition of *Contre une maison sèche,* first published in 1971 in *Le Nu perdu.* In 1980 Zao illuminated the manuscript of *Effilage du sac de jute* (Fraying the Coarse Sack). Other artists, such as Alexandre Galpérine, joined Char's circle and produced drawings and illuminations to accompany his poems.

Char had some major personal setbacks during this period. His former wife, Georgette, died in 1978, as did Lévis-Mano, his longtime friend and publisher. Char again had heart problems that year in August, in the wake of which he relinquished the apartment in Paris where he had lived the preceding twenty years, on the rue de Chanaleilles near the Rodin Museum. Thereafter, he lived in a country house acquired in the early 1960s, Les Busclats, between Fontaine-de-Vaucluse and L'Isle-sur-la-Sorgue.

In 1985 Gallimard published Char's penultimate collection, *Les Voisinages de Van Gogh* (Van Gogh's Proximity). Van Gogh stands, in one sense, for poetry that Char felt to be just as misunderstood as the painter's works had originally been. *Les Voisinages de Van Gogh* comprises only nineteen poems, but it holds pleasant surprises. The first poem, "L'Avant-Glanum" (Before Glanum), refers directly to Van Gogh's Arles period, which, though brilliant, ended in his self-mutilation, but alludes as well to the vast amount of work the painter accomplished during his subsequent stay in the asylum in Saint-Rémy, a town east of the Rhone river in the Alpilles region of Provence. (Saint-Rémy contains the ruins of the ancient Roman town of Glanum.) Although the reader can certainly find allusions to Van Gogh's work in each of the poems of this collection, it is perhaps best to focus on the spiritual affinities that the poet shares with the painter. In "Pierres vertes" (Green Stones) poetry is described as "l'accrue du mot" (the word's rising tide), and poetry helps Char regain the intensity he sees in Van Gogh's colors, as related in "L'irréflexion": ". . . nous nous sommes emplis d'un souffle précipité jusqu'à l'extinction de la dernière couleur" (. . . we filled ourselves with a quickened breath until the last color was extinguished). A high, almost plaintive note marks several poems in *Les Voisinages de Van Gogh.* In "La longue partance" (The Long Moment Before Departure) Char writes as if he were already beyond the verge of death and could cast a retrospective glance on his own life: ". . . j'ai oublié l'essentiel des restes de ma vie là-bas, là-bas, magnétisant encore" (. . . I have left the essential vestiges of my life down there, down there, still attracting).

Char suffered another heart attack in October 1985, six months after the publication of *Les Voisinages de Van Gogh.* He was married for a second time, on 17 October 1987, a month before he submitted to Gallimard the final version of his last poetry collection, *Eloge d'une Soupçonnée* (1988).

After Char's death from heart failure on 19 February 1988, his second wife, Marie-Claude de Saint-Seine, oversaw the preparation and publication of two other important works. The first, *René Char: Faire du chemin avec . . .* (René Char: Walk the Path With . . . , 1992), is the catalogue of an exhibit devoted to Char at the Papal Palace in Avignon. (This work should not be confused with the short book and poem with a similar title.) *René Char: Faire du chemin avec . . .* includes much biographical material, including photographs of the author, his friends and family, and his illuminated manuscripts. Marie-Claude Char also edited the selection of Char's poetry and prose published in the Gallimard "Quarto" collection, *Dans l'atelier du poète: René Char* (In the Poet's Studio, 1996), which has a rich iconography. *Dans l'atelier du poète* complements the Gallimard Bibliothèque de la Pléiade edition of Char's works, the second edition of which, in 1995, was considerably augmented and included *Les Voisinages de Van Gogh* and *Eloge d'une Soupçonnée*.

The posthumous collection *Eloge d'une Soupçonnée* is relatively sparse–twenty pages, thirteen poems–but includes works with interesting biographical and aesthetic implications. The opening poem, "Riche de larmes" (Rich with Tears), is arguably the masterpiece of the volume, and its quality is commensurate with Char's best poems. The landmark traits of his ethics and poetic style are present, and the tone is nostalgic and tragic. Two of Char's exemplary figures of creativity and suffering, Staël and Mandelstam, make a final appearance in the poet's gallery. His intermittent muse, first represented in the guise of Artine in 1930, reappears at the beginning of "Riche de larmes" as the "Passante" (Passerby) and the "Aimée" (Beloved) who accompanies and protects Char's "fruits tardifs" (late fruits), that is, his late poems. Not surprisingly, site plays a large role in "Riche de larmes." At the midpoint of the poem, Char depicts an elevated plateau that his creative energy attains as if in ecstasy and then abandons in search of new landscapes and further poems. The poet must seek a release in writing, since at death no transcendence beyond the word awaits the poet: "Laissons l'énergie et retournons à l'énergie" (Let us leave energy, and let us return to energy), he says in a semblance of materialism.

Char did not particularly welcome queries about his life but "Riche de larmes" shows that he saw his career as a lifelong devotion to poetry, the *soupçonnée* or "Suspected One." Suffering and ecstasy, loyalty to friends, and resistance against a society hostile to art and poetry, are restated here as the tenets, or rich tears, of Char's poetics. Other poems in *Eloge d'une Soupçonnée* evoke the impending loss of poetry, life, and the spectacle of nature that Char so enjoyed. Poetry, "the one under suspicion," must resist the fate of extinction that befell the wolves of Mont Ventoux, as related in the poem "Bestiaire dans mon trèfle" (Bestiary in My Clover). "L'Amante" (The Mistress) closes the collection on a typical note of defiance: the force of love temporarily dulls death's edge. *Eloge d'une Soupçonnée* gives a last image of René Char that is appropriate to his life work. Love and poetry coalesce against an outer world that resists their vivid forces.

Letters:
Correspondance 1935–1970: René Char, Jean Ballard, edited by Jeannine Baude (Mézière-sur-Issoire: Rougerie, 1993).

Interviews:
Jacques Charpier, "Une matinée avec René Char," *Combat,* 16 February 1950, p. 4;

Pierre Berger, "Conversation avec René Char," *La Gazette des lettres,* 8 (15 June 1952): 8–14;

Pierre de Boisdeffre, "Poésie vivante: René Char," *Les Nouvelles littéraires,* 12 February 1959, p. 7;

René Char and France Huser, "Sous ma casquette amarante. Entretiens avec France Huser," *Le Nouvel observateur,* 3 March 1980; revised version, *Œuvres complètes* by Char (Paris: Gallimard, 1983), pp. 819–838.

Bibliographies:
Pierre-André Benoit, *Bibliographie des œuvres de René Char de 1928 à 1963* (Ribaute-les-Tavernes: Le Demi-Jour, 1964);

Lucie Jamme and Franck André Jamme, "Bibliographie," in *René Char: Œuvres complètes,* second edition (Paris: Gallimard, 1995), pp. 1409–1441.

References:
Anna Balakian, "Se mesurer avec le vent," special Char issue, *Europe,* 705–706 (January–February 1988): 16–23;

Pierre Berger, *René Char: Une Essai,* Poètes d'aujourd'hui, no. 22 (Paris: Seghers, 1951);

Michael Bishop, *René Char: Les Dernières années* (Amsterdam & Atlanta: Rodopi, 1990);

Maurice Blanchot, *La Bête de Lascaux* (Paris: Editions G.L.M., 1958; new edition, Montpellier: Fata Morgana, 1982);

Blanchot, "René Char," in his *La Part du feu* (Paris: Gallimard, 1949), pp. 103–114;

Blanchot, "René Char et la pensée du neutre" and "Parole de fragment," in his *L'entretien infini* (Paris: Gallimard, 1969), pp. 439–455;

Nathan Bracher, "Au–delà du mot: Métaphore et métonymie dans 'Donnerbach Mühle' de René Char," *French Review,* 64, no. 3 (1991): 428–436;

L. C. Breunig, "René Char in English," special Char issue, *World Literature Today,* 51, no. 3 (1977): 396–400;

Mary Ann Caws, *L'Œuvre filante de René Char* (Paris: A.-G. Nizet, 1981);

Caws, *The Presence of René Char* (Princeton: Princeton University Press, 1976);

Caws, *René Char* (Boston: Twayne, 1977);

Marie-Claude Char, *René Char: Faire du chemin avec . . .* (Paris: Gallimard, 1992);

Antoine Coron, ed., *René Char: Manuscrits enluminés par des peintres du XXe siècle,* introduction by Georges Le Rider (Paris: Bibliothèque Nationale, 1980);

Mechthild Cranston, *Orion Resurgent: René Char, Poet of Presence* (Madrid: J. P. Turanzas, 1979);

Christine Dupouy, *René Char* (Paris: Belfond, 1987);

Dominique Fourcade, ed., *René Char* (Paris: L'Herne, 1971);

Virginia A. La Charité, *The Poetics and the Poetry of René Char* (Chapel Hill: University of North Carolina Press, 1968);

La Charité, "René Char and the Ascendancy of Night," *French Forum,* 1 (1973): 269–280;

La Charité, "The Role of Rimbaud in Char's Poetry," *PMLA,* 89 (1974): 57–63;

James R. Lawler, *René Char: The Myth and the Poem* (Princeton: Princeton University Press, 1978);

Eric Marty, *René Char,* Les Contemporains, no. 6 (Paris: Seuil, 1990);

Jean-Claude Mathieu, *La Poésie de René Char, ou, Le Sel de la splendeur,* 2 volumes (Paris: José Corti, 1984, 1985);

Jean-Pierre Maulpoix, *Fureur et mystère de René Char* (Paris: Gallimard, 1996);

Philippe Met, *Formules de la poésie: Etudes sur Ponge, Leiris, Char et Du Bouchet* (Paris: Presses Universitaires de France, 1999);

Charles D. Minahen, ed., *Figuring Things: Char, Ponge, and Poetry in the Twentieth Century* (Lexington, Ky.: French Forum, 1994);

Georges Mounin, *La Communication poétique, précédé de Avez-vous lu Char?* (Paris: Gallimard, 1969);

Edmond Nogacki, *René Char, Orion pigmenté d'infini, ou, De l'écriture à la peinture (enluminures, illustrations, poèmes-objets)* (Valenciennes: Presses Universitaires de Valenciennes, 1992);

Carrie Noland, "*Messages personnels:* Radio, Cryptography, and the Resistance Poetry of René Char," in *Poetry at Stake: Lyric Aesthetics and the Challenge of Technology* (Princeton: Princeton University Press, 1999), pp. 141–162;

Jean Pénard, *Rencontres avec René Char,* Collection En lisant en écrivant (Paris: José Corti, 1991);

Paule Plouvier, ed., *René Char 10 ans après* (Paris: L'Harmattan, 2000);

Jean-Dominique Poli, *Pour René Char: La Place de l'origine,* foreword by Yves Battistini (La Rochelle: Rumeur des Ages, 1997);

Georges Poulet, "René Char: De la constriction à la dissémination," special Char issue, *L'Arc,* 22 (1963): 33–45;

Greta Rau, *René Char ou, La Poésie accrue* (Paris: José Corti, 1957);

Jean-Pierre Richard, "René Char ou la contradiction résolue," in his *Onze études sur la poésie moderne* (Paris: Seuil, 1964), pp. 67–103;

Jean Starobinski, "René Char et la définition du poème," special Char issue, *Liberté,* 10, no. 4 (1968): 13–28; translated by Minahen as "René Char and the Definition of the Poem" in *Figuring Things: Char, Ponge, and Poetry in the Twentieth Century,* edited by Charles D. Minahen (Lexington, Ky.: French Forum, 1994), pp. 113–127;

Serge Velay, *René Char: L'Eblouissement et la fureur* (Paris: Editions Olbia, 1998);

Paul Veyne, *René Char en ses poèmes* (Paris: Gallimard, 1990);

Jean Voellmy, *René Char, ou, Le Mystère partagé* (Seyssel: Champ Vallon, 1989).

Papers:

A significant collection of René Char's manuscripts and letters is in the Fonds René Char, Bibliothèque Littéraire Jacques Doucet, Paris. The Bibliothèque Nationale, Paris, has a major collection of Char's manuscripts illustrated by artists.

Paul Claudel
(6 August 1868 – 23 February 1955)

Paul Matthieu St-Pierre
Simon Fraser University

See also the Claudel entry in *DLB 192: French Dramatists, 1789–1914.*

BOOKS: *Tête d'or,* anonymous (Paris: Librairie de l'Art Indépendant, 1890; revised edition, as Claudel, in *L'Arbre,* Paris: Mercure de France, 1901); revised edition translated by John Strong Newberry as *Tête d'or: A Play in Three Acts* (New Haven: Yale University Press / London: Milford, 1919);

La Ville, anonymous (Paris: Librairie de l'Art Indépendant, 1893; revised edition, as Claudel, in *L'Arbre,* Paris: Mercure de France, 1901); translated, based on both editions, by Newberry as *The City: A Play* (New Haven: Yale University Press, 1920);

Connaissance de l'Est (Paris: Mercure de France, 1900; enlarged, 1907); enlarged edition translated by Teresa Frances and William Rose Benét as *The East I Know* (New Haven: Yale University Press, 1914);

L'Arbre (Paris: Mercure de France, 1901)—comprises *L'Echange, Le Repos du septième jour, Tête d'or* (revised edition), *La Ville* (revised edition), and *La Jeune Fille Violaine* (revised edition);

Connaissance du temps (Fou-Tchou, China: Rozario, 1904);

Ode: Les Muses (Paris: Bibliothèque de l'Occident, 1905); translated by Edward Lucie-Smith as *The Muses* (London: Turret, 1967);

Partage de midi (Paris: Bibliothèque de l'Occident, 1906; republished, with a new preface, Paris: Mercure de France, 1948; revised edition, Paris: Gallimard, 1949); translated by Wallace Fowlie as *Break of Noon* (Chicago: Regnery, 1960);

Art poétique (Paris: Mercure de France, 1907); translated by Renée Spodheim as *Poetic Art* (New York: Philosophical Library, 1948);

Cinq grandes odes, suivies d'un processionnal pour saluer le siècle nouveau (Paris: Bibliothèque de l'Occident, 1910); translated by Lucie-Smith as *Five Great Odes* (Lon-

Paul Claudel (photograph Paris-Match)

don: Rapp & Carroll, 1967; Chester Springs, Pa.: Dufour, 1970);

Théâtre, first series, 4 volumes (Paris: Mercure de France, 1910–1912)—volume 4 (1912) comprises *Le Repos du septième jour, L'Agamemnon d'Eschyle,* and *Vers d'exil;*

L'Otage: Drame en trois actes (Paris: Editions de la Nouvelle Revue Française, 1911); translated by Pierre Chavannes as *The Hostage: A Drama* (New Haven: Yale University Press, 1917 / London: Oxford University Press, 1917);

Le Chemin de la Croix (Brussels: Durendal, 1911; Paris: Librairie de l'Art Catholique, 1914); translated by

126

John J. Burke as *Stations of the Cross* (New York: Paulist Press, 1937);

L'Annonce faite à Marie: Mystère en quatre actes et un prologue (Paris: Editions de la Nouvelle Revue Française, 1912); translated by Louise Morgan Sill as *The Tidings Brought to Mary: A Mystery* (New Haven: Yale University Press, 1916; London: Chatto & Windus, 1916);

Cette heure qui est entre le printemps et l'été: Cantate à trois voix (Paris: Editions de la Nouvelle Revue Française, 1913);

Deux poèmes d'été: La Cantate à trois voix; Protée: Drame satirique (Paris: Editions de la Nouvelle Revue Française, 1914);

Corona benignitatis anni Dei (Paris: Editions de la Nouvelle Revue Française, 1915); translated by Sister Mary David as *Coronal* (New York: Pantheon, 1943);

La Nuit de Noël 1914 (Paris: Librairie de l'Art Catholique, 1915);

Trois poèmes de guerre (Paris: Editions de la Nouvelle Revue Française, 1915); translated by Edward J. O'Brien as *Three Poems of the War*, introduction by Chavannes (New Haven: Yale University Press, 1919 / London: Oxford University Press, 1919);

Autres poèmes durant la guerre (Paris: Editions de la Nouvelle Revue Française, 1916);

Sainte Thérèse (Paris: Beltrand, 1916);

L'Homme et son désir (Paris: Editions de la Nouvelle Revue Française, 1918);

Le Pain dur: Drame en trois actes (Paris: Editions de la Nouvelle Revue Française, 1918); translated by John Heard as *Crusts* in *Three Plays: The Hostage, Crusts, The Humiliation of the Father* (Boston: J. W. Luce, 1945);

Sainte Cécile: Poème (Paris: Librairie de l'Art Catholique, 1918);

La Messe là-bas (Paris: Editions de la Nouvelle Revue Française, 1919);

Protée: Drame satyrique en deux actes (Paris: Editions de la Nouvelle Revue Française, 1919);

L'Ours et la lune: Farce pour un théâtre de marionnettes (Paris: Editions de la Nouvelle Revue Française, 1919);

Introduction à quelques œuvres: Conférence faite le 30 mai 1919 au Théâtre du Gymnase pour la maison des amis des livres (Paris: Adrienne Monnier, 1920);

Le Père humilié: Drame en quatre actes (Paris: Editions de la Nouvelle Revue Française, 1920; revised edition, Paris: Gallimard, 1945); original edition translated by Heard as *The Humiliation of the Father*, in *Three Plays: The Hostage, Crusts, The Humiliation of the Father* (Boston: J. W. Luce, 1945);

Ode jubilaire: Pour le six-centième anniversaire de la mort de Dante (Paris: Editions de la Nouvelle Revue Française, 1921);

Verlaine (Paris: Editions de la Nouvelle Revue Française, 1922);

Un Coup d'œil sur l'âme japonaise: Discours aux étudiants de Nikko (Paris: Editions de la Nouvelle Revue Française, 1923);

Sainte Geneviève (Tokyo: Chinchiocha, 1923);

A travers les villes en flammes: Note d'un témoin (Paris: E. Champion, 1924);

Morceaux choisis, avec un portrait et un autographe de l'auteur (Paris: Gallimard/Editions de la Nouvelle Revue Française, 1925);

Feuilles de saints (Paris: Editions de la Nouvelle Revue Française, 1925);

L'Endormie (Paris: E. Champion, 1925);

Le Soulier de satin, première journée (Paris: Plon, 1925); revised and enlarged as *Le Soulier de satin, ou le pire n'est pas toujours sûr: Action espagnole en quatre journées*, 4 volumes (Paris: Gallimard, 1928–1929); translated by John O'Connor and Claudel as *The Satin Slipper; or, The Worst Is Not the Surest* (New York & London: Sheed & Ward, 1931);

La Jeune fille Violaine, original version, preface by Jean Royère (Paris: Excelsior, 1926);

La Parabole du festin, as Delachapelle (Paris: Ronald Davis, 1926); republished as *La Sagesse ou La Parabole du festin* (Paris: Gallimard, 1939);

La Philosophie du livre (Maastricht, The Netherlands: Stols, 1926; Paris: Aveline, 1926);

Cent Phrases pour éventails (Tokyo: Koshiba, 1927; Paris: Gallimard, 1942);

L'Oiseau noir dans le Soleil Levant, engravings by Foujita (Paris: Excelsior, 1927; enlarged edition, Gallimard/Editions de la Nouvelle Revue Française, 1929);

Le Viellard sur le mont Omi (Paris: Le Livre, 1927);

Deux farces lyriques (Paris: Gallimard, 1927)—comprises *Protée* (revised version) and *L'Ours et la lune;*

Sous le rempart d'Athènes (Paris: Gallimard/Editions de la Nouvelle Revue Française, 1928);

Positions et propositions: Art et littérature, 2 volumes (Paris: Gallimard, 1928, 1934); volume 1 translated by O'Connor and Claudel as *Ways and Crossways* (New York & London: Sheed & Ward, 1933);

Le Livre de Christophe Colomb (Vienna: Edition Universelle, 1929; enlarged edition, Paris: Gallimard, 1935); original edition translated by Claudel, Agnes Meyer, and Darius Milhaud, as *The Book of Christopher Columbus: A Lyrical Drama in Two Parts* (New Haven: Yale University Press / London: Oxford University Press, 1930);

Le Voleur volé, suivi du Bon Samaritain (Paris: Emile-Paul Frères, 1930);

Cantate à trois voix; suivie de Sous le rempart d'Athènes, et de traductions diverses (Paris: Gallimard, 1931);

Sur la présence de Dieu (Vienna & Liguré: Aubin, 1932);

Jean Charlot (Paris: Gallimard, 1933);

Note sur l'art chrétien (Paris: Desclée de Brouwer, 1933);

Le Jardin aride: Parabole (Paris: Editions de la Nouvelle Revue Française, 1934);

Ecoute, ma fille (Paris: Gallimard, 1934);

La Légende de Prâkriti (Paris: Gallimard, 1934);

Conversations dans le Loir-et-Cher (Paris: Gallimard, 1935);

Introduction à la peinture hollandaise (Paris: Gallimard, 1935);

Figures et paraboles (Paris: Gallimard, 1936);

Les Aventures de Sophie (Paris: Gallimard, 1937);

Introduction au Livre de Ruth (Paris: Desclée de Brouwer, 1938);

Un Poète regarde la Croix (Paris: Gallimard, 1938); translated by Fowlie as *A Poet Before the Cross* (Chicago: Regnery, 1958);

La Mystique des pierres précieuses (Paris: Cartier, 1938);

Jeanne d'Arc au bûcher (Paris: Gallimard, 1939);

L'Epée et le miroir (Paris: Gallimard, 1939);

La Sagesse ou La Parabole du festin (Paris: Gallimard, 1939);

Contacts et circonstances (Paris: Gallimard, 1940);

Ainsi donc encore une fois (Paris: Gallimard, 1940);

L'Histoire de Tobie et de Sara: Moralité en trois actes (Paris: Gallimard, 1942);

Présence et prophétie (Fribourg, Switzerland: Editions de la Librairie de l'Université, 1942; Paris: Egloff, 1947);

Seigneur, apprenez-nous à prier (Paris: Gallimard, 1942); translated by Ruth Bethell as *Lord, Teach Us How to Pray* (London: Dobson, 1947; New York: Longmans, Green, 1948);

Prière pour les paralysés, suivie des Quinze Psaumes graduels CXIX à CXXIII (Paris: Horizons de France, 1944);

Poèmes et paroles durant la guerre de trente ans (Paris: Gallimard, 1945);

Visages radieux (Paris: Egloff, 1945; revised, 1947);

Dodoitzu: Poèmes de Paul Claudel, illustrated by Rihakou Haradu (Paris: Gallimard, 1945);

Le Livre de Job (Paris: Plon, 1946);

Les Révélations de la Salette (Paris: Table Ronde, 1946);

Un Hommage à la poésie (Nantes: Editions de Fleuve, 1946);

L'Œil écoute (Paris: Gallimard, 1946); translated by Elsie Pell as *The Eye Listens* (New York: Philosophical Library, 1950);

Introduction à l'Apocalypse (Paris: Egloff, 1946);

La Rose et le rosaire (Paris: Egloff, 1946);

Chine, photographs by Hélène Hoppenot (Geneva: Skira, 1946);

Saint François (Paris: Gallimard, 1946);

Discours et remerciements (Paris: Gallimard, 1947);

Du côté de chez Ramuz (Neuchâtel, Switzerland: Ides et Calendes, 1947);

Laudes (Brussels: Editions de la Girouette, 1947);

Vézelay (Paris: Challamel, 1948);

Paul Claudel interroge le Cantique des cantiques (Paris: Egloff, 1948);

Sous le signe du dragon (Paris: Table Ronde, 1948);

Paul Claudel répond les psaumes (Neuchâtel, Switzerland: Ides et Calendes, 1948);

Accompagnements (Paris: Gallimard, 1949);

Emmaüs (Paris: Gallimard, 1949);

Œuvres complètes, 26 volumes, edited by Robert Mallet (Paris: Gallimard, 1950–1967);

Une Voix sur Israël (Paris: Gallimard, 1950);

Saint Thérèse de Lisieux vous parle, edited by the Benedictines of L'Abbaye Notre-Dame-du-Pré (Lisieux: L'Abbaye Notre-Dame-du-Pré, 1950);

L'Evangile d'Isaïe (Paris: Gallimard, 1951);

Paul Claudel interroge l'Apocalypse (Paris: Gallimard, 1952);

Le Symbolisme de la Salette (Paris: Gallimard, 1952);

Trois Figures saintes pour le temps actuel: Le Frère Charles, Sainte Thérèse de Lisieux, Eve Lavallière (Paris: Amyot-Dumont, 1953);

L'Echange, revised edition (Paris: Mercure de France, 1954); original edition translated by Donald L. Holley and Jean-Pierre Krémer as *The Trade/ L'Echange* (Woodbridge, Ont.: Editions Albion Press, 1995);

Mémoires improvisés, edited by Jean Amrouche (Paris: Gallimard, 1954);

J'aime la Bible (Paris: Arthème Fayard, 1955); translated by Wade Baskin as *The Essence of the Bible* (New York: Philosophical Library, 1957);

Conversation sur Jean Racine (Paris: Gallimard, 1956);

Qui ne souffre pas . . . réflexions sur le problème social (Paris: Gallimard, 1958);

Cahiers Paul Claudel, 13 volumes (Paris: Gallimard, 1959–1990)–includes volume 4, *Claudel, diplomate* (1962);

Je crois en Dieu, edited by Agnès du Sarment (Paris: Gallimard, 1961); translated by Helen Weaver as *I Believe in God: A Meditation on the Apostles' Creed,* edited by du Sarment (New York: Holt, Rinehart & Winston, 1963; London: Harvill, 1965);

Bréviare poétique (Paris: Gallimard, 1962);

Sainte Agnès, et poèmes inédits (Paris: Wesmael-Charlier, 1963);

Mes idées sur le théâtre, edited by Petit and Jean-Pierre Kempf (Paris: Gallimard, 1966); translated by Christine Trollope as *Claudel on the Theatre* (Coral Gables: University of Miami Press, 1972);

Le Figure d'Israël (Paris: Gallimard, 1968);

Journal, 2 volumes, edited by François Varillon and Petit (Paris: Gallimard, 1968, 1969);

Magnificat, bilingual edition, Spanish version by Alfonso Rubic (Monterrey, Mex.: Ediciones Sierra Madre, 1969);

Poésies (Paris: Gallimard, 1970);

Les Agendas de Chine, edited by Houriez (Lausanne, Switzerland & Paris: L'Age d'Homme, 1991);

Œuvres diplomatiques: Ambassadeur aux Etats-Unis, 1927–1933, edited by Lucile Garbagnati (Lausanne, Switzerland & Paris: L'Age d'Homme, 1994);

L'Arsenal de Fou-Tchéou: Œuvres consulaires, Chine 1895–1905, edited by Jacques Houriez (Lausanne, Switzerland & Paris: L'Age d'Homme, 1995);

Conversations écologiques, edited by Jean Bastaire (Cognac: Le Temps Qu'Il Fait, 2000).

Editions and Collections: *Poèmes de guerre, 1914–1916* (Paris: Editions de la Nouvelle Revue Française, 1922)–comprises *Trois poèmes de guerre, Autres poèmes durant la guerre,* and *La Nuit de Noël 1914;*

Paul Claudel dans ses plus beaux textes (Montreal: Varin, 1940);

Pages de prose, compiled and edited by André Blanchet (Paris: Gallimard, 1944);

La Perle noire, edited by Blanchet (Paris: Gallimard, 1947);

Théâtre, second series, 2 volumes, edited by Jacques Madaule (Paris: Gallimard, 1947, 1948);

La Bestiaire spirituel (Lausanne, Switzerland: Mermod, 1949);

Œuvre poétique, edited by Jacques Petit (Paris: Gallimard, 1957);

Réflexions sur la poésie, Collection Idées, no. 29 (Paris: Gallimard, 1963);

Œuvres en prose, edited by Petit and Charles Galpérine (Paris: Gallimard, 1965);

Au milieu des vitraux de l'Apocalypse, edited by Pierre Claudel and Petit (Paris: Gallimard, 1966);

Poèmes de Paul Claudel: Le Monde de Vézelay (Saint-Léger-Vauban: Zodiaque, 1967);

Le Poëte et le Shamisen; Le Poëte et le vase d'encens; Jules, ou, L'Homme-aux-deux-cravates, edited by Michel Malicet (Paris: Les Belles Lettres, 1970);

Richard Wagner: Rêverie d'un poète français, edited by Malicet (Paris: Les Belles Lettres, 1970);

Paul Claudel en verve, compiled and edited by Hubert Juin (Paris: Horay, 1971);

Supplément aux Œuvres complète, edited by Jacques Houriez and others, 4 volumes (Lausanne, Switzerland & Paris: L'Age d'Homme, 1990–1997);

Partage de midi: Un Drame revisité, 1948–1949, edited by Gérald Antoine (Paris: L'Age d'Homme, 1997).

Edition in English: *Two Dramas: Break of Noon, The Tidings Brought to Mary,* translated by Wallace Fowlie (Chicago: Regnery, 1960).

PLAY PRODUCTIONS: *L'Annonce faite à Marie,* Paris, Théâtre de l'Œuvre, 20 December 1912;

L'Otage, London, Scala Theatre, 1913; Paris, Théâtre de l'Œuvre, 2 June 1914;

L'Echange, Paris, Théâtre du Vieux-Colombier, 15 January 1914;

Protée, music by Darius Milhaud, Salzburg, 1914;

La Nuit de Noël 1914, read by Eve Francis, Paris, Université des Annales, March 1915;

Tête d'or, Paris, Théâtre du Gymnase, 30 May 1919; second version, Paris, Laboratoire de Théâtre, 25 April 1924;

Le Pain dur, act 2, scene 2, read by Francis and Jean Hervé, Paris, Théâtre du Gymnase, 30 May 1919; full theatrical version, Canada, 1943; Paris, Théâtre de l'Atelier, 12 March 1949;

L'Homme et son désir, music by Milhaud, Paris, Théâtre des Champs-Elysées, 6 June 1921;

Partage de midi, Paris, Groupe Art et Action, 12 November 1921; revised version, Paris, Théâtre Marigny, 17 December 1948;

La Femme et son ombre, Tokyo, Imperial Theater of Tokyo, 16 March 1923;

La Ville, reading at "Palais de Bois," 1926; translated into Dutch by Urbain Van de Voorde, Brussels, Salle Patria, 25 February 1931; French original, Paris, Théâtre National Populaire, 1955;

Sous le rempart d'Athènes, music by Germaine Tailleferre, Paris, Opéra, 26 October 1927;

Le Père humilié, Dresden, Schauspielhaus, 26 November 1928; Paris, Théâtre de l'Œuvre, 1941;

Christophe Colombus, music by Milhaud, Berlin, Staatsoper Unter den Linden, 30 June 1930; Paris, Salle Gustave Doré, 1937; as *Le Livre de Christophe Colomb,* without music, Paris, Vieux Colombier, 1947;

L'Agamemnon d'Eschyle, Les Choéphores d'Eschyle, Les Euménides d'Eschyle, adapted from Aeschylus's *Agamemnon, Choephoroi, Eumenides,* Brussels, Théâtre de la Monnaie, 27–28 March 1935; music by Milhaud, Berlin, Berlin Opera, 1963;

Jeanne d'Arc au bûcher, translated into German, Basel, 12 May 1938; original version, music by Arthur Honegger, Orléans, Théâtre Municipal d'Orléans, 6 May 1939;

La Danse des morts, music by Honegger, Paris, Claudel's home, 2 February 1939;

Le Soulier de satin, Paris, Comédie-Française, 23 November 1943;

Claudel in 1883

La Jeune Fille Violaine, Paris, Salle d'Iéna, 14 March 1944;

L'Histoire de Tobie et de Sara: Moralité en trois actes, Roubaix, Central Théâtre, 28 February 1947;

L'Ours et la lune, Algiers, 2 May 1948;

Le Festin de la sagesse, music by Milhaud, Rome, 15 February 1950;

La Cantate à trois voix, Marseille, Groupe Théâtral Universitaire d'Aix-Marseille, 27 May 1955.

PRODUCED SCRIPTS: *Les Eumenides d'Eschyle,* radio, Radio Belge, 18 November 1929;

Le Repos du septième jour, radio, music by Darius Milhaud, Radio Marseille, 2 November 1942;

Le Soulier de satin, radio, Radiodiffusion Française, 1942;

L'Otage, radio, Radiodiffusion Française, April 1947;

Les Choéphores d'Eschyle, radio, music by Milhaud, Radiodiffusion Française, 29 March 1949;

Tête d'or, radio, music by Arthur Honegger, Radiodiffusion Française, 24 January 1950;

L'Echange, radio, Radiodiffusion Française, 14 February 1950;

Protée, radio, music by Milhaud, Radiodiffusion Française, 16 May 1950;

Le Livre de Christophe Colomb, radio, music by Milhaud, Radiodiffusion Française, 10 October 1950;

L'Histoire de Tobie et de Sara, radio, music by Gaston Litaize, Radiodiffusion Française, 13 December 1951;

Jeanne d'Arc au bûcher, radio, Radiodiffusion Française, 26 September 1952;

L'Agamemnon d'Eschyle, radio, music by Jean Wiener, Radiodiffusion Française, 13 December 1952.

OTHER: Aeschylus, *L'Agamemnon d'Eschyle,* translated by Claudel (Fou-Tchou, China: Rozario, 1896);

Aeschylus, *Les Choéphores d'Eschyle,* translated by Claudel (Paris: Editions de la Nouvelle Revue Française, 1920);

Aeschylus, *Les Euménides d'Eschyle,* translated by Claudel (Paris: Editions de la Nouvelle Revue Française, 1920);

*Vitraux des cathédrales de France, XII*ᵉ *et XIII*ᵉ *siècles,* edited by H. M. Zbinden, preface by Claudel (Paris: Plon, 1937);

Les Sept psaumes de la pénitence: Traduit librement, avec un Examen de conscience (Paris: Seuil, 1945);

L'Europe: Paysages et civilisations (Paris: Egloff, 1947);

Le Mal est parmi nous, by Claudel and others (Paris: Plon, 1948);

Psaumes: Traductions 1918–1959, translated by Claudel, edited by Renée Nantet and Jacques Petit (Paris: Desclée de Brouwer, 1966).

Paul Claudel brought high distinction to France in his two careers as a writer and a politician. His collected works fill twenty-six volumes; his notebooks take up seven volumes; and his correspondence comprises twenty-one collections. He wrote poetry; plays; novels; essays; treatises; biographies; literary, art, and theater criticism; biblical commentary and exegesis; hagiography; and devotional works. He served in the French consular and diplomatic service in New York and Boston (1893–1895), Shanghai (1895–1905), Peking (1906–1909), Prague (1909–1911), Frankfurt and Hamburg (1912–1914), Paris and Rome (1915–1916), Rio de Janeiro (1917–1918), and Copenhagen (1919–1921). In the 1920s and 1930s he was the French ambassador to Japan (1921–1927), the United States (1927–1933), and Belgium (1933–1935). He managed to interweave both careers, writing about politics and politicizing the act of writing, without compromising his professional ambidexterity or conflicting his interests in political ideology and literary ideas. He was a loyal career diplomat and prolific academician. Had Claudel been only a consul and an ambassador, however, his exemplary life's work would have been recorded only in French government archives and a few publications. It is as the author of more than one hundred works of literature and criticism, several of them already established as classics of French letters, that Claudel will be read, performed, studied, discussed, and imitated for as long as the Republic survives.

Paul-Louis-Charles-Marie Claudel was born 6 August 1868 in the village of Villeneuve-sur-Fère, in the province of Aisne, northeast of Paris, the third child of Louis-Prosper Claudel, a government-employed mortgage conservator, and Louise-Athenaïs Cerveaux, a homemaker. Paul Claudel grew up in several nearby villages, wherever his father's work took him. In 1881 Louise-Athenaïs Claudel moved with the children to Paris, so that Paul's eldest sister, Camille, a sculptor, could attend art school. Prosper Claudel stayed behind to work. His parents' separation was Paul Claudel's second emotional crisis, coming as it did after he had attended the death from stomach cancer of his maternal grandfather, Athanase Cerveaux, that same year. In Paris, Claudel attended the Lycée Louis-le-Grand, where he found the competition fierce compared to what he had known in country schools.

In 1883 he failed the first part of the *baccalauréat,* the secondary-school examination giving university-entrance qualification, although he came first in French discourse, receiving the prize from the great philologist and historian Ernest Renan. Upon completing the *baccalauréat* in 1884, Claudel began to set his mind on writing and scholarship. After completing his year of philosophy and graduating with a license in law, he decided not to prepare for *le Conceil d'Etat,* but instead continued his studies at the Ecole Libre des Sciences Politiques, with plans to pursue a career in the foreign service. He received his diploma in 1888, and in 1890 took first place in his entrance examination for the diplomatic service, after the director of the Ecole Libre had encouraged Claudel to specialize in oriental languages. Meanwhile, he was awakening to the imaginative possibilities of literature and language. Reading Arthur Rimbaud's *Les Illuminations* (translated as *Illuminations,* 1953) when it was first published in 1886, Claudel was deeply moved, and he decided to become a writer. Between 1886 and 1888 he wrote his first play, *L'Endormie* (The Sleeper, 1925), a verse drama about a poet enamored with a sleeping beauty, who, when he goes to wake her, turns into *une femme terrible* (a dreadful woman). In 1887 he befriended the French Symbolist poet Stéphane Mallarmé, whose weekly artists' gatherings he attended, and who gave him encouragement in his writing. In 1889 he wrote the play *Tête d'or* (Head of Gold; translated, 1919), published in 1890, about a golden-headed boy who sets out to conquer the spiritual universe and the unknown spirit within himself. Claudel's own

tête-à-tête with God paralleled this drama, as in 1886 at the Christmas Day mass at Notre-Dame Cathedral he had experienced a mystical revelation and felt a renewal of his Roman Catholic faith, returning thereafter to sacramental observance. Throughout his diplomatic and literary careers from this point, Catholicism was his constant inspiration. In his 1890 play *La Ville* (translated as *The City,* 1920), first published in 1893 and republished in a revised version in 1901, he symbolically depicts some of the evils he had experienced as a country boy growing up in Paris. In his vision, the city is a depersonalizing creature, robbing free French citizens of their identities. Upon entering the foreign service, Claudel carried this vision with him to New York, where he served as vice consul in 1893, and to Boston, where he headed the consulate from 1893 to 1895, and where, as a Frenchman, he felt uprooted. As well as conducting his consular duties in New York, he wrote a play, *L'Echange* (The Exchange), about the exchanges of fidelity and betrayal, and of life and death. The dominant mood of the play is that of the Old Testament Book of Lamentations, as characters voice their collective ennui, at once existentialist and spirited, as in this exchange:

LECHY ELCERNON. –Il est midi et la journée est partagée en deux.
Le soleil dévore l'ombre de nos corps, marquant l'heure qui n'est point l'heure: midi.
Et voici que l'ombre tourne, changeant de côté.

LOUIS LAINE. –Si cette brise ne tombe pas, nous pourrions faire une jolie promenade ce soir dans le bateau.

(LECHY ELCERNON. –It's noon and the day is cut in two.
The sun devours the shadow of our bodies, marking the hour that is not an hour at all: midday.
And here the shadow turns, changing sides.

LOUIS LAINE. –If this breeze doesn't die down, we could have a nice sail this evening in the boat).
(translation by St-Pierre)

L'Echange first appeared in the magazine *L'Ermitage* (1900) and was later published in the collection *L'Arbre* (The Tree, 1901), along with *Tête d'or* and *La Ville.* Claudel's next consular appointment took him to Shanghai in 1895, where he researched and wrote *Connaissance de l'Est* (1900; translated as *The East I Know,* 1914), in which Claudel measures Buddhism by the yardstick of his Catholicism and the Aristotelian and Thomistic philosophy he was then studying, and finds it wanting, as in the dialectic "Le Poète et le vase d'encens" (The Poet and the Vessel of Incense):

Louis-Prosper Claudel (standing at left) with Paul Claudel (on his left); directly in front of him is Paul's eldest sister, Camille; in front of her is their mother, Louise-Athenaïs, and their sister, Louise, circa 1886–1887; the other people in the photograph are not identified.

LE VASE D'ENCENS. —Si tu suis ton idée avec logique, tu finiras par tout retrouver. Je t'aiderai. Et je commence par poser la question: Qu'est-ce que l'étang?

LE POËTE. —L'étang, c'est l'eau immobile.

LE VASE D'ENCENS. —Le miroir. L'eau qui commence à refléter dès qu'elle s'arrête. Pareille au néant, image du vide et reflet du tout.

LE POËTE. —L'eau thésaurisée et stagnante, exactement adéquate à son cadre. A l'état de niveau. Immobile. Consciente d'elle-même, jouissant d'elle-même, communiquant avec elle-même, totalisée dans le poids, échappant à l'éternité par le moment.

(THE VESSEL OF INCENSE. —If you follow your idea logically, you will end up seeing everything again. I will help you. And I start by asking the question: What is the pool?

THE POET. —The pool is still water.

THE VESSEL OF INCENSE. —The mirror. Water that starts to reflect the minute it comes to rest. Just like nothing, image of emptiness and reflection of all.

THE POET. —Water hoarded up and stagnant, appropriate to its surroundings. In a level state. Still. Conscious of itself, taking pleasure in itself, in communication with itself, adding up to its own weight, escaping eternity in the moment).
(translation by St-Pierre)

Here the poet disturbs the tranquil surface of Buddhist philosophy and measures the symbol of the pond against the principles of Aristotelian unity and Thomistic self-consciousness.

Claudel wrote two other plays while in China: *La Jeune fille Violaine* (The Young Girl Violaine, 1901) and *Le Repos du septième jour* (The Rest of the Seventh Day, 1901). But his Chinese work with the greatest application to his body of work as a whole is *Art poétique* (1907; translated as *Poetic Art,* 1948). A Scholastic manifesto and mission statement, it is simultaneously an epistemology of time, a discourse on the secular world, and a salvation history of the Roman Catholic Church. His discussion of the art of poetry, however, is philosophically and theologically heterodox:

Dieu, étant toute l'existence, ne peut permettre à rien d'exister aussi, qu'à la condition de s'exclure à sa mode de Lui. L'homme, ce témoin vertical, ne peut constater, en fin d'analyse de la matière, que le fait pur mathématique, le mouvement. Tout *périt*. L'univers n'est qu'une manière totale de ne pas être ce qui est. Que disent donc les sceptiques et quelle n'est pas la sécurité de notre connaissance! Certes, et nous avec, le monde existe; certes, il est, puisqu'il est ce qui n'est pas.

(God, being the whole of existence, cannot permit anything else to exist also, except as it is excluded from Him, each in its own way. Man, this upright witness, can see, in the final analysis, only the purely mathematical fact, movement. Everything *perishes*. The universe is just a total manner of not being what is. What then do the skeptics say and how secure is our knowledge! Most certainly, and together with us, the world exists; indeed, it is, since it is what is not).
(translation by St-Pierre)

In this passage Claudel combines the Buddhist concept of nothingness, of everything at once present and absent, with the Christian theology of omnipresence and exclusivity, to produce his own negating heterodoxy of existence, that-who-is as that-which-is-not.

In China, Claudel developed his skills as a dramatist and as a poet. He worked on two versions of his medieval mystery play *La Jeune fille Violaine*. He drafted the first version in 1892 and a revised version from 1899 to 1900, which was published in *L'Arbre*. The first version was published in 1926, with a preface by Jean Royère. Violaine's stilted death speech in the first version, "Emportez-moi d'ici, car ce n'est point ici ma maison. / J'ai cédé ma part" (Carry me away from here, since this is not my home. / I have given up my part), becomes poetic in the second version: "Mais est-ce qu'il n'est pas bon aussi de mourir? Alors que tout est fini et que s'étend sur nous / L'obscurcissement, comme d'un ombrage très obscur" (But is it not good also to die? When it's all over and the twilight stretches out over us, like a very dark shade [translations by St-Pierre]). A third version of the play, which he wrote in 1911, became his masterpiece *L'Annonce faite à Marie* (1912; translated as *The Tidings Brought to Mary*, 1916). In 1896 or 1897 he wrote *Le Repos du septième jour,* which was first published in *L'Arbre*. This play, a funerary drama, is set in two "other worlds": the eternal day of the dead–the afterlife–and China, a country of mystery to most outsiders. In *Vers d'exil*, a sequence of eleven numbered monologue poems, he expressed something of his own sense of exile and deracination. Yet, his exilic mood is also playful, as in the poem "II":

> Je ne sais plus jouer! je n'ai plus de plaisir
> A travailler, je n'ai plus de plaisir à rire!
> Comme un homme inquiet le mot qu'il vient d'écrire,
> J'oublie et mon attente est longue et mon loisir.
>
> (I don't know how to play anymore! I no longer enjoy
> Working, I no longer enjoy laughing!
> Like a restless man the word comes to be written,
> I forget and my wait is long and my spare time).
> (translation by St-Pierre)

Writing the poems in *Vers d'exil* helped Claudel survive his isolation and his long stay in China, and it also helped him refine his poetics. He published most of the poems in the periodical *L'Ermitage* (15 July 1905), and these poems were collected in volume four of the first series of his *Théâtre* (1912), but the collection in its entirety appeared first in volume one of his *Œuvres complètes* (1950).

Upon returning to France in 1900, Claudel attempted to give up both his diplomatic and his literary careers, becoming a postulant at L'Abbaye Saint-Martin de Ligugé, the great Benedictine monastery. Although his spiritual directors eventually ruled he did not have a religious vocation, his six months at Ligugé, including his crisis over being rejected, were important both to his spiritual formation and also to his formation as a writer who saw himself, and whom France came to see, as distinctively Roman Catholic. Returning to

China in 1901, he had a shipboard romance with a married Polish woman, Rose Vetch, which developed into a three-year affair and included the birth of a child. China was then at the height of the Boxer Rebellion and, as a diplomat, Claudel was the target of some Chinese antiforeigner sentiment. Over the next four years his Benedictine training gave him courage to draw on in the face of rancor and violence. It also gave him the discipline and resolve to continue with his mainly self-directed training as a writer. During this time he developed what proved to be a lifelong friendship with Philippe Berthelot, a fellow French diplomat.

Returning to France in 1905, Claudel resumed his career as a dramatist and a poet, writing *Partage de midi* (translated as *Break of Noon,* 1960), which was published in 1906 but not produced until 1948, when it premiered, in a slightly altered version, in a production by Compagnie Madeleine Renaud–Jean-Louis Barrault, in Paris. His first sustained play, it reflects not only the self-discipline he learned during his sojourn in China but also the spirit of abandon he felt in his relationship with Vetch. It is a stylized four-character play comprising the six possibilities of two-person dialogues in protracted conversations and fervently enacted speeches, as well as some of Claudel's greatest confessional poetry, such as "Cantique de Mesa" (Mesa's Canticle), in which Mesa, having recently left the seminary, wavers between his longing for God and for Ysé, with whom he is voyaging to China:

> Pourquoi cette femme? pourquoi la femme tout d'un coup
>   sur ce bateau?
> Qu'est-ce qu'elle s'en vient faire avec nous? est-ce que
>   nous avions besoin d'elle? Vous seul!
> Vous seul en moi tout d'un coup à la naissance de la Vie,
> Vous avez été en moi la victoire et la visitation et le nom-
>   bre et l'étonnement et la puissance et la merveille et le
>   son!
> Et cette autre, est-ce que nous croyions en elle? et que le
>   bonheur est entre ses bras?
>
> (Why this woman? why the woman all of a sudden on the
>   boat?
> What does she come along to do with us? did we need
>   her? You alone!
> You alone and me suddenly at the origin of Life,
> You have been the victory in me and the visitation and the
>   number and the wonder and the power and the marvel
>   and the sound!
> And this other, did we believe in her? and that goodness is
>   in her arms?)
> (translation by St-Pierre)

Throughout the play Mesa responds to Ysé not as to a temptress but–in spite of the fact that her husband and children accompany her on board–as to a goddess who has taken the place of God, who has rejected him as a

Page from the manuscript for the first draft (1890) of Claudel's 1893 play, La Ville *(Bibliothèque Nationale, Paris)*

priest. In dramatic discourse Claudel acts out his own spiritual crises of faith and of love. He resolved both crises in his own life when, in 1906, with the blessing of his spiritual adviser, he married Reine Sainte-Marie Perin, and the couple settled in Peking, where Paul Claudel had his next consular appointment and where Reine Claudel gave birth to a daughter, Marie, in 1906, the first of their five children. A son, Pierre, was also born in China in 1908. Leaving Peking in 1909, Paul Claudel and his family moved to his next appointment, in Prague, where their daughter Reine was born the following year. Another son, Henri, was born in Hamburg two years later, and their third daughter, Renée, was born in Rio de Janeiro in 1917.

Although he resolved his crises of faith and love, Claudel left unresolved the issue of passion common to faith and love, which he continued to explore in the trilogy comprising *L'Otage: Drame en trois actes* (1911; translated as *The Hostage: A Drama,* 1917), composed in 1908–1910; *Le Pain dur: Drame en trois actes* (Hard Bread: Drama in Three Acts, 1918; translated as *Crusts,* 1945), written in 1913–1914; and *Le Père humilié: Drame en quatre actes* (1920; translated as *The Humiliation of the Father,* 1945), written in 1915–1916. *L'Otage,* which Claudel wrote in Peking and Prague, first appeared, act by act, in three issues of the *Nouvelle Revue française* (1910–1911), and was published in book form in 1911. It premiered in 1913 at the Scala Theatre, London, and was produced in Paris at the Théâtre de l'Œuvre the following year. The play is set in 1812, in the old Cistercian monastery of Coûfontaine, which one of the protagonists, Sygne de Coûfontaine, has recently purchased. The hostage of the title is Le Pape Pie (Pope Pius; modeled on the historical Pius VII), whom Napoleon had imprisoned, and whom Georges Coûfontaine, Sygne's cousin, manages to free and to hide on the estate. To preserve the secrecy of the Pope's asylum, Sygne is forced to marry Baron Toussaint Turelure, a villain who had been instrumental in sacking the abbey during the French Revolution. Her mixed allegiances to her cousin and her husband, and to her church and her country, provide the melodramatic impasse in this historical tragedy. Here Sygne shows a dark, Jeanne d'Arc–like defiance:

SYGNE. –Je n'épouserai point Toussaint Turelure!

MONSIEUR BADILON. –La vie de Georges aussi est en sa puissance.

SYGNE . –Qu'il meure, comme je suis prête à mourir! Sommes-nous éternals?
Dieu m'a donné la vie et me voici prompte à la rendre.

Mais le nom est à moi! mon honneur de femme est à moi seule!

(SYGNE. –I will not marry Toussaint Turelure!

MONSIEUR BADILON. –Georges' life also is in his power.

SYGNE. –Let him die, as I am ready to die! Are we eternal?
God gave me my life and here I am ready to give it back.

But my name is mine! my woman's honor is mine alone!).
(translation by St-Pierre)

Later she recants, makes her confession to le Curé Badilon, and marries Turelure, but her protestation in this passage, like her name, is *un signe* (a sign) that stays with her throughout her marriage, even after she gives birth to a son, until her death, which reveals her to have been the hostage of Turelure and to history. Claudel represents her tragic vindication in a deathbed confession scene with Badilon: twice Sygne refuses to forgive Turelure, indicating her position not in words but in signs, in a dramatic gesture, a sweep of the hand, and the stage direction *"Signe que non"* (sign in the negative). Badilon acknowledges her triumph, while she is still alive, when he calls her, like Jeanne d'Arc, "Sygne, soldat de Dieu" (Sygne, soldier of God).

In *Le Pain dur,* first produced in Canada in 1943 and then in Paris in 1949, the protagonist is Sygne's son, Louis, now an adult. Bankrupt after the failure of his colonial enterprises in Africa, Louis blames his father, Turelure, who is partly responsible for the failure of Louis's plantation, and whose mistress, Sichel Habernichts, is in love with Louis. Louis, however, is engaged to Lumîr, a Polish entrepreneur who spirited money from the Polish treasury to fund Louis's plantation and now needs to take it back. In his depiction of the give-and-take of entrepreneurs and enterprises, Claudel satirizes human propensities toward avarice and exploitation. He also tries to subvert colonialism by blurring the lines that separate servants from masters in French colonial history and thereby undermining the official version of that history. The Senegalese poet Léopold Sédar Senghor acknowledged Claudel's anticolonial stance when he wrote in 1973 that "il y a des *convergences* entre la parole claudélienne et la parole négro-africaine" (there are *convergences* between Claudel's speech and Black African speech [St-Pierre's translation]). Claudel voices much of his anticolonial discourse through Lumîr. Addressing Louis as "soldat de la Légion étrangère" (soldier of the Foreign Legion),

Tous les deux nous avons servi sur la terre
d'Afrique, sous un drapeau qui n'est pas le

nôtre, pour une cause qui ne nous intéresse pas
    Pour l'honneur du Corps,
Sans amis, sans argent, sans famille, sans
maître, sans Dieu
Estimant que ce n'est pas trop de l'esclavage pour payer
    cette demi-liberté!

(We have both served in Africa, under a flag that is not
    our own, for a
cause that does not interest us,
    For the honor of the Corps,
Without friends, without money, without family, without
master, without God,
Estimating that it is no more than slavery
to pay for this half-freedom!)
(translation by St-Pierre)

Lumîr is *une lumière* (a light) that exposes imperialism as enslavement, and the profiteering mentality of colonial endeavor as the moral debt of slave masters who fancy themselves "sans maître" (without master) and who act as if "sans Dieu" (without God).

The final volume of the "Otage" trilogy is *Le Père humilié,* which premiered in Dresden in 1928 before its first major production in Paris in 1941. In this play Le Pape Pie is the center of the dramatic action. The play is set in 1869. Louis Turelure, now le Comte de Coûfontaine, is an old man and the French ambassador in Rome, where he lives with his wife, Sichel, and their daughter, Pensée, who, physically blind, is prescient, flexible, perceptive, and, as her name suggests, thoughtful. Pensée is the object of affection of two brothers, nephews of the Pope: Orian, with whom she is in love, and Orso, who loves her secretly, by the code of courtly love, in which the unrequited lover resigns himself to loving from a distance. After Orian and Orso go off to fight in the Franco-Prussian War, Pensée learns that she is pregnant, but when Orian, the father, is killed in battle, she agrees to marry Orso, because, according to Orso, it was his brother's wish, and to legitimize the birth and give the child a family, though still under the conditions of courtly love. The Pope has frowned on the idea of her marrying either of his nephews, because Turelure is his enemy, a threat to the Vatican, and because Pensée is Jewish. The "humiliated father" of the title is at once the Holy Father, whose papal authority is undermined, Orian, whose fatherhood ends in his death, and Orso, whose parenthood is only apparent. But, at the end of the play, the promise of their marriage of convenience seems less remarkable than Pensée's resolve and independence within nature, like that of the hearty flower (*la pensée* or "pansy") after which she is named. Pensée is in control of the marriage rite, and Claudel leaves open at the end of the play whether Orso will return and marry Pensée or will fall in battle. But his suggestion that,

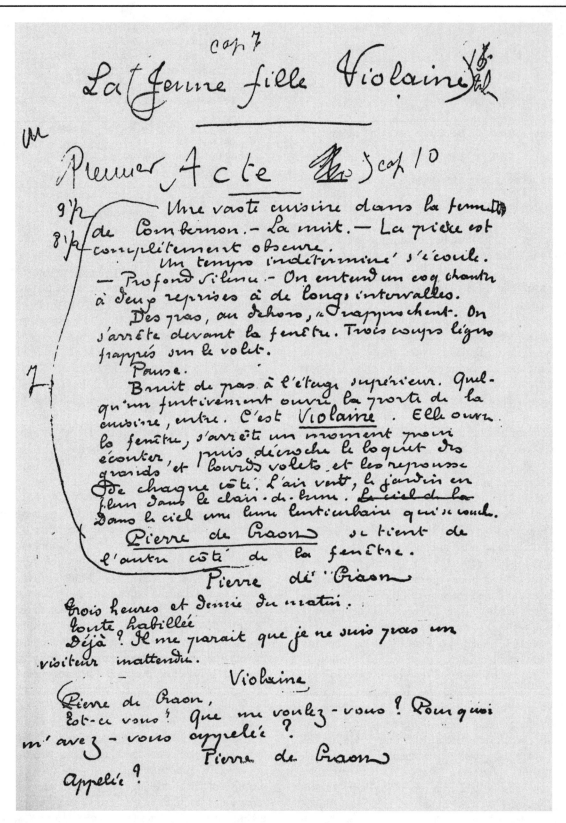

First page of the manuscript for Claudel's 1901 play set during the Middle Ages (from Louis Chaigne, Vie de Paul Claudel et genèse de son œuvre, *1961)*

metaphysically, Pensée will be married to both Orso and Orian brings the trilogy if not to resolution, then certainly to conclusion.

Claudel's greatest play of the 1910s was *L'Annonce faite à Marie,* which he had been working on since 1892. The play was first published in five numbers of the journal *Nouvelle Revue française* (1911–1912), with the prologue and each of the four acts appearing in consecutive issues, then the whole published in book form by Editions de la Nouvelle Revue Française in 1912. Claudel transforms the events of *La Jeune fille Violaine* into a sort of historicized hagiology of an egalitarian fifteenth-century French society in which anyone could be the Virgin Mary and anyone could apprehend the annunciation of the Angel Gabriel, not just people highly favored by class or sainthood. In *L'Annonce faite à Marie* Claudel creates a drama that could pass for a lost narrative from Jacobus de Voragine's *Legenda Aurea* (Golden Legends, circa 1267), his collection of 182 "golden legends" of sainthood. Claudel's legend concerns Violaine and her relationships with two men who love her, Pierre de Craon and Jacques Hury. The first part of the legend is told through antecedent action, as in the prologue Pierre and Violaine discuss their encounter of a year ago, when he assaulted her and made a small cut on her arm with his knife, though she prevented him from raping her. Although their dialogue now seems friendly, the memory of violence, of the confrontation between Violaine and her would-be violator, intensifies the mood, notably in Violaine's chilling remark, "Pauvre Pierre! vous n'avez même pas réussi à me tuer. Avec votre mauvais couteau!" (Poor Pierre! you even failed to kill me. With your bad knife! [translations by St-Pierre]). The mood changes again, to pathos, as Pierre explains he has been absent from Combernon since he discovered, a year ago, that he had contracted leprosy. For the rest of the long prologue, Violaine encourages Pierre to cope with his disease and not to see it as divine retribution, yet Claudel leaves an opening for spectators and readers to consider that perhaps leprosy is an appropriate punishment for a would-be rapist.

As the play moves through its four-act sequence, Claudel develops his heroine's relationship with her fiancé, Jacques. Violaine comes under the influence of her sister, Mara; her father, Anne Vercors; and her mother, Elisabeth Vercors. On the pretext of visiting Jacques's mother, Violaine goes to the leper colony at Le Géyn to see Pierre, but she arouses her fiancé's suspicions. Finally, Violaine confronts Jacques as she has confronted Pierre, and she reveals to him that she has contracted leprosy. Disease becomes a condition of love, as Violaine likens *l'annonce d'une maladie* (the

announcement of an illness) to *l'annonce d'un mariage* (the publication of wedding banns).

In the end, Violaine tells a saintly story of life and death, when, at the point of death, she says "Que c'est beau de vivre!" (It's good to be alive!) and, with her last breath, "Mais que c'est bon aussi / De mourir alors que c'est bien fini et que s'étend sur nous peu à peu / L'obscurcissement comme d'un ombrage très obscur" (But it's good also / To die when it's all over and the twilight slowly stretches out over us, like a very dark shade). Violaine's negative question in *La Jeune fille Violaine,* "is it not good also to die?" has become in *L'Annonce faite à Marie* her angelic annunciation to Claudel's audience "it's good also to die." The statement marks her sainthood as clearly as leprosy marks her flesh, and it is evidence of Claudel's evolution and accomplishment as a dramatist.

The first major sign of his accomplishment as a poet was *Cinq grandes odes, suivies d'un processionnal pour saluer le siècle nouveau* (Five Grand Odes, with a Processional to Salute the New Century, 1910; translated as *Five Great Odes,* 1967). The first ode was published earlier as *Ode: Les Muses* (1905; translated as *The Muses,* 1967), and the third, "Magnificat," first appeared in *La Nouvelle Revue française* (May 1910). The implied speaker is "Le poëte dans la captivité des murs de Pékin" (the poet in the captivity of the walls of Peking), but the odes themselves document the speaker's *ex claustral* (outside the walls) liberation, as in the fourth ode, "La Muse Qui Est la Grace" (The Muse Who Is Grace):

Comme l'antique poëte parlait de la part des dieux privés de présence,
Et moi je dis qu'il n'est rien dans la nature qui soit fait sans dessein et propos à l'homme adressé,
Et comme lumière pour l'œil et le son pour l'oreille, ainsi toute chose pour l'analyse de l'intelligence,
Continuée avec l'intelligence qui la
Refait de l'élément qu'elle récupère,
Que ce soit la pioche qui le dégage, ou le pan du prospecteur et l'amalgame de mercure,
Ou le savant, la plume à la main, ou le tricot des métiers, ou la charrue.
Et je puis parler, continu avec toute chose muette,
Parole qui est à sa place intelligence et volonté.
Je chanterai le grand poëme de l'homme soustrait au hasard!

(As the ancient poet spoke on behalf of gods without presence,
I say in my turn that nothing is made in nature without design and purpose towards man,
And, as the light is made for his eyes, and sound for his ears, so all things are made for analysis by his intelligence,
Which is continuous with the intelligence that
Remakes them from the recovered element,

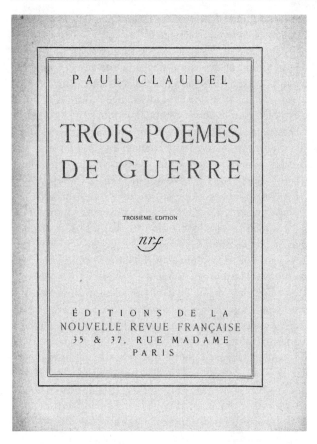

*Cover for Claudel's 1915 collection of poetry about World War I
(Thomas Cooper Library, University of South Carolina)*

Freeing it with the pick, or the prospector's sieve, or with
   the amalgam of mercury,
Through the scholar, pen in hand, with the plough, or the
   looms weaving.
And I can speak, being continuous with all silent things,
Words which in their place are intelligence and will,
I shall sing the great song of man set free from chance!)
(translation by Edward Lucie-Smith)

This poem is Claudel's declaration of personal freedom, his poetics of purposeful design, and his aesthetic
of sense and will. The sequence of five odes is his introspective look at the position of men and women in the
theocentric universe, a beatific meditation and hymn in
the spirit of such Old Testament cantors as Isaiah and
Daniel. Finally, his "Processional pour saluer le siècle
nouveau" constitutes a kind of conciliar document, as
of the Vatican councils: a recessional hymn designed to
follow the dismissal at Mass, but also a procedural song
to utter while undertaking the rite of passage from the
Liturgy into a "new" century—a rite that is, in 1910,
already ten years overdue—and a litany of saints whom
Claudel seems to bid his readers join as they leave Mass
to reenter the world:

Voici devant moi depuis le commencement
du monde jusqu'à nos jours en une procession
Tous les patriarches et les saints suivant
l'ordre de leurs générations.

(A single procession before me from the beginning
of the world until today
All the patriarchs and the saints according
to their generations).
(translation by Lucie-Smith)

This coda to *Cinq grandes odes* is visionary at the theological level and symbolist at the poetic level, but it is also
Claudel's simple act of faith, his challenge to his readers
to join the procession of the blessed, rather than yielding to the process of the world.

   Throughout the following decade, Claudel
refined this poetic of theology and song, as in "La Cantate à trois voix" (Cantata for Three Voices), a monastic plainsong as well as a theatrical cantata, which was
first published in *La Revue de Paris* (March 1913), collected in *Cette heure qui est entre le printemps et l'été: Cantate à
trois voix* (This Hour at the Beginning of Spring and
Summer: Cantata for Three Voices, 1913), and then
republished in *Deux poèmes d'été: La Cantate à trois voix;
Protée: Drame satirique* (Two Poems of Summer: Cantata
for Three Voices; Proteus: Satiric Drama, 1914); and in
Corona benignitatis anni Dei (1915; translated as *Coronal*,
1943), a series of sacramentals (apostolic portraits, spiritual meditations, feast-day prayers, and the Way of the
Cross), all related in spirited verse. His exemplary commentary on the prayers and meditations associated with
viewing the stations of the cross was previously published in book form as *Le Chemin de la croix* (1911; translated as *Stations of the Cross*, 1937) and was approved by
the Church as a guide for French-speaking Catholics.

   Claudel had to draw deeply on his religious
teachings twice in 1913, when he learned of his father's
death, and that his eldest sister, Camille, the sculptor,
had been committed to a psychiatric institution. The
outbreak of World War I the following year added universal calamity to these family tragedies. He drew on
his skills as a dramatist and a poet to comment on the
war. In his 1915 play, *La Nuit de Noël 1914* (Christmas
Eve 1914), which first appeared in the newspaper *Le
Correspondant* (10 April 1915), he mixes theological satire
and political propaganda, as when M. le Curé observes,
"C'est le Seigneur Dieu qui fait silence pour écouter les
Allemands qui vont tirer sur sa maison. Et nous tous,
faisons silence avec lui" (The Lord God has made
silence for listening to the Germans who are going to
shoot at his house [the Cathédrale de Rheims]. And we
all make silence with him [translation by St-Pierre]). In
Trois poèmes de guerre (1915; translated as *Three Poems of
the War*, 1919) and *Autres poèmes durant la guerre* (Other

Poems During the War, 1916), which were both republished, with *La Nuit de Noël 1914*, as *Poèmes de guerre, 1914–1916* (1922), Claudel displays his talent for contextualizing or collapsing the events of war in eschatology. In "La Vierge à Midi" (The Virgin at Midday), which first appeared in *Cahiers Vaudois* (1915) and was collected in both *Autres poèmes durant la guerre* and *Poèmes de guerre,* war is implicit in the collapse of time and events, as a soldier stops to pray at a statue of the Virgin Mary:

Il est midi. Je vois l'église ouverte. It faut entrer.
Mère de Jésus-Christ, je ne viens pas prier.
Je n'ai rien à offrir et rien à demander.
Je viens seulement, Mère, pour vous regarder.
Vous regarder, pleurer de bonheur, savoir cela
Que je suis votre fils et que vous êtes là.
Rien que pour un moment pendant que tout s'arrête.
Midi!
Etre avec vous, Marie, en ce lieu où vous êtes.
Ne rien dire, regarder votre visage,
Laisser le cœur chanter dans son propre langage,
Ne rien dire, mais seulement chanter parce qu'on a le cœur
    trop plein,
Comme le merle qui suit son idée en ces espèces de cou-
    plets soudains.

(It is midday. I see the open church. I must go in.
Mother of Jesus Christ, I do not come to pray.
I have nothing to offer up and nothing to ask for.
I come only, Mother, to look at you.
To look at you, to weep for happiness, to know it
That I am your son and that you are there.
Just for a moment during which everything stops.
Midday!
Being with you, Mary, in this place where you are.
Nothing to say, to look at your face,
To let my heart sing in your own language,
Nothing to say, but only to sing because one's heart is
    overflowing,
Like the blackbird that follows its idea in this
kind of sudden song).
(translation by St-Pierre)

If, as Lechy Elcernon observes in *L'Echange,* midday is "l'heure qui n'est point l'heure" (the hour that is not an hour at all), being neither morning nor afternoon, and thus in a sense "no time," then "La Vierge de midi" transcends time, especially the events of war that deprive soldiers of life. By stepping into the church and looking at the Virgin, the soldier-speaker briefly steps out of the theater of war.

Claudel makes another telling temporal allusion to war in "La Grande Attente" (The Big Wait), which appeared in both *Autres Poèmes durant la guerre* and *Poèmes de guerre:*

La mort qui est dure pour nous aussi et dont nous aurions
    su comme vous nous passer,
    La fin qui est tellement injuste à notre âge!
La valeur de ce grand héritage pour vous dont nous som-
    mes débarrassés,
Nous y avons engagé notre vie, pensez-y et si ce n'était pas
    assez,
    Du moins nous ne pouvions faire davantage.

(Death which is cruel for us too and which like you we
    could have done without,
    The end which is so very unjust at our age!
The value of this great heritage for you from which we are
    released,
We have pledged our life on it, we think about it and if
    that wasn't enough,
    At least we could not have done more).
(translation by St-Pierre)

Here Claudel's parallels around "la mort qui est dure" (death which is cruel) and "la guerre qui dure" (the war that continues) and "la vie qui dure" (life that goes on) emphasize that "la grande attente"–the kind of existential wait that later preoccupied Samuel Beckett in his *En attendant Godot* (Waiting for Godot, 1952)–is both the ontological burden of human beings (that is, death) and an illogical sliver of time during which the war seems to come to a stop. To Claudel "poèmes de guerre" serve not only propagandistic and documentary purposes but also the pacifist purpose of letting him hint that "la fin de guerre est tellement juste à notre âge" (the end of war is so right in our generation).

During the war Claudel also completed his translation of the *Oresteia* trilogy (458 B.C.) of Aeschylus that he had begun in 1892 with *Agamemnon,* which appeared in volume four of his *Théâtre* (1912) as *L'Agamemnon d'Eschyle.* In 1915, while stationed in Rome, he translated both *Choephoroi* (Libation Bearers) and *Eumenides* (The Kind Goddesses), as *Les Choéphores d'Eschyle* (1920) and *Les Euménides d'Eschyle* (1920), respectively. Around the same time he was writing his own "Greek" tragedies. He wrote the three-act play *Protée* (Proteus) in Frankfurt in 1913, publishing it in two issues of the *Nouvelle Revue française* (April and May 1914), and then that same year in his *Deux poëmes d'été* and, in an edited version, in *Deux farces lyriques: Protée; L'Ours et la lune* (Two Lyrical Farces: Proteus; The Bear and the Moon, 1927). Darius Milhaud, Claudel's frequent collaborator, set *Protée* to music in 1922. His piecework during the war also inspired Claudel to write the Hellenic dialogue *Sous le rampart d'Athènes* (Under the Ramparts of Athens), which first appeared in the *Nouvelle Revue française* (December 1927) and was published in book form the following year. He completed his wartime diplomatic service in Rio de Janeiro, where in 1917 he wrote the farce *L'Ours et la lune,* a play for three

Claudel's wife, Reine Sainte-Marie Perin Claudel, with their children Marie, Reine, Henri, and Pierre in 1916

actors and seven marionettes, to which Milhaud contributed a three-page musical score. The play is set variously in a German prison camp, in a puppet theater in a children's bedroom, in the salon of an old woman, and at a mountain summit, together a mise-en-scène of child-like absurdity. This play is Claudel's only venture into *le théâtre dadaïste* (Dadaist theater), epitomized by the Cabaret Voltaire performances (1916) and Jean Cocteau's play *Parade* (1917), both of which use marionettes. In Claudel's play, La Lune, a marionette, speaks in a sort of untranslatable Dadaist nonsense idiom, interrupted, the stage directions read *"à chaque mot par les moulinets et reproduisant en désordre sur sa figure les différentes phases de notre satellite telles qu'elles son décrites dans les traités de cosmographie"* (at each word by the wires and reproducing in confusion on her figure the different phases of our satellite such that they are depicted in treatises on cosmography): "Flic . . . flouc . . . trac . . . bloc . . . hic . . . haec . . . hac . . . hoc. . . . " With this lunar language, Claudel conducted his most daring and comical theatrical experiment, lacking only the shock elements characteristic of Dada.

He began writing his play *Le Soulier de satin, ou le pire n'est pas toujours sûr a été* (translated as *The Satin Slipper; or, The Worst Is Not the Surest*, 1931) in Paris in 1919, drafting it when he was the French consul in Copenhagen from 1919 to 1921, and completing it in Tokyo between 1921 and 1924 during his tenure as French ambassador to Japan. The composition process was not without hardship, as the Tokyo earthquake of 1923 destroyed some of his manuscripts. His promotion in the diplomatic service seemed to take him to a higher level of dramaturgy also, in that *Le Soulier de satin* is by far his most complex play, thematically and structurally. He published the first act as *Soulier de satin, première journée* (1925), and the complete play in four volumes as *Le Soulier de satin, ou le pire n'est pas toujours sûr: Action espagnole en quatre journeés* (The Satin Slipper; or, The Worst Is Not the Surest: Spanish Action in Four Days, 1928–1929). Set in Spain in 1600, it historicizes the grand narratives of the Renaissance, the Protestant Reformation, and the Spanish colonization of Africa and of the New World, and weaves them into a masque that is part romance, part melodrama, and part tragedy (informed also by the death of his mother in 1929). The story concerns the heroine, Doña Prouhèze, who is married to Don Pélage but is in love with Don Rodrigue. Aware of her attraction to Rodrigue, Pélage sends Prouhèze to Mogador, Morocco, on the pretext of overseeing his colonial interests there, but really as a test of her fidelity. He enlists Don Camille to accompany her, fully aware that he too is in love with his wife. Her first test of constancy comes when Rodrigue follows Prouhèze to Morocco and implores her to leave Mogador and run away with him. She manages to resist him, both through her own resolve and also because she has seen fit to consecrate her marriage to the Virgin Mary, presenting one of her satin slippers as her oblation. When Pélage dies, however, Prouhèze writes to Rodrigue, who is now in the Americas as a viceroy of the king of Spain. But when she fails to hear back from him—her letter, in a melodramatic twist, takes a decade to arrive—Prouhèze marries Camille, and they have a daughter, Sept-Epées. When Rodrigue finally arrives in Mogador, it is under siege by the Moroccans. This time she rejects his offer to deliver her from danger, entrusts Doña Sept-Epées to his care, and then dies. Eventually, Rodrigue helps Sept-Epées to renounce social convention and follow her heart. Then, as the play ends, he hears a disembodied woman's voice crying "aidez-moi" (help me) and decides to serve Prouhèze, and through her all women, by helping a nun to raise funds to build a convent. With *Le Soulier de satin* Claudel established himself as one of the most important dramatists of twentieth-century France.

In his fervor during the war and his exuberance after its end, an exuberance inspired by his ambassadorial position in Tokyo, Claudel wrote several hagiographical and biographical studies: the saints' lives *Sainte Thérèse* (Saint Theresa, 1916), *Sainte Cécile* (Saint Cecilia, 1918), *Sainte Geneviève* (Saint Genevieve, 1923), and *Feuilles de saints* (Leaves of the Saints, 1925); the sociospiritual studies *La Messe là-bas* (Low Mass Over There, 1919) and *Un Coup d'œil sur l'âme japonaise: Discours au étudiants de Nikko* (A Good Judgment on the Japanese Soul: Speech to the Students of Nikko, 1923); and the life-writings *Verlaine* (1922), about nineteenth-century French symbolist poet Paul Verlaine; *A travers les villes en flammes: Note d'un témoin* (Through the Cities in Flames: Note of a Witness, 1924), about postwar France; and *Morceaux choisis, avec un portrait et un autographe de l'auteur* (Extracts, with a Portrait and an Autobiography of the Author, 1925), a selection of Claudel's writings. In these works he developed from an apprentice of the politician-writer's life to a master of life-writing.

While French ambassador to the United States from 1927 to 1933, Claudel addressed himself to some New World literary themes, notably in *Le Livre de Christophe Colomb* (translated as *The Book of Christopher Columbus,* 1930), which appeared in the autumn 1929 issue of the review *Commerce* before it was published in book form in Vienna that same year. It is *un livre* not only because it is a book, the fictional autobiography and explorer's journal of Christopher Columbus, but also because it is *le livret,* or the libretto, of an opera, for which Milhaud wrote the music, and which had its premiere on 30 June 1930 at the Staatsroper Unter den Linden, Berlin, the orchestra under the direction of Erick Kleiber. Pierre Boulez conducted the second production, at the 1953 Festival de Bordeaux.

The bipartite text takes the form of a reading by a narrator, "L'Explicateur" (The Analyst), of "Le Livre de la Vie et des voyages de Christophe Colomb qui a découvert l'Amérique!" (The Book of the Life and the Voyages of Christopher Columbus Who Discovered America). The narrator also sets up a series of scenes in which Columbus converses with other characters: specific, such as La Reine Isabelle (Queen Isabella) and Le Roi d'Espagne (the King of Spain); generic, such as Le Défenseur (The Champion), L'Opposant (The Opponent), and Matelot (Sailor); and collective, such as Le Chœur (The Chorus) and Les Hommes Sages (The Wise Men).

Claudel's other main literary undertaking in Washington, D.C., was to expand upon his first collection of critical articles, *Morceaux choisis.* The resultant two-volume work was *Positions et propositions: Art et littérateur* (Positions and Propositions: Art and Literature, 1928, 1934), a retrospective anthology of art criticism comprising articles Claudel originally published in periodicals, newspapers, and anthologies in the 1910s and 1920s, on subjects such as writers (Arthur Rimbaud, Dante Alighieri), artists (Camille Claudel, José-Maria Sert), literature (French verse, the philosophy of the book), religion (Catholic theater, the Eucharist), and politics (justice, liberty).

In 1934, during his tenure as French ambassador to Belgium (1933–1935), Claudel wrote the dramatic oratorio *Jeanne d'Arc au bûcher* (Joan of Arc at the Stake, 1939), which had its first performance, in German, at Bâle, Switzerland, 12 May 1938. His narrative concerns St. Joan, less the historical figure and Fabian player of George Bernard Shaw's play *Saint Joan* (1924), than the Christian martyr, the witness for France, "Jeanne d'Arc en flammes" (Joan of Arc in flames), at the stake. At the point of death, she is comforted by the Virgin Mary, the French people, a dramatic chorus, a priest, St. Marguerite, a voice in heaven, and a voice on the earth, but her voice is dominant until the end, quelling even the voice of God. Throughout the oratorio, only Jeanne, Frère

The Claudels with their daughters Renée and Reine in Tokyo, where Claudel was ambassador from 1921 to 1924

Dominique, Le Chœur, and La Vierge sing in verse, whereas the other characters use prose. Verse seems to be Claudel's signifier (his "stake," or marker) for the woman of true faith and her supporters, whose order of discourse is elevated, as are the flames that consume her.

After his ambassadorial term in Brussels ended in 1935, Claudel retired from the French diplomatic service and took up residence in Paris and in a castle that he had purchased in 1927, in Brangues, Isère, located in the Rhône-Alpes. His retirement allowed him to become a full-time writer for the first time. He continued to offer up prayers around *le bûcher de Jeanne d'Arc,* such as in the devotional works *Un Poète regarde la Croix* (1938; translated as *A Poet Before the Cross,* 1958), *La Mystique des pierres précieuses* (The Mystique of Precious Stones, 1938), and *L'Epée et le miroir* (The Sword and the Mirror, 1939). In the 1940s he wrote a series of spiritual commentaries inspired by the carnage of World War II, especially by the death of his sister Camille in 1943: *Présence et prophétie* (Pres-

ence and Prophesy, 1942); *Seigneur, apprenez-nous à prier* (1942; translated as *Lord, Teach Us How to Pray,* 1947); *Prière pour les paralysés, suivie des Quinze Psaumes graduels CXIX À CXXXIII* (Prayer for Paralytics, Followed by Fifteen Gradual Psalms CXIX–CXXXIII, 1944); and *Poèmes et paroles durant la guerre de trente ans* (Poems and Words During the Thirty Years' War, 1945), a series of psalms on war and peace. Other works of this period include *Le Livre de Job* (The Book of Job, 1946) and two books on the Marian shrine of La Sallette, *Les Révélations de La Salette* (The Revelations of La Salette, 1946) and *Le Symbolisme de La Salette* (The Symbolism of La Salette, 1952). Claudel also wrote many biblical and hagiographic studies: *Emmaüs* (1949) about Christ's appearance to two disciples after the Resurrection; *Saint Thérèse de Lisieux vous parle* (Saint Theresa of Lisieux Speaks to You, 1950); *L'Evangile d'Isaïe* (The Gospel of Isaiah, 1951); *Paul Claudel interroge l'Apocalypse* (Paul Claudel Examines the Apocalypse, 1952); *Trois Figures saintes pour le temps actuel: Le Frère Charles, Sainte Thérèse de Lisieux, Eve Lavallière* (Three

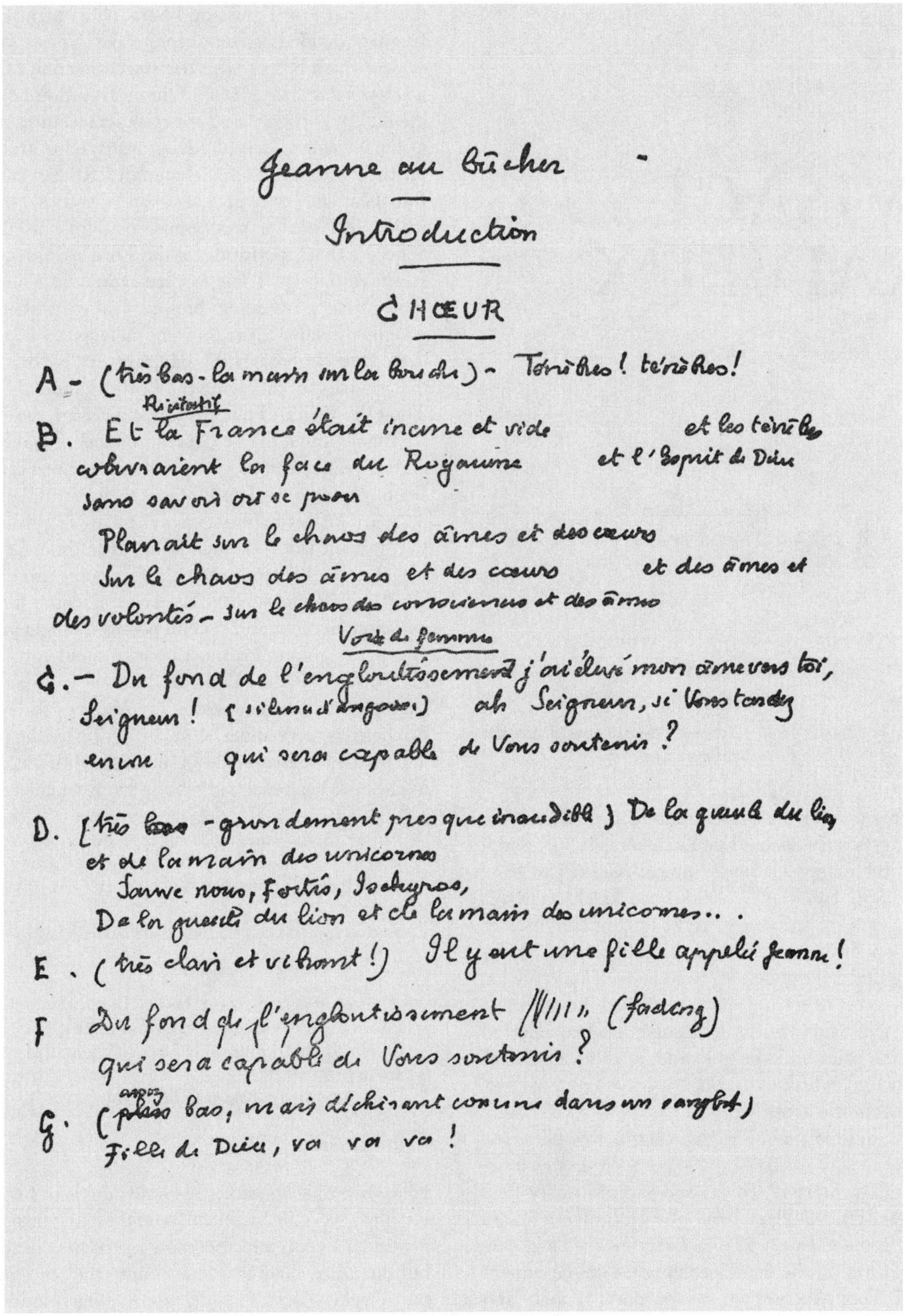

Jeanne au bûcher

Introduction

CHŒUR

A - (très bas - la main sur la bouche) - Ténèbres! ténèbres!

Récitatif

B. Et la France était informe et vide   et les ténèbres
couvraient la face du Royaume   et l'Esprit de Dieu
sans savoir où se poser
   Planait sur le chaos des âmes et des cœurs
   Sur le chaos des âmes et des cœurs   et des âmes et
des volontés - sur le chaos des consciences et des âmes

Voix de femmes

C. - Du fond de l'engloutissement j'ai élevé mon âme vers toi,
Seigneur! (silence d'angoisse) ah Seigneur, si Vous tombez
encore   qui sera capable de Vous soutenir?

D. (très bas - grondement presque inaudible) De la gueule du lion
et de la main des unicornes
   Sauve nous, Fortis, Ischyros,
   De la gueule du lion et de la main des unicornes...

E. (très clair et vibrant!) Il y eut une fille appelé Jeanne!

F   Du fond de l'engloutissement //////" (fadang)
qui sera capable de Vous soutenir?

G. (plus bas, mais déchirant comme dans un sanglot)
Fille de Dieu, va va va!

First page of the manuscript for Claudel's 1939 dramatic poem, Jeanne d'Arc au bûcher *(from Louis Chaigne,*
Vie de Paul Claudel et genèse de son œuvre, *1961)*

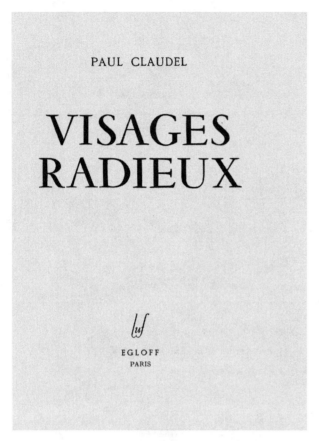

PAUL CLAUDEL

VISAGES RADIEUX

luf

EGLOFF
PARIS

Title page for Claudel's 1945 collection of religious poetry (Robert W. Woodruff Library, Emory University)

Saintly Figures for the Present Day: Brother Charles, Saint Theresa of Lisieux, Eve Lavallière, 1953); and a book of Bible appreciation, *J'aime la Bible* (I Love the Bible, 1955). He wrote religious works through his twenty years of retirement, right up until his death; withdrawn from the world in the religious sense, by devoting his retirement to writing religious books, Claudel, in his heart and spirit, reentered the novitiate at L'Abbaye Saint-Martin de Ligugé that had rejected him for the priesthood in 1900 and lived out his life as a Benedictine, who carried out his *ora et labora* (prayer and work) in the act of writing.

His most distinguished writing of this period is found in the play *L'Histoire de Tobie et de Sara: Moralité en trois actes* (The Story of Tobias and Sara: Morality Play in Three Acts, 1942) and the poem sequence *Visages radieux* (Radiant Faces, 1945). *L'Histoire de Tobie et de Sara,* drawing on the deuterocanonical Old Testament Book of Tobit, focuses on the prophets Tobias and Sara, and Tobit and Anna, who are in exile in Nineveh during the regime of King Shalmaneser of Assyria. Claudel tells the story of the Hebrew deportation, Tobit's blindness and its cure, Sara's demonic possession, Tobias's encounter with the angel Raphael, and

the marriage of Tobias and Sara, all in highly stylized language and mises-en-scène. Like *Jeanne d'Arc au bûcher,* which begins with the stage direction "*On entend un chien hurler dans la nuit*" (One hears a dog howling in the night), *L'Histoire de Tobie et de Sara* features a dog as a character: le Chien (the Dog) leads Tobit and Tobias on their journey from Echatana to Rhages in Media. But Claudel, drawing also on theatrical tradition, makes le Chien a pantomime dog that, as does the angel Raphael, performs as the Lord's messenger and scout, who drags Tobie le Vieux (the Old Tobias) into center stage, revealing him to his wife, Anna, and daughter-in-law, Sara. As a morality play, *L'Histoire de Tobie et de Sara* retells the biblical story by dramatizing the goodness of following the Lord. Claudel shows that Tobie le Vieux, Tobie le Jeune (Tobias the Young), Sara, and Anna, like le Chien, *ont du chien* (have get-up-and-go). They get up and go when the Lord calls them out of Nineveh, and goodness is their eternal reward.

In *Visages radieux* Claudel traces in poetic meter the "radiant faces" of such saints as Jérôme, Catherine, Thérèse de Lisieux, and Martin; some fundamental Christian events, such as Easter, confession, Judgment, and circumcision; and several poems on night and sleep that figure among his most poignant and comical writing. In "L'Invitation à dormir" (Invitation to Sleep), for example, which he wrote at Abbaye St-André de Lophem, 13 September 1932, he addresses the plight of a retreatant (either male or female) who keeps watch over his or her sick child who is trying to fall asleep:

> Pauvre enfant à mes pieds sur ce lit de torture
> Je veux t'envelopper dans mon manteau d'azur!
> Si ton front est brûlant et si ta lèvre est
> sèche,
> Si tu as soif, je veux t'apporter de l'eau
> fraîche!
>
> (Poor child at my feet on this bed of torture
> I want to wrap you up in my azure cloak!
> If your forehead is burning hot and if your lips
> are dry,
> If you are thirsty, I want to bring you fresh
> water!)
> (translation by St-Pierre)

Here the implied speaker responds to his or her nurturing impulse. The "manteau" could be a man's cloak or a woman's coat, and the child's gender is unspecified, but the azure cloak is an allusion to the blue mantle of the Virgin Mary. Claudel shows that kindness and compassion make a parent's face radiant, just as the child's face radiates a fever, and that the radiance of unconditional love blinds people to gender differences.

In "Dans la nuit" (During the Night) the speaker shares a mantra that could either put one to sleep or

Claudel during the 1950s

prevent one from sleeping: "Je dors. Est-ce que je dors? / Mais non je ne dors pas. J'adore" (I am sleeping. Am I sleeping? But no I am not sleeping. I adore [translation by St-Pierre]). This simple pun ("Je dors/J'adore") is another subtle reminder of Dada.

Claudel was elected to the French Academy in 1946. He died on 23 February 1955, after suffering a heart attack the evening before, and his funeral was held at Notre-Dame Cathedral in Paris. Since his death, many new editions of his works have appeared, and several previously unpublished works, notably his fifty years of correspondence, with people ranging from Jacques Rivière, André Gide, and Milhaud to his daughter Reine and his diplomatic colleagues while he was ambassador to Japan. Completing the collected works published or begun in his lifetime—*Introduction à l'œuvre de Paul Claudel avec des textes* (Introduction to the Work of Paul Claudel with the Texts, 1926) and *Œuvres complètes,* 26 volumes (1950–1967)—several collections have appeared posthumously: *Œuvre poétique* (Poetic Work, 1957); *Œuvres en prose* (Works in Prose,

1965); *Supplément aux Œuvres complète* (Supplement to the Complete Works, 1990–1997); *Œuvres diplomatiques: Ambassadeur aux Etats-Unis, 1927–1933* (Diplomatic Works: Ambassador to the United States, 1927–1933, 1994); and *L'Arsenal de Fou-Tchéou: Œuvres consulaires, Chine 1895–1905* (The Arsenal of Fuchow: Consular Works, China 1895–1905, 1995). Some editors of the posthumous works have tried to reshape Claudel, for example, Jean Bestaire in his postmodernizing edition, *Conversations écologiques* (Ecological Conversations, 2000), presents Claudel as an ecologist. Claudel's voice comes out most clearly, however, in the books he was working on in the years leading up to his death: *J'aime la Bible,* which he wrote between 1949 and 1954; his translations of and commentaries on the Psalms (published in full in 1966 as *Psaumes: Traductions 1918–1959*), which he worked on from 1918 until his death; and in the notebooks that he began keeping in 1905, published in thirteen volumes as *Cahiers Paul Claudel* (1959–1990). As an octogenarian writing these books, the subjects of his lifelong passion—the Bible and his own spirit, greater even than his passions for government, theater, and literature—Claudel must have resembled an Old Testament sage, patriarch, and prophet. Yet, as in religion, in life he proved himself a sagacious diplomat, a father of French theater, a poet who was his own muse and the voice of modernist French verse, and a seer who could look with compassion on his readers as his "pauvres enfants"(poor children) as he spread over them the azure cloak of his imagination, his morality, his élan, his mots justes, and *un œuvre complète qui est tellement juste à notre âge* (a complete oeuvre that is so right in our generation).

Letters:

Paul Claudel et Jacques Rivière, Correspondance, 1907–1914 (Paris: Plon, 1926); translated by Henry Longan Stuart as *Letters to a Doubter* (New York: Boni, 1927; London: Burns Oates & Washbourne, 1927);

Correspondance, 1899–1926: Paul Claudel et André Gide (Paris: Gallimard, 1949); translated by John Russell as *The Correspondence, 1899–1926, Between Paul Claudel and André Gide,* edited by Robert Mallett (London: Secker & Warburg, 1952; Boston: Beacon, 1952);

Correspondance, 1897–1938: Paul Claudel, Francis Jammes, Gabriel Frizeau, preface and notes by André Blanchet (Paris: Gallimard, 1952);

Lettres de P. Claudel sur la Bible au R. P. R. Paroissin (17 août 1949–11 octobre 1954) (Paris: Nouvelles Editions Debresse, 1955);

Lettres inédites de mon parrain Paul Claudel, compiled by Agnès du Sarment (Paris: Gabalda, 1959); translated by William Howard as *Letters from My Godfather, Paul Claudel* (Dublin: Clonmore & Reynolds, 1964);

Correspondance Paul Claudel–Darius Milhaud, 1912–1953, edited by Jacques Petit (Paris: Gallimard, 1961);

Claudel and Aurélian François Lugné-Poe, *Claudel, homme de théâtre: Correspondance avec Lugné-Poe, 1910–1928,* edited by Pierre Moreau, Jacques Robichez, and René Farabet, with an introduction by Moreau, preface by Robichez, and notes by Farabet, Cahiers Paul Claudel, no. 5 (Paris: Gallimard, 1964);

Claudel, Jacques Copeau, Charles Dullin, and Louis Jouvet, *Claudel, homme de théâtre: Correspondance de P. Claudel avec Copeau, Dullin, Jouvet,* edited by Henri Micciollo and Jacques Petit, Cahiers Paul Claudel, no. 6 (Paris: Gallimard, 1966);

Paul Claudel and Agnes Meyer, *Claudel et l'Amérique II: Lettres de Paul Claudel à Agnès Meyer, 1928–1929: Note-book d'Agnès Meyer, 1929,* edited, with an introduction and notes, by Eugène Roberto (Ottawa: Editions de l'Université d'Ottawa, 1969);

Lettres inédites de Paul Claudel, introductions by Maurice Zundel and Jacques Madaule (La Pierre-qui-Vire: Presses Monastiques, 1970);

Claudel and Martha Bibescu, *Echanges avec Paul Claudel: Nos lettres inédites* (Paris: Mercure de France, 1972);

Paul Claudel, Louis Massignon (1908–1914): Correspondance, edited by Michel Malicet (Paris: Desclée de Brouwer, 1973);

Correspondance: Paul Claudel, Jean-Louis Barrault, edited by Michel Lioure, Cahiers Paul Claudel, no. 10 (Paris: Gallimard, 1974);

La Tristesse d'un automne sans été: Correspondance de Gabrielle Vulliez avec André Gide et Paul Claudel (1923–1931), edited by Wanda Vulliez (Bron: Centre d'Etudes Gidiennes, Université Lyon II, 1981);

Correspondance Paul Claudel–Jacques Rivière: 1907–1924, edited by Auguste Anglès and Pierre de Gaulmyn, Cahiers Paul Claudel, no. 12 (Paris: Gallimard, 1984);

Lettres de Paul Claudel à Elisabeth Sainte-Marie Perrin et à Audrey Parr, Cahiers Paul Claudel, no. 13 (Paris: Gallimard, 1990);

Claudel, *Lettres à sa fille Reine,* edited by Malicet (Lausanne, Switzerland: L'Age d'Homme, 1991);

Correspondance, 1911–1954: Paul Claudel, Gaston Gallimard, edited by Bernard Delvaille (Paris: Gallimard, 1995);

Correspondance diplomatique: Tokyo, 1921–1927, edited by Lucile Garbagnati, preface by Malicet, Cahiers Paul Claudel, no. 14 (Paris: Gallimard, 1995);

Claudel and Jacques Madaule, *Connaissance et Reconnaissance: Correspondance 1924–1954,* edited by Andrée Hirschi and Pierre Madaule (Paris: Desclée de Brouwer, 1996);

Paul Claudel, Stanislas Fumet, Correspondance 1920–1954: Histoire d'une amitié, edited by Marianne Malicet (Lausanne, Switzerland: L'Age d'Homme, 1997).

Interview:

Mémoires improvisés: Quarante et un entretiens avec Jean Amrouche, edited by Louis Fournier (Paris: Gallimard, 1969).

Bibliographies:

René Lacote, "Bibliographie des Œuvres de Paul Claudel," in *Paul Claudel: Une Etude,* by Louis Perche, Poètes d'aujourd'hi, no. 10 (Paris: Seghers, 1958), pp. 201–215;

Paul-André Lesort, "Bibliographie," in his *Paul Claudel par lui-même* (Paris: Seuil, 1963), pp. 172–190;

André Alter, "Bibliographie," in his *Textes de Claudel: Points de vue critiques, temoignages, bibliographie* (Paris: Seghers, 1968), pp. 185–189;

Stanislas Fumet and M. P. O. Walzer, "Bibliographie," in *Claudel*, by Fumet, second edition (Paris: Gallimard, 1968), pp. 225–252;

Jacques Petit and Andrée Hirschi, eds., *Bibliographie des œuvres de Paul Claudel* (Paris: Les Belles Lettres, 1973).

Biography:

Louis Chaigne, *Vie de Paul Claudel et genèse de son œuvre* (Paris: Mame, 1961).

References:

André Alter, *Textes de Claudel: Points de vue critiques, témoignages, bibliographie* (Paris: Seghers, 1968);

Louis Barjon, *Paul Claudel*, preface by Claudel, Classiques du XXe siècle, no. 9 (Paris: Editions Universitaires, 1953);

Maryse Bazaud, Claudine Lang, and Marianne Malicet, eds., *Catalogue de la bibliothèque de Paul Claudel* (Paris: Les Belles Lettres, 1979);

Ernest Beaumont, *The Theme of Beatrice in the Plays of Paul Claudel* (London: Rockliff, 1954);

Jean-Claude Berton, *Shakespeare et Claudel: Le Temps et l'espace au théâtre* (Geneva: La Palatine, 1958);

Lynne L. Gelber, *In/stability: The Shape and Space of Claudel's Art Criticism* (Ann Arbor, Mich.: UMI Research Press, 1980);

Introduction à l'œuvre de Paul Claudel avec des textes (Paris: Bloud & Gay, 1926);

Bettina L. Knapp, *Paul Claudel* (New York: Ungar, 1982);

Paul-André Lesort, *Paul Claudel par lui-même* (Paris: Seuil, 1963);

Jacques Madaule, *Claudel et le langage* (Paris: Desclée de Brouwer, 1968);

Marianne Mercier-Campiche, *Le Théâtre de Claudel; ou, La Puissance du grief et de la passion* (Paris: Pauvert, 1968);

Henri Micciollo, *"L'Oiseau noir dans le soleil levant" de Paul Claudel: Introduction, variantes et notes* (Paris: Les Belles Lettres, 1981);

Adrianna M. Paliyenko, *Mis-Reading the Creative Impulse: The Poetic Subject in Rimbaud and Claude, Restaged* (Carbondale & Edwardsville: Southern Illinois University Press, 1997);

Louis Perche, *Paul Claudel: Une Etude*, Poètes d'aujourd'hui, no. 10 (Paris: Seghers, 1958);

Jacques Petit, *"Le Pain dur" de Paul Claudel: Introduction, fragments inédits, variantes et notes* (Paris: Les Belles Lettres, 1975);

Petit, *Le Premier drame de Claudel, "Une Mort prématurée": Commentaire thématique* (Paris: Les Belles Lettres, 1970);

Léopold Sédar Senghor, *La Parole chez Paul Claudel et chez les Négro-Africains* (Dakar: Les Nouvelles Editions Africaines, 1973);

Harold A. Waters, *Paul Claudel* (New York: Twayne, 1970);

Harold Watson, *Claudel's Immortal Heroes: A Choice of Deaths* (New Brunswick, N.J.: Rutgers University Press, 1971).

Papers:

Some of Paul Claudel's letters and manuscripts, including the manuscript for *L'Annonce faite à Marie*, are held by the Bibliothèque Nationale, Paris; Claudel's letters and postcards to Audrey Parr are on deposit as Add. MS 9591, Cambridge University Library.

Jean Cocteau
(5 July 1889 – 11 October 1963)

Glenn Moulaison
University of Lethbridge

See also the Cocteau entry in *DLB 65: French Novelists, 1900–1930.*

BOOKS: *La Lampe d'Aladin: Poèmes* (Paris: Société d'Editions, 1909);

Le Prince frivole (Paris: Mercure de France, 1910);

La Danse de Sophocle: Poèmes (Paris: Mercure de France, 1912);

Le Coq et L'arlequin: Notes autour de la musique, Collection des tractes, no. 1 (Paris: Editions de la Sirène, 1918); translated by Rollo Hugh Myers as *Cock and Harlequin: Notes Concerning Music* (London: Egoist Press, 1921);

Le Cap de Bonne-Espérance: Poème (Paris: Editions de la Sirène, 1919);

L'Ode à Picasso: Poème 1917 (Paris: A La Belle Edition, 1919);

Le Potomak, 1913–1914: Précédé d'un Prospectus, 1916, et suivi des Eugènes de la guerre, 1915 (Paris: Société Littéraire de France, 1919; revised edition, Paris: Stock, 1924);

Carte Blanche: Articles parus dans "Paris-Midi" du 31 mars au 11 août 1919 (Paris: Editions de la Sirène, 1920);

Escales, by Cocteau and André Lhote (Paris: Editions de la Sirène, 1920);

Poésies, 1917–1920 (Paris: Editions de la Sirène, 1920);

La Noce massacrée (Souvenirs): 1. Visites à Maurice Barrès (Paris: Editions de la Sirène, 1921);

Le Secret professionnel (Paris: Stock, 1922); enlarged as *Le Secret professionnel; suivi des Monologues de l'Oiseleur* (Paris: Au Sans Pareil, 1925);

Vocabulaire: Poèmes (Paris: Editions de la Sirène, 1922);

Dessins (Paris: Stock, 1923);

Le Grand Ecart: Roman (Paris: Stock, Delamain & Boutelleau, 1923); translated by Lewis Galantière as *The Grand Ecart* (New York & London: Putnam, 1925);

Les Mariés de la Tour Eiffel (Paris: Editions de la Nouvelle Revue Française, 1923); enlarged as *Antigone; Les Mariés de la Tour Eiffel* (Paris: Gallimard/Editions

Jean Cocteau in 1922 (photograph by Man Ray; © 2002 Man Ray Trust/Artists Rights Society [ARS], N.Y./ADAGP, Paris)

de la Nouvelle Revue Française, 1927 [i.e., 1928]);

Picasso (Paris: Stock, 1923);

Plain-Chant: Poème (Paris: Stock, 1923);

La Rose de François: Poème inédit, Collection Alter ego, no. 5 (Paris: A La Belle Edition, 1923);

Thomas l'Imposteur: Histoire (Paris: Editions de la Nouvelle Revue Française, 1923; New York: Macmillan, 1964); translated by Galantière as *Thomas the Imposter: A Story* (New York & London: Appleton, 1925);

Férat (Paris: Crès, 1924);

Poésie, 1916–1923 (Paris: Editions de la Nouvelle Revue Française, 1924)–includes "Le Discours du grand sommeil";

Cri écrit (Montpellier: Imprimerie de Montane, 1925);

Le Mystère de Jean l'Oiseleur: Monologues, 1924 (Paris: E. Champion, 1925);

Prière mutilée, Collection de l'horloge: Une heure, un poète, no. 1 (Paris: Editions des Cahiers Libres, 1925);

L'Ange Heurtebise: Poème, with a photograph by Man Ray (Paris: Stock, 1926);

Lettre à Jacques Maritain (Paris: Stock, 1926);

Maison de santé (Paris: Editions Briant-Robert, 1926);

Le Rappel a l'ordre: Le Coq et l'Arlequin; Carte Blanche; Visites à Maurice Barrès; Le Secret professionnel; D'un ordre considéré comme une anarchie; Autour de l'imposteur; Picasso (Paris: Stock, 1926); translated by Myers as *A Call to Order: Written Between the Years 1918 and 1926 and Including "Cock and Harlequin," "Professional Secrets," and Other Critical Essays* (London: Faber & Gwyer, 1926; New York: Holt, 1926);

Roméo et Juliette: Prétexte à mise en scène par Jean Cocteau d'après le drame de William Shakespeare (Paris: Au Sans Pareil, 1926);

Opéra, œuvres poétiques, 1925–1927 (Paris: Stock, Delamain & Boutelleau, 1927);

Orphée: Tragédie en un acte et un intervalle (Paris: Stock, Delamain & Boutelleau, 1927); translated by Carl Wildman as *Orphée: A Tragedy in One Act and an Interval* (London: Oxford University Press, 1933);

Le Pauvre Matelot: Complainte en trois actes, with music by Darius Milhaud (Paris: Heugel, 1927);

Le Livre blanc, anonymous (Paris: Maurice Sachs & Jacques Bonjean, 1928); enlarged, with a preface and illustrations by Cocteau (Paris: Editions du Signe, 1930); translated as *The White Paper* (Paris: Olympia Press, 1957; enlarged as *Le Livre blanc, suivi de quatorze textes érotiques inédits,* introduction by Milorad (Paris: Persona, 1981);

Le Mystère laïc (Giorgio de Chirico): Essai d'étude indirecte (Paris: Editions des Quatre Chemins, 1928); enlarged as *Essai de critique indirecte: Le Mystère laïc; Des Beaux-arts considérés comme un assassinat,* introduction by Bernard Grasset (Paris: Grasset, 1932);

Œdipe-roi; Roméo et Juliette (Paris: Plon, 1928);

25 Dessins d'un dormeur (Lausanne & Geneva: Mermod, 1928);

Les Enfants terribles: Roman (Paris: Grasset, 1929); translated by Samuel Putnam as *Enfants Terribles* (New York: Brewer & Warren, 1930);

Une Entrevue sur la critique avec Maurice Rouzaud, Les Amis d'Edouard, no. 145 (Paris: E. Champion, 1929);

Carnet de l'amiral (Paris: Grasset, 1930);

La Voix humaine: Pièce en un acte (Paris: Stock, Delamain & Boutelleau, 1930); translated by Wildman as *The Human Voice* (London: Vision Press, 1951);

Opium: Journal d'une désintoxication (Paris: Stock, Delamain & Boutelleau, 1930); translated by Ernest Boyd as *Opium: The Diary of an Addict* (London & New York: Longmans, 1932; London: Allen & Unwin, 1933);

La Machine infernale: Pièce en 4 actes (Paris: Grasset, 1934; London: Nelson, 1944); translated by Wildman as *The Infernal Machine: A Play in Four Acts* (London: Oxford University Press, 1936);

Mythologie, lithographs by Giorgio de Chirico (Paris: Editions des Quatre Chemins, 1934);

Soixante dessins pour "Les Enfants terribles" (Paris: Grasset, 1934 [i.e., 1935]);

Portraits-Souvenir, 1900–1914 (Paris: Grasset, 1935); translated by Margaret Crosland as *Paris Album, 1900–1914* (London: W. H. Allen, 1956);

Le Fantôme de Marseille (Paris: Gallimard, 1936);

Les Chevaliers de la Table Ronde: Pièce en trois actes (Paris: Gallimard, 1937);

Mon Premier Voyage (Tour du monde en 80 jours) (Paris: Gallimard, 1937); translated by Stuart Gilbert as *Round the World Again in Eighty Days* (London: Routledge, 1937);

Les Parents terribles: Pièce en trois actes (Paris: Gallimard, 1938);

Enigme: Poème (Paris: Editions des Réverbères, 1939);

La Fin du Potomak (Paris: Gallimard, 1940);

Les Monstres sacrés: Portrait d'une pièce en trois actes (Paris: Gallimard, 1940);

Allégories (Paris: Gallimard, 1941);

Dessins en marge des Chevaliers de la Table Ronde (Paris: Gallimard, 1941);

La Machine à écrire: Pièce en trois actes (Paris: Gallimard, 1941); translated by Ronald Duncan as *The Typewriter: A Play in Three Acts* (London: Dobson, 1947);

Le Gréco (Paris: Au Divan, 1943);

Renaud et Armide: Tragédie (Paris: Gallimard, 1943);

Serge Lifar à l'Opéra, by Cocteau and Paul Valéry (Paris: Champrosay, 1944);

Léone (Paris: Gallimard, 1945); translated by Alan Neame as *Leoun,* in *Agenda,* 2, nos. 1 and 2 (1961);

Portrait de Mounet-Sully: Prose inédite, illustrated by Cocteau (Paris: Bernouard, 1945);

L'Aigle à deux têtes: Trois actes (Paris: Gallimard, 1946); translated and adapted by Duncan as *The Eagle Has Two Heads* (London: Vision Press, 1948; New York: Funk & Wagnalls, 1948);

La Belle et la Bête, Journal d'un film (Paris: Janin, 1946); translated by Duncan as *Diary of a Film (La Belle et la Bête)* (London: Dobson, 1950; New York: Roy, 1950);

La Crucifixion: Poème (Paris: Morihien, 1947); translated by Jack Hirschman as *The Crucifixion* (Bethlehem, Pa.: Quarter Press, 1976);

Deux Travestis, illustrated by Cocteau (Paris: Fournier, 1947)–comprises *Le Fantôme de Marseille* and *Le Numéro Barbette;*

Le Difficulté d'être (Paris: Morihien, 1947); translated by Elizabeth Sprigge as *The Difficulty of Being* (London: Owen, 1966; New York: Coward-McCann, 1967);

L'Eternel retour (Paris: Nouvelles Editions Française, 1947);

Le Foyer des artistes (Paris: Plon, 1947);

Ruy Blas: Adapté pour l'écran par Jean Cocteau (Paris: Morihien, 1947);

Œuvres complètes de Jean Cocteau, 11 volumes (Lausanne, Switzerland: Marguerat, 1947–1951);

Drôle de ménage: Textes et dessins (Paris: Morihien, 1948);

Poèmes: Jean Cocteau (Paris: Gallimard, 1948)–comprises *Léon, Allégories, La Crucifixion,* "Neiges," and "Un ami dort";

Reines de la France, by Cocteau and Guillaume, illustrated by Christian Bérard (Paris: Maurice Darantière, 1948; republished, with only Cocteau's text, Paris: Grasset, 1952);

Le Sang d'un poète, film, photographs by Sacha Masour (Paris: Marin, 1948); translated by Lily Pons as *The Blood of a Poet: A Film* (New York: Bodley Press, 1949);

Dufy (Paris: Flammarion, 1949);

Lettre aux Américains (Paris: Grasset, 1949);

Maalesh: Journal d'une tournée de théâtre (Paris: Gallimard, 1949); translated by Mary C. Hoeck as *Maalesh: A Theatrical Tour in the Middle-East* (London: Owen, 1956; Westport, Conn.: Greenwood Press, 1978);

Théâtre de Poche (Paris: Morihien, 1949); enlarged as *Nouveau Théâtre de Poche* (Monaco: Editions du Rocher, 1960);

Modigliani (Paris: Hazan, 1950);

Orphée: Film, photographs by Roger Corbeau (Paris: La Parade, 1950);

Jean Marais (Paris: Calmann-Lévy, 1951);

Bacchus: Pièce en trois actes (Paris: Gallimard, 1952);

Le Chiffre sept (Paris: Seghers, 1952);

Gide vivant: Paroles de Jean Cocteau, edited by Jean-Claude Colin-Simard (Paris: Amiot-Dumont, 1952);

Journal d'un inconnu (Paris: Grasset, 1952); translated by Alec Brown as *The Hand of a Stranger* (London: Elek Books, 1956; New York: Horizon, 1959);

La Nappe du Catalan: Soixante-quatres poèmes et seize lithographies en couleurs, by Cocteau and Georges Hugnet (Paris: Imprimerie Fequet & Baudier, 1952);

Appogiatures (Monaco: Editions de Rocher, 1953);

Démarche d'un poète: Der Lebensweg eines Dichters, bilingual edition, with German translation by Friedhelm Kemp (Munich: Bruckmann, 1953);

Dentelle d'éternité (Paris: Seghers, 1953);

Clair-Obscur: Poèmes (Monaco: Editions de Rocher, 1954);

Colette: Discours de réception à l'Académie royale de langue et de littérature française (Paris: Grasset, 1955);

Discours de réception à l'Académie Française et Réponse d'André Maurois (Paris: Gallimard, 1955);

Le Dragon des mers, illustrated by Foujita (Paris: Georges Guillot, 1955);

Adieu à Mistinguett (Liège, Belgium: Editions Dynamo, 1956);

Le Discours de Strasbourg (Metz, France: Imprimerie de la S.M.E.I., 1956);

Le Discours d'Oxford, edited by Jean Seznec (Paris: Gallimard, 1956); translated by Jean Stewart as "Poetry and Invisibility," in *London Magazine* (January 1957);

Poèmes, 1916–1955 (Paris: Gallimard, 1956);

Témoignage (Flers-de-l'Orne, France: Bertrand, 1956);

La Chapelle Saint-Pierre, Villefranche-sur-Mer (Monaco: Editions du Rocher, 1957);

La Corrida du Premier Mai (Paris: Grasset, 1957);

Erik Satie (Liège, Belgium: Editions Dynamo, 1957);

Paraprosodies, précédées de 7 dialogues (Monaco: Editions du Rocher, 1958);

La Salle des mariages, Hôtel de Ville de Menton (Monaco: Editions du Rocher, 1958);

La Canne blanche (Paris: Editions Estienne, 1959);

Gondole des morts (Milan: All'Insegna del Pesce d'oro, 1959);

Poésie critique, 2 volumes (Paris: Gallimard, 1959, 1960);

Guide à l'usage des visiteurs de la chapelle Saint-Blaise-des-Simples (Monaco: Editions du Rocher, 1960);

Le Testament d'Orphée, Brimborions, no. 63 (Liège, Belgium: Editions Dynamo, 1960);

Notes sur "Le Testament d'Orphée," Brimborions, no. 71 (Liège, Belgium: Editions Dynamo, 1960);

Cérémonial espagnol du Phénix; suivi de La Partie d'échecs (Paris: Gallimard, 1961);

Le Cordon ombilical: Souvenirs (Paris: Plon, 1962);

Discours à l'Académie royale de langue et de littérature françaises, Brimborions, no. 99 (Liège, Belgium: Editions Dynamo, 1962);

L'Impromptu du Palais-Royal: Divertissement (Paris: Gallimard, 1962);

Picasso de 1916 à 1961 (Monaco: Editions du Rocher, 1962);

Le Requiem (Paris: Gallimard, 1962);

La Comtesse de Noailles: Oui et non (Paris: Librairie Académique Perrin, 1963);

Entre Picasso et Radiguet, edited by André Fermigier (Paris: Hermann, 1967);

Faire-Part, edited by Pierre Chanel, preface by Claude Michel Cluny (Paris: Chambelland, 1968); republished as *Faire-Part: Poèmes 1922–1962,* new introduction by Jean Marais (Paris: Saint-Germain-des-Prés, 1969);

La Belle et la Bête/Beauty and the Beast, edited by Robert M. Hammond, bilingual edition of the shooting script (New York: New York University Press, 1970);

Du Cinématographe, edited by André Bernard and Claude Gauteur (Paris: Belfond, 1973);

Paul et Virginie, by Cocteau and Raymond Radiguet (Paris: Edition Spéciale, 1973);

Poésie de journalisme, 1935–1938, edited, with an introduction and notes, by Chanel (Paris: Belfond, 1973);

Mes monstres sacrés: Jean Cocteau, compiled by Edouard Dermit and Bertrand Meyer, introduction by Milorad (Paris: Encre, 1979);

Le Passé défini: Journal, 3 volumes, edited by Chanel (Paris: Gallimard, 1983–1989); volumes 1 and 2 translated by Richard Howard as *Past Tense: Diaries,* introduction by Ned Rorem (2 volumes, San Diego & New York: Harcourt Brace Jovanovich, 1987; volume 1, London: Hamilton, 1987; volume 2, London: Methuen, 1990);

Embarcadères: Poèmes inédits, edited by Pierre Caizergues (Fontfroide: Fata Morgana, 1986);

Journal: 1942–1945, edited, with an introduction and notes, by Jean Touzot (Paris: Gallimard, 1989);

Œuvres poétiques complètes, edited by Michel Décaudin and others, Bibliothèque de la Pléiade, no. 460 (Paris: Gallimard, 1999).

Editions and Collections: *Morceaux choisis: Poèmes* (Paris: Gallimard, 1932);

Théâtre, 2 volumes (Paris: Gallimard, 1948);

Orphée: The Play and the Film, edited, with an introduction in English, by Edward Freeman (Oxford: Blackwell, 1976);

Le Mystère de Jean l'Oiseleur, edited by Milorad (Paris: Persona, 1983);

La Machine infernale: Pièce en 4 actes, edited, with an introduction, notes, and commentary, by Gérard Lieber (Paris: Librairie Générale Française, 1992);

Carnet de l'amiral X, edited, with an introduction, by Pierre Caizergues (Saint-Clément-de-Rivière: Fata Morgana, 1997);

La Machine infernale, edited, with notes and commentary, by Thanh-Vân Ton-That (Paris: Larousse-Bordas, 1998);

Le Livre blanc et autres textes, edited, with an introduction, by Bernard Benech, preface by Dominique Fernandez (Paris: Librairie Générale Française, 1999);

Le Potomak: 1913–1914; précédé d'un Prospectus 1916, preface by Serge Linares (Paris: Passage du Marais, 2000).

Editions in English: *Children of the Game,* translated by Rosamund Lehmann (London: Harvill, 1955); republished as *Les Enfants Terribles* (London: Harvill, 1955); republished as *The Holy Terrors* (Norfolk, Conn.: James Laughlin, 1957);

The Journals of Jean Cocteau, edited and translated, with an introduction, by Wallace Fowlie (New York: Criterion Books, 1956; London: Museum Press, 1957);

The Imposter, translated by Dorothy Williams (London: Owen, 1957; New York: Citadel, 1960);

Opium: The Diary of a Cure, translated by Margaret Crosland and Sinclair Road (London: Owen, 1957; New York: Grove, 1958); republished, with a new introduction by Crosland, as *Opium: The Illustrated Diary of His Cure* (London: Owen / Chester Springs, Pa.: Dufour, 1990);

The Miscreant, translated by Williams (London: Owen, 1958; republished, with an introduction, by Serena Thirkell, London: Brilliance Books, 1986);

My Journey Round the World, translated by W. J. Strachan (London: Owen, 1958);

Five Plays: Jean Cocteau (New York: Hill & Wang, 1961); abridged as *Four Plays: Jean Cocteau* (London: MacGibbon & Kee, 1962)—comprises *Antigone,* translated by Carl Wildman; *Intimate Relations (Les Parents terribles),* translated by Charles Frank; *The Holy Terrors (Les Monstres sacrés),* translated by Edward O. Marsh; and *The Eagle with Two Heads (L'Aigle à deux têtes),* translated by Wildman;

Orpheus; Œdipus Rex; The Infernal Machine: Jean Cocteau, translated, with a foreword and introductory essay, by Wildman (London & New York: Oxford University Press, 1962);

The Infernal Machine, and Other Plays, translated by Albert Bermel and others (Norfolk, Conn.: New Directions, 1963)—includes *The Infernal Machine,* translated by Bermel; *Orpheus,* translated by John Savacool; *The Eiffel Tower Wedding Party,* translated by Dudley Fitts; *The Knights of the Round Table,* translated by W. H. Auden; and *Bacchus,* translated by Mary C. Hoeck;

The Wedding on the Eiffel Tower, translated by Michael Benedikt, in *Modern French Plays,* edited by Benedikt and George Wellwarth (London: Faber & Faber, 1965);

My Contemporaries, edited and translated, with an introduction, by Crosland (London: Owen, 1967; Philadelphia: Chilton, 1968);

Two Screenplays: The Blood of a Poet; The Testament of Orpheus, translated by Carol Martin-Sperry (New York: Orion, 1968; London: Calder & Boyars, 1970);

Le Livre blanc, translated, with an introduction, by Crosland (London: Owen, 1969);

Professional Secrets: An Autobiography of Jean Cocteau Drawn from His Lifetime Writings, edited by Roger Phelps, translated by Richard Howard (New York: Farrar, Straus & Giroux, 1970; London: Vision Press, 1972);

Beauty and the Beast: Diary of a Film, translated by Ronald Duncan, new introduction by George Amberg (New York: Dover, 1972);

Three Screenplays: L'Eternel Retour, Orphée, La Belle et la Bête, translated by Martin-Sperry (New York: Grossman, 1972; London: Lorrimer, 1972);

Cocteau's World: An Anthology of Writings by Jean Cocteau, edited and translated by Crosland (London: Owen, 1972; New York: Dodd, Mead, 1973)–includes *Professional Secrets;*

The White Paper, introduction by Kevin Lane (London: Brilliance Books, 1983);

Souvenir Portraits: Paris in the Belle Epoque, translated by Jesse Browner (New York: Paragon House, 1990; London: Robson, 1991);

Les Parents Terribles, translated by Jeremy Sams, introduction by Simon Callow (London: Hern, 1994);

Round the World Again in 80 Days, translated by Stuart Gilbert, introduction by Callow (London: Tauris Parke, 2000).

PLAY PRODUCTIONS: *Le Dieu bleu,* ballet, scenario by Cocteau and Frédéric de Madrazo, music by Reynaldo Hahn, Paris, Théâtre du Châtelet, June 1912;

Parade, ballet, scenario by Cocteau, music by Erik Satie, Paris, Théâtre du Châtelet, 18 May 1917;

Le Bœuf sur le toit, musical spectacle, scenario by Cocteau and music by Darius Milhaud, Paris, Théâtre des Champs-Elysées, 21 February 1920;

Les Mariés de la Tour Eiffel, Paris, Théâtre des Champs-Elysées, 18 June 1921;

Antigone, adapted by Cocteau from Sophocles' play of that title, music by Arthur Honegger, Paris, Théâtre de l'Atelier, 20 December 1922;

Roméo et Juliette, adapted by Cocteau from William Shakespeare's play *Romeo and Juliet,* Paris, Théâtre de la Cigale, 2 June 1924;

Le Train bleu, ballet, scenario by Cocteau, music by Milhaud, Paris, Théâtre des Champs-Elysées, 20 June 1924;

Orphée, Paris, Théâtre des Arts, 17 June 1926;

Œdipus-Rex, opera-oratio, libretto adapted by Cocteau from Sophocles' play of that title, music by Igor Stravinsky, Paris, Théâtre Sarah-Bernhardt, 30 May 1927;

La Voix humaine, Paris, Comédie-Française, 17 February 1930;

La Machine infernale, Paris, Théâtre des Champs-Elysées, 10 April 1934;

Œdipe-roi, Paris, Nouveau Théâtre Antoine, June 1937;

Les Chevaliers de la Table Rond, Paris, Théâtre de l'Œuvre, 14 October 1937;

Les Parents terribles, Paris, Théâtre des Ambassadeurs, 14 November 1938;

Les Monstres sacrés, Paris, Théâtre Michel, 17 February 1940;

Le Bel indifférent, Paris, Théâtre des Bouffes-Parisiens, 1940;

La Machine à écrire, Paris, Théâtre Hébertot, 29 April 1941; Paris, Théâtre Français, Salle Luxembourg, 21 March 1956;

Renaud et Armide, Paris, Comédie-Française, 13 April 1943;

Le Jeune homme et la mort, ballet, scenario by Cocteau, music by J. S. Bach, Paris, Théâtre des Champs-Elysées, 25 June 1946;

L'Aigle à deux têtes, Paris, Théâtre Hébertot, November 1946;

Un Tramway nommé Désir, adapted by Cocteau from Paule de Beaument's translation of Tennessee Williams's *A Streetcar Named Desire,* Paris, Théâtre Edouard VII, 17 October 1949;

Bacchus, Paris, Théâtre Marigny, 20 December 1951;

La Dame à la Licorne, ballet, libretto by Cocteau, music by Jacques Chailley, Munich, Theaters am Gärtnerplatz, 9 May 1953; Paris, L'Opéra, 28 January 1959;

L'Impromptu du Palais-Royal, Tokyo, 1 May 1962.

PRODUCED SCRIPTS: *Le Sang d'un poète,* motion picture, Vicomte de Noailles, 1932; subtitled English version released as *The Blood of a Poet,* Edward T. Ricci, 1933;

Ecco la felicità, motion picture, adapted by Cocteau, André Cerf, and Marcel L'Herbier from a play by Nicolas Evreinoff, Scalera Film S.p.a/DisCina, 1940; released in France as *La Comédie du bonheur,* 1942;

L'Eternel retour, motion picture, Films André Paulvé, 1943; subtitled English version released in the

United States as *The Eternal Return,* DisCina International, 1948, in Britain as *Love Eternal,* n.d.;

Le Baron fantôme, motion picture, by Louis Chavance and Serge de Poligny, additional dialogue by Cocteau, Consortium de Productions de Films, 1943; subtitled English version released as *The Phantom Baron,* n.d.;

Les Dames du Bois de Boulogne, motion picture, adapted by Robert Bresson from Denis Diderot's novel *Jacques le Fataliste et son maître,* additional dialogue by Cocteau, Les Films Raoul Ploquin, 1945; subtitled English version released in the United States as *The Ladies of the Bois de Boulogne,* Brandon Films, 1964, elsewhere as *The Ladies of the Park,* n.d.;

La Belle et la Bête, motion picture, Films André Paulvé, 1946; subtitled English version released as *Beauty and the Beast,* Lopert Pictures, 1948;

L'Aigle à deux têtes, motion picture, Les Films Vog, 1947; subtitled English version released as *The Eagle Has Two Heads,* 1948;

Ruy Blas, motion picture, adapted by Cocteau from Victor Hugo's play of that title, Pierre Billon, 1947; subtitled English version released as *Ruy Blas,* DisCina International, 1948;

Les Parents terribles, motion picture, adapted by Cocteau from his play of that title, Films Ariane, 1948; subtitled English version released as *The Storm Within,* DisCina International, 1950;

Ce siècle a cinquante ans, motion picture, by Cocteau, Marcel Achard, Françoise Giroud, and André Roussin S.E.P.I.C./UGC Images, 1949; dubbed English version released in the United States as *Days of Our Years,* Souvaine Selective Pictures, 1951, elsewhere as *The Century Is Fifty,* n.d.;

Orphée, motion picture, Films André Paulvé/Films du Palais Royal, 1950; subtitled English version released as *Orpheus,* DisCina International, 1950;

Les Enfants terribles, motion picture, adapted by Cocteau and Jean-Pierre Melville from Cocteau's novel of that title, Melville Productions, 1950; subtitled English version released as *The Strange Ones,* Arthur Mayer–Edward Kingsley, 1952;

La Corona negra, motion picture, adapted by Cocteau, Luis Saslavsky, and Charles de Peyret-Chappuis from a story by Cocteau, Spanish dialogue by Miguel Mihura Suevia Films S. A., 1951; French version released as *La Couronne noire,* n.d.; English version released as *Black Crown,* n.d;

Le Bel indifférent, motion picture, by Jacques Demy, scenario and dialogue by Cocteau, 1957;

Le Testament d'Orphée, motion picture, Editions Cinégraphiques, 1960; subtitled English version released as *The Testament of Orpheus,* Films Around the World, 1962;

Princesse de Clèves, motion picture, adapted by Cocteau and Jean Delannoy from Marie-Madeleine de La Fayette's novel of that title, Enalpa Film/Produzioni Cinematografiche Mediterranee/Silver Films, 1960; English version released as *Princess of Cleves,* n.d.;

Thomas l'imposteur, motion picture, adapted by Cocteau, Georges Franju, and Michel Worms from Cocteau's novel of that title, Filmel, 1964.

OTHER: Jean Desbordes, *J'adore,* preface by Cocteau (Paris: Grasset, 1928);

Tennessee Williams, *Un Tramway nommé Désir,* translated by Paule de Beaument and adapted by Cocteau (Paris: Bordas, 1949).

Jean Cocteau's role in twentieth-century French poetry is not unlike that of the rather too talkative Sphinx in his play, *La Machine infernale* (1934; translated as *The Infernal Machine,* 1936), who asks of Oedipus the well-known, oft-repeated riddle but then gives the answer away. On the one hand, were one to ask most people what kind of artist Cocteau was, a "poet" would not be the first thing to come to mind: celebrated works such as his play *Orphée* (Orpheus, 1927; translated, 1933) or his motion picture *La Belle et la Bête, Journal d'un film* (1946; released as *Beauty and the Beast,* 1948) have made Cocteau more familiar to most people as dramatist or *cinéaste* (film producer). On the other hand, "poet" is something of a given, since Cocteau always insisted he was nothing but a poet, calling whatever he did, in fact—and he did nearly everything—poetry: cinema was *poésie cinématographique* (cinematic poetry); criticism, *poésie critique* (critical poetry); novels, *poésie de roman* (novelistic poetry); drama, *poésie de théâtre* (theatrical poetry), and so on. Then again, were it up to many of his contemporaries, Cocteau's contribution to twentieth-century French poetry, and to French literature in general, would best be forgotten: conservatives such as André Gide considered him a frivolous *mondain* (worldling) whose talent was mainly one of a superficial *bricolage,* or pottering; radicals such as André Breton considered him a bourgeois dandy who belonged in the salons, rubbing shoulders with fawning socialites. And yet, to ignore Cocteau, in particular his poetry, would be to do an injustice to one of the more original—in the sense of distinctive and individualized—bodies of work of the first half of the twentieth century. For while many of his contemporaries, such as Breton, were leaders of movements or hangers-on, identifying themselves as Dadaists, Surrealists, Existentialists and the like—that is to say, as spokesmen for, or as members of, various literary factions or schools—Cocteau followed his own path, remaining all his life something of

Cocteau (left) at the Lycée Condorcet during the 1901–1902 school year

a movement unto himself. Of course, this independence was often not by choice, as Cocteau's larger-than-life personality, or stranger-than-fiction persona, was for many cause enough for alienation.

Jean-Maurice Eugène Clément Cocteau was born on 5 July 1889, the youngest of three children of Georges Cocteau and Eugénie Cocteau (née Lecomte). His family, at least on his mother's side, the Lecomtes, was wealthy, and though the Cocteaus lived for most of the year in Paris, at 45 rue La Bruyère, Jean Cocteau was born in Maisons-Laffitte, where the family spent its summers. Maisons-Laffitte was a bourgeois suburb, twenty kilometers from the city; with luxurious parks, gardens, a castle, and a racecourse, it was an enchanting place for a child to grow up. The Paris home, which, as did the Maisons-Laffitte property, belonged to the maternal grandparents, was a world equally magical: it had secret passageways and mysterious nooks and recesses; and the grandfather, Eugène Lecomte, an accomplished cellist, filled his house with a wild, eclectic assortment of paintings (some by the nineteenth-century Romantic Eugène Delacroix), Greek busts, and other artifacts, both ancient and modern, the most intriguing of which must have been a wig belonging to the Italian composer Gioacchino Antonio Rossini,

whom the elder Lecomte had known and from whom he had inherited a piano. Rue La Bruyère, in the heart of the city, also offered the often outlandish spectacles of the music hall, the circus, and, especially, the theater, where names such as Madame Rétane and Sarah Bernhardt enthralled the imagination of an entire generation.

The wonder of Cocteau's childhood, spent as it was in a world of privilege and indulgence, of fantasy and adolescent freedom, which must have contributed to the overdeveloped sense of self-importance and the narcissism that plagued him throughout his life, was shattered by two things. The first, not surprisingly, was school, whose dreariness could hardly compete with the excitement he knew at home. If one accepts as autobiographical *Le Livre blanc* (1928; translated as *The White Paper,* 1957), an anonymous work, but generally attributed to him, the only appeal of school-going for Cocteau seemed to be its homoeroticism, notably in the form of a fascination with bullies, strong males of an almost animal beauty, who often make an appearance in his fictional and dramatic works and to whom he was attracted later on in real life. The prime example of the bully is Dargelos in the novel *Les Enfants terribles* (1929; translated as *Enfants Terribles,* 1930), named after a schoolmate at the Lycée Condorcet, Pierre Dargelos. Cocteau was known by his teachers to be a bright young man, but he lacked the discipline needed for success: after attending the Lycée Condorcet, he went to l'Ecole Fénélon, where he twice failed the *baccalauréat* (secondary-school examination giving university entrance qualification)—the second failure, in 1907, in spite of private tutoring, was largely as a result of an infatuation with the music-hall star Mistinguett, to whom he brought flowers after her afternoon performances.

The second thing which shattered the wonder of Cocteau's childhood was the suicide of his father on 5 April 1898 at the age of fifty-five. Georges Cocteau was trained as a lawyer; however, he abandoned his practice not long after marrying and lived as a *rentier,* or person of independent means, thereafter. He was endowed with some musical talent, but he was a rather uninteresting fellow, and his influence on Cocteau, compared to the influence of his doting mother and of her side of the family, seems negligible. No one is quite sure why he committed suicide, and Cocteau rarely spoke publicly of the incident, which occurred at 45 rue La Bruyère, only saying much later that his father killed himself under circumstances that would not make someone kill themselves "today" (he was speaking in a television interview in 1963). Rumors abound, of course, and there is a story of a financial disaster, and another of an illicit affair his wife had had with an unknown, exotic diplomat of which Jean would have been the offspring. This latter rumor was the version apparently spread by Jean Cocteau himself, most likely to give himself a more interesting paternal background. The absence of strong fatherly figures in Cocteau's work—*Thomas l'Imposteur* (1923; translated as *Thomas the Imposter,* 1925), *Les Enfants terribles, Le Grand Ecart* (1923; translated as *The Grand Ecart,* 1925)—is often interpreted as the consequence of Cocteau's fatherlessness.

Were it not for his mother's indulgence, Cocteau's lack of academic success, combined with a frail constitution and an ever-increasing appetite for independence and the "abundant" life (he claims, for example, to have spent a year in the brothels and opium dens of Marseilles), would have seriously limited his prospects of finding "respectable" work. At the death of her father in 1906, Eugénie Cocteau inherited a considerable fortune, and since her daughter, Marthe, had married and her older son, Paul, had followed in his grandfather's footsteps and found work in the stock market, her youngest child, Jean, was now alone at home and free to do as he pleased. Through his mother, who knew the wife of Alphonse Daudet, he was introduced to the Parisian literary milieu, and it was about this time that he started to write poetry. Given the nature of Cocteau's later production and the artistic background of his family, which was essentially musical and nonliterary—literature had been seen performed on stage rather than read—poetry may seem like

an unusual choice for him as a first attempt at creative activity. In all likelihood this decision was influenced by his new friendships, as well as by the many works he voraciously read on his own, by authors such as Oscar Wilde, Maurice Barrès, Edmond Rostand, Anna de Noailles, Charles Baudelaire, and Paul Verlaine.

In any case, Cocteau's public career as a poet began on 4 April 1908, at the age of eighteen. This debut came in the form of a recital of his poems at the Théâtre Femina on the Champs-Elysées, which was organized and paid for by Edouard de Max, a popular and flamboyant actor in the Comédie-Française. As had many young men (much to the chagrin of their mothers), Cocteau had been introduced to de Max as an adulating fan two years before. De Max's influence drew a large, distinguished crowd, and he even persuaded some of his fellow actors to participate in the recital. Laurent Tailhade, the poet and satirist, lent his prestige to the event by agreeing to give a lecture on contemporary poets, condemning all but Cocteau. Understandably, Cocteau's star rose quickly: critics raved and the doors to the literary and social circles of Paris were immediately flung wide open. He became linked with the most influential artists and personalities of his day, including Catulle Mendès, Lucien Daudet, Jules Lemaître, de Noailles, Marcel Proust, Charles Péguy, and François Mauriac. In 1909, with Maurice Rostand, the son of the dramatist, whose obsession with the actress Sarah Bernhardt led him to bleach his hair and paint his face like hers, Cocteau started *Schéhérazade,* a literary magazine that was published at irregular intervals, for a total of six issues, until 1911. In 1912, while still living with his mother, Cocteau rented space in the Hôtel Biron, where the sculptor Auguste Rodin lived.

The poems that were read and sung that April afternoon in 1908 before *le Tout-Paris* (the whole of Paris) were included in Cocteau's first published work, *La Lampe d'Aladin* (Aladdin's Lamp, 1909). These poems, as well as the two collections that quickly followed, *Le Prince frivole* (The Frivolous Prince, 1910) and *La Danse de Sophocle* (The Dance of Sophocles, 1912), were repudiated by Cocteau years later as silly and immature, and he never permitted them to be republished. Critics tend to agree with the author's lack of enthusiasm for his earliest works, as it is generally admitted that though they reveal signs of some genuine talent, they represent, more than anything, the output of an ambitious young man eager to please and impress his friends and benefactors. *La Lampe d'Aladin,* for instance, includes a hundred or so poems, many of which give some evidence of technical virtuosity, especially in the case of the many pastiches, but there is little sign of the originality or innovation found in his later works. An example of the tenor of the poems can be seen in these lines from "Les Bruits" (The Noises):

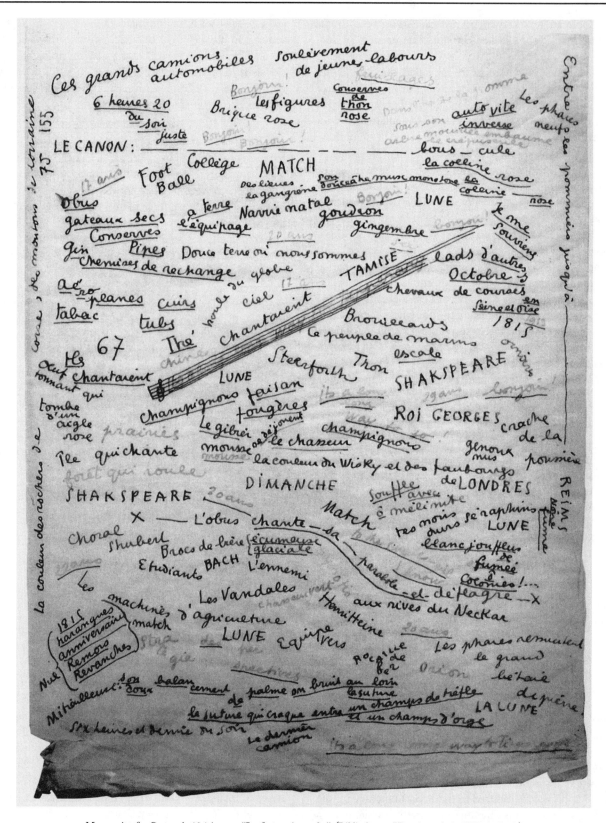

Manuscript for Cocteau's 1914 poem "La forêt qui marche" (Bibliothèque Historique de la Ville de Paris)

Avez-vous entendu l'appel hurlant et long,
L'appel, dans le fracas d'une mer glauque et flasque,
Et les volets mal clos claqués par la bourrasque,
L'appel désespéré du bateau moribond?

(Have you heard the call howling and long,
The call, in the crash of a sea glaucous and slack,
And the half-open shutters slammed about by the squall,
The desperate call of the dying ship?)

This quatrain of alexandrines would have surely rattled the casements of the Théâtre Femina as declaimed by some barrel-chested actor from the Comédie-Française, but it is rather too derivative to be of interest to modern readers. Most of the poems in *La Lampe d'Aladin* bear dedications to celebrated Parisian figures, including some of the performers from the Opéra or the Comédie-Française who had recited them at the Théâtre Femina; Alfred Vallette, director of the *Mercure de France,* who later published *Le Prince frivole* and *La Danse de Sophocle;* and Pierre Lafitte, owner of *Je Sais Tout,* the magazine in which "Les Façades" (Facades), the poem dedicated to him, first appeared.

Because of what they seem to reveal about Cocteau's character and about a life-pattern that he established early on, perhaps the most significant poems in *La Lampe d'Aladin* are those that deal with an event that occurred a few months after the Théâtre Femina recital. On 25 September 1908 in Venice, Cocteau's traveling companion and lover, Raymond Laurent, committed suicide—apparently over Cocteau's involvement with another man, Langhorn Whistler. In "Souvenir d'un soir d'automne au jardin Eaden" (Memory of a Fall Evening in the Eaden Garden), Cocteau tells of a stroll with three others taken before the incident and then after:

Un geste . . . un coup de revolver,
Du sang rouge à des marches blanches,
Des gens accourus qui se penchent,
Une gondole . . . un corps couvert...
Un geste . . . un coup de revolver,
Du sang rouge à des marches blanches...

Et ce fut tout! . . . Quelques effrois,
Quelques amicales paroles,
Et dans les joyeuses gondoles,
L'ennui de n'être plus que trois!

(A gesture . . . a gun shot,
Red blood on white stairs,
People flocking and leaning over,
A gondola . . . a covered body . . .
A gesture . . . a gun shot,
Red blood on white stairs . . .

And that was all! . . . Some fright,
Some friendly words,

And in the joyful gondolas,
The boredom of being only three now!)

The last line seems to refer to the "boredom" of no longer being a foursome in the "joyful gondolas" after a frightful, bloody incident. Perhaps the apparent indifference expressed in this verse is a whistling in the dark, a deliberate effort to cloak a real horror. In any case, what is also apparent is something that often recurred in Cocteau's life, the sense of tragedy—mostly for others—surrounding his dangerous friendship.

Le Prince frivole, Cocteau's second collection of poetry, bears more than any other, as the title may suggest, the traces of his conquest of the fashionable literary salons of Paris. In "Les Sonnets de l'hôtel Biron" (Sonnets Composed at the Hotel Biron) the reader sees Cocteau acting the host to his friends and admirers in his new apartment. Of Reynaldo Hahn, the composer, he writes:

Reynaldo, vous chantiez, cigarette à la bouche,
Des airs vénitiens langoureux et troublants;
Et vos doigts souples qui volaient de touche en touche,
Sur un chemin d'ivoire étaient dix danseurs blancs.

(Reynaldo, you sang, cigarette in mouth,
Langorous and troubling Venetian airs;
And your supple fingers that flew from key to key,
On an ivory road were ten white dancers).

Filled with references to the fashionable shops of the day that sold such things as artificial flowers, perfumes, and hats, the verse in *Le Prince frivole* gives the impression that at this time poetry for Cocteau was a *jeu de société* (parlor game) designed to please the countesses, duchesses, and mesdames who enjoyed nothing more than to host soirees attended by charming, good-looking young poets.

Just after the publication of *Le Prince frivole,* Cocteau met the Comtesse de Noailles, the famed poet and reigning queen of the Paris literary salons, whose sublime style, aristocratic manner, and never-ending complaints about failing health he quickly adopted as his own. Hence, *La Danse de Sophocle,* published two years after *Le Prince frivole,* is reminiscent of the countess's work: poems on insomnia and death; echoes of Pierre de Ronsard, Verlaine, and Victor Hugo; and titles such as "Le Délire matinal" (Morning Delirium) and "Le Cœur éternel" (The Eternal Heart). The most significant thing about the publication of *La Danse de Sophocle* is the review of it that appeared in the September 1912 issue of the *Nouvelle Revue Française.* It was signed by Henri Ghéon, but it is generally accepted that Gide, founder of the journal and Ghéon's companion at the time, had a large part in the writing. The gist of the

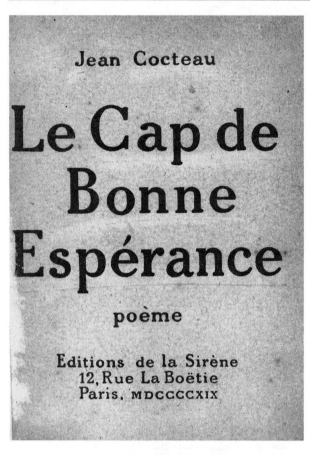

Cover of the collection of poetry that Cocteau dedicated to Roland
Garros, a French pilot who was shot down and killed on
5 October 1918 (Perkins Library, Duke University)

review is that Cocteau is something of a legend in his own mind, and his identifying himself with Sophocles, the great tragedian, is the very height of hubris. For Ghéon (read Gide), Cocteau is an immature poet who may one day reveal his gifts, but whose facile success as of yet rests on nothing but posing. This review marks the beginning of a lengthy, strained relationship between Cocteau and Gide, who was twenty years his senior and who mounted a lifelong cabal against him.

Cocteau's meeting in 1912 with Serge Diaghilev, founder of the Ballets Russe that was dazzling Parisian audiences, marks a significant turning point in his life. Diaghilev was a formidable character whose ruthlessness and despotism were matched only by his extraordinary talent for surrounding himself with the most brilliant and innovative of artists: his lover-protégé, the great dancer Vaslov Nijinsky, whom "Jeanchik," as Diaghilev called Cocteau, found irresistible on and off stage; and composers such as Claude Debussy, Maurice Ravel, Francis Poulenc, and Igor Stravinsky, whose Le Sacre du printemps (Rite of Spring) was a succès de scandale when Diaghilev produced it in May 1913.

What Cocteau learned from Diaghilev, especially from the experience of Stravinsky's Le Sacre du printemps, which put all of Paris in an uproar, was the supreme importance of the artistic endeavor: the goal of art was not to please the countesses of the literary salons; its merit was not to be found in the adulation of the public. The greatness of art, Cocteau discovered while in Diaghilev's company, was not in its frivolity, but in its depth; great art comes from toil, not from play, and especially from the willingness of the artist to break with the conventions of his medium and of his society. "Astound me!" Diaghilev told Cocteau, a command that Cocteau tried to fulfill during the rest of his career. The first work to come out of this renewed sense of vocation was the highly original Le Potomak, 1913–1914 (The Potomac, 1913–1914), a collection of drawings, poetry, and prose dedicated to Stravinsky, written in seclusion in 1913 and 1914 from Cocteau's former milieu, but not published until 1919.

At the outbreak of war in 1914, because of his ardent patriotism as well as his hunger for novel experiences, Cocteau volunteered for military service but was considered medically unfit for duty. Nonetheless, he did manage to make his way to the Belgian front illegally, as an ambulance driver, where he experienced firsthand the horror of war. He witnessed, for instance, the despair of the starving, dying wounded of Rheims, which he describes in his novel Thomas l'imposteur. Another experience during this time that he incorporated in his later works was his meeting the famed aviator Roland Garros and accompanying him on experimental flights over Paris. Garros was working on a way to time the firing of a fixed gun through the propeller of a plane, a feat of engineering that he managed to accomplish and use successfully in three battles before being shot down behind enemy lines in April 1915 and spending nearly three years in prisoner-of-war camps before a spectacular escape in February 1918. Cocteau, of course, never one to miss an opportunity to associate himself with greatness, later said that Garros figured out his method while visiting him in his mother's apartment and staring at a fan. In 1919 Cocteau published Le Cap de Bonne-Espérance (The Cape of Good Hope), his first volume of poetry in seven years, as a sort of tribute to his aviator friend; its dedication reads: "A Roland Garros, prisonnier en Allemagne" (For Roland Garros, Prisoner in Germany). Garros, who had returned to combat duty after his escape, was shot down and killed 5 October 1918, while the book was being printed.

Le Cap de Bonne-Espérance is a collection of poems whose resemblance to the poetry in Cocteau's first three collections lies only in its use of French words—most of the time, for in some poems in Le Cap de

Bonne-Espérance, words give way to simple syllables, as in "Tentative d'évasion" (Escape Attempt):

> Au fil du bol
>   éol
>   ien   oé   ié
>
>   mon doigt mouillé
>
>   éveille
>   un astre
>
> éo   ié   iu   ié
>
> é   é   ié   io   ié
>
> ui   ui   io   ié
>
> (At the edge of the airy
>   firm
>   ament . . .
>
>   my wet finger
>
>   awakens
>   a star
> . . . .
> . . . .
> . . . .).

Diaghilev's injunction to astound or astonish is not the only thing responsible for this revolution in poetic style: since *La Danse de Sophocle,* Cocteau had been exposed to the new aesthetics being developed not in the conservative salons but in the more "leftist" international milieu of Montparnasse. He was introduced to Pablo Picasso and Cubism with its emphasis on the purely formal elements of art; to Guillaume Apollinaire, whose typographical experiments in *Alcools, poèmes 1898–1913* (1913; translated, 1964) and *Calligrammes, poèmes de la paix et de la guerre, 1913–1916* (1918; translated as *Calligrammes, Poems of Peace and War 1913–1916,* 1980) had had a profound effect on French poetry; and to poets associated with Surrealism and with its precursors, Dadaism and Futurism, such as Max Jacob, Pierre Reverdy, and Blaise Cendrars, whose radical techniques of composition, including automatic writing, wreaked havoc on syntactic and semantic conventions. The influence of this avant-garde milieu on Cocteau is evident in the formal aspect of *Le Cap de Bonne-Espérance.* It is also evident in the collaborative effort that produced the ballet *Parade* (1917), with Cocteau creating the argument, Léonide Massine the choreography, Erik Satie the score, and Picasso the set design and the costumes. In a note for the program of the ballet, Apollinaire coined the term "surréalisme" (Surrealism) to describe *Parade.*

Despite this influence, *Le Cap de Bonne-Espérance* does testify to Cocteau's profound originality in the use he

makes of all the technical possibilities available to him. The central image of the collection is an airplane, and with a dazzling array of images the poet manages to portray its dizzying flight as it soars above the countryside, as in "Préambule" (Preamble):

> Il n'y a pas une minute à perdre
>
> Les coqs
> ce brouhaha de limbes
> ces
> aboiements de fantômes en fuite
> autour de l'église   angélus
>
> Le hameau
> accouche   il
>   est pâle   il a peur
>
> (There is not a minute to waste
>
> The cocks
> that hurly-burly of limbo
> those
> bayings of phantoms in flight
> around the church   angelus
>
> The hamlet
> is in labor   it
>   is pale   it is afraid).

The accumulation of acoustic effects and the arrangement of words on the page give the impression of having one's voice intermittently drowned out by the motor of the plane:

> Enfin
>
> voir ce gibier
> face à face
> Halète   coqs
> pèse   coqs
> herbe   coqs
> ring d'ombre   coqs
>
> Jacob lutta contre l'ange
> toute la nuit
>
> Au matin
>
> il était seul
>
> Talus   Enclumes   Angélus
>
>   Les   coqs
> l'aube mouille
>
> (At last
>
> to see that game
> face to face

Cocteau in 1920

Pant   cocks
weigh   cocks
grass   cocks
ring of shadow   cocks

Jacob wrestled with the angel
all night

In the morning

he was alone

Talus   Anvil   Angelus

    The   cocks
dawn moistens).

The airplane in *Le Cap de Bonne-Espérance* is for Cocteau the symbol of the poet. In spite of being dragged down by matter, it surges upward, into the airy realm of sky, and the solitude it experiences is the price it must pay for the possibility of exploration and discovery and for the feeling of absolute freedom, as in "Tentative d'évasion": "Cogne les métaux des planètes / je vibre en réponse aux planètes / incroyable de solitude / et de musique / fraternité" (Strike the metals of planets / I vibrate in response to the planets / incredible of solitude / and of music / fraternity). This conception of the poet is a universe away from the poet as "prince frivole."

Another volume of poetry written during the war, a cycle of eleven poems called "Le Discours du grand sommeil" (The Discourse of the Great Sleep), was published in his 1924 collection, *Poésie, 1916–1923* (Poetry, 1916–1923). Unlike *Le Cap de Bonne-Espérance*, these poems deal more directly with Cocteau's experience of the horrors of war, and in their formal aspect they reflect a more subdued attitude toward technical experimentation, as in "Prologue":

J'ai emporté le capitaine.
La voiture bascule
sur la route défoncée par les marmites.
Je lui tenais le bras
et je ne m'apercevais pas qu'il était mort
parce que son bracelet-montre
continuait de vivre dans ma main.

(I took the captain.
The car teeters
on the road broken up by shells.
I was holding his arm
not realizing that he was dead
because his wrist-watch
kept ticking in my hand).

Cocteau, whose seemingly frivolous demeanor had subjected him to criticism for a perceived indifference to his war experiences, brings the reader with him to the front in this poem to see the horror that humanity is capable of inflicting upon itself. In brilliant, intense images he shows the ruins, the disease, the dying, the cold, the torture. Mankind, in this situation, is reduced to its most "natural," instinctual, uncivilized brutality. In the title poem of the collection, "Discours du grand sommeil," the reader discovers an "angel" who seems to be the poet's Muse, telling the poet to "go," presumably to the war front and as a witness to the folly:

> Tu verras l'Eden infect.
> L'homme nu,
> L'homme inconnu.
> S'il rentre parmi les siens
> son regard remplit sa femme de détresse.
> Il asseoit son corps
> qui fume la pipe;
> mais la pensée,
> prise aux détours du labyrinthe,
> reste lointaine
>
> (You will see Eden diseased.
> Man naked,
> Man unknown.
> If he returns among his own
> his gaze fills his wife with distress.
> He seats his body
> which smokes the pipe;
> but thought,
> stuck in the windings of the labyrinth,
> remains distant).

"Le Discours du grand sommeil" includes an interesting prose piece, "Visite" (Visit), written from a point of view with a long literary history–that of a dead man. The dead man, perhaps a soldier, though it is never clearly stated, speaks matter-of-factly and rather predictably about things on the other side–how the concepts of time and space have different meanings over there, for instance, and how at the moment of death it is like seeing oneself next to a set of clothes discarded the night before. However, he does say something rather intriguing about poetry, namely that it is like death, and consequently, that the poet is continuously between two worlds, teasing the void: "Cette nausée d'architecte toujours taquinant le vide, voilà le propre du poète. Le vrai poète est, comme nous, invisible aux vivants" (That nausea of the architect always teasing the void, therein lies the nature of the poet. The true poet is, like us, invisible to the living).

With *Vocabulaire* (Vocabulary), a collection of poems written during the years 1918–1919, but published only in 1922, Cocteau moves further away from the formal experimentation that characterized his earlier work. This move is perhaps because of the contemplative tone of the collection, which requires a more classical restraint. As the title of one poem indicates, *Vocabulaire* is the work of "Le Poète de trente ans" (The Poet at Thirty), who finds himself halfway through the seasons of life, worried about what the future has in store:

> Me voici maintenant au milieu de mon âge,
> Je me tiens à cheval sur ma belle maison;
> Des deux côtés je vois le même paysage,
> Mais il n'est pas vêtu de la même saison
>
> (Here I am in the middle of my years
> I am sitting astride my beautiful house;
> On both sides I see the same landscape,
> But it is not clothed in the same season).

The poet has had a good life until now, a "belle maison" (beautiful house), but what he fears most is death, ever-present and inevitable, which spares nothing and nobody. It is the inseparable other side ("l'envers") of life ("l'endroit"), and even in the midst of one's greatest pleasures it is impossible to forget its grip:

> Nous ne pouvons te voir et te sentons mêlée
> Aux plaisirs, à l'amour don't [*sic*?] la chaleur ailée
> Fait les cœurs les plus durs, comme neige dissous;
> Bien que tes habitants reposassent dans l'herbe,
> Nous marchions sans souci sur l'étoffe superbe,
>   Et, soudain, nous sommes dessous
>
> (We cannot see you but feel you mixed
> To the pleasures, to love whose winged warmth
> Makes the hardest hearts like snow dissolve;
> Even though your inhabitants repose in the grass,
> We walked without care on the superb cloth,
>   And, suddenly, we are beneath).

In a series of "tombeaux" (tomb) poems, Cocteau shows that even the great poets and lovers of myth and history–Sappho, Socrates, Narcissus, Don Juan–could not escape. Nonetheless, the possibility of poetry and love, or beauty, is what allows "Le Poète de trente ans," atop his "maison," to cheat death, momentarily to be sure, and to find in this worldly existence something for which to live:

> Je veux bien, tu me dis encore que tu m'aimes,
> Vénus. Si je n'avais pourtant parlé de toi,
> Si ma maison n'était faite avec mes poèmes,
> Je sentirais le vide et tomberais du toit
>
> (I'm prepared to believe you still love me,
> Venus. But if I hadn't written about you,
> If my house wasn't built of my poems,
> I would feel the void and fall from the roof).

The literary scene that served as the background for Cocteau's creative activity during the next decade was of a nature to intimidate all but the most serious and committed of artists. Feuding among competing literary magazines, such as Pierre Albert-Birot's *Sic,* Reverdy's *Nord-Sud,* Francis Picabia's *391,* and Breton's *Littérature,* led to brutal attacks against one another's contributors and editors. Often the feuding turned into infighting, as the artist featured in one issue was snubbed or even became the target of abuse in the following one. The rise and fall of Futurism, with its sympathies for Italian fascism, and of the nihilistic Dadaism, and the establishment of Surrealism as their more enduring successor, created several lingering factions, often linked with a particular magazine, which clashed not only on the literary scene but also on the political. Assuredly the most formidable personality of this time was Breton, the self-appointed "Pope"–as he was called by his detractors–of the Surrealists, who spent most of his time in apologetics defending his movement and excommunicating from it members who were not "orthodox."

Cocteau did not thrive within this environment, more for personal rather than literary reasons. As he was becoming more well known, he was drawing more and more attention to himself, most of it bad. *Sic,* for instance, never published anything by Cocteau–it is said because of his friendship with Apollinaire–except a cruel fake alluding to the death of his brother. Reverdy, a fervently religious man who grew weary of Cocteau's lack of faith, published only one article of his in *Nord-Sud.* Picabia continuously rejected Cocteau's poems for publication in *391* until Picabia's break with Dada, at which point he printed a few. In spite of Cocteau's great show of interest in *Littérature,* he was banned from contributing anything to it by Breton, whose hatred of him was based on a mixture of envy for his rising stardom and scorn for his dandyism as reflected in his manners and dress. At the *Nouvelle Revue Française* Cocteau had no more luck given the presence of Gide, whose barely veiled hostility toward him had turned into an almost murderous rage over an incident that had fueled his homosexual jealousy. In spite of all this opposition Cocteau managed to continue working feverishly; for example, he wrote weekly articles on the artistic scene in Paris for the newspaper *Paris-Midi,* collected in 1920 in *Carte Blanche: Articles parus dans "Paris-Midi" du 31 mars au 11 août 1919* (Carte Blanche: Articles Appearing in *Paris Midi* from 31 March to 11 August 1919); produced *Le Bœuf sur le toit* (The Ox on the Roof, 1920), a farcical spectacle set in the United States; *Les Mariés de la Tour Eiffel* (The Wedding on the Eiffel Tower, 1921), a tragicomedy; an adaptation of Sophocles' *Antigone,* which opened in late 1922 (published in 1928); and two short novels, both published in 1923, *Le Grand Ecart* and *Thomas l'Imposteur.* Cocteau

was quickly establishing himself as one of the most versatile artists of his generation.

The main reason for Cocteau's incredible creative output at this time was his meeting in 1919 of the sixteen-year-old Raymond Radiguet, who quickly came to play Arthur Rimbaud to his Verlaine. Radiguet was, on a personal level, a thoroughly unpleasant young man–extremely introverted and of an unkempt appearance–but he was a poet prodigy with strong and original ideas, and Cocteau fell madly in love with him. Radiguet encouraged Cocteau to renew his art by giving up his facile popularity, based on what had already become by then the fashionable demand for hermetism and revolution in style. A proponent of a new classicism, Radiguet even persuaded Cocteau to turn away from modernism, from the irrational approach to literature inspired by such techniques as the Surrealists' automatic writing. Under his influence Cocteau wrote two volumes of poetry, *Poésies, 1917–1920* (Poems, 1917–1920), published in 1920, and *Plain-Chant* (Plain-Song), published in 1923.

The sixty-three poems that make up *Poésies* are, from the point of view of design, a departure from what readers of Cocteau had been used to in the past few volumes, that is, a series of long poems, in the sense that shorter lyrical pieces, such as "Orageux" (Stormy; six lines) and "Lourdes" (eight lines), are organized into different sections, such as "Premières larmes" (First Tears) and "Le voyage en Italie" (Voyage to Italy). The reader can see a more classical approach to form in these poems; however, in some poems, there is still the presence of the modernist, experimental influence, notably in its typography, such as in "Espagne" (Spain):

La procession se déroulera toute la nuit;
Le taureau,
Comme la vierge nègre, fleuri
de sept couteaux,
s'a
genouille
dans le tonnerre du sud Chine.
  Guitare,
    ô
   trou de la mort.

(The procession will go on all night;
The bull,
Like the black virgin, decorated
with seven daggers,
kneels
in the thunder of south China.
  Guitar,
    o
   hole of death).

In many other poems, however, the reader finds traditional rhyme schemes and classical quatrains and

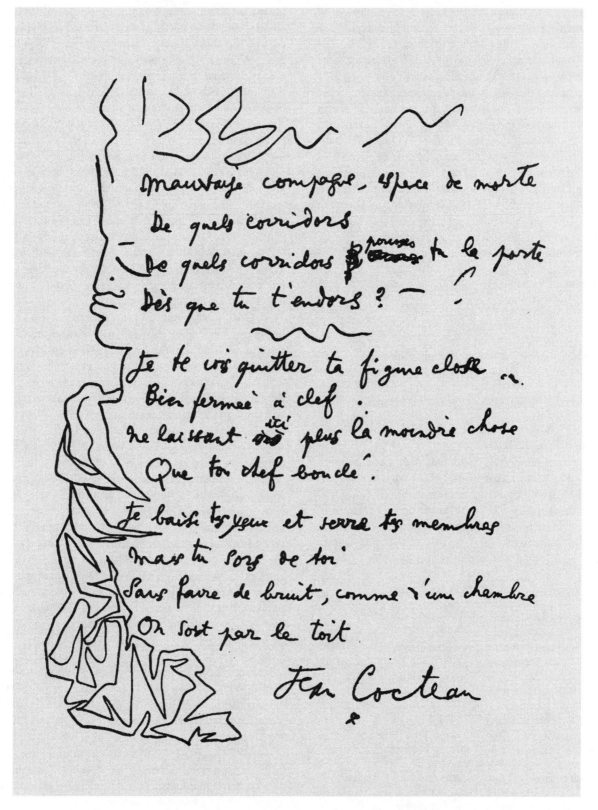

Page from the manuscript for Cocteau's 1923 book of poetry, Plain-Chant: Poème *(from Robert Phelps, ed.,*
Professional Secrets: An Autobiography of Jean Cocteau Drawn from His Lifetime Writings, *1970)*

rhythms. "La Maison de Cézanne" (The House of Cézanne), for example, is a sonnet, complete with alternating feminine and masculine rhymes.

What is most characteristic of this collection is its introduction of a new set of themes and motifs, such as the circus and the clown, the athlete, the sailor, and the dancer; however, as is often the case in Cocteau's works, these new images constellate around the role of the artist, especially in the section "L'Ode à Picasso" (Ode to Picasso), in which the painter is depicted as a tamer of Muses ("dompteur de muses"), as Orpheus, as Guignol, and as a guillotine. On the one hand, the artist is a powerful spirit capable of mastering the forces of inspiration and illuminating the mysteries of creation. On the other hand, the artist is a solitary figure who must pay the price for his talent:

> Rien dans les manches   Rien dans les poches
> Un monsieur
> voudrait-il prêter son chapeau
> à l'arlequin de Port-Royal.

> (Nothing up his sleeves   Nothing in his pockets
> Would a gentleman
> want to lend his hat
> to the Harlequin of Port Royal).

Like the monks of Port-Royal, he is a poor clown secluded from the living.

It is generally accepted that *Plain-Chant* includes some of Cocteau's best poetry and that it is the most directly inspired by Radiguet. It is a short collection of thirty or so poems. In verse reminiscent of the most classical French style, the poet expresses his intense love for his "angel," and reveals his terrible fear of death, which would take him forever from his beloved:

> Je n'aime pas dormir quand ta figure habite,
> La nuit, contre mon cou;
> Car je pense à la mort laquelle vient si vite
> Nous endormir beaucoup.
> Je mourrai, tu vivras et c'est ce qui m'éveille!
> Est-il une autre peur?
> Un jour ne plus entendre auprès de mon oreille
> Ton haleine et ton cœur

> (I do not like to sleep when your face rests
> At night, against my neck;
> For I think of death which comes so quickly
> To send us much to sleep.
> I will die, you will live and that is what awakens me!
> Is there any other fear?
> One day to no longer hear next to my ear
> Your breath and your heart).

As in these stanzas, the poet often portrays his beloveds asleep or contemplates the death of one of them: the poems in *Plain-Chant* are less about reciprocal love than about desire. The poet's passion is fueled by the knowledge or fear that it is not a shared experience: "Si je meurs premier, dans tes rêves j'entre; / Je verrai comment, / Lorsque je dormais, la main sur ton ventre, / Tu changeais d'amant" (If I die first, in your dreams I enter; / I will see how, / When I was sleeping, my hand on your stomach, / You were changing lovers). This anguish is also fed by the reality of being past his youthful prime; and yet, in spite of the suffering that is mixed with this desire, it is what comforts him when all, even the Muses, desert him, as can be seen in the final poem: "Que me laissez-vous donc? Amour, tu me pardonnes, / Ce qui reste, c'est toi: l'agnelet du troupeau. / Viens vite, embrasse-moi, broute-moi ces couronnes, / Arrache ce laurier qui me coupe la peau" (What then do you leave me? Love, you forgive me, / What remains is you: lambkin of the flock. / Come quickly, embrace me, graze on these crowns, / Take this laurel which is cutting into my skin).

Cocteau's fame was quickly growing at this point in his career, extending beyond the borders of France. Enthusiastic articles in the American *Vanity Fair* were being written by such people as Edmund Wilson Jr. and Ezra Pound. There was also a cult of Cocteau beginning to develop among young men coming from all over France and from abroad to attend the performances of his works and then throw themselves at his feet. However, a huge setback soon occurred: in December 1923, Radiguet, already weakened by the excesses of his way of life–alcoholism, insomnia–died from typhoid, which he probably contracted by eating oysters. His death at the age of twenty-one drove Cocteau into a state of despair so unbearable that while trying to regain his strength during his stay with Diaghilev in Monte Carlo in January 1924, he began smoking opium. There is doubt as to the amount of his intake, given his fragile constitution, and it has been said that the occasional and sometimes highly publicized cures he underwent were only pretenses to give him the opportunity to write undisturbed, but in any case he was addicted to the drug for the rest of his life. The projects that he undertook at this time, such as *Roméo et Juliette* (produced 1924; published 1926), his loose adaptation of William Shakespeare's play, were carried through only halfheartedly. Worried by his increasing ill health, his friends suggested that he retire to a villa at Villefranche-sur-Mer, near Nice.

What happened next is considered to be one of the oddest chapters in Cocteau's life. Jacques Maritain, the neo-Thomist philosopher and admirer of many modern artists, including Radiguet and Cocteau, was introduced to Cocteau by a mutual friend and tried to persuade him to return to his childhood Catholicism in order to lift him out of his despair. Encouraged also by Jacob and Reverdy, Cocteau did indeed accept the sacraments and in March of the following year, 1925, he entered the Thermes Urbains, a private hospital in Paris. He stayed for six weeks—because of liver problems, he told his mother. Out of this entire experience came an edifying pamphlet, *Lettre à Jacques Maritain* (Letter to Jacques Maritain), begun a few months after his cure and published in 1926, which describes his return to religion and to health—though it is said that he had already started smoking opium again before finishing the work. In any case, for the first time since the death of Radiguet, Cocteau felt renewed and filled with a sense of purpose.

Poems that he had begun writing at this time were included in a volume of verse published in 1927, *Opéra, œuvres poétiques, 1925–1927* (Opera, Poetic Works, 1925–1927). Understandably, given the biographical context, one can read in this collection, still quite classical in form, the fantastic, yet predictable, experiences of an opium addict, as in the first of the series, "Par lui-même" (By Himself):

> J'ai donné le contour à des charmes informes;
> Des ruses de la mort la trahison m'informe;
> J'ai fait voir, en versant mon encre bleu en eux,
> Des fantômes soudain devenus arbres bleus.
>
> (I have given shape to formless charms;
> Of death's tricks betrayal tells me;
> I have revealed, by pouring my blue ink in them,
> Ghosts suddenly become trees).

In "Prairie légère" (Light Meadow), written in the treatment center, the poet even talks of regretting the loss of the superhuman flights his spirit took under the influence of the drug:

> On veut me changer d'ailes en somme.
> J'avais à mon esprit des ailes de fumée;
> On veut que repoussent mes ailes d'homme,
> Ce qui fait mal, surtout à la fin des journées.
>
> (They want me to change wings in sum.
> I had in my mind wings of smoke;
> They want that my man-wings grow again,
> Which is painful, especially at the end of day).

In spite of the fact that many of the poems in *Opéra* were written during Cocteau's so-called conversion, there is no real sense that this experience in any way affected his approach to the symbolism and imagery he had been borrowing for a long time from Christianity, and from Catholicism in particular. Cocteau was never an orthodox writer in the manner of Paul Claudel, who wrote almost devotional verse; nor did he become with his conversion like Verlaine, whose own return to religion after years of hard living and a prison sentence for trying to kill his lover Rimbaud led to an infusion into

Cocteau and Pablo Picasso in the south of France during the early 1950s

his poetry of a pious spirituality, as in his *Sagesse* (Wisdom, 1880). Although in *Opéra* Cocteau makes use of "Christ," of "God," of "heaven," of "prayer," especially of "angels," and so on, these concepts belong to his private mythology rather than to Church doctrine or to an orthodox spirituality. In "Prière mutilée"(Mutilated Prayer), for example, the poet may ask for help from "God," but surely, this God is not the personal, all-powerful God of the Christian tradition, who is fully involved in human history and sends liberating grace into the world. In fact, this "God" is, like the poet himself, a lower being, subject to the impersonal laws of the universe, including blind fate and necessity:

> Venez à mon secours, astres de ma naissance!
> J'ai perdu le secret des lignes de la main;
> Dieu se déplace toujours dans le même sens
> Et la foudre espiègle déshabille les humains.
>
> (Come help me, stars of my birth!
> I have lost the secret of palmreading;
> God always moves in the same way
> And the mischievous lightning undresses humans).

It is clear, despite what Cocteau says in *Lettre à Jacques Maritain*–namely, that art should be for God–that the personal experience that most influenced the writing of *Opéra* was not the return to Catholicism, but still the loss of Radiguet, which puts the opium poems and the "spiritual" poems in a certain light. The lingering despair that Cocteau feels over his beloved and that drives him into wanting to escape or transcend his earthly existence is what brings all the poems together and is what constellates all images. In other words, in this collection, art is not for God but still for Radiguet, and nowhere is this dedication more visible than in the most significant poem of the volume, *L'Ange Heurtebise* (The Angel Heurtebise), a poem in which God, Jesus, and all the angels, "soldats de Dieu" (soldiers of God), make an appearance but only as a cast of supporting characters in Cocteau's real spiritual drama.

L'Ange Heurtebise is one of Cocteau's most celebrated poems and one of his personal favorites. It was written before his hospitalization (and, therefore, before his conversion) and first published in May–June 1925 in the magazine *Feuilles libres* and republished in book form, with a photograph by Man Ray, in 1926. Cocteau claimed that he got the name "Heurtebise" from a plaque in the elevator in Picasso's building during a moment of "angelic"–so to speak–illumination, although, given his opium habit at the time, it is more likely to have been a case of simple drug-induced, hallucinatory nonsense. The poem is essential Cocteau, with its wordplay, sound associations, puns, and the like–all of which, of course, had always led his critics to accuse him of being superficial and his poetry of being merely verbal. The fourth stanza reads:

> L'ange Heurtebise et l'ange
> Cégeste tué à la guerre–quel nom
> Inouï–jouent
> Le rôle des épouvantails
> Dont le geste *non* effraye
> Les cerises du cerisier céleste,
> Sous le vantail de l'église
> Habituée au geste *oui*.

> (The Angel Heurtebise and the angel
> Cégeste killed in war–what an unheard of
> Name–play
> The role of scarecrows
> Whose gesture *no* scares
> The cherries of the celestial cherry tree,
> Under the door of the church
> Accustomed to the gesture *yes*).

The poem itself is a fantasy, sixteen stanzas long, and its subject is the sort of intellectual ravishing by their muse that artists often write or speak of–in such terms as enthusiasm, inspiration, and possession–except that in this case the entering of the muse into the poet's mind or imagination is a highly eroticized event, and in the expected direction:

> L'ange Heurtebise, d'une brutalité
> Incroyable saute sur moi. De grâce
> Ne saute pas si fort,
> Garçon bestial, fleur de haute
> Stature.
> Je m'en suis alité. En voilà
> Des façons. J'ai l'as; constate.
> L'as-tu?

> (The Angel Heurtebise, of an incredible
> Brutality, jumps on me. Oh please
> Do not jump so hard.
> Beastly boy, flower of great
> Stature.
> I am bed-ridden because of it. What sort of
> Behavior is this. I have the ace; notice.
> Do you have it?)

The angel lives within the poet for a while and causes great suffering: "L'ange Heurtebise me pousse; / Et vous roi Jésus, miséricorde"(The Angel Heurtebise pushes me; / And you King Jesus, mercy). But in the end the poet accepts his fate and the reward is creation: "Heurtebise ne t'écarte / Plus de mon âme, j'accepte, / Fais ce que dois, beauté" (Heurtebise do not part / From my soul anymore, I accept, / Do what you must, beauty).

"Angelism" is one of the most common themes in Cocteau's works: it appears in his poetry as early as *Le Cap de Bonne-Espérance,* in reference to Garros's plane; but the identification Heurtebise-Radiguet is not a difficult one to see in this poem, especially since Radiguet had already been described as an angel in *Plain-Chant,* in which, as in this poem, the (passive) desire to be possessed is the dominant image. The poem is a testimony to the young poet's fertilizing influence on Cocteau, and the pain of his death was with him for a long time afterward.

The period that followed Cocteau's conversion and his rehabilitating stay at Villefranche-sur-Mer was one of his most productive. Inexhaustible, he wrote some of his best-known works, such as the libretto for Stravinsky's *Œdipus Rex* (1927); the play *Orphée,* produced in 1926 and published in 1927; the novel *Les Enfants terribles,* published in 1929; and *Opium: Journal d'une désintoxication* (1930; translated as *Opium: The Diary of an Addict,* 1932), a diary recounting his second attempt at being cured of his addiction, at a clinic in Saint-Cloud, near Paris, from December 1928 to April 1929. He tried his hand at a new medium, cinema, with the screenplay for his first movie, *Le Sang d'un poète* (1932; U.S. release as *The Blood of a Poet,* 1933), which remains a classic. Cocteau was quickly achieving international acclaim; however, during this time, an incident occurred that also brought him some more scandalous notoriety at home. Cocteau had lately replaced Radiguet with another young protégé, Jean Desbordes, whose literary talent and personality were nowhere near as remarkable as Radiguet's had been. In the fall of 1928 Desbordes published his first book, *J'adore* (I Love), with a preface by Cocteau. It was a lurid work, describing all manner of sexual fantasies in graphic detail, and Cocteau's association with such a book shocked the conservative set with whom he had been keeping company, especially Maritain.

The 1930s represent something of an artistic setback for Cocteau. Although he wrote voluminously, including a series of plays that guaranteed his popularity with the public at large, critics generally acknowledge that his creative output at this time did not match either the quality of his past work or the quality of his later work. This dullness could doubtlessly be attributed to his opium addiction, which, in spite of treatments in 1933 and 1936, was getting worse. Among the more interesting works of this period are those that came under the guise of journalism. *Portraits-Souvenir, 1900–1914* (1935; translated as *Paris Album, 1900–1914,* 1956), a series of articles written for *Le Figaro,* recounts his early childhood years and his early years as an artist in Paris. *Mon Premier Voyage (Tour du monde en 80 jours)* (My First Voyage [Around the World in 80 Days],1937; translated as *Round the World Again in Eighty Days,* 1937) is the log of a journey circumnavigating the globe, the result of a bet with the newspaper *Paris Soir* that he could match the exploit of the fictional hero of Jules Verne's book *Tour du monde en quatre-vingt jours* (1873). Other than the first of many facelifts in 1935, the most "Coctelian" thing that happened to Cocteau during this time was his becoming the manager of a down-and-out former bantamweight boxing champion, Panama Al Brown. Having lost the world title in 1935, Brown was discovered in a Paris night club by Cocteau, who got him off drugs and trained him back into top physical form. In Paris on 4 March 1938 Brown won back the title from the opponent to whom he had lost it three years before.

Cocteau's published poetic output during the 1930s was limited to a dozen or so poems, later collected in *Allégories* (Allegories, 1941) along with poems written in the early 1940s. There is a haunting quality to this peculiar volume, with its mixture of predictable Coctelian characters–angels, clowns, and the dying artist-gods Orpheus and Apollo–and a pervasive medieval imagery: knights, feudal hordes, and beating drums. In a sense, this combination anticipates the darkness and brutality that were on the horizon and the impossibility

Cocteau and British poet W. H. Auden on 12 June 1956, when Cocteau received an honorary doctorate from Oxford University (photograph by Roger-Viollet)

of creativity of any kind. Some of these poems were written during another one of Cocteau's attempts at rehabilitation, at the Lyautey clinic in 1940; one of these is "Clinique" (Clinic):

> Mes calembours furent ceux de l'oracle grec
> J'ai tordu le poème et fait un masque avec
> J'ai chanté le sommeil et la fuite des muses
> Du théâtre j'aimai les surprenantes ruses
> L'amour n'en parlons pas, car c'était du joli!
> Et la douleur borde mon lit.

> (My puns were those of the Greek oracle
> I have twisted the poem and made a mask of it
> I have sung of the sleep and of the flight of the Muses
> Of theatre, I loved the surprising tricks
> Love, let us speak of it no longer, for it was a fine mess!
> And pain lines my bed).

The general impression one gets from reading *Allégories* is that of anguish and apprehension: something is wrong with the world and with the poet. Two poems in this collection are noteworthy because they bear the mark of Jean Marais: one, "L'incendie" (The Fire), is dedicated to him; the other, "L'acteur" (The Actor), is about him:

L'acteur crie et murmure, mû par les yeux
De la salle, à l'ancre sur ses vagues.
Hérissé de rayons, de cornes et de dagues,
Il insulte les dieux.

(The actor screams and whispers, moved by the eyes
Of the room, anchored to his waves.
Spiked with rays, horns and daggers,
He insults the gods).

Cocteau had first met Marais in 1937, when the beautiful young actor was auditioning for his play *Œdipe-roi* (translated as *Oedipus Rex,* 1962). They rapidly became close companions, and Marais became Cocteau's lead actor, featured in many of his stage plays and in the motion picture *La Belle et la Bête.* Completely opposed to drugs, he was the one responsible for getting Cocteau into the Lyautey clinic.

Biographers and critics write with some ambivalence about the role Cocteau played during World War II. On the one hand, there is much evidence to support the claim that Cocteau's notorious narcissism and callousness did not serve him well. It seems that at the beginning of hostilities, for example, his greatest concern was the anticipated loss of his opium supply. In May 1940 he was more upset about a hostile article by Claude Mauriac in Gide's *Nouvelle Revue Française* than about the impending invasion of France by German forces. Whereas many of his friends worked in the Resistance, such as Maurice Sachs, Marcel Khill, Max Jacob—and especially Jean Desbordes, who died heroically after being tortured for thirteen hours by the Gestapo without revealing any relevant information about his Resistance work—Cocteau was busily writing movies, such as *La Belle et la Bête* and *L'Eternel retour* (1943; released in the United States as *The Eternal Return,* 1948); and trying to put on his plays, such as *La Machine à écrire* (1941; translated as *The Typewriter,* 1947), *Renaud et Armide* (1943), and *Les Parents terribles* (The Terrible Parents, 1938; translated as *Intimate Relations,* 1957) in Occupied Paris. He also wrote a newspaper article on a Paris exhibition by Adolf Hitler's favorite sculptor, Arno Breker, and he socialized with high-ranking, Francophile officers of the German occupying forces.

There is also much evidence to be found, however, if one wanted to make the case that Cocteau did the best he could under the most extreme of circumstances and suffered greatly because of it. His homosexuality and the nature of the plays he produced during the Occupation—*Les Parents terribles* seemed to be about

incest—made him an easy prey for the moralistic Vichy regime. Yet, as early as 5 December 1940, he published in *La Gerbe* a front-page article, "Adresse aux jeunes écrivains: Les territoires de l'esprit" (Address to Young Writers: The Territories of the Mind), in which he lamented the state of literature under Vichy, with the regime celebrating the classics—such as Pierre Corneille, Jean Racine, and Molière—in the name of French "purity," and censuring anything new; he asked young writers to do their best to defend the freedom of their art before their small-minded compatriots; he even honored his old nemesis, Gide. As he says in the last paragraph: "Pensez, écrivez, adorez, détruisez, fondez de petites revues. Montez des spectacles. Piétinez-nous, si possible" (Think, write, worship, destroy, found small journals. Put on shows. Trample us underfoot, if possible). In 1942 he testified on behalf of the writer Jean Genet, a thief and a homosexual, who was arrested for stealing a volume of Verlaine's poetry, arranged for him to have a good lawyer, and helped to get him acquitted. He was once beaten by Vichyites for failing to salute the French flag borne by volunteer troops on their way to serve with the German army on the Eastern Front. Whichever interpretation of Cocteau's wartime activities one prefers, there is little doubt that at the end of the hostilities, Cocteau was not left untouched. In addition to being filled with a profound feeling of guilt at having survived in the midst of all the horror, which was probably the psychological cause for the chronic eczema from which he began to suffer at this time, he became more and more the target of attack by some of his artistic contemporaries, such as Mauriac, whose *Jean Cocteau; ou, La Vérité du mensonge* (Jean Cocteau; or, The Truth Behind the Lie, 1945) was the first book written on him.

The one work of poetry to come out of this period is *Léone* (translated as *Leoun,* 1961), a long poem of 120 stanzas, published for the first time in 1945 by Gallimard, with two lithographs by the author. The autobiographical, even narcissistic, nature of the poem typifies Cocteau's problematic wartime activity—or inactivity. Once again, in this poem Cocteau presents something of an "angelic" figure, Léone, who wanders through a world which is part dream and part reality—the reality being Cocteau's life and work:

Sur le pont transbordeur du théâtre des ombres
La lumière égorgeait les coqs et les colombes.
On jouait *Antigone* et Léone en passant
Vit les acteurs couverts des mantilles du sang.

(On the transporter bridge of the theatre of shadows
The light was slitting the throat of roosters and doves.
Antigone was being performed, and Léone in passing
Saw the actors covered with mantillas of blood).

There are, of course, references to the historical situation, but rather than being the context for Léone's wandering or Cocteau's work, they are the objects of contextualization, if not trivialization: "Ainsi de l'Opéra j'ai vu les duels illustres / Les spadassins cruels excités par le lustre. Depuis la guerre hélas ces combats n'ont plus cours" (Thus of the Opera I have seen the famous duels / The cruel assassins excited by the chandelier. / Since the war alas these fights are no longer current). But perhaps there is irony, or paradox, in the poem, as there was in Cocteau's life. Near the end of the poem, the reader learns that Léone is the poet's Muse: "Léone était la muse ou la muse Léone" (Léone was the muse or the muse Léone).

During the next decade or so, Cocteau devoted his time to his career as *poète de cinéma* (cinematic poet), producing such motion pictures as *La Belle et la Bête*, filmed in 1945 and released in 1946, *L'Aigle à deux têtes* (1947; U.S. release as *The Eagle Has Two Heads,* 1948) and *Orphée* (1950; U.S. release as *Orpheus,* 1950). These post-Liberation years were not easy ones, and finding the resources required for major motion-picture productions was a difficult task. The stress involved in this task, in addition to his chronic skin condition, had something to do with his return to using opium in 1946 or 1947. It also had something to do with his doctor's advice to get some mountain air for a change of pace. During his stay in the Swiss Alps in 1946 Cocteau wrote one of his best poems, *La Crucifixion* (translated as *The Crucifixion,* 1976), which was published in 1947. In twenty-five stanzas of varying length and meter, the poet meditates on the death of Christ. To be sure, the reader still finds in this poem the by now well-known "Coctelian" wizardry of puns, sound associations, play on words, and so on, but in this context, this merely verbal aspect of Cocteau's poetry seems to be called forth like the anguished outpouring of the witness to horror:

Cocteau (on ladder) and painter Jean-Paul Brusset in 1956 at the Chapel Saint-Pierre, Villefranche-sur-Mer, working on one of the many murals Cocteau painted during the last decade of his life (New York World-Telegram and Sun Collection, Library of Congress)

Il y avait les coups. Les coups
du fer sur le fer. La vieille rose
des vents. Les coups. La rouille
des coups sur l'éventail en os
des pieds. Sur la natte
en orteils. Sur les planches. Sur
l'exquise enluminure du missel
des nerfs où la douleur court
plus vite que la douleur
dans le corail des tortures.

(There were the blows. The blows
of iron on iron. The old rose
of the winds. The blows. The rust
of the blows on the bony fan
of the feet. On the mat
of toes. On the boards. On

the exquisite illumination of the missal
of nerves where pain runs
faster than the pain
in the coral of tortures).

This meditation on the Crucifixion won the approval of Claudel, which is understandable, for, unlike the poems Cocteau wrote following his "conversion," *La Crucifixion* does not try to make Christ's "passion" a metaphor for the poet's own. In fact, at the end of the poem, Cocteau seems to be saying something that would please the most orthodox, that Christ's death has freed him from his personal pain and weakness. *La Crucifixion* is the work of a maturing man, who had seen death and destruction, and who was now thinking concretely of his own mortality; it is also the work of a maturing poet, whose experience of life could now be expressed and absorbed by poetry rather than the other way around.

In spite of the personal and professional difficulties, Cocteau later said that these were some of the best years of his life, and not since the early days of his association with the Diaghilev company had he experienced such collective dedication to an artistic enterprise. Given the popular and critical success of his motion pictures, his fame was growing quickly, with honors coming from home and abroad. In 1945 the Swiss publisher Marguerat offered to publish an edition of his complete works (which appeared in eleven volumes from 1947 to 1951), and the second book on Cocteau, by one of his friends, Roger Lannes, was published as a sort of obsequious response to Mauriac's almost abusive assessment. In 1949 he was made Chevalier de la Légion d'honneur. His triumphal *Orphée* won the International Critic's Prize at the Venice Film Festival in 1950, and the following year, at Cannes, it was voted the best motion picture by the public. In 1949 he was invited to speak at a preview of *L'Aigle à deux têtes* in New York, though he managed to offend many of his hosts by his Parisian air and condescending behavior. He was also offered the possibility of lecturing on cinema at Harvard University as the prestigious Charles Eliot Norton Professor of Poetry, but he had to respectfully decline, given the production schedule of *Orphée*.

Cocteau was now more than sixty years old. In the spring of 1950 he went as a guest with Edouard "Dou-Dou" Dermit, his companion since the filming of *L'Aigle à deux têtes,* in which he appeared, to the villa of Francine Weisweiller at St. Jean Cap Ferrat, near Villefranche. Weisweiller, who was separated from her wealthy husband, Alec Weisweiller, was a huge fan of Cocteau's and had offered him financial assistance for his productions. Cocteau and Dermit's first visit lasted for several months, and though he kept his Paris apartment and another house, in Milly, Cocteau spent most of the rest of his life at Weisweiller's luxurious villa. Despite his celebrity and the success of his motion pictures, Cocteau was not in good financial shape, and the generosity of his benefactress was most welcome. At her villa, for the next ten years, he indulged in—or rather, was indulged in—his last new activity, for which he seemed to have significantly more enthusiasm than talent: wall decorating (frescoes, murals, and tapestries). As for his literary production, critics generally consider the works written during this time, such as *Jean Marais* (1951) and the play *L'Impromptu du Palais-Royal* (The Impromptu at the Royal Palace, 1962), to be minor ones.

The years 1955–1956 brought Cocteau the most prestigious of honors, consecrating his long career. On 10 January, he was elected to the Académie royale de Langue et de Littérature françaises of Belgium, occupying the seat, left vacant by the death of Colette, that was once held by de Noailles. Two months later, on 3 March, he was elected to the Académie Française, the most eminent and the most aristocratic of French literary institutions. Unlike the Académie Royale, the Académie Française requires that its members undergo the process of a true election, complete with a formal application and campaign. Why Cocteau would want to become one of the forty *Immortels* (Immortals, as the members are known) is understandable, given his age and his desire to have his work taken seriously. Cocteau managed to gain quickly the support of the more conservative and scholarly set, including that of Claudel and, surprisingly, of Mauriac; but his candidacy was helped by the fact that his main competitor was Jérôme Carcopino, who had been a high-ranking minister in the Vichy regime. In his election speech delivered on 20 October in front of one of the most distinguished audiences ever assembled for an Academician's reception—two queens were in attendance—he expressed the wish that the Academy protect those "personnes suspectes d'individualisme" (persons suspected of individualism). On 12 June 1956 Cocteau, who had never completed his baccalaureate, received a doctorate *honoris causa* from Oxford University. In his presentation of the degree to Cocteau, Jean Seznec, professor of All Souls College, said how fitting it was that Cocteau was delivering his "Discours d'Oxford" (Oxford Speech) in a place where Verlaine had read his poems, and where both Stephané Mallarmé and Paul Valéry had spoken.

In 1962, a year before his death, Cocteau's last book of poetry, *Le Requiem,* was published. It is a work of 170 pages or so, divided into seven *périodes* (periods), and it opens with a preface in which the poet explains that he is writing after a serious illness, "pendant les suites d'une hémorragie profonde" (in the aftermath of a severe hemorrhage)—and apparently, on the ceiling from his bedridden position: "Couché sur le dos, je devais écrire au plafond comme marchent les mouches" (Lying on my back, I had to write on the ceiling, just as flies crawl). *Le Requiem* is often said to be Cocteau's poetic testament (he calls it his "chant de cygne" [swan song] in the sixth "période"), and as such it has the unmistakable air of François Villon's *Testament* (1461), complete with private associations, metrical variations, songs, the *ubi sunt* (literally, "where are") convention, and a closing "Epitaphe" (Epitaph).

It is, nonetheless, a highly "Coctelian" work, written in an unreflective, almost automatic style, in which the poet adopts all possible tones and modes of expressions. He is at times confessional, regretting especially his lost friends, at times unrepentant, reveling in the memories of his past existence: "Larrons larrons je vous préfère / Larrons mes semblables, mes frères" (Thieves thieves I prefer you / Thieves my equivalents, my brothers). What gives continuity to the collection is the fiction of a guided,

Dante-like, journey, which begins ostensibly with the third "période." In the "univers aux multiples / Dimensions" (universe of multiple / Dimensions) he is being shown, Cocteau sees wonders that he claims to be unable to describe though he does his best to do so:

> Et cette impuissance à traduire
> En notre langage un séjour
> D'une stupéfiante audace
> Sauf par exemple un roc couvert
> De rides s'approchant un peu
> Des empreintes digitales
> A pic sur une mer rouge
> Qui n'était ni rouge ni mer
> Et ce roc point un roc et cette
> Route qui n'en était pas une
> Car cette route se déroule
> Sous notre immobilité

> (And this powerlessness to translate
> In our language a stay
> Of a stunning audacity
> Except for example a rock covered
> With wrinkles approaching a little
> Fingerprints
> Straight down on a red sea
> Which was neither red nor a sea
> And this rock not a rock and this
> Trail which was not one
> For this trail unfolds itself
> Under our immobility).

Le Requiem is the summing up of how Cocteau saw the role of the poet during his entire life as an artist: the journey with his difficult "compagne" (companion), the "Muse froide amazone" (cold, driving Muse), is a lonely but necessary one, and the miraculous things he is allowed to see, or dream, are what give him a glimpse of the divine in this sublunar world:

> Fils d'un monde insensible où j'eus tort de naître
> J'ai voulu saluer ce qu'il avait de mieux
> Et grâce au verbe obscur où je suis passé maître
> Une rose cueillir sur la tombe des dieux

> (Son of an unfeeling world into which I was mistakenly born
> I had wanted to salute the best it had
> And thanks to the obscure word of which I am a past master
> To pluck a rose from the tomb of the gods).

On Friday, 11 October 1963 at the age of seventy-four, Jean Cocteau, who had been in poor health for some time, suffered a heart attack and died. That same morning reporters had been calling him for comments on the death of the singer Edith Piaf. French-American novelist and playwright Julien Green, who saw him just before he died, later said that there was a crucifix on the table beside Cocteau's bed and an image of the Virgin

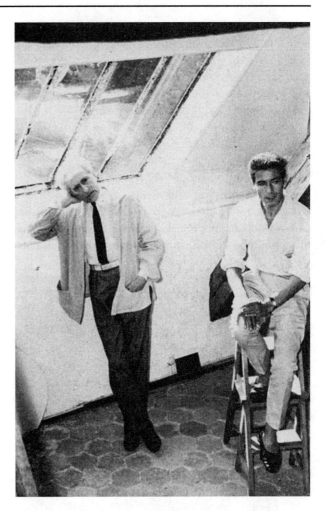

Cocteau and his companion, Edouard "DouDou" Dermit, 1962 (photograph by Sygma)

Mary over his head. Although some were expecting a national funeral, a simple ceremony was performed at Milly, attended by friends, villagers, and representatives of the Académie Française, the Belgian Académie, and the Comédie-Française.

In *Le Discours d'Oxford* (1956), delivered on the occasion of his being granted the doctorate *honoris causa* from Oxford University, Cocteau chose as his title "La Poésie ou l'invisibilité" (Poetry or Invisibility). The point he wanted to make in his lecture was that the true poet is the one who tries to be "invisible," who turns away from the crowd, from facile success; the one who works at his craft in solitude and who suffers for his art: "la poésie est une solitude effrayante, une malédiction de naissance, une maladie de l'âme" (Poetry is a frightful solitude, a curse from birth, a malady of the soul). Surely, this was a most Coctelian occasion, as Cocteau spent most of his lecture talking about himself, and it typifies the irony of his entire career as a poet. On the one hand, his art speaks of the necessity of solitude, of "invisibility": the poet is a lonely figure, a "maudit" (one accursed), who must break from society in order to create. On the other hand, his life speaks of a man who endlessly sought the front stage, who was one of the most photographed men of his time. One of his biographers recounts the anecdote about the photographer who complained that were he to take a picture of a country wedding, Cocteau would doubtlessly appear between the happy couple. As with poets such as Rimbaud and Baudelaire, with whom he liked to compare himself, it is difficult to separate the irritating, narcissistic, over-the-top *homme* (man) from the *œuvre* (work), and the appreciation of his work has suffered from the association. Of course, most of Cocteau's poetry does not compare favorably with that of many other twentieth-century poets, such as Valéry, Mallarmé, and Apollinaire, but it is the remarkable expression of a singular genius who throughout his life fought for the independence and integrity of his art, in spite of all the competing claims that were placed upon it.

Letters:

Lettres à Milorad: 1955–1963, edited by Milorad (Paris: Editions Saint-Germain-des-Prés, 1975);

Correspondance avec Jean-Marie Magnan, introduction by Jean-Marie Magnan (Paris: Belfond, 1981); republished as *Mots et plumes: Sept ans d'amitié, 1956–1963: Lettres à Jean-Marie Magnan,* preface by Jacques Lovichi (Marseilles: Autres temps, 1999);

Correspondance: Jean Cocteau, Anna de Noailles, edited by Claude Mignot-Ogliastri (Paris: Gallimard, 1989);

Lettres à sa mère, volume 1, *1898–1918,* edited by Pierre Caizergues and Pierre Chanel (Paris: Gallimard, 1989).

Interviews:

André Fraigneau, *Entretiens autour du cinématographe* (Paris: A. Bonne, 1951); translated by Vera Traill as *Cocteau on the Film, A Conversation Recorded by André Fraigneau* (London: Dobson, 1954; New York: Roy, 1954);

Entretiens sur le musée de Dresde, by Cocteau and Louis Aragon (Paris: Editions Cercle d'Art, 1957); translated by Francis Scarfe as *Conversations on the Dresden Gallery* (New York: Holmes & Meier, 1982);

Fraigneau, *Jean Cocteau: Entretiens avec André Fraigneau* (Paris: Union Générale d'Editions, 1965);

Fraigneau and Claude Gauteur, eds., *Entretiens sur le cinématographe* (Paris: Belfond, 1973).

Biographies:

Margaret Crosland, *Jean Cocteau: A Biography* (London: Nevill, 1955; New York: Knopf, 1956);

Frederick Brown, *An Impersonation of Angels: A Biography of Jean Cocteau* (New York: Viking, 1968; Harlow, U.K.: Longmans, 1969);

Elizabeth Sprigge and Jean-Jacques Kihm, *Jean Cocteau: The Man and the Mirror* (London: Gollancz, 1968; New York: Coward-McCann, 1968);

Francis Steegmuller, *Cocteau: A Biography* (Boston: Little, Brown, 1970; London: Macmillan, 1970);

Julie Saul, ed., *Jean Cocteau: The Mirror and the Mask: A Photo-Biography,* with an essay by Steegmuller (Boston: Godine, 1992).

References:

Clément Borgal, *Cocteau, Dieu, la mort, la poésie* (Paris: Editions du Centurion, 1968);

Borgal, *Cocteau: Poète de l'au delà* (Paris: Tequi, 1977);

Danielle Chaperon, *Jean Cocteau: La Chute des angles* (Lille: Presses Universitaires de Lille, 1990);

Lydia Crowson, *The Esthetic of Jean Cocteau* (Hanover: Published for the University of New Hampshire by the University Press of New England, 1978);

Wallace Fowlie, *Jean Cocteau: The History of a Poet's Age* (Bloomington: Indiana University Press, 1966);

André Fraigneau, *Cocteau par lui-même* (Paris: Seuil, 1957); translated by Donald Lehmkuhl as *Cocteau,* Evergreen Profile Book, no. 24 (New York: Grove/London: Evergreen, 1961);

Jean-Jacques Kihm, *Cocteau* (Paris: Gallimard, 1960);

Roger Lannes, *Jean Cocteau: Une Etude,* Poètes d'aujourd'hui, no. 4 (Paris: Seghers, 1945);

Claude Mauriac, *Jean Cocteau; ou, La Vérité du mensonge* (Paris: Lieutier, 1945).

Papers:

A collection of Jean Cocteau's manuscripts are in the Archives Jean Cocteau, Milly-la-Forêt, Esone, France.

Robert Desnos

(4 July 1900 – 8 June 1945)

Karen Humphreys
Trinity College

BOOKS: *Deuil pour deuil* (Paris: Editions du Sagittaire, 1924); translated by Terry Hale as *Mourning for Mourning* (London: Atlas, 1992);

C'est les bottes de 7 lieues cette phrase "Je me vois," with four watercolors by André Masson (Paris: Editions de la Galerie Simon, 1926);

La Liberté ou l'amour! censored version (Paris: Editions du Sagittaire, 1927); unexpurgated version published in *La Liberté ou l'amour! Suivi de Deuil pour deuil* (Paris: Gallimard, 1962)–includes revised edition of *Deuil pour deuil; La Liberté ou l'amour!* translated and introduced by Hale as *Liberty or Love!* (London: Atlas, 1993);

The Night of loveless nights, illustrated by Georges Malkine (Anvers, Belgium: Privately printed, 1930); translated by Lewis Warsh as *Night of Loveless Nights,* The Ant's Forefoot, no. 10 (New York: Coach House Press, 1973);

Corps et biens (Paris: Gallimard/Editions de la Nouvelle Revue Française, 1930);

Les Sans-cou, with two watercolors by Masson (Paris: Privately printed, 1934);

Fortunes (Paris: Gallimard, 1942);

Etat de veille, illustrated with ten engravings by Gaston-Louis Roux (Paris: Robert-J. Godet, 1943);

Le Vin est tiré (Paris: Gallimard, 1943);

Contrée, with watercolor frontispiece by Pablo Picasso (Paris: Robert-J. Godet, 1944); translated by William Kulik in *Contrée = Country: Twenty-Five Poems,* bilingual edition (Iowa City: Windover Press/ University of Iowa, 1994);

Le Bain avec Andromède, illustrated by Félix Labisse (Paris: Editions de Flore, 1944);

30 chantefables, pour les enfants sages, à chanter sur n'importe quel air, illustrated by Olga Kowalewsky (Paris: Gründ, 1944);

Félix Labisse (Paris: Sequana, 1945);

La Place de l'Etoile, antipoème (Paris: Collection Humour, 1945);

Robert Desnos

Choix de poèmes, preface by Georges Hugnet, L'Honneur des poètes, no. 1 (Paris: Editions de Minuit, 1946);

Rue de la Gaîté; Voyage en Bourgogne; Précis de cuisine pour les jours heureux; with watercolors by Lucien Coutaud (Paris: Editions Les 13 Epis, 1947);

Les Trois solitaires, lithographs by Yvette Alde (Paris: Editions Les 13 Epis, 1947)–includes "Poème pour Marie," "A la Hollande," and "Mon Tombeau";

Les Regrets de Paris, poèmes posthumes; suivis de Réflexions sur la poèsie et d'un poème de Henri de Lescoët (Brussels & Antibes: Collection des îles de Lérins/Cahiers du Journal des Poètes, 1947);

Chantefables et chantefleurs, illustrated by Christiane Laran (Paris: Gründ, 1952); translated by Carl Little as *Songfables and Songflowers: Sixteen Poems* (E. Holden, Me.: Backwoods Broadsides, 1995);

De L'Erotisme: Considéré dans ses manifestations écrites et du point de vue de l'esprit moderne (Paris: Editions du Cercle des Arts, 1953);

Domaine Public, preface by René Bertelé (Paris: Gallimard, 1953)–includes *Corps et biens, Fortunes,* and previously uncollected poems and essays;

Mines de rien, engravings by Masson, Miroir du poète, no. 6 (Paris: Broder, 1957)–comprises seven poems;

De tous les spectacles (Alès: Editions P.A.B., 1960);

Calixto, suivi de Contrée (Paris: Gallimard, 1962);

Cinéma, edited, with an introduction, by André Tchernia (Paris: Gallimard, 1966);

Les Pénalités de l'enfer; ou, Les Nouvelles Hébrides, illustrated by Joan Miró (Paris: Maeght, 1974);

Destinée arbitraire, preface and notes by Marie-Claire Dumas (Paris: Gallimard, 1975)–includes *C'est les bottes de 7 lieues cette phrase "Je me vois," Le Bain avec Andromède, Etat de veille, Mines de rien,* and previously uncollected poems and poem cycles: "Prospectus," "Peine perdue," "Youki 1930 poésie," "Les Nuits blanches," "Bagatelles," *La Ménagérie de Tristan,* "Le Parterre d'Hyacinthe," "La Géométrie de Daniel," "Sens," "A la caille," and "Ce cœur qui haïssait la guerre";

Récits, nouvelles, et poèmes (Paris: Roblot, 1975)–includes *La Rue de la Gaîté;*

Nouvelles Hébrides et autres textes, 1922–1930, preface and notes by Marie-Claire Dumas (Paris: Gallimard, 1978)–includes *De l'Erotisme, La Place de l'Etoile,* and previously uncollected articles;

La Ménagerie de Tristan, illustrated by Patrick Couratin, Collection Enfantimages (Paris: Gallimard, 1978);

Ecrits sur les peintres: Robert Desnos, preface by Dumas (Paris: Flammarion, 1983)–includes *Félix Labisse;*

Mines de rien, edited, with a preface, by Dumas, introduction by Alain Brieux (Cognac: Le Temps qu'il fait, 1985)–comprises Desnos's contributions to *Aujourd'hui;*

Les Voix intérieures: Chansons et textes critiques, edited, with a preface, by Lucienne Cantaloube-Ferrieu (Nantes: Editions du Petit Véhicule, 1987);

Les Rayons et les ombres: Cinéma, edited, with a preface and notes, by Dumas and Nicole Cervelle-Zonca (Paris: Gallimard, 1992);

Le Bois d'amour (Paris: Editions des Cendres, 1995);

Le Livre secret pour Youki (Paris: Editions des Cendres, 1999).

Editions: *Corps et biens,* edited, with a preface, by René Bertelé (Paris: Gallimard, 1968);

Chantefables et chantefleurs: A chanter sur n'importe quel air, illustrated by Ludmila Jirincová (Paris: Gründ, 1970);

Robert Desnos: Un poète, edited by Michel Cosem; preface by Dumas, Collection Folio Junior en Poèsie, no. 13 (Paris: Gallimard, 1980; revised by Sylvie Florian-Pouilloux, Collection Folio Junior en Poèsie, no. 8, 1998);

Le Vin est tiré, Collection L'Imaginaire, no. 273 (Paris: Gallimard, 1992);

Œuvres: Desnos, edited, with an introduction and notes, by Dumas (Paris: Gallimard, 1999).

Editions in English: *22 Poems: Robert Desnos,* translated, with an introduction, by Michael Benedikt, prints by Jacqueline Airamé (Santa Cruz, Cal.: Kayak Books, 1971);

The Voice: Selected Poems, translated by William Kulik and Carole Frankel (New York: Grossman, 1972);

The Night of Loveless Nights, translated by Fred Beake; illustrated by Naomi Tilston (Bristol: Xenia Press, 1974);

The Selected Poems of Robert Desnos, edited, with an introduction, by Kulik; translated by Carolyn Forché and Kulik (New York: Ecco Press, 1991);

The Circle and the Star: Selected Poems of Robert Desnos, bilingual edition, translations by Todd Sanders (Pittsburgh, Pa.: Air and Nothingness Press, 2000);

The Secret Book for Youki: And Other Poems by Robert Desnos, bilingual edition, translations by Sanders (Pittsburgh, Pa.: Air and Nothingness Press, 2001).

PLAY PRODUCTION: *Cantate pour l'inauguration du Musée de l'homme,* music by Milhaud, Lille, 11 October 1937.

PRODUCED SCRIPTS: *L'Etoile de mer,* motion picture, scenario adapted by Desnos and Man Ray from Desnos's poem of that title, produced by Ray, 1928;

"Initiation au surréalisme," radio, *Arts,* Radio-Paris, 14 June 1930;

La Musique cubaine, radio, by Desnos and Alejo Carpentier, Radio-Paris, 5 January 1931;

La Grande complainte de Fantômas, radio, by Desnos and Paul Deharme, Radio-Paris, 3 November 1933;

Desnos, circa 1925, in one of the self-induced hypnotic trances during which he wrote Surrealist poetry

Le Salut au monde, radio, Poste Parisien, 4 July 1936;

Records 37, motion picture, segment on aviation by Desnos, Cinéfi, 1937;

La Clef des songes, radio series, Radio-France, 11 February 1938–June 1939;

Bonsoir mesdames, bonsoir messieurs, motion picture, screenplay and dialogue by Desnos, Henri Jeanson, and Claude Marcy, 1944.

Robert Desnos is perhaps best known today, as he was in the 1920s, for the poetry he composed in the Surrealist milieu of Paris. He is also recognized for the children's songs and rhymes that thrive in the memories of those who grew up in France in the last half of the twentieth century. Current appraisal of his work celebrates an extensive collection of poems and essays written during the early years of World War II. Desnos's work, ranging from impassioned love poetry to witty satire and tribute to humanism, retains throughout the visionary and lyrical qualities that capture the erotic desires of human experience. His multifaceted poetic achievement places Desnos among the most versatile poets of the twentieth century.

His poetry during the 1920s reflects a rebellious and adventurous spirit that tested the limits of social convention and creative expression. For many artists at the time, liberating the unconscious from the yoke of traditional logic was the key to revealing the true, uninhibited processes of thought; the Surrealist movement seemed to offer the possibility of an unhindered and genuinely original means of artistic creation. Desnos embraced the Surrealist poetics of spoken thought and quickly proved to be a virtuoso at giving voice to his creative vision. He was famous for his intriguing ability to fall into a self-induced trance and recite poetry in a semiconscious state. These poetry recitations performed under hypnosis were considered by other poets to represent the ultimate quest into the depths of poetic imagination. In his *Manifeste du surréalisme* (Surrealist Manifesto, 1924) André Breton said of Desnos, "Il lit en lui à livre ouvert et ne fait rien pour retenir les feuillets qui s'envolent au vent de sa vie" (He reads in himself like an open book and does nothing to retain the sheets flying away in the wind of his life).

Analysis of Desnos's work by such critics as Marie-Claire Dumas, Katherine Conley, and Mary Ann

Caws traces the complex transformations of his poetry from the early Surrealist adventure through the form-conscious verse of the 1930s to his Resistance writings during World War II. His fascination with language and the spoken word also led Desnos to explore his talents in journalism, radio, and cinema, though he continued to write poetry until his death. In the 1930s Desnos began experimenting with more traditional forms while simultaneously pursuing his attraction to popular culture. Although these areas of interest appear somewhat contradictory, they in fact illustrate an underlying characteristic of his work—both colloquial and eloquent language articulate a poetics of paradox, uniting spontaneity with longing and bringing together a matrix of opposing elements. Desnos maintained in *Destinée arbitraire* (1975) that the aim of poetry was "unir le langage populaire, le plus populaire, à une atmosphère inexprimable, à une imagerie aiguë" (to fuse popular language, the most colloquial, with an indescribable atmosphere, with a vital imagery). The combination of colloquial and oratorical language projected through the magical landscape of his mind's eye creates a lyrical and symphonic overture to love and liberty.

Born in Paris on 4 July 1900, Robert Pierre Desnos spent his childhood at 11 rue Saint-Martin in the Marais. His father, Lucien Desnos, worked as a poultry merchant and later became a sales agent at Les Halles, the central covered fruit, vegetable, and meat market that served most of Paris until it was torn down in 1969. The job of sales agent there was an appointed and prestigious position. Lucien Desnos was eager to establish himself in the local community; he also served as deputy-mayor in the Fourth Arrondissement (district) of Paris from 1920 to 1941. Robert Desnos's mother, Claire Guillais Desnos, was a native Parisian whose father was also a merchant. The old neighborhood where Desnos grew up was animated by the lively interaction of local merchants and successful tradesmen. In addition it was imbued with nostalgia and legends of magicians and alchemists—medieval alchemist Nicolas Flamel had resided nearby. Memories of these old streets could well have influenced the young poet's active imagination and may have helped shape such poems as "La Ville de Don Juan" (Don Juan's City, 1934) and "La Prophétie" (The Prophecy, 1942).

As a boy Desnos attended the Communal School and then the Turgot commercial school from age thirteen through sixteen. Lucien Desnos had encouraged his son to pursue good grades and a solid career path, but the maverick Desnos had little interest in school. One report, quoted by Marie-Claire Dumas in her 1980 biography of Desnos, reproaches him for being "bavard, désordonné, désobéissant, dissipé, négligent,

inattentif, trompeur et paresseux" (talkative, disorganized, disobedient, scatterbrained, negligent, inattentive, deceitful and lazy). Instead, Desnos, inspired by daydreams, fantasy, and his own whimsical nature, was attracted to poetry, myth, and adventure. While he cultivated a passion for literature, he flaunted a dandyish contempt for the bourgeois education that his father wanted for him. Gerard de Nerval, Arthur Rimbaud, and Victor Hugo were among the early literary heroes whose spiritual and poetic voyages influenced Desnos's imagery of marine landscapes and dreamworlds.

Little is known of Desnos's early literary production. His earliest extant attempts at poetry, dated July 1915, were not published until 1918 in *La Tribune des Jeunes* (The Young People's Tribune), a small review with a more sociopolitical bent than literary orientation. Desnos, as part of the editorial board, wanted to convert it to a literary journal, to be titled "La Brocante aux chimères" (Secondhand-Shop of Dreams). In any case, the journal heralded the beginning of Desnos's literary career with three poems, "Aquarelle" (Watercolor), "Casqués du heaume" (Armored Helmets), and "Chanson" (Song), that illustrate his early penchant for the symbolist aesthetic. Desnos claimed that at this time he began to record his dreams in detail, an interest that culminated in his mysterious expertise in poetic creation through hypnotic trance, for which he became notorious among Surrealists.

Desnos held various jobs from 1916, the year he left the Lycée Turgot, until he began his compulsory military service in 1920. He was a druggist in the rue Pavée for a brief period and later translated medical prospectuses for the Darasse pharmaceutical laboratories. His appointment in 1919 to the position of personal secretary to Jean de Bonnefon marked a turning point in Desnos's life. Bonnefon was a freethinker and man of letters who ran a publishing firm in the Latin Quarter and another in Nice. Bonnefon's personal library and access to the Bibliothèque Nationale could well have provided Desnos with considerable opportunity to broaden his literary horizons. During these years Desnos became acquainted with Georges Limbour, Paul Smara, Roger Vitrac, and Stéphane Manier, who were associated with the Dada movement or Surrealist circles. He met Benjamin Péret in 1919 and hoped that Péret could facilitate a meeting with Breton and other poets such as Francis Picabia, whose work he had recently discovered. Péret, perhaps somewhat timid and unsure himself, declined; the disappointed Desnos did not meet Breton until 1921. In his correspondence with Jacques Doucet, Desnos alluded to an awkward encounter he had with Breton, Tristan Tzara, and Louis Aragon arranged by Péret at the Certà, a favorite bar and meeting place of the Dadaists. This

J'habite quand il me plaît un ravin,
ténébreux au dessus duquel le ciel se découpe
en un losange déchiqueté par les ombres des
sapins, des mélèzes et des rochers qui
couvrent les pentes escarpées.
Dans l'herbe du ravin poussent d'étranges
tubéreuses et, des ancolies et des colchiques
troublés par des libellules et des
mantes religieuses et si pareils sans
cesse le ciel, la flore et la
faune où succèdent aux insectes
les corneilles moroses et les rats
musqués que je ne sais quelle
immuable saison s'est abattue
sur ce toujours nocturne ravin
avec son dais en losange constellé
que ne traverse aucun nuage
Sur les troncs des arbres deux initiales
toujours les mêmes sont gravées.
Par quel couteau, par quelle main,
pour quel cœur?

Page from the manuscript for The Night of loveless nights, *which was completed in 1928 and published in 1930 (Camille Dausse - Paul Eluard Collection, Museum of Modern Art, New York)* brief and uncomfortable introduction developed into an enthusiastic and dynamic partnership the following year. In 1921 Desnos left for Morocco to complete his military service. Although he did not find himself particularly suited for military life, he developed an affinity for the people and culture of Morocco. He departed for Paris early in 1922 for a forty-day furlough, at the end of which he was discharged from his military duty and subsequently decided to stay in Paris. The reasons for this decision are unclear, but some critics speculate that he remained in Paris because of its literary appeal.

Desnos returned home and rented a room from his father at 9 rue de Rivoli. He was employed at various jobs, mostly for brief periods. The ideal job situation for Desnos was one that would provide a means of subsistence as well as enough free time to indulge his whims and fancies. He resumed his post as secretary and researcher for Bonnefon in 1923. His research work soon led him to a position with La Librairie Baillière, a publishing house for scholarly journals, where he quickly became assistant editor for the medical journals *Paris-Médical* and *Les Archives des maladies du cœur.*

After his return from Morocco he sought out friends that he had made several years earlier–in particular Péret, Vitrac, and René Crevel. Péret had sent letters keeping Desnos abreast of the literary scene and the Dada wave in Paris while he was in Morocco. By 1922 the Dada movement was already history and the literary avant-garde seemed eager to find new blood to sustain the momentum of Dadaist enthusiasm. The opportunity for new artists to invigorate the literary scene, combined with Desnos's place on the fringe of Dadaist activities, might have worked to his advantage. Circumstances surrounding Desnos's introduction to Breton and his entourage remain somewhat nebulous. The ice was finally broken a year after that first awkward meeting at the Certà in 1921. Desnos had sent Breton copies of two of his poems, "Le Fard des Argonautes" (Blush of the Argonauts) and "L'Ode à Coco" (Ode to Coco), both of which were first published in 1919 and later collected in *Corps et bien* (1930). Breton had agreed to meet with the eccentric newcomer, who in little time came to be part of the "nucleus" of contributors to the journal *Aventure.* In her 1980 biography Dumas quotes Breton's remarks made at a conference in Barcelona in the autumn of 1922, "il n'y a a qu'un homme libre de toute attache comme Robert Desnos qui pour cela saura porter assez loin le feu" (Only a man free of all attachments like Robert Desnos, because of this, will know to carry on the torch quite far). For Desnos, always a free spirit, it was the genesis of his own creative quest.

Once he had entered into the Surrealist milieu, Desnos resolved to understand the mission of the Surrealist movement. He sought to catch up on works published while he was in Morocco in such journals as *Littérature, Action, Aventure,* and *Dada 2. Les Champs magnétiques* (1919; translated as *The Magnetic Fields,* 1985) by Breton and Philippe Soupault profoundly influenced Desnos's own experiments with automatic writing and drawing. He began to explore his personal dreamscapes by transforming visions of the subconscious into lyric poetry. His poetry of the early 1920s emphasizes the role of the unconscious in the creative process and moves to the staccato cadence of automatic writing. The imagery reflects the chaos and incoherence of an effervescent dreamworld. "Pénalités de l'Enfer"–republished in book form as *Les Pénalités de l'enfer; ou, Les Nouvelles Hébrides* (Penalities of Hell; or, New Hebrides, 1974)– appeared as Desnos's first publication in the journal *Littérature* in September 1922 and reflects this unbridled venture into the creative reservoirs of dream states and hypnotic trances. The following issue of *Littérature* (1 October 1922) featured three brief dream narratives, a eulogy to Marcel Duchamp by Breton, and the debut of Desnos's persona Rrose Sélavy, which was also the name taken by the cross-dressing Duchamp for his feminine alter ego. It was the sixth issue of *Littérature,* however, that launched Desnos onto center stage of the Surrealist spectacle. In this issue Breton describes in an article, "Entrée des Médiums" (Entry of the Mediums), how Desnos, under the influence of self-hypnosis, responded with oracular alexandrines or cryptic drawings to questions posed by Péret, Paul Eluard, and Max Ernst. Desnos's eloquent articulations of the liminal space between sleep and consciousness left a profound impression on Breton and his coterie. The excitement was contagious and projected the Surrealist experiment further onto the uncharted ground of the creative unconscious. In his *Une Vague de rêves* (A Wave of Dreams, 1924) Aragon recalls the astonishing effect that Desnos had on his onlookers: "Au café, dans le bruit des voix, la pleine lumière, les coudoiements, Robert Desnos n'a qu'à fermer les yeux, et il parle; et au milieu des bocks, des soucoupes, tout l'Océan s'écroule avec ses fracas prophétiques et ses vapeurs ornés de longues oriflammes" (In a café, amid the sound of voices, the bright light, the jostlings, Robert Desnos need only close his eyes, and he talks, and among the steins, the saucers, the whole ocean collapses with its prophetic racket and its vapors decorated with long silk banners). Thus was born what came to be known as the "époque des sommeils"–the era of hypnotic sleeps.

The famous telepathic communication with Duchamp (alias Rrose Sélavy) was featured in the

December issue of *Littérature*. The collection of 138 phrases reflects Desnos's spontaneous wit as well as the Surrealists' tendency to use ambiguity as a means to liberate thought from convention. When it was published in *Corps et biens,* "Rrose Sélavy" (which is a deformation of "Eros, c'est la vie" or "Eros, it's life") included 150 word puns, including spoonerisms, neologisms, and anagrams. Translation of these prophetic and quirky maxims is difficult since much of their effect lies in the internal rhyme and syntactical juxtaposition—for example, "Les lois de nos désirs sont des dés sans loisir" (the laws of our desires are dice without leisure). The playfulness of these aphorisms is typical of two other poems in *Corps et biens,* "Langage cuit" (Cooked Language, 1923) and "L'Aumonyme" (1923), the title of the latter is itself a play on the word "homonym." Desnos had planned to publish "Rrose Sélavy" together with "Langage cuit" and "L'Aumonyme" (1923) under the title "Désordre formel" (Formal Disorder), but the project was never realized, possibly because of time and financial constraints. These earlier collections reveal language as a liberating force as well as a symbolic system with a logic of its own. Through them Desnos experiments with the alchemy of language and its power to signify in the context of an ordered chaos.

Within months of Desnos's newfound fame, enthusiasm for his mediumistic talents waned, and at times the "authenticity" of the trances or telepathic sessions was questioned by cohorts such as Blaise Cendrars or Eluard. The extraordinary facility with which Desnos transformed his fertile imagination might have seemed too glib for some members of the Surrealist circle. Moreover, on occasion, the sessions spun out of control, such as an episode when Desnos chased Eluard with a kitchen knife. Breton eventually called a stop to the practice altogether. Authentic or not, the dramatic effect of the sleeps was certainly real, and the resulting lyrical outpouring, whether deliberately crafted, unconsciously murmured from a dream state, or a complex combination of both, still revealed Desnos's early work as a passionate homage to erotic adventure and freedom.

Shortly after his involvement with *Littérature,* Desnos embarked on a journalistic career, which he followed to varying degrees for the rest of his life. Breton, Aragon, Picabia, and others were also involved with literary reviews such as *La Vie moderne* and *Paris-Journal.* Desnos, however, continued to write articles and essays for different kinds of journals, beginning with *Paris-soir.* The earlier articles reflect the lightheartedness typical of his Surrealist writings. His contributions provided a small source of income, but more importantly they connected him to contemporary popular culture, which played a more influential role on his literary production in the years to come.

At this time Desnos also began writing reviews and essays on contemporary cinema. His interest in motion pictures became a lifelong passion—for Desnos, movies seemed to capture the very stuff of which dreams are made. In her preface to *Les Rayons et les ombres* (Beams and Shadows, 1992), a collection of his writings on cinema and his screenplays, Dumas quotes Desnos's comment in "De L'Erotisme" (On Eroticism), a piece published in *Paris-Journal* (20 April 1923): "nous chercherons à l'entreacte celui ou celle parmi nos voisins qui pourra nous entraîner dans une aventure égale au rêve crépusculaire du cinématographe" (During the intermission we look for the one around us who can take us away into an adventure similar to the twilight dream of the cinematographer). The dynamic presentation of images that cinema offers provided yet another creative outlet for his brimming imagination. Desnos composed motion-picture scenarios, of which three were completed during his lifetime. Other projects included adaptations of Stendhal's *La Chartreuse de Parme* (The Charterhouse of Parma, 1839), Alexandre Dumas *père*'s *Le Comte de Monte-Cristo* (The Count of Monte Cristo, 1845), and Honoré de Balzac's *Le Succube* (The Succubus).

Desnos's first published work, *Deuil pour deuil* (translated as *Mourning for Mourning,* 1992), appeared in 1924. The title is reminiscent of the expression "l'art pour l'art" (art for art's sake) and accordingly evokes the idea of sorrow for its own sake. Throughout the lyric prose of the novel, he continued to experiment with psychic automism. The work is a paradoxical composition in that it can be read as a fragmentary single text, or as twenty-four separate texts. A single voice narrates a series of brief dream narratives that have no chronology or centrality of plot. The shifting of pronouns, verbs, and adjectives resists the reader's assigning a single identity to what is a seemingly androgynous narrator. The work is nonetheless consistent in its density and complex imagery. The frenetic changes in setting mimic the polymorphism typical of dreams and also characterize another lyric novel, *La Liberté ou l'amour!* (1927; translated as *Liberty or Love!* 1993), written in 1925.

Much of *C'est les bottes de 7 lieues cette phrase "Je me vois"* (It's Seven-League Boots, This Sentence "I See Myself," 1926) was actually written before *Deuil pour deuil* and contemporaneously with "Langage cuit." *C'est les bottes de 7 lieues cette phrase "Je me vois"* exhibits a playfulness with language similar to that of some of the earlier poems, such as "Le Fard des Argonautes" and "L'Ode à Coco." At the same time, it departs from Desnos's earlier work by adopting a more seri-

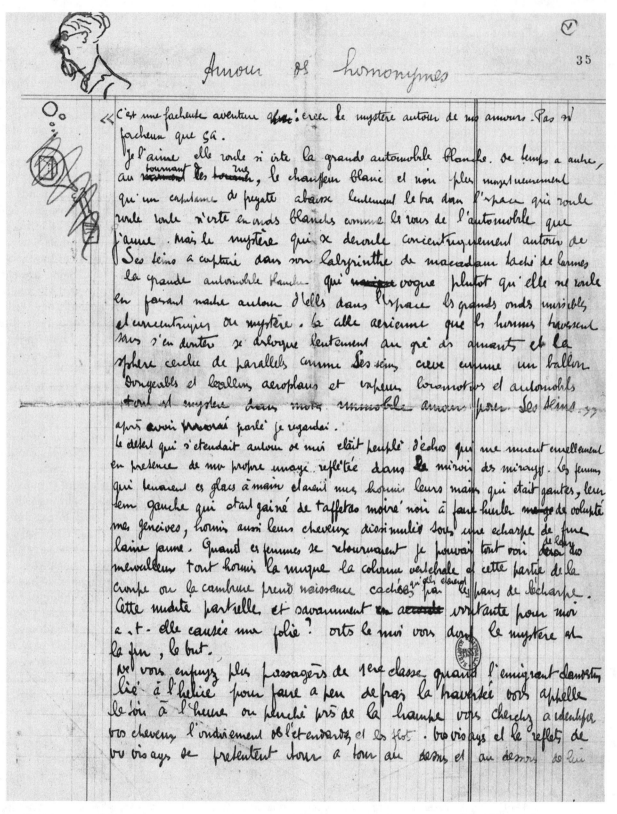

Page from the manuscript for "Amour des Homonymes," included in the 1930 collection Corps et biens *(Bibliothèque Nationale, Paris)*

ous tone. Violent images evoking fear and death (such as weapons, skeletons, and coffins) emerge from a dark marine backdrop. This menacing imagery is a result of, in part, the Surrealist penchant for shock tactics—"pour épater le bourgeois" (to shock middle-class attitudes)—but, more importantly, it announces the imminent change in Desnos's own poetics. These poems illuminate a new gaze into the self and awareness of poetic transformation. In "Destinée Arbitraire" (Arbitrary Destiny), one of the poems in the collection, he claims "je sens que mon commencement est proche" (I know that my beginning is near). By reversing the conventional phrase, "I know that my end is near," he remains true to his playful style but turns toward a new creative horizon.

Some critics, such as Terry Hale, maintain that *La Liberté ou l'amour!* is Desnos's masterpiece. The plot of this lyric novel is loosely structured around the fictional travels of the Corsaire Sanglot and his erotic escapades with Louise Lame. His earlier essay "De l'Erotisme" reveals Desnos's theory on the erotic "as an individual science." In *La Liberté ou l'amour!,* however, Desnos frees his imagination through the erotic fantasy played out by his protagonists, thus dismantling bourgeois attitudes toward love. The book was condemned by the Tribunal Correctional de la Seine, which ordered that it be heavily censored. In fact, several complete sections, including the episode of the "Club des Buveurs de sperme" (the Sperm Drinkers Club) were cut from the first edition and were not published until 1962, when *La Liberté ou l'amour!* appeared in a Gallimard edition, in one volume with the revised edition of *Deuil pour deuil.* As is *Deuil pour deuil,* the 1927 novel is unrestricted by rules of time and space, representing freedom from the laws and logic of the world. The work incarnates the Surrealist desire to know the unknown, represented by the aloof and taciturn Louise Lame. Her relationship with Corsaire Sanglot evokes the struggle between silence or immanence and the fluid mobility of poetic expression, as well as the potential reconciliation between love and freedom. The title itself presents a choice between love or liberty but, paradoxically, it also evokes the two as one and the same—"liberty or love."

Belgian singer and actress Yvonne George was a crucial inspiration to Desnos's love poetry of the late 1920s. He first encountered her while he was reviewing one of her performances for *Le Journal littéraire.* The article, "Yvonne George à l'Olympia," was later included in the 1978 collection *Nouvelles Hébrides et autres textes, 1922–1930* (New Hebrides and Other Texts, 1922–1930). In it Desnos claimed that she sang in the name of love and desire: "Je l'ai vue dans un concert, réléver aux mélomanes par la seule vertu de chansons de marins, que la musique n'est jamais que de l'art quand la parole peut être poésie" (I saw her in concert reveal to music lovers by the sole virtue of her sailor songs that music is never just art when the spoken word can be poetry). Many of the female figures in Desnos's poetry of this period are avatars of Yvonne George and appear transformed as stars, both celestial and marine, or flames, that correspond to his own passion for her and to her luminous presence.

Desnos's poetry of the late 1920s reveals a somber, almost tragic, vein. "A la Mystérieuse" (To the Mysterious Woman) is a 1926 cycle of seven poems (collected in *Corps et biens*) that on the surface appears to be love poems to an unattainable woman; however, in each of these poems the isolation evoked by the poetic voice is more a testimony to Desnos's solitary dream adventure rather than a lament for unrequited love. The woman, transfigured as the ideal expression of his inner vision, is elusive, shadowy, like Eurydice, and disappears under the poet's contemplative gaze. Amid the impossibility and despair, however, a hopeful chord resonates throughout the collection. Along with *Les Ténèbres* (Darkness, 1927), also collected in *Corps et Biens,* these poems constitute some of Desnos's most intense and hauntingly beautiful lyric poetry, as in "J'ai tant rêvé de toi" (I've Dreamt So Much of You):

J'ai tant rêvé de toi, tant marché parlé, couché avec ton fantôme qu'il ne me reste plus peut-être, et pourtant, qu'à être fantôme parmi les fantômes et plus ombre cent fois que l'ombre qui se promène et se promènera allégrement sur le cadran solaire de ta vie.

(I've dreamt so much of you, walked so much, spoken and lain with your phantom that perhaps nothing more is left me than to be a phantom among phantoms and a hundred times more shadow than the shadow that walks and will joyfully walk on the sundial of your life).

Some critics, such as Caws and Dumas, claim that *Les Ténèbres* is unmistakably Desnos's most successful and most complex work. Twenty-four poems of various length and form evolve into a more self-reflexive questioning of the creative process and poetic language. The solitude and isolation of the lyric voice seem to emphasize the impossibility of any reconciliation between love and poetic adventure. The tensions produced by this opposition reinforce a desire for fulfillment, which is the emotional core of the collection and why the poems seem to rest on the precarious cusp of anticipation. In *Second Manifeste du surréalism* (1930) Breton referred to these poems as narcissistic; and yet, this self-reflexive aspect also illuminates the topography of Desnos's poetic universe. The shipwreck evoked in "Il fait nuit" (Nightfall)—"Le naufrage s'accentue sous la

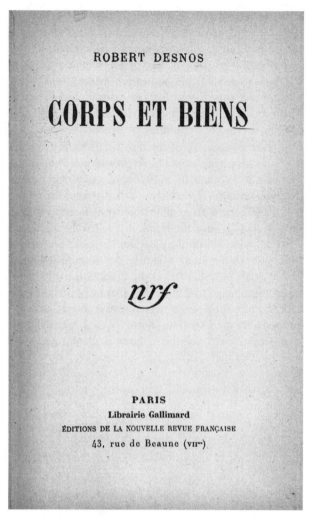

Title page for the collection that includes Desnos's "Rrose Sélavy," the punning prose poem he claimed was written while in telepathic communication with artist Marcel Duchamp

paupière / Je conte et décris le sommeil" (the shipwreck is accentuated under the eyelid / I tell stories describing sleep)—is juxtaposed with the novelty and promise of another voyage as articulated in "Le Désespoir du Soleil"(The Sun's Despair): "Rêvons acceptons de rêver c'est le poème du jour qui commence" (Dream accept dreaming it's the poem of a new day).

Desnos also composed *La Place de l'Etoile* (The Place of the Star) in 1927; in 1944 he reworked it, and it was published the following year. Much in the spirit of his earlier work, *La Place de l'Etoile* juxtaposes humor, the absurd, desire, and romantic longing. Although Desnos subtitled the piece *antipoème* (antipoem), it is a dramatic comedy centered around Maxime, his passion for collecting starfish, and the interactions of a zany cast of characters. The title *La Place de l'Etoile* alludes not only to the spaces where Maxime keeps his starfish (on

the mantelpiece or in jars) but also to Yvonne George and the geographical heart of Paris.

The Night of loveless nights (1930; translated, 1973) corresponds to a period of experiment and transition in Desnos's work. Written in 1920 and 1928, it is a lyric collage-like text composed of fragments of prose poetry and occasional alexandrines linked together by references to the creative process: love, dreams, stars, and mermaids refer to inspiration; swords, pens, and plumes allude to instruments of writing; and prisons, manacles, and chains evoke struggle with creative expression. As do the earlier collections, *A la Mystérieuse* and *Les Ténèbres,* this poem evokes a complex emotional network composed of doubt, fulfillment, love, and cruelty.

Desnos frequented the booming nightlife of Montparnasse, the artistic center of Paris, during these years. In 1926 he had moved to 45 rue Blomet, an overgrown lot with three dilapidated buildings, where the artists Joan Miró and André Masson had once had their studios. Sculptor André de la Rivière and Desnos's friend, painter George Malkine also moved to the same address. The site became a social headquarters that fueled a spirit of community and collective creativity for a new generation of artists. Desnos's sole motion-picture role, a cameo, resulted in part from this festive and collaborative environment. Prior to his departure for a conference on journalism in Havana, Desnos read his poem "L'Etoile de mer" (Starfish) after a farewell dinner with the artist and photographer Man Ray, model and cabaret performer Kiki de Montparnasse, and Yvonne George. Impressed by what he perceived as the visual and cinematic images of the poem, Ray resolved to make a movie of Desnos's "L'Etoile de mer." As Ray later recalled in his autobiography, *Self Portrait* (1963): "Desnos's poem was like a scenario for a film, consisting of fifteen or twenty lines, each line presenting a clear, detached image of a place or of a man and woman." Desnos appears in the movie with Kiki and André de la Rivière; it premiered on 13 May 1928 at the Studio des Ursulines. A trio of musicians played the accompaniment—a selection of Cuban songs that Desnos had brought back from Havana.

Desnos also encountered model and free spirit Youki Foujita (née Lucie Badoud) in the lively world of Montparnasse. When he first met her in 1928, she was married to the Japanese painter Tsuguharu Foujita, who had nicknamed her "Youki" (the Japanese word for snow). The three became close friends and often traveled together. *Le Voyage en Bourgogne* (Travels in Burgundy, 1947) was inspired by a carefree and picturesque excursion they took through the region. Desnos's amicable relationship with Youki soon turned into ardent passion and eternal love. They never married but were deeply devoted to each other throughout their lifetimes. For Desnos, Youki represented the confluence of desire and reality. In his iconography, she often appears as a mermaid or seahorse; invigorated by the frothy tide of the ocean, she is a swimmer, a survivor. Rediscovery of love through her inspiration is inscribed in the 1931 poem "Siramour" (1931), the title of which is a combination of the words *sirène* (mermaid) and *amour* (love). "Siramour" was later republished in the 1942 collection *Fortunes.*

The year 1930 was a time of radical change in Desnos's personal and professional life. Relations between Desnos and Breton had been strained as early as 1927, when Breton, Aragon, Eluard, and Péret joined the French Communist Party. Despite their encouragement, Desnos refused to follow suit. Although he continued to consider himself a Surrealist, he did not believe in following a prescribed doctrine that would inevitably inhibit his own creativity. Tensions surfaced when Breton censured Desnos in his *Second Manifeste du surréalisme* (Second Manifesto of Surrealism, 1930). Breton accused Desnos of lowering himself to the plane of reality and of sacrificing his literary talent to trivial journalism. In March of 1930 Desnos published "Le Troisième Manifeste du Surréalisme" (The Third Manifesto of Surrealism) in *Le Courrier Littéraire;* the article was later included in *Neuvelles Hébrides.* In it Desnos calls Breton a hypocrite quick to criticize others from his ivory tower while consumed by his own envy of their talent. At the end of the essay Desnos affirms that Surrealism had finally and rightfully come into the public domain. In April of that year Yvonne George died from tuberculosis, which was accelerated by her habitual use of opium and morphine. Although he was already deeply devoted to Youki at this point, Desnos still loved the singer. *Corps et biens* appeared in bookstores the following month and featured the two early poems he had shared with Breton, as well as "Rrose Sélavy," *L'Aumonyme, Langage cuit, A la Mystérieuse,* and *Les Ténèbres,* in addition to five new poems. The title carries a double meaning: first of all, the phrase refers to "perdu corps et biens," the nautical term describing a ship that has been lost at sea with all of its crew and cargo. Secondly, it transforms the expression "corps et âme" (body and soul): the soul has been replaced by material belongings, possessions–*biens.* The collection charts his activity with the Surrealist movement and is perhaps his most widely read work today. At the time of its publication, however, the Surrealists–Aragon in particular–responded with scathing commentary in "Corps, âme, et biens" from the first volume of *La Surrealisme au service de La revolution* and accused Desnos of verbosity and "complaisence verbale" (verbal compla-

cency). It signaled the end of Desnos's association with the Surrealist movement.

Although Desnos continued to write poetry during the 1930s, he became increasingly involved with radio over the decade. His first experience with radio was a program on Surrealist painting sponsored by Radio-Paris and aired in June of 1930. Two years later Paul Deharme, a pioneer in broadcasting, hired him at Radio-Paris. The poet was fascinated by "l'art radiophonique" (the art of radio) and saw the new medium both as a way to influence the public and to bring art into the realm of popular culture. Desnos wrote advertising slogans for toothpaste, soap, chocolate, coffee, and salt among a myriad of other products totaling more than three thousand. He brought to these jingles the sparkle of his humor and his poetry. In the postface to *Etat de veille* (Waking State, 1943), he writes of this period of his life, "je me livrai avec passion au travail quasi mathématique mais cependant intuitif de l'adaptation des paroles à la musique, de la fabrication des sentences, proverbes et devises publicitaires, travail dont la première exigence était un retour aux règles proprement populaires en matière de rythme" (I threw myself passionately into the almost mathematical, yet intuitive, work of adapting words to music, of fabricating sentences, proverbs, and slogans for advertising, work whose primary exigency was a return to the people's taste in the way of rhyme and rhythm). The most celebrated shows of his radio career include *La Grande complainte de Fantômas* (Song of Fantomas, 1933), a detective story in verse written by Desnos and directed by Antonin Artaud; *Le Salut au monde,* an adaptation of the poem by Walt Whitman (1936); and *La Clef des songes* (The Key to Dreams, 1938–1939). The latter was a weekly broadcast starring Desnos, who read and interpreted dreams sent in by listeners. Radio for Desnos was yet another venue into the world of dreams; only now his desire was to connect with others, to understand their dreams.

Les Sans-cou (1934) is Desnos's only collection of poetry published during the decade. With a title translatable as either "The Headless" or "The Neckless," the work comprises sixteen poems that reveal Desnos's candid questioning of personal growth and middle age, as well as a growing concern with the rise of fascism in Europe. Unlike the earlier poetry of *A la Mystérieuse* and *Les Ténèbres,* which illuminates creative introspection, these poems express an outward-bound mission to expose hypocrisy and social struggle. Poems such as "Camarades" (Comrades) and "Aux Sans-cou" (To the Headless) are a eulogy to fraternal solidarity as well as a warning against the dangers of ignorance and blind faith. The contemplative aspect of Desnos's poetry is

Desnos and his lover, Lucie Foujita, known as Youki, during the 1930s

still clear, only the focus shifts from the inner self to human interaction in a larger social context.

The same year that *Les Sans-cou* was published, Desnos and Youki moved to 19 rue Mazarine. Their apartment, stacked with piles of books and objects collected from various trips, was decorated with paintings by Foujita and Desnos's collection of curios–objects such as a crystal sword, glass bowls, ceramic pottery, and oddly shaped bottles–that appear transfigured throughout his poetry. The early 1930s were marked by financial difficulty for the couple. Desnos often felt compelled to write more to keep up with Youki's expensive tastes, as evidenced in "Comme" (Like). The poem evokes awe at and also frustration with the transformative power of metaphor, which can turn water into wine–or put wine on the table.

Desnos's later works reveal the break with the earlier efforts of navigating the unconscious and focus on form, rhythm, and language. Much of the poetry he composed during the 1930s is assembled in *Fortunes* and *Destinée Arbitraire* and illustrates Desnos's appeal to a wider readership. These poems celebrate the meaningful details of daily life such as the ripple of water under a bridge, in relation to the broader question of camaraderie among human beings. Desnos's poetry of this period conveys through an earthy simplicity the personal, professional, and creative changes he had experi-

enced to that point. In 1936 Desnos decided to undertake the rigorous endeavor of writing a poem a day for a year. An exercise in discipline and mastery, it did not yield the success that he had hoped, although he maintained that ultimately it was a worthwhile experiment. Many of the poems written as a result are included in the cycle of poems *Les Portes Battantes* (Swinging Doors) in *Fortunes*. *Fortunes* features several other poems written during the decade, in addition to "Siramour," *The Night of loveless nights,* and *Les Sans-cou*. Desnos also composed several cantatas, including *Cantate pour l'inauguration du Musée de l'homme* (Cantata for the Inauguration of the Museum of Man), which was set to music by composer Darius Milhaud and performed in 1937.

During the 1930s Desnos also wrote *Le Livre secret pour Youki* (The Secret Book for Youki, 1999), a volume of love poetry for Youki, illustrated by gouaches that he had painted. *Les Nuits Blanches* (White Nights, or Sleepless Nights), published in *Destinée arbitraire,* comprises dream narratives combined with songs he wrote. In addition, he wrote poems for the children of friends, such as "Le Parterre d'Hyacinthe" (The Hyacinth Bed), composed in 1932 for the children of Lise and Paul Deharme; and "La Géométrie de Daniel" (Daniel's Geometry), written in 1939 for the son of Madeleine and Darius Milhaud. Along with *La Ménagerie de Tristan*

(Tristan's Menagerie, 1978), these poems were originally illustrated with gouaches by Desnos and were collected in *Destinée Arbitraire*.

After France declared war on Germany in September 1939, Desnos was mobilized as a sergeant and consequently discontinued his work with radio. He continued to write but published less frequently, his work appearing in such journals as *Europe, Commune,* and *Ce-Soir.* He also contributed to reviews such as *Poésie 42, L'Honneur des poètes,* and *L'Eternelle Revue.* Beginning in 1940 Desnos also wrote for the newspaper *Aujourd'hui,* which played a pivotal role in his life, as it politicized his value as a journalist and as a poet. When Desnos first joined *Aujourd'hui,* he had envisioned, along with the founders and other contributors, an independent voice that would not be controlled by the Occupation authorities. However, this hope was never realized, and, as a result, Desnos limited his contributions mainly to literary reviews and critiques on contemporary music. Although he was recognized as part of the intellectual Left that voiced concern about the spread of fascism in Europe, Desnos was obliged to observe a modicum of caution (which was not his forte). In the years following 1941, the threat to free speech was such that he rarely signed his work and instead used pseudonyms such as Pierre Andier, Lucien Gallois, Valentin Guillois (all variations of family names), and Cancale.

On 16 and 17 July 1942, French policemen carried out what became known as "La Grande rafle du Vel'd'Hiv" (The Great Raid [or Roundup] of the Vel'd'Hiv), when some 13,000 Jewish men, women, and children were rounded up and held in an indoor sports arena, the Vélodrome d'Hiver, before being turned over to the German authorities for eventual deportation to Auschwitz. Desnos's articles in *Aujourd'hui* from 1940 on reveal a contempt he felt for the Occupation all along; the raid seems to have been decisive, however, in leading him to begin work with the Agir (Act) network of the French Resistance. Through his position with *Aujourd'hui,* he could easily acquire and transmit information. He also participated in clandestine publishing and helped to supply forged identity papers for Jews and other members of the network. During these endeavors Desnos made little attempt to conceal his hostility toward Nazism, making him suspicious in the eyes of the collaborationist Vichy authorities.

His 1943 collection *Etat de veille* includes poems that are essentially songs of struggle and courage. Even the title of the collection shifts from the oneiric settings of his earlier poetry and insists on a state of consciousness, awareness. The poem "Demain" (Tomorrow, 1942), included in *Etat de veille,* attests to this call to attention:

Or, du fond de la nuit, nous témoignons encore
De la splendeur du jour et de tous ses présents.
Si nous ne dormons pas c'est pour guetter l'aurore
Qui prouvera qu'enfin nous vivons au présent.

(Meanwhile, from the depths of night we still bear witness
To the splendor of the day and all its gifts.
If we do not sleep, it is to watch for the dawn,
Which will prove that at last we are living in the present).

The work also includes some of the "poèmes forcés" (forced poems) written between 1936 and 1937—many of which have been carefully and sometimes completely reworked. *Etat de veille* also yielded the lyric classical verses that were later set to music by Marcel Delannoy in his song cycle *Etat de veille: Cinq mélodies sur des poèmes de Robert Desnos, op. 48* (Waking State: Five Melodies After the Poems of Robert Desnos, Op. 48, 1946), which includes "Je n'aime plus la rue St. Martin" (I Don't Love St. Martin Street Anymore) and "Le Soleil de la rue de Bagnolet" (The Sun on Bagnolet Street). The collection is the result of Desnos's attempt to ally freedom of expression with the laws of form; it is the test to which he put his own talent, thus revealing a continual and deliberate reworking of his poetic experiment.

The novel *Le Vin est tiré* (The Wine Has Been Tapped, 1943) bears little resemblance to his earlier novels. The story chronicles the tragic downfall of its drug-addicted heroes—a group of young bohemians in Paris. It is a lament documenting the dangers of the excessive drug use he had witnessed in friends, particularly Yvonne George. Desnos's own experience with opium was brief and largely motivated by his psychic exploration during the 1920s. The realistic style of the novel reflects Desnos's growing concern with the social realities of the time.

In the early 1940s Desnos reorganized various poems that had already been published in journals along with new creations and prepared them for publication in book form. Among these projects were *30 chantefables, pour les enfants sages* (Thirty Song-fables for Good Children, 1944), *Le Bain avec Andromède* (The Bath with Andromeda, 1944), and *Contrée* (Country, 1944). These works, composed of a mixture of prose and poetry, weave together popular language and traditional form. *Calixto* (1962), like *Le Bain avec Andromède,* features a classical figure resurrected in measured verse seasoned with vernacular.

Contrée was the last work Desnos published before his arrest. Comprised of twenty-five poems, many of which are alexandrines or sonnet-like, the collection alternates between country scenes and meditations on the place of the self in the world. Some of the poems, such as "Le Cimetière" (The

Desnos (far right) with fellow soldiers at the Taillebourg army base, awaiting demobilization on 26 June 1940, the day after the Franco-German armistice took effect

Cemetery), "Le Souvenir" (The Memory), "La Prophétie" (The Prophecy), "La Route" (The Road), and "La Maison" (The House), were also published in literary journals in the early 1940s. Other poems written during these years that later became famous include "Ce Cœur qui haissait la guerre" (This Heart that Hated War, 1943), "Maréchal Ducono" (1944)—a satirical allusion to Marshal Philippe Pétain, leader of the Vichy government)—and "Le Veilleur du Pont au Change" (Watchman of the Pont-au-Change, 1944). Several of these poems, often referred to as his Resistance writings, were republished in *Choix de poèmes* (Selected Poems, 1946), *Domaine Public* (Public Domain, 1953), and *Destinée arbitraire*.

Desnos was arrested by the Gestapo on 22 February 1944 at his rue Mazarine apartment. At the time of his arrest, he was working on an underground journal titled "Les Nouveaux Taons" (The New Gnats), a satirical reference to the collaborationist journal *Les Nouveaux Temps* (The New Times). Following his arrest he embarked on an arduous and tragic journey. He was first interred at the prison Fresne, where he stayed for several weeks before being transferred to the transit camp of Royal-Lieu at Compiègne. Here he found a group of kindred souls who met to discuss poetry and

literature when they could. His experience here inspired the well-known poem "Sol de Compiègne" (Soil of Compiègne). Youki was warned of his next transfer, and on 27 April she arrived in time to call out goodbye before he was deported to Auschwitz with 1,700 other men. On 12 May, Desnos was moved to Buchenwald; within two weeks he and approximately 1,000 inmates were transferred to Flossenberg, which served as the site for a munitions factory. Soon afterward Desnos and about 185 other men were moved yet again to a camp in Flöha, where an abandoned textile factory had been converted for manufacturing aircraft fuselage. They worked at Flöha under horrendous conditions for eleven months, until the news arrived on 14 April 1945 that the Allies were closing in. The camp was subsequently emptied, and the few remaining inmates were sent on a forced march to a camp near Terezin, Czechoslovakia, then known as Theresienstadt. The men arrived on 8 May, after the Nazis had already left, informed of the imminent Allied arrival. At this point Desnos was suffering from typhus and dehydration. A medical student who had been sent to Desnos's barracks recognized his name on a list of ailing inmates. In her 1980 biography Dumas reports that the student, Josef Stuna, asked him "Connaissez-vous le poète Robert Desnos?" (Do you know the poet Robert Desnos?), and he answered, "Robert Desnos, le poète français mais c'est moi" (Robert Desnos, the French poet, why, that's me!) Over the next three days Stuna conversed at length with Desnos about poetry, Surrealism, and poets Breton, Eluard, Péret, Tanguy, and Tzara. Desnos's condition worsened and he died at 5:30 A.M. on 8 June 1945–after having said, Stuna later recalled, "C'est mon matin le plus matinal" (It's my earliest morning).

Details of Desnos's life and writings in the concentration camps are scarce. The few stories that have surfaced about him are moving and reflect his sensitivity toward fellow prisoners as well as an indomitable strength of spirit. Testimonies of survivors report that he read the palms of other inmates and told them their fortunes, which he prophesied with hope and humor. Supposedly a tin box that contained some of his writings was either lost or disposed of at the time of his death. Stuna testified, however, that the only object that Desnos possessed at the time of his death was a pair of glasses. It is perhaps fitting that Desnos's death acquired a mythical significance that originated with one of his own poems. In her essay "The Myth of the 'Dernier Poème'" (1999) Katharine Conley traces the story of this myth, revealing the complexities of the French cultural memory of World War II as well as the popularity of the poem. After Desnos died, word quickly spread that a poem–"Le Dernier Poème" (The Last Poem)–had been found with his body. The poem, a version of "J'ai tant rêvé de toi" (I Have Dreamt of You So Much), is inscribed on the Mémorial des Martyrs de la Déportation, dedicated in Paris in 1962 to the memory of the more than two hundred people deported from France to German concentration camps during World War II. The new rendition of the poem was written for Youki and evokes a similar sentiment as the original:

J'ai rêvé tellement fort de toi,
J'ai tellement marché, tellement parlé,
Tellement aimé ton ombre,
Qu'il ne me reste plus rien de toi.
Il me reste d'être l'ombre parmi les ombres
D'être cent fois plus ombre que l'ombre
D'être l'ombre qui viendra et reviendra dans ta vie
ensoleillée.

(I have dreamt so very much of you
I have walked so much, talked so much,
Loved your shadow so much,
That nothing more is left to me of you.
All that is left to me is to be the shadow among shadows
To be a hundred times more of a shadow than the
shadow

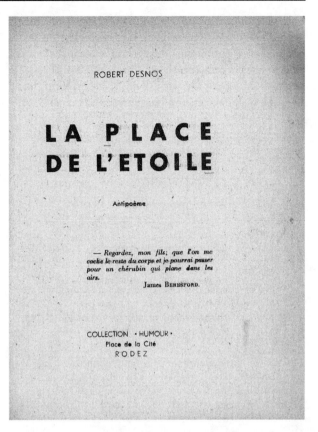

ROBERT DESNOS

LA PLACE DE L'ETOILE

Antipoème

— Regardez, mon fils; que l'on me cache le reste du corps et je pourrai passer pour un chérubin qui plane dans les airs.
James BERESFORD.

COLLECTION · HUMOUR ·
Place de la Cité
RODEZ

Title page for the revised edition (1945) of Desnos's absurdist 1927 comedy about a starfish collector (Main Library, University of California, Irvine)

To be the shadow that will come and come again into your sunny life).

In part, the confusion arose from a misleading headline "Le Dernier Poème de Robert Desnos" (The Last Poem of Robert Desnos) in an article that was printed two months after his death. Despite repeated efforts by critics during the 1960s to set the record straight, the myth persists. Conley points out that the last poem Desnos actually wrote is "Printemps" (Spring). Although the poem was composed at Compiègne and is dated 6 April 1944, it was not discovered until 1969 by Pierre Lartigue. The poem begins with a reference to Rrose Sélavy and ends with "le soleil fleurira les buissons" (the sun bursting the bushes into bloom). The poem incarnates in verse the different aspects of Desnos's poetic career–from the errant Rrose Sélavy to the burst of vernal optimism in the face of adversity. The hopeful tone of the ending resonates with the poet's desire for renewal and freedom reinforced by his passion for life.

New discoveries and studies of Desnos's life and poetry continue to enrich the body of scholarship and artistic representation of his work. Many sound recordings of his poems set to music and adaptations of his cantatas are available worldwide. His poetry has been translated into English, Russian, Spanish, Hebrew, German, Czech, Italian, and Turkish. He influenced such contemporaries as the composers Francis Poulenc and Milhaud and the singers Yves Montand and Juliette Greco; he continues to inspire artists with such creative innovations as "window books," that is, plexiglass etchings. Desnos himself wrote in 1944 in "Rélféxions sur la Poésie" (Reflections on Poetry), published posthumously in 1947:

> Les plus grands noms de notre époque (je parle des poètes) ne sont pas encore assurés d'une place supérieure au troisième rayon de la bibliothèque d'un érudit curieux de l'an 2000. Cela n'a d'ailleurs aucune importance. La grande poésie peut être nécessairement actuelle, de circonstances . . . elle peut donc être fugitive.

> (The greatest names of our time–I am speaking of poets–are still not assured of a prominent place on the third shelf of a curious scholar of the year 2000. This isn't important, though. Great poetry may be of the present moment, of current circumstances . . . therefore, it may be short-lived).

Perhaps it is the very ephemeral and contemporary nature of Robert Desnos's poetry that continues to stir the hearts and minds of readers and artists alike in the twenty-first century, where he still emerges as a visionary bard and dream weaver.

Letters:
Robert Desnos, edited by Marie-Claire Dumas, Roger Dadoun, and others, Cahiers de l'Herne, no. 54, second edition (Paris: Fayard, 1999)–includes selected correspondence.

Bibliography:
Œuvres: Desnos, edited, with an introduction and notes, by Marie-Claire Dumas (Paris: Gallimard, 1999), pp. 1371–1377.

Biographies:
Marie-Claire Dumas, *Robert Desnos ou L'exploration des limites* (Paris: Klincksieck, 1980);

Dumas, *Etude de "Corps et biens" de Robert Desnos* (Paris: Champion, 1984);

Dominique Desanti, *Robert Desnos, le roman d'une vie* (Paris: Mercure de France, 1999);

André Bessière, *Destination Auschwitz avec Robert Desnos,* preface by Marie-Claire Dumas (Paris: L'Harmattan, 2001).

References:
Pierre Berger, *Robert Desnos: Une Etude,* Collection Poètes d'aujourd'hui, no. 16 (Paris: Seghers, 1949);

Mary Ann Caws, *The Surrealist Voice of Robert Desnos* (Amherst: University of Massachusetts Press, 1977);

Katharine Conley, "The Myth of the 'Dernier Poème': Robert Desnos and French Culural Memory,'" in *Acts of Memory: Cultural Recall in the Present,* edited by Mieke Bal, Jonathan Crewe, and Leo Spitzer (Hanover, N.H.: Dartmouth College/University Press of New England, 1999), pp. 134–147;

Conley, "Silence in the Heart: The Feminine in Desnos's *La Liberté ou L'amour!" French Review,* 63, no. 3 (1990): 475–484;

Conley, "The Woman in the Bottle of Robert Desnos's Surrealist Dreams," *French Forum,* 16, no. 2 (1991): 199–208;

Youki Desnos, *Les Confidences de Youki,* second edition (Paris: Fayard, 1999);

Dumas, ed., *"Moi qui suis Robert Desnos": Permanence d'une voix: Onze études* (Paris: José Corti, 1987);

Laurent Flieder, ed., *Poétiques de Robert Desnos: En hommage à Marie-Claire Dumas: Actes de la Journée d'études du 25 novembre 1995* (Fontenay-aux-Roses: ENS Editions, 1996);

Man Ray, *Self Portrait* (Boston: Little, Brown, 1963; London: Deutsch, 1963);

Pierre Seghers, *La Résistance et ses poètes: France, 1940–1945* (Paris: Seghers, 1974).

Papers:
The major collection of Robert Desnos's manuscripts, letters, and iconography is in the Archives of the Bibliothèque Jacques Doucet, Paris; a smaller collection of manuscripts and letters is held by the Bibliothèque Nationale, Paris; drawings and notes for Man Ray's motion picture *Etoile de mer* and Desnos's *The Night of loveless nights* are located at the Museum of Modern Art, New York.

Paul Eluard

(14 December 1895 – 18 November 1952)

Kenneth W. Meadwell
University of Winnipeg

BOOKS: *Premiers poèmes,* as Paul-Eugène Grindel (Paris & Lyons: Nouvelle Edition Française, 1913);

Dialogues des inutiles, as Grindel (Paris: Les Œuvres Nouvelles, 1914);

Le Devoir: Poèmes (Paris: Privately printed for P. E. Grindel, 1916);

Le Devoir et l'inquiétude: Poèmes, suivis de, Le Rire d'un autre, with a frontispiece by André Deslignères (Paris: Gonon, 1917);

Poèmes pour la Paix (Mantes: Imprimerie du Petit Mantais, 1918);

Les Animaux et leurs hommes; Les Hommes et leurs animaux, illustrated by André Lhote (Paris: Au Sans Pareil, 1920);

Les Nécessités de la vie, et, Les Conséquences des rêves: Précédé d'Exemples, preface by Jean Paulhan (Paris: Au Sans Pareil, 1921);

Répétitions, illustrated by Max Ernst (Paris: Au Sans Pareil, 1922);

Les Malheurs des immortels, by Eluard and Ernst (Paris: Librairie Six, 1922); translated by Hugh Chisholm as *Misfortunes of the Immortals* (New York: Black Sun Press, 1943);

Mourir de ne pas mourir, with a portrait by Ernst (Paris: Editions de la Nouvelle Revue Français, 1924);

152 Proverbes mis au goût du jour, by Eluard and Benjamin Péret (Paris: La Révolution Surréaliste, 1925); translated by John Robert Colombo and Irène Currie in *Cent cinquante-deux proverbes mis a goût du jour=152 Proverbs Adapted to the Taste of the Day,* trilingual edition, with Spanish version by Susana Wald and Ludwig Zeller (Toronto: Oasis, 1977);

Au défaut du silence, anonymous, illustrated by Ernst (Paris, 1925);

Capitale de la douleur (Paris: Editions de la Nouvelle Revue Français, 1926; revised, 1946); translated by Richard M. Weisman as *Capital of Pain* (New York: Grossman, 1973);

Les Dessous d'une vie, ou, La Pyramide humaine (Marseilles: Les Cahiers du Sud, 1926);

Défense de savoir, with a frontispiece by Giorgio de Chirico (Paris: Editions Surréalistes, 1928);

L'Amour la Poésie (Paris: Gallimard, 1929);

Ralentir travaux, by Eluard, André Breton, and René Char (Paris: Editions Surréalistes, 1930); translated by Keith Waldrop as *Ralentir, travaux = Slow, Under Construction* (Cambridge, Mass.: Exact Change, 1990);

A toute épreuve (Paris: Editions Surréalistes, 1930);

L'Immaculée conception, by Eluard and Breton (Paris: José Corti, 1930); translated by Jon Graham as *The Immaculate Conception,* introduction by Antony Melville (London: Atlas, 1990);

La Vie immédiate (Paris: Editions des Cahiers Libres, 1932);

Comme deux gouttes d'eau (Paris: José Corti, 1933);

La Rose publique (Paris: Gallimard, 1934);

Nuits partagées, with two drawings by Salvador Dalí (Paris: Editions G.L.M., 1935);

Facile, photographs by Man Ray (Paris: Editions G.L.M., 1935);

Notes sur la poésie, by Eluard and Breton, with a drawing by Dalí (Paris: Editions G.L.M., 1935);

La Barre d'appui, with three engravings by Pablo Picasso (Paris: Editions des Cahiers d'Art, 1936);

Les Yeux fertiles, illustrated by Picasso (Paris: Editions G.L.M., 1936);

Appliquée: Prose, illustrated by Valentine Hugo (Paris: Printed by Henri Jourde, 1937);

Quelques-uns des mots qui jusqu'ici m'étaient mystérieusement interdits (Paris: Editions G.L.M., 1937);

Cours naturel (Paris: Editions du Sagittaire, 1938);

Médieuses, with lithographs by Hugo (Paris: Dorfinant, 1939);

Chanson complète (Paris: Gallimard, 1939);

Donner à voir (Paris: Gallimard, 1939);

Le Livre ouvert, 2 volumes (Paris: Editions des Cahiers d'Art, 1940, 1942)–comprises volume 1, *I. 1938–1940* and volume 2, *II. 1939–1941;* enlarged as *Le Livre ouvert (1938–1944),* 1 volume (Paris: Gallimard, 1947)–includes *Chanson complète, Le Livre ouvert,* and *Le Lit, La Table;*

Moralité du sommeil, illustrated by René Magritte (Antwerp: Editions de l'Aiguille Aimantée, 1941);

Sur les pentes inférieures, preface by Paulhan (Paris: Librairie La Peau de Chagrin, 1941);

Choix de poèmes, 1914–1941 (Paris: Gallimard, 1941; revised and enlarged, 1946);

La dernière nuit, frontispiece by Henri Laurens (Paris: Editions des Cahiers d'Art, 1942);

Poésie et Vérité 1942 (Paris: Editions de la Main à Plume, 1942; enlarged edition, Neuchâtel, Switzerland: Editions de La Baconnière, 1943); revised edition republished with *Au rendez-vous allemand* as *Au rendez-vous allemand* (Paris: Editions de Minuit, 1945);

Les Sept poèmes d'amour en guerre, as Jean du Haut (Saint-Flour: Bibliothèque Française, 1943);

Les Armes de la douleur (Toulouse: Comité National des Ecrivains, Centre des Intellectuels, 1944);

A Pablo Picasso, Collection Les Grands peintres par leurs amis, no. 1 (Geneva: Editions des Trois Collines, 1944; Paris & Geneva: Editions des Trois Collines, 1945); translated by Joseph T. Shipley as *Pablo Picasso* (New York: Philosophical Library, 1947);

Pour vivre ici, clandestine edition, Collection Le Lapin et Le Chat (The Hague: H. van Krimpen, 1944);

Au rendez-vous allemand (Paris: Editions de Minuit, 1944);

Le Lit La Table (Geneva & Paris: Editions des Trois Collines, 1944);

En avril 1944, Paris respirait encore! illustrated by Jean Hugo (Paris: Editions de la Galerie Charpentier, 1945);

Doubles d'ombre, illustrated by André Beaudin (Paris: Gallimard, 1945);

Poésie ininterrompue (Paris: Gallimard, 1946);

Souvenirs de la maison des fous, illustrated by Gérard Vulliamy (Paris: Editions Pro Francia, 1946);

Le Dur désir de durer, with twenty-five original drawings and a frontispiece by Marc Chagall (Paris: Editions Arnold-Bordas, 1946); republished as *Le Dur désir de durer = The Dour Desire to Endure,* bilingual edition, translation by Stephen Spender and Frances Cornford (Philadelphia: Grey Falcon Press / London: Trianon Press, 1950);

Le Temps déborde, as Didier Desroches, photographs by Dora Maar and Ray (Paris: Editions Cahiers d'Art, 1947);

Corps mémorable, as Brun, with a drawing by Valentine Hugo (Paris: Seghers, 1947; enlarged, as Eluard, 1948);

Premiers poèmes (1913–1921), Collection le Bouquet, no. 40 (Lausanne, Switzerland: Mermod, 1948);

A l'intérieur de la vue, illustrated by Ernst (Paris: Seghers, 1948);

Poèmes politiques, preface by Louis Aragon (Paris: Gallimard, 1948);

Perspectives, illustrated by Albert Flocon (Paris: Maeght, 1948);

Une Leçon de morale (Paris: Gallimard, 1949);

Léda, Collection les Amoureuses, no. 7 (Lausanne, Switzerland: Mermod, 1949);

Grain-d'aile, illustrated by Jacqueline Duhème (Paris: Editions Raisons d'Etre, 1951);

Le Phénix, with eighteen drawings by Hugo (Paris: Editions G.L.M., 1951);

Pouvoir Tout dire, illustrated by Françoise Gilot (Paris: Editions Raison d'Etre, 1951);

Le Visage de la paix, with twenty-nine lithographs by Picasso (Paris: Editions de la Cercle d'Art, 1951);

Marines (Alès: P.A.B., 1951);

Paul Eluard: Choix de poèmes, portraits, facsimilé, documents, inédits, edited by Louis Parrot (Paris: Seghers, 1952);

Picasso, with sixteen drawings by Picasso (Paris: Braun, 1952);

Les sentiers et les routes de la poésie, edited by Alain Trutat (Lyons: Les Ecrivains Réunis, 1952;

Poésie ininterrompue, II (Paris: Gallimard, 1953); translated by Gilbert Bowen as *Unbroken Poetry II – Poésie ininterrompue II,* bilingual edition, introduction by Jill Lewis (Newcastle upon Tyne: Bloodaxe, 1996);

Le Poète et son ombre, edited by Robert D. Valette (Paris: Seghers, 1963).

Editions and Collections: *La Jarre peut-elle être plus belle que l'eau?* (Paris: Gallimard, 1951)–comprises *La Vie immédiate, La Rose publique, Les Yeux fertiles,* and *Cours naturel;*

Poèmes pour tous: Choix de poèmes, 1917–1952, preface by Jean Marcenac (Paris: EFR, 1959);

Derniers poèmes d'amour de Paul Eluard, preface by Lucien Scheler (Paris: Club des Libraires de France, 1962)–comprises *Le Dur désir de durer, Le Temps déborde, Corps mémorable,* and *Le Phénix;* bilingual edition published as *Last Love Poems of Paul Eluard,* translated, with an introduction, by Marilyn Kallet (Baton Rouge: Louisiana State University Press, 1980);

Choix de poèmes, preface by Alain Bosquet (Paris: Livre de Poche, 1963);

Capitale de la douleur, suivi de L'Amour la poésie, preface by André Pieyre de Mandiargues (Paris: Gallimard, 1966);

Œuvres complètes, 2 volumes, edited by Marcelle Dumas and Scheler, Bibliothèque de la Pléiade, nos. 200 and 201 (Paris: Gallimard, 1968);

Poésies, 1913–1926, preface by Claude Roy (Paris: Gallimard, 1971);

Capitale de la douleur, suivi de L'Amour la poésie, preface by Max-Pol Fouchet (Paris: Bibliothèque des Chefs-d'œuvre, 1979);

L'Immaculée conception, by Eluard and André Breton, edited by Marguerite Bonnet and Etienne-Alain Hubert (Paris: José Corti, 1991).

Editions in English: *Paul Eluard: Selected Writings,* translated by Lloyd Alexander, with introductory notes by Louis Aragon, Louis Parrot, and Claude Roy (New York: New Directions, 1951; London: Routledge & Kegan Paul, 1952); republished as *Uninterrupted Poetry: Selected Writings of Paul Eluard* (Westport, Conn.: Greenwood Press, 1977);

Liberté, translated by Teo Savory (Greensboro, N.C.: Unicorn Press, 1977);

Eluard and Helena Diakonova (known as Gala) in the tuberculosis sanitorium at Calvadel, 1913

Selected Poems: Paul Eluard, bilingual edition, edited and translated by Gilbert Bowen, introduction by Max Adereth (London: Calder / New York: Riverrun Press, 1988);

Ombres et soleil=Shadows and Sun: Selected Writings of 1913–1952, translated by Alexander and Cicely Buckley (Durham, N.H.: Oyster River Press, 1995);

Liberty, translated by Alan Dixon (Peterborough, U.K.: Spectacular Diseases, 1999).

OTHER: Man Ray, *Les Mains libres,* drawings, with poems by Eluard (Paris: Editions Jeanne Bucher, 1937);

Federico García Lorca, *Ode à Salvador Dali,* translated by Eluard and Louis Parrot (Paris: Editions G.L.M., 1938);

Charles Baudelaire, *Choix des textes,* preface by Eluard, (Paris: Editions G.L.M., 1939);

Poésie involontaire et poésie intentionnelle, edited by Eluard (Villeneuve-les-Avignon: Seghers, 1942);

André Frénaud, *Les Mystères de Paris,* preface by Eluard (Paris: Seuil, 1943);

Gisèle Prassinos, *Le Feu maniaque,* foreword by André
 Breton, preface and afterword by Eluard (Paris:
 R. J. Godet, 1944);

Angèle Vannier, *L'Arbre à feu: Poèmes,* preface by Eluard
 (Paramé, Brittany: Editions du Goéland, 1950);

Première anthologie vivante de la poésie du passé, 2 volumes,
 edited by Eluard (Paris: Seghers, 1951);

Anthologie des écrits sur l'art, 3 volumes, edited by Eluard
 (Paris: Editions Cercle d'Art, 1952–1954);

Paul Eluard holds a special place in the hearts of
fellow French patriots. He is known, appreciated, and
remembered for his great compassion in the face of the
suffering and human adversity caused by wars and dictatorships; as a poet supremely inspired by the three
women who, consecutively, became his wives; and,
finally, for his contribution to the Surrealist movement,
which he abandoned later in life to concentrate on a
less abstract and more humanistic approach to poetry.
Eluard's poetry shines with refined and luminous
imagery evoking ordinary objects that take on new
images and meaning.

Born in Saint-Denis, a small working-class industrial center north of Paris, on 14 December 1895,
Paul-Eugène Grindel was the only child of Clément
Eugène Grindel, an accountant who later became a successful real estate developer, and Jeanne Marie Cousin, a
seamstress. Initially, the small family lived in polluted
and overpopulated Saint-Denis, in extremely modest
conditions, until about 1899 when they moved to Aul-
nay- sous-Bois, a smaller city northeast of Paris, which
offered a more salubrious environment in which to raise
a child. In about 1908 the Grindels moved to the tenth
arrondissement (district) in Paris. Here, Paul-Eugène Grindel, known by the nickname of Gégène, attended school.
Especially proficient in English, he spent two months in
Southampton at the age of fifteen to further his English
studies. During this period the adolescent poet composed
such poems as "Culte" (Cult) and "Ballade de l'inspiration" (Ballad of Inspiration), collected in *Premieres poèmes*
(First Poems, 1913), in which he evoked the concepts of
religion and poetic inspiration and practiced refined versification reminiscent of the postsymbolist tradition. At
this young age he was already exploring the mysteries of
language and the power of poetry to transcend the banal-
ities of everyday life.

In July 1912, while vacationing with his mother
in a small village close to Montreux, Switzerland, he fell
ill with a serious pulmonary infection that necessitated
a stay in a sanatorium in Davos, Switzerland, from the
winter of 1912 to the spring of 1914. Here, surrounded
by breathtaking alpine scenery and fresh air, Grindel
tended to his tuberculosis by taking frequent daily
walks in the pure mountain air and by eating regularly

to strengthen his weakened body; he wrote, read, and
contemplated life. His bedside book was *Feuilles d'herbe*
(1909), Léon Bazalgette's French translation of Walt
Whitman's *Leaves of Grass* (1855), and he also read
avidly from the works of such symbolist or avant-garde
writers as Arthur Rimbaud, the Comte de Lautréamont
(pseudonym of Isidore Lucien Ducasse), Charles
Baudelaire, Gérard de Nerval, and Guillaume Apollinaire. From his sickbed the young man, not yet nineteen, pondered the creation of poetry, contemplated his
solitude, and compensated for the silence around him
with the fullness of sustained introspection.

In Davos he met a slightly older young Russian,
Helena Diakonova, who later became known as Gala,
with whom he fell deeply in love. The daughter of a
Muscovite lawyer, Gala was an avid reader of Fyodor
Dostoevsky, Leo Tolstoy, and the Russian symbolists.
She captivated Grindel with her charm, literary culture,
and expressive presence. Grindel returned to Paris in
the spring of 1914, having been pronounced cured by
his physician; Gala returned to Russia. The young couple's desire to remain together was thwarted by his
mother; however, they did eventually marry in Paris in
February 1917.

Grindel joined the army at the outbreak of World
War I in 1914. His war experience had a profound and
enduring effect on his personal philosophy and fed his
desire to help those oppressed by military force, political
power, or social constraints. A member of the medical
corps and then of the infantry, he saw firsthand the horror
and devastation of military action; he was himself gassed,
which caused great harm to his already fragile lungs. Following the birth of his daughter, Cécile Simone Antonyle
Grindel, on 11 May 1918, he was posted to a military
supply store, one and a half hours from Paris by train.

In 1918 his *Poèmes pour la Paix* (Poems for Peace)
were published under the name Paul Eluard, the surname of his maternal grandmother, which he had taken
as a pseudonym in 1914. Written during the war years,
one of his most beautiful poems, "Pour vivre ici" (In
Order To Live Here), was intended to form a suite to his
Poèmes pour la Paix but was not published in its entirety as
a five-part work until 1940, when it was included in *Le
Livre ouvert, I* (The Open Book, I). The poem includes
the profound and symbolic imagery that became characteristic of his later poetry. Its title is evidence of Eluard's
desire to invite and create peace and to construct and for-
tify one's own metaphorical space in the darkness of wartime destruction:

Je fis un feu, l'azur m'ayant abandonné,
Un feu pour être son ami,
Un feu pour m'introduire dans la nuit d'hiver,
Un feu pour vivre mieux.

Je lui donnai ce que le jour m'avait donné:
Les forêts, les buissons, les champs de blé, les vignes,
Les nids et leurs oiseaux, les maisons et leurs clés,
Les insectes, les fleurs, les fourrures, les fêtes.

(I made a fire, the sky having abandoned me,
A fire to be its friend,
A fire to lead me into the winter night,
A fire to live better.

I gave it what the day had given me:
Forests, bushes, fields of grain, vines,
Nests and their birds, houses and their keys,
Insects, flowers, furs, holidays).

The absurdity of war, the absence of a divine presence that might alleviate suffering, and the horrific images encountered during Eluard's war experiences lend a poignant voice to this piece. Longing for light, warmth, and human kindness is expressed through universal imagery derived from nature and intimate and sensual objects. The mellifluous cadence of the lines reinforces the melancholy that permeates the subjectivity of the narrative voice, creating a rhythm that seems to follow the systematic feeding of the fire. Memories, objects, vistas, nature—all serve to fuel the fire by which the poet wishes to replace the blackness that had descended upon humankind during the war years. *Poèmes pour la Paix* earned Eluard critical attention and entry into Parisian literary circles, in which he met such writers as André Breton, author of *Le Premier Manifeste du surréalisme* (The First Manifesto of Surrealism, 1924), the novelist and poet Louis Aragon, and the Romanian poet Tristan Tzara, the creator of Dadaism.

It was the heyday of avant-garde thought and practice and of the Dadaist movement, which through literature, art, and music strove to repudiate artistic and social conventions as well as the conventional use of language. Founded in Switzerland in 1916, a neutral country during World War I, Dadaism was embodied by a group of artists and intellectuals who congregated in Zurich. Profoundly troubled by the atrocities of war, Tzara and his Dadaist compatriots believed in scandalizing the bourgeois. They mixed art forms in Dadaist performance pieces that incorporated recitation, music, and art; they created word games, practiced unusual uses of language, and revolted against the tenets of traditional representational art. For example, *dada,* in French, is baby talk for "horse," the equivalent of "horsey" in English. An example of the Dadaist attempt to foster an iconoclastic attitude toward art is Marcel Duchamp's work *L.H.O.O.Q.* (1919)—a cheap reproduction of Leonardo da Vinci's painting *Mona Lisa* (1503–1506) to which Duchamp added a moustache and goatee; the letters of Duchamp's title, when read rap-

André Breton, Eluard, and René Char in 1930

idly in French, sound like "Elle a chaud au cul"(she has a hot ass).

In 1919 Tzara created the avant-garde review *Littérature,* which was also directed by Breton, Aragon, and Philippe Soupault. Eluard, having been released from the army on 10 May 1919—just before the first birthday of Cécile—joined the ranks of the Parisian Dadaists. But Dadaism, as a counterculture aesthetic, was necessarily doomed to disappear before it could become a convention. And so Surrealism was born. Its first manifesto, published by Breton in 1924, proclaimed that logical rational thought was only one part—and by no means the most significant part—of human thought processes. Freudian psychoanalysis, the voice of the subconscious, dream imagery, dark humor, the free association of language: these were aspects of the new aesthetic proposed by the Surrealists. In Cologne in 1920 the Surrealist movement brought together Eluard and Max Ernst, an intellectual artist who denied the existence of art in the traditional sense and who exploited the ambiguity of objects and structures in order to puzzle the viewer. In essence, his art turned against the familiar, placing it in innovative or enigmatic situations.

Eluard and Ernst collaborated on various projects, such as *Répétitions* (Repetitions, 1922), which Ernst illustrated and is one of many examples of Eluard's systematic rejection of rhyme and his commitment to the exploration of language. In "Parfait" (Perfect) he writes:

> Un miracle de sable fin
> Transperce les feuilles les fleurs
> Eclôt dans les fruits
> Et comble les ombres.
>
> Tout est enfin divisé
> Tout se déforme et se perd
> Tout se brise et disparaît
> La mort sans conséquences.
>
> (A miracle of fine sand
> Runs through the leaves the flowers
> Blooms in the fruits
> And fills the shadows.
>
> Everything is at last divided
> Everything becomes misshapen and lost
> Everything breaks and disappears
> Death without consequence).

It is, of course, impossible to overlook a salient feature of Eluard's use of language, exemplified in these lines: the simplicity and directness of his style. While he does not create elaborate and textured contexts, such as Rimbaud does in his "Le Bateau ivre" (1884; translated as "The Drunken Boat," 1931), the summit of nineteenth-century French symbolist poetry, Eluard does offer images of unremarkable things transposed in such way as to be found in extraordinary situations. "Parfait" speaks of the passing of time, sand filling in shadows, but also of sand that blooms, of the inevitability of destruction. These lines, through their suggested meaning derived from an individualistic use of language, recall La Pléiade, the group of French Renaissance poets who were inspired by the notion that "tout est vanité" (all is vanity), that one day all will disappear, but that nature will reincarnate itself in forms that underline the permanence of the natural world. Eluard's poetry at this time endeavored to dislocate conventional language and meaning without subverting the purpose of poetry: to suggest ways of perceiving, visually and through other senses, the multiple dimensions of physical existence apprehended in a way that is guided, if not dictated, by social and aesthetic norms.

His poem "L'Invention" (Invention) also speaks of the possibility of metamorphoses:

> La droite laisse couler du sable.
> Toutes les transformations sont possibles.

> Loin, le soleil aiguise sur les pierres sa hâte d'en finir.
> La description du paysage importe peu,
> Tout juste l'agréable durée des moissons
>
> (The right side lets the sand slip away.
> All transformations are possible.
>
> Far off, on the rocks, the sun sharpens his haste to be done with it.
> The description of the landscape matters little,
> Just the pleasant duration of harvests).

Finality, termination, the cycle of nature: such are the themes evoked in these sparse yet rich lines, as Eluard's simple image of a sunset over a field conjures up the universal theme of the inevitable passing of time, a recurring motif in literature. The originality of the manner in which this motif is evoked suggests the poet's expressive subtlety. If all transformations are possible, language must endeavor to depict them.

In 1924 Eluard published *Mourir de ne pas mourir* (Dying Not to Die), with a dedication to Breton that indicated that this book was to be Eluard's last work. In *Mourir de ne pas mourir* Eluard expresses his fatigue and need for fulfilling human relationships, thus adumbrating the themes of love and mutual understanding in his future works. His "Nudité de la vérité" (Nakedness of Truth) conveys the poet's despair through its bleak tone:

> Le désespoir n'a pas d'ailes,
> L'amour non plus,
> Pas de visage,
> Ne parlent pas,
> Je ne bouge pas,
> Je ne les regarde pas,
> Je ne leur parle pas
> Mais je suis bien aussi vivant que mon amour et que mon désespoir
>
> (Despair does not have wings,
> Nor does love,
> Faceless,
> They do not speak,
> I do not move,
> I do not look at them,
> I do not speak to them
> But I am just as alive as my love and my despair).

The narrative voice of the poem is clearly troubled by the permanence of despair but comforted by the presence of love. There is, however, a troubling note of uneasiness in this text, the consequence of solitude and silence.

In the same year, just before the publication of *Mourir de ne pas mourir,* Eluard's personal life took a dramatic turn. During the preceding months he had received stinging criticism from his father for allowing an unusual artistic and romantic relationship to develop between Gala and Ernst. His father protested vehemently, particularly incensed that Ernst was living with the couple. Eluard was largely supported financially by his father, who had prospered in the business of land development and had bought his son a house in Eaubonne, to the north of Paris. In March of 1924 Eluard disappeared. Relatives and friends were unable to locate him; obituaries appeared in the press. Leaving Gala and Cécile, whom his parents refused to help, Eluard had left Paris for the port of Marseilles, where he caught the first ship leaving France. He sent his father a letter stating that he intended to travel around the world, visiting Malaysia, India, the Caribbean, New Zealand, Java, and Singapore. This moment was one of personal crisis, a trip that Eluard himself called a "voyage ridicule" (ridiculous trip), and curiously, one that did not seem to influence his future work, which bears no trace of the exotic locales that he visited. Eluard's escapade, which was never fully understood by anyone but himself, ended seven months later in Singapore, where he was met by Gala. The couple returned to France in September of 1924.

That same year Breton's *Le Premier manifeste du surréalisme* was published, an event that heralded the birth of this aesthetic movement from the ashes of Dadaism. The word *surréaliste* had first been used by Apollinaire in his program notes for *Parade* (1917), a ballet directed by Serge Diaghilev, with a scenario by Jean Cocteau, music by Erik Satie, and design by Pablo Picasso. Apollinaire used the term again in the subtitle of the published version of his 1917 play, *Les Mamelles de Tirésias: Drame surréaliste en deux actes et un prologue* (The Breasts of Tiresius: Surrealist Drama in Two Acts and One Prologue, 1918). Breton affirmed that Surrealism is meant to describe a psychic automatism that comes close to a dream state, and he endeavored to promote the systematic exploration and study of the unconscious, its repression through social taboos, and its creations in dreams. Breton wished thus to liberate the superior reality of certain previously neglected forms of intellectual association. Louis Aragon, René Crevel, Robert Desnos, and Benjamin Péret, as well as Eluard, became associated with the Surrealist movement. Eluard played an important role as a supporter of the movement, appearing in the first issue of the flagship review of the movement, *La Révolution surréaliste,* as well as in nine of the remaining ten issues. The singular work *152 Proverbes mis au goût du jour* (1925; translated as *152 Proverbs Adapted to the Taste of the Day,* 1977), written by Eluard in collaboration with Péret, is an amusing example of the attempt by Surrealists to reconceptualize certain preconceived notions fitted into the structure of

Louis Aragon, Elsa Troilet, André Breton, Eluard, and Maria Benz (known as Nusch), 1931

a saying, such as "A bird in the hand is worth two in the bush" or "The early bird catches the worm." The goal of *152 Proverbes mis au goût du jour* is to recast the mode of the proverb, which the Surrealists deemed to have been created through too narrow a system of rationalization. The results are sometimes striking, as in "4. Les éléphants sont contagieux" (Elephants are contagious); "13. Quand un œuf casse des œufs, c'est qu'il n'aime pas les omelettes" (When an egg breaks eggs, it's because it doesn't like omelettes); "60. Il y a toujours un squelette dans le buffet" (Every buffet has a skeleton inside); and "142. Un rêve sans étoiles est un rêve oublié" (A dream without stars is a forgotten dream). This attempt to subvert the institutionalization of thought, as exemplified by traditional proverbs, not only underlines the Surrealist quest for new expressions and new ideas but also Eluard's love of language.

In *Capitale de la douleur* (1926; translated as *Capital of Pain,* 1973), which had the working title of "L'Art d'être malheureux" (The Art of Being Unhappy), Eluard found a maturity of thought evidenced in an emotional vitality whose goal is to carry the poet beyond the experience alluded to in the title. *Capitale de la douleur* is considered to be his first great collection of poetry. Some of the poems in it had been previously published in *Mourir de ne pas mourir,* while others were collected for the first time. Originally published in *La Revue européenne* in 1925, "Paris pendant la guerre" (Paris During the War) evokes a nostalgia for the past, the violence of war and its apocalyptic devastation:

> Les bêtes qui descendent des faubourgs en feu,
> Les oiseaux qui secouent leurs plumes meurtrières,
> Les terribles ciels jaunes, les nuages tout nus,
> Ont, en toute saison, fêté cette statue.
>
> Elle est belle, statue vivante de l'amour.
> Ô neige de midi, soleil sur tous les ventres,
> Ô flammes du sommeil sur un visage d'ange
> Et sur toutes les nuits et sur tous les visages.
>
> (The animals which flee the flaming suburbs,
> The birds which shake their deadly feathers,
> The terrible yellow skies, the clouds in their nakedness
> Have in all seasons celebrated this statue.
>
> It is beautiful, a living statue of love.
> Oh noontime snow, sun shining on all chests,
> Oh flames of sleep on the face of an angel
> And on all nights and all faces).

The trauma of war was indelibly engraved on Eluard's psyche, translating his concern for nature into one for humanity. It is noteworthy that the image most closely resembling a human figure, the statue, is literally a living statue of love, an icon of fraternity that was a gathering point for celebration in days of peace. Eluard's concern for humankind, his rejection of bourgeois smugness and French colonialism, as well as his abiding desire to improve the human condition for all, led him to join the French Communist Party in 1926, as did eventually other Surrealists. While *Capitale de la douleur* expresses a collective grief, it also conveys Eluard's intensely personal desire to achieve inner peace and balance through love. The last piece in this work, "Celle de toujours, toute" (She, Always, Everything) closes on an intimate note expressing the poet's need to love and his dependence on the woman in his life to sustain him with the creative forces of love:

> Je chante la grande joie de te chanter,
> La grande joie de t'avoir ou de ne pas t'avoir,
> La candeur de t'attendre, l'innocence de te connaître,
> Ô toi qui supprimes l'oubli, l'espoir et l'ignorance,
> Qui supprimes l'absence et qui me mets au monde,
> Je chante pour chanter, je t'aime pour chanter
> Le mystère où l'amour me crée et me délivre

> Tu es pure, tu es encore plus pure que moi-même.
>
> (I sing the great joy of celebrating you,
> The great joy of having you or of not having you,
> The candor of waiting for you, the innocence of knowing you,
> Oh you who chases away forgotten memories, hope and ignorance,
> Who abolishes absence and delivers me into the world,
> I sing to celebrate, I love you in order to celebrate
> The mystery wherein love creates and delivers me.
>
> You are pure, even more pure than I).

The conclusion of this work is resolutely optimistic; through the image of the couple, Eluard emphasizes his belief that love is the source of life, creativity, and all that can be accomplished for the good of society.

In May 1927 Eluard's fifty-seven-year-old father, Clément Grindel, died suddenly after unsuccessful surgery for an unknown ailment. As Grindel's only child, Eluard inherited slightly less than half of his father's considerable estate; his mother received the remaining portion. It is, of course, curious from an ideological perspective that the poet, having recently joined the Communist Party, should become a millionaire, owning shares in a gold mine, a Congo railway line, and rubber plantations. Unskilled in finance and prone to making large expenditures in developing his collection of contemporary art, Eluard dissipated nearly all of his fortune within four years.

Given Eluard's need for love, both as the inspiration for his creativity and also as the reason for political action undertaken in the name of compassion, it is unsurprising that his poetry was the vehicle by which he expressed his communist ideology. In an untitled poem in *L'Amour la poésie* (Love, Poetry, 1929), a slogan-like title that was suggested to him by his ten-year-old daughter, Cécile, he writes: "Je sors des caves de l'angoisse / Des courbes lentes de la peur / Je tombe dans un puits de plumes" (I leave the cellars of anguish / From slow curves of fear / I fall into a well of feathers). If, as these lines suggest, the poet has found freedom and peace in his personal and family life, he has also found a language, distinctly his own, that captures the fundamental notion of Surrealism. For example, in the oft-quoted verse "La terre est bleue comme une orange" (The earth is blue like an orange), from another untitled poem in *L'Amour la poésie,* Eluard has taken a conventional poetic technique, the simile, and stripped it of its traditional association: the sun is round like an orange. It is, of course, *blue* that disturbs the reader. While one might say that the earth is round like an orange, the likening of *blue* to *orange* seems illogical. It is, however, an eminently logical idea: when the

Manuscript for Eluard's 1936 poem "Grand Air," with marginal illustrations by Pablo Picasso
(from Louis Parrot, Paul Eluard: Une Étude, *1944)*

roundness of the earth is seen, the planet takes on a bluish color; the earth can, therefore, resemble a blue orange, as odd as this object might at first seem. Closely linked to Eluard's desire to create innovative imagery and to encourage original thought is his ardent hope that his work will offer strength and unity in an often hostile and confusing world. As he writes in another untitled piece in *L'Amour la poésie:* "Il fallait bien qu'un visage / Réponde à tous les noms du monde" (It was quite necessary that one face / Answer to all the names in the world). The social mission of the poet was one in which Eluard truly believed.

At the end of the 1920s Eluard's fragile health required frequent stays in the Parksanatorium in Arosa, Switzerland, where both he and Gala received therapy for their pulmonary conditions. Their relationship deteriorated markedly, and ultimately ended in a breakup. Gala was an impulsive creature, given to capricious behavior that exhibited her need for personal freedom within an already unconventional marriage. Eluard was less high-strung than his wife, though he did at times engage in extramarital affairs, in keeping with the Surrealist opposition to oppressive "bourgeois" dogmatism. After a partnership of more than fifteen years the couple separated and were divorced in 1930. Eluard received custody of their daughter. By August of 1929 Gala had become Salvador Dalí's lifelong muse, collaborator, and companion; they wed in 1934. Gala died in 1982, at the age of eighty-seven, and Dalí in 1989, at the age of eighty-four.

In 1930 Eluard, for whom the Surrealist ideal of *amour fou* (blinding erotic passion) was a guiding principle toward the discovery and development of one's emotional and physical being, met and fell in love with an Alsatian woman ten years his junior, Maria Benz, known as Nusch, who became his second wife in 1934. Nusch's presence is evident in Eluard's *La Vie immédiate* (Life Here and Now, 1932), which also alludes to the personal crisis he endured after the separation from Gala. The title evokes the joy and sadness experienced by Eluard at this time: the immediacy and spontaneity of life. Separation and union, exile and belonging, are the themes communicated in this work. "Nusch" expresses the complicity of touch, the union of love, and the ideal of desire that is frequently present in Eluard's work:

Les sentiments apparents
La légèreté d'approche
La chevelure des caresses.

Sans souci sans soupçons
Tes yeux sont livrés à ce qu'ils voient
Vus par ce qu'ils regardent.

Confiance de cristal
Entre deux miroirs
La nuit tes yeux se perdent
Pour joindre l'éveil au désir.

(Clear feelings
Softness of your approach
Hair of caresses.

Without care or suspicions
Your eyes are fixed on what they see
Seen by what they look upon.

Crystal confidence
Between two mirrors
At night your eyes become lost
In order to unite awakening with desire).

Essentially a poem expressing desire, "Nusch" is not only an idealized sketch of Benz's luminous face and expressive eyes but also conceptually an affirmation of the quest for purity and frankness in the shape of an unencumbered love shared by two lovers. It also elaborates a complex system of light and dark, the luminous crystal reflected in the darkness of night. These opposites serve to bolster an aesthetic framework in which the poet contemplates the beauty of his companion's face.

"En exil" (In Exile) offers the image of a woman who is the antithesis of Nusch, one whose eyes are saddened, full of doubt: "Elle est triste elle fait valoir / Le doute qu'elle a de sa réalité dans les yeux d'un autre" (She is sad she shows / The doubt she holds about her own reality in the eyes of another). The marvelous singularity of this once-magical life is no more:

La perle noire n'est plus rare
Le désir et l'ennui fraternisent
Manège des manies
Tout est oublié
Rien n'est sacrifié
L'odeur des décombres persiste.

(The black pearl is no longer rare
Desire and boredom are brothers
Carousel of obsessions
Everything is forgotten
Nothing is sacrificed
The smell of rubble persists).

The loss of uniqueness, the fatigue that haunts desire, the offensive odor of debris hinting at a battle, all of these images and concepts suggest to the reader a love that has lost its luster, the burden of exile, and the difficulty of freeing oneself and moving into the future. This "here and now" is, however, transitional in Eluard's life as it leads to the second major period of his adult life, the one spent with Nusch.

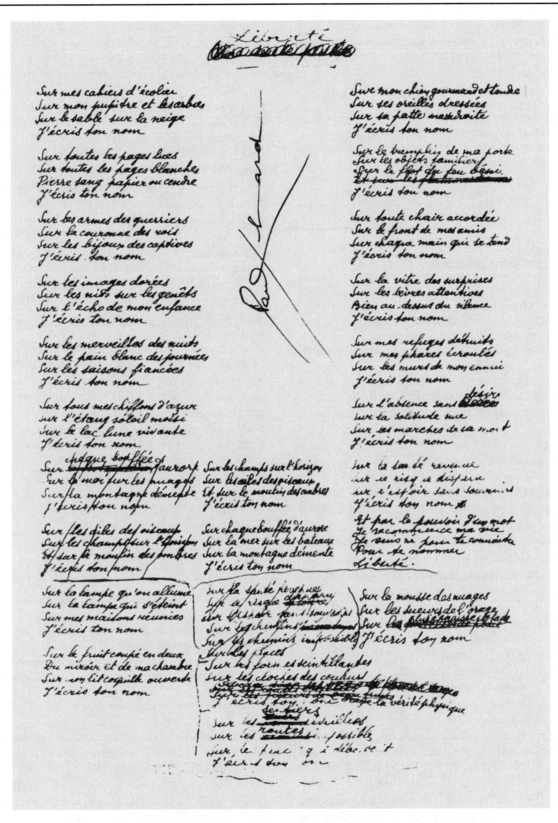

Page from the manuscript for Eluard's best-known poem, "Liberté," which was widely circulated by the French Resistance during World War II (from Raymond Jean, Paul Eluard, *1968)*

In the final piece in *La Vie immédiate,* titled "Critique de la poésie" (Critique of Poetry), Eluard states in the clearest possible terms his personal commitment to Communism:

C'est entendu que je hais le règne des bourgeois
Le règne des flics et des prêtres
Mais je hais plus encore l'homme que ne le hait pas
Comme moi
De toutes ses forces.

Je crache à la face de l'homme plus petit que nature
Qui à tous mes poèmes ne préfère pas cette *Critique de la poésie*

(It is understood that I hate the reign of the bourgeois
The reign of cops and of priests
But I hate even more he who doesn't hate it
As I do
With all his force.

I spit in the face of he, smaller than normal,
Who doesn't prefer to all my poems this *Critique of Poetry*).

These provocative and violent lines reveal a seldom-seen side of Eluard. Profoundly committed to his communist ideals, he is nonetheless enigmatic in other aspects of his personal life. A collector of Surrealist and African art, for example, he traveled constantly, sometimes at considerable expense, yet his *Critique de la poésie* questions the social relevance of his poetry, over which he purports to prefer ideological discourse, and suggests that subversion and revolt are of greater importance than aesthetic contemplation.

Eluard, Breton, and Crevel were expelled from the French Communist Party in 1933. They had been in disagreement since 1930 with Aragon's denunciation of Freudianism, idealism, and Trotskyism, which they believed to be compatible with fundamental Surrealist tenets. Aragon accused Breton of undermining the Communist Party, and this disagreement eventually led to the exclusion of the three Surrealists from the ranks of the French Communist Party.

In 1936, while in Spain for a lecture tour on the art of his friend Picasso, Eluard was galvanized into action by the Spanish Civil War. The Nationalists, led by General Francisco Franco, were supported by the conservatives and the army and received weapons and troops from Nazi Germany and Fascist Italy. Extensive aid from the Soviet Union was received by the opposing side, the Loyalists, also known as the Republicans, who were also assisted by foreign nationals motivated by their hatred for fascism, as exemplified in the governments of Germany and Italy, and an idealistic commitment to communism. During the war about one million people perished–approximately six hundred thousand of these casualties were battle-related deaths. A friend of Dalí, the Spanish poet Federico García Lorca was murdered by Franco's troops in the early days of the conflict. Immensely moved by the events of the war and by the death of García Lorca, Eluard sought to renew contact with the Communist Party, the only organization in his eyes that took the appropriately humane stance in the context of the Spanish Civil War. This renewed contact caused an irreconcilable rift between Eluard and Breton.

Originally published in 1936 in the official French Communist newspaper, *L'Humanité,* and later in *Au rendez-vous allemand* (At the German Meeting Place, 1944), "Novembre 1936" praises the resistance of the citizens of Madrid to Franco and speaks of the horror of aerial bombings and mass destruction, and the impossibility of accepting war: "On s'habitue à tout / Sauf à ces oiseaux de plomb / Sauf à leur haine de ce qui brille / Sauf à leur céder la place" (We get used to anything / Except to those leaden birds / Except to their hatred for that which shines / Except to yielding to them). The triple anaphora underscores the relentless destruction and hatred, as well as the unyielding opposition to fascism. Eluard's style is sparse, conveying his profound bewilderment. The eerie image of a leaden bird menacingly dropping from the sky subverts that of the bird as a universal symbol of aspiration and idealism. The final lines express the hope that this absurd time will end, that reason will prevail and that grimaces will be replaced by smiles:

Que la bouche remonte vers sa vérité
Souffle rare sourire comme une chaîne brisée
Que l'homme délivré de son passé absurde
Dresse devant son frère un visage semblable

Et donne à la raison des ailes vagabondes.

(Would that our mouth turn up to truth
Rare breath a smile like a broken chain
Would that man delivered from his absurd past
Show his brother such a smile

And give to reason vagabond wings).

The conclusion of "Novembre 1936" is a hymn of hope, juxtaposing the images of chains and wings, oppression and freedom, and conveying, above all else, Eluard's belief that the collectivity is capable of improving the human condition through creative, unfettered reason. As a *poète engagé* (committed poet), Eluard was dedicated to advancing the common good. His growing political awareness eventually led him further away from Surrealism. By the end of 1938 Breton's insistence on the separation of political action and aesthetic revolution caused

Eluard and Picasso in Wrocław, during a 1948 visit to Poland

Eluard to abandon the ideology and practice of Surrealism altogether.

Eluard's participation in Surrealism was born in part from his desire to harness the energy and spirit of subversion inherent in the Surrealist movement, with a view to undertaking a type of proletarian revolution. Poetry allowed him to express freely his political convictions. He was an idealist who held to a humanitarian vision of a fraternal society wherein the burden of the individual's solitude would be tempered by ideological affiliation.

Eluard's convictions were put to the test by the outbreak of World War II. He contributed to the resistance movement in France by producing, printing, and distributing anti-Nazi leaflets. He led resistance activities undertaken by groups of intellectuals in the occupied zone of northern France. The first volume of his *Le Livre ouvert* (2 volumes; 1940, 1942) was the first collection of poetry to appear in occupied Paris. Written

in the winter of 1940–1941, the seven poems that constitute *Sur les pentes inférieures* (On the Bottom Slopes, 1941) are his first Resistance poems. "La Halte des heures" (The Stopping Place of Time) evokes the stillness of life, silent hope, and the potential for movement forward in time and space:

> Immenses mots dits doucement
> Grand soleil les volets fermés
> Un grand navire au fil de l'eau
> Ses voiles partageant le vent
> . . . .
> Le rêve des innocents
> Un seul murmure un seul matin
> Et les saisons à l'unisson
> Colorant de neige et de feu
>
> (Immense words said softly
> Large sun closed shutters
> A big ship on the water
> Its sails sharing the wind

. . . .
The sole dream of the innocent
A lone murmur a lone morning
And the seasons in unison
Coloring with snow and fire).

"La Halte des heures" is exemplary of Eluard's mature style, unencumbered by punctuation. Symbolically and prophetically the awaiting ship promises physical liberation from the emptiness of *la vie immédiate,* depicted in "Courage" (Courage), which was first published in 1943 in the clandestine newspaper *Les Lettres françaises* and was later collected in *Les Armes de la douleur* (The Weapons of Pain, 1944):

Paris a froid Paris a faim
Paris ne mange plus de marrons dans la rue
Paris a mis de vieux vêtements de vieille
Paris dort tout debout sans air dans le métro
. . . .
Ne crie pas au secours Paris
Tu es vivant d'une vie sans égale
Et derrière la nudité
De ta pâleur de ta maigreur
Tout ce qui est humain se révèle en tes yeux
Paris ma belle ville

(Paris is cold Paris is hungry
Paris no longer eats chestnuts in the street
Paris has put on old women's clothing
Paris sleeps upright in the airless subway
. . . .
Do not cry for help Paris
You are alive a life without equal
And behind the bleakness
Of your pallor and thinness
Everything that is human is revealed in your eyes
Paris my beautiful city).

Through his Resistance poems, his efforts to secure contributors for *Les Lettres françaises,* and his participation in the creation of Les Editions de Minuit, a clandestine publishing firm founded in 1941, Eluard came to be known and admired as a humanitarian poet and patriot dedicated to the pursuit of social ideals.

Eluard's most famous poem by far is "Liberté" (Liberty), many copies of which were dropped by parachute into occupied Europe by the British Royal Air Force as part of its anti-Nazi propaganda campaign. The poem was collected in 1942 in *Poésie et Vérite 1942* (Poetry and Truth 1942). Other poems were broadcast in the evening by clandestine anti-Nazi radio stations throughout occupied Europe. "Liberté" quickly became known internationally and is considered a classic in the French school system. Comprising twenty-one four-line stanzas and ending with the lone verse "Liberté," this poem is often memorized by French schoolchildren in

honor of Eluard and the patriots who resisted the Germans. The first two stanzas are:

Sur mes cahiers d'écolier
Sur mon pupitre et les arbres
Sur le sable sur la neige
J'écris ton nom

Sur toutes les pages lues
Sur toutes les pages blanches
Pierre sang papier ou cendre
J'écris ton nom

(On my school exercise books
On my desk and the trees
On the sand on the snow
I write your name

On all pages read
On all blank pages
Stone blood paper or ash
I write your name)

Written as an apostrophe to liberty, the poem is in keeping with the Surrealist tendency to put disparate objects into unexpected contexts. The anaphoric style and lyric tone convey both Eluard's political commitment and his need for intimacy. Characteristically, the closing lines transcend physical reality to embrace idealism; the last verse is the only one that carries any punctuation:

Et par le pouvoir d'un mot
Je recommence ma vie
Je suis né pour te connaître
Pour te nommer

Liberté.

(And by the power of the word
I begin my life again
I was born to know you
To name you

Liberty).

In Eluard's work the power of the written word goes far beyond the simple transcription of reality; it serves to establish communication between and among individuals, to reach out in moments of solitude and pain, to protest against those ideologies that threaten human rights and freedoms, and, ultimately, to invite the reader to explore uncommon perceptions of reality. Following the Liberation, Eluard received the Médaille de la Résistance from the government of France in honor of his inspiring patriotism and his support of the French people during the Occupation.

Eluard and his third wife, Dominique Eluard, in Leningrad during their 1950 visit to the Soviet Union

In 1942 Eluard renewed his ties with the French Communist Party. After the war international recognition of his talent and name was at its pinnacle. In 1944 Louis Parrot inaugurated the critical series *Poètes d'aujourd'hui* (Poets of Today) with his *Paul Eluard,* published by the Parisian publishing house of Pierre Seghers. As a cultural ambassador of postwar France, Eluard traveled extensively, to Italy, Greece, Poland, Czechoslovakia, and Yugoslavia. In all of these countries he was greeted, celebrated, and acclaimed by the intelligentsia and the general public. The idealistic Eluard strove to make Europe a vast site of cultural exchange, a geographical entity without borders, united in solidarity and compassion.

In 1946 Eluard published *Poésie ininterrompue* (Uninterrupted Poetry). Totaling 674 lines, the introductory title poem is essentially a recounting of Eluard's evolution as a man, patriot, social activist, and poet, underscoring once again the close relationship between personal happiness and political and social activism in his conception of life and poetry. The title

itself conveys the idea of constant and unbroken creation fundamental to both his literary production and his life. In "Poésie ininterrompue" Eluard evokes his past, his present, and his future, taking stock of his life:

> Je rends compte du réel
> Je prends garde à mes paroles
> Je ne veux pas me tromper
> Je veux savoir d'où je pars
> Pour conserver tant d'espoir
> Mes origines sont des larmes
> Et la fatigue et la douleur
> Et le moins de beauté
> Et le moins de bonté
>
> (I take stock of reality
> I am careful with my words
> I don't want to be mistaken
> I want to know from whence I leave
> In order to preserve so much hope
> My origins are tears
> And fatigue and pain

And the least beautiful
And the least bountiful)

Although his past has not been without pain, Eluard affirms: "Je n'ai pas de regrets / Plus noir plus lourd est mon passé / Plus léger et limpide est l'enfant que j'étais"(I have no regrets / Heavier and darker is my past / Lighter and more limpid is the child that I was). He has been able, therefore, to transcend the suffering endured in life here and now, for as a living, conscious being he knows the power of thought and word, the supreme inspiration of love and peace-oriented idealism:

Et j'écris pour marquer les années et les jours
Les heures et les hommes leur durée
Et les parties d'un corps commun
Qui a son matin
Et son midi et son minuit
Et de nouveau son matin
Inévitable et paré
De force et de faiblesse
De beauté de laideur
De repos agréable et de misérable lumière
Et de gloire provoquée

(And I write to mark the years and the days
The hours and the men their duration
And the parts of the common body
Which has its morning
And its noon and its midnight
And again its morning
Inevitable and equipped
With strength and weakness
With beauty and ugliness
With pleasant rest and miserable light
And provoked glory).

A recurring trait of Eluard's poetry is exemplified here: the use of antithesis. For example, the lines "De force et de faiblesse" (With strength and weakness) and "De beauté de laideur" (With beauty and ugliness) are indicative of his conceptualization based on opposites, a type of reasoning that is classical in that it encompasses all possibilities between the two poles.

A further recurring trait is luminous imagery, as in "Pour vivre ici." The central image of the fire built by the speaker of the poem and sustained by his memories of special objects and momentous occasions in that poem is rekindled in an equally striking image in "Poésie ininterrompue":

Par toi je vais de la lumière à la lumière
De la chaleur à la chaleur
C'est par toi que je parle et tu restes au centre
De tout comme un soleil consentant au bonheur

(Through you I go from light to light

From heat to heat
It is through you that I speak and you remain in the centre
Of everything like a sun consenting to happiness).

Eluard's World War I experience, as reflected in the dark imagery of "Pour vivre ici" invites comparison with the context described in "Poésie ininterrompue." In the latter poem the poet has found the solace and inspiration of the *tu*, the familiar and intimate form of *you* in French. It is difficult not to see the reflection of Nusch in this evocation. The last lines of the poem point to the complementariness of the couple:

Nous deux toi toute nue
Moi tel que j'ai vécu
Toi la source du sang
Et moi les mains ouvertes
Comme des yeux

Nous deux nous ne vivons que pour être fidèles
À la vie

(The two of us you entirely naked
I as I have lived
You the source of blood
And I with open hands
Like eyes

The two of us live only to be faithful
To life).

In his poetry Eluard thus continued to search for and praise the image of the unified couple, the woman signifying light and life, the man, observation and action. A celebration of life and love, constants in Eluard's life, "Poésie ininterrompue" is the high point of his introspective, antithetical style.

But the personal and professional summit on which Eluard stood at this time collapsed with the sudden death of his companion of sixteen years, his beloved Nusch, from a stroke on 28 November 1946. Eluard was devastated. Begun before Nusch's death and published in 1947 under the pseudonym Didier Desroches, his collection *Le Temps déborde* (Time Overflows) includes fourteen poems divided into two groups—those written before and those after her death—as well as photographs of Nusch taken by Dora Maar and Man Ray. The title is taken from the first lines written after his wife's death:

Vingt-huit novembre mil neuf cent quarante-six
Nous ne vieillerons pas ensemble
Voici le jour
En trop: le temps déborde.
Mon amour si léger prend le poids d'un supplice.

(November twenty-eighth nineteen hundred and forty-six
We will not grow old together
This is the day

So unwelcome: time overflows.
My love so light carries the weight of torture).

Eluard's profound sense of loss colored the next several months of his life. As a public figure of heroic dimension he was revered by the public as well as by his peers; in the 6 December 1946 issue of *Les Lettres françaises* the Comité National des écrivains published a declaration of their support: "A Paul Eluard: Notre ami Paul Eluard n'est pas seul. Nous demeurons autour de lui. Nous savons ce que nous lui devons et ce que lui doit la France. Nous comptons sur lui" (To Paul Eluard: Our friend Paul Eluard is not alone. We remain at his side. We know what we owe him and what France owes him. We are counting on him). Eluard was a man of the people and of the intelligentsia alike and a prominent figure in European antifascist movements; thus his tragedy elicited an outpouring of sympathy from all who knew him, directly or indirectly. Haggard, insomniac, and already suffering from fragile health, Eluard wrote to Gala in a March 1947 letter that he thought he might never write poetry again.

Although it was clear that he was close to complete nervous exhaustion, he did continue his work, publishing in 1947 (under the single pseudonym, Brun) *Corps mémorable* (Memorable Body). In this small collection, as is suggested by the title, the poet celebrates the physical presence of Nusch. In "Entre la lune et le soleil" (Between Moon and Sun) he writes:

Je te le dis, gracieuse et lumineuse,
Ta nudité lèche mes yeux d'enfant.
Et c'est l'extase des chasseurs heureux
D'avoir fait croître un gibier transparent
Qui se dilate en un vase sans eau
Comme une graine à l'ombre d'un caillou.

Je te vois nue, arabesque nuée,
Aiguille molle à chaque tour d'horloge,
Soleil étale au long d'une journée,
Rayons tressés, nattes de mes plaisirs.

(I say to you, graceful and luminous,
Your nakedness licks my child eyes.
And there is the ecstasy of happy hunters
For having raised transparent game
Which throbs in a waterless vase
Like a seed in the shade of a stone.

I see you naked, knotted arabesque,
Soft hand with each revolution of the clock,
Sun spreading along the day,
Plaited rays, my pleasure's braids).

Time is thus situated in an undefined manner between darkness and light, perhaps the time of introspection, of solitary grief; a time when one is confined to a solitude

Illustration by Valentine Hugo in Le Phénix *(1951), the last of Eluard's books published before his death*

that is, however, also a time of memory and re-creation of the past. Eluard creates a compelling metaphor in this work, one that captures the presence of Nusch, her graceful body splendid in its nakedness, the source of ecstasy for men, and symbolically associated with the passage of time and the brilliance of sunbeams. A celebration of all that Nusch brought to his life, this luminescent image is one that undoubtedly shone in on Eluard's darkness as he gathered the strength to continue his literary and political work.

During the period immediately following Nusch's death, the enormous void left in Eluard's life was filled by brief liaisons, including one with a beautiful trapeze artist named Diane Deriaz and another with Jacqueline Duhême, who requested Eluard's autograph at a book fair and who soon thereafter became an assistant to the artist Henri Matisse. The poet also sought solace in his political activism; as a Communist he had always endeavored to remain close to ordinary people, in whose name he attempted to promote an ideal world based, somewhat naively, some would say, on generosity, love, and fraternity.

Many months later at the 1949 World Peace Council meeting in Mexico, Eluard, who was a delegate, met thirty-five-year-old Dominique Laure, born Odette Lemort. The mother of a young girl, she had studied law in Bordeaux and was in the process of divorcing her husband. She became Eluard's third wife in 1951 after twenty-one months of companionship. With her, Eluard found once again the happiness of partnership, mutual inspiration, and shared ideology. In April 1950 the couple visited Prague, Sofia, the Black Sea, Moscow, Leningrad, and Stalingrad. This trip was Eluard's first visit to the Soviet Union, and his most optimistic expectations of the success of Communism were surpassed; he believed the generosity of his reception was an indication of the socioeconomic achievements of the Soviet Union. Eluard was oddly untouched by Joseph Stalin's ruthless expansion of communism in Eastern Europe, his campaigns of political terror and purges of those who opposed him, or such deeds as the starvation of three million farmers in Ukraine in the early 1930s. Although a Communist herself, Dominique Eluard returned to France less than inspired by the example of the Soviet Union. A romantic idealist, Eluard only saw in the Soviet Union what he believed to be manifestations of the greatest value he sought in life: the fellowship that can overcome solitude and estrangement. Universal fellowship remained Eluard's political ideal and he endeavored to attain it through his poetry.

In *Le Phénix* (The Phoenix, 1951), the last of his books published before his death, Eluard offered seventeen poems in which he expressed his joy at having found, once again, a love that sustained him and restored his faith in humankind. From the desolate times following Nusch's death to the gloriously full life he was leading with Dominique, Eluard had endured and overcome a great personal crisis that had threatened a loss of faith in the power of poetry and the strength of love. *Le Phénix* is a song of love lost and found again. Eluard writes in "Dominique aujourd'hui présente" (Dominique Present Today):

Tu es venue j'étais triste j'ai dit oui
C'est à partir de toi que j'ai dit oui au monde
Petite fille je t'aimais comme un garçon
Ne peut aimer que son enfance

Avec la force d'un passé très loin très pur
Avec le feu d'une chanson sans fausse note
La pierre intacte et le courant furtif du sang
Dans la gorge et les lèvres

Tu es venue le voeu de vivre avait un corps
Il creusait la nuit lourde il caressait les ombres

Pour dissoudre leur boue et fondre leurs glaçons
Comme un oeil qui voit clair

(You came I was sad I said yes
It was beginning with you that I said yes to the world
Little girl that I loved like a boy
Can love only his childhood

With the strength of a past very far away and very pure
With the fire of a flawless song
The unmoved stone and the furtive flow of blood
In the throat and lips

You came the wish to live had a body
It penetrated the heavy night it caressed the shadows
To dissolve their mud and melt their ice
Like an eye that sees clearly).

An example of Eluard's mature style, without punctuation to inhibit his free-flowing sentiments, this text speaks of Dominique's strength of character and conviction, of her desire to engage Eluard once again in *la vie immédiate*. Other poems, such as "La Petite enfance de Dominique" (Dominique's Young Childhood) or "Je t'aime" (I love you), express his undying love and gratitude for this blessing.

Throughout his life Eluard sought in the companionship of women the inspiration, support, and love that nourished and sustained him in times of ill health and personal sadness and that enhanced moments of great personal joy. A man of the people, he nevertheless led what most would call a privileged life as an active participant in European cultural and intellectual life during one of the most fascinating times in its modern history.

In September of 1952 Eluard suffered a heart attack. He died from heart failure at his Paris apartment on the morning of 18 November—his last word was "Dominique." His body lay in state for the thousands of admirers who wished to say goodbye, as Claudio Monteverdi's opera *L'Orfeo* (Orpheus, 1607) played over loudspeakers. Eluard's Médaille de la Résistance and a plaster mask of his face made when he was thirty-five years old lay on a cushion beside him. He was laid to rest in the Père-Lachaise cemetery of Paris without national honors, however, the honors being forbidden by the French government because of his membership in the Communist Party.

Eluard left an imposing literary legacy, consistent in its nature, yet varied in its manifestations. Above all, a creator of magnificently simple, sometimes anecdotal poetry, he strove to speak clearly of life and death, love and solitude, and through his pioneering work in Surrealism he helped create a modern poetry that is engaged in the search for truth, that evokes in innovative fashions the human longing for love that enhances exist-

Là se dressent les mille murs
De nos maisons vieillissant bien
Et mères de mille maisons
Là dorment des vagues de tuiles
Renouvelées par le soleil
Et portant l'ombre des oiseaux
Comme l'eau porte les poissons

Ⓓ Là tous les travaux sont faciles
Et l'objet caresse la main
La main ne connaît que promesses
La vie éveille tous les yeux
Le corps a des fièvres heureuses
Nommées la Perle de midi
Ou la Rumeur de la lumière

Là je vois de près ~~et~~ et de loin
Là je m'élance dans l'espace
Le jour la nuit sont mes tremplins
Là je reviens au monde entier
Pour rebondir vers chaque chose

Page from the manuscript for "Ailleurs, ici, partout," published in the 1953 collection Poèsie interrompue, II
(from Roselyne de Ayala and Jean-Pierre Gueno, Belles Lettres, *2001)*

ence. His ultimate break with Surrealism at the end of the 1930s allowed him to reach out from his inherent solitude. Eluard's poetry possesses an attraction that is subtly and skillfully created. The majority of his texts are brief and describe particular phases in the reading process. They draw the reader through a type of centripetal force into the center of the crystallizing image, and then, in a centrifugal motion, lead the reader away from the crystallized image, now frozen in its completeness. This process is much like the cinematic technique whereby the camera gradually reveals certain constitutive parts of an image before revealing the whole, then focuses on other selected parts of the completed image, only to move on to create a new image. This type of visual creation points to Eluard's quest for an ever greater synthesis of vital forces.

Eluard's use of language is also distinctive. A lexical study of his poetry reveals that a large proportion of his vocabulary is drawn from nature and the human body. Nature, the individual, and the collectivity: these are the three focuses of his imagery. In an untitled poem in *Les Armes de la douleur,* Eluard writes: "Je dis ce que je vois / Ce que je sais / Ce qui est vrai" (I say what I see / What I know / What is true). One cannot find a more simple lexicon or a more direct mode of communication. An untitled text in *Poèmes pour la Paix* typifies his use of metaphorical space:

> Toute la fleur des fruits éclaire mon jardin,
> Les arbres de beauté et les arbres fruitiers.
> Et je travaille et je suis en mon jardin.
> Et le Soleil brûle en feu sombre sur mes mains.

> (The entire flower of fruits illuminates my garden,
> The trees of beauty and the fruit trees.
> And I work and I am alone in my garden.
> And the Sun burns in a low fire on my hands).

Eluard's poetry is a chronicle of the aesthetic evolution undergone by French poetry in the first half of the twentieth century as well as a chronicle of his personal life, what one might term the poetic cycles of Gala, Nusch, and Dominique, for each of these women played a fundamental role in his perception of reality.

In speaking of himself Paul Eluard creates a metaphor that is fundamental to his life and work, the image of *homo faber* (man the maker), the individual who endeavors to create, in the poet's case from the richness of language, in order to achieve a sense of personal and collective unity. Ideologically speaking, Eluard worked tirelessly for social betterment and sought an aesthetic means through which to voice his political and social ideals. His conception of poetry is consequently one that eschews the notion of art for art's sake. His abandonment of Surrealism hinged on his belief that poetry must not cultivate obscurity but must

speak clearly, yet evocatively, of the human condition. Even in times of despair Eluard did not offer religious introspection in his poetry. Allusions to a divine or superior presence are entirely absent from his work. His belief in moral duty and his optimism that collective action can achieve social melioration constitute the core of his personal spirituality. Through his poetry he sought to explain the ambient world and the present and future place of humanity within it. His desire to achieve a moral absolute, and to encourage the reader to do so also, guided him in a way that underscores the sincerity of his work. In periods of social and personal disharmony as well as in times of personal fulfillment, Eluard was the voice of love and fraternity, denouncing political repression and encouraging aesthetic innovation. For that, contemporary French poetry has been immeasurably enriched.

Letters:

Lettres de jeunesse, avec des poèmes inédits, edited by Robert D. Valette (Paris: Seghers, 1962);

Lettres à Joë Bosquet, preface and notes by Lucien Scheler (Paris: Editeurs Français Réunis, 1973);

Lettres à Gala, 1924–1948, edited, with notes, by Pierre Dreyfus, preface by Jean-Claude Carrière (Paris: Gallimard, 1984); translated by Jesse Browner as *Letters to Gala* (New York: Paragon House, 1989).

Bibliography:

Luc Decaunes, "Essai de bibliographie," in his *Paul Eluard, biographie pour une approche, suivie de, Notes jointes et d'un Essai de bibliographie des œuvres publiées en langue française* (Rodez: Editions Subervie, 1965), pp. 143–155.

Biographies:

Luc Decaunes, *Paul Eluard, biographie pour une approche, suivie de notes jointes et d'un essai de bibliographie des œuvres publiées en langue française* (Rodez: Editions Subervie, 1965);

Robert D. Valette, *Eluard: Livre d'identité* (Paris: Tchou, 1967);

Roger-Jean Ségalat, *Album Eluard: Iconographie* (Paris: Gallimard, 1968);

Jean-Charles Gateau, *Paul Eluard, ou, Le Frère voyant, 1895–1952,* Collection Biographies sans masques (Paris: Editions Robert Laffont, 1988);

Violaine Vanoyeke, *Paul Eluard: Le Poète de la liberté: Biographie* (Paris: Editions Julliard, 1995).

References:

Anna Balakian, "Post-Surrealism of Aragon and Eluard," in her *Surrealism: The Road to the Absolute* (New York: Noonday Press, 1959), pp. 165–187;

Daniel Bergez, *Eluard, ou, Le Rayonnement de l'être* (Seyssell: Champ-Vallon, 1982);

Guy Besse, *Paul Eluard* (Paris: Editeurs Français Réunis, 1972);

Louise Bogan, "The Poetry of Paul Eluard," in her *Selected Criticism: Prose and Poetry* (New York: Noonday Press, 1955), pp. 157–170;

Nicole Boulestreau, *La Poésie de Paul Eluard: La rupture et le partage, 1913–1936,* Bibliothèque du XXe siècle, no. 20 (Paris: Klincksieck, 1985);

Francis J. Carmody, "Eluard's Rupture with Surrealism," *PMLA,* 86 (September 1961): 436–446;

Michel Carrouges, *Eluard et Claudel* (Paris: Editions du Seuil, 1945);

Mary Ann Caws, "Paul Eluard," in her *The Poetry of Dada and Sur-realism: Aragon, Breton, Tzara, Eluard & Desnos* (Princeton: Princeton University Press, 1970), pp. 136–169;

Jean-Yves Debreuille, *Eluard, ou, Le Pouvoir du mot: Propositions pour une lecture* (Paris: Nizet, 1977);

Heinrich Eglin, *Liebe und Inspiration im Werke von Paul Eluard* (Bern & Munich: Francke, 1965);

Pierre Emmanuel, *Le je universel chez Paul Eluard* (Paris: Editions G.L.M., 1948);

Wallace Fowlie, "Eluard: the Doctrine of Love," in his *Age of Surrealism* (Denver: Swallow Press / New York: Morrow, 1940), pp. 138–156;

Fowlie, ed., "Paul Eluard," in *Mid-Century French Poets: Selections, Translations, and Critical Notices,* edited and translated by Fowlie (New York: Grove, 1955), pp. 170–197;

René Gaffé, *Paul Eluard* (Paris & Brussels: A l'Enseigne du Cheval Ailé, 1945);

Jean-Charles Gateau, *Paul Eluard et la peinture surréaliste, 1910–1939* (Geneva: Droz, 1982);

Marie Renée Guyard, *Le Vocabulaire politique de Paul Eluard* (Paris: Klincksieck, 1974);

Antonin Ingrassia, *Eluard et Baudelaire* (Aix-en-Provence: La Pensée Universitaire, 1962);

Jean-Pierre Jacques, *"Poésies," Eluard: Analyse critique,* Profil d'une œuvre, no. 80 (Paris: Editions Hatier, 1982);

Raymond Jean, *Lectures du désir: Nerval, Lautréamont, Apollinaire, Eluard* (Paris: Editions du Seuil, 1977);

Jean-Pierre Juillard, *Le Regard dans la poésie d'Eluard* (Paris: La Pensée Universelle, 1972);

Atle Kittang, *D'Amour de poésie: Essai sur l'univers des métamorphoses dans l'œuvre surréaliste de Paul Eluard,* Collection Situation, no. 12 (Paris: Editions Minard, 1969);

Maryvonne Meuraud, *L'Image végétale dans la poésie d'Eluard,* Collection Langues et styles, no. 4 (Paris: Lettres Modernes, 1966);

Albert Mingelgrün, *Essai sur l'évolution esthétique de Paul Eluard: Peinture et langage* (Lausanne, Switzerland: Editions l'Age d'Homme, 1977);

Maurice Nadeau, *Histoire du surréalisme, suivie de Documents surréalistes* (Paris: Editions du Seuil, 1964); translated by Richard Howard as *The History of Surrealism,* introduction by Roger Shattuck (New York: Macmillan, 1965);

Robert Nugent, "Eluard's Use of Light," *French Review,* 34 (May 1961): 525–530;

Nugent, *Paul Eluard* (New York: Twayne, 1974);

Louis Parrot and Jean Marcenac, *Paul Eluard: Une étude,* revised edition, Poètes d'aujourd'hui, no. 1 (Paris: Seghers, 1969);

Louis Perche, *Paul Eluard,* Classiques du XXᵉ siècle, no. 63 (Paris: Editions Universitaires, 1963);

Gabrielle Poulin, *Les Miroirs d'un poète: image et reflets de Paul Eluard,* Collection Essais pour notre temps (Brussels & Paris: Desclée de Brouwer / Montréal: Editions Bellarmin, 1969);

Marcel Raymond, *De Baudelaire au surréalisme,* revised edition (Paris: José Corti, 1940); translated as *From Baudelaire to Surrealism* (New York: Wittenborn, Schultz, 1950 [i.e., 1949]; London: Owen, 1957);

English Showalter Jr., "Biographical Aspects of Eluard's Poetry," *PMLA,* 78 (June 1963): 280–286.

Papers:

Some of Paul Eluard's papers and manuscripts are preserved at the Musée Municipal d'art et d'histoire, Saint-Denis, and at the Bibliothèque littéraire Jacques Doucet, Paris; others are held in private collections.

Pierre Emmanuel

(3 May 1916 – 22 September 1984)

Mary Anne O'Neil
Whitman College

BOOKS: *Elégies,* Cahiers des poètes catholiques, no. 24 (Paris: A. Magné / Brussels: Edition Universelle, 1940);

Tombeau d'Orphée (Les Angles, Gard: Seghers, 1941); enlarged as *Tombeau d'Orphée: suivi de Hymnes orphiques* (Paris: Seghers, 1967);

Christ aux enfers, dessin de André Marchand, Ligne de vie, no. 2 (Marseilles: Ars, 1942);

XX Cantos (Algiers: Editions de la Revue Fontaine, 1942); enlarged as *Cantos* (Neuchâtel, Switzerland: Ides et Calendes, 1944); enlarged again as *Chansons du dé à coudre* (Paris: Egloff, 1947);

Jour de Colère (Algiers: Charlot, 1942);

Le Poète et son Christ, 1938, preface by Albert Béguin (Neuchâtel, Switzerland: Editions de La Baconnière, 1942);

Combats avec tes défenseurs (Villeneuve-les-Avignon: Seghers, 1942); enlarged as *Combats avec tes défenseurs, suivi de la Liberté guide nos pas* (Paris: Seghers, 1969);

Orphiques, Collection Métamorphoses, no. 14 (Paris: Gallimard, 1942);

Prière d'Abraham, Les Cahiers du Rhône, série rouge no. 9 (Neuchâtel, Switzerland: Editions de La Baconnière, 1942);

La Colombe, introduction by Pierre Jean Jouve (Fribourg, Switzerland: Edition de la Librarie de l'Université, 1943);

Le Poète fou, illustrated by Léon Zack (Monaco: Editions du Rocher, 1944); enlarged as *Le Poète fou, suivi d'Elégies* (Neuchâtel, Switzerland: Editions de La Baconnière, 1948; Paris: Seuil, 1948); selections from first edition translated by Elliott Coleman as *The Mad Poet,* Contemporary Poetry Library Series, volume 11 (Baltimore: Contemporary Poetry, 1956);

Sodome (Fribourg, Switzerland: Egloff, 1944; Paris: Seuil, 1971)–includes *Prière d'Abraham;*

Memento des vivants (Paris: Seuil, 1944);

La Liberté guide nos pas (Paris: Seghers, 1945)–includes *La Colombe;*

Tristesse, ô ma patrie (Paris: Fontaine, 1946);

Pierre Emmanuel, 1935

Qui est cet homme; ou, Le Singulier universel (Paris: Egloff, 1947); translated by Erik de Mauny as *The Universal Singular* (London: Grey Walls Press, 1950);

Le Je universel chez Paul Eluard, Théorie, no. 2 (Paris: Editions G.L.M., 1948);

Poésie raison ardente (Paris: Egloff, 1948);

Car enfin je vous aime (Neuchâtel, Switzerland: Editions de La Baconnière / Paris: Seuil, 1950; revised and enlarged edition, Paris: Seuil, 1983);

Babel (Paris: Desclée de Brouwer, 1951);

L'Ouvrier de la onzième heure (Paris: Seuil, 1953);

Visage nuage (Paris: Seuil, 1955);

Versant de l'âge (Paris: Seuil, 1958);

Les Jours de la Nativité, edited by Denis Grivot, Les Points cardinaux, no. 2 (Paris: Editions du Zodiaque, 1960);

Evangéliaire (Paris: Seuil, 1961);

Les Jours de la Passion, Les Points cardinaux, no. 6 (Paris: La Pierre qui Vire, 1962);

Le Goût de l'Un (Paris: Seuil, 1963);

La Nouvelle naissance, La Mandragore qui chante, no. 4 (Paris: Seuil, 1963);

La Face humaine (Paris: Seuil, 1965);

Indonesia in Travail, by Emmanuel, Herbert Luethy, and Burton Raffel (New Delhi: Congress for Cultural Freedom, 1966);

Baudelaire, Les Ecrivains devant Dieu, no. 11 (Paris: Desclée de Brouwer, 1967); translated by Robert T. Cargo as *Baudelaire: The Paradox of Redemptive Satanism* (University: University of Alabama Press, 1970); French edition republished as *Baudelaire, la femme et Dieu* (Paris: Seuil, 1982);

La Monde est intérieur: Essais (Paris: Seuil, 1967);

Discours de remerciement et de réception à l'Académie française, by Emmanuel and Wladimir d'Ormesson (Paris: Seuil, 1969);

Notre Père, illustrated by Loo (Paris: Seuil, 1969);

Choses dites (Paris & Brussells: Desclée, De Brouwer, 1970);

Jacob (Paris: Seuil, 1970);

Pour une politique de la Culture (Paris: Seuil, 1971);

Saint-John Perse: Praise and Presence, with a bibliography by Ruth S. Freitag (Washington, D.C.: Published for the Library of Congress by the Gertrude Clarke Whittall Poetry and Literature Fund, 1971);

Sophia (Paris: Seuil, 1973);

La Poésie doit-elle avoir pour but la vérité pratique? (Brussels: Editions du Cercle d'Education Populaire, 1974);

La Révolution parallèle (Paris: Seuil, 1975);

La Vie terrestre (Paris: Seuil, 1976);

Tu (Paris: Seuil, 1978);

Una: ou, La Mort, la vie, volume 1 of *Livre de l'homme et de la femme* (Paris: Seuil, 1978);

Duel, volume 2 of *Livre de l'homme et de la femme* (Paris: Seuil, 1979);

L'Autre, volume 3 of *Livre de l'homme et de la femme* (Paris: Seuil, 1980);

Culture, noblesse du monde: Histoire d'une politique, preface by Jacques Chirac (Paris: Stock, 1980);

L'Arbre et le Vent: Feuilles volantes, 1980–1981 (Paris: Seuil, 1982);

Une Année de grâce: Feuilles volantes, 1981–1982 (Paris: Seuil, 1983);

Le Grand œuvre: Cosmogonie (Paris: Seuil, 1984).

Edition and Collections: *Ligne de Faîte* (Paris: Seuil, 1966);

Autobiographies: Qui est cet homme; L'Ouvrier de la onzième heure (Paris: Seuil, 1970);

Tombeau d'Orphée, suivi de Hymnes orphiques, edited, with an introduction, by Anne-Sophie Andreu (Lausanne, Switzerland & Paris: L'Age d'Homme, 2001).

OTHER: François Villon, *Villon: Choix de textes et préface,* edited, with an introduction, by Emmanuel, Le Cri de la France, no. 9 (Fribourg, Switzerland: Egloff, 1944);

Agrippa d'Aubigné, *Les Tragiques,* edited, with an introduction, by Emmanuel, woodcuts by Léon Zack (Monaco: Editions du Rocher, 1946);

Anne Hébert, *Le Tombeau des rois: Poèmes,* edited by Emmanuel (Québec: L'Institut Littéraire du Québec, 1953);

Jules Monchanin, *De l'ésthetique à la mystique: Précedé de La Loi d'exode,* introductory essay by Emmanuel (Tournai, Belgium: Casterman, 1967);

Alphonse de Lamartine, *Geneviève: Histoire d'une servante,* introduction by Emmanuel (Paris: Vialetay, 1972);

Pope John Paul II, *Poèmes: Karol Wojtyla,* translated by Emmanuel, Constantin Jelenski, and Anna Turowicz (Paris: Cana-Cerf, 1979);

St. John of the Cross, *Poésies complètes: Jean de la Croix,* translated, with an introduction, by Bernard Sesé, preface by Emmanuel (Paris: Obsidiane, 1983).

A prolific writer of both verse and prose and an important intellectual force in France for more than forty years, Pierre Emmanuel ranks among the leading poets of the mid twentieth century because of the variety of his inspiration, his skill in all types of versification (from fixed forms to the prose poem), and the sheer quantity of his poetic production. Emmanuel's understanding of the world and of the human condition is shaped, above all, by the Bible, and all of his poetry asserts that the stories of the Creation, the Fall, and the Redemption found in the Hebrew Scriptures and the New Testament hold fundamental truths that alone can save a secularized, spiritually bereft generation from alienation and even social catastrophe. Far from imposing limits on his poetry, this Christian framework provided Emmanuel with a springboard to the exploration of myriad myths of the Western intellectual tradition: the Eden story, Sodom and Gomorrah, Babel, the Apocalypse, but also the Orphean myth, Romanticism, the Freudian concepts of *Eros* (life-preserving instincts) and *thanatos* (self-destructive tendencies), and Jungian archetypes.

PIERRE EMMANUEL

TOMBEAU D'ORPHÉE

FRAGMENT

" POÉSIE 41 "

Frontispiece and title page for the 1941 epic poem in which Emmanuel retold the myth of Orpheus using images drawn from Christian mysticism and Freudian psychology (Olin Memorial Library, Wesleyan University)

During World War II Emmanuel adapted his biblical imagination to the composition of patriotic verse condemning Nazism and celebrating the French Resistance. While Emmanuel turned to more personal themes in the final decades of his life–the soul's longing for God, the reconciliation of the masculine and feminine experience, the desire to anchor his verse in everyday life, the struggle to create a pure poetic language–criticism of modern culture and intellectual movements is always present in his later poetry. Throughout his career Emmanuel divided his attention between the short lyric and the long narrative poem. Certainly no other French poet of this century wrote as many successful epics. Emmanuel is equally remarkable for the unusual range of his poetic voice: intellectual, hermetic, and rhetorical in the early volumes, and clearer and more lyrical in the later poems. A mystical tendency permeates all of his work. Emmanuel has been compared to John Donne,

Agrippa d'Aubigné, St. John of the Cross, Victor Hugo, T. S. Eliot, Rainer Maria Rilke, and Pierre Jean Jouve. In the 1960s and later, Emmanuel's verse falls much in line with that of other post-Surrealist French poets, especially René Char, in its quest for a concrete, simple language that incarnates the human need for connection to the physical world but also for transcendence. Thus, while Emmanuel's extensive body of work harks back to an earlier tradition of European religious poetry, it is not anachronistic. It represents, rather, the survival and successful reinterpretation of Christian thought in modern French verse.

In two volumes of autobiography, *Qui est cet homme; ou, Le Singulier universel* (Who Is This Man; or, The Universal Singular, 1947; translated as *The Universal Singular,* 1950) and *L'Ouvrier de la onzième heure* (The Laborer of the Eleventh Hour, 1953), which were republished in one volume in 1970, Emmanuel offers a coherent portrait of his youth and early career. He was born Noël Jean Mathieu on 3 May 1916 in Gans, a small Bearnais town near Pau, to Emile Mathieu and Maria Mathieu (née Boulogne), working-class parents who had immigrated to the United States but returned to France to give birth to their children, whom they left in the care of French relatives. Except for a brief stay in the United States from the age of three to six, Mathieu had virtually no contact with his parents and siblings, and he lived a lonely, isolated childhood with his maternal grandmother and aunt under the open skies and rocky crags of the Pyrenees. His precocious intellectual gifts led to his move to Lyon in early adolescence, when his paternal uncle, a teacher, enrolled him in Catholic secondary schools to prepare for an engineering degree, for which he had talent but no inclination. The saving grace of these years was his contact with two priests, Fathers Larue and Monchanin, who encouraged his spiritual and philosophical development. At eighteen he disappointed familial expectations by abandoning the mathematical sciences and enrolling as a student of philosophy at the university of Lyon.

From 1936 until the advent of World War II he worked as a secondary school teacher in northern France. During his studies and teaching, nevertheless, he prepared himself for a literary career by reading voraciously in all areas of Christian thought and European poetry and by writing verse. His first true literary mentor, Jouve, dismissed these early poems as merely imitative and without authentic poetic inspiration. In 1938 the aspiring artist wrote his first real poem, "Christ au Tombeau" (Christ at the Tomb), later included in the 1942 book *Le Poète et son Christ, 1938* (The Poet and His Christ, 1938), which he signed with the pseudonym he used for the rest of his life, Pierre Emmanuel, a name that signified both the solidity of stone and the presence of the living God within him. Over the next decade he published fifteen volumes of poetry, some of which won literary prizes and earned him a reputation as one of the most exciting young poets of France. Emmanuel spent the war years with his first wife, Jeanne Crepy, whom he had married in 1938, and Jouve in the southeastern French town of Dieulefit, where he again taught but also worked actively in the French Resistance.

Emmanuel's first important collection, *Tombeau d'Orphée* (Tomb of Orpheus, 1941), was an immediate success. Inspired by Jouve's *Sueur de sang* (Sweat of Blood, 1933), this short epic attempts to reconcile Christian mysticism and the Freudian theory of sexuality. In frankly erotic language Emmanuel dredges up the darkest secrets of his subconscious, his conflicting needs for God and for woman, his ambivalent desires for destruction but also redemption, by reliving Orpheus's descent to the underworld to retrieve the dead Eurydice. The seven sections of this narrative poem, written principally in blank alexandrines, relate the hero's journey to hell, his battle with God for possession of Eurydice, and his return to the upper world without his beloved. As in the Ovidian legend, the hero's body is torn apart by the Maenads; however, death becomes a liberation from the tormented flesh and offers the possibility of a less selfish passion. In the final section Orpheus joins Christ in the grave. He awaits resurrection not only as lover but also, like the Orpheus of antiquity, as a poet in possession of the gift of song. The popularity of this volume was no doubt a result of its Freudian bent, its dream-like atmosphere that recalls the work of the Surrealists and its erotic re-creation of biblical themes and symbols. Indeed, at one point, the poet-Orpheus looks on as Christ makes love to Eurydice. To modern readers, *Tombeau d'Orphée* may seem overly obsessive and hermetic, too full of idiosyncratic references to allow for definitive interpretation; however, it demonstrates Emmanuel's skill as a reinterpreter of myths and his successful use of images drawn from his own subconscious to reflect universal emotional and artistic concerns.

Le Poète et son Christ, 1938 includes verse written as early as 1938 and best exemplifies Emmanuel's first poetic preoccupations. Another short epic, it retells, in separate pieces written principally in blank alexandrines, the account of the Passion found in the Gospel of John, beginning with the episode of the adulterous woman and ending with the disciples' vision of Christ at Emmaus. Emmanuel is interested in a part of the Passion myth not addressed in the New Testament, namely Christ's sojourn in the grave between Good Friday and Easter Sunday, when he, incomprehensibly, submitted not only to death but also to nothingness. The poem takes the form of a psychodrama in which the poet-narrator assumes the roles of various biblical characters—the Pharisees, Mary Magdalene, Lazarus, Christ dying and Christ resurrected—in order to relive the mystery of the Incarnation. The poem also takes into account both the problem of faith in the twentieth century and the possibility of writing meaningful religious verse in a predominantly secular age. Emmanuel uses symbols drawn from the Scriptures, the Catholic liturgy, and the natural world, preferring those, such as the tree, that bring together all realms of experience. *Le Poète et son Christ, 1938* received less critical attention than *Tombeau d'Orphée*, possibly because of its religious focus, although readers with a Christian bent, such as Albert Béguin, noted Emmanuel's affinities in this poetry with the sixteenth-century Spanish mystics, English Metaphysical poets and French Baroque writers.

In 1944 Emmanuel published *Le Poète fou* (The Mad Poet), which comprises thirty-six short pieces, few of which exceed twenty lines and some of which are regular sonnets, on the life and madness of the early nineteenth-century German Romantic Friedrich Hölderlin. This volume follows in the same vein as *Tombeau d'Orphée* and *Le Poète et son Christ,* since it reexamines a myth, that of the *poète maudit* (accursed poet), who attempts to redeem a fallen humanity by formulating a pure poetic language. As in the two previous poems, Emmanuel reworks Greek and Christian mythology, as well as the Hölderlinian concept of song, to express his personal preoccupations with death, rebirth, and art. This poem may also be considered a short epic, since it narrates the German poet's life from his creative period to the onset of the schizophrenia that resulted in his confinement and his eventual death in poverty, and tells the story of his quest. Initially the poet-hero possesses the secret of divinity, a perfected language, or song, which he must make accessible to his fellow humans. This high conception of language, however, has no real power against evil, and the hero ironically sees his dreams of redeeming society fade in the face of the decline of civilization and the reality of sickness and death. While Emmanuel gives Hölderlin full credit for his attempt to carry out a sacred mission, he ultimately criticizes him for not recognizing Christ as the only true spiritual mediator, as well as for failing to create a poetic language rooted in concrete, everyday experience. As Emmanuel himself had come to understand, in order to speak for the human community the twentieth-century artist must break the mold of the Romantic *poète maudit.* The revised 1948 edition of *Le Poète fou* incorporates Emmanuel's first published volume of poetry, *Elégies* (1940), verse sketches that were later expanded into *Tombeau d'Orphée.*

In 1944 Emmanuel's first long narrative dealing with the Book of Genesis, *Sodome,* was also published. As its title suggests, *Sodome* retells the destruction of the Cities of the Plain, Sodom and Gomorrah, for the sin of homosexuality. This transgression becomes a symbol of contemporary narcissism, which overly encourages individuality and ultimately destroys the possibility of communal life. The poem consists of a preface reviewing the history of sin, beginning with the Creator's separation from humanity as a result of Adam and Eve's transgression, and two parts: part 1 retells the story of Abraham's encounter with the avenging angels through the episode of the Sodomites' assault on the divine messengers and Lot's family; part 2 recounts Lot's flight from the condemned city and ends with his sojourn in Zoar. Most of the second part takes the form of a psychodrama, in which Lot assumes the guilt of his city and attempts to purge himself of individual and com-

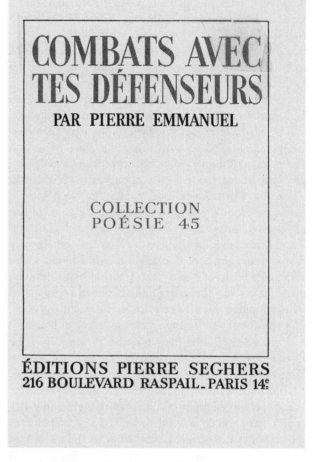

Cover for the 1945 edition of Emmanuel's 1942 collection of poetry, in which he used Old Testament imagery in poems denouncing politicians who collaborated with the Germans (California State University, Northridge, University Library)

munal evil. Emmanuel begins each part with a long prose argument intended to guide the reader through the narration and clarify any hermetic symbolism. *Sodome* remains, however, one of Emmanuel's most difficult works.

Emmanuel published five collections dealing specifically with World War II–*Jour de Colère* (Day of Wrath, 1942), *Combats avec tes défenseurs* (Battles with Your Defenders, 1942), *La Colombe* (The Dove, 1943), *La Liberté guide nos pas* (Freedom Guides Our Steps, 1945), and *Tristesse, ô ma patrie* (Sorrow, Oh My Country, 1946)–as well as many individual pieces, some under his Resistance pseudonym, Jean Amyot. These books mark the high point of Emmanuel's popularity, when he was considered a leader of the French intellectual resistance, a poetic force comparable to Louis Aragon and Paul Eluard. The declamatory tone of this verse earned Emmanuel the reputation of one of the greatest living orators of France. While these books deal with actual historical events, such as Nazi atrocities and the heroism of French fighters, they place these events in a mythical context. *Jour de Colère,* the least cohesive of the volumes, alternates prophetic views of current events with mystical visions of the Second Coming. In *Combats avec tes défenseurs,* Emmanuel approximates the style of the Old Testament prophets Isaiah and Jeremiah by decrying the corruption of modern political leaders and prophesying the downfall of sinful cities, but he also looks forward to the salvation of victims of the war through Christ's mediation. Both *La Colombe* and *La Liberté guide nos pas* interpret the contemporary debacle as a reenactment of the Babel story. Humanity, swollen with pride, has corrupted language to the extent that God has forsaken his creation and plunged the world into chaos. Yet, the poet-prophet foretells the advent of a new Pentecost, when the Holy Spirit will intervene on behalf of the fearful, silenced masses to restore liberty and the power of divinely inspired language. In *Tristesse, ô ma patrie,* Emmanuel assumes the role of a simple witness to the sufferings of his generation. The poetry of this volume almost resembles a series of newspaper articles written in verse; they report Nazi war crimes in a language much more objective and pictorial than that of the previous volumes.

Most of Emmanuel's poetry of the 1940s is challenging to the reader. Sometimes highly rhetorical, it requires that the reader have a good knowledge of the myths the poet reworks and it demands considerable effort to decipher his symbolism. During this decade, however, he also composed a much different form of poetry—brief lyrics, sometimes no more than two lines, in short meters, which he first published as *XX Cantos* (1942), then as *Cantos* (1944), and, finally, in a greatly augmented edition, as *Chansons du dé à coudre* (Songs of the Thimble, 1947). Formally, these poems recall Paul Valéry's *Charmes* (Charms, 1922) in their use of uncommon meters, but the simple, repetitive rhymes employed to paint fleeting moments of experience suggest the influence of Paul Verlaine. Emmanuel treats a variety of subjects, from war to love, from the problems of poetic language to mystical union with God. His themes include the soul's longing for a Pascalian *Deus absconditus* (hidden God) who reveals his presence but refuses to explain his purpose to humanity, the relationship between the human and the sacred word, and the reflection of God's presence in simple objects of nature and everyday life. As the title of the 1947 version suggests, the poet imagines himself as a woman sewing together the realms of experience—the spiritual and the physical, the intellectual and the ordinary—so that verse becomes a means of communication as well as a cure for alienation. This volume fulfills Emmanuel's ambition, outlined in *Le Poète fou,* to fashion a more concrete

language and points in the direction his poetry took in the 1960s.

From 1945 to 1947 Emmanuel worked for the French government radio station, Radiodiffusion Française (RDF), as director of the English Service; from 1947 to 1959 he directed the North American Service of the RDF. His contact with leftist writers during the war, especially Aragon, led to a brief flirtation with communism, which ended abruptly in 1947 after he visited Eastern Europe as a journalist and dared to criticize Soviet policy. This trip had several important consequences: it confirmed his Christian convictions and inspired his most important epic, *Babel* (1951), but also caused a definitive break with the leading French intellectual forces in Paris and probably explains, in large measure, why he lost and never again regained the popularity he enjoyed in his early career. After the war and divorce from his first wife, Emmanuel moved to Paris, where he remarried in 1952. He had two daughters with his second wife, Janine Loo, an artist.

Emmanuel's most important work of the 1950s is undoubtedly *Babel,* one of the outstanding long verse narratives of the twentieth century. This three-hundred-page narrative poem continues in the political vein of his Resistance writings, treating the rise and fall of European totalitarianism. In this work Emmanuel creates a story in which myth and history are so tightly linked that the action takes place simultaneously in biblical times and in contemporary Europe. The subject is the specifically modern phenomenon of totalitarianism, its effect on the individual and the collectivity, and liberation from such regimes. *Babel* is divided into five sections that relate the circumstances surrounding the rise of oppressive government, the construction of a tower that symbolizes political enslavement, a tyrant's reign, the beginnings of communal revolt, and, finally, the fall of the tyrant and his tower. Emmanuel alternates poetry with extensive prose commentaries spoken by "Le Récitant" (The Reciter), the narrator of the poem, who claims to have lived this experience of tyranny as a member of the oppressed multitudes. The reciter's voice alternates with those of the tyrant, a shepherd, and Christ.

Babel is, at once, the culmination of Emmanuel's political obsessions of the previous decade and a new poetic experiment that combines prose and verse into one narration and creates a story through dialogues. Imagery drawn from nature, the Bible, and Catholic liturgy is woven coherently into symbols that mark the poet's move from hermeticism to the world of common, everyday objects. For the verse sections of *Babel,* Emmanuel prefers the blank alexandrine, although several parts are written in rhymed stanzas as well as a looser verse form resembling the parallel structure of the Psalms. *Babel* draws upon the full range of Emmanuel's favorite themes: nature, history, language, and Christian doctrine. *Babel* also stands out as Emmanuel's most prophetic work, for though he did not live to see the fall of the Soviet Union in 1989, his poem had predicted almost forty years earlier that the modern Babel of Eastern European Communism would give way to a spontaneous, communal Pentecost, thanks to the tenacity of the human spirit.

Emmanuel recognized that *Babel* marked the end of his early poetic career. He did not write another long narrative poem for almost twenty years, preferring instead to compose short lyrics in a variety of meters. When he began again to write verse in the mid 1950s after a five-year hiatus, he abandoned his declamatory style of the 1940s for a more musical style, established by the consistent use of end and internal rhymes, alliteration, assonance, and repetition. While the imagery and obsessions of his collections published in the 1950s and 1960s do not change appreciably from those of the 1940s, Emmanuel tries to render his thought as accessible as possible. Inspired by an ambition to create a language faithful both to his personal concerns and to the universal human experience, simple yet capable of multiple levels of interpretation, he situates the question of the poetic word at the center of his work.

The main subject of *Visage nuage* (Face Cloud, 1955) is the poet's struggle to reconcile his imperfect human condition with his endless longing for perfection. Many poems are mystical, presenting God as light, love, transparency, the union of light and darkness. *Visage nuage* is Emmanuel's most popular work published after World War II. Concise, comprehensible, developing a single thought through imagery drawn from the domestic sphere and the four elements, these brief meditations on the spiritual life and art mark Emmanuel as one of the foremost philosophical poets of the century.

Versant de l'âge (Slopes of the Age, 1958), written on the occasion of the poet's fortieth birthday, is more polemical in tone. As the title suggests, Emmanuel sees himself entering the mature phase of his life and work. No longer obsessed by his past, he can declare his Christian faith and reject the notion of the Absurd. Far from permitting a facile optimism, such faith requires that the believer fully live the contradictions of a spirit contained in flesh, a mortal destined for eternity. The poet's principal task is to suppress his individualism in order to become the anonymous voice of every believer. In the short pieces that compose this volume, Emmanuel attempts to cover the spectrum of human experience by meditating upon human mysteries ranging from biblical accounts of the Exodus and the Apocalypse to the deaths of friends and the atrocities of war.

Emmanuel lecturing at Brandeis University, where he was a visiting professor in 1957 (from Alain Bosquet, Pierre Emmanuel, 1959)

The four other volumes of poetry published during this period, *Les Jours de la Nativité* (The Days of the Nativity, 1960), *Evangéliaire* (Evangeliary, 1961), *Les Jours de la Passion* (The Days of the Passion, 1962), and *La Nouvelle naissance* (The New Birth, 1963), are meditations on the Gospels and the Catholic liturgical year, which closely resemble the meditative poetry of the late Renaissance in that they reconstruct vividly the biblical scene, analyze the scene for its theological content or relevance to a contemporary philosophical problem, and conclude with a lesson that offers both the poet and his readers practical spiritual direction. *Les Jours de la Passion* and *Les Jours de la Nativité* are especially interesting because they combine Emmanuel's verse with color and black-and-white reproductions of religious art from the medieval to the modern period.

Emmanuel published his third biblical epic, *Jacob*, in 1970, at a time when he was devoting his principal energies to writing prose essays and had not published a volume of poetry in seven years—the longest break since he began writing in 1940. The first half of the poem retells the story of the Hebrew patriarch Jacob recounted in Genesis 27–32 from his birth and election over Esau to his dream of the ladder ascending into heaven. In a prose confession that concludes the narration, Emmanuel admits that the composition of *Jacob* signified for him a spiritual rebirth after a time when he despaired of ever overcoming his contradictory desires to be at one both with God and with the world. Emmanuel identifies himself with Jacob, who wrestles with the angel and emerges, both vanquished and victorious, as a new man, Israel. This epic is more autobiographical and mystical than *Sodome* or *Babel*, more concerned with the individual's spiritual quest than with communal sin and redemption. As in the earlier epics, in *Jacob* erotic love is an important secondary theme. Emmanuel insists, especially, on the salvific role played by women throughout history and on the artist's need to bring together the masculine and feminine sides of the human soul. The second half of *Jacob* changes from a narrative to a series of short poems on contemporary European life—including pieces on literary criticism and higher education. For Emmanuel, Jacob's struggle is reenacted by all those who confront their limitations. Besides the usual range of free verse and pieces in regular meter, *Jacob* includes two lyrical meditations on New Testament texts: the Lord's Prayer and the Beatitudes.

Sophia (1973) is Emmanuel's first long poem that is not an epic. As the titles of its subsections—"Portal," "Tympanum," "Apse," "Nave"—suggest, this work follows an architectural model. The poet undertakes a pilgrimage to a medieval cathedral in search of *Sophia*, or divine wisdom, which he discovers in the myriad relationships between men and women. Emmanuel's lifelong struggle to understand the value of human love achieves a resolution, as woman replaces language as the means of anchoring the poet's desire for union with God and the world. *Sophia* presents an historical overview of woman, from Eve and the Virgin Mary to contemporary feminists, and examines moral issues connected to women both real and mythical—from original sin in biblical times to pornography and abortion in the twentieth century. In *Sophia* Emmanuel explores not only myth but also his personal experiences with love, such as his longing for the mother who abandoned him as an infant and his physical relations with his wives. It is also possible to interpret this poem as a meditation on the Catholic Church, the spiritual mother of humanity. Indeed, many sections of this work either deliberately re-create prayers appearing in the Mass or imitate litanies or songs used in the Catholic liturgy.

Tu (You, 1978) closely resembles *Sophia* in form and intent. Another thick book comprising long and short poems, some in prose, others in free verse, blank verse, or traditional meters, *Tu* transcribes the poet's quest for the Supreme Other, the "you" whose name is beyond all other names. The goal of this quest is both

spiritual and artistic autonomy, for, Emmanuel explains, he can neither speak confidently as an independent individual nor pass beyond the limits of solipsism until he conquers his fears of addressing God directly, as the "Tu" who inspires language. The sections of this work are arranged like the panels of an altarpiece, each of which presents an example of transcendence: the Creation, the lives of Moses and Elijah, the Christ story. While this clearly mystical work remains firmly rooted in the Bible and Catholic liturgy, Emmanuel also incorporates Eastern religious practices, especially the chanting of mantras or meditation on the *om*, the secret syllable containing the divine essence.

In the same year that he published *Tu*, Emmanuel embarked on yet another poetic experiment, a trilogy titled *Livre de l'homme et de la femme* (Book of the Man and of the Woman) that reverts, surprisingly, to the obsessions of his first literary success, *Tombeau d'Orphée* of 1941. The erotic relationship between man and woman clearly supersedes any religious themes in these volumes. The first book, *Una: ou, La Mort, la vie* (Una, or, Death and Life, 1978) explores the tragedy of a failed love affair. The male poet wishes, perhaps in fantasy, perhaps in reality, to return to the maternal womb in order to be reborn and capable again of love. Unlike in *Tombeau d'Orphée*, no Christ or God the Father emerges as a mediator; the poet finds himself isolated from a feminine universe that he seeks to rejoin. The second book, *Duel* (1979), gives two versions of an intense and cruel love affair—the first from the male point of view, the second from the female. This erotic combat resolves itself in the final section of the book, "Eux" (Them), where the opponents turn to a barely perceived, unnamed God to resolve this conflict that threatens to consume both parties. *L'Autre* (The Other, 1980) concludes the trilogy with yet another interpretation of the Adam and Eve story and the Fall, which, for Emmanuel, is that erotic desire informs all human love.

All three volumes have a nearly identical structure, comprising 160 poems of twelve lines each. *Duel* is divided into a section comprising monologues of equal length, followed by the oncluding dialogue, "Eux," while *L'Autre* is divided in half, with the first 80 poems treating the theme of innocence and the last eighty, that of loss. The identites of the speakers of the individual poems remain purposefully vague, and, as Emmanuel suggests in the short preface to each volume, readers are not only free to identify the speaker of the poems with Pierre Emmanuel himself but also with every human who has ever suffered from desire. Now conceiving of poetry as a collaborative effort, Emmanuel invites his readers to create personal meanings for these poems, which function as mirrors of the universal human psyche.

In his long career Emmanuel wrote not only poetry but also his autobiography and several volumes of prose reflections on art and the spiritual life. He was also a journalist, a frequent contributor to such periodicals as *Christian Témoignage, Réforme, Esprit,* and *La France catholique.* Emmanuel was a popular lecturer, and he held appointments as visiting professor to several English and American universities, including Harvard, Brandeis, and Johns Hopkins. He was awarded honorary degrees from the universities of Oxford, Neuchâtel, Montréal, and Pennsylvania. He served as audiovisual minister of Paris under Mayor Jacques Chirac (from 1974 to 1979) as well as head of a commission on educational reform in the aftermath of the 1968 student riots. Awarded the Grand Prix de Poèsie de l'Academie Française in 1963, Emmanuel was also an Officier de la Légion d'Honneur, a Commandeur des Arts et des Lettres, and a Grand Officier de l'Ordre National du Mérite. On 25 April 1968 he was elected to the Academie Française, taking his place among the *Immortels* (Immortals), as members of the Academie are known, in June of the following year.

Until his death Emmanuel remained politically active. He combated the repression of religion and intellectual freedom in the Soviet Union and became the first *Immortel* to threaten to resign his position when the Academie Française considered the nomination of Félicien Marceau, a writer suspected of Nazi sympathies, to its ranks in 1975. Although Emmanuel tendered his resignation when Marceau was elected to the seat previously held by Marcel Achard, the Academie Française refused to accept his resignation, since members are elected for life. He died of cancer at the age of sixty-eight on 22 September 1984.

Pierre Emmanuel's last collection of poetry, *Le Grand œuvre: Cosmogonie* (The Great Work: Cosmogony, 1984), is both a retrospective and the culmination of a lifetime dedicated to meditation upon the creative process. In this final long work, which combines his deep understanding of the Bible with his study of Oriental religions, Emmanuel elaborates a unified tale tracing the origins of language, God, the physical universe, humanity, and love to end with the story of the liberation of the individual psyche, which learns to overcome isolation from the divinity and to achieve autonomy. *Le Grand œuvre,* a work that draws upon myth as well as personal experience, provides a fitting conclusion to one of the most-prolific poetic careers of the twentieth century in France.

References:

Anne-Sophie Andreu and François Livi, eds., *Lire Pierre Emmanuel,* Cahiers Pierre Emmanuel, no. 1 (Lausanne, Switzerland: L'Age d'Homme, 1994);

Alain Bosquet, *Pierre Emmanuel: Une Etude,* Poètes d'aujourd'hui, no. 67, third edition (Paris: Seghers, 1971);

William Calin, "Pierre Emmanuel," in his *A Muse for Heroes: Nine Centuries of the Epic in France* (Toronto & Buffalo: University of Toronto Press, 1983), pp. 403–423;

Evelyne Frank, *La Naissance du oui dans l'œuvre de Pierre Emmanuel: Oui amen om* (Paris: Presses Universitaires de France, 1998);

Eva Kushner, "L'Evolution des symboles dans la poésie de Pierre Emmanuel," *Ecrits du Canada français,* 13 (1962): 9–70;

Sven E. Siegrist, *Pour et contre Dieu: Pierre Emmanuel, ou la poésie de l'approche; L'expérience du manque et de l'antériorité potentielle* (Neuchâtel, Switzerland: Editions de La Baconnière, 1971).

Léon-Paul Fargue

(4 March 1876 – 24 November 1947)

Craig Monk
University of Lethbridge

BOOKS: *Tancrède* (Paris & Saint-Pourçain-sur-Sioule: Privately printed by A. Raymond, 1911);

Poëmes (Paris: Editions de la Nouvelle Revue Française, 1912); enlarged as *Poëmes: suivis de Pour la musique* (Paris: Editions de la Nouvelle Revue Française, 1919); enlarged as *Poëmes,* illustrated by Alexandre Alexeïeff (Paris: Gallimard, 1931); enlarged as *Poèmes: suivi de Pour la musique* (Paris: Gallimard, 1944);

Pour la musique: Poëmes (Paris: Editions de la Nouvelle Revue Française, 1914);

Banalité (Paris: Editions de la Nouvelle Revue Française, 1928);

Vulturne (Paris: Editions de la Nouvelle Revue Française, 1928);

Epaisseurs (Paris: Editions de la Nouvelle Revue Française, 1928);

Suite familière (Paris: Emile-Paul, 1928);

Les Ludions de Léon-Paul Fargue, illustrated by Marie Monnier (Paris: Fourcade, 1930);

D'après Paris (Paris: Editions de la Nouvelle Revue Française, 1931 [i.e., 1932]);

Sous la lampe (Paris: Gallimard, 1937);

Le Piéton de Paris (Paris: Gallimard, 1939);

Haute Solitude (Paris: Emile-Paul, 1941);

Déjeuners de soleil (Paris: Gallimard, 1942);

Fantôme de Rilke (Paris: Emile-Paul, 1942);

Refuges (Paris: Emile-Paul, 1942);

Trois Poèmes (Paris: Textes Prétextes, 1942);

Composite: Débats, idées bohémiennes, anecdotes, by Fargue and André Beucler (Paris: Ocia, 1944); enlarged as *Composite* (Paris: Ocia, 1945);

Contes fantastiques: Gravures sur cuivre de André Villeboeuf (Paris: Editions de la Galerie Charpentier, 1944);

Lanterne magique (Marseilles: Laffont, 1944); translated by G. Micholet-Coté as *The Magic Lantern* (London: Seagull Press, 1946);

Présentation de 1900 (Paris: Editions Nationales, 1944);

Charme de Paris (Paris: Denoël, 1945);

De la Mode, illustrated by Chériane (Paris: Editions Littéraires de France, 1945);

Léon-Paul Fargue, 1945 (Collection Mediathèque Valery Larbaud, Vichy)

Une Saison en astrologie, illustrated by Demetrius Galanis (Paris: Editions de l'Astrolabe, 1945);

Souvenir de Saint-Exupéry, Brimborions, no. 4 (Liège, Belgium: Editions Dynamo, 1945);

Méandres (Geneva, Paris & Montréal: Editions du Milieu du Monde, 1946);

Poisons, illustrated by Elisabeth Mary Burgin (Paris: Daragnès, 1946);

Rue de Villejust (Paris: Haumont, 1946);

Portraits de famille: Souvenirs (Paris: Janin, 1947);

Les Quat' Saisons: Astrologie poétique (Paris: Editions de l'Astrolabe, 1947);

La Flânerie à Paris (Paris: Commissariat Général au Tourisme, 1948);

Les Grandes heures du Louvre (Paris: Les Deux Sirènes, 1948);

Music-Hall, illustrated by Luc-Albert Moreau (Paris: Les Bibliophiles du Palais, 1948);

Côtes rôties, 1928–1938, illustrated, with an introduction, by André Dunoyer de Segonzac (Paris: Textes Prétextes, 1949);

Etc. (Geneva: Editions du Milieu du Monde, 1949);

Maurice Ravel, Collection Au voilier, no. 4 (Paris: Domat, 1949);

Les XX arrondissements de Paris, photographs by Laure-Albin Guillot (Paris: Editions Vineta, 1951);

Dîners de lune (Paris: Gallimard, 1952);

Illuminations nouvelles, lithographs and drawings by Raoul Dufy (Paris: Textes Prétextes, 1953);

Petit Diagnostic de Paris, illustrated by Gabriel Fournier (Paris: Haumont, 1955);

Pour la Peinture (Paris: Gallimard, 1955);

Fréquentations d'art: 1893–1894 (Paris: Echoppe, 1997);

Vivre ensemble (Cognac: Le Temps qu'il fait, 1999).

Collections: *Sous la lampe; Suite familière; Banalité* (Paris: Editions de la Nouvelle Revue Française, 1929);

Pour la musique: Tancrède, suivi de Ludions, Collection Metamorphoses, no. 18 (Paris: Gallimard, 1943);

Poésies; Tancrède; Ludions; Poëmes; Pour la musique; Espaces; Sous la lampe, preface by Saint-John Perse, Collection Soleil, no. 139 (Paris: Gallimard, 1963);

Poésies; Tancrède; Ludions; Poëmes: Léon-Paul Fargue, preface by Henri Thomas, Collection Poésie (Paris: Gallimard, 1967);

Première vie de Tancrède, edited, with an introduction and notes, by Laurent de Freitas (Fontfroide-le-Haut: Fata Morgana, 2001).

Léon-Paul Fargue established himself as a major literary figure in Paris during the first half of the twentieth century. A poet whose best work could be read as an important precursor to the writings of the Dadaist and Surrealist groups, Fargue first published while he was still a teenager. During his lifetime his name was known throughout France, and he took his place among the most important literary circles in Paris, involving himself with nearly every significant literary magazine published in the city during his adult life. Although relatively little of Fargue's work was translated into English during his lifetime, he was admired by the generation of American expatriates who lived in France between the world wars. In his declining years Fargue became known for contribu-

tions he made to newspapers and popular journals in Paris. His columns on life in the city sustained him professionally during the 1930s and 1940s, even as his reputation as a poet began to wane.

Fargue was born in Paris on 4 March 1876, the illegitimate son of entrepreneur and artisan Léon Fargue. His mother was Marie Aussudre, a dressmaker from a rural, agrarian family. The boy's paternal grandmother opposed the union between his parents, and as a result the couple did not marry until 1907, a year after her death—when her grandson was thirty-one. An only child who was periodically estranged from his father, Fargue had an unsettled, lonely childhood, and he drew upon his memories of these early years in his subsequent writings. The elder Fargue gained some prominence as the proprietor of a ceramics factory, but the family remained relatively impoverished. In his youth Fargue chafed under the strict regimen of formal schooling. While he was by all accounts a bright boy, he was also absentminded, disorganized, and poorly motivated. He enjoyed reading, however, and a variety of fantastic, illustrated texts fostered his imagination during his formative years. Early in life he developed his enduring love for the city: Paris captivated him, and his fascination with the urban also found its way into much of his later work. At the same time, Fargue was drawn to the rural idyll of his mother's rustic background. He was interested in the natural world, and he loved insects: he claimed that the beauty of the countryside inspired him to write. During this time he was moved deeply by the material he discovered in Eugène Crépet's anthology *Les Poètes français* (The French Poets, 1861), and he also grew interested in the works of Gustave Flaubert, Victor Hugo, and Arthur Rimbaud.

Inspired by his reading and drawn to a community of emerging writers in Paris, the adolescent Fargue published his first text, the poem "Idée de Retard" (Idea of Delay) in the magazine *L'Art littéraire* in February 1893. Later that spring, however, his parents sent him to Germany in an attempt to help him finish his education. By this time, Fargue had begun to spend more time with a circle of young artists that at first centered around Alfred Jarry but soon grew to include Maurice Chevrier, Fabien Launay, and Louis Lormel. Fargue's parents believed that these young companions provided a distraction that was detrimental to their son. The young man was deeply unhappy in Germany, however, and after only two months he petitioned his father to allow him to return to France. Fargue was genuinely torn between his interest in writing and his interest in painting, the latter endeavor encouraged by his father. Léon Fargue allowed his son to go to Brittany to paint, but he soon grew restless and was permitted to return to Paris in the summer of 1893.

At this time Fargue's distinctive writing style began to emerge. His concern with the everyday can be seen as a direct extension of the bohemian poetry of the nineteenth century, while his linguistic experimentation anticipates the avant-garde writing of the years following World War I. Fargue delighted in the use of elision, onomatopoeia, tropes, and spoonerisms. He paid close attention to the rules of grammar in an attempt to stretch the limits of orthodox practice, and his combination of verse and prose created uncommon prose poems. His work soon came to the attention of the editors of the *Mercure de France,* and Alfred Vallette invited him to contribute; his first appearance in the magazine was in July 1894. Fargue had been working closely with Jarry since his return to Paris, and an acrimonious dispute between the two young men led Fargue to break off from writing for nearly a year. He returned to it in the magazine *Pan,* which, during a six-month period in 1895 and 1896, published *Tancrède,* a long poem that earned Fargue the admiration of the poet Stéphane Mallarmé and proved itself a most influential text when it appeared in book form in 1911.

Fargue's literary production was arrested once more in the last years of the decade, however, because of his obligatory military service. He entered the army in the autumn of 1897, and he was finally discharged in the autumn of 1900. Fargue later viewed these three years as the worst of his life; he spent many months in the army suffering from a variety of illnesses. But his time in the military was also marked by a romantic liaison with a young woman named Ludivine Létinois. This first significant relationship ended poorly for Fargue, however, and it began a pattern of broken trysts that earned him a reputation for being unlucky in love. When he returned to Paris, Fargue assembled around him another group of young artists, which included Charles Chanvin, Francis Jourdain, Charles-Louis Philippe, and Michel Yell.

In the first years of the twentieth century, Fargue continued to hone his poetic skills, but he also sought to diversify his interests in other creative endeavors. He struck up a friendship with the composer Maurice Ravel, and Fargue began to take music seriously. Building upon his knowledge of painting, he started to write art criticism. During these years of dabbling, Fargue's reputation for poor work habits and peevishness also was established. He arranged to have a book, "Premier Cahier de Poèmes" (First Gathering of Poems), printed in 1907

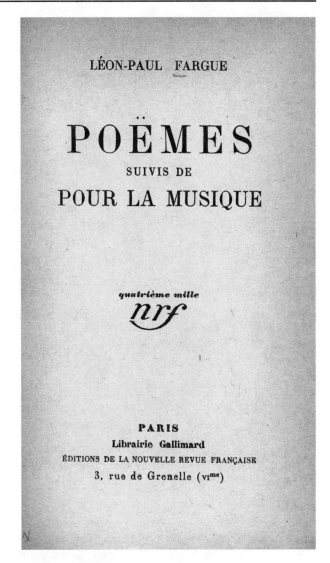

Title page for the enlarged, 1919 edition of Fargue's 1912 poetry collection (Thomas Cooper Library, University of South Carolina)

but because of his frequent disagreements with the publisher, it never actually appeared. Paradoxically, this sort of difficulty was one of the things that inspired Fargue to write with renewed vigor through this period: he began an important collaboration with the *Nouvelle Revue française* in 1909, and by 1914 he had published a great deal of material in that magazine, including the poetry collected in his influential *Poèmes* (1912). But during these years tragedy also touched Fargue. No other event in the first half of his life had as profound an effect on him as did the death of his father in 1909. Over the next two decades he took an active role in the operation of the ceramics factory, an operation he saw as an important part of his father's legacy. This upheaval in his personal life just before World War I led to the development of a strong friendship with Valery Larbaud. Larbaud was

Fargue in 1919

a source of constant encouragement for his friend, and Fargue's reputation for eccentricity continued to grow as the two men spent their evenings deep in conversation, wandering throughout Paris. At about this time Fargue also made the acquaintance of Adrienne Monnier. From the time they met in February 1916, Monnier was an ardent supporter of the poet, and through her famous bookstore, La Maison des Amis des Livres, she helped to promote his work in the interwar period. This most important literary circle, of which Fargue was a central member, was disrupted when Fargue quarreled with Larbaud over a woman in the early 1920s. But the personal estrangement between the two men did not interfere with their professional collaboration with Paul Valéry to publish the magazine *Commerce*. With the backing of Monnier and her bookshop, the publication flourished between 1924 and 1932.

By the late 1920s Fargue was on the verge of gaining international recognition. He met Eugene Jolas, an American newspaperman working for the Paris *Tribune*, the European edition of the *Chicago Tribune*. Jolas had been raised in Europe, and after tak-

ing over the literary column of the newspaper in 1924, he recognized that Paris had become the center of literary activity on the Continent. Jolas was interested in founding in the city a magazine in which artists of all countries would come together, exhibiting to a reading public in Europe and North America the dynamism of literary experimentation that one could encounter in Paris. Between 1927 and 1938 this magazine, *transition*, established itself as the preeminent expatriate American journal in Europe, and Jolas proved his commitment to the support of experimental writing. In Fargue, Jolas found a poet whose work, he maintained, embodied many of the concerns that shaped the editorial direction of the magazine, which published some of the first English translations of Fargue's texts, thus introducing the poet to a new readership in the United States, and hailed him as an influential modern artist worthy of esteem. In an article titled "The Revolution of Language and James Joyce," published in the February 1928 issue of *transition* and subsequently collected in *Man from Babel* (1998). Jolas provided a brief overview of the work of the most important literary mavericks he had encountered in Europe: "Léon-Paul Fargue in his prose poems creates astonishing neologisms, although retaining in large measure the classical purity of French." Jolas writes, "He slashes syllables and transposes them from one word to the subsequent word, builds new words from root vocables and introduces thus an element entirely unknown before in French literature."

Jolas began introducing Fargue to his English-speaking readership, translating "Æternæ Memoriæ Patris" (To the Eternal Memory of My Father) and printing it in the May 1927 issue of *transition*. Originally published in *Nouvelle Revue française* in 1914, this remembrance of Fargue's father includes passages reminiscent of the traditional lyric elegy: "Ah! I see you, my loved ones. My father, I see you. I shall always see you stretched out upon your bed. / Just and pure before the Master as in the times of youth." However, the poem also features Fargue's characteristic hybrid of competing styles and tones. The poem is organized around sharp images suggestive of the purity to which European avant-garde verse aspired: "At the call of the whistle scattering a cold blast beneath the hangars, / Or the smell of a kitchen at evening, / Recalling a silence at table long ago, / Brought by a trifle, / Or like a dry touch of God's fingers on my ashes. . . ."

In the November 1927 issue of *transition* Jolas proclaimed Fargue "one of the great poets of modern France," and he offered as a case in point a translation of the prose poem "Tumult." The piece not only has as its theme flux and change but also reflects tumult through a series of juxtapositions that frame the oppositions that, Fargue believed, defined the modern world. "Here is man. There you are, lil-birdie," he writes. "Good-day Sir, hey stupid fool," he continues. Running throughout the poem is a tangible sense of modern malaise. "You have filled me with your hatred, your quarrels, your outrages," writes Fargue, "with everything about love that seeks and twists itself like a worm." He expresses a concern with art itself, specifically, the role of the artist in modern society; in this respect, the self-reflexiveness of "Tumult" is characteristic of much of the verse written at this time by writers such as Ezra Pound, Hilda Doolittle, and William Carlos Williams. "Poet, will you remain a poet," he asks, "in this turning island scented with the musk of lies and phantoms, that do not return your love." Maria McDonald Jolas, the editor's wife and a gifted linguist in her own right, prepared the translation of the poem for the magazine. The difficulty she had in finding English equivalents such as "poor pawgawkies" and "solitary vroucolacowamp" for Fargue's neologistic phrases encouraged Eugene Jolas to revisit the whole issue of translation. While in the first issue of *transition* (April 1927) Jolas had invited contributors to submit their work "in a language Americans can read and understand," in the eighteenth issue (November 1929) he concedes, in a note accompanying French texts by Robert Desnos, Jacques Prévert, and Roger Vitrac, that "the language itself is of intrinsic interest and would lose by translation." Finally, in the twenty-second issue of *transition* (February 1933), Jolas made the announcement that the magazine had embarked "upon its new policy of tri-lingual publication" (that is, in English, French, and German), arguing that avant-garde poetry could only be effective if it was left untranslated, its "linguistic creative material" still "intact." Fargue's French coinages thus began a debate that raged in American literary magazines for nearly a decade, polarizing views throughout the United States on the nature of experimental verse.

In all, Fargue's writing appeared in *transition* five times. His last contribution, "The Alchemist," published in the twenty-third issue (July 1935), was the text of an introduction he provided for James Joyce at a dinner in the novelist's honor, which was published as a three-page booklet by *Nouvelle Revue Française* under the original French title, *L'Alchemiste,* in 1934. In his speech Fargue called Joyce the "authority and master in everything that concerns literary matters" and "the physician, the dentist of lexicon, of semantics, of syntax." Fargue had been introduced to the

Irish exile by Sylvia Beach and Monnier in the mid 1920s, and Fargue helped Larbaud and Joyce revise the French translation of the latter's 1922 novel, *Ulysses.* Fargue's ability to stretch language was indispensable to that project; beyond that, Joyce admired his use of idiomatic slang and turns of phrase in everyday speech. The men shared a warm admiration for each other: the gregarious Fargue was a suitable complement for the introspective Joyce. At about the same time as he met Joyce, Fargue also began to spend a great deal of time with André Beucler. Beucler replaced Larbaud in the poet's affections, and he also joined Fargue on his nightly journeys through Paris. Fargue began to hire a taxi for a whole day, crisscrossing the city; these excursions were inevitably extended into the small hours of the morning. Published after Fargue's death, Beucler's memoirs, including *Vingt ans avec Léon-Paul Fargue* (1952; translated as *The Last of the Bohemians: Twenty Years With Léon-Paul Fargue,* 1954), were the most heartfelt remembrances of the poet ever to appear.

During his association with *transition*, Fargue was hailed in literary circles as a father of the avant-garde, and the material he published in *Commerce* cemented his reputation throughout France. But critical acclaim alone could not sustain him, and Fargue again turned his attention to securing a living. A burst of activity produced four books published in 1928: *Banalité* (Ordinariness), *Epaisseurs* (Thicknesses), *Suite familière* (Familiar Sequence), and *Vulturne* (Sirocco). But while these texts were well received, they did not earn the sales he desired. The ceramics factory failed in 1926 after years of heavy losses, and Fargue entered into a publishing venture with Jacques Fourcade in 1929. Fargue's erratic work habits contributed to the collapse of that enterprise, which failed in 1932. When, in that same year, *Commerce* ceased publication, Fargue found himself near poverty, and he made several unsuccessful attempts to secure a government appointment. With the encouragement of Beucler, Fargue began to write commissioned pieces for newspapers and commercial magazines in 1934. That this writing was necessitated by financial need is underlined by the fact that Fargue demanded advance payment for his work. These pieces were wildly popular, and Fargue was soon unable to meet the demand for them. This writing earned Fargue more money and gained him a larger readership than had his poetry. Soon, he was contributing to the most popular Parisian magazines: *Le Figaro, Mariane, Paris-Soir,* and *Voilà.* Inspired by the popularity of this writing, he published in 1939 an influential collection of material on the city, *Le Piéton de Paris* (The Pedestrian of Paris).

Fargue, composers Maurice Ravel and Georges Auric, and diplomat-writer Paul Morand, June 1927

Fargue lost his mother in April 1935, and while he was staggered by his bereavement, he resolved to balance his commissioned writing with a new commitment to his creative endeavors. He began to contribute to *Measures,* a new literary magazine. At this time he also met Chériane, an artist, whom he married in 1939. The late 1930s was a happy time for Fargue, and this period culminated with the critical and commercial success of *Haute Solitude* (High Solitude, 1941). But at the end of 1943 he suffered a stroke that left him partially paralyzed. While his failing health kept him bedridden for the rest of his life, the tragedy also facilitated a reconciliation with Larbaud. Reaching out to his old friend suggests that the combative Fargue had finally found peace.

Léon-Paul Fargue died on 24 November 1947. While he scoffed openly at the idea of literary celebrity and maintained that his work would quickly be forgotten, Fargue showed some concern with securing his literary reputation, even before his final illness. Supported in his application by Valéry, he made two unsuccessful attempts to gain election to the Académie Française. But in the 1930s he

obtained such rewards as admission to the Légion d'Honneur, the granting of the Prix de la Renaissance, and election to the Académie Mallarmé. At the end of his life this most devoted citizen of Paris was awarded the Grand Prix de la Ville.

A genuine celebrity in his own lifetime, Fargue was treated poorly by literary history. His career took a strange trajectory. As a young man he published works of an unusually high quality, and yet he never produced such work on a consistent basis. Indeed, his reputation as a poet was not always reinforced by his later work; his commercial writing could be described as mercenary ephemera. While there was little interest in his poetry in the decades following his death, his writings on Paris found their way into several anthologies. But his work failed to capture the imagination of subsequent generations of scholars, and few of his texts were ever marketed effectively by his publishers. His standing among his contemporaries was persistent, however; Fargue's name surfaced once more as a variety of memoirs appeared. In his introduction to *The Last of the Bohemians,* the English translation of Beucler's memoir,

Archibald MacLeish maintains that "Fargue's poems opened doors for many of us in the Twenties and they will go on opening doors for a long time to come." While Fargue's importance to his contemporaries cannot be questioned, his influence on modern literature has been more subtle. Certainly, his confrontation with the urban in all his work is consistent with the preoccupations of international modernism. He solved for himself the vexed question of the relation of art to the world at large: Fargue believed that poets live their poetry in every aspect of their life. Most importantly, perhaps, his questioning of the nature and condition of language itself spoke to many of the deepest-held concerns of modern writers. Indeed, many of his solutions were commensurate with the literary experiments undertaken by writers throughout Europe in the first half of the twentieth century.

Letters:

Léon-Paul Fargue. Valery Larbaud: Correspondance, 1910–1946, edited, with an introduction and notes, by Théophile Alajouanine (Paris: Gallimard, 1971);

Fargue, Marie Monnier, and Paul-Emile Bécaut, *Trente lettres aux Bécat: Léon-Paul Fargue,* edited by Maurice Saillet, introduction and notes by Jean-Paul Goujon (Dolhain, Belgium: Editions Compléments, 1994).

Biographies:

Louise Rypko Schub, *Léon-Paul Fargue,* Histoire des idées et critique littéraire, no. 132 (Geneva: Droz, 1973);

Jean-Claude Walter, *Léon-Paul Fargue; ou, L'Homme en proie à la ville* (Paris: Gallimard, 1973);

Jean-Paul Goujon, *Léon-Paul Fargue: Poète et Piéton de Paris* (Paris: Gallimard, 1997).

References:

Peter Baker, *Obdurate Brilliance: Exteriority and the Modern Long Poem* (Gainesville: University of Florida Press, 1991);

André Beucler, *Dimanche avec Léon-Paul Fargue* (Paris: Editions du Point du Jour, 1947);

Beucler, *Vingt ans avec Léon-Paul Fargue* (Geneva: Editions du Milieu du Monde, 1952); translated by Geoffrey Sainsbury as *The Last of the Bohemians: Twenty Years with Léon-Paul Fargue,* introduction by Archibald MacLeish (New York: Sloane, 1954); translation republished as *Poet of Paris: Twenty Years with Léon-Paul Fargue* (London: Chatto & Windus, 1955);

Richard Ellmann, *James Joyce,* revised edition (New York: Oxford University Press, 1982);

Maurice Imbert and Raphaël Sorin, eds., *Adrienne Monnier et la Maison des Amis des Livres* (Paris: Institut Mémoires de l'Edition Contemporaine, 1991);

Eugene Jolas, *Man from Babel,* edited and annotated, with an introduction, by Andreas Kramer and Rainer Rumold (New Haven: Yale University Press, 1998);

Dougald McMillan, *Transition: The History of a Literary Era, 1927–38* (London: Calder & Boyars, 1975; New York: Braziller, 1976);

Saint-John Perse, *Œuvres complètes: Saint-John Perse* (Paris: Gallimard, 1972);

Edouard Roditi, "A Paris Memoir," *James Joyce Quarterly,* 28, no. 1 (1990): 169–178;

Henri Thomas, *A la rencontre de Léon-Paul Fargue* (Saint-Clément-la-Rivière: Fata Morgana, 1992).

Papers:

Some of Léon-Paul Fargue's correspondence and a few manuscripts and proof copies are held by the Koninklijke Bibliotheek van België/Bibliothèque royale de Belgique, Brussels.

Jean Follain

(29 August 1903 – 10 March 1971)

Frank A. Anselmo
Louisiana State University

BOOKS: *5 poèmes de Jean Follain–5 gravures de Poncet,* engravings by Marcel Poncet (Paris: La Rose des Vents, 1933);

La Main chaude, introduction by André Salmon (Paris: Corrêa, 1933);

L'Année poétique (Paris: Trois Magots, 1934);

Huit poèmes (Paris: Debresse, 1935);

Paris (Paris: Corrêa, 1935);

La Visite du domaine, Repères, no. 5 (Paris: Editions G.L.M., 1935);

Le Gant rouge, Les Feuillets de Sagesse, no. 17 (Paris: Editions Sagesse, 1936);

Chants terrestres: Poèmes (Paris: Denoël, 1937);

L'Epicerie d'enfance (Paris: Corrêa, 1938);

Poètes: Jean Follain, introduction by Yanette Delétang-Tardif, portrait of Follain by Madeleine Dinès (Paris: Beresniack, 1941);

Ici-bas: Poèmes (Brussels: Journal des Poètes, 1941);

Canisy (Paris: Gallimard, 1942); translated by Louise Guiney as *Canisy,* foreword by Robert Morgan (Durango, Colo.: Logbridge-Rhodes, 1981);

Inventaire: Poëms, Cahiers de l'Ecole de Rochefort, second series, no. 3 (Paris: Debresse, 1942);

Usage du temps: Poèmes (Paris: Gallimard, 1943);

Exister: Poèmes (Paris: Gallimard, 1947);

Chef-lieu (Paris: Gallimard, 1950);

Les Choses données (Paris: Seghers, 1952);

Territoires (Paris: Gallimard, 1953);

Palais souterrain (Alès: Editions P.A.B., 1953);

Objets (Limoges: Rougerie, 1955);

Tout instant: Poèmes en prose (Paris: Gallimard, 1957);

Saint Jean-Marie Vianney, curé d'Ars (Paris: Plon, 1959);

Des Heures: Poèmes (Paris: Gallimard, 1960);

Notre Monde (Wülfrath, Germany: R. Atteln, 1960);

Poèmes et proses choisis (Paris: Gallimard, 1961);

Appareil de la terre, illustrated with woodcuts by Charles Lapicque (Paris: Galanis, 1961; revised edition, Paris: Gallimard, 1964);

Le Divorce et la séparation de corps, Contrats ou le droit pratique, no. 23 (Paris: Sirey, 1962);

Jean Follain, circa 1945 (photograph by Yvonne Chevalier)

Cheminements: Poèmes, Poèmes-missives, no. 7 (Geneva: Le Club du Poème, 1964);

Pérou, photographs by Jean-Jacques Languepin and Paul Almasy, L'Atlas des voyages, no. 33 (Lausanne, Switzerland: Editions du Rencontre, 1964);

Nourritures (Groupe Libre Création, 1965);

Célébration de la pomme de terre, Célébration, no. 33 (Revest-Saint-Martin, Basses-Alpes: Robert Morel, 1966);

Petit glossaire de l'argot ecclésiatique (Paris: Pauvert, 1966);

Napoléon (Paris: Editions Hermès, 1967);

Pierre Albert-Birot, Poètes d'aujourd'hui, no. 163 (Paris: Seghers, 1967);

D'après tout (Paris: Gallimard, 1967); translated by Heather McHugh as *D'après tout: Poems* (Princeton: Princeton University Press, 1981);

Approaches, illustrated by Lydie Chantrell, Prestige de la poésie, no. 7 (Basse-Yutz: Vodaine, 1969);

Eclats du temps, illustrated by Ania Staritsky (Puymoyen, Charente: Duchêne, 1970);

Espaces d'instants (Paris: Gallimard, 1971);

Pour exister encore, serigraphs by Claude Maréchal (Paris: Edition Silium, 1972);

Collège, preface by Marcel Arland (Paris: Gallimard, 1973);

Comme jamais (Paris: Editeurs Français Réunis, 1976);

Falloir vivre (Asnières: Editions Commune Mesure, 1976);

Noir des carmes (Asnières: Commune Mesure, 1976);

Le Pain et la boulange (Colombes: La Feugeraie, 1977);

Présent jour, illustrated by Denise Esteban, Collection Ecritures, no. 9 (Paris: Galanis, 1978);

Les Uns et les autres (Mortemart: Rougerie, 1981);

Cérémonial Bas-Normand (Fontfroide-le-Haut: Fata Morgana, 1982);

Piège du temps, introductory poem by Eugène Guillevic (Caen: Le Pavé, 1983);

La Table, introduction by Jacques Réda (Fontfroide-le-Haut: Fata Morgana, 1984);

Ordre terrestre, preface by André Frénaud (Fontfroide-le-Haut: Fata Morgana, 1986);

Le Magasin pittoresque, preface by Hughes Labrusse (Thaon: Amiot-Lenganey, 1991);

Agendas, 1926–1971, edited, with notes, by Claire Paulhan (Paris: Seghers, 1993).

Editions and Collections: *Exister; suivi de, Territoires,* preface by Henri Thomas, Collection Poésie, no. 48 (Paris: Gallimard, 1969);

Trois bois gravés pour trois proses de Jean Follain, woodcuts by Jean Coulon (Paris: Commune Mesure, 1976)–comprises "Nourritures pauvres," "Noir des carmes," and "Viandes vives";

Paris: Jean Follain, edited by Gil Jouanard (Paris: Phébus, 1978);

Canisy; suivi de Chef-lieu (Paris: Gallimard, 1986);

L'Epicerie d'enfance, afterword by Jouanard (Fontfroide-le-Haut: Fata Morgana, 1999).

Editions in English: *Transparence of the World,* edited and translated by W. S. Merwin (New York: Atheneum, 1969);

12 Poems, bilingual edition, translations by Mary Feeney (Tucson: Grilled Flowers Press, 1977);

Poems by Jean Follain, bilingual edition, translations by Clare Sheppard (London: Charles Boase, 1979);

A World Rich in Anniversaries: Prose Poems by Jean Follain, bilingual edition, translations by Feeney and William Matthews (Iowa City: Grilled Flowers Press, 1979);

Selected Prose: Jean Follain, translated by Feeney and Louise Guiney (Durango, Colo.: Logbridge-Rhodes, 1985).

OTHER: Martin Nadaud, *Mémoires de Léonard: Ancien garçon maçon,* introduction by Follain and Georges Duveau (Paris: Egloff, 1948);

Honoré de Balzac, *Le Cousin Pons,* preface and notes by Follain (Paris: Delmas, 1955);

Pierre Albert-Birot, *Grabinoulor: Epopée,* preface by Follain (Paris: Gallimard, 1964);

Agricol Perdiguier, *Mémoires d'un compagnon,* edited by Follain, Livres de toujours, no. 78 (Paris: Club des libraires de France, 1964).

SELECTED PERIODICAL PUBLICATIONS– UNCOLLECTED: *Inventaire,* Cahiers de l'Ecole de Rochefort, 2, no. 3 (1942);

Dessins et poèmes manuscrits, Revue de la Maison de la poésie (Rhone-Alps), 8 (November 1990).

As a result of Jean Follain's poetic independence, it is difficult to place or classify him within any category of twentieth-century poetry. Although he did establish close ties with various members of the Sagesse group in the 1920s and 1930s and of the Ecole de Rochefort in the 1940s, he never truly belonged to any particular school in a strict sense, nor did he profess acceptance of any specific poetic doctrine. Moreover, in spite of his successful career as a lawyer and judge, he kept a guarded distance from the wide spectrum of national and international political events of his time. As Françoise Rouffiat states in her 1996 study of the poet, his life, and his work: "Il n'est pas simple de situer un poète d'une singularité troublante et réputé inclassable, dans l'histoire de la poésie de ce siècle, d'autant que Follain ne s'est pas non plus engagé dans les événements de son temps, n'ayant pas, que l'on sache, fait acte de résistance ni pris position politique comme d'autres poètes, amis proches ou lointains" (It is not easy to situate a poet of a troubling and reputedly unclassifiable singularity in the history of the poetry of this century; this is particularly so because Follain was not engaged in the events of his time, not having, as far as one knows, made any act of resistance or taken a political posi-

Follain at the age of seven

for history and catechism as well as for the literary works of Victor Hugo and Honoré de Balzac. Although he suffered from a muscular and bone illness that prevented him from participating in sporting activities, he later cherished fond memories of his childhood and the countryside, both of which had a profound influence on his future poetic compositions. Follain provides much information about these early years of his life in the autobiographical prose works *Canisy* (1942; translated, 1981) and *Chef-lieu* (County Seat, 1950). He recalls in *Canisy,* for instance, that it was during this period of his life that he began to develop a profound attachment to words, which, he writes, seemed capable of grasping "la beauté du monde" (the beauty of the world). As evidence of this early love for language, he often pretended to deliver scholarly lectures from a wood bin in his grandmother's kitchen, where he would recite from philosophy texts that admittedly made little sense to him at the time. Through these imaginary lectures, he hoped to divine the intrinsic meaning of words "dont les phrases pleines d'incidents dessinaient un filigrane compliqué dans le tissu de vie journalière" (whose rambling phrases wove a complicated filigree into the fabric of everyday life).

Following World War I, Follain's father sent the sixteen-year-old boy to Leeds to learn English. However, as Follain admitted, his English studies were not at all successful because he had grown too attached to the French language and words that represented the various objects around him. His bond with his native tongue was so great that he insisted upon reading a French newspaper every day. Explaining his inability to learn a foreign language, Follain stated: "Quand on lie trop le mot à la chose qu'il designe, on ne peut pas rompre cette union. Par conséquent on ne peut pas apprendre d'autre langue" (When one links the word too much to the thing that it designates, one cannot break this union. Consequently, one cannot learn another language). Perhaps because of his natural perspicacity and the minute attention that he gave to words and their inherent meaning, Follain decided to practice law upon his return to France and enrolled in the law school of Caen in 1921. This rigorous course of studies apparently complimented his predilection for precise details, and he completed the program with high distinctions.

In spite of Follain's profound attachment to his native province of Normandy, he succumbed to the allure of Paris when he was a young boy and spent hours memorizing the precise details of street maps of the capital city that he had yet to visit. In 1923 he finally had the opportunity to travel to Paris, and he decided to move there permanently the following

tion as had some other poets, friends both close and distant). Nevertheless, Follain was in fact deeply touched and troubled by the tumultuous events of the twentieth century, and there is a certain pessimism that permeates much of his work. However, it is primarily Follain's distinctive depiction of time and space and his revelation of the hidden connections that link man to his universe and the objects that make up his physical world that most profoundly mark his work and serve to distinguish him from other twentieth-century poets of "quotidian objects," such as Francis Ponge.

The son of Albert Follain and Berthe Follain (née Heussebrot), Jean René Follain was born on 29 August 1903 in the small town of Canisy, which is located near Saint-Lô, in the province of Normandy. He was raised by loving and caring parents and grandparents within a bourgeois milieu that was faithful to tradition and social conventions. By all accounts, his family was financially comfortable, if not especially wealthy. His paternal and maternal grandfathers were, respectively, a schoolmaster and a provincial notary, and his father was a science instructor at the Saint-Lô school where Follain developed a passion

year under the pretense of pursuing a doctoral degree. He found work instead with a Parisian solicitor and later began to practice law on his own in 1927. Recognized as a brilliant conversationalist and having developed a reputation as a sort of bon vivant and a connoisseur of fine dining in Paris, he became a regular figure in Parisian society. Actively pursuing, under the pretense of having to make himself known professionally, his new *vie mondaine* (worldly life), he always dressed meticulously and never declined an invitation.

Although he had established himself as a promising lawyer, Follain could not abandon his other great passion: composing poetry. Shortly after his arrival in Paris, he started to frequent various literary circles and regularly participated in the gatherings that took place at the Brasserie Courbet (near the Porte d'Orléans), where he forged friendships with such poets as André Salmon, Pierre Reverdy, Max Jacob, Pierre Mac Orlan, and Léon-Paul Fargue, as well as with such painters as Georges Braque, André Masson, and Jean Marembert. Within this circle he met the artist Madeleine Denis (who painted under the pseudonym of Madeleine Dinès in order to distinguish herself from her father, the painter Maurice Denis); Follain and Madeleine Denis married in 1934. Furthermore, as a result of Follain's successful law career and the many contacts that he had established in the literary world of Paris, he legally defended Louis Aragon and Roger-Gilbert Lecomte, as well as the literary journal *Montparnasse* in the 1930s.

One of the most important early friendships of Follain at this time was with Fernand Marc, who, in an attempt to find a viable alternative to the Surrealist movement of André Breton, had founded the literary group *Sagesse* in 1927. Although the members of this group sought a measure of artistic independence from the Surrealists, they never openly declared themselves hostile to this movement. In fact, Follain admitted that he had even attempted to compose Surrealist poetry but was not entirely pleased with the outcome: "Je n'ai jamais eu l'impression de lutter contre le Surréalisme. J'ai admiré le Surréalisme, avec quelquefois la volonté d'en faire; j'ai essayé mais ce n'était pas moi" (I never had the impression of fighting against Surrealism. I admired Surrealism and sometimes had the desire to create such works; I tried, but it was not in me). Follain published his first poems in Marc's literary journal, *Les Feuillets de Sagesse*. He later made poetic contributions to various other literary journals, such as *Dernier carré, Feuillets inutiles, Montparnasse, Nouvelle Revue française, Commerce, Europe,* and *Cahiers du sud*. In 1933 Follain published his first individual collection of poetry, *5 poèmes de Jean Follain–5 gravures de Poncet* (Five Poems by Jean Follain–Five Engravings by Poncet), which was illustrated by Marcel Poncet. Although modest in scope (as the title indicates), it was well received within Parisian poetic circles. This volume was quickly followed the same year by his first substantial collection of poetry, *La Main chaude* (The Warm Hand), which consisted of sixty-three individual poems. In 1937 Follain published *Chants terrestres* (Earth Songs), a collection of fifty-six poems, for which he received the prestigious Prix Mallarmé in 1939.

At the outset of World War II in 1940, Follain was briefly mobilized and served–in spite of his poor physical condition and weak eyesight–as a gunner at Châteaudon in a unit of the Défense Contre Avions (anti-aircraft defense). Following the capitulation of France, Follain distanced himself from national politics; nevertheless, he openly associated with poets who refused to succumb to the difficulties of life in Occupied France and even encouraged many of them, including André Frenaud, to publish their work. He was particularly attracted to the Ecole de Rochefort, a movement inaugurated by Jean Bouhier in western France. Among those who were affiliated with this loosely organized "school" (which had never issued a formal manifesto or developed a clearly defined agenda) were the poets Jean Rousselot, Michel Manoll, Maurice Fombeure, Eugène Guillevic, Luc Bérimont, Paul Chaulot, and René Guy Cadu. Bound more through friendship than in any aesthetic or ethical point of view, these poets maintained a certain sense of creative independence and pursued their own individual poetic endeavors. The adherents of the Ecole de Rochefort did, however, share several artistic principles. Most important among these was their desire to create works of a *réalisme poétique* (poetic realism), which was characterized by their dedication to conscious writing (as opposed to the subconscious writing of the Surrealists) and their advocacy of a renewed *humanisme poétique* (poetic humanism) in which man and his relationship to the physical world would once again play a central role.

In addition to providing support and encouragement to other French poets during the turmoil of World War II, Follain also continued to write and publish much poetry himself. In 1941 he published his third volume of poetry, *Ici-bas* (Here Below), which comprised forty-four new poems. And, though never truly a member of the Ecole de Rochefort in a strict sense, Follain was certainly sympathetic to its principles and contributed a minor collection of sixteen poems titled *Inventaire* (Inventory) to its journal, *Cahiers de l'Ecole de Rochefort,* in January 1942, the same year in which he published his most important prose

Jean Follain

LA MAIN CHAUDE

Introduction d'André Salmon

CRA·

1933
ÉDITIONS R.-A. CORRÊA
8, rue Sarasate, 8
PARIS XVᵉ

Title page for Follain's first major collection of poetry (from André Dhôtel, Jean Follain: Une Etude, *1972)*

work, *Canisy.* One year later, he published *Usage du temps* (Use of Time), which essentially reprised his first three volumes of poetry (*La Main chaude, Chants terrestres,* and *Ici-bas*) in their entirety. The only new section was *Transparence du monde,* which comprised thirty-six poems, twelve of which had already appeared in *Inventaire. Usage du temps* therefore presented only twenty-four new poems; nevertheless, this book is generally considered as Follain's first major collection of poetry, and all four sections are typically read today as a single volume.

These early poems were written in a style that remained remarkably consistent throughout Follain's entire life. All of his poetry (with the exception of his prose poems) is composed in vers libre (free verse) and demonstrates a resolute lack of meter or rhyme as well as a frequent suppression of punctuation. Nevertheless, his poems are finely crafted—one could even say chiseled—and reveal a striking attention to the minute details of form. Referring to the composition

of his poems, Follain once stated: "Si insolite que paraisse son contour, quelle que soit sa dimension, un poème doit être façonné, artisanalement façonné" (No matter how insolent its contours might appear, whatever its dimensions might be, a poem must be fashioned with artisanship). Moreover, most of Follain's poetry is extremely concise; several early poems that sometimes consist of little more than a few lines actually convey remarkably powerful images, such as the untitled poem in *Usage du temps:* "Il y a sous ton cou, / une tranchée sanglante" (There is below your neck / a deep bloody cut). Follain referred to his brief yet finely formulated compositions as a poetry of "concentration," in which he tightened the text and freed it from all discursiveness. The result is a poetry that is practically devoid of metaphors, clichés, and other forms of rhetoric so that the inherent value of language and the simplest meanings of words can be revealed. Unlike that of the earlier Romantics, his poetry is practically devoid of subjectivity and reveals a more meditative and less emotive quality. It is therefore common for critics to compare his poetry to that of Stéphane Mallarmé, whom Follain actually evokes—along with Guillaume Apollinaire and George Gordon, Lord Byron—in "Poème glorieux" (Glorious Poem), the first poem of *Usage du temps.* Follain clarifies the poetic mission in an apostrophe in another poem in *Usage du temps,* "Le Carême de Notre-Dame" (The Fasting of Notre Dame): "Il ne s'agit pas de panégyrique, ô poète / mais de voir les choses / telles qu'elles sont" (It is not a question of panegyric, oh poet / but of seeing things / such as they are).

The poetry of Follain therefore demonstrates a certain measure of realism—Balzac even appears in "Fulgurance"; Jacob once correctly stated that the poetry of Follain was "faite avec des objets" (made with objects). In *Usage du temps,* no item is too obscure for Follain's attention. In a manner that is often compared to that of Francis Ponge, Follain meticulously analyzes and studies quotidian objects of apparent insignificance in an attempt to uncover their hidden or unexpected aspects. Follain perceives the physical object in its entirety: its strangeness, its details, its components, even its placement in space. Unlike Ponge, however, Follain imbues his objects with a certain mobility that, by transcending the limits of both time and space, reveals the mysteries of the physical universe. In the transcendent "instants" that characterize his work, the true essence of the object is rendered comprehensible in a sudden moment of revelation, as Follain explains:

Durant un certain instant privilégié cet objet peut nous paraître en soi si précis qu'il en devient transfiguré, et un élément du mystère du monde, un motif irremplaçable d'appréhension de ce mystère. Ainsi tel objet, fûtil practiquement médiocre ou inutilisable, en devient poétiquement nécessaire, affirmatif de la *nécessité de la poésie* même.

(During a certain privileged instant, this object can appear to us to be so precise in itself that it becomes transfigured; it is an element of the mystery of the world, an irreplaceable motif of apprehension of this mystery. Such an object, be it practically mediocre or useless, becomes poetically necessary, affirmative of the *need of poetry* itself).

Through his meticulous study of these various objects, Follain develops the main theme of his entire poetic creation: all people and things (past, present, and future) are connected in this world through time and space. Follain's intense analysis of these objects eventually reveals the hidden connections; however, it is not always the object in and of itself that acquires importance in Follain's universe but rather its temporal and spatial placement, which can be either expanded or compressed. Man, however, is often incapable of understanding the omnipresent connections that bind him to the universe because of his imperfect perception of time and space. To demonstrate these hidden connections, Follain establishes corollaries between common objects or people and the past and the present as well as the future. Through these apparently unrelated temporal and spatial juxtapositions, man's inability to understand the implications of time is made evident, as in "Atelier de la préhistoire" (Prehistoric Workshop), in which a young woman "songe à vivre / plus d'un demi-siècle" (dreams of living / for more than fifty years) as she contemplates a wheat field for a brief instant of time. Unbeknownst to her, she is standing on a site where prehistoric men once fashioned stone tools; this woman is obviously unaware of the implications of time, which actually seems to stand still at this precise instant as the sun "sertit / à ses pieds l'ombre la plus noir" (casts / at her feet the darkest shadow). The reader is thus made poignantly aware of the implications of time (bells, clocks, watches, pendulums, seasons, and the sun all figure often in Follain's poetry as a measure of its passage) and of the futility of any attempt to conquer it. Man, insects, trees, and even inanimate objects hopelessly resist its ravages, as in "Figures du temps" (Figures of Time): "L'arbre et le bouquet / mendiaient l'existence / feuille par feuille et fleur par fleur" (the tree and the bouquet / fought for existence / leaf by leaf and flower by flower).

Follain imbues these sudden "instants" with much importance, for it is during these unexpected

Follain and his wife, Madeleine, on their wedding day, 1934

moments—which often last no more than a few milliseconds—that one actually confirms one's life and becomes intensely aware of one's existence and place in the material world. As Jean-Yves Debreuille observes in his 1995 monograph, Follain's poems are spaces "où est permise pour un instant la contemplation sereine et intemporelle des éléments contrastés et divergents qui constituent l'existence—tant il est vrai qu'*exister* est l'état non pas de départ, mais auquel permet d'accéder la poésie" (in which is permitted for an instant the serene and timeless contemplation of the contrasted and divergent elements that constitute existence—such that it is true that *to exist* is not the state of departure, but the one to which poetry provides access). Throughout Follain's poetry, verbs such as *trembler* (to tremble), *frémir* (to quake), and *frissonner* (to shiver) thus acquire interesting meaning because shaking or trembling generally accompanies a sudden realization of one's existence, as in "Aux couleurs du monde" (To the colors of the world):

Des servantes écoutent au loin
bouillir des légumes verts,

Follain, poet and dramatist Georges Schéhadé, and poet Max Jacob, during the 1930s

c'est une immense
satiété;
des femmes tremblent en des corsages
couleur de lièvre ou de sang
et l'homme entend battre son cœur.

(Servants listen
to the distant boiling of green vegetables,
it's an immense
satiety;
women tremble in bodices
the color of hare or blood
and the man hears his heart beat).

As these few lines suggest, women figure prominently in Follain's poetry: they are intrinsically linked to the constant cycle of life and death and are often depicted as spouses and mothers as well as lovers or objects of sexual desire. Moreover, Follain's frequent description of their physical qualities undeniably gives an erotic quality to *Usage du temps*. In direct contrast to sexual pleasure, however, it is more often pain and suffering that women experience, and blood frequently accompanies the major events that mark their lives: menstruation, loss of virginity, pregnancy, childbirth. There is thus a certain pessimism that permeates the work. For example, when Follain refers to the chest of "cette fille poitrinaire" (that tubercular

girl) in "Carnaval" (Carnival), it is no longer sexual desire that is evoked but sickness instead. This vague pessimism is undoubtedly related to the horrors of the two world wars, which had profoundly affected Follain. Although he does not refer specifically to either war in *Usage du temps,* war and the hardships it imposes on common people are nonetheless frequently evoked, as in "douleurs d'un sergent" (Grief of a Sergeant), in which a military man must endure "le poids lourd de ses douleurs" (the heavy weight of his sadness), or in the deceptively simple lines of another poem in *Usage du temps,* "Spectacles du monde" (Worldly Shows), in which death lingers sinisterly even in the most apparently peaceful parts of the world:

Beaux soirs que hantait la rumeur de la guerre
et l'atroce comédie du monde
et l'immense imagerie qui pesait sur les choses:
mille soldats buvant l'élixir
avant de bondir fiers et multicolores.
. . . .
Cette fille qui lave ses bras blancs en pleurant
au son des cloches limpides
s'en ira bientôt vers les morts;
. . . .
L'univers toujours changeant
est toujours éperdu

malgré que nul grand houzard constellé
ne s'appuie plus sanglant
sur la meule d'un champ pour y mourir.

(Beautiful evenings that were haunted by the rumor of
         war
and the atrocious comedy of the world
and the immense imagery that was weighing on things:
one thousand proud and multicolored soldiers drinking
         elixir
before springing to action.
. . . .
That girl who is washing her white arms while crying
at the sound of limpid bells
will soon join the dead;
. . . .
The constantly changing universe
is lost
even though a great constellated hussar
no longer supports himself
on the pile of hay in a field to die there).

In 1947, shortly after the conclusion of the war, Follain published *Exister* (Exist). As its title implies, the seventy-six poems of this collection attempt to confirm the existence of things and living beings. Many of the images and themes of *Usage du temps* are repeated. For instance, trembling generally marks a privileged instant when one becomes intensely aware of one's existence, which is often marked by suffering and hardship, as in "Enfantement" (Childbirth):

L'enfant tremblait en elk
au milieu des tissus roses
des veines bleues
du fiel sombre.
On voyait à travers la ville
cette femme dont les yeux
avec tout son corps
exprimaient la résignation
aux épuisantes constructions
de la chair et du sang.

(The child trembled inside of her
in the middle of pink tissues
blue veins
somber bile.
One saw across the city
that woman whose eyes
with her entire body
expressed resignation
to the tiresome construction
of flesh and blood).

The constant struggle of life is also evoked in "Existence," in which an insect struggles to remain alive in the petals of a rose, and in "Natures mortes" (Still Lifes), in which objects selfishly guard their existence as well as their secrets: "chaque chose pourtant veil-

lait et travaillait / pour sauver son éternité" (everything nevertheless kept guard and worked / in order to save its eternity). In spite of the universal desire to achieve eternal existence, time persists—albeit slowly and imperceptibly—in "Les Jardins" (The Gardens); resistance to its inevitable effects is futile:

S'épuiser à chercher le secret de la mort
fait fuir le temps entre les plates-bandes
des jardins qui frémissent
dans leurs fruits rouges
et dans leurs fleurs.
L'on sent notre corps qui se ruine
et pourtant sans trop de douleurs.

(To tire oneself seeking the secret of death
causes time to escape between the flower beds
of gardens that shake
in their red fruit
and in their flowers.
One feels our body fall into ruin
and yet without too much pain).

In many of the poems of *Exister,* death is just as frequently evoked as life, since the two are inextricably linked, as in "La Paix" (Peace), in which a hooligan and his female victim "arrivaient à vivre et mourir" (happened to live and die) in a single block of time. Existence is thus suspended and menaced within one precise instant, and—as a result of the indifference of the physical world in the face of unavoidable and omnipresent death—a poignant sobriety dominates the collection.

In 1950 Follain published his prose work *Chef-lieu,* a continuation of the autobiographical *Canisy.* Of particular interest in *Chef-lieu* is the scene in which Follain describes the photographing of his mother at the age of thirty, for many of the images and themes that commonly appear throughout Follain's verse are repeated in this single passage: the female as mother or object of sexual desire; the passage of time; the spatial and temporal connectedness of people and things; the unexpected juxtaposition of heterogeneous objects. Moreover, it is appropriate that the young Follain of *Chef-lieu* should be intrigued with the actual photographing of his mother; given his astute attention to the minute details of everyday objects in his verse, his poems themselves frequently resemble photographs.

Following the publication of *Chef-lieu,* Follain decided to leave the bar to practice as a judge magistrate in Charleville in the Ardennes, but he continued nevertheless to reside in Paris. During this period he also traveled extensively: to Spain and Portugal in 1953; to Thailand and Japan in 1956; and to Brazil, Peru, and Bolivia in 1960. His trip to Peru resulted in

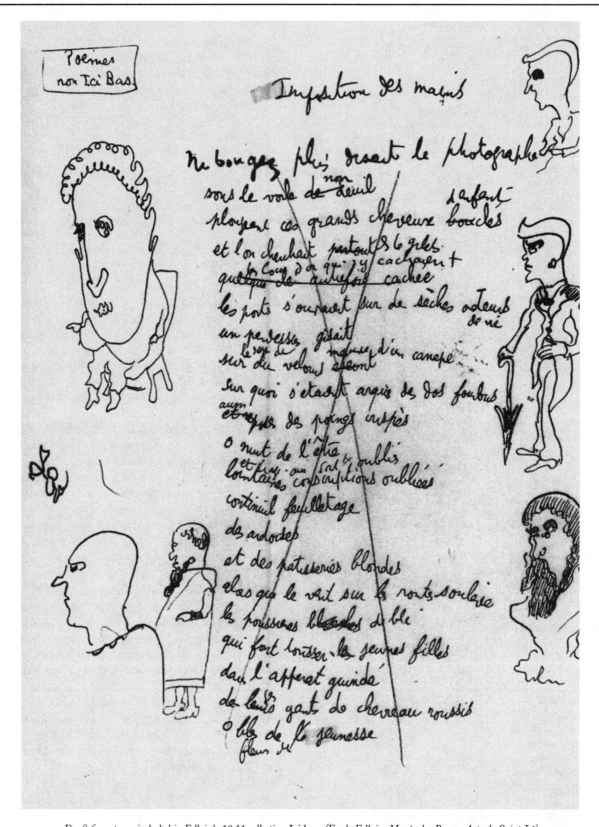

Draft for a poem included in Follain's 1941 collection, Ici-bas *(Fonds Follain, Musée des Beaux-Arts de Saint-Lô)*

the travel book, *Pérou* (1964), with photographs by Jean-Jacques Languepin and Paul Almasy. He also published three new collections of poetry during this period: *Territoires* (Territories) in 1953, *Tout instant* (Every Instant) in 1957, and *Des Heures* (Hours) in 1960. Oddly enough, unlike other contemporary poets such as Paul Claudel, Henri Michaux, and Jean-Claude Renard, who had traveled around the world and were inspired to write about their voyages, none of Follain's travels had any major influence on his poetry; exoticism is absent from his literary production of this period, in which the new poems merely repeat the themes commonly associated with his writing.

Territoires consists of seventy-six poems. Although the expected repertoire of mundane yet significant daily objects is drawn upon in this collection in conjunction with his usual musings on the conditions of women, existence, life, death, and suffering, it is Follain's treatment of time that has been perfected in this collection. In poems such as "Moyen Age" (Middle Ages), "Vie" (Life), "L'Assiette" (The Dish), "Domaine d'homme" (Man's domain), or "La Pomme rouge" (The Red Apple), Follain adroitly focuses on a specific "instant" that has unexpected connections or implications in either the past, present, or future. Perhaps the best example of such an unexpected juxtaposition of apparently unrelated yet suddenly connected objects in all of Follain's body of work occurs in "Les Siècles" (The Centuries), in which the invention of the printing press is signaled in the mark of a horse's hoof:

Follain in 1950

Regardant la marque du sabot
de son cheval de sang
le cavalier dans cette empreinte contournée
où déjà des insectes préparaient leur ouvroir
devina la future imprimerie
puis pour lui demander sa route
il s'approcha du charpentier
qui près d'une rose
en repos contemplait la vallée
et ne lirait jamais de livres.

(Looking at the mark of the hoof
of his thoroughbred horse
the knight in this traced imprint
where insects were already preparing their needlework
glimpsed the future printing press
then in order to ask his way
he approached the carpenter
who next to a rose
contemplated the valley while relaxing
and would never read any book).

With this simple yet powerful image, Follain succeeds in associating several disparate events through an unexpected connection between seemingly unrelated objects. The mark of the horse's hoofprint upon the ground, the carpenter's shaping of wood, and the invention of the printing press are all evoked within a single "instant" whose implications essentially go unnoticed by the main players.

Unlike Follain's earlier collections of poetry, *Tout instant* is a collection of untitled prose poems that is divided into three sections, in which Follain presents and redefines images and themes that the reader is already quite familiar with. In the fourteen poems of the first section, which is titled "Objets" (Objects), items that at first appear to be mundane are actually imbued with great significance (such as broken bowls, dishes, cups, glasses, and pockets filled with forgotten screws, marbles, knives, or handkerchiefs); in the eighteen poems of the second section, titled "Etendues" (Expanses), time and space are either compressed or expanded (as in the second poem, in which centuries, weeks, and the four seasons are all evoked within a ten-square-inch terrain upon which war was once waged and three hundred different species of vegetation have bloomed); in the thirty-seven poems of the third section, "Allées et venues" (Comings and

Follain on the grounds of the Château Cerisy-la-Salle, 1966

remarkably similar to those that preceded it, Follain nevertheless aptly demonstrates the connection of objects and living beings in the present to those of the far-distant past or future, while showing that the duration of an individual's life is short—relatively speaking, of course. Of particular interest are "La Conduite de la bête" (The Behavior of the Beast), in which an animal resembles the thousands of others who have traversed the centuries before her; "Fin de siècle" (End of the Century), in which a child, a fly, and a greedy man live out a New Year's Eve in a city that will continue to exist for the next thousand years; and "Sous des étoiles" (Beneath the Stars), in which the short lives of insects, animals, and men are compared to the eternal existence of the stars. These inconsistencies and intricacies of time and space are meticulously analyzed, as in "Autre temps" (Other Time), in which heterogeneous objects are once again placed in juxtapositions that create surprising connections as well as contradictions:

> Arrière et devant de la maison
> ne s'éclairent pas au même instant
> l'ombre du feuillage clair
> tombe sur un corps
> jusqu'à son dernier jour
> mais peut-être vient le temps
> que le roc seul demeurera
> sous la pluie
> sans que la moindre chair tressaille
> comme dans ce temps des fusillés

> (The back and front of the house
> are not lighted at the same instant
> the shade of the clear foliage
> falls upon a body
> until its last day
> but perhaps the time comes
> when the rock alone will last
> beneath the rain
> without the least bit of flesh quivering
> as in the time of the executed).

Follain resigned his judgeship in 1961 in order to devote more time to travel and writing. He undertook voyages to Hungary in 1962 and 1964, the United States in 1966, the Ivory Coast and Senegal in 1967, and Saint Helena in 1969. During this period he also published two new collections of poetry, *Appareil de la terre* (Apparel of the World) in 1961 and *D'après tout* (After All) in 1967. The poetry in these two volumes retains Follain's usual themes and style, but the poems seem nevertheless to have become more somber. *Appareil de la terre* is divided into three sections; the first two sections consist of poetry in prose, titled "Appareil de la terre" (from a poem in *Des Heures*),

Goings), movement is presented over the course of centuries by means of roads, trains, carriages, planes, and staircases, and in conjunction with man's desire to give meaning to life. The most revealing poems, however, are the first three of the collection, because these best explain the poet's mission as defined by Follain. As he states in the untitled first section of *Tout instant,* an ordinary object can unexpectedly acquire extreme importance: "Il y a un jour où tout à coup j'aperçois cet objet qui, depuis dix ans, était sous mes yeux et qu'en réalité je n'avais jamais véritablement vu" (There comes a day when I suddenly perceive this object that was under my nose for ten years and that I had never truly seen in reality). Once the previously insignificant object reveals itself to the poet, it is then his duty to uncover and explain its hidden essence, as Follain states in the untitled third piece: "La finesse des choses donne sa noblesse à l'univers. Derrière chacune un mot de passe reste caché" (The fineness of things gives its nobility to the universe. Behind each one, a password remains hidden).

Des Heures is a collection of ninety-one poems in which Follain again presents a long inventory of items that allows him to examine the intrinsic implications of time and space. While essentially no new themes are presented in this collection, which remains

which comprises fourteen entries, and "Proses," which comprises twelve entries. The third section, "Poésies," comprises forty-nine entries. Follain's characteristic juxtaposition of physical objects that appear at first to be temporally or spatially unrelated is evident in "Fragment," the first poem of this section:

> Une épaisse chevelure
> jusqu'aux hanches se tord
> le corps qui la possède
> des yeux grands ouverts
> contemple
> l'esprit perdu
> ce fragment du monde
> pour un temps offert
>
> (A thick head of hair
> just to the hips wraps around itself
> the body that possesses it
> with its eyes wide open
> contemplates
> with distracted spirit
> this fragment of the world
> for a moment offered).

So continues Follain's observation of the various objects that populate the world: crows, rain, red meat, signs, flowers, girls, blades of grass, dresses, vases, insects, and so on. And, like the unsuspected murderer who, in "Figure du temps" (Figure of Time), contemplates the body of the woman who serves him as she, in turn, contemplates lush foliage from an open restaurant window, Follain remains detached from the various objects that he observes and imbues with an ability to transcend time and space in their suddenly revealed connectedness. In spite of this detachment, a certain cynicism with regard to human relations is clearly discernible in various poems in which war, massacres, and other violent behaviors are evoked, as in "Saint-Barthélemy," in which murdered children are thrown into the river at the same moment as a wealthy woman contemplates her jewelry, while her pets—"que personne ne tue" (that no one kills)—lie at her feet.

This pessimism is also evident in the eighty-eight poems of *D'après tout;* the first poem, "Le Cri" (The Cry), sets the mood for the entire collection:

> Dans la cité fortifiée
> des quartiers s'abîment
> un homme s'arrête étonné
> d'une voix qui mue
> une à une à l'asile
> il faut laver les folles
> une restant belle s'y prête
> malgré des larmes silencieuses.
> Des chiens s'acharnent
> autour d'un os à lambeaux
> quelqu'un vrainment crie: assez
>
> (In the fortified city
> quarters fall into ruin
> a man stops surprised
> by a pubescent voice that cracks
> one by one at the asylum
> it is necessary to wash the crazy women
> one still beautiful prepares herself
> in spite of silent tears.
> Dogs fight
> over a ragged bone
> someone in vain shouts: enough).

In the somber "univers de fuite" (universe of flight) depicted by Follain in *D'après tout,* the isolation of individuals is stressed: a child's lost voice is heard over the din of a mob; one stays behind to sing in a church as others depart; trapped between "vie et mort" (life and death), a young girl contemplates her naked beauty as another human fears his approaching end; a lonely man walks across a field "comme pour représenter à lui seul / sans vouloir la trahir / toute l'humanité" (as if to represent to himself alone / without desiring to betray it / all humanity). Perhaps man's ultimate inability to adapt to the human condition or societal constraints is best depicted in "Poursuite" (Chase), in which a man is hunted across ruins and through labyrinths (symbols of worldly decay and entrapment created by the hand of man) "car il n'a jamais pu / s'habituer à ce temps" (because he was never able / to grow accustomed to this time).

In June 1970 Follain received the Grand Prix de Poésie de l'Académie Française. This award was followed by the last major collection of his poetry, *Espaces d'instants* (1971), published just days before he lost his life when he was struck by a car on the rue des Tuileries near the Place de la Concorde in Paris on 10 March 1971. The ninety-five poems of this collection show that Follain had perfected his poetry of "concentration"; they are remarkably concise, varying between seven and fifteen lines, yet are shockingly powerful in their imagery. As these poems reveal, Follain was preoccupied with the man-made horrors of the modern world. Cadavers repeatedly appear in poems that depict the atrocities of Napoleonic Wars as well as those of the two World Wars and concentration and prisoner-of-war camps, in which the internees are unaware of time. In this desperate world that always moves "dans son espace" (in its space), in "Le Temps d'un cri" (The Time of a Cry) a child who liked to play with ants dies in 1812 as a "cri de douleur" (cry of pain) pierces the sharp winter wind across the Continent, while in "Sans

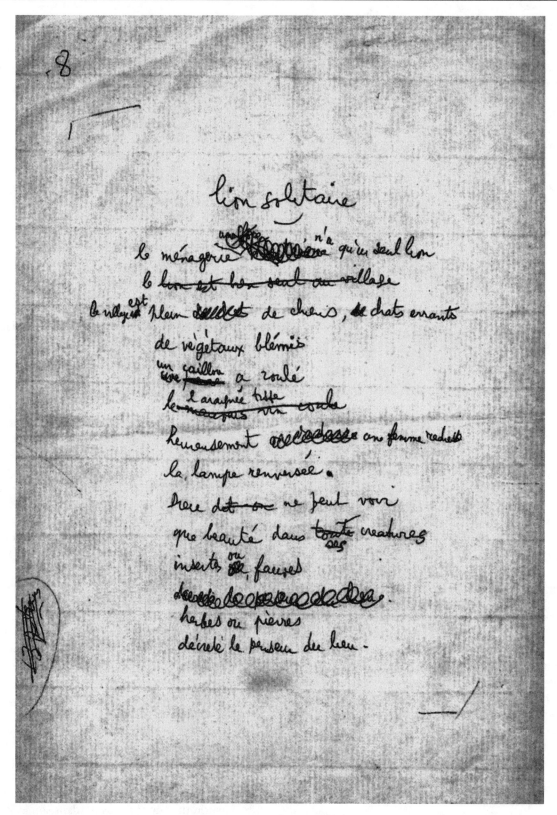

Page from the manuscript for a poem published in the first issue of the review Création *in 1971 (from Arlette Albert-Birot,*
Le Monde de Jean Follain–Lion Solitaire et Autre Poèmes Manuscrits, *1998)*

courage" (Without Courage) "Dieu est mort / l'homme aussi" (God is dead / so is man).

Follain's readership has gradually diminished since his death, and his poetic legacy has been relegated to that of a minor poet. Nevertheless, he was certainly a figure whose talents were appreciated by his contemporaries; shortly after his death, Guillevic qualified Follain as a "un poète majeur" (a major poet), and in his history of modern French literature Pierre de Boisdeffre identifies him as a poet of "une importance exceptionnelle" (an exceptional importance). Although Follain might be generally overlooked today, his contribution to twentieth-century poetry is undeniable. With Guillevic and Frénaud, Follain confirmed that twentieth-century poetry could acquire a certain "réalisme poétique" in which the physical mysteries confronting the senses are given preeminence over metaphysical concerns. As Follain stated, "Plus que personne le vrai poète demeure conscient de réel: *réel matétriel* et *réel du songe*" (More than anyone else, the true poet remains conscious of the real: be it *material reality* or the *reality of the dream*). Twentieth-century French poetry thus returned from the unconscious world of the Surrealists to a preoccupation with conscious man and his place—no matter how distressing—within the physical universe.

Interview:

Serge Gavronsky, "Interview with Jean Follain," in *Poems and Texts: An Anthology of French Poems, Translations, and Interviews with Ponge, Follain, Guillevic, Frénaud, Bonnefoy, DuBouchet, Roche, and Pleynet,* edited by Gavronsky (New York: October House, 1969).

References:

Arlette Albert-Birot, ed., *Le Monde de Jean Follain: Lion solitaire et autres poèmes manuscrits* (Paris: J.-M. Place, 1999);

Pierre de Boisdeffre, *Histoire de la littérature de langue française des années 1930 aux années 1980,* revised edition, volume 2: *Poésie, idées, dictionnaire des auteurs* (Paris: Perrin, 1985);

Les Cahiers bleus: Hommage à Jean Follain, 4 (Spring 1976);

Jean-Yves Debreuille, *Jean Follain: Un Monde peuplé d'attente* (Marseilles: Autre Temps, 1995);

André Dhôtel, *Jean Follain: Une étude,* revised edition, Poètes d'aujourd'hui, no. 49 (Paris: Seghers, 1972);

Serge Gaubert, ed., *Lire Follain* (Lyon: Presses Universitaires de Lyon, 1981);

Eugène Guillevic and Lucie Albertini, *Avec Jean Follain* (Pully: PAP, 1993);

Gil Jouanard, *D'Après Follain* (Montolieu, France: Deyrolle, 1997);

Nouvelle Revue française, 222 (June 1971);

Joseph Rouffanche, *Jean Follain et la passion du temps* (Limoges: Rougerie, 2001);

Françoise Rouffiat, *Jean Follain: Le Même, autrement* (Seyssel: Champ Vallon, 1996);

Sud, special Follain issue (Spring 1979).

Papers:

A substantial collection of Jean Follain's manuscripts, notes, and correspondence is held by the Institut Mémoires de L'Edition Contemporaine, Paris; a smaller archive is housed by the Musée des Beaux-Arts de Saint-Lô.

Max Jacob

(12 July 1876 – 5 March 1944)

David LeHardy Sweet
Columbia University

BOOKS: *L'Histoire du Roi Kaboul Ier et le marmiton Gauwain* (Paris: Pichard & Kahn, 1904);

Saint Matorel, illustrated by Pablo Picasso (Paris: Kahnweiler, 1911); revised and enlarged as *Saint Matorel, roman, suivi des Œuvres burlesques et mystiques du Frère Matorel, mort au convent, et du Siège de Jérusalem, drame céleste* (Paris: Gallimard, 1936);

La Côte: Recueil de chants celtiques (Paris: Max Jacob, 1911; Paris: Crès, 1926);

Les Œuvres burlesques et mystiques de Frère Matorel, mort au couvent, illustrated by André Derain (Paris: Kahnweiler, 1912);

Le Siège de Jérusalem: Grande tentation céleste de Saint Matorel, illustrated by Picasso (Paris: Kahnweiler, 1914);

Les Alliés sont en Arménie (Paris: Imprimerie Artistique C. A. Lembessis, 1916);

Le Cornet à dés (Paris: Max Jacob, 1917; revised and enlarged edition, Paris: Stock, 1922; revised, 1923);

Le Phanérogame (Paris: Max Jacob, 1918);

La Défense de Tartufe: Extases, remords, visions, prières, poèmes et méditations d'un Juif converti (Paris: Société Littéraire de France, 1919; enlarged and annotated edition, Paris: Gallimard, 1929);

Le Cinématoma (Paris: Sirène, 1920; Paris: Gallimard, 1929);

Dos d'Arlequin (Paris: Editions du Sagittaire, 1921);

Le Laboratoire central: Poésies (Paris: Au Sans Pareil, 1921);

Matorel en province: Fragment d'un prologue qui fut enlevé par l'auteur à son roman "Le Terrain Bouchaballe," illustrations by Jules Dépaquit (Paris: Lucien Vogel, 1921);

Le Roi de Béotie (Paris: Editions de la Nouvelle Revue Française, 1921);

Ne coupez pas Mademoiselle; ou, Les Erreurs des P.T.T: Conte philosophique, illustrated with four lithographs by Juan Gris (Paris: Editions de la Galerie Simon, 1921);

Max Jacob

Isabelle et Pantalon: Opéra bouffe en deux actes (Paris: Ménestrel, 1922);

Le Cabinet noir: Lettres avec commentaires (Paris: Librairie de France, 1922; enlarged edition, Paris: Gallimard/Editions de la Nouvelle Revue Française, 1928);

Art poétique (Paris: Emile-Paul, 1922);

Filibuth, ou La Montre en or (Paris: Gallimard, 1922);

Le Terrain Bouchaballe (Paris: Emile-Paul, 1922);

La Couronne de Vulcain: Conte breton, illustrated by Suzanne Roger (Paris: Editions de la Galerie Simon, 1923);

L'Homme de chair et l'homme reflet (Paris: Editions du Sagittaire, 1924);

Visions infernales (Paris: Editions de la Nouvelle Revue Française, 1924);

Les Penitents en maillots roses (Paris: Editions du Sagittaire, 1924);

Le Nom (Liège, Belgium: A la Lampe d'Aladdin, 1926);

Fond de l'eau (Toulouse: Editions de l'Horloge, 1927);

Visions des souffrances et de la mort de Jésus fils de Dieu: Quarante dessins de Max Jacob, Collection Maurice Sachs, no. 1 (Paris: Quatre Chemins, 1928);

Sacrifice impériale (Paris: Emile-Paul, 1929);

Tableau de la bourgeoisie (Paris: Editions de la Nouvelle Revue Française, 1929);

Rivage (Paris: Editions des Cahiers Libres, 1931);

Bourgeois de France et d'ailleurs (Paris: Gallimard, 1932);

Chemin de croix infernal, illustrated by J. M. Prassinos, Repères, no. 13 (Paris: Editions G.L.M., 1936);

Morceaux choisis, edited by Paul Petit (Paris: Gallimard, 1936);

Ballades (Paris: Debresse, 1938);

Derniers poèmes en vers et en prose (Paris: Gallimard, 1945; revised and enlarged, 1961);

Conseils à un jeune poète, suivis de Conseils à un étudiant, introduction by Marcel Béalu (Paris: Gallimard, 1945);

L'Homme de cristal: Poèmes (Paris: Editions de La Table Rond, 1947; revised and enlarged edition, with a preface by Pierre Albert-Birot, Paris: Gallimard, 1967);

Méditations religieuses, edited by Pierre Colle and Maurice Morel, with a preface by Morel (Paris: Gallimard, 1947);

Miroir d'astrologie, by Jacob and Claude Valence (Paris: Gallimard, 1949);

Lettres imaginaires, introduction by Jean Cocteau, Les Cahiers Max Jacob, no. 2 (Paris: Les Amis de Max Jacob, 1952);

Poèmes de Morven le Gaëlique, preface by Julien Lanoë (Paris: Gallimard, 1953);

Théatre I: Un Amour du titien; La Police napolitaine, introduction by Henri Sauguet, Les Cahiers Max Jacob, no. 3 (Paris: Les Amis de Max Jacob, 1953);

Le Cornet à dés, II, introductory note by André Salmon (Paris: Gallimard, 1955);

Romanesques, nouvelles, introduction by François Mauriac, Les Cahiers Max Jacob, no. 4 (Paris: Les Amis de Max Jacob, 1956);

Chroniques d'art, edited by Lawrence A. Joseph (Paris: Lettres modernes, 1987);

L'Echelle de Jacob: Recueil d'inédits, edited by Nicole Cruz and José-Emmanuel Cruz, introduction by Sylvia Lorant-Colle, Collection Pergamine (Paris: Bibliothèque des Arts, 1994);

Editions and Collections: *Le Roi Kaboul Ier et le marmiton Gauwain,* introduction by André Salmon, Les Cahiers Max Jacob, no. 1 (Paris: Les Amis de Max Jacob, 1951);

Ballades (Paris: Nouvelles Editions Debresse, 1954)–includes facsimile of manuscript;

Esthétique de Max Jacob, edited by René Guy Cadou (Paris: Seghers, 1956);

Le Laboratoire central: Poèmes, preface by Yvon Belaval (Paris: Gallimard, 1960);

La Terrain Bouchaballe (Paris: Gallimard, 1964);

La Défense de Tartufe: Extases, remords, visions, prières, poèmes et méditations d'un Juif converti, edited, with an introduction and notes, by André Blanchet (Paris: Gallimard, 1964);

Le Cornet à dés, preface by Michel Leiris (Paris: Gallimard, 1967);

Ballades; suivi de Visions infernales; Fond de l'eau; Sacrifice impérial; Rivage; les Pénitents en maillots roses, preface by Claude Roy (Paris: Gallimard, 1970);

Méditations, edited, with an introduction, by René Plantier (Paris: Gallimard, 1972);

Méditations religieuses: Derniers cahiers 1942–1943, edited, with an introduction, by Henri Sauguet (Quimper: Calligrammes, 1986);

Petite astrologie, introduction by Marcel Béalu (Reims: Le Bibliophile Rémois, 1989);

La Côte: Recueil de chants celtiques, edited, with an introduction, by Pierre Jakez Hélias (Paris: Editions du Layeur, 2001).

Editions in English: *Drawings and Poems by Max Jacob,* edited and translated, with an introduction, by Stanley J. Collier (Leeds: Lotus Press, 1951);

The Dice Cup: Selected Prose Poems, edited, with an introduction, by Michael Brownstein; translated by John Ashbery and others (New York: SUN, 1979)–comprises selections from *Le Cornet à dés* and *Le Cornet à dés, II;*

Double Life and Other Pieces: Thirty Prose Poems From "Le Cornet à dés," translated and introduced by Michael Bullock (London: Oasis, 1988);

Hesitant Fire: Selected Prose of Max Jacob, translated and edited by Moishe Black and Maria Green (Lincoln & London: University of Nebraska Press, 1991);

The Story of King Kabul the First and Gawain the Kitchen-Boy = Histoire du roi Kaboul Ier et du marmiton Gauwain: Followed by Vulcan's Crown = La Couronne de Vulcan, translated by Black and Green (Lincoln: University of Nebraska Press, 1994).

Devout Catholic, converted Jew, homosexual, and a rumored ether addict, Max Jacob seems an unlikely representative of the various avant-garde

Pablo Picasso and Jacob in Montparnasse, 1916

movements with which he has been identified. Although a close friend of Pablo Picasso and Guillaume Apollinaire, as well as such younger writers as Michel Leiris, Jean Cocteau, and Edmond Jabès, whom he encouraged and inspired, Jacob has been accorded only a tangential status in the Orphist, Surrealist, and other postsymbolist movements of the period. His real but eccentric contributions to modernist poetics were eclipsed by those of his contemporaries who assumed the role of modern master with greater facility. Unlike such poets as Apollinaire and Blaise Cendrars, Jacob combined clownish dandyism with deep religious humility in a way that discomfited his avant-garde peers and impeded serious consideration of his achievements. The work itself proved difficult to categorize. His poetic experiments were diverse and far-reaching but also parodic and self-deprecatory. Fellow modernists and their apologists sometimes responded to his writings with condescension, dismissing it as protean or inconsistent. Certain younger writers indebted to Jacob neglected him once they joined the Surrealist movement, whose leader, André Breton, publicly insulted him. Later generations of poets and scholars have been more attentive to Jacob's aesthetics, discovering their own postmodern preoccupations mirrored in his varied accomplishments as a poet, narrator, critic, painter, and mystic. What clearly "situates" Jacob (to borrow a term from his critical lexicon) among the most prominent literary innovators of his day are the early prose poems collected in his *Le Cornet à dés* (The Dice Cup, 1917), a tour de force of "Cubist" poetics, but also indicative of

the aleatory strategies and dream-like juxtapositions the Surrealists later exploited more systematically. At the same time, Jacob also produced a sizable body of religious meditations, satirical prose narratives, and astrological investigations that make similar use of such techniques, intercalating pastiches of popular and specialist discourses in a way that reveals his abiding poetic concerns even in putative acts of religious devotion.

Jacob was born on 12 July 1876, in Quimper, Brittany, the youngest son of Prudence Jacob and Lazare Alexandre, tailors and store owners whose families had moved there from Alsace and Lorraine at the beginning of the nineteenth century. The fifth of six children, Max Jacob grew up in a boisterous middle-class family of freethinking, secularized Jews. Although in most respects he seems to have had a happy childhood, Jacob described himself to his first biographer, Robert Guiette, as sensitive and misunderstood. He suffered from headaches and was sent to a sanatorium in Paris, run by the celebrated doctor Jean-Martin Charcot, with a distinguished clientele. There he encountered something of the beau monde for the first time. Exhilarated by such experiences, he returned to Quimper, where his heretofore mediocre academic performance improved and where he also began drawing and painting. He received high marks in philosophy in the *Concours Générale,* a national examination, in 1894 but remained vulnerable to depression and, by his account to Guiette, attempted suicide three times.

Despite his parents' hope of seeing their son enter the prestigious Ecole Normale to become a civil servant or professor, Jacob enrolled in the Ecole Coloniale, dreaming of faraway countries. The ordeal of military service quickly put an end to such dreams, and, though he earned an additional degree in law, he never took any serious steps to enter the practice. After a false start as a musical accompanist, Jacob, who professed to have no literary pretensions at the time, was introduced to Maurice Méry, director of the *Moniteur des Arts,* who agreed to publish an article the young man had written on the Breton painter Lucien Simon. Jacob pursued a successful career as an art critic, writing under the name of Léon David; his reviews from this period have been collected in *Chroniques d'art,* published in 1987. Although he had been successful, when someone close to him criticized his writing, he quit the review. He resolved, in his own words, as quoted by biographer Pierre Andreu, "d'apprendre à écrire en français" (to learn to write in French) and began a protracted period of odd jobs and almost miserable poverty. At one point he worked at Entrepôt Voltaire, an emporium and stationery store, where he embarked upon a secret love affair with a woman named Cécile. These and other experiences provided material for various short narratives that he later included in his prose works *Saint Matorel* (1911) and *Le Roi de Béotie* (The King of Beotia, 1921). But his first literary endeavor, *L'Histoire du Roi Kaboul Ier et le marmiton Gauwain* (1904; translated as *The Story of King Kabul the First and Gawain the Kitchen-Boy,* 1994), was a social satire in the guise of a children's story about a clever kitchen helper who wins the hand of a princess through his cooking skills, which he wrote for the publishing firm of Picard et Kahn for ƒ 30. He continued in this genre with "Le Géant du soleil"(The Giant of the Sun), written for Librairie Générale, but the publishing house closed in 1904 before the work ever appeared in print; he later reworked this material as *Le Phanérogame,* a novel published in 1918.

At about the same time as he was undertaking these first literary endeavors, Jacob befriended Picasso, whose works he first admired at the Ambrose Vollard gallery in 1901 during his stint as an art critic. Although Picasso could barely speak French and Jacob no Spanish at all, the two soon became inseparable, even living together for a while in Jacob's room on the boulevard Voltaire. Picasso relocated to Montmartre, with Jacob eventually following him, and thus began the legendary epoch of the Bateau-Lavoir, an oddly shaped building on the rue Ravignan that housed, at different times, some of the most important modernist painters and poets, including Picasso, Juan Gris, and Pierre Reverdy. Picassso also introduced Jacob to Apollinaire shortly after himself meeting the poet, and the three developed a vibrant friendship that helped determine the course of modern poetry and painting for years to come.

In a letter to Tristan Tzara many years later, Jacob revealed that he had begun to see himself as a poet only in 1905. Although many of his friends and acquaintances knew he wrote poetry at that time, few were given the chance to read it except Picasso, who declared, Guiette reports, "Tu es le seul poète de l'époque" (you alone are the poet of the age). As hundreds of poems accumulated in a trunk he kept beneath his bed, Jacob drew them out for others to read, but only with the greatest, albeit feigned, reluctance. He steadfastly resisted publication for years, except once when he was persuaded by the poet André Salmon to let him publish a few poems in *Lettres Modernes.* Although generous in giving advice to others on their writing and in expounding his poetic theories, Jacob's hesitation about publishing his own writing later proved detrimental to his literary reputation, as formal discoveries he had made years before emerged in the work of others who did not hesitate to lay claim to them.

Meanwhile, Jacob and Apollinaire began competing in different ways to discover the principles of a truly modernist poetics, which endeavor, in their view, required jettisoning certain qualities of verbal abstrac-

tion and esoteric allusiveness that typified the late symbolist poetry then current. "Encore trop symboliste" (again too symbolist) was Jacob's critical refrain whenever he judged his friend's work to have lapsed into old literary habits. For his part, Apollinaire clearly recognized Jacob's less encumbered modernist sensibility, but responded negatively to the latter's capacity for pastiche, as when Jacob produced his mock-Celtic collection, *La Côte: Recueil de chants celtiques* (The Coast: Collection of Celtic Songs, 1911). Nonetheless, at a conference at the Salon des Artistes indépendants in 1908, where he launched his *Phalange Nouvelle* movement in poetry, Apollinaire generously accorded Jacob high honors as a distinct new talent, as Andreu reports: "La renomée viendra bientôt prendre Max Jacob dans sa rue Ravignan. C'est le poéte le plus simple qui soit et il paraît souvent comme le plus étrange. Cette contradiction s'expliquera aisément lorsque j'aurai dit que le lyrisme de Max Jacob est armé d'un style délicieus, tranchant, rapide, billament et souvent tendrement humoristique" (Renown will soon come to Max Jacob in his rue Ravignan. He is the most simple of poets, and yet he often seems the most bizarre. This contradiction will be easily explained when I will have said that the lyricism of Max Jacob is fortified with a style that is delightful, trenchant, quick, brilliant, and often tenderly humorous).

Shortly after Apollinaire's lecture, Jacob applied himself, as he writes in his brief history of *Le Cornet à dés,* included in the 1943 edition of that volume, "à saisir en moi, de toutes manières, les données de l'inconscient: mots en liberté, associations hasadeuses des idées, rêves de la nuit et du jour, hallucinations" (to seize from within, and by all means, the data of the unconscious: liberated words, free association of ideas, day and night dreams, hallucinations), long before these practices had been codified as either Futurist, Dadaist, or Surrealist procedures. The product of this struggle was his most important work, *Le Cornet à dés.* Although Jacob had already published various short stories, burlesque pieces, celestial dramas, and humorous parodies, his best work did not emerge until 1917, after he finally agreed to assemble the curious prose poems he had been composing for years in his little room in Montmartre. But in the interval, Jacob's overall output was prodigious, including the picaresque, hybrid novel *Saint Matorel* and other works such as *La Côte; Les Œuvres burlesques et mystiques de Frère Matorel, mort au couvent* (The Burlesque and Mystical Works of Brother Matorel, Dead in the Convent, 1912); and *Le Siège de Jérusalem: Grande tentation céleste de Saint Matorel* (The Siege of Jerusalem: Great Celestial Temptation of Saint Matorel, 1914), all of which included elements of verse that anticipated *Le Cornet à dés.*

As the title itself suggests, *Le Cornet à dés* represents a series of verbal tosses from the dice cup of the poet's imagination. Yet, unlike the grand experimental opus of Stéphane Mallarmé to which the title alludes– *Un coup de dès jamais n'abolira le hazard* (A Throw of the Dice Will Never Abolish Chance, 1897)–Jacob's prose poems have the cumulative effect of repeated, finite wagers in which something perhaps more intimate than a symbolist universe of ideas is at stake. Each poem seems to protest its own inadequacy, to call attention to itself as some strangely dwarfed endeavor to surmount the absurdly outsized obstacles to lyric communication in the modern era. They are vignettes of their own misadventures that lead one nowhere but a place of puzzled wonder. Often beginning as a kind of anecdote or pastiche of a particular poetic genre–such as "Poème déclamatoire" (Declamatory Poem), "Poème de la lune" (Poem to the Moon), and "Fable sans moralité" (Amoral Fable)–Jacob's narratives quickly succumb to a sense of verbal play that is distinctly his own. Chance intrudes upon the task of poetic construction in a way that deftly unsettles ordinary communication to invest each effort with qualities of novelty, surprise, humor, and unexpected poignancy. In this way the poems both exemplify and curiously deviate from Cubist notions of aesthetic construction and semiotic play.

Jacob's interest in contemporary art theory and its transposition to literary media is indicated in such titles as "Cubisme et soleil noyés" (Cubism and Drowned Sun), "Le Fond du tableau" (The Picture Ground), and "De la peinture avant toute chose" (Painting First), as well as an untitled poem that once bore the title "Poème simultané avec superposition simple" (Simultaneous Poem With Simple Superimposition) in apparent anticipation of futurist discourse. Many of the poems seem to be informed by a general notion of thwarting traditional, illusory perspectives and their referents in favor of the artificiality of art. Reader expectations based on the titles of the poems or initial narrative procedures are regularly rerouted by way of the most tenuous verbal ambiguities, much as the visual components of Cubist paintings seem to oscillate between perspectival appearance and material surface. A fairly representative example of this rerouting can be seen in "Poème," a dream narrative about passengers on a boat near an island in the Indian Ocean, who find themselves without a map. They go ashore in search of one, climbing a high cliff and hoping the "petits nègres avec des chapeaux melons" (little Negroes with bowler hats) will have some charts. What begins as a third-person narrative suddenly shifts into the first person, culminating in the speaker's arrival at the top of the cliff, only to be directed by his companion, who is strangely both a native and his brother, to "Fais le tour" (Go round, or

double back). He then discovers that everything has disappeared: "Il n'y a plus ni étages, ni passagères, ni bateau, ni petit nègre; il y a le tour qu'il faut faire. Quel tour? C'est décourageant" (There are no more floors, nor passengers, nor boat, nor little Negro; there is a round to do. What round? It's frustrating). The linear narrative has suddenly become a circular one for which there is no map of narrative elements, as it were. The perspective has changed, leaving both author and reader stranded between narrative strategies. In this shift of perspective the poem is not unlike Apollinaire's "Les Fenêtres" ("Windows"), in his *Calligrammes, poèmes de la paix et de la guerre, 1913–1916* (1918; translated as *Calligrammes, Poems of Peace and War [1913–1916]*, 1980), in which "Les Tours ce sont les rues / Puits / Puits ce sont les places" (The towers are roads / Pits / Pits are squares), with vertical objects becoming flat ones that might be found on a map. But Jacob's experiment also takes place in a realm of dreams, the dreamer of which seems distinctly Jacobian: anxious, insecure, slightly ridiculous but strangely endearing.

In this last respect it also helps to see the different poems as acts of simultaneous self-concealment and disclosure. A cast of workers, artists, moralists, theatergoers, and flaneurs people these poems that function as windows onto the urban milieu the poet inhabits. But in many ways these urban types reflect Jacob's own variegated persona, his many encounters on the fringes of Parisian society. Thus, a poem such as "La Rue Ravignan" discreetly enacts an almost magical transference of identity between the poet and the urban populace, described as a sort of feedback flow of people performing their daily rituals and tasks: "Vous tous, passants de la rue Ravignan, je vous ai donné les noms des défunts de l'Histoire!" (All of you, passers-by of Ravignan street, I have given you the names of History's departed!). In this way heroes of history and myth (as well as more mundane historical personages) reappear as Jacob's neighbors, including Ulysses as a milkman and Castor and Pollux as two women of the fifth *arrondissement* (district). But Jacob saves his most glowing tribute for the mendicant ragpicker who comes during the night to rummage through the day's debris like some oneiric sorter of dreamstuffs. Jacob bestows on him the almost sacred name of Dostoevsky. It is the poet's right to confer such literary titles, and yet one can also recognize Jacob's own affinities with both the ragpicker and the novelist Fyodor Dostoevsky, as if some mystic barter in disposable goods was being undertaken between beggar, poet, and literary forerunner on the edges of society and time.

But Jacob's affinities go beyond those he shared with certain contemporaries and precursors. On 22 September 1909, Jacob experienced a life-changing event.

He had a vision that he attributed to the grace of Jesus Christ, as he later describes it in *La Défense de Tartufe: Extases, remords, visions, prières, poèmes et méditations d'un Juif converti* (The Defense of Tartufe: Ecstasies, Remorse, Prayers, Poems and Meditations of a Converted Jew, 1919), which is, as the subtitle indicates, a tearful and ecstatic collection of poems, prayers, and meditations pertaining to his conversion: "j'ai relevé la tête, il y avait quelqu'un sur le mur! . . . Il y avait quelqu'un sur la tapisserie rouge. Ma chair est tombée par terre! J'ai été déshabilleé par la foudre! Oh! Impérissible seconde! Oh! vérité! vérité! Larmes de la vérité! Joie de la vérité! Inoubliable vérité! Le Corps Céleste est sur le mur de la pauvre chambre! Pourquoi, Seigneur?" (I lifted my head and there was someone on the wall! . . . There was someone on the red tapestry. My flesh fell down. I was stripped by lightning. O eternal moment! O truth! truth! tears of truth! joy of truth! unforgettable truth! The heavenly host is on the wall of my poor room! Why me, Lord?). The vision, however, did not come without some preparation on the part of Jacob, who had been assiduously studying astrology, the occult, and the kabbala for many years—even taking drugs to conjure forth demonic images (though he denied ever using ether, at least before his first vision). Although the sincerity of his conversion cannot be questioned, many of his contemporaries did so. Jacob was seen as someone who would do almost anything for a laugh, and this impression did not change, especially insofar as his writing and public behavior remained largely unaffected by his newfound faith. The Catholic Church was also suspicious, albeit primarily because of his Jewish origins, and refused to baptize him. After years of frustrated effort and a second vision in December 1914 (which appeared on a cinema screen), Jacob was directed to Notre-Dame-de-Sion, whose priests specialized in converting Jews. He was finally baptized in 1915, with Picasso acting as godfather, and took the baptismal name of Cyprien.

Throughout the war years Jacob deplored his condition as a sinner and "sodomite sans joie" (joyless sodomite), as he had previously written in *Saint Matorel*. Nonetheless, certain developments greatly improved his material and literary standing. Jacob's poetry had by now appeared in Apollinaire's *Soirées de Paris;* he was a primary collaborator with Reverdy on the review *Nord-Sud;* and he became a regular contributor to Pierre Albert-Birot's *Sic* and, later on, to *Littérature* (that is, before the poets who later founded Surrealism pilloried him in a 1920 literary survey). Furthermore, the gouaches he had been producing for years began to provide a regular, if modest, income. Eventually, the collector Jacques Doucet began purchasing Jacob's manuscripts and urged him to publish *Le Cornet à dés,*

the anticipated appearance of which finally brought Jacob some of the attention Apollinaire seemed to promise long ago. Jacob was also producing a sizable body of prose work, including the novels *Le Terrain Bouchaballe* (The Bouchaballe Property) and *Filibuth, ou La Montre en or* (Filibuth, or The Gold Watch), both published in 1922, and his fragmentary, astrological "memoirs," *Le Cinématoma* (1920). Most importantly, he assembled another collection of poems, *Le Laboratoire central* (The Central Laboratory, 1921), perhaps his most significant work published after *Le Cornet à dés* (though much of it was composed at the same time as was that work). Unlike his other poems, the poems of *Le Laboratoire central* are mostly written in a supple, syncopated verse, usually free but often rhymed. They follow rhythms that elude the metronome, and indeed, according to Yvon Belaval, who wrote the preface for the 1960 edition, "le rhythme fait battre la pensée" (the rhythm makes the thought go faster). But much of the poetics of *Le Cornet à dés* remain operative in *Le Laboratoire central,* as in the famous line "Dahlia, dahlia, que Delila lia" (Dahlia, dahlia, that Delilah tied) with its alliterative rhythms generating novel and surprising configurations of the word.

By this stage of his career Jacob was a middle-aged man and mature poet. He decided, at the urging once again of Doucet, to elaborate his own poetics in a work that was published as *Art poétique* (Poetic Art, 1922). In this book he describes the aims of the modern prose poet: "On n'y es préoccupé que du poème lui-même, c'est-à-dire de l'acccord des mots, des images et de leur appel mutuel et constant" (We are no longer concerned with anything but the poem itself, that is, the interrelations among words and images and their mutual and constant appeal). But these ideas clearly correspond to strategies already employed in *Le Cornet à dés,* where the main outlines of his poetics were presented in his preface of 1916. There Jacob describes two basic principles at work in literature: style and situation. He distinguishes his notion of style from that of Georges Louis Leclerc, the comte de Buffon, who famously remarked in his *Discours sur le style* (Discourse on Style, 1753), that "Le style est l'homme même" (the style is the man). But for Jacob, style is more than the language that an individual uses: "Le style est la volonté de s'extérioriser par les moyens choisis" (style is the will to externalize the self by selected means). It has to do with the individual will and its choice of means, elements drawn from the resources of language but finally going beyond it as an ensemble. As Jacob concedes, the theory is essentially classical. But unlike inherited language or the adherence to tradition, style takes risks by confronting life, by expressing a poet's real vitality (regardless of the particular subject or

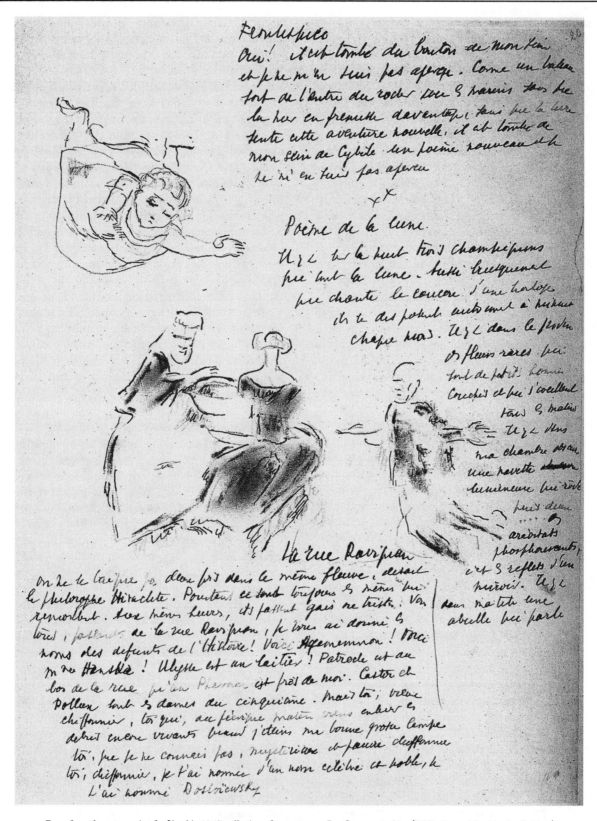

Page from the manuscript for Jacob's 1917 collection of prose poems, Le Cornet à dés *(Bibliothèque Municipale, Orléans)*

mood described). Style, then, is the same as art; it has a distinct effect on the reader or viewer, who is attracted by it and thus "distracted" from the mere subject matter of the work. It is a question of form, the quality of closure or constructedness. This question raises the issue of what is meant by "situation." Situation has to do with aesthetic emotions, the distinctive affect a work has on the one who approaches or engages it. It is a quality of distance, otherness, not unlike Walter Benjamin's idea of "aura," but described without critical disparagement. In his later work and in letters to friends, Jacob identifies it as a special atmosphere or margin between the reader and the work, a product, it would seem, of a mutual preparedness.

Despite the moderate success he was enjoying at this time, or perhaps because of it, Jacob's spirit was in turmoil. Worse than his increasing neglect by a new generation of poets and his miserable convalescence in a municipal hospital after being hit by a car at the Place Pigalle, Jacob feared for his soul on account of what he considered his sinful life. It was a fear, however, that he treated with something akin to humor in "Méditation sur ma mort" (Meditation on My Death), in *La Défense de Tartufe:* "Gourmand. Susceptible. Orgueilleux. Joyeux à l'excès. Triste sans raison, maussade, méprisant, capricieux, bavard, présomptueux, cupide sinon avare, avide de louanges, comédien, amoureux, amoureux, amoureux, amoureux, accessible au vice" (Gluttonous. Sensitive. Arrogant. Excessively happy. Unreasonably sad, morose, contemptuous, capricious, loquacious, presumptuous, greedy if not miserly, eager for praise, comedian, amorous, amorous, amorous, amorous, inclined to vice). In 1921, with the help of a friend, he was placed in a monastery, Saint-Benoît-sur-Loire, outside of Paris. There he remained, with few interruptions, for seven years, free of the distractions of the "poisoned" city. Nevertheless, Jacob frequently received visitors, some of whom raised eyebrows among the other residents. Jacob, however, transformed his writing into a kind of meditation and thus completed several novels, libretti, and books of poetry, including *Le Terrain Bouchaballe, Filibuth,* and *Le Roi de Béotie;* the opera-buffo *Isabelle et Pantalon* (1922); *Le Cabinet noir: Lettres avec commentaires* (The Black Cabinet: Letters with Commentaries, 1922), a collection of fictional letters with astrological commentaries; the moralizing novel *L'homme de chair et l'homme reflet* (The Man of Flesh and the Man of Reflection, 1924); and his *Visions infernales* (Infernal Visions, 1924), which biographer Andreu describes as Jacob's Christian *Le Cornet à dés,* underappreciated but "dramatiquement inspiré" (dramatically inspired). Dedicated to Reverdy, who had also converted to Catholicism, this collection of short prose poems is narrated from the perspective of the sinner who strives to overcome his demons, reminding himself all along of the many errors one can make even on the path to goodness. The collection was later combined with several other books of poetry in verse, including *Les Pénitents en maillots roses* (The Penitents in Pink Tights, 1925), *Fond de l'eau* (Bottom of the Water, 1927), *Rivage* (Coast, 1931) and other newer poems, to create the collection *Ballades* published by René Debresse in 1938. Jacob also wrote pseudonymous poems—most under the name "Morven le Gaëlique"—in the Celtic vein of *La Côte* that were later assembled by Gallimard under the title *Poèmes de Morven le Gaëlique* (1953).

Jacob's effort to lead a pure life according to the Catholic faith ended in 1928 when he returned to Paris and took up residence in the comfortable Hotel Nollet, which housed many young poets and musicians. The period began almost gloriously with the publication of his latest works, the continuing sale of his drawings and gouaches, a series of review issues entirely devoted to his life and work, and the acquisition of many new, young friends in apparent awe of his genius. He was even named a Chevalier de la Légion d'Honneur, in 1932. According to Guiette, this period was one of both frivolity and profundity: "Tout se mettait à vivre par l'imagination, dans un climat d'agilité, de gaîté, d'effervescence, d'humour, de jeu, d'hyperbole . . ." (Imagination brought everything to life in a climate of virtuosity, gaiety, effervescence, humor, play, hyperbole . . .). But Jacob soon abandoned himself, as he saw it, to his vices, certain of which were rudely divulged in 1935 in a book by one of the aging poet's young friends, Maurice Sachs. In it, the author caricatured Jacob's mixed devotion to religion, poetry, and pederasty. Furthermore, his love affair with another poet had gone sour. By 1936 the contradictions of Jacob's life had made Paris, once again, a moral hell for him, and he finally returned, this time for good, to Saint-Benoît-sur-Loire.

Jacob was not particularly welcomed upon his return but was given a modest lean-to in a courtyard that opened onto the garage of the presbytery, not unlike his meager dwellings twenty-five years before in Montmartre. He was so miserable at one point, he bitterly complained of his fate as a writer and artist in a letter to a friend, quoted by Andreu: ". . . avoir tant souffert pour rien pour rien rien rien rien! Que servir de marchepied aux autres!" (To have suffered so much for nothing, for nothing nothing nothing! But to serve as the doormat of others!). Other developments, however, eased his sense of increasing obscurity. A new, enlarged edition of *Saint Matorel* and his *Morceaux choisis* (Selected Pieces) were published in 1936. He participated in several literary conferences, including one in Paris during which he delivered his famous definition:

Jacob painting, 1930 (photograph by Louis Silvestre)

"La poésie, c'est du rêve inventé" (Poetry is invented dream). But most of all, he continued writing, primarily religious meditations (published posthumously) but also maintaining a vast correspondence, through which he cultivated several new friendships with people such as Michel Manoll and Marcel Béalu. This new network of friends later helped him survive the early years of the German occupation, when it became dangerous for Jacob to move about. Another of his new correspondents was Jacques Evrard, a shy, seventeen-year-old poet. Jacob developed a large body of literary aphorisms and advice for Evrard that he gradually combined with other such writings originally included in letters to friends, to assemble his last two works on the art of poetry, *Conseils à un jeune poète,* (translated as *Advice to a Young Poet,* 1976) and *Conseils à un étudiant* (translated as *Advice to a Student,* 1996), published together as *Conseils à un jeune poète suivis de Conseils à un étudiant* in 1945. His primary counsel pertained to the cultivation of "la vie intérieure" (the interior life). Jacob's premise was that if poetry had to do with self-exteriorization, as he had proclaimed in his *Art poétique,* a poet had to have a rich inner or spiritual life before it could be externalized. But while the first of these treatises is characterized by Jacob's fundamental human sympathy for youth, he

increasingly incorporates the lessons of conventional religion in the second, which lapses into tedious sermonizing, with warnings against dining in the city, going to the cinema, even against reading novels. But as Jacob cleaved to his faith, he also grappled with his own erotic disappointment, as evidenced in his final works, particularly *L'Homme de cristal* (The Man of Crystal, 1947), in which sexual desire is poetically transfigured into spiritual love through the crystalline agency of Christian doctrine.

After the collapse of the French army in 1940, at the outset of World War II, and the subsequent German occupation of northern France, Jacob turned to religion with a fervor and desperation that only the terror of divine judgment could inspire. He saw the horror of World War II and even the Holocaust as a form of judgment not only for his own sins but also those he attributed to his countrymen and race. In many of the Last Judgment poems included in his posthumously published *Méditations réligieuses* (Religious Meditations, 1947), however, Jacob begins to identify with the sufferings of his race as a collective sacrifice that mysteriously promises future redemption. His faith could not be wrong, and it remained his abiding consolation in times of increasing hardship and fear, as he was forced to wear a yellow Star of David. Although he was probably spared for a time because of his many influential friends, this protection did not extend to other members of his family, several of whom disappeared into the death camps. His turn came 24 February 1944, when he was suddenly arrested by the Nazis and sent to the Drancy transit camp to await deportation to Auschwitz. A desperate, vigorous effort was made by his friends, particularly Cocteau, to secure his release. The one person whose prestige was such that a few words would have sufficed to release the poet in time failed to assist Jacob when he most needed support. When asked, Picasso simply responded (according to the account given in Andreu's biography), "Ça n'est pas la peine de faire quoi que ce soit. Max est un ange. Il n'a pas besoin de nous pour s'envoler de sa prison" (It's not worth doing anything. Max is an angel. He doesn't need us to escape his prison). By the time release orders were secured, Max Jacob had already died (on 5 March 1944) in the Drancy infirmary of bronchial pneumonia, which he probably caught, frail as he was at sixty-seven years of age, on the night of his arrest. He was buried in a cemetery at Ivry, but his body was exhumed in 1949 to be reinterred at Saint-Benoît.

Letters:

Lettres à Edmond Jabès (Alexandria, Egypt: Editions du Scarabée, 1945);

Lettres inédites du poète à Guillaume Apollinaire (Paris: Seghers, 1946);

Choix de lettres de Max Jacob à Jean Cocteau, 1919–1944 (Paris: Paul Morihien, 1949);

Lettres à un ami, correspondance 1922–1937 avec Jean Grenier, introduction by Jean Grenier (Paris, Lausanne & Basle: Vineta, 1951);

Lettres à Bernard Esdras-Gosse (Paris: Seghers, 1953);

Max Jacob: Correspondance, edited by François Garnier, 2 volumes (Paris: Editions de Paris, 1953–1955)–comprises volume 1, *Quimper–Paris, 1876–1921* (1953) and volume 2, *Saint-Benoît-sur-Loire, 1921–1924* (1955);

Lettres aux Salacrou (août 1923–janvier 1926) (Paris: Gallimard, 1957);

Jacob and Marcel Béalu, *Lettres à Marcel Béalu: Précédées de Dernier visage de Max Jacob* (Lyon: E. Vitte, 1959);

Lettres (1920–1941), edited by Stanley J. Collier (Oxford: Blackwell, 1966);

Jacob and Michel Levanti, *Lettres à Michel Levanti; suivis des Poèmes de Michel Levanti,* edited by Lawrence A. Joseph (Limoges: Rougerie, 1975);

Lettres à René Villard, preface and notes by Yannick Pelletier (Mortemart: Rougerie, 1978);

Lettres à Marcel Jouhandeau: Avec quelques lettres à Mme Marcel Jouhandeau et à Mme Paul Jouhandeau, edited, with an introduction and notes, by Anne Spofford Kimball (Geneva: Droz, 1979);

Jacob and Salomon Reinach, *Lettres à Liane de Pougy,* preface by Jean Chalon and introduction by Paul Bernard (Paris: Plon, 1980);

Lettres à René Rimbert, edited, with notes, by Christine Van Rogger Andréucci and Maria Green (Mortemart: Rougerie, 1983);

Lettres mystiques: 1934–1944, à Clotilde Bauguion (Quimper: Calligrammes, 1984);

Lettres à Michel Manoll, preface by Michel Manoll, edited, with notes, by Green (Mortemart: Rougerie, 1985);

Lettres à Pierre Minet, edited, with an introduction and notes, by Kimball (Quimper: Calligrammes, 1988);

Max Jacob: Lettres à Nino Franck, edited by Kimball (New York: Peter Lang, 1989);

Les Propos et les jours: Lettres 1904–1944, edited by Annie Marcoux and Didier Gompel-Netter (Saint-Léger-Vauban: Zodiaque, 1989);

Lettres à Florent Fels, edited, with notes, by Green (Mortemart: Rougerie, 1990);

Lettres à Roger Toulouse: 1937–1944, edited, with notes, by Patricia Sustrac and Van Rogger Andreucci (Troyes: Librairie Bleue, 1992);

Jacob and Jacques Evrard, *Correspondance entre Max Jacob et un jeune poète: Trois lettres inédites,* introduction by José de Naudor (Sèvres: J. Evrard, 1993);

L'Amitié: Lettres à Charles Goldblatt, edited by André Roumieux (Bègles: Le Castor Astral, 1994);

Jacob and Robert Levesque, *Une Amitié de Max Jacob: Lettres de Max Jacob à Robert Levesque; suivies de Dernière visite à Max Jacob de Robert Levesque,* edited, with commentary and notes, by Pierre Masson (Mortemart: Rougerie, 1994);

Lettres à André Level, edited, with an introduction and notes, by Bernard Duchatelet (Quimper: Bibliothèque Municipale / Brest: Centre d'Etude des Correspondances, Faculté des Lettres, 1994);

Lettres à Jean Colle: 1923–1943, edited by Sylvia Colle-Lorant, notes by Maurice Dirou, and afterword by Lucien Colle (Douarnenez: Mémoire de la Ville, 1996);

Jacob and Jacques Maritain, *Correspondance: 1924–1935,* edited, with an introduction and notes, by Sylvain Guéna (Brest: Centre d'Etude des Correspondances, 1999);

Jacob and Jean Cocteau, *Correspondance: 1917–1944,* edited, with an introduction and notes, by Kimball (Paris: Paris-Méditerranée / Ripon, Québec: Ecrits des Hautes-Terres, 2000);

Lettres à Michel Leiris, edited, with an introduction and notes, by Van Rogger Andréucci (Paris: H. Champion, 2001).

Bibliographies:

Judith Morganroth Schneider and Sydney Lévy, "Max Jacob," in *A Critical Bibliography of French Literature,* volume 6, *The Twentieth Century,* edited by Douglas W. Alden and Richard A. Brooks, part 2, *Principally Poetry, Theater, and Criticism before 1940, and Essay* (Syracuse, N.Y.: Syracuse University Press, 1980), pp. 807–817;

Maria Green, *Bibliographie et documentation sur Max Jacob* (Paris: Association des Amis de Max Jacob, 1988);

Green and Christine Van Rogger Andreucci, eds., *Bibliographie des poèmes de Max Jacob parus en revue* (Saint-Etienne: Publications de l'Université de Saint-Etienne, 1992).

Biographies:

Robert Guiette, *La Vie de Max Jacob* (Paris: A. G. Nizet, 1976);

André Peyre, *Max Jacob quotidien* (Paris: José Millas-Martin, 1976);

Pierre Andreu, *Vie et Mort de Max Jacob* (Paris: La Table Ronde, 1982);

Alain Le Grand-Vélin, ed., *Max Jacob et Quimper* (Quimper: Calligrammes, 1984);

Pierre Jakez Hélias, *Le Piéton de Quimper: Esquisse de Max Jacob* (Paris: Editions de Fallois, 1994).

References:

Georges Auric, *Max Jacob retrouvé* (Paris: Firmin-Didot, 1949);

Marcel Béalu, *Dernier visage de Max Jacob,* enlarged edition, edited, with a preface, by André Salmon (Quimper: Calligrammes, 1994);

Yvon Belaval, "Poèmes d'aujourd'hui," in his *La Recherche de la poésie* (Paris: Gallimard, 1947);

Belaval, *La Rencontre avec Max Jacob* (Paris: Charlot, 1946);

André Billy, "Apollinaire et Max Jacob," *Figaro littéraire* (29 January 1938);

Billy, *Max Jacob,* Poètes d'Aujourd'hui, no. 3 (Paris: Seghers, 1945);

Gabriel Bournoure, "La Poésie de Max Jacob," *Nouvelle Revue française,* 250 (1 July 1934), pp. 109–118;

Leroy Breunig, "Max Jacob et Picasso," *Mercure de France,* 331 (September–December 1957): 581–596;

René Cadou, *Esthétique de Max Jacob* (Paris: Seghers, 1956);

Hubert Fabureau, *Max Jacob: Son œuvre,* Célébrités contemporaines, third series no. 3 (Paris: Editions de la Nouvelle Revue Critique, 1935);

Renée Riese Hubert, "Max Jacob: The Poetics of *Le Cornet à dés,*" in *About French Poetry from Dada to "Tel Quel": Text and Theory,* edited by Mary Ann Caws (Detroit: Wayne State University Press, 1974), pp. 99–111;

Gerald Kamber, *Max Jacob and the Poetics of Cubism* (Baltimore & London: Johns Hopkins University Press, 1971);

Sydney Lévy, *The Play of the Text: Max Jacob's "Le Cornet à dés,"* (Madison: University of Wisconsin Press, 1981)–includes selected translations by Judith Morganroth Schneider;

Neal Oxenhandler, *Looking for Heroes in Postwar France: Albert Camus, Max Jacob, Simone Weil* (Hanover, N. H.: Dartmouth College/University Press of New England, 1996);

René Plantier, *Max Jacob,* Les Ecrivains devant Dieu, no. 32 (Paris: Desclée de Brouwer, 1972);

Plantier, *L'Univers poétique de Max Jacob* (Paris: Klincksieck, 1976);

Christine van Rogger Andréucci, *Max Jacob: Acrobate absolu* (Seyssel: Champ Vallon, 1993);

Jean Rousselot, *Max Jacob au sérieux* (Rodez: Subervie, 1958);

Schneider, *Clown at the Altar: The Religious Poetry of Max Jacob* (Chapel Hill: University of North Carolina Press, 1978);

Annette Thau, *Poetry and Anti-Poetry: A Study of Selected Aspects of Max Jacob's Poetic Style* (Chapel Hill: University of North Carolina Press, 1976).

Alfred Jarry

(8 September 1873 – 1 November 1907)

James Bunzli

and

Rhona Justice-Malloy
Central Michigan University

See also the Jarry entry in *DLB 192: French Dramatists, 1789–1914.*

BOOKS: *Les Minutes de sable mémorial* (Paris: Mercure de France, 1894);

César-Antechrist (Paris: Mercure de France, 1895); translated by James H. Bierman as *Caesar Antichrist* (Tucson, Ariz.: Omen Press, 1971);

Ubu Roi (Paris: Mercure de France, 1896); translated, with a preface, by Barbara Wright as *Ubu Roi: Drama in 5 Acts* (London: Gaberbocchus Press, 1951);

Les Jours et les Nuits, roman d'un déserteur (Paris: Mercure de France, 1897); translated by Alexis Lykiard as *Days and Nights: Novel of a Deserter* (London: Atlas Press, 1989);

L'Amour en visites (Paris: Pierre Fort, 1898); translated by Iain White as *Visits of Love,* introduction by Alastair Brotchie (London: Atlas Press, 1993);

Almanach du Pére Ubu, illustré, lithographs by Pierre Bonnard (Paris: Privately printed, 1899);

L'Amour absolu (Paris: Mercure de France, 1899);

Ubu Enchaîné, précédé de Ubu Roi (Paris: Editions de la Revue Blanche, 1900);

Almanach illustré du Père Ubu (XXᵉ Siècle), lithographs by Bonnard (Paris: Ambroise Vollard, 1901);

Messaline, roman de l'ancienne Rome (Paris: Editions de la Revue Blanche, 1901); translated by Louis Coleman as *The Garden of Priapus,* introduction and notes by Matthew Josephson (New York: Privately printed for subscribers at Coventry House, 1932);

Le Surmâle, roman moderne (Paris: Editions de la Revue Blanche, 1902); translated by Wright as *The Supermale: A Modern Novel* (London: Cape, 1968);

Par la taille: Un Acte comique et moral en prose et en vers, pour esjouir grands et petits (Paris: Sansot, 1906); trans-

Alfred Jarry, 1896 (photograph by Nadar)

lated by Emylou Spears de Alvarez as "Measuring Up!" in *Lawrence, Jarry, Zukovsky: A Triptych, Manuscript Collections at the Harry Ransom Humanities Research Center,* edited by Dave Oliphant and Gena Dagel (Austin: Harry Ransom Humanities

Research Center, University of Texas at Austin, 1987), pp. 61–75;

Ubu sur la Butte (Paris: Sansot, 1906);

Albert Samain: Souvenirs (Paris: Victor Lemasle, 1907);

Le Moutardier du Pape (Paris: Privately printed for subscribers by Imprimerie Bussière, 1907);

Pantagruel: Opéra bouffe en cinq actes et six tableaux, libretto by Jarry and Eugène Demolder, music by Claude Terrasse (Paris: Sociéte d'Editions Musicales, 1910; republished, without music, 1911);

Gestes et opinions du docteur Faustroll, pataphysicien: Roman néo-scientifique; suivi de Spéculations (Paris: Fasquelle, 1911); translated and annotated by Simon Watson Taylor as *Exploits & Opinions of Doctor Faustroll, Pataphysician: A Neo-Scientific Novel,* introduction by Roger Shattuck (Boston: Exact Change, 1996);

Gestes, suivis des Paraliponménes d'Ubu (Paris: Editions du Sagittaire, 1921);

La Dragonne: Roman, preface by Jean Saltas (Paris: Gallimard, 1943);

Ubu Cocu (Geneva: Editions des Trois Collines, 1944);

Alfred Jarry: Œuvres Poétiques Complètes, edited by Henri Parisot, preface by André Frédérique (Paris: Gallimard, 1945);

L'Autre Alceste: Drame en cinq récits, edited by Maurice Saillet (Paris: Fontaine, 1947);

La Revanche de la Nuit, poémes retrouvés, edited by Saillet (Paris: Mercure de France, 1949);

Commentaire pour servir à la construction pratique de la machine à explorer le temps (Paris: Collège de 'Pataphysique, 1950);

Visions actuelles et futures (Paris: Collège de 'Pataphysique, 1950);

Autour d'Ubu, edited by Jean-Hugues Sainmont (Paris: Collège de 'Pataphysique, 1951);

Les Alcoolisés: Opèra-chimique, preface by Sainmont (Paris: Collège de 'Pataphysique, 1952);

Les Nouveaux timbres (Paris: Collège de 'Pataphysique, 1952);

L'Objet aimé: Pastorale en un acte, edited by Shattuck (Paris: Editions Arcanes, 1953);

L'Ouverture de la pêche (Paris: Collège de 'Pataphysique, 1953);

Le Futur malgré lui (Paris: Collège de 'Pataphysique, 1954);

Tatane (Paris: Collège de 'Pataphysique, 1954);

Soleil de Printemps, text by Jarry and illustrations by Bonnard (Paris: Collège de 'Pataphysique, 1957);

Etre et Vivre (Paris: Collège de 'Pataphysique, 1958);

Léda: Fragments de brouillons d'un opérette-bouffe introuvable (Paris: Collège de 'Pataphysique, 1958);

Le Temps dans l'art: Conférence prononcée par Alfred Jarry au Salon des Indépendants en 1901 (Paris: Collège de 'Pataphysique, 1958);

Album de l'Antlium (ou pompe à merdre): Textes et dessins de Jarry enfant (1886) 13 (Paris: Collège de 'Pataphysique, 1964);

Les Antliaclastes: (2e version) (Paris: Collège de 'Pataphysique, 1964);

Saint-Brieuc des Choux: Poésies et comédies tirées d'Ontogénie, edited by Saillet (Paris: Mercure de France, 1964);

Peintures, gravures & dessins d'Alfred Jarry, edited by Michel Arrivé (Paris: Collège de 'Pataphysique/Le Cercle Français du Livre, 1968);

La Chandelle verte, lumiéres sur les choses de ce temps, edited by Saillet (Paris: Le Livre de Poche, 1969);

Résponses à des enquêtes (Paris: Collège de 'Pataphysique, 1970);

Le Manoir enchanté et quatre autres œuvres inédites, edited by Noël Arnaud (Paris: Editions de La Table Ronde, 1974);

Léda, edited by Arnaud and Henri Bordillon (Paris: Christian Bourgois, 1981).

Editions and Collections: *Œuvres Complétes d'Alfred Jarry,* edited by René Massat, 8 volumes (Monte Carlo: Editions du Livre / Lausanne, Switzerland: Kaeser, 1948);

Tout Ubu, edited by Maurice Saillet (Paris: Livre de Poche, 1962);

Œuvres Complétes: Alfred Jarry, 3 volumes, edited by Michel Arrivé and Henri Bordillon, Bibliothèque de la Pleiade, nos. 236, 342, and 347 (Paris: Gallimard, 1972–1988);

Ubu, edited by Noël Arnaud and Bordillon, Collection Folio (Paris: Gallimard, 1978).

Editions in English: *King Turd,* translated by Beverly Keith and George Legman (New York: Boar's Head Books, 1953)–comprises *King Turd, King Turd Enslaved,* and *Turd Cuckolded;*

Selected Works: Alfred Jarry, edited by Roger Shattuck and Watson-Taylor (London: Methuen, 1965; New York: Grove, 1965);

The Ubu Plays, translated by Cyril Connolly and Simon Watson-Taylor (New York: Grove, 1969)–includes *Ubu Rex,* translated by Connolly and Watson-Taylor; *Ubu Cuckolded,* translated by Connolly; and *Ubu Enchained,* translated by Watson-Taylor;

Ubu Rex, translated by David Copelin (Vancouver: Pulp Press, 1973);

Messalina: A Novel of Imperial Rome, translated by John Harman (London: Atlas Press, 1985);

Caesar Antichrist, translated by Antony Melville, introduction and notes by Alastair Brotchie (London: Atlas Press, 1992);

The Antliaclasts & Related Texts, by Jarry and Henry Meyer, translated by Paul Edwards (London: Atlas Press, 1994);

Adventures in 'Pataphysics, translated by Edwards and Melville (London: Atlas Press, 2001).

PLAY PRODUCTIONS: *Ubu Roi,* Paris, Théâtre de l'Oeuvre at the Nouveau Théâtre, 10 December 1896;

Ubu sur la Butte, Montmartre, Guignol des Gueules de Bois at the Théâtre des Quatz'arts, 10 November 1901;

Ubu Enchaîné, Paris, Compagnie Le Diable Écarlate at the Comédie des Champs-Elysées, 22 September 1937;

Ubu Cocu, Reims, Chambre de Commerce, 21 May 1946;

Ubu á l'Opéra, Avignon, Théâtre de l'Est Parisien, 1974;

Ubu aux Bouffes, Paris, Centre International de Créations Théâtrales at Théâtre des Bouffes du Nord, 1977.

TRANSLATIONS: Emmanuel Rhoïdes, *La Papesse Jeanne, roman médiéval,* by Jarry and Jean Saltas (Paris: Fasquelle, 1908);

Samuel Taylor Coleridge, *La Ballade du vieux marin* (Paris: Ronald Davis, 1921).

Alfred Jarry's life and work are both wildly separated and inextricably connected. The varied nature of his writing makes his work as a whole difficult to assimilate. Jarry is widely regarded as an icon of the modern theater. His best-known play is the infamous *Ubu Roi* (King Ubu, 1896; translated, 1951). But Jarry's work and influence extend well beyond the theatrical. Jarry's collected works also include a smattering of poetry, prose, fiction, and critical essays. Just as his plays influenced those whom critic and historian Martin Esslin dubbed the Absurdists and modern theater in general, Jarry's poetry is generally recognized as a driving force in Surrealism and a major influence on poets such as Guillaume Apollinaire, Antonin Artaud, and Roger Vitrac.

Lacking as it does the strong central focus found in his dramatic works, however, Jarry's poetry seems scattered and difficult to conceive of either as an interrelated whole or as part of his overall body of work. Much of his poetic writing predates *Ubu Roi,* though the poetry collected in *Alfred Jarry: Œuvres Poétiques Complétes* (Alfred Jarry: Complete Poetic Works, 1945) was written throughout his career. Much of this work is in the form of prose poems and poetry incorporated in dramatic texts. Overshadowed by *Ubu Roi,* Jarry's poetry has not received universal attention from critics, translators, and anthologists; for example, Roger Shattuck and Simon

Watson-Taylor's *Selected Works: Alfred Jarry* (1965) includes only five poems. Indeed, though Jarry's poems are included in anthologies of French poetry of the period, his importance as a poet is largely viewed in terms of his influence on major poets who followed. And while this influence is widely acknowledged, Jarry's place relative to the Symbolist and Surrealist movements in poetry is a matter of some debate, and the degree to which critics find Jarry's work to be of importance to his successors varies. In the third edition of his *Anthology of Modern French Poetry: From Baudelaire to the Present Day* (1967), C. A. Hackett calls Jarry "a minor, marginal figure whom the Surrealists have placed at the summit of their hierarchy of predecessors"; as depicted by Jacques-Henri Lévesque in his 1951 monograph, by contrast, Jarry is a more direct participant in the Symbolist movement; and André Frédérique, in his preface to Jarry's *Œuvres Poétiques Complétes,* calls him "avant tout un poéte" (above all a poet).

In *Gestes et opinions du docteur Faustroll, pataphysicien: Roman néo-scientifique* (translated as *Exploits & Opinions of Doctor Faustroll, Pataphysician: A Neo-Scientific Novel,* 1996), written in 1898 but not published until 1911, Jarry describes 'Pataphysics, a philosophy that he applied not only in his writing but also in his life: "La pataphysique est la science de ce qui se surajoute à la métaphysique" ('Pataphysics is the science of the realm beyond metaphysics), which seeks to study "les lois qui régissent les exceptions" (the laws which govern exceptions) and to describe "l'univers supplémentaire à celui-ci" (the universe supplementary to this one). He defines 'Pataphysics as "la science des solutions imaginaires, qui accorde symboliquement aux linéaments les propriétés des objects décrits par leur virtualité" (the science of imaginary solutions, which symbolically attributes the properties of objects, described by their virtuality, to their lineaments).

As a practitioner of 'Pataphysics in his life and his art, Jarry reveled in ambiguities, abstractions, and imaginative excess. His willingness to undertake any form of writing—and many forms of poetry—represents a kind of 'Pataphysics in action. His poetry runs the gamut from symbolist composition to popular ditties. It demonstrates an awareness of forms and a willingness to use them freely without ever being bound by rules or expectations. Just as he eschewed no form or style, so too, Jarry undertook almost any subject or theme. There is, however, some consistency in his way of dealing with various themes, stemming from his fascination with duality, horror, humor, and the seamy or sordid, whether in everyday life or in the iconographies of myth and symbol. Hackett credits Jarry's poetry with a "nightmare-by-daylight atmosphere." In each case, Jarry's general approach to life (as epitomized by the

Ubu persona) is reflected in all his work. Indeed, whatever the subject, the specter of the anarchic, adolescent Ubu haunts all his poetry. Embracing the natural and the unnatural, the physical and the ethereal, the real and the imagined, Jarry's poetry is unified not by theme or form but by its relentless challenge to language, art, society, and poetry itself, which challenge endeared him to the French Symbolists and the "anti-realists" who followed them.

Alfred-Henri Jarry was born in Laval on 8 September 1873. His father, Anselme Jarry, was a former traveling salesman who had become a partner in a successful textile factory. His mother, Caroline Jarry (neé Quernest), came from a wealthy family. The Quernest family was marked by a history of insanity, and Caroline Jarry herself behaved somewhat eccentrically, adopting unusual clothing, hairstyles, and makeup. Anselme Jarry's business failed in 1879, forcing him to resume his career as a traveling salesman. Caroline Jarry subsequently left her husband, moving to Saint-Brieuc on the coast of Brittany (where her father lived) with her son and daughter, Charlotte. There Alfred Jarry entered the lycée and undertook his first writing projects, which included poems and short plays, published in 1964 as *Saint-Brieuc des Choux: Poésies et comédies tirées d'Ontogénie* (Saint-Brieuc des Choux: Poetry and Comedies Adapted from Ontogenesis).

The poetry of this period reveals many of Jarry's lifelong fascinations. Although not as linguistically complex as his later poetry, these early pieces make evident Jarry's taste for the macabre and his interest in simple ironies that subvert ideas of heroism, idealism, and faith. "Le Chien D'Ulysse" (Ulysses' Dog, 1887) tells the plaintive story of Ulysses' faithful dog, Argus, who is the only one to recognize the returning traveler. Argus, hearing his master's voice after so many years, runs to Ulysses and dies upon seeing him. In "Enterré Vivant" (Buried Alive, 1888) Jarry paints the horrifying picture of a man buried alive. The epigraph of the poem is Goya's simple "Nada" (nothing). Following this chilling epigraph, Jarry goes on to tell the story, with the ironic twist that the last sound the doomed man hears is the gravedigger's laughter. In both of these poems Jarry adheres to a strict pattern of rhythm and rhyme. In its choice of subjects, its use of epigraphs, and other formal qualities, Jarry's early poetry suggests a well-read individual, one interested in connections between things. While his later poetry became increasingly inscrutable, this early work demonstrates the skill, knowledge, and passion that lie at the core of his writing, which were further evidenced by his early academic achievements. In July 1886, when prizes were distributed at school, Jarry was awarded first prizes in Latin, English, reading, and recitation, and second prize in French composition.

Jarry enrolled in the Lycée de Rennes in October 1888, beginning a period significant to his life and later art. There he befriended the brothers Charles and Henri Morin, who introduced him to the unofficial school tradition of taunting and playing tricks on the physics teacher, Félix Hébert. A fat and ineffectual man, Hébert had long been the target of practical jokes and featured as the grotesque protagonist of many parodies written by the students of Rennes. As Keith Beaumont notes in his 1984 biography, however, Jarry "carried the attack to a new level, harassing Hébert with a grim determination which far surpassed the pranks of the others." Drawing on the existing body of schoolboy parodies, Jarry and Henri Morin collaborated on a play about the exploits of Pére Héb, a monstrous figure with an enormous *gidouille* (belly), who usurps the throne of Poland. The result, *Les Polonais* (The Poles), was staged with marionettes in the attic of the Morin family home in December 1888. Jarry later transformed this play into *Ubu Roi.* Another play, mostly written by Jarry, targeted a fellow pupil named Priou and was also staged with marionettes during the 1888–1889 school term. This play, *Onésime; ou, Les Tribulations de Priou* (Onanism; or, The Tribulations of Priou)–fragments of which were published in *Saint-Brieuc des Choux*–formed the basis for *Ubu Cocu* (1944; translated as *Turd Cuckolded,* 1953).

In June 1891 Jarry took the *concours d'entré* (competitive entry exam) for the prestigious Ecole Normale Supérieure. He did not pass the test, and in the fall of 1891 Jarry enrolled in the Lycée Henri IV in Paris, to prepare for another attempt at the entrance exam. His subsequent attempts to pass the examination were also failures; after three unsuccessful attempts to gain admittance to the Ecole Normale Supérieure, Jarry took the examination for the *licence-ès-lettres* (roughly equivalent to a bachelor of arts degree) at the Sorbonne in March 1894. He failed that exam, as well as a second attempt in October of that year. Jarry was more successful in his social and literary pursuits, befriending Léon-Paul Fargue, who became famous as a poet, and publishing pieces in such reviews as *L'Echo de Paris* and *L'Art Littéraire.* He came to the attention of Alfred Vallette, editor of the *Mercure de France,* and his wife, Marguerite Eymery (who wrote novels under the pen name of Rachilde). Jarry began regular attendance at the couple's weekly literary soirees, and Valette and Rachilde became close friends and supporters of the young man, who was already developing a reputation for his wit and eccentric behavior. He habitually dressed in black bicyclists' clothing and carried a revolver with him.

At the time Jarry arrived in Paris, the French Symbolist movement was taking shape. The artists active at the inception of the movement were fighting to establish a new vision of the world and humanity.

Illustration by Jarry for his Les Minutes de sable mémorial *(1894), a collection of poetry, prose, and short plays*
(from Michel Arrive, ed., Peintures, gravures & dessins d'Alfred Jarry, *1968)*

Jarry joined in this struggle and subscribed to the new vision adherents of the movement espoused. Breaking with Romantic simplicity, this vision focused on inner life and delighted in enigma, the unseen, and the unspoken, in a constant questioning of the "known." Given his fascination with complexity and the subversion of understood truths, Jarry readily adopted this new vision. Between 1893 and early 1895 he met most of the prominent figures of Parisian literary and artistic circles, including such writers, artists, and composers as Stephané Mallarmé, Catulle Mendés, André Gide, Rémy de Gourmont, Gustave Kahn, Pierre Louÿs, Henri de Régnier, Paul Valéry, Paul Gauguin, Henri Rousseau, Henri de Toulouse-Lautrec, and Maurice Ravel. Not everyone was favorably impressed by Jarry's outlandish persona; Gide later described him as "Ce Kobold, à la face plâtrée, accou-

tré en clown de cirque et jouant un personnage fantasque, construit, résolument factice et en dehors de quoi plus rien d'humain ne se montrait (This Kobold, his face plastered white, got up as a circus clown and playing a fantastic, fabricated, resolutely artificial role outside of which no human characteristics could any longer be seen).

In January and March of 1893 Jarry was bedridden by a severe case of influenza; after nursing her son back to health, his mother died 10 March 1893 of the same disease. Jarry never fully recovered from the loss of his mother, but he threw himself back into his writing. He translated Samuel Taylor Coleridge's *The Rime of the Ancient Mariner* (1798), submitting it to Editions du Mercure de France in March 1894, but the manuscript was rejected. The translation was eventually published by Ronald Davis as *La Ballade du vieux marin* (1921). In

1893 and 1894 he was also working on the various texts that were published in October 1894 as *Les Minutes de sable mémorial* (The Minutes of Sand Chronicle), a collection of poems, prose pieces, and dramatic writings. Among the latter is *Haldernablou* (the title formed from the names of the two protagonists, Haldern and Ablou), a short play featuring a duke, his servant, and an invisible chorus.

Haldernablou depicts the homosexual relationship between Duke Haldern and his servant Ablou. Some critics, such as Beaumont, believe that the play is to some degree biographical and that the two male lovers in *Haldernablou* represent Jarry and Fargue, who shared living quarters and worked together off and on until 1895. *Haldernablou,* which Lévesque calls Jarry's first important work, features a chorus that is invisible until the final line of the play. When the chorus speaks, it does so in verse, as in Greek tragedy. The epilogue, a twenty-two-line poem spoken by the chorus, evokes the specter of the hourglass, an image that Jarry draws on in detail in a poem in *Les Minutes de sable mémorial,* "Le Sablier" (The Hourglass), and one that resonates with the title of the collection. Jarry's fascination with time, death, and decay are made manifest in the choral poetry of the piece as a whole. The final line of the play, intoned as the chorus appears, conjures a disturbing image: "Le lombric blanc des enterrements sort de ses tanières" (The white worm of the burials emerges from his lairs).

Jarry began his obligatory military service in the French army in November 1894, but he secured a medical discharge by taking a dose of picric acid, which gave him the appearance of jaundice. In August 1895 Jarry's father died. Jarry returned to Paris after his discharge on 14 December 1895; soon afterward, he and Fargue ended their relationship.

In 1896 the twenty-three-year-old Jarry both achieved his greatest artistic success and began an epic slide into alcoholism, drug abuse, and poverty that ultimately cost him his sanity and his life. With his masterpiece, *Ubu Roi,* Jarry changed modern theater, creating in the gross and blundering Ubu a new literary type, the embodiment of all that is base and venal. In his own life he then seemingly set out to transform himself into his own monstrous creation, through bizarre and self-abusive behavior.

Although the Ubu cycle consists of three plays, *Ubu Roi* was the only one staged during Jarry's lifetime and is generally considered his most important piece of stagecraft. The basic plot of *Ubu Roi* is a farcical parody of William Shakespeare's *Macbeth,* but what makes the play important is not the plot; rather, it is Jarry's subversion of dramatic convention. In the six acts of *Ubu Roi* he carefully avoids creating sympathetic characters, identifiable loca-

tions, or a logical and coherent structure, thus overturning conventions of mimesis and theatrical illusion.

The play revolves around Pére Ubu's rise to power in the mythical kingdom of Poland (not an independent political unit in 1896). Urged on by his wife, Mére Ubu, he uses his "debraining" device to assassinate the king, then proceeds to eliminate his former allies, most of the Polish nobles, the judiciary, and the bankers. King Ubu then roams the countryside collecting taxes, which he has doubled and tripled. The play increasingly loses any semblance of unified action or linear narrative; ultimately, after a cowardly retreat from an army led by the Tsar and surviving an attack by a bear, Ubu and his wife are forced to flee Poland, and the play ends with the two sailing to France.

Sources differ about the dates of the two productions of the play, directed by Aurélien Lugné-Poe, by the Théâtre de l'Œuvre at the Nouveau Théâtre in 1896. In *The Banquet Years: The Origins of the Avant-Garde in France, 1885 to World War I* (1969) Shattuck says the premiere was 11 December, while Beaumont, in his 1984 biography, and Claude Schumacher say there was a public dress-rehearsal on 9 December and the actual premiere was 10 December. Linda K. Stillman also gives 10 December as the date of the premiere, but she seems to conflate the dress rehearsal with the actual premiere. As Beaumont points out, this distinction is one "frequently blurred in the memories of those participants who later recalled the scene (including Lugné-Poe), and perpetuated by many writers on the subject since."

According to Beaumont's recounting of events, the dress rehearsal went smoothly until near the end of act 3, when Ubu, played by Firmin Gémier, visits one of his former coconspirators, whom he has imprisoned: "in place of the door of the prison cell, an actor stood with one arm outstretched; Gémier 'inserted' a key into his hand, made a clicking noise, and turned the arm as if opening a door." Apparently outraged at this assault on theatrical convention, the audience erupted in jeers and catcalls, forcing the performance to halt. Gémier managed to bring the audience around, however, by dancing a comic jig on stage, which pleased the crowd, and the play was able to resume.

While accounts differ, it seems that it was at the actual premiere on 10 December that, as Beaumont observes, "the real explosion occurred." It began with Gémier's first line, "Merdre," an expletive Jarry had invented by adding an extra *r* to the word *merde* (shit). The audience reacted violently, causing such an uproar that the play could not continue for some minutes. On each subsequent repetition of "le mot d'Ubu" (Ubu's word; as *merdre* came to be known), pandemonium ensued, as partisans for and against the play threatened to come to blows.

In the sequel, *Ubu Cocu,* the purposively incoherent plot concerns the cuckolded Père Ubu's desire to enact his

Lithograph by Jarry for the program of the January 1898 marionette production of Ubu Roi *(1896) at the Théâtre des Pantins
(from Michel Arrive, ed.,* Peintures, gravures & dessins d'Alfred Jarry, *1968)*

revenge against his adulterous wife and her lover. In *Ubu Cocu* Jarry was so successful in eliminating the conventions of traditional theater that the play is essentially unstageable, though it has been produced, premiering under the direction of Emmanuel Peillet at the Chambre de Commerce in Reims on 21 May 1946, with Pierre Minet in the role of Père Ubu.

The third play of the cycle, *Ubu Enchaîné* (Ubu Enchained; translated as *Turd Enslaved,* 1953), was published in 1900 but not produced until 22 September 1937, when it premiered at the Comédie des Champs-Elysées. As the play opens, it seems at first that Père Ubu has mended his ways. When Mére Ubu asks him "As-tu donc oublié le mot?" (Have you forgotten the word?), he declares "je ne veux plus prononcer le mot, il m'a valu trop de désagréments" (I don't want to utter the word anymore, it has brought too much trou-

ble upon me). In addition to his renunciation of the use of the "mot d'Ubu," it seems that he no longer wishes to be a despot, as he declares "je vais me mettre esclave, Mère Ubu!" (I'm going to become a slave, Ma Ubu!)

The plot of *Ubu Enchaîné* mirrors that of *Ubu Roi;* however, rather than depicting Ubu's rise to power, as did the first Ubu play, *Ubu Enchaîné* traces Ubu's descent into subjugation, first as a servant, then a prisoner, and finally a galley slave. But Ubu has not really changed; he is still motivated by greed and a desire to dominate others. When at the end of the play he is offered command of the slave galley, he refuses, declaring "Je n'en suis pas moins resté Ubu enchâiné, esclave, et je ne commanderai plus. On m'obéit bien davantage" (I am still Ubu bound, a slave, and I am not giving orders ever again. That way people will obey me even more promptly).

With the Ubu plays Jarry created a character who is at once clownish and sinister, a macabre buffoon whose greed, avarice, and selfishness seem limitless. In *Ubu Roi*, Jarry's intended to create a theater based on abstraction and extreme simplification, one dealing with universal themes and with characters who represented archetypes rather than individuals. Although the play was widely reviled as a monstrosity or a crude hoax upon the public by contemporary reviewers, many later critics have traced the heritage of much of the so-called new or experimental theater of the twentieth century back to the premiere of *Ubu Roi*. Rather than presenting an entertaining diversion, the play directly confronted and provoked the audience from the first line onward. As Shattuck observes, faced with the tumult in the Nouveau Théâtre on that opening night, the actors "waited patiently, beginning to believe that the roles had been reversed and they had come to watch a performance out front." Although Jarry continued to write dramatic pieces, after the production of *Ubu Roi* he essentially ceased his active participation in the theater.

In the absence of an Ubu to make it cohere in the way the dramatic works do, Jarry's poetry may seem difficult to apprehend as a whole and to reconcile with his other writings. In his *Anthologie de la poésie française de XXe siècle* (Anthology of 20th-Century French Poetry, 1983), however, Michel Décaudin notes that Jarry's poems "ont le même caractère et participent au même mouvement que l'ensemble de l'oeuvre, représentant . . . une mise en question du langage et du contenu de la poésie en même temps qu'une restructuration de l'imaginaire" (have the same character and partake in the same movement as the rest of his work, representing . . . a questioning of language and the content of poetry together with a restructuring of the imagination). The wide variety of Jarry's work in form, theme, genre, and approach is the result of a peculiar focus, the kind of thinking and behavior that gave birth to 'Pataphysics. Especially significant is the way in which Jarry uses language; as Shattuck notes: "A random sampling of his poetry may easily disclose texts that seem to come from two different authors, two different countries of the mind. Yet both in the idiom of popular balladry and in a style of contorted symbolism, Jarry used internal rhythm, alliteration, and refrain to build up a monotonous rhythm. The lullaby effect serves to throw into relief the boldness of certain images and to prepare the way for comic effects. With its roots deep in a childhood spent in the French countryside, Jarry's 'symbolist' poetry never departs far from the aural, jocose, yet moving manner of the popular ditty. Not versatility but singleness of vision produced the variety of his writings."

While the bulk of his poetry is found in *Les Minutes de sable mémorial*, Jarry continued to produce poetic writings up to the end of his life. His *Œuvres Poétiques* includes passages from *César-Antéchrist* (1895; translated as *Caesar Anti-*

christ, 1971), *Les Jours et les Nuits, roman d'un déserteur* (1897; translated as *Days and Nights: Novel of a Deserter,* 1989), *L'Amour en visites* (1898; translated as *Visits of Love,* 1993), *Almanach du Pére Ubu, illustré* (Almanac of Father Ubu, Illustrated, 1899), *Le Surmâle, roman moderne* (1902; translated as *The Supermale: A Modern Novel,* 1968), and *Gestes et Opinions du docteur Faustroll, pataphysicien.* Jarry also published poems in the *Revue Blanche* and other journals.

Among the topics dealt with in Jarry's poetry, relationships (with men or women) seem notably marginal. His only poem written to a woman, "Madrigal" (Compliment), is directed to a prostitute. Published in the *Revue Blanche* in 1903, the poem begins "Ma fille ma, car vous êtes àtous" (My girl—my, since you belong to all). Noting that "nous sommes chez nous" (we are at home), the poet urges her to sleep at last. Jarry plays with warring dualities, likening peace to death and evil to purity. The woman, an object for sale, is described as "d'orreilles at d'yeux" (of ears and eyes), and the poet evokes the time when she was a virgin and he had not yet trod her sidewalk. He speaks of their height, her dim garret, their passion: "La bruit terrestre est loin" (the sounds of earth are distant) in altitude and death. He concludes with the couplet:

Et c'est d'avoir mordu dans tout le mal
Qui vous a fait une bouche si pure.

(And it is having bitten into evil
That has given you a mouth so pure).

Composed in the manner of a love song or lullaby, this poem is much more, however, than an homage to a particular woman. The poem asks: "Comment s'unit la double destinée?" (How is a double destiny united?) The duality of tenderness expressed toward a prostitute, evil leading to purity, the mud kissing "La chaussure / De votre pied infinitesimal" (The shoe / On your tiny foot) compels the reader to rethink not only the relationship between prostitute and client but also that between woman and man. Domesticity and affection, rather than passion and sexuality, are what dominate this piece.

In "Une Forme Nue" (A Naked Form) from *Le Surmâle*, Jarry plays with a similar duality of vision: "Une forme nue qui tend les bras, / Qui désire et qui dit: Est-ce possible?" (A naked form who reaches out her arms, / Who wants and who says: Is it possible?). Jarry goes on to praise this figure, her "Yeux illuminés de joie incicible" (eyes lit with inexpressible joy) and "grands yeux si francs, surtout quand ils trompent" (Big eyes so honest, especially when they lie), and asks of her: "Salez moins vos pleurs, car je les boirai" (Salt less your tears, for I will drink them). This poem in praise, at least at first, of a cold, stone statue is more sensual than "Madrigal." He refers to the model as "Un cher oreiller et qui bat un cœur" (A beloved pillow in which beats a heart); their mouths, in his imagination, make a single hideaway, their tongues the bride and groom.

Jarry then goes on at length about Helen of Troy, "Vieux mais éternel nom de la beautié" (Ancient but eternal name for beauty). Helen is painted as a cruel woman, highly physical and sensual, but next to whom hard stone seems warm. Her cruelty is made more salient by the apparently arbitrary, frivolous nature of her affections, and their tragic repercussions. The poem closes by mimicking that whimsicality: "Et puis j'ai souvent une robe verte / Et . . . je ne sais pas . . . ces jour-là, j'aime le rouge" (And then I often get a green dress / And . . . I don't know . . . these days I like red).

In "Je ne sais pas . . ." (I Do Not Know), from *Les Jours et les Nuits,* Jarry addresses a male who is similarly elusive: "Je ne sais pas si mon frère m'oublie" (I do not know if my brother is forgetting me). He speaks tenderly of this figure, especially "sa voix adorable" (his adorable voice). That voice, however, "semble faite fausse expris" (seems made false on purpose). The brother's physicality is called into question by his absence. The speaker of the poem has a photograph of the brother but claims that "Le Double est vide et vain comme un tombeau" (The Copy is empty and hollow as a tomb). Even his recollection of the brother is betrayed by "un souvenir qui ment" (a lying memory).

Subtle dualities, ironies, and juxtapositions of this nature can be found throughout Jarry's poetry. His use of language, however, is often more complex, inasmuch as it challenges both the nature and role of language itself, as in "Les trois meubles du Mage surannés" (Three Antiquated Movables of the Wise Man), in *Les Minutes de Sable mémorial.* The first line—"Vase olivâtro et vain d'où l'âme est envolée" (Sallow bowl, and empty, from which the soul has flown)—makes use, as does much of the poem, of both assonance and alliteration. Jarry also uses personification to frame the first part of this piece. The object he addresses, the first of the three "movables," is a skull. This section, called "Minéral," ends:

Et, presse-papier lourd, sur le haut d'une armoire
Serrant de l'occiput les feuillets du grimoire,
Contre le vent rôdeur tu rechignes, hargneux.

(So, heavy paper-weight, on a high closet shelf
Occipitally pressing the pages of magic spells,
Against the thieving wind you balk, belligerent).

In the second section, "Végétal," Jarry lends anthropomorphic qualities to the parchment on which he writes: "Le vélin écrit rit et grimace, livide." The book itself is described as "un grand arbre émergé des tombeaux" (a large tree rising from the tombs). In the third section, "Animal," Jarry describes a supposed dispenser of wisdom and justice. "Tout vêtu de drap d'or frisé" (Clothed in a sheet of curling gold), this figure is contrasted with a beggar who is revealed to have real wisdom. He has come to understand that life is fleeting and death inevitable: "Car il déchiffre sur les tombes l'avenir" (For he reads the future on tombstones). Jarry then twists the ending with a strong image of death; the beggar dreams "Des longs fémurs croisés en siestes triomphales" (Long thighbones crossed in a triumphal nap).

Jarry's poetry often includes this kind of extravagant imagery, a product of extreme experimentation. "Le Sablier," the final poem in *Les Minutes de Sable mémorial,* plays on a single image, stretching it in all directions. The hourglass is characterized as the heart of time, a heart connected to its own reflection. The speaker in the poem addresses time, admonishing it:

Suspend ton cœur aux trois piliers,
Suspend ton cœur les bras liés,
Suspend ton cœur, ton cœur qui pleure
Et qui se vide au cours de l'heure.

(Hang your heart on the three pillars,
Hang your heart its arms linked,
Hang your heart, your heart which cries
And empties itself in the course of the hour).

The imperative "Suspend ton cœur" occurs several times in the piece, as do "Hausse tes bras" (Raise your arms) and "Verse la sueur" (Pour your sweat). The poet's attitude toward time is mixed. Clearly, time is destructive. Time knows "l'heure où les corps mourront" (the hour when bodies will die), but the poet also urges time on:

Et sur leur sang ineffaçable
Verse on sable intarissable.

(And on their unerasable blood
Pour out your inexhaustible sand).

A strong duality surrounds the key image in the poem. The top and bottom of the hourglass represent the future and the past, life and death, reality and illusion. Time is good and bad but ultimately flows only in one direction. (Until the hourglass is turned upside down.) The construct that contains the hourglass itself is variously described as pillars, stocks, gallows, a charred and blackened arm, and tireless arms. The image is complex and the poet uses it in a way that allows for multiple resonances. Within the rhythmic structure to which he adheres faithfully, Jarry plays on the image of the hourglass with tremendous freedom, creating almost a stream-of-consciousness rant against and about time.

Jarry also experimented with the song, or ditty. "Tatane" (Nookie), which Shattuck has dubbed "a hugely successful obscenity" and "a symbolist barracks-room ballad," was first published in the *Almanach du Pére Ubu, illustrée* and follows a strict pattern of rhythm and rhyme. The story of the song revolves around Ubu's sexual encounter with a black woman. She is alarmed at the whiteness of his penis and asks him to "Colorié / Li blanc bébête / Dans l'encrié." A fairly literal translation of this line might be "Color / That little white creepy-crawly / In the inkwell," but Paul Schmidt captures the spirit and rhythm of the original better in his version, published in Shattuck and Watson-Taylor's edition of *Selected Works:* "Dunk that chile / In an inkwell." The poem describes the encounter in a rather vulgar manner but uses fresh imagery and raises questions that go far beyond the "story" itself. Ubu's wild behavior and dirty legacy are the chief subjects of the piece, but Jarry plays with issues of race and ownership, using image and language to paint a picture of life in keeping with his (and Ubu's) destructive point of view.

In "Trois Grenouilles" (Three Frogs), from *L'Amour en visites,* Jarry subverts the form of the lullaby, creating a kind of "anti-lullaby." This poem, complete with the sweet refrain "Ma mie Oulaine" (My beloved Oulaine), tells the story of three frogs who wish to make a woolen garment for the king. The tone shifts upon the arrival of the executioner:

–Coupez, cousez l'habit d'Elbeuf
Ma mie Oulaine.
C'est plein de sang, mais c'est tout neuf
Est c'est en laine!

(Cut, sew the garment of finest cloth
My beloved Oulaine.
It's full of blood, but it's brand new,
And made of wool!).

The poem ends with the king dying as the singers agree to share his wealth. This "anti-lullaby," which, as Hackett notes, "is intended not to soothe, but to terrify," is as complex as "Tatane"; rather, its very simplicity is the source of terror. In keeping with the antisocietal stance and love for language for its own sake that Jarry espoused in his life and work, this piece works to subvert both form and convention.

While Jarry's poems vary a great deal in style, content, and use of language, they all share certain qualities. Among these is the delight Jarry seems to take in the resonances of language, particularly the way in which words

and phrases can have several, sometimes contradictory, meanings simultaneously. But Jarry's use of language is highly precise and exigent. In "Les trois meubles du Mage surannés," for example, he uses "vélin," which can mean "parchment." *Vélin,* however, can also mean—as does the English cognate, *vellum*–a more-specific writing surface, one made from the skin of stillborn calves.

Jarry's poetry is the direct result of who he was (both by nature and as he "manufactured" himself) and what he was trying to do. His poetry revels in a duality that allows objects and ideas to be what they are (or what one thinks one knows they are) as well as the complete opposite. This duality often takes the form of ironies that call into question the reader's understanding of things. Be it poetry, heroism, or faith, Jarry's twofold vision–much like the image of the hourglass–reveals an underside or shadow to everything. The inner life the Symbolists were trying to express is given form in Jarry's extravagant imagery and resonant use of language.

But while duality and subversion inhabit Jarry's work, this duality is inclusive; Jarry's exploration of good and bad suggests a less clear-cut alternative than that of the Romantics. Similarly, his experiments with form included the original form, using it to further his subversion of the known. The creative/destructive duality of his life is evident in his work; and, Shattuck notes, this duality does not split the work but rather unites it: Jarry's writing "must be taken whole despite its disparity at first glance," the individual works "turn and turn constantly away from a straight line, modulating from grossness to subtle irony to sentiment to metaphysical speculation to blasphemy to anarchism–and come full circle back to grossness. . . . The unity, the center, is the same as for his life: hallucination accepted as reality. In that vividly lit universe all products, base and elevated, of his fertile mind demand equal standing. His writings elude criticism as stubbornly as his life confounds biography."

Weakened by malnutrition and years of substance abuse, Jarry collapsed and was taken to the Hopital de la Charité, where he died of tubercular meningitis 1 November 1907. Dead at the age of thirty-four, he lived what appears to have been a calculatedly monstrous and self-destructive life; toward the end he was known less as a dramatist and poet and more as simply a bizarre figure, seen on drunken or drugged rambles through the streets of Montparnasse with his face powdered white, ranting in his clipped, staccato high-pitched speech. His literary reputation was revived when Artaud and Vitrac founded the Théâtre Alfred Jarry in 1927. Through the efforts of Artaud and his pupil Jean-Louis Barrault, Jarry's dramatic theories survived. A significant portion of his work was not published until after his death, and much of it was not translated into English until the end of the twentieth century. Founded in 1948, the College de 'Pataphysique, a

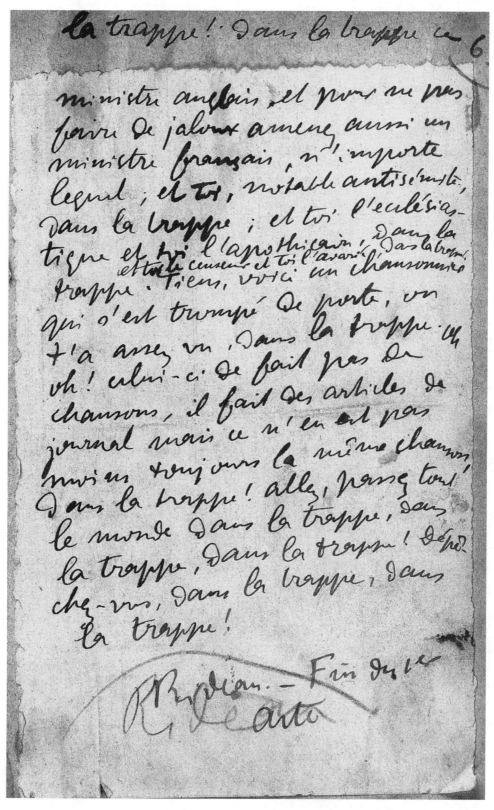

Page from the manuscript for Ubu sur la Butte *(1906), Jarry's two-act musical adaptation for marionette theater of* Ubu Roi *(Bibliothèque Historique de la Ville de Paris)*

group of scholars and thinkers heavily indebted to his groundbreaking work, has kept Jarry's influence alive. The Jarry myth has continued to fascinate readers.

Letters:

Rachilde, *Alfred Jarry; ou, Le Surmâle des lettres* (Paris: Grasset, 1928);

Correspondance avec Félix Féneén, preface by Henri-Bordillon (Paris: Société des Amis d'Alfred Jarry, 1980).

Bibliography:

L. F. Sutton, "An Evaluation of the Studies on Alfred Jarry from 1894–1963," dissertation, University of North Carolina at Chapel Hill, 1970.

Biographies:

Paul Chauveau, *Alfred Jarry; ou, La Naissance, la vie et la mort du Père Ubu, avec leurs portraits* (Paris: Mercure de France, 1932);

Noël Arnaud, *Alfred Jarry d'Ubu Roi au Docteur Faustroll* (Paris: La Table Ronde, 1974);

Keith Beaumont, *Alfred Jarry: A Critical and Biographical Study* (New York: St. Martin's Press, 1984; Leicester: Leicester University Press, 1984);

Nigey Lennon, *Alfred Jarry: The Man with the Axe* (Los Angeles: Panjandrum, 1984);

Patrick Besnier, *Alfred Jarry* (Paris: Plon, 1990);

Christian Soulignac, *Alfred Jarry: Biographie 1906–1962* (Paris: Fourneau, 1995);

Philippe Régibier, *Ubu sur la berge: Alfred Jarry à Corbeil, 1898–1907,* preface by François Caradec (Paris: Presses du Management, 1999).

References:

Daniel Accursi, *Merdre* (Paris: Presses Universitaires de France, 2000);

Accursi, *La Philosophie d'Ubu* (Paris: Presses Universitaires de France, 1999);

Michel Arrivé, *Les Langages de Jarry: Essai de sémiotique littaire* (Paris: Klincksieck, 1972);

Arrivé, *Lire Jarry* (Brussels: Complexe, 1976);

Keith Beaumont, *Jarry, Ubu roi* (London & Wolfeboro, N.H.: Grant & Cutler, 1987);

Beaumont, "The Making of Ubu: Jarry as Producer and Theorist," *Theatre Research International,* 12 (1972): 139–54;

Henri Béhar, *Jarry Dramaturge* (Paris: Nizet, 1980);

Béhar, *Jarry, Le Monstre et la marionnette* (Paris: Larousse, 1973);

François Caradec, *A la Recherche d'Alfred Jarry* (Paris: Seghers, 1974);

Charles Chassé, *Dans les coulisses de la gloire: D'Ubu Roi au douanier Rousseau* (Paris: Editions de la Nouvelle Revue Critique, 1947);

Judith Cooper, *Ubu Roi: An Analytical Study,* Tulane Studies in Romance Languages and Literature, no. 6 (New Orleans: Department of French and Italian, Tulane University, 1974);

Michel Décaudin, ed. and biographical notes, *Anthologie da la poésie française de XXe siécle* (Paris: Gallimard, 1983);

Brunella Eruli, *Jarry: I mostri dell'immagine* (Pisa: Pacini, 1982);

Martin Esslin, *The Theatre of the Absurd* (Garden City, N.Y.: Doubleday, 1961);

Europe, revue littéraire mensuelle, special Jarry issue, nos. 623–624 (1981);

Ben Fisher, *The Pataphysician's Library: An Exploration of Alfred Jarry's "Livres pairs"* (Liverpool: Liverpool University Press, 2000);

C. A. Hackett, *Anthology of Modern French Poetry: From Baudelaire to the Present Day,* third edition (Oxford: Blackwell, 1967; New York: Macmillan, 1968);

Maurice Marc LaBelle, *Alfred Jarry: Nihilism and the Theater of the Absurd* (New York & London: New York University Press, 1980);

André Lebois, *Alfred Jarry, l'irremplaçable* (Paris: Le Cercle du Livre, 1950);

Jacques-Henri Lévesque, *Alfred Jarry: Une Etude,* Poètes d'aujourd'hui, no. 24 (Paris: Seghers, 1951);

Le Magazine Littéraire, special Jarry issue, 48 (1971);

Claude Schumacher, *Alfred Jarry and Guillaume Apollinaire* (Basingstoke, U.K.: Macmillan, 1984; New York: Grove, 1985);

Shattuck, *The Banquet Years: The Origins of the Avant-Garde in France, 1885 to World War I,* revised edition (London: Cape, 1969; Salem, N.H.: Ayer, 1984);

Linda K. Stillman, *Alfred Jarry* (Boston: Twayne, 1983).

Papers:

The chief repository of Alfred Jarry's works and critical studies is the Collège de 'Pataphysique, Paris.

Pierre Jean Jouve

(11 October 1887 – 8 January 1976)

Joseph A. DiLuzio

St. Joseph's University

BOOKS: *Artificiel: Poèmes MCMVII–MCMIX* (Paris: Printed for the author by L. Linard, 1909);

Les Muses Romaines et Florentines (Paris: Messein, 1910);

La Rencontre dans le carrefour: Roman (Paris: Figuière, 1911);

Les Ordres qui changent, poème (Paris: Figuière, 1911);

Les Aéroplanes, poème (Paris: Figuière, 1911);

Présences (Paris: Crès, 1912);

Les Deux forces: Pièce en quatre actes (Paris: Editions de l'Effort Libre, 1913);

Parler (Paris: Crès, 1913);

Vous êtes des hommes, 1915 (Paris: Editions de la Nouvelle Revue Française, 1915);

Poème contre le grand crime, 1916 (Geneva: Editions de la Revue Demain, 1916);

Danse des morts (Geneva: Editions des Tablettes, 1917);

Le Défaitisme contre l'Homme Libre (La Chaux-de-Fonds, Switzerland: Edition d'Action Sociale, 1918);

Hôtel-Dieu: Récits d'hôpital en 1915, illustrated with twenty-five woodprints by Frans Masereel (Geneva: Printed for the authors by Sonor, 1918);

Heures: Livre de la nuit (Geneva: Editions du Sablier, 1919);

Heures: Livre de la grâce (Geneva: Kundig, 1920);

Romain Rolland Vivant: 1914–1919 (Paris: Ollendorf, 1920);

Toscanes (Geneva: Kundig, 1921);

Tragiques; suivis du, Voyage Sentimental (Paris: Stock, 1922);

Prière, engraving by Masareel (Paris: Stock, 1924);

Les Mysterieuses Noces (Paris: Stock, 1925); enlarged as *Noces* (Paris: Au Sans Pareil, 1928); republished as *Les Noces* (Paris: Gallimard, 1931)–includes *Nouvelles Noces* and *La Symphonie à Dieu;*

Paulina 1880 (Paris: Gallimard, 1925; revised edition, Paris: Mercure de France, 1959; revised again, 1963); translated by Rosette Letellier and Robert Bullen as *Paulina 1880* (Indianapolis: Bobbs-Merrill, 1973);

Pierre Jean Jouve, 1946

Nouvelles Noces (Paris: Editions de la Nouvelle Revue Française, 1926);

Beau Regard, illustrated by Sima (Paris: Au Sans Pareil, 1927);

Le Monde désert (Paris: Editions de la Nouvelle Revue Française, 1927; revised edition, Paris: Mercure de France, 1960); translated by Lydia Davis as *The Desert World* (Evanston, Ill.: Marlboro Press/ Northwestern University Press, 1996);

Hécate (Paris: Editions de la Nouvelle Revue Française, 1928); enlarged as *Aventure de Catherine Crachat* (Paris: Librairie Universelle de France / Fribourg, Switzerland: Egloff, 1947)–comprises *Hécate* and *Vagadu;*

Le Paradis Perdu (Paris: Grasset, 1929; revised and enlarged edition, with a preface, "La Faute,"

Paris: Editions G.L.M, 1938; revised again, Fribourg, Switzerland: Librairie Universelle de France/Editions de la Librairie de l'Université de Fribourg, 1942);

La Symphonie à Dieu (Paris: Gallimard, 1930);

Vagadu (Paris: Gallimard, 1931);

Histoires Sanglantes (Paris: Gallimard, 1932; enlarged edition, Paris: Librairie Universelle de France, 1948)–includes a preface, "Considérations sur le sujet"; revised edition includes *La Scène capitale;*

Sueur de Sang (Paris: Editions des Cahiers Libres, 1933; revised and enlarged edition, Paris: Gallimard, 1935; revised again, Paris: Mercure de France, 1955)–1933 introduction, "Inconscient, Spiritualité et Catastrophe," translated by David Gascoyne as *The Unconscious Spirituality Catastrophe* (Child Okeford, U.K.: Words Press, 1987);

La Scène capitale (Paris: Gallimard, 1935; revised edition, Paris: Mercure de France, 1961);

Hélène (Paris: Editions G.L.M., 1936); translated by Lydia Davis as *Hélène* (Marlboro, Vt.: Marlboro Press, 1993);

Matière Céleste (Paris: Gallimard, 1937);

Kyrie (Paris: Gallimard, 1938);

Résurrection des morts (Paris: Editions G.L.M., 1939);

Porche à la Nuit des Saints, introduction by Marcel Raymond (Neuchâtel, Switzerland: Ides et Calendes, 1941);

Le Don Juan de Mozart (Fribourg, Switzerland: Librairie Universelle de France/Editions de la Librairie de l'Université de Fribourg, 1942; revised, 1944; revised again, Paris: Plon, 1953); translated by Eric Earnshaw Smith as *Mozart's Don Juan* (London: V. Stuart, 1957);

Tombeau de Baudelaire (Neuchâtel, Switzerland: Editions de la Baconnière, 1942; revised edition, Paris: Editions du Seuil, 1958);

Vers majeurs (Fribourg, Switzerland: Editions de la Librairie de l'Université de Fribourg, 1942);

Le Bois des pauvres (Fribourg, Switzerland: Librairie Universelle de France/Editions de la Librairie de l'Université de Fribourg, 1943);

Défense et illustration (Neuchâtel, Switzerland: Ides et Calendes, 1943);

Processional de la force anglaise (Fribourg, Switzerland: Librairie Universelle de France/Egloff, 1944);

La Vierge de Paris (Fribourg, Switzerland: Librairie Universelle de France/Librairie de l'Université de Fribourg/Egloff, 1944; revised edition, Paris: Librairie Universelle de France / Fribourg, Switzerland: Egloff, 1946);

L'Homme du 18 juin (Paris: Librairie Universelle de France / Fribourg, Switzerland: Egloff, 1945);

A une soie: Prose et vers (Paris: Librairie Universelle de France / Fribourg, Switzerland: Egloff, 1945);

La Louange (Fribourg, Switzerland: Egloff / Paris: Librairie Universelle de France, 1945);

Apologie du Poète (Paris: Editions G.L.M., 1947);

Hymne (Paris: Librairie Universelle de France, 1947);

Génie (Paris: Editions G.L.M., 1948);

Diadème (Paris: Editions de Minuit, 1949);

Commentaires (Neuchâtel, Switzerland: Editions de La Baconnière, 1950);

Ode (Paris: Editions de Minuit, 1950);

Langue (Paris: Editions de l'Arche, 1952);

Wozzeck; ou, Le Nouvel opéra, by Jouve and Michel Fano (Paris: Plon, 1953); republished as *Wozzeck d'Alban Berg* (Paris: Plon, 1964);

En Miroir: Journal sans date (Paris: Mercure de France, 1954);

Lyrique (Paris: Mercure de France, 1956);

Quatre suites (Paris: Caractères, 1956);

Mélodrame (Paris: Mercure de France, 1957)–includes *Lyrique;*

Inventions (Paris: Mercure de France, 1959);

Proses (Paris: Mercure de France, 1960);

Moires (Paris: Mercure de France, 1962; revised and enlarged edition, 1967);

Ténèbre (Paris: Mercure de France, 1965);

Pierre Jean Jouve Œuvre, 2 volumes, edited by Jean Starobinski, Catherine Jouve, and René Micha, preface by Yves Bonnefoy (Paris: Mercure de France, 1987).

Edition in English: *An Idiom of Night: Poems by Pierre Jean Jouve,* selected and translated by Keith Bosley (London: Rapp & Whiting, 1968; Chicago: Swallow Press, 1968).

OTHER: Friedrich Holderlin, *Poèmes de la folie de Hölderlin,* translated by Jouve and Pierre Klossowski, introduction by Bernard Groethuysen (Paris: J. O. Fourcade, 1927);

"La Langue de Mallarmé," in *Stéphane Mallarmé: Essais et Témoignages* (Neuchâtel, Switzerland: Editions de la Baconnière, 1942);

Joseph Rouget de Lisle, *Le Chant des combats, vulgairement l'hymne des Marseillois,* edited by Jouve and William Kundig (Paris: Librairie Universelle de France / Fribourg, Switzerland: Egloff, 1945);

William Shakespeare, *Shakespeare: Sonnets,* translated by Jouve (Paris: Editions du Sagittaire, 1955);

Giusseppe Ungaretti, *Quattro Poesie,* translated by Jouve (Milan: All'Insegna del Pesce d'Oro, 1960);

Eugenio Montale, *Eugenio Montale,* translated by Jouve (Milan: All'Insegna del Pesce d'Oro, 1966).

Although he himself considered poetry his true vocation, Pierre Jean Jouve is better known as a novelist. His more successful works in this genre include: *Paulina 1880* (1925; translated, 1973), *Le Monde désert* (1927; translated as *The Desert World,* 1996), *La Scène capitale* (Capital Scene, 1935), and *Hélène* (1936; translated, 1993). In addition to his own creations, Jouve was interested in the poetry of others, translating many sonnets from William Shakespeare, poems from Friedrich Hölderlin, and several from his near-contemporaries Giuseppe Ungaretti and Eugenio Montale.

Jouve was born 11 October 1887 in Arras, the middle-class agricultural environment of which did not suit him, as he recalls in the autobiographical *En Miroir: Journal sans date* (In the Mirror: Journal without a Date, 1954): "Dans Arras je revois une enfance généralement triste" (In Arras I look back on a rather sad childhood). His father, Alfred Jouve, was a businessman and his mother, Aimee Rose Jouve, a music teacher. The exposure to music, the opportunity to improvise at the piano, first brought out his creative imagination. As a student in Arras and Lille, Jouve was rather contemptuous of literature, especially poetry, but after he left the lycée in 1905 he was converted after reading works by symbolist poets Stephané Mallarmé and Arthur Rimbaud. He began writing poetry himself, and in 1907 he cofounded, with Paul Castiaux, the literary magazine *Les Bandeaux d'or,* in which he published his first poems.

A 1910 trip to Italy marked an important turning point in Jouve's life. His travels there, highlighted by a trip to Rome and its environs, produced a short poem, "Ode à la Villa d'Adrien," an ode to Emperor Hadrian's eponymous villa. Overwhelmed by the remnants of ancient Rome and the art of the Renaissance set against the sunny landscape of Italy, Jouve wrote the poems published in *Les Muses Romaines et Florentines* (The Roman and Florentine Muses, 1910). Lofty and reverential in tone, these early poems, with their callow earnestness, give little indication of the deeply inward and hermetic style to come:

O Monument brûlé de lumière auguste,
Et dont la claire nuit, dans un silence juste,
D'une ombre colossale arrête les contours . . .

(O Monument burning with august light
And of which the clear night, in worthy silence,
Interrupts the contours with a colossal shadow . . .).

In 1910 Jouve married Andrée Charpentier, an older woman of powerful intelligence and a well-known suffragist. He volunteered for service as an orderly in a military hospital at the outbreak of World War I, but he contracted a severe respiratory infection and was forced to resign. After he went to Switzerland

Illustration by Balthus (Balthazzar Klossowski de Rola) for Jouve's 1937 poetry collection, Matière Céleste *(from René Micha,* Pierre-Jean Jouve, *1956)*

to recover from his illness, Jouve and his wife developed a close relationship with the novelist and pacifist Romain Rolland and his intellectual circle. Influenced by Rolland and having seen the effects of war firsthand in the hospital, Jouve wrote many pacifist poems, published in such books as *Vous êtes des hommes, 1915* (You Are Men, 1915), *Poème contre le grand crime, 1916* (Poem Against the Great Crime, 1916), and *Danse des morts* (Dance of the Dead, 1917).

In 1924 Jouve underwent an artistic transformation that deeply influenced his poetic development. He called it his "Vita Nuova," in allusion to *La Vita nuova* (The New Life, circa 1293) of Dante Alighieri, a work in which the Florentine poet, like Jouve, asks himself "perché altro parlare è stato lo mio" (why the speech of others was once my own). This same period coincided with the dissolution of his marriage to Andrée Jouve, and his involvement with another older and intellectual woman, Blanche Reverchon, a psychoanalyst whom he subsequently married in 1925. The fact that Rolland and his followers took the side of Jouve's first wife throughout the crisis must have affected Jouve. Crisis and change are apparent in his rejection of what he had previously written and published and in his conversion to what he calls in *En Miroir* "l'Idée religieuse la plus inconnue, la plus haute et la plus humble et tremblante, celle que nous pouvons à peine concevoir en ce temps-ci, mais hors laquelle notre vie n'a point d'existence" (the most unknown religious Idea, the highest and humblest and trembling, one which we can hardly conceive of in this day and age, but one outside of which our life has no existence).

This conversion marked an intensification of Jouve's Catholicism rather than a sudden change from one creed to another; in essence, the "Vita Nuova" pointed to an exploration and deepening of "des valeurs spirituelles de poésie, valeurs dont je reconnaissais l'essence chrétienne" (spiritual values of poetry, values whose Christian essence I recognized), as he recounts in *En Miroir*.

Theory met practice in Jouve's great poetic undertaking *Le Paradis Perdu* (The Lost Paradise), published in 1929. His affirmation of "the Christian essence" necessitated an encounter with Original Sin, as he explained,

Par le poème dramatique LE PARADIS PERDU je devais rencontrer "la faute." La faute, la nostalgie d'une innocence, et tout ce qui s'ajustait à la crise morale que je traversais.

(It was through the dramatic poem LOST PARADISE that I would encounter "The Fall." The Fall, the nostalgia of an innocence, and all that went with the moral crisis I was going through).

Le Paradis Perdu is divided into a prologue and two books. The work represents a literary journey back to Eden, where Jouve explores humankind's relationship with God and Satan, Beauty and Evil. The opening depiction of the prelapsarian state or condition is characteristically Jouvian:

Par confuses douceurs d'engendrements
Rayons encor sauvages ou sages pour toujours
Les Lueurs passent l'une en l'autre. Les durs espaces
S'échangent et se créent sans vouloir une fin
Pareils au sein qui s'agrandit en respirant.

(In confused sweetness of births
Rays yet wild or forever mild
The Lights pass one into another. The hard spaces
Alternate and create themselves without desiring an end
Like the bosom that swells in breathing).

But sin enters the universe and pristine nature is forever corrupted. At the end of *Le Paradis Perdu*, Jouve leaves the reader with a powerful image of sinful Earth and Man in the form of Adam and Eve transmogrified:

. . . Sous le pleur de la nuit
Le sommeil les prend tête à tête posés
Deux pierres appuyées au grand désert.

(. . . Under the tears of the night
Sleep gathers them poised face to face
Two stones leaning in the great desert).

Jouve's preoccupation with sin continues in *Sueur de Sang* (Sweat of Blood), a work marked by the evolving materiality of Jouve's imagery. First published in 1933 and then in an enlarged and revised edition in 1935, the collection features tangible signs of a corrupt world:

Je voyais une nappe épaisse d'huile verte
Ecoulée d'une machine et je songeais
Sur le pavé chaud de l'infame quartier
Longtemps, longtemps au sang de ma mère.

(I saw a thick cloth of green oil
Flowing from a machine and I thought
On the hot pavement of that vile quarter
Long and hard of the blood of my mother).

Juxtapositions suggestive of the unconscious make up much of the poetry. These images recall the introduction to *Sueur de Sang,* "Inconscient, Spiritualité et Catastrophe" (translated as *The Unconscious Spirituality Catastrophe,* 1987), in which Jouve writes, "Nous sommes au mystère de la sublimation, pour reprendre le mot dont Freud a désigné toute une espèce dynamique" (We have arrived at the mystery of sublimation, to take up the word that Freud used to designate an entire dynamic concept).

Part of the distinctiveness of Jouve's poetry is indeed suggested by the term "sublimation." It refers, of course, to the Freudian theory with all of its implications of rechanneled libido, but for Jouve it also signifies an essentially Christian form of transcendence. *Sueur de Sang* is in great measure a volume about materiality. Yet, there are hints of the sublime, which culminate in the final poem of the collection, "A la Fin" (At the End), describing a wondrous transformation:

A la fin la clarté devient folle d'octobre
Le paysage est transparent et décharné
Les ombres percent le sol jusqu'au cœur
Les glaciers touchent les yeux et quelle brûlure
L'exquise aurore bleue ne quitte pas le jour
Vraiment on tremble d'irisations et d'amour
Devant cette blonde
Maîtresse transparente des hauteurs.

(At the end the brightness becomes mad with October
The landscape is transparent and lean
The shadows penetrate the earth to its heart
The glaciers touch the eyes and what burning

Jouve in 1938

The exquisite blue dawn does not leave the day
Truly there is a trembling of iridescence and of love
Before that blond
Transparent mistress of the lofty heights).

Despite his interest in Sigmund Freud and the unconscious, Jouve was careful to distance himself from the Surrealists. He writes specifically, and dismissively, about automatic writing: "Tout automatisme doit être banni (le hasard, disait Mallarmé) d'autant plus que la vie inconsciente le produit avec facilité" (All automatic writing must be outlawed [chance, Mallarmé called it] especially as our unconscious life produces it so easily).

Jouve's preoccupation with terrestrial materiality is counterbalanced by an obsession with that which is not of Earth. This obsession is apparent in *Matière Céleste* (Celestial Matter, 1937), in which the figure of Hélène, in the poem of the same title, becomes a symbol both of human sexuality and transfiguration through death:

Que tu es belle maintenant que tu n'es plus
La poussière de la mort t'a déshabillée même de l'âme
Que tu es convoitée depuis que nous avons disparu

(How beautiful you are now that you are no more
The dust of death has undressed you even of your soul
How coveted you are now that we have gone).

In a later untitled poem, the reader is directed toward a more cosmic, mystical vision:

Le cœur divin en haut
Tout devenant immense et irradié
En haut plus près du bas
Seulement si l'on est à l'intérieur et si l'on joue
Tout pour le tout.

(The divine heart on high
Everything becoming immense and radiating
On high nearer than down below
Only if one is inside and if one plays
Everything for everything).

Jouve spent World War II in Geneva, where he produced a different kind of poetry in *La Vierge de Paris* (The Virgin of Paris, 1944). During World War I his pacifism, his antichauvinistic stance, and his association with Rolland had made Jouve firmly believe in the prophetic role of the poet, whose mission was international in scope. Similarly, between 1939 and 1944 Jouve once again concerned himself in his poetry with the more global and spiritual repercussions of conflict. He had not been indifferent to the evils of the period before World War II, however, as he writes:

Quand la guerre de 1939 éclata, la préparation de ma pensée était complètement achevée. Le principe fasciste, placé à l'imitation du marxisme sur les valeurs et avec les buts de "l'homme planétaire"–idolâtrie, démagogie, servitude–m'avait très bien fait comprendre son diabolisme.

(When the war broke out in 1939, the preparation of my thinking was already complete. The Fascist principle, based in imitation of Marxism on the values and goals of "planetary Man"–idolatry, demagogy, slavery–had made me understand very well its diabolical nature).

Despite Jouve's antipathy for Adolf Hitler and the Nazis, readers in search of direct references to the war or the Holocaust in *La Vierge de Paris* will undoubtedly be disappointed. What the reader will find, instead, are material evocations of evil mixed in with apostrophes and allusions to "Hélène," "La Vierge," and "l'Agneau" (The Lamb). Typically, the cataclysmic event elicited a deeply personal reaction from Jouve, one that reached out to a higher plane and spiritual authority. Jesus Christ and the Virgin Mary are the central figures in *La Vierge de Paris:*

HUMANITÉ DU CHRIST, à l'époque parjure
Dans les églises où Jésus est pollué
Dans les états où Jésus est injure
Dans les combats où Jésus mort est forniqué . . .
Humanité du Christ! en faiblesse et en ombre
Tu veux que j'aie connu l'ivresse singulière
De mon sang qui a vie et ressource première
Dans ta perfection hors du temps le plus sombre.

(HUMANITY OF CHRIST, in this era of perjury
In the churches where Jesus is defiled
In the states where Jesus is blasphemy
In the battles where the dead Jesus is fornicated . . .
Humanity of Christ! in weakness and in shadow
You wanted me to know the rare drunkenness
Of my blood which has life and first source
In your perfection outside of the darkest hour).

Here is a rather idiosyncratic example of Jouvian chiaroscuro, in which the overwhelmingly dark and sexual imagery finally gives way to glimmers of hope. The constant tension between dark and light, material and immaterial, despair and faith, and death and resurrection, which became such a definitive aspect of his poetry, reaches its climax in the untitled final poem of this long collection:

O Vierge de Paris c'est à présent que l'art
Obscur emplit l'abîme alors que tous les plis
Disparaissent, que tu n'es plus la vierge mère,
C'est à présent que nous voyons le vent du temps
Mêlant nos murs cassés à nos tristes parvis
Demander durement si nous sommes Lazare.

(O Virgin of Paris it is now that obscure art
Fills the abyss at a time when all the folds
Disappear, that you are no more the virgin mother,
It is now that we see the wind of time
Mingling our broken walls with our sad courtyards
Ask harshly if we are Lazarus).

"Hardness" is a good epithet both for Jouve's poetic style and his view of the creative act itself. In *Le Don Juan de Mozart* (1942; translated as *Mozart's Don Juan,* 1957) he writes: "De la polyphonie de Mozart, il apparaît que la substance soit en acier, quelque chose d'extrêmement dur" (About Mozart's polyphony, it appears that the substance is of steel, something extremely hard). For Jouve, art requires a form somehow adamantine in character, one whose "hardness" gives it a perfection and a duration.

Don Juan de Mozart, En Miroir, Tombeau de Baudelaire (Tomb of Baudelaire, 1942), and a work cowritten with Michel Fano, *Wozzeck; ou, Le Nouvel opéra* (Wozzeck; or, The New Opera, 1953), show another important side of Jouve's creativity. In these works Jouve the literary critic and aesthete emerges. Whether analyzing poetry, art, or music, he attempts to describe the creative act and to discuss the form peculiar to a given work and how it makes its effect upon the reader, viewer, or listener. A good example of his approach can be found in his *Tombeau de Baudelaire:* "Le secret de Baudelaire, dont il ne connaît pas lui-même l'étendue, est la recherche de l'inconsient comme moteur de la Poésie" (Baudelaire's secret, the extent of which he himself could not have known, is the search for the unconscious as the driving force of Poetry). In *En Miroir* he offers this definition of poetry:

La Poésie est établie sur le mot; sur la tension organisée entre les mots, c'est le "chant"; sur les mystères de l'association des idées et des colorations, entre souvenirs, émotions et désirs, provoquées par les mots; et enfin, j'oserai dire, sur le pouvoir occulte du mot de créer la chose.

(Poetry is established on the word; on the organized tension between the words, it is the "chant"; on the mysteries of association of the ideas and the colorations, between memories, emotions and desires, provoked by the words; and finally, I dare say, on the hidden power of the word to create the thing).

As Jouve grew older, his poetry tended to be characterized by an unearthly quality, a reaching out for an immaterial realm. Paradoxically, however, it was often through hard, material imagery that this quality was achieved. In "Fairy," from *Diadème* (Diadem, 1949), this tension between the material and the immaterial also signals the self-reflexity of his poetry:

> Impénénatrable vœu des charnelles douceurs
> D'être avec Dieu selon Dieu reconnues!
> Des miracles vivants fermant les avenues
> De la honte, et en diamants changés les pleurs.
>
> (Impenetrable wish of carnal delights
> Of being with God according to God recognized
> Of living miracles closing the avenues
> Of shame, and into diamonds to transform tears).

The poet's call for a communing with God and a transmuting of tears into diamonds coincides with Jouve's conception of the creative act. In *Mélodrame* (Melodrama, 1957), he writes succinctly: "Le mystère engendreur baisant conscience noire a fait la fleur absurde où le parfum est art" (The creative mystery kissing black consciousness has made the absurd flower whose fragrance is art). Jouve's "parfum" is the Baudelairian "correspondance," or analogue, to his own song. That Jouve's poetics includes elements of the divine should come as a surprise to no one. Earlier, in his foreword to *Sueur de Sang,* Jouve had concluded:

> La révolution comme l'acte religieux a besoin d'amour. La poésie est un véhicule intérieur de l'amour. Nous devons donc, poètes, produire cette "sueur de sang" qu'est l'élévation à des substances si profondes, ou si élevées, qui dérivent de la pauvre, de la belle puissance érotique humaine.
>
> (The revolution as religious act needs love. Poetry is an internal vehicle of love. We must therefore, poets, produce this "sweat of blood" which is the elevation to the deepest substances or the most elevated, those deriving from our poor, from our beautiful human erotic power).

Thus, despite his insistence on Freudian terminology, Jouve's desire to delve into the unconscious is clearly rooted in a religious context. In the poem "Adieu," from *Mélodrame,* the reader finds perhaps the most beautiful example of this religious and artistic faith:

> Tout poème a Dieu pour témoin et cœur et réceptacle
> Tout chant est substance à Dieu et même si Dieu absent:
> Harmonie avec le torrent de dissonance dans l'orchestre
> Cri exultant de l'univers en son voyage adorant.
>
> (Every poem has God as witness and heart and receptacle
> Every chant is substance to God even with God absent:
> Harmony with the torrent of dissonance in the orchestra
> Exultant cry of the universe in its voyage of adoration).

Here Jouve's characteristic hermeticism yields to a luminous transparency. And yet, in keeping with his poetics, he retains the essential antithetical couplings

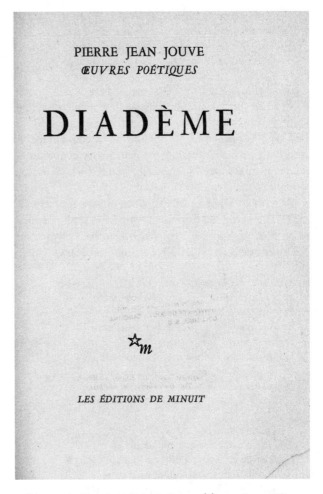

Title page for Jouve's 1949 book of poetry (Thomas Cooper Library, University of South Carolina)

that, in his view, are alone capable of translating mysteries of faith and the cosmos.

Jouve continued to write poetry well into his late seventies. His last major collection, *Moires* (Watered Silk), was published in 1962 and republished in a revised and enlarged edition in 1967. In this final work of poetry, there are many signs of a poetic valediction. As in previous volumes, especially *Mélodrame,* music is evoked and apostrophized, even to the point of including bar lines. This intertextuality greatly enriches Jouve's text, giving new meaning to the intrinsic complexity built into the poet's architecture of hardness. In "Chant de la terre" (Song of the Earth), an allusion to Gustav Mahler's symphony of the same title, Jouve describes the aural impression of the composition on the listener:

> Ce contrepoint des douleurs et des chairs
> Des timbres des soubassements noirceur profonde
> Des féroces et lourds chevauchements des cors
> Aux trombones–la voix alors voix déchirante!

(This counterpoint of grief and of flesh
Of timbres of underpinnings deep blackness
Of fierce and heavy galloping from the horns
To the trombones—the voice then heart-rending voice!)

Jouve includes six bars of music as part of his poem. And below the bar lines he adds Mahler's name for that section of the score, "Der Abschied" (The Farewell), as well as the one word to be sung in accompaniment: "ewig" (eternal or forever). The valedictory character of the poem, and indeed of the collection as a whole, is juxtaposed to the idea of permanence.

This constant tension between opposites reaches a high point in the last two poems of *Moires*. In the penultimate text, an untitled composition, Jouve's mysticism coincides perfectly with his reflections on his own work:

TRÈS PEU COMPRENDRONT. Que le feu de la chair
Et la blancheur du ciel, le refus de la honte
Et la tentation bienheureuse du désir
Se sont toujours montrés en la même lumière,
Se sont heurtés se sont aimés
Du même corps à travers cent angoisses
Mais aucun n'a cédé de ses forces sacrées
A l'adversire, ni le péché ni la folle espérance.

(VERY FEW WILL UNDERSTAND. That the fire of the flesh
And the whiteness of the sky, the rejection of shame
And the blissful temptation of desire
Have always shown themselves in the same light,
Have collided into have loved each other
From the same body through one hundred torments
But not one has yielded its sacred forces
To its adversary, neither sin nor mad hope).

Pessimism and optimism coexist in these verses. The images are held in tight opposition, as if inextricably bound.

The epigraph of *Moires* consists of only six words: "ET LE SEL DANS LES LARMES" (AND SALT IN TEARS). This line is a distillation of *Moires,* and in many ways, a distillation of Jouve's writing as a whole. A *moire* is a cloth that has a watered or wavy pattern, and in *Mélodrame,* Jouve declares: "L'essence arrive à Dieu dans la langue des ondes" (The essence comes to God in the language of the waves.) Water constitutes an important metaphor for Jouve, translating the mystical correspondence of "le chant" and "le parfum."

Moreover, besides Jouve's characteristically mystical language, there is the poet who foresees that his poetry will go unappreciated. In Jouve's poetry the reader finds elements of the living artist struggling with his creation where the text itself reflects the struggle and comments on it.

Pierre Jean Jouve died on 8 January 1976. Despite his enormous talent and output, he remains a somewhat enigmatic figure, a writer more esteemed than well-known. Although Margaret Callander's critical study, *The Poetry of Pierre Jean Jouve* (1965), includes much biographical information presented chronologically, there is no real biography of Jouve. Perhaps the next-to-last poem of *Moires* provides a clue to the puzzle and an appropriate epitaph for the poet: TRÈS PEU COMPRENDRONT.

References:

Charles Bachat, Daniel Leuwers, and Etienne-Alain Hubert, eds., *Bousquet, Jouve, Reverdy: Colloques poésie, Cerisy* (Marseilles: Sud, 1981);

Christiane Blot-Labarrère, ed., *Jouve et ses curiosités esthétiques* (Paris: Lettres Modernes, 1988);

Blot-Labarrère, *Relation de la faute de l'Eros et de la mort dans l'œuvre romanesque de P.J. Jouve* (Aix-en-Provence: La Pensée Universitaire, 1962);

Yves Bonnefoy, *Le Nuage rouge: Essais sur la poétique* (Paris: Mercure de France, 1977);

Martine Broda, *Jouve* (Lausanne, Switzerland: L'Age d'Homme, 1981);

Margaret Callander, *The Poetry of Pierre Jean Jouve* (Manchester: Manchester University Press, 1965);

Leuwers, *Jouve avant Jouve; ou, La Naissance d'un poète (1906–1928)* (Paris: Klincksieck, 1984);

Leuwers, ed., *Jouve poète de la rupture* (Paris: Lettres Modernes, 1986);

Leuwers, "Pierre Jean Jouve et Le Tasse," *Argile,* 41 (Summer 1978);

Kurt Schärer, *Thématique et poétique du mal dans l'œuvre de Pierre Jean Jouve* (Paris: Lettres Modernes, 1984);

Jean Starobinski, *Pierre Jean Jouve, poète et romancier* (Neuchâtel, Switzerland: La Baconnière, 1946).

Patrice de La Tour du Pin

(16 March 1911 – 28 October 1975)

Toby Garfitt
University of Oxford

BOOKS: *Lys et violettes: Premiers essais de deux jeunes cousins,* by La Tour du Pin and Louis d'Hendecourt, with a preface by Pierre de La Gorce (Paris: Les Gémeaux, 1926);

La Quête de Joie (Paris: La Tortue, 1933); enlarged as *La Quête de Joie, suivi de Petite Somme de poésie,* preface by Maurice Champagne (Paris: Gallimard, 1967);

D'un aventurier (Paris: Debresse, 1935);

L'Enfer: Poème (Tunis: Editions de Mirages, 1935);

Le Lucernaire: Livre I, Les Cahiers de Barbarie, no. 13 (Tunis: Editions de Mirages, 1936);

Le Don de la Passion, suivi de Saint Élie de Gueuce, Cahiers des poètes catholiques, no. 2 (Paris: La Pléiade / Brussels: Edition Universelle, 1937);

Psaumes (Paris: Gallimard, 1938);

La Vie recluse en poésie, suivi de Présence et poësie, par Daniel-Rops, by La Tour du Pin and Daniel-Rops (Paris: Plon, 1938); translated, with "Correspondance de Laurent de Cayeux," by G. S. Fraser as *The Dedicated Life in Poetry and The Correspondence of Laurent de Cayeux,* introduction by Stephen Spender (London: Harvill, 1948);

Les Anges (Tunis: Monomotapa, 1939);

Deux chroniques intérieures (Paris: Seghers, 1945);

La Genèse, Idées poétiques, no. 8 (Neuchâtel, Switzerland: Ides et Calendes, 1945);

Le Jeu du Seul (Paris: Gallimard, 1946);

Les Concerts sur terre (Paris: Robert Laffont, 1946);

Une Somme de poésie (Paris: Gallimard, 1946)–includes "Correspondance de Laurent de Cayeux"; revised as *Une Somme de poésie I: Le Jeu de l'homme en lui-même* (Paris: Gallimard, 1981);

Les Contes de Soi, illustrated by Charles-Emile Pinson (Paris: Robert Laffont, 1946);

Bestiaire fabuleux, illustrated by Jean Lurçat (Paris: Darantière, 1947);

La Contemplation errante (Paris: Gallimard, 1948);

Noël des eaux (Neuchâtel, Switzerland: Ides et Calendes, 1951);

Patrice de La Tour du Pin as a prisoner of war, 1940
(from Jacques Gauthier, Patrice de la Tour du Pin, quêteur du Dieu de joie, *1987)*

Pépinière de sapins de Noël, par deux sylviculteurs, text by La Tour du Pin and illustrations by Jacques Ferrand (Paris: Gallimard, 1957);

Une Somme de poésie: Le Second Jeu (Paris: Gallimard, 1959); revised as *Une Somme de poésie II: Le Jeu de l'homme devant les autres* (Paris: Gallimard, 1982);

Une Somme de poésie III, première partie: Petit Théâtre crépusculaire (Paris: Gallimard, 1963); revised and enlarged as *Une Somme de poésie III: Le Jeu de l'homme devant Dieu* (Paris: Gallimard, 1983)–includes revised version of *Une Lutte pour la vie;*

Lieux-dits (Paris: Société de Saint-Eloy, 1967);

Une Lutte pour la vie (Paris: Gallimard, 1970);

Concert eucharistique (Paris: Desclée, 1972);

Psaumes de tous mes temps: Textes nouveaux (Paris: Gallimard, 1974);

Carnets de route, preface by Joseph Gelineau (Paris: Plon/Mame, 1995);

Chemin de croix (des rapatriés en pèlerinage à Lourdes), illustrated by Paul Monnier (Saint-Maurice, Switzerland: Editions Saint-Augustin, 1998);

Du vierge–De la Vierge, edited by Marc Gsell (Saint-Maurice, Switzerland: Editions Saint-Augustin, 1999).

Edition: *Daniel-Rops: L'Œuvre grandissante de Patrice de la Tour du Pin. Suivi d'un poème de Patrice de la Tour du Pin: "Les Anges,"* introductory essay by Daniel-Rops, Cahiers des poètes catholiques, no. 41 (Paris: Desclée de Brouwer / Brussels: Edition Universelle, 1942).

OTHER: Yves Noulant, *Exil: poèmes,* preface by La Tour du Pin (Nancy: Privately printed, 1946);

Irène-Carole Reweliotty, *Journal d'une jeune fille,* preface by La Tour du Pin (Paris: La Jeune Parque, 1946);

Jean-Claude Renard, *Cantiques pour des pays perdus,* preface by La Tour du Pin, Sous le signe d'Arion, no. 15 (Paris: Robert Laffont, 1947);

Jean de Frotté, *Le Sculpteur de son espérance,* introductory poem by La Tour du Pin (Paris: Plon, 1953);

Henry Clairvaux, *Quand le diable a soif: Vignettes de l'auteur,* introduction by La Tour du Pin (Paris: Oswald, 1956);

"Lettre aux confidents," in *Patrice de La Tour du Pin,* by Eva Kushner, Poètes d'aujourd'hui, no. 79, (Paris: Seghers, 1961), pp. 195–217;

Prière du temps présent: Le Nouvel office divin, with several prayers and hymns by La Tour du Pin (Paris: Cerf/Desclée de Brouwer/Desclée/Mame, 1971);

Conférence francophone cistercienne, *La Nuit, le jour: Hymnes et tropaires par un groupe de moines et de moniales,* preface by La Tour du Pin (Paris: Desclée/Cerf, 1973);

Jean Trémolières, *Partager le pain,* with a preface by La Tour du Pin (Paris: Robert Laffont, 1975);

Antoine Trémolières, *Chants de la lumière qui tremble,* preface by La Tour du Pin (Paris: Privately printed, 1980).

SELECTED PERIODICAL PUBLICATIONS–UNCOLLECTED: "Comment je suis venu au théâtre," *Le Figaro littéraire,* 2 June 1956: 1;

"L'écrivain et la liturgie," *La Maison-Dieu,* 91 (1967): 145–159;

"Une question de sève vitale," *Liturgie et vie chrétienne,* 68 (1969): 104–107;

"Poétique et liturgie," *Christus,* 67 (1970): 392–415;

"Langage poétique et liturgie," *Lumière et vie,* 100 (1970): 121–140;

"Travaillé par la Parole," *Aujourd'hui la Bible,* 62 (1971): 3;

"La fonction poétique et liturgique," *La Maison-Dieu,* 121 (1975): 81–97;

"Deux lettres à Ernest Dutoit," *Création,* 16 (1979): 12–13;

"Deux lettres à Hugues de Kerret," *Les Cahiers Obsidiane,* 3 (1981): 51–52;

"Chanter Dieu, chanter pour Dieu," *La Maison-Dieu,* 150 (1982): 163–166.

Patrice de La Tour du Pin is a major Catholic poet, and indeed a major poet by any reckoning. Much of his life was devoted to the elaboration of a single work in three volumes, *Une Somme de poésie* (A Summa of Poetry), which was published in its definitive form in three volumes in 1981–1983, but fragments of which had appeared over the preceding half-century, with the first major portion published as *Une Somme de poésie* (1946).

Patrice Arthur Elie Humbert de La Tour du Pin Chambly de La Charce was born in Paris on 16 March 1911, the eve of St Patrick's Day: hence the name Patrice. His mother, born Brigitte O'Connor, was the great-granddaughter of Arthur O'Connor, an Irish parliamentarian who defended Catholic rights, later joining Napoleon's army and rising to the rank of general. Arthur O'Connor married Elisa de Condorcet, the daughter of the political philosopher and revolutionary statesman Marie Jean Antoine Nicolas Caritat, Marquis de Condorcet. Part of his wife's dowry was the estate of another revolutionary, Honoré Gabriel Victor Riqueti, Comte de Mirabeau, where O'Connor settled, taking French citizenship. Patrice de La Tour du Pin's father was François de La Tour du Pin Chambly de La Charce, a member of an extensive noble family with roots in the Dauphiné. A great-uncle, René Charles Humbert, Marquis de La Tour du Pin Chambly de La Charce (1834–1924), was a leading figure in Catholic social thought at the turn of the century and the author of *Vers un ordre social chrétien, Jalons de Route, 1882–1907* (Toward a Christian Social Order, Milestones along the Way, 1882–1907, 1907). Patrice de La Tour du Pin was the youngest of three children. After his father was killed in the first month of World War I, the boy was raised by his mother and his maternal grandmother, Marguerite O'Connor (née de Ganay), partly in Paris but mainly on the family estate of Le Bignon-Mirabeau, seventy miles to the south. When he was fifteen, his sister, Phylis, joined the Dominican convent at Sens, but they remained in close contact throughout his life, and the influence of her and his brother, Aymar, on him was considerable. He was educated at the Collège Sainte-Croix in Neuilly, several years behind the writer Henry de Montherlant, and completed his *baccalauréat* (secondary-school examination giving university entrance qualification) at the Lycée Janson-de-Sailly, where he was in the same class as the politician Maurice Schumann. He studied briefly at the Sorbonne and the Ecole des Sciences Politiques, but he already knew that his real calling was to be a poet. He had no career in the normal sense of the word, but devoted the rest of his life to his poetry, his family, and his estate. He served as a *conseiller municipal* (town councilman) and then as mayor of the local village for more than twenty years from 1947 until his death.

Lys et violettes: Premiers essais de deux jeunes cousins (Lilies and Violets: First Ventures by Two Young Cousins), a volume of poetry by La Tour du Pin and his cousin Louis d'Hendecourt, was privately printed in 1926, but La Tour du Pin's first real breakthrough came in 1931 when the prestigious *Nouvelle Revue française* published his poem "Les Enfants de Septembre" (Children of September), on the recommendation of Jules Supervielle. In 1933 the volume *La Quête de Joie* (The Quest for Joy) was published privately in Paris in an edition of six hundred copies. The book elicited a large and enthusiastic critical response, encouraged in 1934 by the appearance of a special issue of Armand Guibert's review, *Mirages,* devoted to La Tour du Pin. Guibert himself wrote several articles in which he compared La Tour du Pin to Dante Alighieri, John Milton, John Keats, the French Romantics, William Blake, and William Morris, as well as the great Christian mystics. The novelist and critic Robert Brasillach saw La Tour du Pin as the spiritual heir of Emily Brontë and Edgar Allan Poe. Novelists André Gide and Montherlant were among those who wrote to congratulate him.

La Quête de Joie is not an anthology but rather a cycle of poems, or possibly even a single poem with many constituent parts, whose theme is the quest for true spiritual joy. This quest is portrayed both in terms of a wildfowling expedition and as the quest for the Holy Grail. The naturalness with which La Tour du Pin draws on his own daily life as a countryman saves his writing from the artificiality of the French Symbolist topos of the swan-hunt, for instance, while his use of such features as twilight,

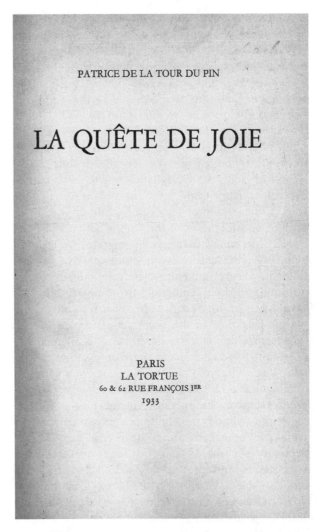

PATRICE DE LA TOUR DU PIN

LA QUÊTE DE JOIE

PARIS
LA TORTUE
60 & 62 RUE FRANÇOIS Iᵉʳ
1933

Title page for the cycle of poems in which La Tour du Pin employed a wildfowling expedition as an allegorical representation of the quest for spiritual joy (Case Library, Colgate University)

mist, and starlight helps to create a powerful air of mystery, reminiscent not only of the plays of Belgian Symbolist Maurice Maeterlinck but also of the pre-Romantic tradition associated with the third-century Irish warrior-poet Ossian, as presented by James MacPherson in the eighteenth century. There are several characters: the mysterious princely figure of Ullin, with his cold intelligence; the more human leader Lorenquin; a couple of beautiful young girls, Laurence and Gemma; and Christ, appearing enigmatically as a passive, crucified figure, yet one who is central to the action. The visual element is strong in *La Quête de Joie:* La Tour du Pin was much influenced by Albrecht Dürer, Mathias Grünewald, and Sandro Botticelli, particularly the latter's illustrations of the works of Dante. The unnamed poetic persona plays the major part in the unfolding saga, which is an essentially personal quest.

The opening poem of *La Quête de Joie,* "Prélude," displays many of the characteristic features of La Tour du Pin's verse. It is in regular lines— decasyllables in the opening section, then mainly alexandrines, with some *vers impairs* (irregular verse; with an uneven number of syllables) with careful but not entirely regular rhyme patterns. The poem begins with a memorable couplet: "Tous les pays qui n'ont plus de légende / Seront condamnés à mourir de froid" (A land without a legend is condemned / To die of cold). A solitary landscape at dawn is then evoked, which is at the same time a landscape of the soul. The mention of the cry of a hunted bird leads on to a consideration of the "anges sauvages" (wild angels), described in terms of migratory birds and evidently representing the yearning for love and fulfillment. Desire, adventure, heroism, death, poetic vocation, spiritual ambition, the unattainability of divine perfection, and the idea of a training school for the discipline of the quest are all touched on in this poem, culminating in the image of a solemn commissioning ceremony somewhere on a snowy mountain slope. The volume then proceeds in a series of overlapping cycles in which these and other themes are developed. "Enfants de Septembre" comes early on in the volume: the child-poet leaves his room at dawn and follows the prints left by a magical child of September, a sort of "ange sauvage" that has been separated from the rest of the flock. At first he imagines how the child will welcome him as a brother, but then he foresees a long, tiring chase, after which he will caress his almost-dead prey and gently bring it home. At the end the vision fades. This poem appealed strongly to early readers because, as in *Le Grand Meaulnes* (Big Meaulnes, 1913) by Alain-Fournier (pseudonym of Henri Alban Fournier), "les sortilèges de l'enfance y étaient restitués dans toute leur fraîcheur" (the magic of childhood was restored in all its freshness), as Pierre de Boisdeffre puts it in his *Histoire vivante de la littérature française d'aujourd'hui* (Living History of French Literature of Today, 1958). In the rest of *La Quête de Joie* La Tour du Pin explores various approaches to the quest, ranging from the uncompromisingly cerebral gaze of Ullin to the natural sensuality of Laurence, and from the elevated tone of "Hulmaune," reminiscent of Victor Hugo and Poe, to the simple lyricism of "La Plaie" (The Wound). The central poems in the volume, "Le Christ voilé" (The Veiled Christ) and "Banquet," express a sense of failure, at least in terms of the high spiritual and poetic aspirations that have been implied. Failure leads not to despair, however, but to a fresh appreciation of modest, human values such as compassion. The final poem, "Epilogue," is again set

in a misty dawn landscape of lakes and woods that recalls La Tour du Pin's own region of the Gâtinais: the poet encounters an unidentified interlocutor, a former companion in the quest, evidently representing aspects of himself, who has returned to die. The implication is that the quest will go on but in a different form.

La Quête de Joie is only a fragment of what was always intended to be a much longer and more comprehensive work. For the critics it has tended to overshadow the rest of La Tour du Pin's writings because of its freshness and richness, and no doubt also because many of them encountered it at an impressionable age. Here was a poet who was completely untouched by Surrealism and who had both a high ideal of poetry and a distinctively personal voice. "Il est rare de voir naître un poète" (It is rare to witness the birth of a poet), Brasillach writes with admiration, in his *Les Quatre Jeudis: Images d'avant-guerre* (The Four Thursdays: Pre-War Images, 1944). In a 1938 article, collected in volume two of his *Littérature du XXe siècle* (Literature of the Twentieth Century, 1939), André Rousseaux claims that La Tour du Pin had challenged the whole of the French Symbolist tradition from Gérard de Nerval and Charles Baudelaire onward, and that henceforth he would be a force to be reckoned with. *La Quête de Joie* was republished by Gallimard in 1939, and again in the "Poésie" series in 1967 (with a selection of later poems). It is still considered of central importance by La Tour du Pin scholars, and a major study of it by Luca Pietromarchi was published in Italian in 1995 and in French in 2001.

The larger work of which *La Quête de Joie* was intended to be a part was originally titled "Saul," after Saul of Tarsus, Saint Paul's preconversion, Jewish name. Partly under the influence of his reading of Dante, La Tour du Pin was planning to have Saul visit Hell—another possible title for the book was "L'Enfer" (Hell). By 1933, however, La Tour du Pin had decided on "Une Somme," as a homage to the *Summa theologiæ* (Summa of Theology, circa 1265 or 1267–1273) of St. Thomas Aquinas: the title eventually became specifically *Une Somme de poésie,* but the theological aspect was always important. Important sections of *Une Somme de poésie* were published during the 1930s: *D'un aventurier* (The Adventurer, 1935), *L'Enfer* (1935), *Le Lucernaire* (1936), *Le Don de la Passion, suivi de Saint Elie de Gueuce* (The Gift of the Passion, Followed by Saint Elie of Gueuce, 1937), *Psaumes* (Psalms, 1938), *La Vie recluse en poésie, suivi de Présence et poésie, par Daniel-Rops* (1938; translated as *The Dedicated Life in Poetry,* 1948), and *Les Anges* (1939). *La Vie recluse en poésie*—published together with

La Tour du Pin and his wife, Anne, in 1944

a critical essay by Daniel-Rops (pseudonym of Henri Petiot)—is a treatise in prose attributed to Laurent de Cayeux, the successor to Lorenquin (their names are deliberately similar). It sets out the philosophy of the Ecole de Tess, a quasi-monastic community of singers or poets. They are encouraged to go back to first principles and learn to express the simplest things in life before raising their sights to the higher poetic goal of the quest. They will then need to devote all their intelligence to the task, but intelligence alone will never be sufficient: as Rainer Maria Rilke had foreseen, love is essential to the poetic quest. Critics such as Henri Massis applauded the attempt, while others found the idea of a modern *Ars Poetica* unpalatable. La Tour du Pin's friend Claude Mauriac later revealed, in his *La Terrasse de Malagar* (The Terrace of Malagar, 1977), that he was deeply moved by certain passages of *La Vie recluse en poésie*. In an essay

included with an unauthorized 1942 edition of *Les Anges,* "L'Œuvre grandissante de Patrice de La Tour du Pin" (Patrice de La Tour du Pin: A Work of Growing Importance), one of several pieces that he devoted to the poet, Daniel-Rops takes a broader view, explaining the overall plan of the forthcoming *Somme de poésie.*

For at least a part of the reading public on the eve of World War II, then, La Tour du Pin held out the promise of nothing less than a renewal of the French poetic tradition. His supernaturalism, his humanism, and his championing of regular but unstuffy verse was refreshing. Rousseaux expressed the feelings of many when he wrote in 1938 that while it was too early to judge whether La Tour du Pin was the leading poet of the century, his work was destined either to be truly epoch-making or at least to leave "quelques vestiges inouïs de grand poème manqué" (extraordinary traces of a great poem manqué). When the poet was mistakenly reported killed in action in October 1939 (he later enjoyed showing friends an invitation to a memorial mass), there was a particularly poignant sense of loss among his readers. After it was discovered that he had not been killed but had been wounded and taken prisoner after a valiant show of resistance (for which he was awarded the Légion d'Honneur in 1942), he was quickly seized on by the press as an emblematic figure representing the best of French youth. François Mauriac wrote an influential article in *Temps présent* (24 November 1939), which was reprinted in *Le Figaro littéraire,* a sonnet written by Maurice Rostand titled "Un Poète prisonnier" was published in *L'Œuvre,* and there were tributes on the radio. La Tour du Pin was compared to two great poets associated with World War I, Charles Péguy and Guillaume Apollinaire.

He spent three years in captivity, first in the Saarland, at Spangenberg (Oflag IXA), and then in Silesia, at Hoyerswerda (Oflag IVD), where one of the other prisoners was Jean Guitton. He was able to carry on working on the first volume of *Une Somme de poésie,* the later parts of which are strongly colored by his recent near-death experience and by the pressures of life in confinement. He was also able to reread the works of Michel de Montaigne and Paul Valéry, two of the most enduring influences on his work (he saw them as sparring partners).

La Tour du Pin had the strange honor of being elected president in absentia of the Jeune France group of poets and musicians that gathered at Lourmarin in September 1941. Inspired by Emmanuel Mounier, the movement included such individuals associated with *Poésie 41* and *Fontaine* as Pierre Emmanuel, Max-Pol Fouchet, and Pierre Seghers. La Tour du Pin kept the poetry he wrote in captivity to himself until the *Somme de poésie* was complete. A release of prisoners was finally arranged, and he returned to France in 1942. In October of the following year he married his first cousin, Anne de Pierre de Bernis-Calvière. They had four children, Marie-Liesse, Anne-Dauphine (or Dauphinelle), Aude, and Laurence. La Tour du Pin's discovery of human love supplied some of the missing elements for his *Somme de poésie.*

The first substantial part of *Une Somme de poésie* finally appeared in 1946. It is a volume of more than six hundred pages and consists of nine books separated by eight interludes, which usually take the form of a prose narrative or a short play. The first volume of the definitive edition, published in 1981, has the same format, but many of the texts have been extensively revised. There is clearly a progression from the "Genèse" (Genesis) of book 1 to the "Enfer" (Hell) of book 9, but it is hardly a straightforward one, though the last book explains much of what has gone before, in that all the colorful characters who people its pages—such as the unnamed kings, Ellor, Jean de Flaterre, Lorenquin, Laurent de Cayeux, Gorphoncelet, Le Cortinaire, Borlonge, and Fauln—are ultimately rejected for overemphasizing one aspect or another of the quest, and the poet has to leave them behind if he is to make any real artistic or spiritual progress. In book 1 the poet indulges his creative desires, using material drawn from the depths of his inner self that he externalizes to form a world inhabited by fascinating creatures such as the collared Bareuls (further explored in some witty prose poems in book 6). He creates three bird-like species, the Enfants Paradisiers (Children of Paradise), the Enfants Chanteurs (Song-Children), and the Enfants Sauvages (Wild Children), which represent between them the whole range of the poetic voice; these are later joined by a fourth species, the more intellectual Planistes. "La Genèse" gives rise to the dangerously solipsistic "Jeu du Seul" (Play of the Solitary One) of book 2 and the early human kingdoms of book 3, but the interlude that follows, "L'Aventure de Jean de Flaterre" (The Adventure of Jean de Flaterre), introduces the insight that "Tout homme est une histoire sacrée" (Every man is a sacred history), which paves the way for the account in book 4 of the Ecole de Tess. Lorenquin there attempts to move the emphasis away from the self and provide an external focus: the Chapel of the Virgin is at the center of the school, so that Tess stands as a contrast both to François Rabelais's self-indulgent Abbey of Thélème, in his *La Vie inestimable du grand Gargantua* (The Inestimable Life of the Great Gargantua, 1534), and to the arid rationalism of Valéry's Monsieur Teste, protagonist of such works as *La Soirée avec M. Teste* (1919; translated as *An Evening with Mr. Teste,* 1925). Book 4 also includes a revised version of Lorenquin's treatise "La Vie recluse en poésie," which does not, as might have been expected, constitute the center of the volume: that honor is reserved for "La Quête de Joie," which occupies the whole of book 5. Book 6 is dominated by a cycle of fifty-one psalms, but also includes further material on the Ecole de Tess, ending with the moving "Poème de l'agonie du Cortinaire" (Poem of the Agony of Le Cortinaire). Book 7 then takes up the theme of death, this time in the context of war, with "La Mise à l'autre monde" (Into the Other World) and the "Chronique de Borlonge" (Chronicle of Borlonge). Love makes its appearance in book 8, with the cycle of thirty-three poems dedicated to the poet's wife, Annie, under the title "Le Monde d'amour" (The World of Love). Book 9, with "L'Enfer," constitutes a principled rejection of much of what has come before. The two parts of the poem titled "Thème" (Theme), which open and close the whole volume, make explicit La Tour du Pin's project. The exuberance of self-discovery and unbridled creation has had to be confronted with the grim realities of war and death and tempered by the responsibilities of friendship, love, marriage, and fatherhood. At the same time, there has been a constant disciplined commitment to study the inner life and to give it adequate poetic expression, balancing the intellectual and the emotional in a song of joy that will also be a hymn to the love of God. This discipline is evident in the architectural qualities of *Une Somme de poésie;* it is reflected not only in the attention given to the account offered by the architect Lydiverquen of the physical architecture of Tess but also in the careful structure of the volume as a whole and its constituent parts. In a letter to Anne-Henri de Biéville-Noyant (published in *Les Cahiers bleus* in 1987) La Tour du Pin described three of the nine books (the second, fifth, and eighth) as "livres-piliers" (pillars), giving support and structure to the whole: they represented "la base, le mouvement et le but cherché" (the basis, the dynamic, and the goal).

Rousseaux, in an article written in 1946 and included as a supplement to his 1938 piece in the revised edition (1948) of his *Littérature du XXe siècle,* acknowledges that until the publication of *Une Somme de poésie* he had failed to grasp the deeper meaning of La Tour du Pin's enterprise. He says that he would now call it a drama rather than a legend, and he defines it in terms of a fervent *angélisme,* passionately religious but unlike the angelism of Stéphane Mallarmé, Valéry, and Jean Giraudoux. Biéville-Noyant, a close friend of La Tour du Pin, objected to the term: there were many angels in *Une Somme de poésie,* but "l'angélisme ressortit à une esthétique douteuse que le poète réprouve" (angelism belongs to an erroneous aesthetic which the poet censures). In his *Patrice de La Tour du Pin: Document pour l'histoire de la littérature française* (1948), Biéville-Noyant chronicled the poet's career from an early age up to the publication of *Une Somme de poésie,* quoting extensively from private letters, and then gave a masterly analysis of the work itself, finishing with a one-hundred-page "résumé anthologique" (anthological summary) of the work. He makes it clear that though the 1946 book was originally conceived as complete in itself, it would have to be completed by further volumes.

Another important critical assessment to appear in 1948 was Stephen Spender's introduction to *The Dedicated Life in Poetry and The Correspondence of Laurent de Cayeux,* G. S. Fraser's translation of "La Vie recluse en poésie" and the "Correspondance de Laurent de Cayeux" (from the 1946 volume of *Somme du poésie*). His essay makes a distinction between those modern poets who "are more interested in the poetic experience to which they feel they must remain true," and those "who are concerned with limiting their poetic experience in order to write aesthetically complete poems." In line with the statement in "La Vie recluse en poésie" that "notre base n'est pas la poésie, notre base est l'homme" (our basis is not poetry but man), Spender places La Tour du Pin in the first category, alongside Paul Claudel, Rilke, and William Butler Yeats, while placing Valéry, T. S. Eliot, and Stefan George in the second. For Spender, La Tour du Pin reintegrates the separate functions of poetry, resembling Walt Whitman's "Song of Myself" (in his *Leaves of Grass,* 1855), but with much different results: his egotism is "profounder, wiser and richer than that of Whitman," though La Tour du Pin lacks Whitman's clarity and uniformity of style and purpose. Spender suggests that La Tour du Pin "is in some ways a curiously un-French poet who has a good deal in common with modern English poets, and who may for that reason have a special value for English readers." He points out the many parallels with the early Yeats: "legendary qualities with a certain consciousness of purpose which the mistiness never quite obscures," anticipation of wider responsibilities to come, and an element of spiritual pride.

Rousseaux recognized that in *Une Somme de poésie* La Tour du Pin had "jeté à pleines mains des morceaux de toutes sortes dont beaucoup sont des joyaux" (thrown in poems by the handful, many of which were jewels) and that "des fragments resteront sans doute acquis à la mémoire des hommes" (some fragments will no doubt remain fixed in the memory of mankind), but he felt that the poet's spiritual concerns had been unfavorable to his lyricism, and he found the ending rather flat. Henri Clouard, in his *Histoire de la littérature française 1915–1940* (History of French Literature 1915–1940, 1949), was more critical: "Voilà une grande barque démâtée sur un océan de soliloques sans rivages" (This is a great ship drifting without a mast on a shoreless ocean of soliloquy). La Tour du Pin himself had no doubt that he must take a new direction. The "jeu de l'homme seul" (play of man by himself) of the first volume–the subtitle in the definitive version of volume one is "Le Jeu de l'homme en lui-même" (The Play of Man in Himself)–must be followed by "Le Jeu de l'homme

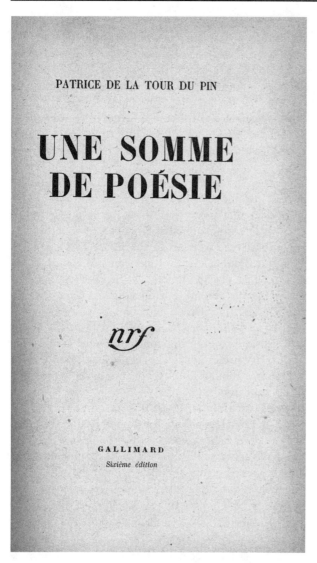

Title page for the first full-length volume (1946) in the body of work La Tour du Pin called "théopoésie" (theopoetry), in which he attempted to express the organic unity of religious faith and poetry (Howard-Tilton Memorial Library, Tulane University)

devant les autres" (The Play of Man before His Fellows), as the definitive version of volume two is subtitled. Initially, he saw this change as a move toward greater involvement with his contemporaries, to whom he could bring a *témoignage* (testimony); but how could he pass on a message that he himself had not yet fully grasped? He found poetry increasingly difficult to write and indeed went through a period of comparative sterility until it became clear that that very experience of blockage was to be the subject of the second volume.

The second volume was published as *Une Somme de poésie: Le Second Jeu* (A Summa of Poetry: The Second Play, 1959). The main character of *Le Second Jeu,* as the work is known, is called André Vincentenaire

(that is, man of the twentieth century). He has an ambiguous relationship with his father, whose name he shares, and to whom the authorship of the first volume of *Une Somme de poésie* is attributed. Questions of identity and the subject are clearly central, and the work is more obviously autobiographical than the first volume; in describing the book, Serge Doubrovsky's term "autofiction," that is, works that encompass both autobiographical and novelistic expression, seems appropriate. André's first, rather overconfident attempt to strike out on his own is a failure—the episode is recounted in *La Contemplation errante* (Wandering Contemplation), published separately in 1948—but eventually he sets out again, at his father's urging, into the "désert de l'âme" (desert of the soul); or rather, one part of him does (having been reconciled to his father to the extent of recognizing him as his own "profondeur" or inner depth), while the other part continues to live a perfectly normal domestic life, in order to avoid becoming unhealthily unbalanced. This crossing of the desert is depicted from the outset in terms of the biblical Exodus, and there are strong echoes of the Bible throughout. In "L'Assassinat au bord d'une mare" (Assassination beside a Pool) André relives Adam's original sin, reinterpreted as a refusal to embrace the totality of his being, and as a result he experiences an inner desert. He glimpses the solution to his dilemma in the underground water that suggests baptism and rebirth but persists in his quest, trying to put into practice the ten commandments passed on to him by his father. His whole enterprise is called into question in the temptation scene, which occurs in "Le Plan de l'échiquier" (The Chessboard), but he manages to reach the Mount of the Passion, in the company of three new companions, who represent three of the four tendencies of the poetic voice as outlined in the first volume, with himself as the fourth. When they eventually scale the mountain, the expected sign is absent: but they realize that their four exhausted bodies make the sign of the Cross and that the baptized are already the sign of God in the world. Refreshed by a rest in the Cave of the Virgin, which resembles a tomb, André goes down the mountain but is swept away by a river and receives a wound to the head. The imagery of blood connotes both the lifeblood of the world and the blood of the Lamb. André has an epiphany in which he pictures the Red Sea (of the Exodus) as the sea of humanity in its corporeal aspect. He himself is a cell of the "corps d'humanité" (body of humanity) that is called to be the Bride of Christ, and his contact with the rest of mankind will be fruitful only if he is prepared to surrender his fierce independence and identify himself with the Church, which is the chosen locus for the nuptials ("noces") of

Christ with humanity. In "Le Contrat dans une masure" (Contract in a Hovel) he signs his own death warrant with a cross. He can then return to his ordinary existence, bringing with him a report that sums up the insights he has gained. The next step takes a while to become clear, but then the launch of the first *Sputnik* in 1957 provides the key image: he will launch a satellite, propelled by the power of the Eucharist, on a reconnaissance mission around the mystery of God, following the orbit of the liturgy through the whole of human life. That will be the program for the third and final volume. In the meantime *Le Second Jeu* ends with a hymn to God the Father: its paradoxical title, "Préface," is explicable in that it not only announces the sequel but also reminds the reader that all human achievements can be seen as belonging to the first part of the Mass, up to the preface, and must give way to the divine Eucharist.

Le Second Jeu is largely in prose, though it includes at least 130 poems scattered throughout the text, 81 of which form a single (but fragmented) numbered sequence. The lyrical facility of the first volume has largely disappeared. The alexandrine is still the preferred line, and rhyme is still sometimes present, but some poems are in free verse, and elsewhere alexandrines are written out almost as if they were prose, with dashes rather than line-breaks. One model is the psalms (already used in the first volume), whose poetic form, while important, is less obtrusive than that of traditional French verse. The status of poetic language is a central question in *Le Second Jeu*. In the important early chapter "L'Accession à l'esprit" (Accession to the Spirit), the father says: "il ne s'agit pas de lever la poésie du monde pour trouver Dieu, mais de tirer de la Révélation autant de poésie que tu le pourras pour revêtir peut-être le monde, mais en tout cas pour tenir Dieu" (it is not a question of raising poetry from the world to find God, but rather of drawing from Revelation as much poetry as you can, maybe to clothe the world, but in any case to grasp God). The "peut-être" (maybe) is significant: the outward show of poetic language, while desirable, is not essential. Poems are sometimes described as "stèles" (wayside inscriptions) or, in photographic terms, as snapshots of a particular moment or state of mind; in either case the journey itself is more important than the disposable record. In her book *Patrice de La Tour du Pin: Biographie spirituelle* (Patrice de La Tour du Pin: A Spiritual Biography, 1992), Isabelle Chamska draws attention to the remarkable architecture of *Le Second Jeu,* emphasizing that the term "poème" applies to the whole, in the sense of a carefully constructed work of art. Of course, the true poem is that of God's glorious redemption, "un seul Poème avec l'écho des hommes"

(a single Poem with the echo of men), and God is the true poet. The human poet, for his part, recognizes that he is "d'abord une prière en Toi" (first and foremost a prayer in You). To the outside world, and indeed to the poet, it will seem as though his poetic (lyrical) gift has simply dried up, and that is, in fact, one of the major satanic temptations confronted in "Le Plan de l'échiquier." In "Mémoires d'un jardinier" (Memoirs of a Gardener), which draws on botanical imagery, the poet puts his faith in future fruitfulness: "Et je suis plus heureux, Seigneur, avec mes balbutiements et malgré l'aridité de mon cantique, que si j'étais arrivé à produire un poème satisfaisant à mon goût, mais sans crainte de Dieu. Je mise sur ce qu'il se simplifiera et s'enrichira un jour" (I am happier, Lord, with my stammerings and despite the aridity of my song, than if I had managed to produce a poem that satisfied my taste but lacked the fear of God. I am wagering that one day it will become simpler and richer). In the meantime his writing is by no means always as arid as it might at first seem. There is room for the whimsical playfulness already seen in the interludes of the first volume, as for instance in two charming stories La Tour du Pin wrote for his children, *Noël des eaux* (A Watery Christmas Tale), separately published in 1951 and included in *Le Second Jeu,* and *Pépinière de sapins de Noël* (A Christmas-Tree Nursery), separately published in 1957.

When *Le Second Jeu* was published in 1959, it aroused little critical interest. Some reviewers, such as Philippe Jaccottet writing in the *Nouvelle Revue française* (January 1960), found it uncongenial. While applauding the poet's honesty and noting "l'accent vigoureux et noblement simple des psaumes bibliques" (the strong, noble simplicity of the Psalms), Jaccottet regretted that "à la place d'un chant nouveau, nous n'entendons alors qu'un écho émouvant, mais affaibli, d'une très ancienne parole, insuffisamment ravivée" (instead of a new song, we hear only a moving but faint echo of a very distant word whose vitality has not been restored). That judgment is echoed by Robert Sabatier in his monumental *Histoire de la poésie française.* In the volume *Métamorphoses et modernité* (Metamorphoses and Modernity, 1988) Sabatier writes, apropos *Le Second Jeu,* "Là où l'homme de foi trouvera pâture en des lieux d'exigence, le simple amateur de poésie pourra regretter que les poèmes, les moments de poésie apparaissent perdus, peu nombreux, avec, çà et là, le souvenir de la grâce du premier livre, celui où le poème nu resplendissait" (Where the man of faith will find fodder in harsh places, the mere lover of poetry may regret that the poetic moments appear few and far between, with just the occasional reminder of the lightness of the First

La Tour du Pin and Pierre Emmanuel (from Jacques Gauthier, Patrice de la Tour du Pin, quêteur du Dieu de joie, *1987)*

book where the poem shone pure and bright). Catholic critics were more favorable, citing parallels with Saint John of the Cross and Saint Teresa of Avila. Jean Mambrino, writing in *Etudes* (October 1960), went so far as to claim that "ce livre calciné, d'une beauté amère et pure, . . . rejoint par un détour inattendu l'*alittérature* de certains écrivains d'aujourd'hui" (the ashes of this book, with its bitter, pure beauty, . . . link it unexpectedly with the *aliterature* of certain contemporary writers). La Tour du Pin was not interested in situating his own work in relation to that of his contemporaries. He wanted to keep moving forward. The award of the Grand Prix de Poésie of the Académie Française in 1961, while an important honor, was inevitably backward-looking.

Toward the end of *Le Second Jeu,* André Vincentenaire murmurs to a friend: "Je rêve, oui je rêve, d'une forme qu'on pourrait appeler théopoésie" (I dream, yes I dream, of a form that might be called theopoetry). The word *théopoésie* (theopoetry) was coined by La Tour du Pin to express the organic union of the life of faith

and the craft of poetry. As Jacques Gauthier puts it in his theological study *La Théopoésie de Patrice de La Tour du Pin* (1989), it is "la chair de l'expérience spirituelle du poète et le souffle de son contact avec le grands corps eucharistique du Christ pascal" (the flesh of the spiritual experience of the poet together with the breath of his contact with the great eucharistic body of the Paschal Christ). The third and final volume of *Une Somme de poésie* is an exercise in *théopoésie,* using almost entirely liturgical patterns.

It was originally published in two parts: the first book, *Une Somme de poésie III, première partie: Petit Théâtre crépusculaire* (A Summa of Poetry III, First Part: Little Twilight Theater), was published in 1963 as a substantial volume of 330 pages. It offers two short texts for each day of the liturgical year from the beginning of Advent to the end of Epiphany, one in verse and one in prose. It is thus based on the alternation of "chant" and "réflexion," "orientés vers le même mystère" (focused on the same mystery), while the "nuit des intervalles" (night of the gaps) between the texts is illuminated by "ce qui descend continuellement de Dieu" (that which continually comes down from God). God is the origin of time and truth rather than the goal of human thought, and this inversion of habitual ways of thinking changes the relationship of humans both to God and to the universe.

Shortly after the publication of *Petit Théâtre crépusculaire,* La Tour du Pin was invited to join the commission, set up as a direct outcome of the Second Vatican Council, to translate the Latin Missal into French. He was the only lay member of the commission, which included Joseph Gelineau and Didier Rimaud, well-known authors and composers of metrical psalms. La Tour du Pin had already had some experience in translating liturgical texts in the early 1950s, when he teamed up with Adalbert Hamman to produce French versions of early eucharistic prayers. He found considerable satisfaction in the work, which involved the translation of more than 1,200 prayers and 90 proper prefaces, as well as the four eucharistic prayers; there were also the baptismal and marriage services, and the psalms for the ecumenical Psalter. These translations were team efforts, and the texts are not attributable to individual translators, but La Tour du Pin also composed several hymns and prayers, some of which were incorporated into subsequent editions of the Missal—twenty-one in the 1980 edition of *Prière du temps présent* (Prayer for Today); ten of the hymns are reproduced, with commentaries, in Gauthier's *Que cherchez-vous au soir tombant?* (What Are You Looking for As Night Falls? 1995). Most also appear in *Une Lutte pour la vie* (A Struggle for Life, 1970), the second part of the third volume of *Une Somme de poésie.* This book begins with *Lieux-dits* (Places), a group of twelve poems—previously published separately in 1967—reminiscent of some of the pieces in the first volume of La Tour du Pin's magnum opus, particularly "Hameaux" (Hamlets) in *La Quête de Joie.* There is similar material in later sections, "Le Voyage vers la ville" (Journey toward the City) and "Le Pâtis de la création" (Grazing-Land of Creation); the latter is a reworked version of *Bestiaire fabuleux* (Mythical Bestiary, 1947), in which La Tour du Pin's text accompanied illustrations by Jean Lurçat. These poem cycles are balanced by several brief liturgical cycles and by four long letters explaining the poet's conception of his work, beginning with "Lettre à des citadins à propos de 'théopoésie'" (Letter to Some Townsfolk about "Theopoetry"). "Cinq petites liturgies de carême" (Five Short Easter Liturgies) and "Veillée pascale" (Paschal Vigil), which close the volume, stress the importance for the poet of Easter and in particular of the night that immediately precedes the joy of Easter morning.

La Tour du Pin had now moved toward a full identification of poetry with prayer. The object of poetry being to translate life into language in order to present it to God, it cannot do that adequately if the poet seeks "poetic" effects; that is, if poetry is cut off from faith and the workings of the Spirit of God on the one hand, or from the life and language of the world on the other. The poem "Le Laboratoire" (The Laboratory) in *Une Lutte pour la vie* sums up the patient work of the poet-experimenter to take words—he himself is "rien qu'un mot de notre histoire" (but a word of our common history)—and present them to the "petit falot / Brûlant derrière ma mémoire" (tiny flame / Flickering at the back of my memory). Biological metaphors have obvious advantages here, and La Tour du Pin was naturally drawn to them, in any case, because of his interest in botany and because of his longstanding friendship with biologist Jean Trémolières. Thus, the relationship of the individual to Christ is seen in terms of *exposition* and *retournement,* both terms borrowed from biology: the first refers to the exposure of green plants to the light of the sun, which enables them to derive nourishment from photosynthesis, while the second refers to the inversion of causality whereby a future flower may have an influence on the seed from which it grows. La Tour du Pin was constantly probing the resources of language and forcing words to reveal latent meanings and connections: "sauveteur," for example, with its connotations of lifesaving in water, suggested itself as a helpful modern alternative to the fossilized religious word *Sauveur* (Savior).

One of the characteristics of the new *théopoésie* is that the texts have meaning only in relation to one other and to the whole. Another is that there is a constant double focus, on Christ and on the self. This duality saves La Tour du Pin from having to strive to prove a point or to force the poetry into an unpoetic framework, which is what Gaëtan Picon, in his *Panorama de la nouvelle littérature française* (Panorama of New French Literature, 1949), had objected to in the 1946 volume of *Une Somme de poésie.* This new freedom no doubt helped La Tour du Pin to win not only the Grand Prix de la Littérature Catholique in 1971 but also the Grand Prix de la Société des Poètes Français in 1972. He had never made any secret of being a Catholic poet but, at least in the 1946 volume, as Gonzague Truc points out in his *Histoire de la littérature catholique contemporaine* (History of Contemporary Catholic Literature, 1961), "si l'univers de ce poète est un univers chrétien, il ne laisse pas de le tirer tout entier de lui-même et le colore de ses propres couleurs" (if this poet's universe is a Christian one, he nevertheless draws it all from his own inner being and

*La Tour du Pin at his family estate, Le Bignon-Mirabeau,
1973 (from Jacques Gauthier,* Patrice de la Tour
du Pin, quêteur du Dieu de joie, *1987)*

(Poets of Today), was the first important study of La Tour du Pin to be published since Biéville-Noyant's pioneering work. It introduced him to a wider public and offered a helpful reading of the first two volumes of *Une Somme de poésie,* as well as an indication of the aims of the third. It also included a selection of published texts (mainly, but not exclusively, drawn from the first volume) and an important unpublished text, "Lettre aux confidents" (Letter to the Confidants), dated 1960–not to be confused with the "Lettre aux confidents à propos d'*Une Lutte pour la vie*" (Letter to the Confidants about *A Struggle for Life*), included in the 1970 book–that sums up the poet's own understanding of the elaboration of the whole trilogy. Published in 1962, *De Baudelaire à Mauriac: L'Inquiétude contemporaine* (From Baudelaire to Mauriac: The Contemporary Restlessness) by Jesuit scholar Louis Barjon includes a twenty-page chapter on La Tour du Pin titled "Le Monde du recueillement" (The World of Quiet Recollection). Despite his admiration for the poet, Barjon echoes other critics' doubts about the literary value of *Une Somme de poésie:* but he scarcely takes *Le Second Jeu* into account and had no inkling of what the third volume might comprise. The new edition of *La Quête de Joie,* published in 1967 in the "Poésie Gallimard" series, which included a brief summary of the rest of the first volume titled "Petite Somme de poésie" (Little Summa of Poetry), might have had the adverse effect of focusing attention on the poet's earliest work at the expense of what followed, but for the memorable preface, "Tout homme est une histoire sacrée," by Maurice Champagne. Champagne, who soon thereafter defended his (unpublished) thesis at the University of Nice, "De la poésie à la "théopoésie" chez Patrice de La Tour du Pin," and to whom "L'Auberge de l'agonie" (The Agony Inn) in *Une Lutte pour la vie* was later dedicated, was careful to put *La Quête de Joie* in the context of the poet's development.

From 1971 onward, La Tour du Pin applied himself to the major task of revising the whole of *Une Somme de poésie,* which task he completed shortly before his death. The definitive, three-volume edition was finally published by Gallimard in 1981, 1982, and 1983. Many sections were extensively rewritten, though others, such as *La Quête de Joie* and the verse poems of *Une Lutte pour la vie,* were left almost entirely untouched. The main outcome of the revisions was to tighten up the text (*Le Second Jeu* shrank by more than a quarter of its length, with the sequence of numbered poems falling from eighty-one to fifty-eight pieces), thus responding to criticism of the diffuseness of the original, and making the theopoetic dimension clear from the outset, in keeping

gives it his own colors). In the 1938 book *Psaumes,* La Tour du Pin had included the important disclaimer: "Le poète amoureux du Christ a dit à ceux qui l'écoutaient:–je ne suis pas le poète christique. / Ceux qui m'appellent de ce nom me font du tort" (The poet in love with Christ said to those who listened:–I am not the Christ-poet. / Those who call me so do me wrong). The process of refinement chronicled in *Le Second Jeu,* however, and the bolder stance of the *théopoète,* together with La Tour du Pin's work with the Liturgical Commission, made it natural to see him as a fully Catholic poet, happy to be closely associated with the Church. But though he was much appreciated by Catholics, particularly by religious communities, his focus remained resolutely universal. As Eva Kushner writes in her *Patrice de La Tour du Pin* (1961), "c'est bien au nom de tous que Patrice de La Tour du Pin demande l'espérance" (it is in the name of all that Patrice de La Tour du Pin calls for hope).

Kushner's book, which appeared in the popular Editions Pierre Seghers series "Poètes d'aujourd'hui"

with the idea of *retournement,* in that the later flower of theopoetry appears to influence the seed from which it has grown. The architecture of the whole work could now be appreciated in its entirety. The three volumes acquired new subtitles: "Le Jeu de l'homme en lui-même," "Le Jeu de l'homme devant les autres," and "Le Jeu de l'homme devant Dieu" (The Play of Man before God). The theme of the "jeu" had, of course, been present earlier, but the dramatic interludes of the first volume, which had baffled some commentators, benefited from the fuller context. The implicit references to the twelfth-century semiliturgical drama *Le Jeu d'Adam,* and to Dante's fourteenth-century verse epic, *The Divine Comedy,* also became clearer. What is being staged is both the inner life of the poet and, by extension, that of all humanity, and the process of poetic creation.

The death of Patrice de La Tour du Pin on 28 October 1975 called forth tributes to him, and he warranted an entry in the 1976 *Universalia* volume of the *Encyclopædia Universalis.* A proper reassessment of his work and of his significance as a poet had to wait until 1981, when a conference was organized at the Sorbonne to mark the seventieth anniversary of his birth and the publication of the first volume of the definitive edition of *Une Somme de poésie.* Yves-Alain Favre, who was largely responsible for the conference, also launched the Société des Amis de Patrice de La Tour du Pin in 1982 with its annual *Cahiers Patrice de La Tour du Pin* and edited a special issue of *Les Cahiers bleus* devoted to the poet in 1987. There have been several important studies of La Tour du Pin since his death, and several texts have been posthumously published: these include his correspondence with André Romus, published in 1981; the first volume of the *Carnets de route* (Travel Notebooks), representing only two-thirds of the contents of a single notebook out of a total of ninety-seven whose composition extended over the poet's entire working life, published in 1995; and *Chemin de croix (des rapatriés en pèlerinage à Lourdes)* (Way of the Cross [of the Repatriated on Pilgrimage to Lourdes]), with illustrations by Paul Monnier of stained-glass windows, composed for the 1946 pilgrimage to Lourdes of repatriated prisoners of war, published in 1998. Previously unpublished pieces continue to appear in *Cahiers Patrice de La Tour du Pin.* There has also been activity on the liturgical front, with the commissioning by the French government of a setting by Christian Villeneuve of *Comme un reflet: Office de la Vierge* (As a Reflection: Office of the Virgin, 1997), based on the "Office de la Vierge" from the revised first volume of *Une Somme de poésie.*

Early in his career La Tour du Pin was recognized as an important new voice in French poetry.

Having escaped the influence of Surrealism, he seemed well placed to inherit the mantle of Rimbaud, Claudel, and Valéry. There was enough obscurity and apparent unevenness in his early work to make critics hesitate to pronounce judgment on his future prospects, and many of them were frankly disappointed at his failure to continue to exploit the lyrical vein. The increasingly Catholic orientation of La Tour du Pin's work merely compounded what Jaccottet saw as his unwarranted isolation from modern trends. Most positive appreciations of La Tour du Pin have been by those who sympathize with his religious position; however, as Albert Camus wrote in his untitled, two-paragraph presentation in an undated program for *Catherine Aulnaie* and *Saint Elie de Gueuce* (two of the dramatic interludes from the first volume of the *Somme de poésie,* performed in 1956 at the Théâtre de Poche): "Comment . . . n'écouterions-nous pas avec reconnaissance et amitié ce langage qui, sans jamais rien maudire, nous venge de tant de médiocrités par la vertu d'une simple grandeur?" (How . . . can we fail to listen with gratitude and friendship to this language which never stoops to cursing and yet avenges us on so much mediocrity by virtue of its simple grandeur?). His deep humanity and his skill as a poetic architect can be appreciated by all readers, as can his practical outworking of an impressively ambitious philosophy of poetry, while the third volume of *Une Somme de poésie* has surely answered Boisdeffre's plea that "l'architecte des grands ensembles théologiques laisse une petite place à l'enfant musicien d'autrefois!" (the architect of these great theological constructions should leave a little room for the child-musician of yesteryear!). These dauntingly large volumes include many little gems and richly repay browsing as well as more sustained reading. La Tour du Pin ranks with and probably above Jean-Claude Renard and Pierre Emmanuel, both of whom grew in his shadow, as the leading representative of spiritual poetry in France in the mid twentieth century.

Letters:

Lettres à André Romus, edited by Luc Estang, introduction by André Romus (Paris: Seuil, 1981).

Interviews:

"Rencontre de Patrice de La Tour du Pin," *Promesses,* 17 (1966): 46–51;

"Entretien avec Patrice de La Tour du Pin," *Connaissance des hommes,* 36 (1970): 14–15;

"Qu'est-ce qui vous fait vivre?" *Rive gauche,* 1973: 5;

J. -J. Marchand, "Interview avec Patrice de La Tour du Pin," *Archives du XXe siècle* (1974).

References:

Louis Barjon, "Le Monde du recueillement," in his *De Baudelaire à Mauriac: L'Inquiétude contemporaine* (Paris: Casterman, 1962), pp. 197–217;

Anne-Henri de Biéville-Noyant, *Patrice de La Tour du Pin: Document pour l'histoire de la littérature française* (Paris: Editions de la Nouvelle Revue Critique, 1948);

Robert Brasillach, "Patrice de La Tour du Pin," in his *Les Quatre Jeudis: Images d'avant-guerre* (Paris: Editions Balzac, 1944), pp. 486–490;

Les Cahiers bleus, special La Tour du Pin issue, edited by Yves-Alain Favre, 40 (1987);

Isabelle Chamska, *Patrice de La Tour du Pin: Biographie spirituelle* (Paris: Desclée, 1992);

Favre, ed., *Colloque Patrice de La Tour du Pin: Tenu à la Sorbonne le 21 et le 22 novembre 1981* (Paris: Nizet, 1983);

Toby Garfitt, "Ecriture du mal dans l'économie poétique selon Patrice de La Tour du Pin," in *Le Mal dans l'imaginaire littéraire français (1850–1950),* edited by Myriam Watthée-Delmotte and Metka Zupancic (Paris: L'Harmattan / Orléans, Ont.: Editions David, 1998), pp. 385–395;

Jacques Gauthier, *Patrice de La Tour du Pin, quêteur du Dieu de joie* (Montréal: Editions Paulines / Paris: Médiaspaul, 1987);

Gauthier, *Que cherchez-vous au soir tombant? Dix hymnes de Patrice de La Tour du Pin* (Paris: Cerf / Montréal: Médiaspaul, 1995);

Gauthier, *La Théopoésie de Patrice de La Tour du Pin* (Montréal: Bellarmin / Paris: Cerf, 1989);

Eva Kushner, *Patrice de La Tour du Pin,* Poètes d'aujourd'hui, no. 79 (Paris: Seghers, 1961);

Marie-Josette Le Han, *Patrice de La Tour du Pin: La Quête d'une théopoésie* (Paris: H. Champion, 1996);

La Maison-Dieu, special La Tour du Pin issue, 150 (1982);

Claude Mauriac, *La Terrasse de Malagar* (Paris: Grasset, 1977);

Mirages, special La Tour du Pin issue, edited by Armand Guibert (1934);

Gaëtan Picon, *Panorama de la nouvelle littérature française* (Paris: Gallimard, 1949);

Luca Pietromarchi, *La Quête de Joie di Patrice de La Tour du Pin* (Trento, Italy: Università degli Studi, Dipartimento di scienze filologiche e storiche, 1995); French version published as *Les Anges sauvages: La Quête de Joie de Patrice de La Tour du Pin* (Paris: Champion, 2001);

André Rousseaux, "La Légende mystique de Patrice de La Tour du Pin," in his *Littérature du XXe siècle,* volume 2 (Paris: Albin Michel, 1948), pp. 148–164;

Robert Sabatier, *Histoire de la poésie française,* volume 6, *La Poésie du XXe siècle: III, Métamorphoses et modernité* (Paris: Albin Michel, 1988): 59–62;

Transversalités, special La Tour du Pin issue, *Ecriture et prière chez Patrice de La Tour du Pin,* edited by Isabelle Renaud-Chamska, 61 (1997);

Gonzague Truc, *Histoire de la littérature catholique contemporaine* (Paris & Tournai, Belgium: Casterman, 1961).

Papers:

All of Patrice de La Tour du Pin's notebooks, manuscripts, and other personal papers are at the family estate, Le Bignon-Mirabeau, Ferrières-en-Gâtinais, France.

Henri Michaux
(24 May 1899 – 19 October 1984)

Jean-Xavier Ridon
University of Nottingham

BOOKS: *Les Rêves et la jambe: Essai philosophique et littéraire* (Antwerp: Ça Ira, 1923);

Fables des origines (Brussels: Editions du Disque Vert, 1923);

Qui je fus (Paris: Editions de la Nouvelle Revue Française, 1927);

Ecuador: Journal de voyage (Paris: Gallimard, 1929; revised, 1968); translated by Robin Magowan as *Ecuador: A Travel Journal* (Seattle: University of Washington Press, 1970; London: Owen, 1970);

Mes propriétés (Paris: Editions Fourcade, 1929);

Un Certain Plume (Paris: Editions du Carrefour, 1930);

Un Barbare en Asie (Paris: Gallimard, 1933; revised, 1967); translated by Sylvia Beach as *A Barbarian in Asia* (New York: New Directions, 1949);

La Nuit remue (Paris: Gallimard, 1935; revised, 1967);

Voyage en Grande Garabagne (Paris: Gallimard, 1936);

Entre centre et absence (Paris: Matarasso, 1936);

Sifflets dans le temple (Paris: Editions G.L.M., 1936);

La Ralentie (Paris: Editions G.L.M., 1937);

Plume, précédé de Lointain intérieur (Paris: Gallimard, 1938; revised, 1963);

Peintures: Sept poèmes et seize illustrations (Paris: Editions G.L.M., 1939);

Au pays de la magie (Paris: Gallimard, 1941; London: Horizon, 1946);

Arbres des Tropiques (Paris: Gallimard, 1942);

Tu vas être père, as Plume (Paris: Pierre Bettencourt, 1943);

Exorcismes (Paris: R. Godet, 1943);

L'Espace du dedans (Paris: Gallimard, 1944; revised, 1966); translated by Richard Ellman as *Henri Michaux, Selected Writings: The Space Within* (New York: New Directions, 1951);

Labyrinthes (Paris: R. Godet, 1944);

Le Lobe des monstres (Lyons: L'Arbalète, 1944);

Liberté d'action (Paris: Fontaine, 1945);

Apparitions (Paris: Editions du Point du Jour, 1946);

Peintures et dessins (Paris: Editions du Point du Jour, 1946);

Ici, Poddema (Lausanne, Switzerland: Mermod, 1946);

Henri Michaux, 1939

Meidosems (Paris: Editions du Point du Jour, 1948);

Nous deux encore, 1948 (Paris: J. Lambert, 1948);

Poésie pour pouvoir (Paris: René Drouin, 1949);

La Vie dans les plis (Paris: Gallimard, 1949; revised, 1979);

Arriver à se réveiller (Saint-Maurice d'Etelan: Pierre Bettencourt, 1950);

Lecture par Henri Michaux de huit lithographies de Zao Wou-Ki (Paris: Editions Euros & R. Godet, 1950);

Tranches de savoir, suivi du Secret de la situation politique (Paris: Librairie Les Pas Perdus, 1950);

Passages: 1937–1950 (Paris: Editions du Point du Jour, 1950); revised and enlarged as *Passages: 1937–1963* (Paris: Gallimard, 1963);

Veille (Paris: G. A. Bolloré, 1951);

Quelque part, quelqu'un (N.p., 1951);

Mouvements (Paris: Gallimard, 1951);

Nouvelles de l'étranger (Paris: Mercure de France, 1952);

Misérable miracle: La Mescaline (Monaco: Editions du Rocher, 1956; revised and enlarged, Paris: Gallimard, 1972); translated by Louise Varèse as *Miserable Miracle: Mescaline* (San Francisco: City Lights Books, 1963);

Quatre cents hommes en croix (Saint-Maurice d'Etelan: Pierre Bettencourt, 1956);

L'Infini turbulent (Paris: Mercure de France, 1957; revised and enlarged, 1964); translated by Michael Fineberg as *The Turbulent Infinite* (London: Calder & Boyars, 1970);

Vigies sur cibles (Paris: Editions du Dragon, 1959);

Paix dans les brisements (Paris: Flinker, 1959);

Connaissance par les gouffres (Paris: Gallimard, 1961; revised, 1967); translated by Haakon Chevalier as *Light Through Darkness* (New York: Orion Press, 1963);

Vents et poussières (Paris: Flinker, 1962);

Les Grandes Epreuves de l'esprit et les innombrables petites (Paris: Gallimard, 1966); translated by Richard Howard as *The Major Ordeals of the Mind, and the Countless Minor Ones* (New York: Harcourt Brace Jovanovich, 1974; London: Secker & Warburg, 1974);

Vers la complétude: (Saisie et dessaisies) (Paris: Editions G.L.M., 1967);

Façons d'endormi, façons d'éveillé (Paris: Gallimard, 1969);

Poteaux d'angle (Paris: L'Herne, 1971; enlarged edition, Montpellier: Fata Morgana, 1978); translated by Lynn Hoggard as *Tent Posts* (Copenhagen: Green Integer, 1997);

Emergences-Résurgences (Geneva: Albert Skira, 1972; Geneva: Albert Skira / Paris: Flammarion, 1987); translated by Richard Sieburth as *Emergences–Resurgences* (Milan: Skira Editore / London: Thames & Hudson, 2001);

En rêvant à partir de peintures énigmatiques (Montpellier: Fata Morgana, 1972);

Bras cassé (Montpellier: Fata Morgana, 1973);

Moments: Traversées du temps (Paris: Gallimard, 1973);

Quand tombent les toits (Paris: Editions G.L.M., 1973);

Par la voie des rythmes (Montpellier: Fata Morgana, 1974);

Coups d'arrêt (Paris: Le Collet de Buffle, 1975);

Face à ce qui se dérobe (Paris: Gallimard, 1975);

Henri Michaux: Peintures (Paris: Maeght, 1976);

Les Ravagés (Montpellier: Fata Morgana, 1976);

Jours de silence (Saint-Clement: Fata Morgana, 1978);

Saisir (Montpellier: Fata Morgana, 1979);

Une Voie pour l'insubordination (Montpellier: Fata Morgana, 1980);

Affrontements (Montpellier: Fata Morgana, 1981; enlarged edition, Paris: Gallimard, 1986);

Chemins cherchés, chemins perdus, transgressions (Paris: Gallimard, 1981);

Comme un ensablement (Montpellier: Fata Morgana, 1981);

Les Commencements: Dessins d'enfants, essais d'enfants (Fontfroide-le-Haut: Fata Morgana, 1983);

Le Jardin exalté (Saint-Clément: Fata Morgana, 1983);

Par surprise (Fontfroide-le-Haut: Fata Morgana, 1983);

Fille de la montagne (Le Pontet: M.D., 1984);

Par des traits (Fontfroide-le-Haut: Fata Morgana, 1984);

Déplacements, dégagements (Paris: Gallimard, 1985); translated by David and Helen Constantine as *Spaced, Displaced* (Oxford: Alden Press, 1992);

A distance: Poèmes, edited by Micheline Phankim and Anne-Elisabeth Halpern (Paris: Mercure de France, 1996).

Collections: *Epreuves, exorcismes, 1940–1944* (Paris: Gallimard, 1945);

Ailleurs (Paris: Gallimard, 1948; revised, 1967);

Face aux verrous (Paris: Gallimard, 1954; revised, 1967);

Henri Michaux, Œuvres complètes, 3 volumes projected, edited by Raymond Bellour and Ysé Tran, Bibliothèque de la Pléiade (Paris: Gallimard, 1998–)—includes volume 1, Bibliothèque de la Pléiade, no. 444 (1998) and volume 2, Bibliothèque de la Pléiade, no. 475 (2001).

Editions in English: *Henri Michaux: A Selection,* translated by Michael Fineberg (Norwich, U.K.: Embers, 1979);

Darkness Moves: An Henri Michaux Anthology, 1927–1984, edited and translated by David Ball (Berkeley: University of California Press, 1994).

PRODUCED SCRIPT: *Images du monde visionnaire,* motion picture, scenario by Michaux, 1963.

OTHER: "Quelques renseignements sur cinquante-neuf années d'existence," in *Michaux,* edited by Robert Bréchon, La Bibliothèque Idéale, volume 4 (Paris: Gallimard, 1959).

Henri Michaux, for many years known only to a small circle of poetry lovers and connoisseurs, has become one of the major figures of contemporary francophone poetry. During his life Michaux hid behind his work, avoiding fame, rarely giving interviews or allowing photographs of himself to be taken. He broke this self-imposed silence in 1959, when he published an autobiographical sketch titled "Quelques renseignements sur cinquante-neuf années d'existence" (Some Information on Fifty-Nine Years of Existence). This brief and often elliptical text, in which he refers to himself in the third person, remains the only reliable document originating from the author himself that recounts the important events in his life. Michaux's work has come to be recognized only gradually, through an ever-increasing appreciation of its qualities by critics and contemporary poets. From his first writings he exposes the limitations of language, subjecting its structure to a multitude of metamorphoses. He invents words, some full of humor, some full of despair, that ultimately reveal the poet's revolt against the limitations of existence. This manipulation of words highlights his difficulty in finding and defining his place in the world. Feeling trapped within words, Michaux increasingly turned to painting, an art that he describes in *Emergences-Résurgences* (1972; translated as *Emergences-Resurgences,* 2001), a book about his own development as a painter, as a more appropriate medium to express the ever-changing states of one's inner self.

Henri Eugène Marie Ghislain Michaux was born 24 May 1899 in Namur, Belgium, the second son of Jeanne Blanke and Octave Michaux, a shopkeeper who came from a relatively well-off family. Henri's elder brother, Marcel, was born in 1896. In 1901 the whole family left Namur and moved to Brussels. Five years later Michaux was sent to the Van Der Borgt boarding school in Putte Grasheide in the Belgian countryside. In his autobiographical sketch he describes himself at this period of his life as a lonely and fragile child who is more inclined to reject the world than to engage it with curiosity or open-mindedness: "Il boude la vie, les jeux, les divertissements et la variation. Le manger lui répugne" (He turns away from life, from games, from entertainment, from variety. Eating disgusts him). This feeling of not belonging subsided temporarily when he returned to Brussels in 1910 to enter the Jesuit *collège* (secondary school) of Saint-Michel. His first interests led him to study Latin and the great Christian mystics. During this time Michaux avoided writing, concerned as he was that it might drive him away from the "essential." Although as an adult Michaux never belonged to any particular religion, his works display a continuous fascination with mysticism as a way of transcending everyday existence as well as the limits of language.

After finishing his secondary education, Michaux had to wait two years to attend university because of the German occupation of parts of Belgium during World War I. In 1919 he enrolled as a first-year student in medicine at the Université Libre de Bruxelles. He abandoned his studies before the end of his first year, but his interest in medicine remains detectable in the incisive descriptions of disease symptoms and bodily dysfunction found in his works. Between 1920 and 1921 Michaux joined the merchant navy as a simple sailor. He made the first

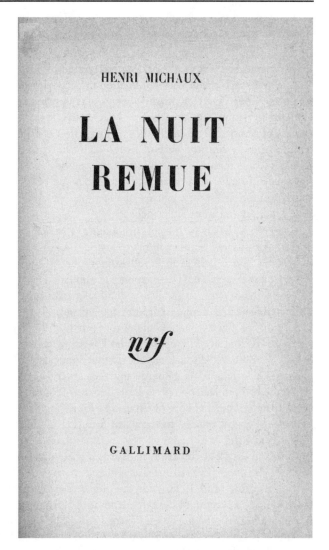

Title page for Michaux's second book of poetry (John C. Hodges Library, University of Tennessee, Knoxville)

of a long series of trips in which he not only discovered for himself the ports of North and South America but also a geographic "elsewhere," images of which permeate almost all his writings.

Michaux returned to Belgium in early 1921 but was unable to find more work as a sailor. In April he was obliged to enter military service as a reserve officer in the Belgian army; the following year, after a month in a military hospital, he applied for discharge on grounds of a heart condition. He was granted a leave of absence until the approval of his discharge in August 1922. As he later explained to Franz Hellens in a letter of 16 March 1923, it was during this period that he began writing, around the same time that he first read *Les Chants de Maldoror* (Songs of Maldoror, 1869), by the Comte de Lautréamont (pseudonym of Isidore Lucien Ducasse). As they did for the Surrealists, Lautréamont's verbal excesses and radical revolt against mankind provided the creative trigger that enabled Michaux to begin writing. His first texts were published in 1922 in the Belgian literary review *Le Disque vert,* edited by Hellens. These early texts defy conventional categories of genre, shifting between prose, poetry, and aphorism, sometimes within the same piece. This elusive style is typical of almost all of Michaux's writing. In 1924 he left Belgium, a country he had never really liked and that he always mentioned with bitterness, and he settled in Paris. There he became acquainted with some of the most prominent literary figures of the time, including Jean Paulhan and Jules Supervielle.

In 1927 Michaux began negotiating a series of exclusive contracts binding him to Gaston Gallimard's publishing house, which included Editions de la Nouvelle Revue Française. These contracts stipulated that Michaux, while free to publish individual works with other publishers in limited editions, had to publish his collections of poetry with Gallimard, even if only as reprints. His first book, *Qui je fus* (Who I Was), was published by Editions de la Nouvelle Revue Française in August 1927. This book gathered together several texts that had been published in periodicals between 1923 and 1927. *Qui je fus* remained out of circulation for a long time because Michaux refused to republish it during his lifetime. With the exception of six poems that were reprinted in his 1944 collection, *L'Espace du dedans* (translated as *The Space Within,* 1951), its contents were generally unavailable until 1998, with the publication of the first volume of Raymond Bellour's edition of Michaux's works in the Bibliothèque de La Pléiade series. The most striking aspect of *Qui je fus* is the variety of styles adopted by the poet; this first book already includes many of the writing techniques later explored by Michaux. In the title piece, for example, the poetic persona has a dialogue with "Qui-je-fus," an imaginary personification of his own self; Michaux makes similar use of imaginary beings to explore notions of identity in such later pieces as "Plume" and "La Ralentie" (Woman in Slow Motion). Torn between the expression of the poet's ego and the sense of his self as other, Michaux's narratives highlight the impossibility of defining the self as a unified entity. In the section titled "Poèmes" Michaux attacks the structure of language itself with poems that are partly onomatopoeic, such as "Glu et Gli" and "Le Grand Combat" (The Big Fight). In these poems he does not use words for their referential value but reduces them to units of sound that suggest certain actions. Michaux returned to this device on many occasions in order to express the energy of voice and sound.

On 28 December 1927 Michaux left for the Equator, on the invitation of his friend and travel companion, Peruvian poet Alfredo Gangotena. Michaux traveled across the South American continent from west to east and sailed down the Napo and Amazon Rivers. In 1929, soon after his return to France, he published *Ecuador: Journal de voyage* (translated as *Ecuador: A Travel Journal,* 1970), a book composed mostly during his yearlong trip. Written and presented as a travel narrative, *Ecuador* questions and redefines the conventions of this literary genre. First, Michaux challenges the idea that a traveler must be a lover of exoticism. He insists that he is not seeking a geographic "elsewhere," as typical of all adventure and escapist literature. As he warns his reader from the beginning: "Non, je l'ai déjà dit ailleurs. Cette terre est rincée de son exotisme" (No, as I already said elsewhere. This land is emptied of its exoticism). Michaux challenges the accounts of Western travelers who return from faraway trips with much to relate but whose vision has more to do with their own fantasies than with the different world they have "discovered." Michaux denounces the ethnocentrism of this type of discourse. In his own travel narrative Michaux refuses at first to talk about the native South Americans, whose absence in the text is somewhat unsettling. Instead he exposes the inadequacy of language to express his discoveries; words are merely tools on which he has to rely for want of anything better: "Je n'ai écrit que ce peu qui précède et déjà je tue ce voyage. Je le croyais si grand. Non, il fera des pages, c'est tout" (I've written only a few words, and already I am destroying this trip. I thought it so grand. No, it will consist of pages, that is all). Michaux defines himself essentially as a bad traveler, one who does not accept all the inconvenient material problems inherent in traveling. He highlights his disappointments rather than his discoveries. As he explains in his preface: "Un homme qui ne sait ni voyager ni tenir un journal de voyage a composé ce journal de voyage" (A man who knows neither how to travel nor how to keep a travel journal has written this travel journal). Because of his inability to express the differences of the world revealed to him, Michaux redirects his writing toward himself in order to analyze his own reactions to traveling. A large part of the book is thus about the poet's physical weakness and his confrontation with the image of his own death. Once again, however, he finds language inadequate: his own essential being proves as inexpressible as the world he experiences while traveling. *Ecuador* is therefore an anti-travel narrative that questions ideological and literary preconceptions of otherness.

In the early 1930s Michaux continued to travel, first in Europe and North Africa. As he writes of himself in a fragment from "Quelques renseignements": "Il voyage *contre.* Pour expulser de lui sa patrie . . . et ce qui s'est en lui et malgré lui attaché de culture grecque ou romaine ou germanique ou d'habitudes belges" (He travels *against.*

In order to expel from himself his fatherland . . . and everything within him that is, despite himself, attached to Greek or Roman or German culture, or Belgian ways). This statement reveals his search for a space that would enable him to escape from a cultural heritage he feels entrapped by, a space he was not able to find on his travels in South America. Michaux found something of this space at last during a trip to Asia in 1932, when he traveled across India, Nepal, Ceylon, China, Japan, and Indonesia. This eight-month trip constituted the basis of his next book, *Un Barbare en Asie* (1933; translated as *A Barbarian in Asia,* 1949). As justification for his writing Michaux asks, "Comment n'écrirait-on pas sur un pays qui s'est présenté à vous avec l'abondance des choses nouvelles et dans la joie de revivre?" (How could I forego writing about a country that offered itself to me with an abundance of new things and in the joy of rebirth?). Unlike *Ecuador, Un Barbare en Asie* is written in a style that aims to represent the different cultures the poet encounters. Michaux, moving beyond the inadequacy of words, elaborates a descriptive style that at times comes close to journalistic writing. Everything seems to attract his attention: men, arts, animals, and languages, as well as details from everyday life such as walking and praying. He is particularly fascinated by Hindu religious rituals, in which he claims to have discovered a way of thinking that dissolves the opposition between inward and outward life. His text establishes a series of comparisons between Europeans and Asians that cast the former in an unfavorable light. Michaux is thus the "barbarian" referred to in the title of the work, a word that signals his distance from an Asia he desperately tries to understand, but where he remains a plain traveler. He later came to regard some of his hasty judgments as dated and somewhat naive, and he felt a certain embarrassment with each republication of the text. In his preface to the 1967 revised edition he asks himself, "N'avais-je rien vu, vraiment? Pourquoi? Ignorance? Aveuglement de bénéficiaire des avantages d'une nation et d'une situation momentanément privilégiés?" (Had I failed to see anything? Why? Was it ignorance? Or a blindness resulting from my momentarily privileged position as a member of a wealthy nation?) Nevertheless, the East as described in *Un Barbare en Asie* was a significant part of Michaux's dream of finding a form of otherness that would allow him to conceive of his existence in new ways.

Between 1934 and 1935, still apparently in search of his own space, Michaux spent time in Spain, the Canary Islands, and Portugal. In 1935 Gallimard published his second volume of poetry, *La Nuit remue* (Night Moves). Henceforth abandoning his travel writing, Michaux offers in this volume a kind of introspective writing that includes all the great preoccupations that characterize his work. The most striking feature of these

Cover by Michaux for his 1948 collection of lithographs depicting the imaginary creatures he called Meidosems (from Henri Michaux, Œuvres complètes, *edited by Raymond Bellour and Ysé Tran, 2001)*

poems is the way in which Michaux uses his own body as a writing topic. The body of the poet is represented as a space to investigate in order to understand its mechanisms in a deeper way. Through his body, the primary home of his being, the poet attempts to understand not only his relation to the world but also the uncanny inner places where his consciousness of the world was born. The outlook he offers on the symptoms of particular diseases is characteristic of this perspective; the poet uses the dysfunctions of his body to explore its unknown spaces. As he explains in "Saint": "En circulant dans mon corps maudit, j'arrivai dans une région où les parties de moi étaient fort rares et où pour vivre, il fallait être saint" (While exploring my accursed body, I arrived in a territory where there was hardly any part of me and where I had to be a saint to survive). The body appears as if an infinite space, an immense labyrinth where the poet sometimes loses his way. Elsewhere in *La Nuit remue* Michaux elaborates what could be called his "intervention" poems. Here the poet's goal is to use his imagination to subvert the notion of external reality. In a piece appropriately titled "Intervention" he explains: "Autrefois, j'avais trop le respect de la nature. Je me mettais devant les choses et les paysages et je les laissais faire. Fini, maintenant *j'interviendrai*" (In the past I used to pay too much respect to nature. I would stand before objects and landscapes, and I would simply let them be. But that is through, now I will *intervene*). The poet goes on to explain how one day he decided to populate the city of Honfleur with camels in order to overcome his boredom. This wild and amusing piece illustrates the poet's reflections on the power of the mind and of the imaginary. Texts such as "Contre!" (Against!), "Mes occupations" (My Occupations), and "L'Age héroïque" (The Heroic Age) make use of writing as a form of catharsis. Through representations of violence and fighting, Michaux exteriorizes and overcomes the obstacles and tensions of his life. Describing his motivation for writing one section of his collection, he states in his postface, "Par hygiène, peut-être, j'ai écrit 'Mes propriétés,' pour ma santé" (I wrote "Mes propriétés" for my health, out of a concern for hygiene maybe). *La Nuit remue* established Michaux as one of the most original voices of poetry in his day.

Around 1935 Michaux met Marie-Louise Ferdière, whom he married on 15 November 1943. In 1936 he became a contributor to *Hermès,* a journal devoted to the study of mysticism, later editing some of its issues. In July of the same year Michaux left once more for Latin America, in order to participate in the Fourteenth International PEN Colloquium in Buenos Aires. There he met Jorge Luis Borges, who in 1941 translated *Un Barbare en Asie* into Spanish. Although Michaux had been experimenting with painting since 1925, his first exhibition was not until 1937. This showing at the Paul Magné Ancienne Pléiade gallery in Paris was a major step in his search for expression through painting, an activity he later found difficult to separate from his writing. In 1938 he published one of his best-known works, *Plume, précédé de Lointain intérieur* (Plume, Preceded by Distant Interior), parts of which had previously appeared in 1930 as *Un Certain Plume* (A Certain Plume). It was republished in a final, revised version with four new chapters in 1963. Plume was a character through whom the poet could project himself into an imaginary world specific to fiction, one who could allow him to forget the problems encountered during his travels. In "Observations," a text from his 1950 collection *Passages: 1937–1950,* Michaux explains that "Mes 'Emanglons,' 'Mages,' 'Hivinizikis' furent tous des personnages-tampons suscités par le voyage. (Plume disparut le jour même de mon retour en Turquie où il était né)" (My "Emanglons," "Mages," "Hivinizikis" were all buffer-characters that emerged from my travels. [Plume disappeared on the day of my return to Turkey, where he was born]). The character of Plume develops over the course of thirteen consecutive texts arranged into chapters, thus leading the poet to remark in *Passages* that it was in this book that he came

closest to novel writing. In this disjointed story the reader follows Plume through a series of problematic, if not outright absurd, situations. He is often a victim of the ill will of others: in "Plume voyage" (Plume Travels), for instance, the reader witnesses the ways in which Plume is refused the bed, the food, and the train he needs. The chapter closes with these words: "Mais il ne dit rien, il ne se plaint pas" (But he doesn't say anything, he doesn't complain). At other times, however, Plume becomes the tyrant. In chapter 5, "La Nuit des Bulgares" (The Night of the Bulgarians), Plume does not hesitate to kill the Bulgarians who overcrowd his train compartment and to dispose of their bodies by throwing them out the window. Plume is a fluctuating and self-contradictory being whose indecisiveness and mutability make his identity difficult to grasp. Other voices in the volume that represent the author's experiments with notions of identity can be found in "La Ralentie" and "Je vous écris d'un pays lointain" (I Write to You from a Distant Country). The latter takes the form of a letter in which a woman confides to the addressee her doubts about the world and her life. The woman writing may be understood to represent the feminized "I" of the poet addressing the reader. As Michaux states in his postscript to the volume: "Il n'est pas un moi. *Il n'est pas dix mois. Il n'est pas de moi. MOI n'est qu'une position d'équilibre*" (There isn't one "I." *There aren't ten "I"s. There is no I. I is only a balancing point*). All of his characters and personas have to be seen as the expression of the poet's consciousness of being trapped in a movement where his "I" can be expressed only in terms of a difference from himself.

Peintures: Sept poèmes et seize illustrations (Paintings: Seven Poems and Sixteen Illustrations) was published in 1939, just before the outbreak of World War II. This volume is the first in which Michaux pairs his poetry with his paintings. An exchange is established between texts and black and white reproductions of his paintings, each medium echoing and completing the other. It is impossible to know whether Michaux's texts inspired the images or vice versa. In this sense, the images in *Peintures* are more than mere illustrations: they present a dialogue between two different modes of expression, each aiming for a common resolution. Michaux's painting is not representational; it is invested in a space outside of words, where emotions may be freed. It enables the poet to find, through a game of colors and forms, another means of investigating his inner self while trying to grasp the fleeting sensations described by words. This kind of painting comes close to a form of pictorial automatism, since the process through which the drawing is produced matters more than the result.

During the German occupation of France, Michaux and his wife lived mostly in Le Lavandou. This period was a dark one for the poet, who as a foreign resi-

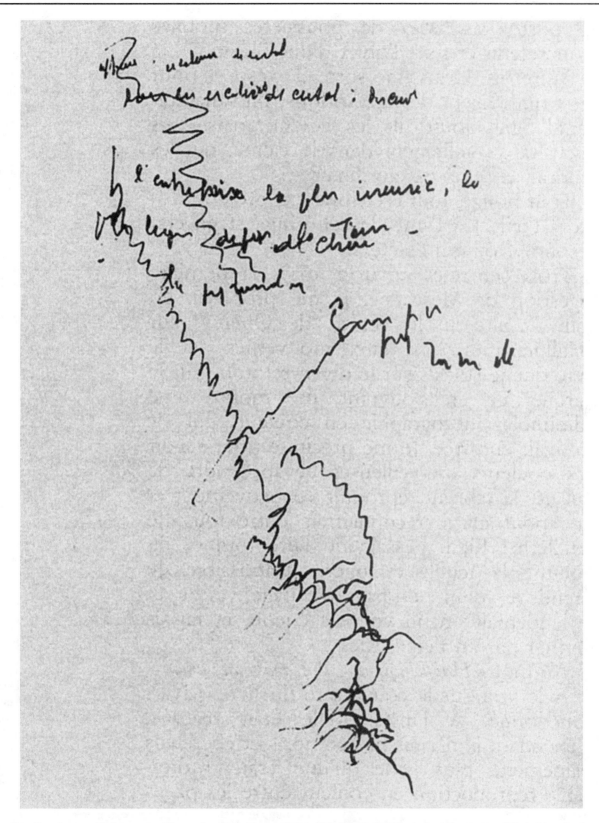

Page from the notes Michaux took while experimenting with mescaline, published in his 1956 book about his experience, Misérable miracle:
La Mescaline *(from* Henri Michaux, Œuvres complètes, *edited by Raymond Bellour and Ysé Tran, 2001)*

dent did not possess the authorization papers required to travel. Michaux took refuge in his creative activities. In May 1941 André Gide organized a conference on Michaux, but it was immediately banned. In July 1941 Gide proceeded to publish *Découvrons Henri Michaux* (Discovering Henri Michaux), a book that contributed to the recognition of Michaux as one of the most important writers of poetry at the time. In it Gide underlines Michaux's unconventional spirit and discusses the way in which he plays with the boundaries between the imaginary and the real. In 1944 Michaux published a collection of selected texts under the title of *L'Espace du dedans*. Revised and completed in 1966, this volume included, in chronological order, extracts from all his books except *Un Barbare en Asie*. Published in 1945, *Epreuves, exorcismes, 1940–1944* (Ordeals, Exorcisms, 1940–1944) is an anthology of works dealing with his experience of the war. Unlike the Resistance poems of writers such as Louis Aragon and Paul Eluard, Michaux's poems do not make any explicit references to historical events of the time. Instead, the situation created by the war is transferred to a far more allegorical plane representative of the traps life set for him, all the events or beings that fettered his existence. In his preface to the book Michaux explains what he means by "exorcism": "L'exorcisme, réaction en force, en attaque de bélier, est le véritable poème du prisonnier" (Exorcism, a forceful reaction, with a battering ram, is the prisoner's only poem). In *Epreuves, exorcismes*, in contrast to his "intervention" poems, the poet uses the forces of imagination not only to escape a painful situation but also to produce a form of saving energy. Through repetition games and the careful use of the sound of certain words, the poet thus elaborates a new form of opposition to the difficulties life presents, as in "Epervier de ta faiblesse, domine!" (Sparrowhawk of Your Weakness, Dominate!):

Je romps
Je plie
Je coule
Je m'appuie sur les coups que l'on me porte
Je gratte
J'obstrue
J'obnubile

(I break
I bend
I sink
I lean against the blow I receive
I scratch
I obstruct
I obsess).

This use of words as a pragmatic form of acting upon the world is associated by the poet with a form of

"magic," in which words and thought disturb habitual perceptions of reality.

The end of the war did not mark the end of painful years for Michaux. In 1945 his brother died in Brussels. The following year Michaux and his wife, who had been diagnosed with tuberculosis, spent a few months in the Pyrenees. The same year, Editions Pierre Seghers published a book by René Bertelé on Michaux, in its series Poètes d'Aujourd'hui (Poets of Today). This critical edition, which offers a wide range of selections from Michaux's works, helped make his poetry accessible to a general readership. Later Michaux collaborated with Bertelé on editing books of his paintings and organizing exhibitions of his works. In 1948 Michaux's wife died from burns she had suffered in a domestic accident when her nightgown caught on fire. Michaux wrote about her death the same year, in *Nous deux encore, 1948* (Still the Two of Us, 1948), a short text he subsequently refused to republish. In 1948 he also published *Ailleurs* (Elsewhere), a collection that brought together texts previously published separately in three small volumes, *Voyage en Grande Garabagne* (Travel in Grand Garabagne, 1936), *Au pays de la magie* (In the Land of Magic, 1941), and *Ici, Poddema* (Here, Poddema, 1946). In these texts Michaux develops a form of motionless travel in which he describes imaginary countries and peoples. Placing his imaginary travels on the same level as those undertaken in real life, Michaux opens his preface with the statement, "L'auteur a vécu très souvent ailleurs: deux ans en Garabagne, à peu près autant au pays de la Magie, un peu moins à Poddema" (The author has very often lived elsewhere: two years in Garabagne, about as long in the land of Magic, a little bit less in Poddema). To accentuate the authenticity of his trips, Michaux does not hesitate to adopt the style of an ethnologist, describing with great precision the customs of the strange peoples he invents, as well as the climates and geography of their lands. He wants to show that reality depends on the way in which it is shaped through language. Ridiculing travel narratives, Michaux demonstrates an often amusing capacity for inventing words, as when the names of the peoples he describes correspond to their sometimes absurd customs. Thus the reader encounters the Hacs, the Orbus, the Omanvus, the Ecovarettes, the Anardis, and so on. One should not be misled, however; through the cruelty and the absurdity of the places he creates, Michaux is in fact invoking the real world and the alienation of a civilization just coming out of a deadly war. His following book, *La Vie dans les plis* (Life in the Folds, 1949), uses the same inspiration. The beings he describes in it have simply lost all consistency. They are the Meidosems, imaginary and evanescent creatures who are at times reduced to mere strands of rope or string: "Appuyée contre un mur, un mur du reste que personne ne reverra jamais,

*Michaux (wearing sunglasses) and publisher Claude Gallimard at a conference on
Jorge Luis Borges, 1983 (photograph by Roger-Viollet)*

une forme faite de corde est là. Elle s'enlace. C'est tout. C'est une Meidosemme" (Leaning against a wall that no one will ever see again there is a shape made of string. It is intertwined. That is all. It is a Meidosem). These beings on the verge of nonexistence bring the poet back from his exterior "elsewhere" to his inner space, to his feeling of "peu d'être" (scarce being), to the weakness he has always thought of as inherent in him. In *Ecuador* he had already written that he was built on a "colonne absente" (absent column). These travels in an "elsewhere" lead the poet back to meditate on his own existence, through a writing that cannot help but crumble little by little. The text is made of small fragments surrounded by blank spaces that seem to work to erase the Meidosems' fragile life.

In 1950 Michaux published *Passages*. This collection, revised and enlarged in 1963, comprises poetic reflections on the art forms with which Michaux had experimented and which inspired him, as well as occasional commentary on the artistic creations of others. "Aventure de lignes" (Adventure of Lines), a piece in the 1963 edition, is a sort of reverie about the significance that lines in Paul Klee's paintings had taken for him, lines, he explains, that introduced him to the world of painting. Michaux's interest in music is also revealed in this volume. Music is represented as a liber-

ating activity, a form of movement that, like the strokes of a paintbrush, opposes the inertia of words: "Musique, opération du devenir, opération humaine la plus saine." (Music, a function of becoming, the most wholesome human activity). *Passages* includes Michaux's most direct revelations on his creative preoccupations and innovations.

In 1951 the first retrospective exhibition of his works was organized, at the Rive Gauche gallery in Paris. The same year, Michaux published *Mouvements,* another book in which poems and images alternate. *Mouvements* was subsequently reprinted as part of the collection *Face aux verrous* (Facing the Locks, 1954). The pieces in this anthology, all previously published between 1949 and 1952, redevelop and provide more depth to some of the writing techniques used in prior works: exorcism poems in the section "Poésie pour pouvoir" (Poetry for Power), originally published as a separate work in 1949; aphorisms in "Tranches de savoir" (Slices of Knowledge), which was first published in 1950; and the creation of imaginary places in "La Situation politique," first published as *Le Secret de la situation politique* (The Secret of the Political Situation), a companion piece to *Tranches de savoir*. The poet continues to experiment with different literary genres, subverting them as he changes their parameters and boundaries.

In 1955 Michaux became a French citizen. Around the same time he began to experiment with drugs, though not out of a desire for any artificial paradise that might enable him to escape the world. Michaux wished to find through drugs a new dimension of knowledge about the workings of human consciousness. *Connaissance par les gouffres* (Knowledge through the Abysses, 1961; translated as *Light Through Darkness,* 1963) opens, "Les drogues nous ennuient avec leur paradis. Qu'elles nous donnent plutôt un peu de savoir. Nous ne sommes pas un siècle à paradis" (Drugs bore us with their paradise. I wish they would give us a little knowledge instead. This is not a century for paradise). This exploration of alternative modes of perception occupied ten years of the poet's life and resulted in a series of four books: *Misérable miracle: La Mescaline* (1956; translated as *Miserable Miracle: Mescaline,* 1963), *L'Infini turbulent* (1957; translated as *The Turbulent Infinite,* 1970), *Connaissance par les gouffres,* and *Les Grandes Epreuves de l'esprit et les innombrables petites* (1966; translated as *The Major Ordeals of the Mind, and the Countless Minor Ones,* 1974). Experimenting with mescaline, psilocybin, LSD, and hashish, Michaux set out to compare their effects on him. He writes in *Connaissance par les gouffres* that his first attempt to use psilocybin (a hallucinogenic drug extracted from a Mexican mushroom) took place in a scientific setting at the Hôpital Sainte-Anne in Paris, in the presence of four psychiatrists. The poet was thus simultaneously the object of these experiments and the subject describing their effects. As a result his texts emphasize the tension between his desire to give an objective and scientific description and the impossibility of his achieving this aim. In *Misérable miracle* and *L'Infini turbulent* Michaux, finding it difficult to grasp the multiple dysfunctions induced by the drugs, decided to include notes in the margin of the main text, in an attempt to make sense of the turmoil that overcame him. Both works are accompanied by a few drawings, and *Misérable miracle* includes facsimiles of some handwritten pages, though the distorted script often comes across as no more than lines on a page. Under the influence of the drugs, Michaux experienced a complete alienation that upset and destroyed his consciousness by disarticulating time and space and distorting his perception of speed. Words would begin to spin and jostle each other, unable to keep up with the continuous flux of the world, and the poet would lose the sense of his body's limits. These dangerous adventures at times brought Michaux to states close to madness.

In 1959 the critic Robert Bréchon published his book *Michaux,* for which Michaux wrote "Quelques renseignements sur cinquante-neuf années d'existence." In 1961 Michaux met Micheline Phankim, who became his lifelong companion and his literary executor. One year later he applied himself to a new medium, writing the scenario for director Eric Duvivier's documentary *Images du monde visionnaire* (Images of the Visionary World), which illustrates his experiments with drugs. Though Michaux had always been interested in the possibilities of cinema, he was not completely satisfied with Duvivier's final product (released in 1963), and he never again participated in the making of a movie. During the early 1960s Michaux exhibited his paintings at least once a year and resumed his travels. On 30 November 1965 he was offered the Grand Prix National des Lettres, which he turned down. His refusal was not so much an act of provocation as a sign of the author's mistrust of the literary world (he also refused the Fertinelli prize in 1982). Michaux had never thought of himself as a poet or a painter. For him these two activities were a means of doing research on himself, not a way of succeeding on an artistic level. Michaux had always refused to make of himself a public figure; nevertheless, his fame began to spread at an international level, as evinced by Bellour's 1966 study *Henri Michaux,* written for the series Les Cahiers de l'Herne. Bellour's critical study documents the reception of Michaux's work by such foreign writers as Borges, Mounir Hafez, Paul Celan, and Allen Ginsberg. In 1969 Michaux published *Façons d'endormi, façons d'éveillé* (Modes of Sleeping, Modes of Waking). In it the poet, without engaging in psychoanalysis, investigates the world of his dreams, studying the links between his nocturnal and daily experiences. He examines with great precision how experiences throughout the day are transformed or transposed in his dream space. In these fascinating reflections he establishes a distinction between dreams and daydreams: "Le contraire du rêve qui, n'importe où il mène, vous y mène attaché et sans que vous puissiez rien, la rêverie dispose de liberté" (The opposite of dreaming, which no matter where it takes us, takes us there bound and powerless, daydreaming consists of freedom). Daydreaming, a form of mind-wandering associated with games and the fulfillment of desires, therefore allows the poet to find a richer space than that of dreams.

First published in 1971 and enlarged in 1978, *Poteaux d'angle* (translated as *Tent Posts,* 1997) is the only book of Michaux's that is composed exclusively of aphorisms. Using this concise style that he particularly loved, he presents the reader with countertruths and paradoxes. Some of his aphorisms are reminiscent of Zen koans, short questions or anecdotes used by Buddhist masters in order to test and train their disciples. Koans aim to trigger something in the listener's mind beyond the principle of deductive thinking. Passionate about Eastern thought, Michaux was inspired by its method of "non-teaching" through mysterious and paradoxical formulas, as is evident in the following aphorisms: "Tu sors du lac, tu rentres dans un lac, portant bandeau noir, mais tu crois toujours voir clair!" (You get out of the lake. You get back into the lake wearing a blindfold, but you still think you can see!); "Ne te livre pas comme un paquet ficelé. Ris avec tes cris; crie avec tes rires" (Don't hand yourself over like a ticd package. Laugh with your screams; scream with your laughs). The poet does not set himself the goal of delivering ready-made truths but instead creates a situation in which everyday language must be transcended.

Emergences-Résurgences (1972) includes many illustrations of Michaux's pictorial works, revealing his different painting techniques. The writer-painter offers a history of his journey through images. He speaks of his first abortive attempts at drawing, which he viewed as a direct means of participating in the world. From the beginning, painting represented for the poet a way of finding a space beyond knowledge. Not affiliated with any school, Michaux proceeded by personal experimentation. In this compilation the reader can follow his different experiments with diluted gouache, with black sheets of paper on which vague silhouettes appear, and with Indian inkblots used to portray strange visions of battles. Michaux explains how he tried to transpose to paper the disruptive phenomena induced by mescaline. What painting brought Michaux was essentially a place of uncertainty and surprise that he defines as a site of "aventures" (adventures).

Moments: Traversées du temps (Moments: Crossings of Time), published in 1973, is a collection of some of Michaux's sparest poems. In pieces such as "The Thin Man" and "Iniji," sentences fall to pieces, giving way to a juxtaposition of terms that aim to depict fleeing beings. Thus, Iniji is ultimately a form of sputtering, carried away by the very sounds of the name that is supposed to identify her:

> Anania Iniji
> Annan Animha Iniji
> Ornanian Iniji
> et Iniji n'est plus animée
>
> (Anania Iniji
> Annan Animha Iniji
> Ornanian Iniji
> and Iniji is no longer animated).

Michaux reduces the sentence to a minimum, as if subjects and verbs were being absorbed by the white sheet of paper, or as if the words themselves were destined to disappear. This poem, which inspired novelist J. M. G. Le Clézio in his *Vers les icebergs* (Toward the Icebergs, 1978), shows Michaux's influence on a later generation of writers, which included also the poet Jean-Pierre Verheggen and the poet-novelist Jean-Michel Maulpoix.

In *Bras cassé* (Broken Arm, 1973), reprinted in the 1975 collection *Face à ce qui se dérobe* (Facing What Is Disappearing), Michaux writes about his fractured right

Michaux with some of his paintings (photograph by Giselle Freund / Agence Nina Beskow)

arm. The writer explains that the event gave him the opportunity to discover a part of himself, namely the left side of his body, which his right-handed habits had made him ignore for many years. Michaux explores pain in order to gain new insight into how one lives with one's body.

In 1978 the Musée Nationale d'Art Moderne at the Centre Georges Pompidou held a retrospective exhibition of all of Michaux's pictorial works. A catalogue was subsequently published, and the exhibition traveled to the Guggenheim Museum in New York. The last collection of poetry published by Michaux before his death was *Chemins cherchés, chemins perdus, transgressions* (Paths Searched For, Paths Lost, Transgressions, 1981). One of its sections, *Les Ravagés* (first published separately in 1976), was inspired by drawings made by mental patients. In it Michaux writes as if on a journey through images of madness, wandering through the paintings of others. Rather than attempt to explain these paintings, Michaux shows how they came to inhabit his imagination. Through this exchange he seeks to show the necessity of listening to madness in order to gain a better understanding of the functioning and limits of one's own consciousness.

Michaux died of a heart attack in Paris on 19 October 1984. His body was cremated four days later at the Père Lachaise cemetery in Paris. Two more volumes of his works, comprising texts he had published during the final years of life, were printed posthumously: *Déplacements, dégagements* (1985; translated as *Spaced, Displaced,* 1992) and *Affrontements* (Confrontations, 1986), an enlarged edition of a work first published in 1981. In 1996 Michaux's literary executor, Phankim, edited and published *A distance* (At a Distance), a volume of previously unpublished poems.

Henri Michaux's poetry does not belong to any particular school, nor did he write in a particular genre. In his works language is seized, ill-treated, and coerced, so that it is impossible to pin down his poems as either poetry or prose, tale or allegory, cries of pain or scientific discourse. Michaux questions the boundaries between the real and the imaginary, so much so that genres can no longer occupy a fixed place. Ultimately, Michaux does not really care about literature: words are there not to enable the poet to construct some kind of self-identity but to explore the unsettling sites of disequilibrium and otherness where words meet the strokes of the paintbrush.

Letters:

Correspondance Adrienne Monnier & Henri Michaux: 1939–1955, edited, with an introduction, by Maurice Imbert (Paris: La Hune, 1995);

Sitôt lus: Lettres à Franz Hellens, 1922–1952, edited, with an introduction, by Leonardo Clerici (Paris: Fayard, 1999);

A la minute que j'éclate: Quarante-trois lettres à Hermann Closson, edited by Jacques Carion (Brussels: D. Devillez, 1999).

Interviews:

Alain Jouffroy, *Avec Henri Michaux* (Monaco: Editions du Rocher, 1992);

Jean-Dominique Rey, *Henri Michaux* (Creil: Dumerchez, 1994).

Bibliographies:

Maurice Imbert, *Bibliographie des livres et plaquettes d'Henri Michaux* (Paris: M. Imbert, 1993);

Raymond Bellour, bibliography, *Magazine Littéraire,* special Michaux issue, *Henri Michaux: Ecrire et peindre,* no. 364 (April 1998);

Bellour and Ysé Tran, "Tableau synoptique des publications d'Henri Michaux (1922–1946)," in *Henri Michaux, Œuvres complètes,* edited by Bellour and Tran, volume 1 (Paris: Gallimard, 1998), pp. 1385–1396;

François d'Argent, "Bibliographie," in *Henri Michaux,* third edition, edited by Bellour, Les Cahiers de l'Herne, no. 8 (Paris: Editions de l'Herne, 1999), pp. 463–526;

Bellour and Tran, "Tableau synoptique et chronologie des publications d'Henri Michaux (1947–1959)," in *Henri Michaux, Œuvres complètes,* edited by Bellour and Tran, volume 2 (Paris: Gallimard, 2001), pp. 1379–1384.

References:

Marianne Béguelin, *Henri Michaux, esclave et démiurge* (Lausanne: L'Age d'Homme, 1974);

Raymond Bellour, *Henri Michaux ou Une Mesure de l'être* (Paris: Gallimard, 1965);

Bellour, ed., *Henri Michaux,* Les Cahiers de l'Herne, no. 8 (Paris: Editions de l'Herne, 1966);

René Bertelé, *Henri Michaux,* Poètes d'Aujourd'hui, no. 5 (Paris: Seghers, 1946);

Anne Le Bouteiller, *Michaux: Les Voix de l'être exilé* (Paris & Montreal: L'Harmattan, 1997);

Malcom Bowie, *Henri Michaux: A Study of His Literary Works* (Oxford: Clarendon Press, 1973);

Robert Bréchon, *Michaux* (Paris: Gallimard, 1959);

Peter Broome, *Henri Michaux* (London: Athlone Press, 1977);

Michel Butor, *Improvisations sur Henri Michaux* (Montpellier: Fata Morgana, 1985);

Roger Dadoun, ed., *Ruptures sur Henri Michaux* (Paris: Payot, 1976);

Laurie Edson, ed., *Henri Michaux* (Baton Rouge: Louisiana State University, 1986);

Claude Fintz, *Expérience esthétique et spirituelle chez Henri Michaux* (Paris & Montreal: L'Harmattan, 1996);

André Gide, *Découvrons Henri Michaux* (Paris: Gallimard, 1941);

Anne-Elisabeth Halpern, *Henri Michaux: Le Laboratoire du poète* (Paris: S. Arslan, 1998);

Magazine Littéraire, special Michaux issue, no. 85 (February 1974);

Jean-Pierre Martin, *Henri Michaux: Ecritures de soi, expatriations* (Paris: J. Corti, 1994);

Jean-Claude Mathieu and Michel Collot, eds., *Passages et langages d'Henri Michaux: Actes de la troisième "Rencontre sur la poésie moderne"* (Paris: J. Corti, 1987);

Jean-Michel Maulpoix, *Henri Michaux, passager clandestin* (Seyssel: Champ Vallon, 1984);

Brigitte Ouvry-Vial, *Henri Michaux* (Lyons: La Manufacture, 1989);

Jean-Xavier Ridon, *Henri Michaux, J. M. G. Le Clézio: L'Exil des mots* (Paris: Kimé, 1995);

François Trotet, *Henri Michaux ou La Sagesse du vide* (Paris: A. Michel, 1992).

Anna de Noailles

(15 November 1876 – 30 April 1933)

Catherine Perry
University of Notre Dame

BOOKS: *Le Cœur innombrable* (Paris: Calmann-Lévy, 1901);

L'Ombre des jours (Paris: Calmann-Lévy, 1902);

La Nouvelle Espérance (Paris: Calmann-Lévy, 1903);

Le Visage émerveillé (Paris: Calmann-Lévy, 1904);

La Domination (Paris: Calmann-Lévy, 1905);

Les Eblouissements (Paris: Calmann-Lévy, 1907);

De la rive d'Europe à la rive d'Asie (Paris: Dorbon-Ainé, 1913); enlarged as *Exactitudes* (Paris: Grasset, 1930);

Les Vivants et les Morts (Paris: Fayard, 1913);

Les Forces éternelles (Paris: Fayard, 1920);

Poésies (Paris: Payot, 1920);

A Rudyard Kipling, Les Amis d'Edouard, no. 38 (Paris, 1921);

Parmi les lettres qu'on n'envoie pas, Les Œuvres libres, no. 14 (Paris: Fayard, 1922);

Poésies, romans (Paris: Crès, 1922);

L'hommage à Paul Valéry, by Noailles and others (Paris: Le Divan, 1922);

Les Innocentes; ou, La Sagesse des femmes (Paris: Fayard, 1923);

Poème de l'amour (Paris: Fayard, 1924);

Passions et Vanités (Paris: Cité des Livres, 1926);

Hommage à Marcel Proust, by Noailles and others (Paris: Gallimard, 1927);

L'Honneur de souffrir (Paris: Grasset, 1927);

Poèmes d'enfance (Paris: Grasset, 1928);

Choix de poésies (Paris: Fasquelle, 1930; republished, 1963; republished, with a preface by Jean Rostand, Paris: B. Grasset, 1976);

Le Livre de ma vie (Paris: Hachette, 1932; Paris: Mercure de France, 1976);

Derniers Vers (Paris: Grasset, 1933);

L'Offrande, edited by Philippe Giraudon (Paris: Orphée / La Différence, 1991).

Edition: *Derniers Vers et Poèmes d'enfance,* edited by Constantin Photiadès (Paris: Grasset, 1934).

OTHER: Henri Franck, *La Danse devant l'Arche,* preface by Noailles (Paris: Nouvelle Revue Française, 1912);

Anna de Noailles, 1931

Sadī, *Le Jardin des Roses,* translated by Franz Toussaint, preface by Noailles (Paris: Fayard, 1912; revised edition, Paris: L'Edition d'Art H. Piazza, 1965);

Marie Lenéru, *La Paix,* preface by Noailles (Paris: Grasset, 1922);

Sabine Sicaud, *Poèmes d'enfant,* preface by Noailles (Poitiers: Cahiers de France, 1926);

Pierre Weiss, *L'Espace,* preface by Noailles (Paris: Querelle, 1929);

"Portrait de Marcel Proust," "Un souvenir de Marcel Proust," and "Quand Marcel Proust nous eut quittés," in Marcel Proust, *Correspondance générale,* volume 2: *Lettres à la comtesse de Noailles, 1901–1919,* edited by Robert Proust and Paul Brach (Paris: Plon, 1931), pp. 1–14, 15–19, 217–223;

"Discours de réception de la Comtesse de Noailles à l'Académie Royale de Belgique," in Jean Cocteau, *La Comtesse de Noailles Oui et Non* (Paris: Perrin, 1963), pp. 183–193.

SELECTED PERIODICAL PUBLICATIONS– UNCOLLECTED: "Apologie pour Victor Hugo," *Les Nouvelles littéraires* (30 June 1923): 1;

"Gloire de l'été: l'Assomption," *Le Gaulois* (15 August 1923);

"Les Chefs d'œuvre inconnus," *Le Gaulois* (18 August 1923);

"Ronsard," *Le Gaulois* (2 February 1924); republished, *La Muse française* (February 1924): 138–140;

"Colette," *Le Capitole* (January 1925); republished in Colette, *Lettres à ses pairs,* edited by Claude Pichois and Roberte Forbin (Paris: Flammarion, 1973), p. 59;

"Poésie des repas," *Vogue* (1 June 1926): 33;

"Etre juste envers soi-même," *Vogue* (1 July 1926): 31;

"Travailler," *Vogue* (1 August 1926): 29;

"Les Enfants, les étrangers," *Vogue* (1 September 1926): 35;

"Azur et lucidité," *Vogue* (1 October 1926): 33;

"Notre Famille et nos amis," *Vogue* (1 November 1926): 27;

"A la mémoire d'une grande figure française: pour le monument de Maurice Barrès," *Le Figaro,* 358 (24 December 1926): 1;

"Victor Hugo," *Les Nouvelles littéraires* (23 April 1927): 1;

"Les Secrets du poète," *Les Feuilles libres* (June 1927): 21–23;

"Ma Chambre et la fidélité," *Vogue* (September 1930): 63;

"L'Automobile, oiseau terrestre," *Les Annales politiques et littéraires* (1 November 1930): 389–390;

"Adieux aux Ballets Russes," *La Revue musicale,* 110 (December 1930): 3–7;

"Confidences à l'ami inconnu," *Les Annales politiques et littéraires* (15 November 1931): 423–424;

"Savoir dessiner une rose," *Vogue* (1 December 1931): 43;

"Avec le concours du cœur," *Les Annales politiques et littéraires* (1 September 1932): 183–185;

"Rencontre à Palerme," edited by Claude Mignot-Ogliastri, *Nouvelle Revue des Deux Mondes* (October–December 1976): 372–380.

With her first book, *Le Cœur innombrable* (The Innumerable Heart, 1901), Anna de Noailles became the most popular and celebrated female poet in early-twentieth-century France. Admired by writers, thinkers, artists, and politicians of many nationalities, this literary "star" of the Belle Epoque was the only woman writer of her time in France to receive the highest public recognition: in 1921 the Academie Française bestowed on her its Grand Prix de Littérature. The following year she became the first female member of the newly instituted Belgian Academy of French Language and Literature, and in 1931 she was the first woman ever to be elevated to the rank of Commandeur in the Legion of Honor. Poetry, which had gradually removed itself from the public with the Parnassians' cultivation of art for art's sake and with the linguistic complexities of the decadents and the symbolists, became popular again to a large extent through her influence. As Tama Lea Engelking puts it, Noailles "brought pleasure back into reading and writing." Her work also had a strong influence on other contemporary poets; in his 1959 biography of Marcel Proust, George Painter stresses that Noailles's "voluptuous, anguished and truly 'dazzling' poems"–a term taken from her 1907 volume, *Les Eblouissements* (Dazzling Lights)–"by their technical influence during the next few years upon Valéry and Cocteau, were to help to bridge the gap between symbolism and the twentieth century."

Among her contemporaries, perhaps no one captured Noailles's character with greater sympathy and insight than Proust in his early unfinished novel, *Jean Santeuil* (1952; translated, 1955); the chapter "La Vicomtesse Gaspard de Réveillon" explains her social personae as so many veils designed to shield an intimate poetic vocation, when poetry was still a favored genre but the notion of inspiration was increasingly considered naive and deluded, if not presumptuous. Proust also wrote one of the most perceptive essays on Noailles's poetry, observing in 1907 that her poetic self represents not "le moi social, contingent" (the social, contingent self) but one that bears no trace of the caste or class to which she belonged; it is "le moi profond qui individualise les œuvres et les fait durer" (the deep self that personalizes works and makes them endure).

Although her popularity decreased after World War I as modernism gained ground with poets such as Guillaume Apollinaire and Paul Valéry, and although her readership declined dramatically after her death in 1933, later critical judgments confirm that she deserved her early recognition. A discrepancy between form and content, reflecting Noailles's position at the cusp of the antithetical worldviews of nineteenth-century Romanticism and twentieth-century modernism, characterizes her poetry, in which dynamic concepts and images strive to dissolve a largely classical structure. By actively engaging with her French literary heritage, while also finding inspiration in Greek paganism and in the thought of Friedrich Nietzsche, Noailles constructed an original poetic world that often emerges as modern in spite of its Romantic trappings and that sets her apart from literary practices of the previous century. The term "Dionysian" best describes her work, as in Nietzsche's use of it: ecstatic, sensual, erotic, playful, sometimes violent, and marked by a tragic undercurrent that becomes magnified in her later poetry.

Noailles published nine volumes of poetry, three novels, a book combining novellas with meditations on gender issues, a collection of prose poems, an autobiography spanning her childhood and adolescence, essays, articles, and book prefaces. Despite the extensiveness and diversity of her writings, and despite the recognition she received earlier in the century, the critical consensus until recently seems to have been that Noailles was a second-rate poet who owed her success to extraliterary factors, the most significant being her social class. Such an assessment originated in a general misperception of Noailles's life, personality, and thought that has been corrected by biographies such as Claude Mignot-Ogliastri's thoroughly researched and exhaustive *Anna de Noailles: Une Amie de la Princesse Edmond de Polignac* (1986), complemented by her 1994 edition of Noailles's previously undisclosed correspondence with Maurice Barrès.

Anna Elisabeth de Brancovan was born in Paris on 15 November 1876 to a fifty-year-old Romanian expatriate, Prince Grégoire Bassaraba de Brancovan, and Princess Rachel Musurus, twenty-one years his junior, an accomplished pianist of Greek origins who had been born in Constantinople (today Istanbul, Turkey) and reared in London. Along with her older brother, Constantin, and her younger sister, Hélène, Anna de Brancovan led a life of privilege in her youth. Educated almost entirely at home, she spoke English and German in addition to French and was raised to appreciate the arts—particularly music and poetry. The family spent the winter in Paris and the rest of the year at their estate, Amphion, near Evian on the south shore of Lake Geneva.

The park-like setting of Amphion impressed the child: Noailles's poetry bears witness to a preference for the calm beauty and exuberance of the natural world over the urban environments in which she subsequently had to live. The estate remained in her memory as an earthly paradise that she sought to re-create in her poetry; in her autobiography, *Le Livre de ma vie* (The Book of My Life, 1932), she recalls: "Si parfaites de transparence, de pureté, de bonheur sans inquiets désirs furent de telles journées de Savoie qu'elles devaient me servir de modèle définitif pour la figure du monde, selon mon choix" (So perfectly transparent, pure, and joyful without anxious desires were those days in Savoy that they would serve me as a definitive model for the configuration of the world as I chose it to be).

Noailles's husband, Count Mathieu Fernand Frederic Pascal de Noailles

In the poems of Victor Hugo's *Les Contemplations* (1856), dedicated to his drowned daughter Léopoldine, Anna de Brancovan discovered a language that enabled her both to express her grief over her father's death in October 1886 and to overcome it through representation. Although she disapproved of Hugo's patriarchal values, she remained faithful to the man Charles Du Bos correctly perceived as her poetic father, who was, perhaps, closer to her through his words than the biological father for whom she had felt, as she says in her autobiography, both "un grand amour et une peur extrême" (great love and extreme fear). In 1887 she visited Romania and Turkey and observed the subjection of women there; in her autobiography Noailles deplores such "femmes enfantines qui ont toujours levé les yeux vers l'homme, ont vénéré sa tyrannie tutélaire et n'ont pas cherché à se mesurer contre lui" (childish women who have always looked up to man, have venerated his protective tyranny, and have not sought to measure themselves against him).

Brancovan's adolescence was frequently marred by illness. When she was about eighteen, the study of science and the thought of atheists such as Hippolyte Taine, Ernest Renan, Charles-Marie Leconte de Lisle, Emile Zola, Anatole France, and Arthur Schopenhauer resulted in the loss of her religious faith; in her unpublished notebooks she recorded: "Ne plus croire c'est une épouvante qui touche à la folie.–C'est la conscience perpétuelle d'une fragilité sans secours, d'un agissement sans résultats d'une fin sans avenir" (To believe no longer is a terror that borders on madness.–It is the perpetual awareness of a frailty without recourse, of actions without results of an end without a future). Her poetry translates this personal experience into a combination of metaphysical anguish, proclaimed atheism, deep sympathy for suffering, and insights into the human condition that, Mari H. O'Brien argues, anticipate existentialism. Poetry for Noailles became the sole means of replenishing the ontological and epistemological void left by the absence of God, a situation concisely described in the last stanza of a poem in her 1913 collection, *Les Vivants et les Morts* (The Living and the Dead):

J'aspire à vous, Splendeur, Raison éblouissante!
Mais je ne vous vois pas, ô mon Dieu! et je chante
   A cause du vide infini!

(I aspire to you, Splendor, dazzling Reason!
But I do not see you, o my God! and I sing
   Because of the infinite void!)

On 18 August 1897, with her marriage to Count Mathieu Fernand Frederic Pascal de Noailles, Anna de Brancovan became a member of one of the most prominent families of the old French nobility. By then she was familiar with the radical thought of Nietzsche through the essayist and novelist Augustine Bulteau, who had been her mentor since 1896 and whom she considered her spiritual mother; when she began to read the philosopher's works around 1900, Noailles was conquered by his aphoristic, poetic style. A confirmed and despairing atheist, she was probably rescued from nihilism by Nietzsche's affirmation of the Stoic concept of *amor fati* (acceptance of one's fate); she decided that she would seek, as Nietzsche says in *Die Geburt der Tragödie* (1886; translated as *The Birth of Tragedy,* 1909), "metaphysical comfort" in the notion that "life is at the bottom of things, despite all the changes of appearances, indestructibly powerful and pleasurable." Her poetry increasingly affirms every instant of existence against a permanent backdrop of pessimism.

Following the birth of her only child, her son Anne-Jules, on 18 September 1900, Noailles underwent a depression that led her in-laws to confine her from December 1900 to February 1901 to a psychiatric clinic run by the neurologist Paul Sollier. Unpublished documents reveal that this experience, which Noailles concealed from all but her closest friends, was extraordinarily traumatic: given permission to write, on 10 January 1901 she described its effects to Bulteau: "Je crois qu'on reste marqué du malheur; j'ai dans l'âme un pli de dureté et de méfiance, un regard oblique vers la vie que je ne connaissais pas. J'ai vécu seule dans l'abandon et dans l'horreur des heures si terribles que la cendre amère m'en reste dans la bouche" (I believe that one remains marked by misfortune; my soul bears a crease of hardness and distrust, an oblique gaze toward life which I did not know before. I have endured, in abandonment and horror, such terrible hours that their bitter ashes remain in my mouth).

Several of Noailles's poems, composed at eighteen mostly under the decadent influence of Charles Baudelaire, Jules Laforgue, Paul Verlaine, and Albert Victor Samain, had appeared in periodicals and had attracted critical approbation. With her first collection, *Le Cœur innombrable,* she pulled away from these early models and resolved to abandon constraining forms such as the sonnet; thenceforth she alternated among a variety of forms–for the most part alexandrine and octosyllabic verse, often set in distichs, tercets, and quatrains. In contrast to poets who were beginning to experiment with open forms, Noailles upheld traditional patterns of rhythm and rhyme; she did so, she claimed in a 1913 interview with André Arnyvelde, because only such versification could ensure a precise rendition of the poet's perceptions, as well as readers' participation in the poet's world: "La plupart d'entre ces jeunes poètes négligent la rime, se croient libérés. . . . Mais la rime est la pointe, l'épine, qui accroche, fixe la sensation. . . . La forme traditionnelle et la rime sont comme la palpitation générale où tous les cœurs peuvent s'entendre" (Most of these young poets neglect rhyme, they believe that they are liberated. . . . But rhyme is the crest, the thorn, that catches and fixes sensation. . . . Traditional form and rhyme are like the general palpitation where all hearts can understand one another). Apart from a few Hugolian poems on social justice, which constitute an exception in her corpus, the main inspirations for *Le Cœur innombrable* were *The Greek Anthology;* Stoic treatises; and works by Nietzsche, Schopenhauer, and the historian Jules Michelet, along with her own obsessive awareness of suffering and death.

Serving to introduce and explain her poetry of nature, "Le Pays" (The Country), the prefatory poem of the collection, subtly raises issues that a woman who was also a foreigner striving for poetic recognition in France had to confront. In the context of the growth of right-wing nationalism that followed the 1894 court-martial conviction of Alfred Dreyfus, a Jewish army officer, on false charges of selling secrets to the Germans, Noailles stood out as an alien—all the more so because she defiantly took the side of the "other," meaning non-French, that Dreyfus came to symbolize. In the context of French poetry, which remained largely a masculine domain at the turn of the century, Noailles faced a similar challenge in establishing her legitimacy as a poet. In response to critics who dubbed her "une poétesse," she maintained that she was "un poète."

From the first verse of "Le Pays," in which she carefully avoids revealing her sex, Noailles takes hold of France with the possessive adjective "ma" (my), while simultaneously reaching for a universal voice through the impersonal pronoun "on" (one): "Ma France, quand on a nourri son cœur latin / Du lait de votre Gaule . . ." (My France, when one has nourished one's Latin heart / With the milk of your Gaul . . .). Not only does her Latin heart both extend beyond and incorporate France's boundaries; she also addresses the country through its origins as Gaul, the Latin name given to France by the Romans. Noailles thereby asserts her right to a place among French poets because she partakes of the same cultural origins in the cradle of Occidental civilization. By inferring through the image of the nourishing milk that Gaul is also her own mother, she further stresses her lineage with the French. She then declares that she has settled on the banks of the Seine to construct her home—a metaphor for her work. Noailles thus implies that her will to write in French proceeds not only from her cultural birthright but also from a deliberate choice that emphasizes her freedom.

The conventional theme of the poet's will to overcome individual transience through art is present with a peculiar insistence in Noailles's early poetry. *Le Cœur innombrable* frequently asserts the poet's survival through her verse, often by representing her as nature itself. The opening stanza of the second piece in the volume, "L'Offrande à la Nature" (The Offering to Nature), a poem composed in January 1901 at Sollier's clinic and the most applauded work in the collection at the time of its publication, depicts her as a poet who has loved nature with such passionate devotion that she will remain unequaled:

Nature au cœur profond sur qui les cieux reposent,
Nul n'aura comme moi si chaudement aimé
La lumière des jours et la douceur des choses
L'eau luisante et la terre où la vie a germé.

(Deep-hearted Nature upon whom the skies recline,
None more than I will have loved with such warmth
The light of day and the sweetness of things,
The shimmering water and the nurturing earth).

Noailles in 1899

The future-perfect tense of the verb *"aimer"* (to love) suggests that Noailles is composing her own eulogy. The poem establishes an intimate correspondence between the poet and the natural world. In typical Romantic fashion, fusion with nature's continued life guarantees her immortality.

With "L'Offrande à la nature" Noailles proceeds out of France to a universal territory that the now clearly feminine speaker claims for herself. More than the banks of the Seine, nature appears as her true site of election, for it grants her the possibility of constructing a poetic identity unhampered by restrictive concepts of nation, ethnicity, or propriety. Human beings are kept at a safe distance: "La forêt, les étangs et les plaines fécondes / Ont plus touché mes yeux que les regards humains" (The woods, ponds, and fertile plains / Have touched my eyes more than human gazes). Echoing Nietzsche, the speaker renounces reason as the faculty that legislates absolute moral values in favor of an unshackled, animal nature that has become the criterion for her own values:

Je suis venue à vous sans peur et sans prudence
Vous donnant ma raison pour le bien et le mal,

Ayant pour toute joie et toute connaissance
Votre âme impétueuse aux ruses d'animal.

(I have come to you without fear or prudence,
Giving you my reason for good and evil,
Embracing as my only joy and knowledge
Your impetuous soul with animal cunning).

"L'Offrande à la nature" introduces ideas that Noailles's poetry went on to modulate in many variations over most of her career.

Le Cœur innombrable had an immediate and resounding success, receiving thirty reviews in a few months and going through more than twenty editions in twenty years. It was awarded the Archon-Despérouses prize of the French Academy in 1902. The energy that appeared to flow through Noailles's words corresponded to the vitalist currents of thought exemplified by the philosophy of Henri Bergson. A diffuse movement known as "Naturisme" was then in vogue, although Noailles did not specifically participate in it; a literary analogue of impressionism in painting, it advocated a sensory approach to reality as the primary means of knowledge and as the basis of art. The cult of sensuality, Roger Charbonnel explained in "La Renaissance du Paganisme" (1909), was part of an aesthetics grounded in the body, understood as "la source première de toutes nos joies et même . . . la condition initiale de toute esthétique combinant avec harmonie des sensations vécues et non de froides idées" (the primary source of all our joys and even . . . the necessary condition for all aesthetics, combining harmoniously experienced sensations rather than lifeless ideas). Noailles's work appealed to a readership that had lost its ties with religion and with traditional morality. Here was a female poet who praised the body and the senses without a trace of Christian shame, brazenly substituting Eros for the biblical God, as in the poem "L'Amour": "Amour, qui dès l'aube du temps, / Flottais sur la terre et les eaux" (Love who, from the dawn of time / Moved upon the earth and the waters).

After *L'Ombre des jours* (The Shadow of Days, 1902), a relatively somber collection in which nature provides less reassurance and the speaker often appears divided into conflicting selves or "âmes désordonnées" (disorderly souls), Noailles published three novels. *La Nouvelle Espérance* (New Hope, 1903) is about a woman who strives for fulfillment through love in and out of marriage and decides to commit suicide when she finds men's love to be an illusion. Though admired for its poetic prose and its candid revelations about the feminine psyche, the novel shocked readers such as Charles Maurras, the founder of the nationalist party L'Action Française, who in *Minerva* (1 May 1903) castigated Noailles for her immoralism. *Le Visage émerveillé* (The

Marveling Face, 1904), which narrates in diary form the sensual awakening of a novice who welcomes a lover into her convent and then renounces him, was even more audacious. Both novels were successful, going through many reprints over approximately twenty years. Noailles's final novel, *La Domination* (Domination, 1905), recounts from a masculine perspective the will to power, fixation on death, and amorous adventures of a protagonist modeled on Barrès. Because she was criticized for using a Barresian style in the novel, Noailles refused to allow it to be republished.

Initiated in 1903, Noailles's relationship with Barrès remained platonic until 1917–five years after Noailles legally separated from her husband. Throughout his career after 1903 Barrès oscillated between attaching a symbolic significance to Noailles as an incarnation of Romantic, Dionysian values and rejecting her as a poet whose inspiration clashed with his philosophy of nationalist action. Noailles's presence can be detected in every work Barrès composed after 1903, except his patriotic treatises of World War I.

Published on 24 April 1907, *Les Eblouissements* is the first volume of Noailles's mature poetry and the one that had the greatest immediate impact: it went through five reprints in less than two weeks and received more than fifty reviews, most of them laudatory. The 420 pages of the book are divided into four sections: "Vie-joie-lumière" (Life-Joy-Light), "Beauté de la France" (The Beauty of France), "Les Jardins" (The Gardens), and "La Douleur et la Mort" (Pain and Death). Among the important themes it explores are a Nietzschean reverence for life, energy, heroism, and a predilection for the "Orient" inspired in part by Noailles's background and childhood memories and in part by her friendship with Barrès. The most exalted poems in the collection are directed not to a human lover but to nature, which is perceived as a constant source of wonder. In her autobiography Noailles explains her relationship with nature, inaugurated in her childhood, as a mutual one: "je me suis abandonnée à elle et je l'ai attirée sur mon cœur" (I abandoned myself to it and I drew it upon my heart); this "union passionnée" (passionate union) inspired her to compose a poetry of her own, "une harmonie hardie et neuve, soutenue par la tradition et les réminiscences, mais qui ne recueillait les conseils d'aucune école et ne voulut reproduire que ce qui est vif et frémissant" (a daring new harmony, sustained by tradition and reminiscences, but which took advice from no school and wanted to reproduce only that which is alive and throbbing). But in her work, as in Nietzsche's, nature progressively emerges as a fearful power demanding the death of individuals for its perpetuation. Adopting the concept of *amor fati,* Noailles recovers even the most terrifying aspects of existence through love, which turns what might otherwise be a bitter confrontation with the

Page from the manuscript for "L'empreinte," included in the 1901 collection Le Cœur innombrable *(Bibliothèque Nationale, Paris)*

forces of dissolution into the intense pleasure of an imagined union, as in the long poem "La Prière devant le Soleil" (Prayer before the Sun):

> J'ai tenu contre moi si serré le flambeau,
> Que le feu merveilleux ayant pris à mon âme,
> J'ai vécu, exaltée et mourante de flammes. . . .
>
> (I have held the torch so close to me,
> That the marvelous fire taking hold in my soul,
> I have lived exalted and dying in flames . . .).

In "Adoration," dedicated to the beauty of nature, the poet joins Zarathustra on his mountain peak, and the two transcend through laughter the anguish of mortality:

> O vous louer avec l'or liquide et le sang
>   Du soleil sur la cime,
> Et le rire enflammé d'une âme qui descend
>   Dans le Hadès sublime . . .
>
> (O to praise you with the liquid gold and the blood
>   Of the sun on the peak,
> And the flaming laughter of a soul that descends
>   Into sublime Hades . . .).

Noailles was gifted with acute perceptions, which she often translates into dynamic and synesthetic images in her poetry. The poet strives to encounter the natural world through every sense rather than through vision alone, and she gladly yields to an intoxicated loss of control. In "Bondissment" (Leaping) she makes no distinction between abstract beauty and concrete sensation: "Ainsi je puis goûter, respirer, toucher, mordre / La beauté du matin, la gomme des bourgeons" (Thus I can taste, breathe, touch, bite into / The morning beauty, the gum of buds). In Noailles's conception the spirit is inseparable from the body. A playful, irreverent poem, "Le Faune" (The Faun) demonstrates that spirituality is only a sublimation of the desiring body, and several poems eroticize the sky as though to contest its traditional identification with the spirit. In three short, uninhibited stanzas, "Azur" (Azure) illustrates a close interconnection between eroticism and aesthetic creation; with images drawn from her beloved "double azure"–the lake and the sky at Amphion–Noailles implies that her poetry is born from sexual pleasure, nature's gift to the body:

> Comme un sublime fruit qu'on a de loin lancé,
> La matinée avec son ineffable extase
> Sur mon cœur enivré tombe, s'abat, s'écrase,
> Et mon plaisir jaillit comme un lac insensé!
>
> (Like a sublime fruit, thrown from afar,
> The morning with its ineffable ecstasy

> On my drunken heart falls, collapses, presses down,
> And my pleasure gushes like a crazed lake!)

No less concerned than before with her literary destiny, in "Offrande" (Offering) the poet bequeaths to future generations "mon cœur faible et doux, qui eut tant de courage / Pour ce qu'il désirait" (my vulnerable and gentle heart, which had so much courage / For that which it desired). The title figure of "La Danseuse persane" (The Persian Dancer) delights in the innocence of her sensuality and discloses a feminine subjectivity far removed from the world of male dominance:

> Que t'importait, ange farouche,
> Ardent, faible et voluptueux,
> Ce que, loin de ta douce bouche,
> Les vieux sages disaient entre eux.
>
> Pendant leur morne promenade,
> Sur les bords du Tigre, en été
> Roulant leurs chapelets de jade,
> Ils maudissaient la volupté.
> . . . .
>
> —Mais toi, danseuse au clair délire,
> Gâteau de miel, de lis et d'or,
> Tu ris et dédaignes de lire
> Leurs manuscrits où l'on s'endort.
> . . . .
>
> Tu danses, grave comme un prêtre,
> Chaude comme les animaux!
> . . . .
>
> Tu dis que c'est l'heure de vivre,
> Que le moment de vivre est court,
> Que ton Dieu veut que l'on s'enivre
> De parfum, de vin et d'amour!
>
> (Of what concern to you, untamed angel,
> Ardent, weak, and voluptuous,
> Were, far from your sweet mouth,
> The words spoken by old pundits.
>
> In the course of their bleak meanderings
> On the banks of the Tigris, in summer,
> Rolling their jade rosaries,
> They cursed voluptuous pleasure.
> . . . .
>
> —But you, clear frenzied dancer,
> Honeycomb wrapped with lilies and gold,
> You laugh and disdain to read
> Manuscripts that put us to sleep.
> . . . .
>
> You dance, grave as a priest,
> Hot as an animal!
> . . . .

You say that now is the time to live,
That the hour of life is all too brief,
That your God wants us to revel
In fragrance, wine, and love!)

Just as significant in this poem as the Dionysian value of the dance, which appears repeatedly in Noailles's poetry, is the suggestion of the resurgence of a feminine power that male-dominated culture has repressed and that the poet, as the interpreter of the dancer's words, now reclaims. By opposing the dancer's mouth to the words of the sages, Noailles implies that an independent language of female desire and pleasure has always existed, one that was not recorded in writing but was experienced in the body. The body and the spirit are inseparable, for the dancer is simultaneously a wild "animal," an "untamed angel," and a "priest." In Noailles's imagination she seems to play the role of a goddess, corresponding to Zarathustra's declaration in Nietzsche's *Also sprach Zarathustra: Ein Buch für Alle und Keinen* (1883–1885; translated as *Thus Spake Zarathustra: A Book for All and None*, 1896), which she copied in a 1907 notebook: "Je ne pourrai[s] croire qu'à un dieu qui danserait" (I would believe only in a god who could dance). With a touch of irony, the poem shows the old sages serenely unaware of the mighty river roaring at their side: "Tigre" is French not only for "Tigris" but also for "tiger," a figure epitomizing for Nietzsche vital energy and the fearful aspects of existence.

While Noailles's poetry sustained liberating values for many readers, among them the poets Lucie Delarue-Mardrus and Gérard d'Houville (pseudonym of Marie de Régnier), it was offensive to others. Some critics overlooked revisionary poems such as "Le Vallon de Lamartine" (Lamartine's Vale) and regarded her poetry as a throwback to outdated themes and techniques of French Romanticism. Others saw an expression of confused emotions and unrestrained egocentrism cast in unruly language. Because she emphasized the value of the body, many critics tended to recognize little more in her work than the received view of woman as representing the instincts and the senses, whereas man represents the intellect. In his influential 1909 study of women's literature Jules Bertaut judged Noailles's poetry as a "monstrous" intensification of sensations paradoxically directed toward the most paltry of natural settings, such as gardens. The garden is a recurring site in Noailles's work: in "La Consolation de l'été" (Summer Solace), from *Les Eblouissements,* she says that "Un jardin est secret, profond, inépuisable" (A garden is secret, profond, inexhaustible). Misunderstanding the import of the symbol, some critics derided this original aspect of Noailles's poetry; in their eyes she was "la muse potagère" (the muse of the vegetable patch). As late as 1923 the Spanish

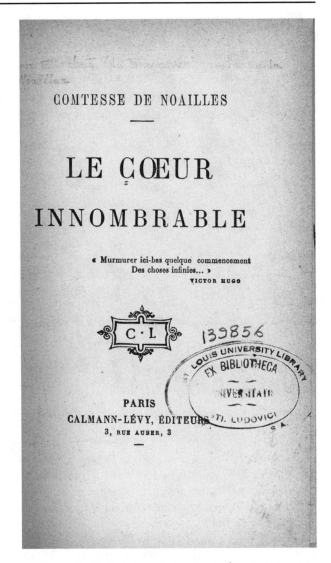

COMTESSE DE NOAILLES
—

LE CŒUR
INNOMBRABLE

« Murmurer ici-bas quelque commencement
Des choses infinies... »
VICTOR HUGO

PARIS
CALMANN-LÉVY, ÉDITEURS
3, RUE AUBER, 3
—

Title page for Noailles's first collection of poetry (Pius XII Memorial Library, Saint Louis University Library)

philosopher José Ortega y Gasset reduced her to a "plant-like genius, divinely blind like a camellia."

Others, on the contrary, perceived a philosophical idealism in Noailles's poetry. For Proust it demonstrated that "l'univers se représente au sein de la pensée" (the universe is represented in thought). According to Jules de Gaultier, Noailles gave artistic form to the metaphysics of a generation impressed by nineteenth-century German philosophy; and because she recognized that there is no object without a subject, she intentionally projected her own thoughts, emotions, perceptions, and sensations onto the natural world to stimulate the reader's imagination.

Following a series of dramatic episodes related to her friendship with Barrès, Noailles and her husband separated in the fall of 1908. Noailles's next collection,

Noailles and her son, Anne-Jules, 1913

Les Vivants et les Morts, marks a decisive turn from the love of nature toward human love, a turn justified in the poem "La Prière" (Prayer): "aucun cœur ne bat derrière le soleil" (no heart beats behind the sun). The volume recapitulates Noailles's friendship with Barrès, who had been estranged from her since 1909 because he held her responsible for the suicide of his nephew Charles Demange, apparently done out of unrequited love for Noailles. It also celebrates a more harmonious platonic relationship with the poet and philosopher Henri Franck, who had died of tuberculosis in 1912 at twenty-three. Both men account for some of Noailles's most poignant verses on separation and loss, such as the Proustian emphasis in the opening poem, "Tu vis, je bois l'azur . . ." (You live, I drink the azur . . .), on the irrevocable movement of time: "Quelque chose de toi sans cesse m'abandonne, / Car rien qu'en vivant tu t'en vas" (Something of you constantly abandons me, / For merely in living you depart). Rainer Maria Rilke, an early admirer of Noailles's work, translated this poem into German and later echoed it in his *Duineser Elegien* (1923; translated as *Duineser Elegien: Elegies from the Castle of Duino,* 1931; translated as *Duino Elegies,* 1939). New images appear from a series of travels and prolonged stays in Italy, Sicily, Germany, Switzerland, and the German-occupied province of Alsace, all of which she visited in a mood of loss and

errancy: "Solitaire, nomade et toujours étonnée, / Je n'ai pas d'avenir et je n'ai pas de toit" (Solitary, nomadic, and forever amazed, / I have no future and I have no roof).

Noailles's quarrel with religious dogma culminates in poems grouped under the heading "Les Elévations" (Elevations). As in Franck's Judaic poetry, the Judeo-Christian God often functions as the lyric addressee of these meditative pieces, which led some readers to assume that Noailles had renounced paganism for Christianity. But she had corrected this misinterpretation in an interview with Alain-Fournier (pseudonym of Henri Alban Fournier) in 1911, when the poems appeared in periodicals: "je ne suis pas chrétienne. Ou plutôt, je suis désespérée, chrétienne, comme j'étais désespérée, païenne" (I am not Christian. Or rather, I am a despairing Christian just as I was a despairing pagan). The collection includes the only poem indicating Noailles's preoccupation with madness, "L'Ile des folles à Venise" (The Insane Women's Island in Venice), in which the speaker identifies with incarcerated madwomen and translates their silence or their nonsense words into poetry, thereby endowing them with dignity. Despite an overabundance of long poems in alexandrine verse, *Les Vivants et les Morts* was hailed by many as a masterpiece; in a review in the *Times* (London) of 16 July 1913, Mary Duclaux declared Noailles "the greatest poet that the twentieth century has produced in France–perhaps in Europe."

Plagued by poor health, after 1911 Noailles often remained in her bedroom, where she wrote and received guests. Present-day visitors to the Musée Carnavalet in Paris can see, facing the display of Proust's bedroom, a reconstitution of the modest room in which Noailles's friendship with such figures as Jean Cocteau and Colette developed; "L'amitié est mon second métier" (Friendship is my second career), she once declared.

During World War I Noailles devoted what energy she had to hospital work, while the poems she composed were mostly patriotic and supportive of the troops. But a poet who had so energetically opposed life to death could not fail to be ambivalent about the war, as in the last line of "Verdun," written after a visit in October 1916 to the most destructive battlefields of the war and collected in *Les Forces éternelles* (The Eternal Powers, 1920): "Contemple, adore, prie, et tais ce que tu sens" (Contemplate, adore, pray, and silence what you feel). In her biography of Noailles, Elisabeth Higonnet-Dugua reproduces letters from soldiers expressing appreciation not only for her hospital work but also for her poetry, which enabled them to rise, if only for brief moments, above the horrors of the war.

In 1917 Barrès and Noailles secretly resumed their relationship, this time as lovers. Barrès resurfaces as an

General Charles Marie Emmanuel Mangin and Noailles near Soissons on the western front, June 1918

interlocutor in the poems in the final section of *Les Forces éternelles*. Although her love poetry had become more audacious, Noailles's major innovation in this volume consists in titling a section "Poèmes de l'esprit" (Poems of the Spirit). Several of the poems in this section commemorate the origins of her vocation through her matrilineal connection with Greece, the birthplace of Western thought. Other poems attempt to provide formerly silent feminine figures with a voice and presence, while yet others claim to speak on behalf of women. Thus, her poetry now aims to integrate the feminine sensual realm with the masculine intellectual realm.

In *Le Temps retrouvé* (1927; translated as *The Past Recaptured*, 1932) Proust remarks that writers often move toward a greater use of the intellect as their work matures. This progression can be seen in Noailles's career. The short stories she wrote after 1920, collected in *Les Innocentes; ou, La Sagesse des femmes* (The Innocents; or, The Wisdom of Women, 1923), critique romantic love through

lucid analyses of the amoralism of passion. More tellingly, a sequence of short poems published as *Poème de l'amour* (Poem of Love, 1924) reveal an evolution in both inspiration and poetic practice: breaking away from the cult of nature and its accompanying Dionysian frenzy, the poems are laconic and often end with epigrammatic twists that exemplify a new, demystified self. Apart from readers such as Bergson, who told Noailles in a 9 September 1924 letter that he perceived in the new collection a whole "metaphysics of sensation," and François Mauriac, who declared in the *Nouvelle Revue française* (1 October 1924) that the "incomparable dimension in this poet is not her sensibility . . . but her intelligence," this shift bewildered Noailles's public. But it signaled a decisive turn: in the last months of 1923 Noailles's mother and two of her most intimate friends, including Barrès, had died. From then on she composed more than a hundred poems concentrating exclusively on death, most of which were collected in *L'Honneur de souffrir* (The Honor of Suffering, 1927).

Albert Einstein, Noailles, physicist Jean-Baptiste Perrin, and mathematician Paul Painlevé, 1929

Adopting Antigone as her model and gazing on the graves of those who have preceded her, the poet, described in poem "XII" as "Habitante éthérée et fixe des tombeaux, / Dont l'âme a soulevé les portes funéraires" (Ethereal and steadfast inhabitant of the graves / Whose soul has lifted the funereal gates), strives to identify with the dead and rejects her own life:

> –Je ne commettrai pas envers votre bonté,
> Envers votre grandeur, secrète mais charnelle,
> O corps désagrégés, ô confuses prunelles,
> La trahison de croire à votre éternité.
> Je refuse l'espoir, l'altitude, les ailes,
> Mais étrangère au monde et souhaitant le froid
> De vos affreux tombeaux, trop bas et trop étroits,
> J'affirme, en recherchant vos nuits vastes et vaines,
> Qu'il n'est rien qui survive à la chaleur des veines!

> (–I will not commit, against your goodness,
> Against your secret, but carnal, greatness,
> O disintegrated bodies, o dissolved eyes,
> The treason of believing in your eternity.
> I refuse hope, loftiness, wings,
> But a stranger to the world and wishing for the cold
> Of your horrible, too low and too narrow tombs,
> I affirm, while probing your vast, empty nights,
> That nothing survives the warmth of the veins!)

This thoroughly materialistic poetic testament sets itself apart from the elegiac tradition by affirming the reality of death in images of the body's decomposition. The repudiation of immortality for the poet's loved ones corresponds to a repudiation of her own immortality, or literary survival. In choosing an epigraph from Sophocles' *Antigone* for the volume, Noailles appears to have foreseen her literary destiny: "J'aurai plus longtemps à plaire à ceux qui sont sous terre qu'à ceux qui sont ici" (The time in which I must please those that are dead is longer than I must please those of this world). At the very moment she disavowed the power of her art, however, Noailles created some of her most powerful poems; and at a time when her prestige was waning, many readers considered this collection her greatest literary achievement. Quoting Jean Rostand in the final sentence of her preface to a collection of poetic prose, *Exactitudes* (1930), she gave the most convincing account of her significance for literature: "Seul importe dans l'œuvre le peu qu'on est seul à pouvoir écrire" (All that matters in your work is the little that only you could write). After years of painful migraines for which no cause was found, Anna de Noailles died in her Paris home on 30 April 1933, surrounded by her husband (who had reconciled with her), their son, and their daughter-in-law.

Letters:

Colette, *Lettres à ses pairs,* edited by Claude Pichois and Roberte Forbin (Paris: Flammarion, 1973), pp. 58–103;

Marcel Proust, *Correspondance,* volumes 2–12, 19–20, edited by Philip Kolb (Paris: Plon, 1976–1992);

Correspondance André Gide–Anna de Noailles (1902–1928), edited by Claude Mignot-Ogliastri (Lyon: Centre d'Etudes Gidiennes, 1986);

Jean Cocteau et Anna de Noailles: Correspondance 1911–1931, edited by Mignot-Ogliastri, *Cahiers Jean Cocteau,* 11 (Paris: Gallimard, 1989);

Anna de Noailles–Maurice Barrès: Correspondance 1901–1923, edited by Mignot-Ogliastri (Paris: L'Inventaire, 1994).

Interviews:

Paul Acker, *L'Echo de Paris* (1 April 1903);

André Arnyvelde, "Une heure chez Mme de Noailles," *Les Annales politiques et littéraires* (13 April 1913): 310–311;

Frédéric Lefevre, "Une heure avec la comtesse de Noailles," *Les Nouvelles littéraires,* 205 (18 September 1926): 1–3;

Claude-André Puget, "Chez la Comtesse de Noailles: à propos des Souvenirs qu'elle écrit pour 'Les

Annales,'" *Les Annales politiques et littéraires* (January 1931): 173–174.

Bibliography:

Claude Mignot-Ogliastri, *Anna de Noailles: Une amie de la Princesse Edmond de Polignac* (Paris: Méridiens-Klincksieck, 1986), pp. 429–436.

Biographies:

Lucien Corpechot, "La Comtesse de Noailles," in his *Souvenirs d'un journaliste,* volume 3 (Paris, Plon, 1936), pp. 105–186;

Charles Fournet, *La Comtesse de Noailles* (Geneva: Roulet, 1950);

Claude Mignot-Ogliastri, *Anna de Noailles: Une Amie de la Princesse Edmond de Polignac* (Paris: Méridiens-Klincksieck, 1986);

François Broche, *Anna de Noailles: Un mystère en pleine lumière* (Paris: Robert Laffont, 1989);

Elisabeth Higonnet-Dugua, *Anna de Noailles: Cœur innombrable: biographie, correspondence* (Paris: Editions Michel de Maule, 1989);

Arthur Conte, "Anna de Noailles, la poétesse," in his *Grandes Francaises du XX siècle* (Paris, Plon, 1995), pp. 71–82;

Patricia Ferlin, "Anna de Noailles," in her *Femmes d'encrier* (Etrépilly: Christian de Bartillat, 1995), pp. 5–45.

References:

Romeo Arbour, *Henri Bergson et les lettres françaises* (Paris: José Corti, 1955), pp. 261–266;

Angela Bargenda, *La Poésie d'Anna de Noailles* (Paris: L'Harmattan, 1995);

Maurice Barrès, "Un grand poète: La Comtesse Mathieu de Noailles," *Le Figaro,* 9 July 1904: 1;

Jules Bertaut, *La Littérature féminine d'aujourd'hui* (Paris: Librairie des Annales politiques et littéraires, 1909);

Geneviève Bianquis, *Nietzsche en France: L'Influence de Nietzsche sur la pensée française* (Paris: Félix Alcan, 1929), pp. 56–57, 70–78;

Léon Blum, "Madame de Noailles: *La Nouvelle Espérance,*" in *L'Œuvre de Léon Blum,* volume 1 (Paris: Albin-Michel, 1954), pp. 94–102;

Blum, "L'Œuvre poétique de Madame de Noailles," in *L'Œuvre de Léon Blum,* volume 2 (Paris: Albin-Michel, 1962), pp. 407–424;

Marthe Borely, *L'Emouvante Destinée d'Anna de Noailles* (Paris: Editions Albert, 1939);

Henri Clouard, "La Poésie de Madame de Noailles," *Revue Critique des Idées et des Livres,* 22 (10 August 1913): 257–271;

Jean Cocteau, *La Comtesse de Noailles Oui et Non* (Paris: Librairie Académique Perrin, 1963);

Colette, *Discours à l'Académie royale de langue et de littérature françaises de Belgique* (Paris: Grasset, 1936);

Rubén Darío, "Una musa: La condesa de Noailles," in *Escritos dispersos de Rubén Darío (recogidos de periódicos de Buenos Aires),* volume 1 (La Plata: Universidad Nacional de la Plata, 1968), pp. 353–358;

Darío, "A Propósito de Mme. de Noailles," in his *Opiniones* (Madrid: Fernando Fé, 1906), pp. 89–98;

Michel Décaudin, *La Crise des valeurs symbolistes: 20 ans de poésie française. 1895–1914* (Toulouse: Privat, 1960), pp. 155–165;

Charles Dédéyan, *L'Image de la France dans l'œuvre de Rilke* (Paris: Société d'Edition d'Enseignement Supérieur, 1962), pp. 289–314;

Charles Du Bos, *La Comtesse de Noailles et le climat du génie* (Paris: Table Ronde, 1949);

Mary Duclaux, "The Countess of Noailles: 'le grand poète,'" *The Times Literary Supplement,* 10 July 1913; republished in her *Twentieth Century French Writers (Reviews and Reminiscences)* (New York: Scribners, 1920), pp. 178–192;

Tama Lea Engelking, "Anna de Noailles Oui et Non: the Countess, the Critics and *la poésie féminine,*" *Women's Studies,* 23 (1994): 95–110;

Léon-Paul Fargue, "Presence d'Anna de Noailles," in his *Portraits de famille* (Paris: J. B. Janin, 1947), pp. 7–17;

A. Favre-Gilly, "Mysticisme païen: Comtesse Mathieu de Noailles," *Annales de philosophie chrétienne,* 14 (August–September 1912): 475–495, 587–611;

Ida-Marie Frandon, *L'Orient de Maurice Barrès* (Genève: Droz / Lille: Giard, 1952), pp. 95–123;

Rosa Galli-Pellegrini, "Le Courage de le dire: les rêveries végétales dans la poésie d'Anna de Noailles," *Travaux de Littérature,* 9 (1996): 217–228;

Jules de Gaultier, *La Vie mystique de la nature* (Paris: Grès, 1924), pp. 214–221;

Jean de Gourmont, *Muses d'aujourd'hui: Essai de physiologie poétique* (Paris: Mercure de France, 1910);

Gourmont, "Les Nietzschéennes," *Mercure de France* (July 1903): 101–111;

Fernand Gregh, *La Comtesse de Noailles* (Abbeville: F. Paillart, 1933);

Francis Jammes, "L'Evolution spirituelle de Mme la comtesse de Noailles," in his *Œuvres,* volume 5 (Paris: Mercure de France, 1926), pp. 203–227;

Robert Jardillier, "La Musique dans l'œuvre de la comtesse de Noailles," *Revue musicale,* 112 (February 1931): 97–124;

Walter Lacher, *L'Amour et le divin: Marceline Desbordes-Valmore, Anna de Noailles, David-Herbert Lawrence, Charles Morgan* (Geneva: Perret-Gentil, 1962);

Gustave Lanson, "Les Vivants et les Morts," *Le Matin* (9 July 1913);

Jean Larnac, *Comtesse de Noailles: Sa vie, son œuvre* (Paris: Sagittaire, 1931);

Edmée de La Rochefoucauld, *Anna de Noailles* (Paris: Editions Universitaires, 1956);

Pierre Lasserre, "Madame de Noailles," in his *Portraits et Discussions* (Paris: Mercure de France, 1914), pp. 266–278;

Yves-Gérard Le Dantec, "La Place d'Anna de Noailles dans la poésie contemporaine," *Mercure de France,* 244 (1933): 276–298;

Georges-Armand Masson, *La Comtesse de Noailles, son œuvre: Portrait et autographe* (Paris: Editions du Carnet-Critique, 1922);

François Mauriac, "*Poème de l'amour,* par la comtesse de Noailles," *Nouvelle Revue française,* 133 (1 October 1924): 486–489;

Charles Maurras, "Le Romantisme féminin: allégorie du sentiment désordonné," in his *L'Avenir de l'intelligence* (Paris: Flammarion, 1927), pp. 145–234;

Louis de Mondadon, "Les Inexactitudes de Mme la comtesse de Noailles," *Les Etudes: Revue catholique d'intérêt général,* 205 (20 December 1930): 706–713;

Les Nouvelles littéraires, 551, special Noailles issue (6 May 1933);

George Norman, "Comtesse de Noailles," *Blackfriars,* 14 (October 1933): 846–853;

Mari H. O'Brien, "Muse de l'angoisse: Anna de Noailles as Modernist Romantic," *Utah Foreign Language Review,* 1997 (1997): 129–143;

Victoria Ocampo, "Anna de Noailles y su poesía," in her *Testimonios,* volume 1 (Madrid: Revista de Occidente, 1935), pp. 295–333;

José Ortega y Gasset, "La Poesía de Ana de Noailles," *Revista de Occidente,* 1 (July 1923)–collected in his *Obras completas,* volume 3 (Madrid: Revista de Occidente, 1963), pp. 429–435;

Ortega y Gasset, "El Rostro maravillado," in his *Obras completas,* volume 1 (Madrid: Revista de Occidente, 1963), pp. 33–36;

Louis Perche, *Anna de Noailles* (Paris: Seghers, 1964);

Catherine Perry, "Celles par qui le scandale arrive: Ethique de l'innocence chez Gérard d'Houville et Anna de Noailles," *El Imparcial* (25 July 1904)–collected in *Le Mal dans l'imaginaire littéraire français (1850–1950),* edited by Metka Zupančič and

Myriam Watthee-Delmotte (Paris: L'Harmattan / Ottawa: Editions David, 1998), pp. 275–289;

Perry, "In the Wake of Decadence: Anna de Noailles' Revaluation of Nature and the Feminine," *L'Esprit Créateur,* 37 (Winter 1997): 94–105;

Perry, *Persephone Unbound: Dionysian Aesthetics in the Works of Anna de Noailles* (Lewisburg, Pa.: Bucknell University Press, 2002);

Perry, "Retour au mythe païen dans l'œuvre d'Anna de Noailles," *Religiologiques,* 15 (Spring 1997): 75–89;

Marcel Proust, "Les *Eblouissements* par la comtesse de Noailles," in his *Essais et Articles,* edited by Pierre Clarac and Yves Sandre (Paris: Gallimard, 1971), pp. 229–241;

Proust, "La Vicomtesse Gaspard de Réveillon," in his *Jean Santeuil,* volume 2 (Paris: Gallimard, 1952), pp. 304–313;

Rainer Maria Rilke, *Les Amantes,* edited and translated by Maurice Betz (Paris: Emile-Paul, 1944), pp. 77–84;

Rilke, *Gesammelte Werke,* volume 6 (Leipzig: Insel, 1927), pp. 340–344;

Christopher Robinson, "The Comparison of Greek and French Women Poets: Myrtiotissa, Maria Polydoure, Anna de Noailles," *Journal of Modern Greek Studies,* 2 (May 1984): 23–38;

Nicolas Ségur, "Madame de Noailles," in his *Le Génie européen* (Paris: Fasquelle, 1926), pp. 145–176;

Anthony Stephens, "Das Gedichtbuch der Anna de Noailles: Ein Dokument aus Rilkes mittlerer Periode," in *Rilke Heute: Beziehungen und Wirkungen,* edited by Ingeborg H. Solbrig und Joachim W. Storck (Frankfurt am Main: Suhrkamp, 1975), pp. 155–182;

André Thérive, "L'Enseignement de Madame de Noailles," *Revue Critique des Idées et des Livres,* 31 (10 February 1921): 257–269;

Jean-Louis Vaudoyer, "*Les Forces éternelles* de la comtesse de Noailles," *La Revue hebdomadaire* (December 1920): 444–460.

Papers:

Most manuscripts of Anna de Noailles's childhood writings are at the Bibliothèque de l'Arsenal in Paris. Most manuscripts of her mature works, as well as her notebooks, her correspondence with Edmond Rostand, and her letters to Augustine Bulteau, are at the Bibliothèque Nationale in Paris. Other manuscripts and letters are in the archives of Princess Eugénie Bassaraba de Brancovan. The remainder of her voluminous correspondence is at the Bibliothèque de l'Institut de France in Paris.

Marie Noël
(Marie-Mélanie Rouget)
(16 February 1883 – 23 December 1967)

Paul Matthieu St-Pierre
Simon Fraser University

BOOKS: *Poésies et chansons de guerre* (Poitiers: Bousrez, 1918);

Les Chansons et les heures (Paris: Sansot, 1921);

La Muse dans les ruines (Monte Carlo: Estival, 1921);

Les Chants de la merci (Paris: Crès, 1930);

Le Rosaire des joies (Paris: Crès, 1930; revised and enlarged edition, Paris: Stock, 1937; revised and enlarged, 1948; revised and enlarged again, 1950);

Poèmes choisis (Paris: Magné, 1939);

Contes (Paris: Stock, 1944; revised and enlarged, 1949);

Chants sauvages pour chant et piano (Paris: Philippo, 1946);

Chants et psaumes d'automne (Paris: Stock, 1947);

Le Voyage de Noël et autres contes (Paris: Stock, 1949);

Petit-jour: Souvenirs d'enfance (Paris: Stock, 1951);

L'Ame en peine (Paris: Stock, 1954);

Le Jugement de Don Juan: Miracle (Paris: Stock, 1955);

Notes intimes: Suivies de souvenirs sur l'abbé Bremond (Paris: Stock, 1959); excerpts translated by Howard Sutton as *Notes for Myself,* foreword by François Mauriac (Ithaca, N.Y.: Cornell University Press, 1968);

La Rose rouge, L'Ame en peine, et autres contes (Paris: Stock, 1960);

Chants d'arrière-saison (Paris: Stock, 1961);

Petits-jour et souvenirs du beau mai (Paris: Stock, 1962);

Marie Noël: Choix de textes, bibliographie, portraits, facsimilés, edited by André Blanchet Poetes d'aujourd'hui, no. 89 (Paris: Seghers, 1962; revised, 1970);

Le Cru d'Auxerre (Paris: Stock, 1967);

Chants des quatre-temps (Paris: Stock, 1972);

Œuvres en prose, edited by Elise Autissier (Paris: Stock, 1977);

Auxerre et Marie Noël (Auxerre: Société des sciences historiques et naturelles, 1992).

Collections: *L'Œuvre poétique* (Paris: Stock, 1956; corrected, 1971; corrected again, 1975);

Les Chansons et les heures; Le Rosaire des joies (Paris: Gallimard, 1983).

Marie Noël

Edition in English: *Reflected Light: Poems of Marie Noël,* translated by Sara Elizabeth Woodruff (New York: Pageant, 1964).

PLAY PRODUCTION: *Le Jugement de Don Juan, miracle,* Paris, Eglise Saint-Germain-des-Près, May 1976.

Self-cloistered in her home in Auxerre in the Burgundy region, Marie Noël wrote poems, songs, short stories, and a journal that documented the struggles of a devout Catholic with questions of dogma and belief. Though she was neither a nun nor an academic, Noël proved herself a capable theologian who could hold her own in discussions with her spiritual adviser, the Abbé Arthur Mugnier, the Parisian priest who was an associate of such writers as Marcel Proust and Joris Karl Huysmans. Her poems have been set to music by Paul Berthier (1948), Roger Boutry (1963), and Marcel Landowski (1982).

Marie-Mélanie Rouget was born on 16 February 1883 in Auxerre, the first of four children and the only daughter of Louis and Emilie Barat Rouget. Her father taught philosophy at the boys' lycée and art history at the girls' lycée in Auxerre. The family moved into her grandfather's home when she was two years old; they remained there until 1894, when they purchased an eighteenth-century manor house in the Rue des Milliaux, near the Cathedral of Saint-Etienne. Marie Rouget lived there until her death seventy-three years later.

Because of her delicate constitution, Rouget attended school irregularly. She was mostly educated at home by her parents and through her own reading of the Bible; *Imitatio Christi* (*The Imitation of Christ,* written between 1390 and 1440), attributed to Thomas à Kempis; the medieval chansons de geste; the folktales of Jean de la Fontaine and Hans Christian Andersen; and the novels of Charles Dickens. In 1901, she recalls in her journal, *Notes intimes: Suivies de souvenirs sur l'abbé Bremond* (Intimate Notes: Followed by Recollections of the Abbé Bremond, 1959; excerpts translated as *Notes for Myself,* 1968): "A dix-huit ans, j'ai vendu mon esprit à Dieu come d'autres vendent leur âme au Diable. En ce temps-là j'étais gauche, laide, chétive, honteuse comme 'le vilain petit canard,' mais j'avais de l'esprit . . . un esprit clair, gai, vif, aigu qui piquait, mordait sans miséricorde" (At eighteen, I sold my spirit to God as others sell their soul to the Devil. Then I was clumsy, plain, sickly, as shy as "the ugly duckling," but I had spirit . . . a clear, cheerful, lively, keen spirit that would sting and bite without mercy). She composed her first collection of poems, "Les Chansons de Cendrillon" (Songs of Cinderella), between 1903 and 1905; some of them commemorate her brother Eugène, whom she discovered dead in his bed on 27 December 1904. She suppressed publication of these poems throughout her life, recognizing the work as juvenilia, and they remain unpublished.

In 1918 Rouget made the acquaintance of Mugnier when he paid a pastoral visit to Auxerre, and he encouraged her to write. She adopted the pseudonym Marie Noël, in commemoration of the birth of Jesus, for her first publications, which were responses to the destruction of World War I: *Poésies et chansons de guerre* (Poems and Songs of War, 1918) and *La Muse dans les ruines* (The Muse in the Ruins, 1921). In 1920, prompted by Mugnier, Noël started keeping the journal that became *Notes intimes*.

Noël's first important volume of verse, *Les Chansons et les heures* (Songs and Hours, 1921), is divided into "songs" of young women and the "hours" of the Divine Office that are chanted by priests and members of religious orders. The songs are mainly in the voices of ordinary peasant girls and women, who had seldom been heard previously in French verse. In "Ronde" (Roundelay) the speaker breaks the silence of generations of women "bound" by the patriarchy:

> Mon père me veut marier,
> Sauvons-nous, sauvons-nous par les bois et la plaine,
> Mon père me veut marier,
> Petit oiseau, tout vif te lairas-tu lier?
>
> (My father wants to marry me off,
> Fly, fly through the woods and over the plain,
> My father wants to marry me off,
> Little bird, so alive, will you let yourself be bound?)
> (translation by Paul Matthieu St-Pierre)

Another song, "Berceuse de la Grand'Mère" (Grandmother's Lullaby) begins with the traditional bidding of the child to go to sleep: "Dors maintenant, dors" (Sleep now, sleep), "Dors, ne crains rien, dors" (Sleep, don't be afraid, sleep), "Dors, n'attends rien, dors" (Sleep, wait for nothing, sleep). But by the end, the poem has become antithetical to the mood of a lullaby as the grandmother tells the child, "Dors, laisse en aller l'amour qui t'abandonne" (Sleep, let go the love that deserted you) and, in the final line, "On n'a pas besoin de bonheur pour être heureux" (One doesn't need happiness to be happy). The reader is prompted to wonder why the grandmother would offer such worldly admonitions to a child who, even if old enough to understand them, must be asleep. Why is the child unloved? Has its mother abandoned it? What has the grandmother experienced to make her so cynical about happiness?

The poems tracing the hours of the Divine Office–Matins, Lauds, Prime, Terce, Sext, None, Vespers, and Compline–are pseudo-psalms that, in their insistent assonance and respiratory cadences, demand to be chanted. "A Tierce" (Terce), traditionally sung at nine o'clock in the morning, opens with the stanza:

> Mon Maître, enseignez-moi dans notre solitude
> Ce qu'il faut que je fasse, où je dois me plier . . .
> Je ne sais rien. Daignez me mener à l'étude,
> Donnez une leçon à ce pauvre écolier.

(My Master, teach me in our solitude
What I must do, where I must bend my will to yours . . .
I know nothing. Deign to lead me to study,
Teach this poor scholar a lesson).
(translation by St-Pierre)

Among the admirers of *Les Chansons et les heures* were such literary figures as Edouard Estaunié, Raymond Escholier, Robert Kemp, André Billy, and the Abbé Henri Bremond, author of the twelve-volume *Histoire littéraire du sentiment religieux en France depuis la fin des guerres de religion jusqu'à nos jours* (Literary History of Religious Thought in France from the End of the Wars of Religion until Today, 1923–1936).

The death of her father in 1923 forced Noël to take on more family responsibilities. It also led her deeper into her private world of journal keeping, spiritual examination, and theological speculation.

Noël continued to pursue orthodox themes with original variations in her next two collections, *Les Chants de la merci* (Songs of Thanks, 1930) and *Le Rosaire des joies* (Rosary of Joys, 1930). One of the poems in *Les Chants de la merci* is "Bataille" (Battle), in which the speaker represents the peace that can rise from a battlefield:

Et me voilà gisant, mais je ne suis past mort . . .
Prends garde à toi, douleur, à peine est-ce une trêve,
Prends garde à toi, douleur, déjà je me relève,
Prends garde à toi, demain je serai le plus fort.

(And here I am lying helpless, but I am not dead . . .
Watch out for yourself, sorrow, hardly is it a truce,
Take care of yourself, sorrow, I'm already getting up,
Look out for yourself, tomorrow I will be the stronger).
(translation by St-Pierre)

Another poem in *Les Chants de la merci*, "Poème du lait" (Poem of Milk), starts out with a woman nursing her child: "Bois, mon petit, à ma poitrine qui coule" (Drink, my little one, at my abundant breast). As the poem unfolds, the speaker identifies the child as Adam:

Adam! Adam! la douceur d'être mangée,
Qui la savait? Qui savait le cher surplice
D'être la gorgée émouvante qui glisse
Et m'entraîne toute en mon petit changée? . . .

(Adam! Adam! the sweetness of being eaten,
Who knew it? Who knew the dear surplice
Of being the moving mouthful that slips
And takes me along completely into my changed little
    boy? . . .).
(translation by St-Pierre)

The speaker nourishes Adam and, through him, all people. In the poem "Adam et Eve" Noël asks why it

Marie-Mélanie Rouget in 1898, twenty years before she adopted the pseudonym Marie Noël

was necessary for God to arrange things so that humans have to prey on animals, and animals on each other, to survive.

"Annonciation" (Annunciation), a poem in *Le Rosaire des joies,* is a simple recitation of the first decade of joyful mysteries on the rosary: "Le ciel a poussée la porte, / La porte a chanté, un Ange est entré" (Heaven pushed the door open, / The door sang, an Angel has come in [translation by St-Pierre]).

After Noël's father's death, the family had to subdivide the house into rental apartments. In 1931 Noël reflected on her situation in her journal:

Je suis de plus en plus victime d'un désordre de choses auquel je ne puis porter remède: ma vielle maman malade tout l'hiver, une domestique anormale, une grande maison d'autrefois–Douze chambres!–Et dans plusiers autres maisons nous avons douze locataires. Je gère le tout. Très mal.

(More and more I am the victim of a disorderly situation which I am powerless to remedy: my elderly mother ill all winter, a neurotic servant, a big old-fashioned house–Twelve bedrooms!–And we have twelve tenants in several other houses. I am the sole

MARIE NOEL

LES CHANSONS
ET LES HEURES

1938

ÉDITIONS STOCK
DELAMAIN ET BOUTELLEAU
6, *rue Casimir Delavigne*
PARIS

Title page for a later edition of Noël's 1921 collection of poetry
(Thomas Byrne Memorial Library, Spring Hill College)

manager. A very poor one).
(translation by St-Pierre)

During the 1930s several of Noël's friends died, including Bremond, Estaunié, and Mugnier. She recorded in her journal the German invasion of France in 1940; the deaths in 1941 of her brother Peter and her mother; life in Auxerre under German occupation: "Vint le jour où les Juifs furent traqués, persécutés. Persécutés? Exterminés! où des Français furent fusillés, déportés . . . pour mourir plus cruellement encore" (The day came when the Jews were hounded, persecuted. Persecuted? Exterminated! when Frenchmen were shot, deported . . . to die still more cruelly [translation by Howard Sutton]); her renewed hope when the United States entered the war in 1942; and the Allied bombardment of Auxerre in 1944.

Noël's first collection of short stories, *Contes* (Tales), appeared in 1944. Some of the stories are anachronistic retellings of Gospel narratives. "Le Noël du riche honteux" (The Christmas of the Uncomplain-

ing Rich) begins, "La veille de Noël, cette année-là, la vielle Mère Rachel se prépara comme tous les ans à conduire ses fils à la Crèche" (On Christmas Eve that year old Mother Rachel got ready, as she did every year, to take her sons to see the Crèche [translation by St-Pierre]). The journey Rachel and her sons take is not to a crèche in a church, however, but to the original Nativity scene in Bethlehem. Similarly, in "Saint Joseph cherchant les Trois Rois" (Saint Joseph Seeking the Three Kings), which appeared in the enlarged edition of the collection in 1949, the biblical Joseph goes out, as he does every year, to find three people to come to the manger and act out the drama of Epiphany. Unable to find any kings in modern France, he seeks for "une Juste" (a just person), "un Doux" (a gentle person), and "un Pauvre" (a poor person) but finds that he must settle for "une 'imbécile,' une 'archi-folle,' une 'empotée.' . . . Mais l'imbécile est franc comme l'or, la folle est si douce qu'elle a donné pour du fiel sa robe de fête et, des mains de l'empotée, l'encens monte à Dieu toute la journée" (a "fool," a "total madwoman," a "klutz." . . . But the fool is free like gold, the madwoman is so gentle that she gave her party dress in exchange for gall, and the hands of the klutz raise up incense to God all day long). At the end of the story la Vièrge Marie (the Virgin Mary) tells Jesus, "Réveille-toi! Réveille-toi! ô mon Fils, voici les trois Rois!" (Wake up! Wake up! O my Son, the Three Kings are here!), and readers recognize that the last have, indeed, become first. Other stories in *Contes* are in the folktale genre, such as "Les Sabots d'or" (The Golden Clogs), in which "Les animaux étaient toujours aussi jeunes, la vielle toujours aussi vieille, mais la petite Espérance poussa comme une fleur et elle devint jeune fille" (The animals also were always young, the old ones also always old, but little Hope shot up like a flower and she became a young woman), and "Lise changée en lis" (Lise Turned into a Lily), in which "la jeune fille de brouillard" (the maid of the mist) instructs Lise: "Ferme les yeux et change. Change comme l'eau qui devient nuage, comme la terre qui devient herbe, comme le ver dans son cocon qui devient ailes. Serait-ce moi qui'ils appellent Mort? Dors et change" (Close your eyes and change. Change like water that becomes snow, like earth that becomes a plant, like the worm in its cocoon that takes on wings. Would it be I that they call Death? Sleep and change). Both editions of the collection also include the charming "L'Oeuvre du sixième jour" (The Work of the Sixth Day), in which God, having created the dog, believes that he has achieved his masterpiece. The dog, however, begs for a master that he can love and obey; God, against his better judgment, creates humanity on the sixth day, and all of the world's troubles begin. Noël's other stories are collected in *Le Voyage de Noël et autres contes* (The Christmas Journey and Other Tales, 1949), *L'Ame en peine* (The Troubled Soul, 1954), and *La Rose rouge, L'Ame en peine, et autres contes* (The Red Rose, The Soul in Pain, and Other Tales, 1960).

In 1947 appeared *Chants et psaumes d'automne* (Songs and Psalms of Autumn), a collection of darker poems that Noël had written in earlier years but had withheld from publication. One of the finest pieces in this collection is "Jugement," which Noël wrote for and read to Mugnier—the first of her poems she ever read aloud. The speaker defends herself before God but ultimately appeals to his mercy: "Juge-moi! / Mais sauve-moi comme Tu m'aimes." (Judge me! / But save me since You love me [translation by St-Pierre]). Divided into "Appel" (appeal), "Accusation" (accusation), and "Défense" (defense), the poem reveals the dramatic skill that Noël also demonstrated in her play with a similar theme, *Le Jugement de Don Juan, miracle* (The Judgment of Don Juan: Miracle Play), which was published in 1955 and performed at the Eglise Saint-Germain-des-Prés in Paris in May 1976, almost nine years after her death.

Noël kept her journal from 1920 to 1958 and published it as *Notes intimes* in 1959. The book includes her comments on her own writing and her methods of composition. Perhaps only in a journal not originally intended for publication would she express such pleasure in her work:

> Quand j'écris, par moment je tombe sur un vers ou deux dont le charme m'ensorcelle, m'enivre, me berce, m'endort. Je suis tellement emmusiquée qu'il n'y a plus moyen de penser outre, de forcer les mots à venir. Il faut m'arrêter, me distraire, faire un grand effort pour me dégager du chant où je reste prise et ressaisir le sens de mon ouvrage, sans quoi tout se dissoudrait en silence.

> (When I write, I occasionally come upon a verse or two whose charm captivates me, intoxicates me, soothes me, rests me. I am so much under the spell of the music that it is impossible to go on thinking, to force the words to come. I am obliged to stop, to shake myself, to make a great effort to free myself from the magic of the song, and to regain control of the direction of my work, without which everything would melt into silence).
> (translation by Sutton)

She comments on how she had to find the time to write: "Elle, ma poésie, avait besoin d'heures—Je la repoussais— Elle n'aura rien eu que les restes des autres. Sauf au temps de maladie, le meilleur de tous, celui qu'on ne pouvait pas me prendre" (My poetry called for leisure—I pushed it aside—It has had only what others left. Except when I was ill, the best time of all, for no one could take that from me). She is proud that she found time to write every day, although she did not always manage two full hours: "J'ai toujours pu garder un bout de matin, deux

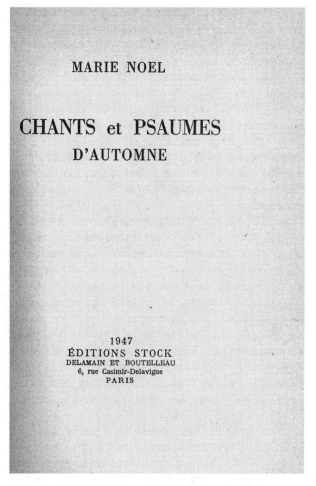

MARIE NOEL

CHANTS et PSAUMES
D'AUTOMNE

1947
ÉDITIONS STOCK
DELAMAIN ET BOUTELLEAU
6, rue Casimir-Delavigne
PARIS

Title page for the collection that includes Noël's "Jugement," the first of her poems Noël read in public (Knight Library, University of Oregon)

heures presque respectée, pour prendre régulièrement ma peine de poète" (I was always able to set aside a portion of the morning, two hours almost respected, to labor at my poetry with regularity). In a comment recorded between 1934 and 1936 she says that "L'artiste créateur doit être à la fois mâle et femelle" (The creative artist must be at once male and female [translation by St-Pierre]). In 1942 she confesses that "Je n'ai jamais rien *réussi*, accompli, sans faute. Ni mon âme, ni ma vie, ni mon oeuvre" (I have never *managed*, never accomplished anything, without failing. Not my soul, nor my life, nor my work [translation by St-Pierre]).

As a spiritual exercise commissioned by Mugnier, *Notes intimes* features orthodox examinations of conscience and recitations of dogma; but it also includes some original and daring ideas of Noël's, such as the meditation titled "La Pauvre Communion" (Poor Communion): "Mon Dieu, je ne Vous aime pas, je ne le désire même pas, je m'ennuie avec Vous. Peut-être même que je ne crois pas en Vous" (My God, I do not love you, I don't even want to, I'm bored with you. Maybe I don't even believe in you [translation by St-Pierre]). But she counters such shocking outbursts with ejaculations of orthodoxy: "Quand je pense trop douloureusement, je m'attache pour nous sauver à la grandeur de Dieu, j'accepte tout" (When my thoughts are too painful, I become devoted to the grandeur of God for our salvation, I accept everything). In the same entry, for November 1929, she reminds herself, "Mais éviter habituellement les gens d'Eglise" (But make a habit of avoiding men and women of the cloth). On the other hand, she notes with approval that "Certains clercs novateurs tendent de plus en plus à s'écarter de la liturgie traditionelle pour ouvrir l'avenir, de plus en plus, à une religion discoureuse qu'ils pensent devoir parler mieux, avec plus de fruit, à l'âme du peuple" (Some innovative clerics deviate more and more from the traditional liturgy to open the future, more and more, to a discursive religion which they think will speak better, with more purpose, to the soul of the people).

Noël's final volume of new poetry was *Chants d'arrière-saison* (Late Autumn Songs, 1961). In "La Morte et ses mains tristes" (Dead Girl with Sorrowful Hands) God tells a young woman who has died because her lover left her for another that he will send an angel to bring the lover to be with her in heaven; the woman begs him not to do it: "Las! et faudra, s'il pleure / Sans elle jour et nuit / Que de nouveau je meure / D'en avoir trop souci." (Alas! if he were to weep day and night without her, I would die again from caring too much for him [translation by St-Pierre]). Marie Noël died on 23 December 1967 and was widely mourned.

Letters:

Marie Noël au Canada français, edited by Olivier Durocher (Québec: Garneau, 1974).

Biography:

Raymond Escholier, *Marie Noël: La Neige qui brûle* (Paris: Stock, 1957); republished as *La Neige qui brûle: Marie Noël* (Paris: Fayard, 1957).

References:

Anne-Claire, ed., *La souffrante, l'aimante, la fervente Marie Noel: Poete authentique. Conference* (Cournon d'Auvergne: Orionis, 1989);

Claudine Bernier, "Originalité de Marie Noël," *Revue Générale,* 132 (February 1997): 51–55;

Paul Berthier, *Trois chansons de Marie Noël, pour chant et piano avec chœurs* (Nice: Delrieu, 1948);

Roger Boutry, *Le Rosaire des joies: Pour récitante, soprano, choeur mixte et orchestre* (Paris: Salabert, 1963);

Yves-Alain Favre, ed., *Actes du Colloque Marie Noël: tenu à la Sorbonne le 8 et le 9 novembre 1985,* special issue of *Cahiers Marie Noël,* no. 17 (May 1986);

Henri Forestier, *Les Traditions populaires des pays de l'Yonne: Bibliographie critique avec des chansons populaires, paroles et musique recueillies par Marie Noël et Paul Berthier* (Dijon: Centre d'Etudes Bourguignonnes, 1940);

René Fourrey, *Oraison funèbre de Marie Noël . . . aux obsèques célébrées en l'église Saint-Pierre d'Auxerre, le 27 décembre 1967* (Auxerre: Imprime Moderne, 1968);

Henri Gaston Gouhier, *Le Combat de Marie Noël* (Paris: Stock, 1971);

Marcel Landowski, *Un enfant appelle–: Concerto pour soprano violincelle seul et orchestre* (Paris: Salabert, 1982);

Benoit Lobet, *"Mon Dieu, je ne nous aime pas": Foi et spiritualité chez Marie Noël* (Paris: Stock, 1994);

Michel Manoll, *Marie Noël* (Paris: Editions Universitaires, 1962);

Manoll, *Sur le chemin de Marie Noël* (Troyes: Librairie Bleue, 1993);

Aurélie de Faucamberge Mortier, *La Conscience embrasée* (Paris: Radot, 1927);

Marie Tharsicius, *L'Experience poètique de Marie Noël d'après* Petit-jour *et* Les Chansons et les heures (Montreal: Fides, 1962).

Charles Péguy

(7 January 1873 – 5 September 1914)

Camille René La Bossière
University of Ottawa

BOOKS: *De la Cité socialiste,* as Pierre Deloire (Paris: Librairie de la Revue Socialiste, 1897);

Jeanne d'Arc, by Péguy (as Pierre Baudouin) and Marcel Baudouin (Paris: Librairie de la Revue Socialiste, 1897);

Marcel, as Pierre Baudouin (Paris: Georges Bellais, 1898);

Notre Jeunesse (Paris: Ollendorff, 1910);

Le Mystère de la charité de Jeanne d'Arc (Paris: Librairie Plon, 1910; Paris: Emile-Paul, 1910; revised and enlarged edition, notes by Albert Béguin, Paris: Club du Meilleur Livre, 1956); original edition translated by Julian Green as *The Mystery of the Charity of Joan of Arc* (New York: Pantheon, 1950; London: Hollis & Carter, 1950);

Le Porche du Mystère de la deuxième vertu (Paris: Emile-Paul, 1911); translated by Dorothy Brown Aspinwall as *The Portico of the Mystery of the Second Virtue* (Metuchen, N.J.: Scarecrow Press, 1970);

Œuvres choisies, 1900–1910 (Paris: Grasset, 1911); republished as *Le Choix de Péguy: Œuvres choisies, 1900–1910* (Paris: Gallimard, 1952);

Le Mystère des Saints Innocents (Paris: Emile-Paul, 1912); translated by Pansy Pakenham as *The Mystery of the Holy Innocents, and Other Poems,* introduction by Alexander Dru (London: Harvill, 1956; New York: Harper, 1956);

Morceaux choisis des œuvres poétiques, 1912–1913 (Paris: Ollendorff, 1914);

Note sur M. Bergson et la philosophie bergsonienne (Paris: Emile-Paul, 1914);

Notre Patrie (Paris: Gallimard, 1915);

Œuvres complètes de Charles Péguy, 1873–1914, 20 volumes (Paris: Gallimard, 1916–1955)—includes volume 3, *Œuvres de prose:* includes *De la Situation Faite à l'Histoire et à la Sociologie dans les Temps Modernes, De la Situation Faite au Parti Intellectuel dans le Monde Moderne,* and *De la Situation Faite au Parti Intellectual dans le Monde Moderne devant les Accidents de la Gloire Temporelle;* volume 7, *Eve* (1925); volume 8, *Clio: Dialogue de l'histoire de l'âme païenne* (1917); volume

Charles Péguy (portrait by Pierre Laurens; from Daniel Halévy, Péguy and Les Cahiers de la Quinzaine, 1946)

9, *Note conjointe sur M. Descartes, précédée de la note sur M. Bergson* (1924); volume 11, *Polémique et dossiers: Textes politiques, I* (1940)—includes *La Préparation du Congrès Socialiste Nationale* and *De la raison;* volume 12, *Polémique et dossiers: Textes politiques, II* (1944)—includes *De la Situation Faite à l'Histoire et à la Sociologie et de la Situation Faite au Parti la Situation Faite à l'Histoire et à la Sociologie et de la Situation Faite au Parti Intellectuel dans le Monde Moderne;* volume 16, *Par ce demi-clair matin* (1952); volume 17, *L'Esprit de système* (1953); volume 18, *Un Poète l'a dit* (1953);

volume 19, *Deuxième élégie XXX* (1955); and volume 20, *La Thèse* (1955);

Morceaux choisis: Poésie (Paris: Gallimard, 1927);

Morceaux choisis: Prose (Paris: Gallimard, 1928);

Alfred de Vigny (Paris: Editions Saint-Michel, 1930);

Pierre, commencement d'une vie bourgeoise (Paris: Desclée de Brouwer, 1931);

L'Argent, suivi de L'Argent (suite) (Paris: Gallimard, 1932);

Prières (Paris: Gallimard, 1933 [i.e., 1934]);

Victor-Marie, comte Hugo (Paris: Gallimard, 1934);

Les Tapisseries (Paris: Gallimard, 1936);

Un Nouveau théologien, M. Laudet (Paris: Gallimard, 1937);

De Jean Coste (Paris: Gallimard, 1937);

Pensées (Paris: Gallimard, 1936 [i.e., 1937]);

Souvenirs (Paris: Gallimard, 1938);

La France (Paris: Gallimard, 1939);

Situations (Paris: Gallimard, 1940);

Œuvres poétiques complètes: Charles Péguy, introduction by François Porché, chronology by Pierre Péguy, and notes by Marcel Péguy, Bibliothèque de la Pléiade, no. 60 (Paris: Gallimard, 1941; revised editions, 1948, 1954, 1957);

Saints de France (Paris: Gallimard, 1941);

Notre Dame (Paris: Gallimard, 1941);

Notre Seigneur (Paris: Gallimard, 1943);

La République . . . Notre royaume de France, edited by Denise Mayer (Paris: Gallimard, 1946);

Cinq prières dan la cathédrale de Chartres (Paris: Gallimard, 1947);

Pascal (Paris: L'Amitié Charles Péguy, 1947);

Péguy et les Cahiers: Textes concernant la gérance des Cahiers de la quinzaine, edited by Mme. Charles Péguy (Paris: Gallimard, 1947);

Lettre à Franklin-Bouillon (Paris: L'Amitié Charles Péguy, 1948);

Sainte Geneviève (Paris: Gallimard, 1951);

Les Enfants (Paris: Gallimard, 1952);

Pages choisies, edited by Jacques Bonnot (Paris: Librairie Hachette, 1952);

Notes politiques et sociales, edited by André Boisserie (Paris: L'Amitié Charles Péguy, 1957);

Charles Péguy: Œuvres en prose, 2 volumes edited by Marcel Péguy, Bibliothèque de la Pléiade, nos. 122 and 140 (Paris: Gallimard, 1957, 1959)—comprises volume 1, *Œuvres en prose, 1898–1908* (1959) and volume 2, *Œuvres en prose, 1909–1914* (1957); revised and enlarged by Robert Burac as *Œuvres en prose complètes: Charles Péguy,* 3 volumes, Bibliothèque de la Pléiade, nos. 122, 140, and 389 (Paris: Gallimard, 1987–1992);

Les Œuvres posthumes de Charles Péguy, edited by Jacques Viard (Paris: L'Amitié Charles Péguy, 1969);

Véronique: Dialogue de l'histoire de l'âme charnelle (Paris: Gallimard, 1972);

La Ballade du cœur: poème inédit, edited by Julie Sabiani (Paris: Klincksieck, 1973);

Péguy tel qu'on l'ignore, edited by Jean Bastaire, Collection Idées, no. 291 (Paris: Gallimard, 1973);

La Chanson du roi Dagobert, edited by Robert Burac (Paris: H. Champion, 1996).

Editions: *Le Mystère de la charité de Jeanne d'Arc* (Paris: Gallimard, 1918);

Le Porche du Mystère de la deuxième vertu (Paris: Gallimard, 1929);

Le Mystère des Saints Innocents (Paris: Gallimard, 1929);

Notre Jeunesse (Paris: Gallimard, 1933);

Jeanne d'Arc (Paris: Gallimard, 1948);

Marcel: Premier dialogue de la cité harmonieuse, accompagné d'une série d'articles publiés en 1897 et 1898 dans la Revue Socialiste (Paris: Gallimard, 1973).

Editions in English: *Basic Verities: Prose and Poetry,* translated by Anne Green and Julian Green (New York: Pantheon, 1943; London: Kegan Paul, 1943);

Men and Saints: Prose and Poetry, translated by Green and Green (New York: Pantheon, 1944; London: Kegan Paul, 1947);

God Speaks: Religious Poetry, translated by Julian Green (New York: Pantheon, 1945);

Temporal and Eternal, translated by Alexander Dru (London: Harvill, 1958; New York: Harper, 1958).

The generously inclusive achievement of poet, dramatist, philosopher, editor, pamphleteer, amateur medievalist, revolutionary socialist, and pious mystic Charles Péguy bespeaks an integrity that understandably remains difficult to identify in conventional political terms. A heretic among Marxists, what Simone Fraisse calls, in the introduction to his *Les Critiques de notre temps et Péguy* (The Critics of Our Time and Péguy, 1973), a "half-rebellious son" of the Roman Catholic Church, and an ardent patriot who kept his distance from nationalism of the kind preached by Maurice Barrès and Charles Maurras, he achieved in his life and writings a coherence and independence of moral action based on faith, hope, and charity, virtues that he understood to be inherently consistent with the secular ideals of liberty, equality, and fraternity. The examples of Joan of Arc and St. Vincent de Paul helped inspire Péguy's own mission in defense of the oppressed, the suffering, the destitute; and, in sympathy with the toilers of the world, he made his own the Benedictine principle that "to work is to pray." The 229 volumes of his *Cahiers de la Quinzaine* (Fortnightly Journal), published from January 1900 to July 1914, the 20 volumes of the *Œuvres complètes de*

Péguy and Charlotte Françoise Baudouin at the time of their marriage in October 1897

Charles Péguy, 1873–1914 (Complete Works of Charles Péguy, 1873–1914; 1916–1955), and the more than eight thousand items in the collection of his correspondence held at the Centre Charles Péguy d'Orléans provide some indication as to just how resolutely he worked to share his thoughts with others. But the writer Péguy is most often remembered for his poetry—*Le Mystère de la charité de Jeanne d'Arc* (1910; translated as *The Mystery of the Charity of Joan of Arc*, 1950) in particular. Auguste Martin and Georges Dalgues quote the mayor of Orléans René Thinat as comparing the "phrases simples et touchantes" (simple and touching phrases) of this work to the language of the Synoptic Gospels, which makes it naturally suitable for popular, communal dissemination. Péguy's Christian sense of *mysterium* (mystery) invites comparison with that of existential philosopher Gabriel Marcel.

Charles Pierre Péguy was born at Orléans 7 January 1873 to Cécile Péguy (née Quéré), a chair-seat mender from a line of impoverished Bourbonnais farm laborers, and to her husband, Désiré

Péguy, a cabinetmaker often unable to work because of poor health. Widowed within a year of her only child's birth, some six months after his baptism at the Church of St. Aignan, Cécile Péguy eked out a living by working sixteen hours a day while her mother, Etienette Quéré, attended to the boy. From the vivid stories he heard from his illiterate grandmother, who had never married, Charles Péguy learned something of "the Devil, Hell, and Damnation," as he puts it in his autobiographical *Pierre, commencement d'une vie bourgeoise* (Pierre, the Beginning of a Middle-Class Life, 1931); from the tireless efforts of his mother, who taught him his letters in what little free time she had, he learned the virtue of perseverance in a task. Although not churchgoers themselves, Madame Quéré and Cécile Péguy also took care to encourage a sense of religious observance in the young boy by regularly sending him to Sunday Mass with a neighboring family.

The lessons in "concentration, seriousness and industry" that Charles Péguy learned at home assured the development of his talents at school. Outstanding achievement at the primary school annexed to the local Ecole Normale (1879–1884) and at the Ecole Municipale Professionnelle d'Orléans (1884–1885) earned him a municipal government scholarship to the Lycée d'Orléans. The assiduity of young Péguy likewise showed itself in his quick mastering of catechism lessons from the curate of St. Aignan. And Péguy continued to work hard during his years at the Lycée d'Orléans (1885–1891), where he soon came to establish himself as the most promising student of the school. He won prizes in all academic subjects, most notably in Latin, philosophy, and French composition, and gained further recognition for his leadership in athletics and army cadet exercises: "bon soldat" (good soldier) Péguy served as founding president of the Société de Jeux et Exercices de Plein Air at the Lycée d'Orléans in 1891. Other memorable events from Péguy's early youth include the making of his First Communion in June 1885 and his sympathetic reading of Victor Hugo's *Les Misérables* (1862), in a copy provided by blacksmith and homespun philosopher Louis Boitier, who lived near Péguy's childhood home. With his *bachelier ès lettres* degree from the Lycée d'Orléans in hand, he garnered yet another scholarship, to the Lycée Lakanal at Sceaux, a boarding school in the suburbs of Paris for aspirants to admission to the Ecole Normale Supérieure.

The promise of impending professional success held out by that scholarship was not realized. Péguy continued to practice due discipline in his year at Lakanal, winning a prize for Latin and continuing to attend Sunday Mass. But, much to Cécile Péguy's disappointment, her son failed in his entrance examinations for the Ecole Normale Supérieure in 1892. Putting that failure behind him, Péguy withdrew from Lakanal to enlist in the 131st Régiment d'Orléans. His decision to do so affected more than just his academic prospects. He returned from his year of military service an apparently changed man, a self-professed "atheist" committed to the spirit of "brotherhood in humanity" that he had come to deem irreconcilable with official Catholic dogma regarding damnation: in *Toujours de la Grippe* (Always the Grippe), a work published in the 5 April 1900 issue of *Cahiers de la Quinzaine* and collected in volume one (1916) of *Œuvres complètes de Charles Péguy, 1873–1914,* Péguy explains the grounds for his conversion in the year after Lakanal, "For Christianity to be able to accept, side by side, a Church Triumphant and a Hell, a vision of beatitude and a house of death . . . there must be in the roots of Christian feeling some monstrous . . . partnership with death and disease" (translated by Margaret Villiers). Now devoted more

to soldiering for practical brotherhood than to maintaining his place in good standing with academic or ecclesiastical authority, Péguy again came up short in his bid to qualify for the Ecole Normale Supérieure in September 1893, two weeks after his discharge from the 131st with the rank of corporal.

Another moving experience of fellowship in action almost immediately followed. A group of his Lakanal schoolmates from well-to-do families gained Péguy yet another chance to prepare for the entrance examinations by using their influence discreetly to advance his name for a scholarship at the prestigious Sainte-Barbe, a residential college located in the heart of Paris that numbered John Calvin and St. Ignatius Loyola among its distinguished alumni. Péguy's year at Sainte-Barbe was in many ways a happy one: it was marked by the beginning of his intimate and enduring friendship with Louis Baillet (who soon entered the Benedictine Order); the first stages in his outlining of a socialist utopia–"the Harmonious City"–in collaboration with Marcel Baudouin; his election (his policy of absenting himself from "prayers" notwithstanding) to the presidency of the student branch of the St. Vincent de Paul Society chaplained by the Abbé Battifol; his completion of a "dissertation française en philosophie" (French thesis in philosophy) titled "Instinct et Intelligence"; and, in July 1894, his admission to the Ecole Normale Supérieure. Péguy's mother was more pleased with her son's official progress than she was with his new-found disposition to give away what little pocket money and winter clothing he had to the poor he sought out, "pour l'amour de l'humanité" (for the love of humanity), on the streets of Paris.

Enrolled as a philosophy major at the Ecole Normale Supérieure in November 1894, Péguy chose to study in company with the *anti-talas* (the word *talas* is derived from "ceux qui vont *à la* messe"–those who attend Mass), whose *mot d'ordre* (watchword) was "Utopia," and began preparing a formal academic thesis on Immanuel Kant and social duty. But the appeal of regular scholarly progress soon waned as he came to concern himself more with writing a life of the mystic-in-action Joan of Arc and with such immediately practical matters as the strike at Carmaux and the case of Captain Alfred Dreyfus. Cognizant though he was of the vagaries and problems that must attend any effort to put the ideal of a perfectly just society into practice, Péguy was able unambiguously to distinguish the principle of "la mystique" (mysticism; action in accordance with a disinterested ethic) from the ostensible practicality of "la politique" (politics; action from mere expediency, in accordance with *raisons d'état* [matters of state]): "A single dishonorable action is sufficient to dishonor a nation," as he rigorously maintains in *Notre Jeunesse* (Our Youth), published as the 17 July 1910 issue of *Cahiers de la Quinzaine* (and reissued, with a cancel title page, as a book by Emile-Paul frères later that year). Convinced of the need for fidelity to the truth of "la mystique," Péguy was granted the yearlong leave of absence from the Ecole Normale Supérieure that he requested in the fall of 1895. He used the time to found a socialist cell in Orléans, advance his work on the life of Joan of Arc, learn the craft of typesetting, and help his mother mend chairs. Again, Cécile Péguy was chagrined by her son's want of worldly prudence and ambition.

A few months after his return to the Ecole Normale Supérieure in November 1896, Péguy requested a second leave of absence. He ostensibly needed the time to prepare for his marriage the following October to Charlotte Françoise Baudouin, his friend Marcel Baudouin's sister. From a strongly socialist family, Charlotte Baudouin had stipulated that their wedding be sanctioned by civil authority only and that any children born of their union not be baptized. The couple had four children: Marcel (born September 1898), Germaine (born September 1901), Pierre (born June 1903), and Charles-Pierre (born February 1915). If Péguy retreated from the prospect of acquiring a teaching certificate that still remained open to him during the year leading up to his marriage with Charlotte in October 1897, he did so to the benefit of his own spiritual and intellectual advancement, by using the leave to read works by Alfred de Vigny, Blaise Pascal, and Henri Bergson, and to bring the manuscript of his first book to virtual completion. Nor did his spotty attendance at university lectures in the last months of 1897 indicate a lapse in attention to matters of essential import: in their introduction to *Basic Verities: Prose and Poetry* (1943), translators Anne and Julian Green record Bergson's recollections of Péguy as his student at the Ecole Normale Supérieure: "he had a marvelous gift for stepping beyond the materiality of beings, going beyond it and penetrating to the soul. Thus it is that he knew my most secret thought, such as I have never expressed it, such as I would have wished to express it." That "capacity for stepping beyond" in sympathetic spiritual discernment found further expression in Péguy's *Jeanne d'Arc* (Joan of Arc), published in December.

The resistance to rationalist materialism–and, therefore, to "l'esprit capitaliste" (the capitalist spirit)–that Péguy found so congenial in the teachings of Bergson is amply reflected in *Jeanne d'Arc,* a play in three acts ("Domrémy," "Les Batailles" [The

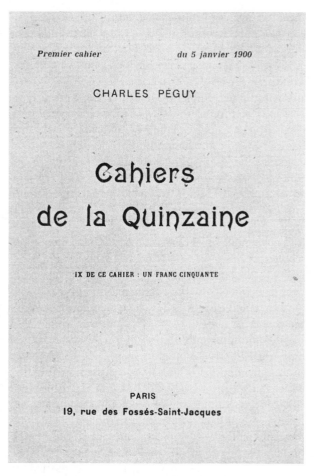

Cover for the first issue of the journal that Péguy published and edited (from Daniel Halévy, Péguy and Les Cahiers de la Quinzaine, *1946*)

Battles], "Rouen") dedicated to "all those women and men who have lived . . . and died trying to find a cure for our universal ill [of oppression, poverty, destitution]" (translated by Villiers). Designed to evoke the abiding vitality of a patriotism in service to all of downtrodden humanity, *Jeanne d'Arc* opens with a scene of unsentimental almsgiving–with its heroine in the act of feeding two starving children, even as she remains acutely aware of the limits of her charity, humbled by the "thought of all the other hungry people in this world who have nothing to eat . . . of all the unhappy people who have no one to comfort them" (translated by Villiers). The very production of *Jeanne d'Arc* as an *objet d'artisanat* (artisanal object) matched the communal, radically democratic character of its ideal conception. A contribution of ƒ2,000 from fellow students at the Ecole Normale Supérieure provided necessary assistance; and Péguy appended to the octavo volume of 752 pages (unnumbered, with some left blank so as to invite creative reader participation) a list of the compositors, printers, proofreaders, and bookbinders to whose collective craftsmanship the beautifully finished product as a whole tacitly attested. Proceeding in a way again consistent with socialism as he understood it, Péguy refused to have the book advertised anywhere but on neighborhood streets, and only in person, by word of mouth. *Jeanne d'Arc* accordingly received little market response indeed: it sold but one copy within the first month of its publication and garnered but one published notice, in the *Revue Socialiste,* which limited itself to remarking on the adherence of the book to "party" doctrine. Villiers quotes from Louis Gillet's long commentary, written for *Le Sillon* but unpublished, in which Gillet characterizes the author of *Jeanne d'Arc* as "a brother to *all* who suffer."

In May 1898, with what little money remained from his wife's dowry, Péguy purchased a lease to the Librairie Georges Bellais, a Parisian bookshop on the corner of the rue Cujas. His aim was to launch a truly communal publishing enterprise respectful of individual liberty—as he puts it in *Lettre du Provincial* (Letter from the Provincial), published in the first issue of *Cahiers de la Quinzaine* (5 January 1900) and collected in volume one of the complete works, "un coup de révolte de publier ce que ces amis sentaient, disaient, pensaient, voulaient, croyaient" (a revolutionary blow to publish what these friends feel, say, think, wish, believe)—in which he would participate not only as author on occasion but also as editor, typesetter, printer, and proofreader. Books published by the firm within the first year of its operation under Péguy's direction included his own *Marcel,* subtitled on the interior of the volume *Premier dialogue de la cité harmonieuse* (First Dialogue on the Harmonious City), a poetic dream-vision of complete earthly felicity subsequent to the triumph of universal socialism, and Romain Rolland's *Les Loups* (The Wolves), an allegory of "conflict between justice and patriotism" (translated by Villiers) based on the Dreyfus controversy. The fundamentally Christian sense of the socialism that subtends *Marcel* is reiterated in *Pierre, commencement d'une vie bourgeoise,* a recollection of his boyhood years composed in the same year as *Marcel* but published posthumously: "la dignité du travail est le plus beau de tous les honneurs, le plus chrétien" (the dignity of labor is the noblest and most Christian of all honors).

Péguy's commitment to an apostolate of writing for "the people" involved a choice, of course, and one that in several respects cost him dearly. His preoccupation with the work of the Librairie virtually closed off the possibility of completing his *agrégation* (highest competitive teachers' examination) even as

his unconcern with actually making money from book sales made for one financial crisis after another: "Ce sont des idées [que Péguy] . . . vend dans sa boutique, des idées qui . . . le ruinent" (Ideas are [what Peguy] . . . sells in his shop, ideas that . . . ruin him)—as biographer Marc Tardieu quotes Henri Alain-Fournier as observing. In August 1899, alarmed at the prospect of impending bankruptcy faced by his bookstore, Georges Bellais arranged for a takeover of the shop by a company of socialists, the Société Nouvelle de Librairie et d'Editions, managed by a board of directors that included Lucien Herr, Léon Blum, Mario Roques, Henri Boivin, and François Simiand. The directors, committed as they were to the principle of class warfare in accordance with official party doctrine, and Péguy, convinced as he was that the coming of the Harmonious City depended not on strict adherence to party discipline but on individual spiritual conversion, soon came to a parting of ways. In the words of Rolland, Péguy found "the tyrannical and sectarian point of view of his colleagues . . . intolerable," only too much like the position from which "a Minister of the Empire" would be expected to "operate" (quoted and translated by Villiers). The very idea of class warfare, Péguy had come to conclude, was inherently "bourgeois," as he puts it in the eighth issue of *Cahiers de la Quinzaine* (20 April 1900): "Nous voulons la Révolution, mais nous ne voulons pas la haine éternelle" (What we want is Revolution, not endless hatred). Late in 1899 he resigned from his editorship with the Librairie and established his periodical *Cahiers de la Quinzaine,* with its office on the rue des Fossés-Saint-Jacques. Two works published in the first issues of the periodical, *Lettre du Provincial* and *La Préparation du Congrès Socialiste Nationale* (Exercise for the National Socialist Congress), published in the second issue (20 January 1900) and collected in volume eleven (1940) of the complete works, made clear at once his opposition to the edict of the National Congress of the Socialist Party that "the press will refrain from all communications which might damage the organisation," and his conviction that the materialist division of society into warring classes does "not represent a classification of hearts and consciences." He found the edicts of the Party entirely "too despotic," in contravention of the principle of real justice. The purpose of the *Cahiers de la Quinzaine,* as he envisioned it, was to tell the unvarnished truth, whole and unembellished, as he puts it in *Lettre du Provincial:* "Dire la vérité, toute la vérité, rien que la vérité, dire bêtement la vérité bête, ennuyeusement la vérité ennuyeuse, tristement la vérité triste" (To speak the truth, the whole truth, and nothing but the truth; to

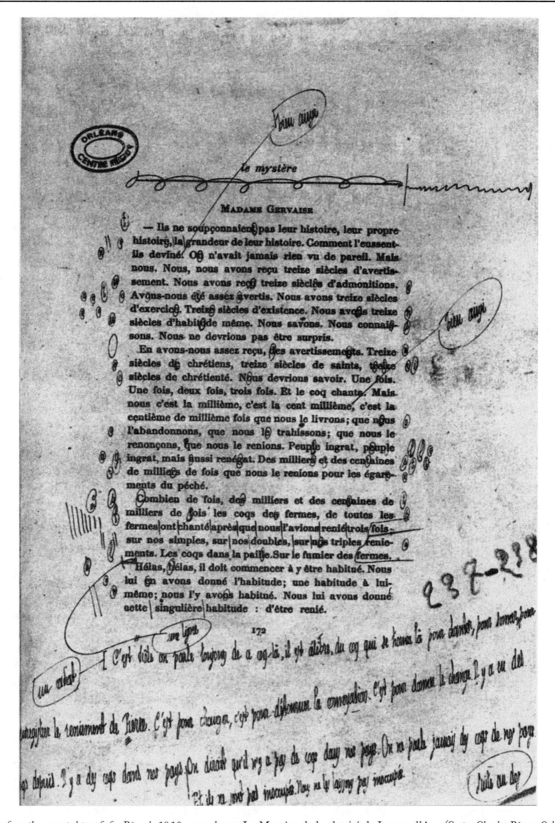

Page from the corrected proofs for Péguy's 1910 verse drama, La Mystère de la charité de Jeanne d'Arc *(Centre Charles Péguy, Orleans)*

speak the foolish truth foolishly, the tedious truth tediously, the sad truth sadly).

In the fall of 1901, confident that, as he writes in *Notre Jeunesse,* "tout ce qu'il y avait de mystique, de fidèle, de croyant, dans le Dreyfusisme, s'est refugié dans les Cahiers" (all there was of mysticism, of faith, of belief, in Dreyfusism, was preserved in the Journals), Péguy moved his publishing enterprise to 8 rue de la Sorbonne, its last home. Once again his disregard for established commercial practices had its natural effect. For all their limited circulation, though, the first issues of the *Cahiers de la Quinzaine* succeeded in attracting several distinguished and influential subscribers, among them Jean Jaurès, Raymond Poincaré, Etienne Millerand, Anatole France, André Gide, the Library of the Senate and the *Bulletin de l'Union pour l'Action.* The considerable minatory criticism that various issues of *Cahiers de la Quinzaine* met with, even from subscribers, normally had to do with apparent lapses from the *bienséances* (proprieties) dear to Gallic high literary culture. Rolland's response to that line of criticism, as reported by Villiers, remains telling: "You can criticise . . . the authors, the editor, anything except the production. You may say that we don't know French, that we lack common sense, that we are bores, but to say that the paper of the *Cahiers* is poor and the printing is bad shows poor judgment." And Péguy prized judgment as much as practical beauty. If analysis by reason, as he explained in his *De la raison* (On Reason), published in the 5 December 1901 issue of *Cahiers de la Quinzaine* and collected in volume eleven of the complete works, neither exhausts nor represents the best of life ("nous savons que la raison n'épuise pas la vie et même le meilleur de la vie" [we know that reason does not exhaust all that there is in life, nor even its better part]), the life of reasoned discipline stands as a necessary condition for all genuine, humane craftsmanship.

Péguy subsequently distanced himself from what Villiers quotes him as calling "the Socialist hunger" for "pure fame" that he was saddened to detect in the political maneuvering of his friend Jaurès, for example, since such a hunger, in his view, signed a disposition to "dictatorship," augured the triumph of the bourgeois spirit resentful of difference and genuine independence: "It is slaves who do not differ, or who differ less." In a series of four formidably titled works published in *Cahiers de la Quinzaine* and collected in *Œuvres complètes de Charles Péguy, 1873–1914–De la Situation Faite à l'Histoire et à la Sociologie dans les Temps Modernes* (The Predicament of History and Sociology in Modern Times), appearing in the 30 October 1906 issue and collected in volume three;

De la Situation Faite au Parti Intellectuel dans le Monde Moderne (The Predicament of the Intellectual Party in the Modern World), published in the 27 November 1906 issue and also collected in volume three; *De la Situation Faite à l'Histoire et à la Sociologie et de la Situation Faite au Parti Intellectuel dans le Monde Moderne* (The Predicament of History and Sociology and of the Intellectual Party in the Modern World), published in the 29 January 1907 issue and collected in volume twelve (1944); and *De la Situation Faite au Parti Intellectual dans le Monde Moderne devant les Accidents de la Gloire Temporelle* (The Predicament of the Intellectual Party in the Modern World in the Face of the Accidents of Temporal Glory), published in the 30 October 1907 issue and collected in volume three–Péguy characterized the Ecole Normale Supérieure as a "seminary" for the training of a new clergy inimical to intellectual freedom. His assailing of "the Socialist Church" had a paradoxical double effect: Socialist Party members suspected him of being a Catholic and closet anarchist, while the Catholic establishment regarded him as an atheistic revolutionary.

Péguy suffered intensely during the years that immediately followed. A crushing workload left him exhausted, prone to illness; and his parting from old friends and cohorts in the cause of social justice left him isolated. But with suffering came a blessing: in the autumn of 1908, while recovering from a bout of influenza, Péguy announced to Joseph Lotte that he had come to discover himself "un Catholique" (a Catholic). As Villiers records his description of his "conversion," it represented not so much "a return" as a moving forward: "We did not find the high road of Christianity by turning back . . . we found it at the end." The news of Péguy's conversion was spread by Raïssa and Jacques Maritain, recent converts to Roman Catholicism who did all that they could to induce him to return to the fold of institutional orthodoxy. But Péguy's fidelity to the promises he had made to his wife, Charlotte, made it impossible for him to go to confession, attend weekly Mass, and have his marriage "blessed" and his children baptized. Nor did he turn away from the Maritains, whose sometimes meddling actions on his behalf he magnanimously understood as prompted by charity.

Three *mystères* (mystery plays) register some of the genuinely theological effects attendant on Péguy's recognition of himself as a traveler along "the high road of Christianity." The first, a poetic drama titled *Le Mystère de la charité de Jeanne d'Arc* (first published in *Cahiers de la Quinzaine,* 16 January 1910), opens with a Joan beset by anxiety and inspired by hope as she prays to "Notre Père" (Our Father) for the coming of his kingdom: "Notre Père,

Péguy in his bookshop at 8 rue de la Sorbonne, which served as the offices of the Cahiers de la Quinzaine *from 1901 until 1914*

notre père qui êtes aux cieux, de combien il s'en faut que votre volonté soit faite; de combien il s'en faut que nous ayons notre pain de chaque jour. De combien il s'en faut que nous pardonnions nos offenses; et que nous ne succombions pas à la tentation; et que nous soyons délivrés du mal. Ainsi soit-il" (Our Father, our father who art in heaven, how far is your will from being done; how far are we from being given our daily bread. How far are we from forgiving those who trespass against us; and not succumbing to temptation; and being delivered from evil. Amen [translated by Green and Green]). What consolation Joan finds is in working toward the actualizing of that kingdom: "orare est laborare" (to work is to pray). *Le Mystère de la charité de Jeanne d'Arc* found an enthusiastic reader in Gide, who wrote a review in praise of Péguy's style—it reminded him of "very old litanies"—and who sent copies of the book to Paul Claudel, Francis Jammes, and Emile Verhaeren. The two subsequent *mystères,* both first published in *Cahiers de la Quinzaine* and immediately thereafter published as books by Emile-Paul frères—*Le Porche du Mystère de la*

deuxième vertu (first published in the 22 October 1911 issue; translated as *The Portico of the Mystery of the Second Virtue,* 1970), on the virtue of hope as encouraged by the parables of the Lost Sheep and the Prodigal Son; and *Le Mystère des Saints Innocents* (first published in the 24 March 1912 issue; translated as *The Mystery of the Holy Innocents,* 1956), a paean to a child-like spirituality reckoned dearer to God than a spirituality born of the complexities of experience—met with little or no immediate reader response. Their simplicity and homely tenor seem to have confused such sophisticated intellectual sympathizers as Claudel, Maritain, and Gide, leaving them with nothing much to say.

The poet in Péguy also came alive with his renewed sense of Christian allegiance. In the period 1910–1912 he composed 1,500 sets of quatrains centered on a comparison of the theological virtues (of faith, hope, and charity) with the cardinal virtues (of prudence, justice, fortitude, and temperance): "Les quatre Cardinales / Viennent des dieux, / Les trois Théologales / Viennent du Dieu" (The four Cardinals /

Come from the gods, / The three Theologicals / Come from God). Péguy's substantial concern in these quatrains is with the corruption of the "Theologicals" when the authority of these is derived from the "Cardinals," virtues only too attractive to the worldliness of a politicized spirituality. His conviction of the abidingly mystical, theological character of the human condition is further indicated in a work first published in the 1 December 1912 issue of *Cahiers de la Quinzaine* and collected in *Les Tapisseries* (The Tapestries, 1936), *Tapisserie de Sainte Geneviève et de Jeanne d'Arc* (Tapestry of St. Genevieve and Joan of Arc), a series of poems in nine parts inspired by his several pilgrimages to Chartres in the summer of that year:

> Mais c'est l'esprit qui mène et l'esprit qui nourrit
> Et la lettre n'est là que comme un mot écrit;
> Et la lettre n'a jamais fait qu'un peut de bruit,
> C'est elle qui séduit et c'est elle qui nuit.
> Et la lettre et l'esprit, c'est le jour et la nuit.

> (It is the spirit that leads and the spirit that feeds
> And the letter is only there as a written word,
> And the letter has never made much stir.
> And it is the letter that seduces and it is she who harms
> And the letter and the spirit are as night to day).

But such a disjoining of "the letter" from "the spirit" hardly accorded with Péguy's own practice. He kept to the letter of his word. In the first months of 1913 Péguy prayed to the Virgin Mary for the deliverance of his son, who was afflicted with typhoid, promising that he would make yet another pilgrimage to Chartres should his prayer be answered. The boy recovered, and Péguy kept his promise, making several pilgrimages (on foot) to the Cathedral of Chartres during the following summer. Initially published in the 11 May 1913 issue of *Cahiers de la Quinzaine* and collected in *Les Tapisseries,* the sequence of poems *La Tapisserie de Notre Dame de Chartres* (The Tapestry of Our Lady of Chartres) provides a prayerful testimony to its author's coming to peace and reconciliation in a place and a spirit of veneration, simplicity, reconciliation:

> Voici le lieu du monde où tout devient facile,
> Le regret, le départ, même l'évènement,
> Et l'adieu temporaire et le détournement,
> Le seul coin de la terre où tout devient docile. . . .
> Voici le lieu du monde où tout est revenu
> Après tant de départs, après tant d'arrivées. . . .
> Voici le lieu du monde où tout rentre et se tait,
> Et le silence et l'ombre et la charnelle absence,
> Et le commencement d'éternelle présence,
> Le seul réduit où l'âme est tout ce qu'elle était.

> (Here is the one place on earth where all becomes easy,
> The regret, the going away, even the event itself,

> And the temporary goodbye and the turning away;
> The only place on earth where all becomes docile. . . .
> Here is the one place on earth to which all has returned
> After so many departures, so many arrivals. . . .
> Here is the one place on earth to which all comes home
>   and in which all keeps silence,
> The silence and the shadow and the physical absence
> And the beginning of everlasting presence,
> The only retreat in which the soul is fully what it was).

For all of the piety and respect for Christian tradition that it evinces, though, the poem failed to convince the Catholic establishment of its author's full orthodoxy. Villiers reports that the Benedictine monk Baillet, an old friend of Péguy's from his days at Sainte-Barbe, expressed his fear that the writer of *La Tapisserie de Notre Dame de Chartres* "would make a heretic."

And Baillet, attentive as he was to the politics of ecclesiastical thinking, had reason to be so concerned. The anticlericalism of *Véronique: Dialogue de l'histoire de l'âme charnelle* (Veronica: Dialogue on the History of the Carnal Soul, 1972) and *Clio: Dialogue de l'histoire et de l'âme païenne* (Clio: Dialogue on the History of the Pagan Soul, 1917), works from Péguy's last years, was anything but oblique. Since "it is the ligature of the eternal and the temporal . . . which constitutes Christianity," as he observes in *Véronique,* the effects produced by the "lay-curés who deny the eternal aspect of the temporal" and by the "ecclesiastical curés who deny the temporal in the eternal" have been equally disastrous for genuine Christianity. That critique is extended in *Clio,* which stresses the "inorganic," dissociative character of a modern culture founded on a Cartesian-style "dualism" and an economy of "money" (translated by Villiers).

With *Eve,* a poem of some two thousand quatrains, first published in *Cahiers de la Quinzaine* (28 December 1913) and republished as volume seven (1925) of *Œuvres complètes de Charles Péguy, 1873–1914,* Péguy's belief in the coincidence of the temporal and the eternal in bona fide Christianity found explicitly constructive expression. In his 1970 anthology of critical responses to Péguy's writing, Fraisse includes Jean Onimus's description of the story that *Eve* tells as one of "life confronted by the forces of destruction and placing its ultimate hope in grace." The mystery of the Incarnation essential to Christian belief in grace and reconciliation naturally provides the essential point of reference of the poem:

> Car le surnaturel est lui-même charnel
> Et l'arbre de la grâce est racine profonde,
> Et plonge dans le sol et cherche jusqu'au fond
> Et l'arbre de la race est lui-même éternel.

> (For the supernatural itself is carnal
> And the tree of grace has deep-thrusting roots

And drives through the soil and searches the depths
And the tree of the stock is itself eternal).

Rooted in such a faith, Péguy could hardly help but continue to sympathize with the Bergsonian resistance to any philosophy that would radically sever matter from spirit, "idea" from "extension."

But politically speaking, Peguy's anticipation, shared with Baillet, that he would come to be deemed by the Church as something of "a heretic" was only too well founded. His *Note sur M. Bergson et la Philosophie Bergsonienne* (Note on M. Bergson and Bergsonian Philosophy), first published in *Cahiers de la Quinzaine* (26 April 1914), republished that same year with a cancel title page and collected in volume nine (1924) of *Œuvres complètes de Charles Péguy, 1873–1914,* was clearly anti-Cartesian but was also taken to be anti-Thomist by Catholic critics of Bergson, most notably Peguy's good friend Jacques Maritain. When Bergson's books were placed on the Index of Forbidden Books in the early summer of 1914, Maritain implored Péguy to turn his back on his old teacher. Péguy declined to do so, on the grounds that such an action would contravene the dictates of his own conscience and constitute a betrayal of his commitment to "la mystique."

Péguy's Bergsonianism seems also to have played a role in his decision, at the age of forty-one, to volunteer for army service in August 1914, when World War I broke out. Yet again, his position was as much philosophical as practical in its justification: the war against Germany was "une juste guerre" (a just war) since it represented, in his view, a struggle against the forces of scientism and industrialism, ever enemies at once to the principle of élan vital, the justice of Christian socialism and the humane ideals of liberty, equality, and fraternity. In the late summer of 1914, on the Feast of the Assumption of the Blessed Virgin Mary, Lieutenant Charles Péguy of the 276th Regiment attended Mass for the first and last time since his "conversion." And true to his commitment to the spirit of élan vital that he shared with his commanding officers, he urged his troops to move forward whenever the occasion to do so presented itself. According to most accounts, he died suddenly, standing up, from a single shot in the forehead, as he led an attack against retreating German troops in the vicinity of Villeroy, on the river Marne. His last words, heard on 5 September 1914, were reportedly "Tirez, tirez, nom de Dieu" (Fire, fire, in God's name), an oath or an imprecation or a prayer directed to the men under his command, who prudently continued to lie low and keep their heads down. Not long after hearing the news of her husband's death, Charlotte Péguy became a Catholic and had her children baptized. In 1920, after much official hesitation, Péguy was made a Chevalier de la Légion d'Honneur and was awarded the Croix de Guerre.

Many other signs of Péguy's recognition followed. His writings and the example of his life inspired French prisoners of war and members of the Resistance during World War II; and the society L'Amitié Charles Péguy was founded in 1946. *Feuillets,* a bio-bibliographical newsletter published by that society, dates from 1948. Commemorations of the fiftieth anniversary of his death included the establishment of the Centre Charles Péguy d'Orléans and the holding of an international symposium in honor of his achievement, also at Orléans. Martin and Dalgues's 1973 exhibition catalogue presenting Péguy's manuscripts, and Fraisse's edition of *Les Critiques de notre temps et Péguy* figure among the many still highly useful scholarly works published in celebration of the centenary of Péguy's birth. The long list of writers influenced by his works includes Rolland, Gide, Louis Aragon, Julian Green, Georges Bernanos, and May Sarton. Radical Christian theologians since the Second Vatican Council have increasingly come to value Péguy's achievement. Urs von Balthasar, for one, has ranked the author of *Le Mystère de la charité de Jeanne d'Arc* among the "ten essential Christians since Jesus."

Letters:

Lettres et Entretiens: Charles Péguy (Paris: Artisan du Livre, 1927);

Maurice Reclus, *Le Péguy que j'ai connu: Avec cent lettres de Charles Péguy, 1905–1914* (Paris: Hachette, 1951);

Une Amitié française: Correspondance de Charles Péguy et Romain Rolland, edited by Alfred Saffrey (Paris: Albin Michel, 1955);

Correspondance Charles Péguy-André Suarès, edited by Saffrey, Cahiers de L'Amitié Charles Péguy, no. 14 (Paris: Cahiers de L'Amitié Charles Péguy, 1961);

Alain-Fournier et Péguy: correspondance, 1910–1914 (Paris: Fayard, 1973);

Pour l'honneur de l'esprit: Correspondance entre Charles Péguy et Romain Rolland, 1898–1914, edited, with an introduction and notes, by Auguste Martin, Cahiers Romain Rolland, no. 22 (Paris: Albin Michel, 1973).

Bibliography:

Feuillets–L'Amitié Charles Péguy (Paris), 1948–   .

Biography:

Marc Tardieu, *Charles Péguy: Biographie* (Paris: François Bourin, 1993).

References:

Albert Béguin, *L'Eve de Péguy: Essai de lecture commentée,* Cahiers d'Amitié de Charles Péguy, nos. 3 and 4 (Paris: Labergerie, 1948);

Joseph Bonenfant, *L'Imagination du mouvement dans l'œuvre de Péguy* (Montréal: Centre Educatif et Culturel, 1969);

Victor Boudon, *Avec Charles Péguy de la Lorraine à la Marne, août-septembre 1914,* preface by Maurice Barrès (Paris: Hachette, 1916); republished as *Mon lieutenant Charles Péguy (juillet-septembre 1914),* with additional material by Romain Rolland (Paris: Albin Michel, 1964);

Georges Cattaui, *Charles Péguy* (Paris: Seuil, 1964);

Albert Chabanon, *La Poétique de Charles Péguy* (Paris: Laffont, 1947);

Lucien Christophe, *Les Grandes heures de Charles Péguy, du fleuve à la mer, 1905–1914* (Brussels: Renaissance du Livre, 1964);

Christophe, *Le Jeune homme Péguy, de la source au fleuve (1897–1905)* (Brussels: Renaissance du Livre, 1963);

Simone Fraisse, ed., *Les Critiques de notre temps et Péguy,* Les Critiques de notre temps, no. 12 (Paris: Garnier, 1973);

Henri Guillemin, *Charles Péguy* (Paris: Seuil, 1981);

Daniel Halévy, *Péguy et les Cahiers de la Quinzaine,* revised edition (Paris: Grasset, 1941); translated by Ruth Bethell as *Péguy and Les Cahiers de la Quinzaine* (London: Dobson, 1946);

René Johannet, *Vie et mort de Péguy* (Paris: Flammarion, 1950);

Auguste Martin and Georges Dalgues, eds., *Manuscrits de Péguy: Exposition pour le centième anniversaire de sa naissance: Ville d'Orléans, Centre Charles Péguy, musée, bibliothèque: septembre 1973,* introduction by René Thinat (Orléans: Centre Charles Péguy, 1973);

Jean Onimus, *Introduction aux Quatrains de Péguy,* Cahiers de l'Amitié Charles Péguy, no. 9 (Paris: L'Amitié Charles Péguy, 1952);

Rolland, *Péguy,* 2 volumes (Paris: Albin Michel, 1944);

Roger Secrétain, *Péguy, soldat de la liberté* (New York: Brentano's, 1941);

Yvonne Servais, *Charles Péguy: The Pursuit of Salvation* (Cork, Ireland: Cork University Press, 1953; Westminster, Md.: Newman Press, 1953);

Jérôme Tharaud and Jean Tharaud, *Notre cher Péguy,* 2 volumes (Paris: Plon-Nourrit, 1926);

Jacques Viard, *Philosophie de l'art littéraire et socialisme selon Péguy* (Paris: Klincksieck, 1970);

Robert Vigneault, *L'Univers féminin dans l'œuvre de Charles Péguy: Essai sur l'imagination créatice d'un poète* (Bruges & Paris: Desclée de Brouwer / Montréal: Les Editions Bellarmin, 1967);

Marjorie Villiers, *Charles Péguy: A Study in Integrity* (London: Collins, 1965; New York: Harper & Row, 1966).

Papers:

A large collection of Charles Péguy's manuscripts and correspondence is held by the Centre Charles Péguy d'Orléans.

Saint-John Perse

(31 May 1887 – 20 September 1975)

Camille René La Bossière
University of Ottawa

BOOKS: *Eloges,* as Saintleger Leger (Paris: Editions de la Nouvelle Revue Française, 1911; revised and enlarged edition, as St-J. Perse, Paris: Editions de la Nouvelle Revue Française/Gallimard, 1925; revised and enlarged edition, Paris: Gallimard, 1948); 1925 edition translated by Louise Varèse as *Eloges and Other Poems,* introduction by Archibald MacLeish (New York: Norton, 1944; revised edition, based on 1953 French edition, Bollingen Series, no. 55, New York: Pantheon, 1956);

Amitié du prince (Paris: Ronald Davis, 1924);

Anabase (Paris: Gallimard, 1924; revised and enlarged, 1948); translated, with an introduction, by T. S. Eliot as *Anabasis,* bilingual edition (London: Faber & Faber, 1930; revised edition, New York: Harcourt, Brace, 1938; revised and enlarged edition, based on 1948 French edition, New York: Harcourt, Brace, 1949; London: Faber & Faber, 1959);

Poème pour Valery Larbaud, Bahut des aromates, no. 10 (Liège: A la Lampe d'Aladdin, 1936);

Exil: Poème (Marseilles: Editions Cahiers du Sud, 1942; revised edition, Buenos Aires: Les Editions Lettres Françaises, 1942);

Pluies (Buenos Aires: Les Editions Lettres Françaises, 1944);

Quatre poèmes, 1941–1944 (Buenos Aires: Les Editions Lettres Françaises, 1944); republished as *Exil, suivi de Poème à l'étrangère, Pluies, Neiges* (Paris: Gallimard, 1945); revised as *Exil, suivi de Poèmes à l'étrangère, Pluie, Neiges* (Paris: Gallimard, 1946); translated by Denis Devlin as *Exile and Other Poems,* bilingual edition, Bollingen Series, no. 15 (New York: Pantheon, 1949);

Vents (Paris: Gallimard, 1946); translated by Hugh Chisholm as *Winds,* bilingual edition, Bollingen Series, no. 34 (New York: Pantheon, 1953);

Amers (Paris: Gallimard, 1957); translated by Wallace Fowlie as *Seamarks,* bilingual edition, Bollingen Series, no. 67 (New York: Pantheon, 1958);

Saint-John Perse (photograph by Dorothy Norman)

Chronique (limited edition, Marseilles: Cahiers du Sud, 1959; trade edition, Paris: Gallimard, 1960); translated by Robert Fitzgerald as *Chronique,* bilingual edition, Bollingen Series, no. 69 (New York: Pantheon, 1961);

Poésie: Allocution au Banquet Nobel du 10 décembre 1960 (Paris: Gallimard, 1961); translated by W. H. Auden as *On Poetry by St.-John Perse, Speech of Acceptance upon the Award of the Nobel Prize for Literature*

Delivered in Stockholm December 10, 1960 (N.p., Bollingen Foundation, 1961);

Hommage à Rabindranath Tagore, Collection Brimborions, no. 89 (Liège, Belgium: Editions Dynamo, 1962);

L'Ordre des oiseaux, illustrated by Georges Braque (Paris: Sociéte d'Editions d'art, 1962); republished, without illustrations, as *Oiseaux* (limited edition, Paris: Sociéte d'Editions d'art, 1962; trade edition, Paris: Gallimard, 1963); translated by Robert Fitzgerald as *Birds,* bilingual edition, Bollingen Series, no. 82 (New York: Pantheon, 1966);

Valéry Larbaud; ou, L'Honneur littéraire, Collection Brimborions, no. 95 (Liège, Belgium: Editions Dynamo, 1962);

Silence pour Claudel, Collection Brimborions, no. 116 (Liège, Belgium: Editions Dynamo, 1963);

Au souvenir de Valery Larbaud, Collection Brimborions, no. 122 (Liège, Belgium: Editions Dynamo, 1963);

Pour Dante (Paris: Gallimard, 1965);

Chanté par celle qui fut là . . . (Paris: Privately Printed by Robert Blanchet, 1969); translated by Howard as *Chanté par celle qui fut là . . . ("Sung by One Who Was There")* (Princeton: Princeton University Press, 1970);

Œuvres Complètes: Saint-John Perse, Bibliothèque de la Pléiade, no. 240 (Paris: Gallimard, 1972);

Chant pour un équinoxe (Paris: Gallimard, 1975); translated by Howard as *Song for an Equinox,* bilingual edition, Bollingen Series, no. 69 (Princeton: Princeton University Press, 1977).

Editions and Collections: *Œuvre Poétique: Saint-John Perse* (2 volumes, Paris: Gallimard, 1953–1960; revised and enlarged, 3 volumes, 1967–1970)—comprises volume 1, *Eloges, La Gloire des Rois, Anabase, Exil, Vents* (1953)—includes revised edition of *Eloges;* volume 1 revised as *Eloges, La Gloire des Rois, Anabase, Exil* (1960; revised, 1967); volume 2, *Vents, Amers, Chronique* (1960; revised, 1967); revised as *Vents, suivi de Chronique* (1968); and volume 3, *Amers, suivi d'Oiseaux et de l'Allocution au banquet Nobel* (1970);

Amitié du prince de Saint-John Perse, edited by Albert Henry, Publications de la Fondation Saint-John Perse, no. 3 (Paris: Gallimard, 1979);

Anabase de Saint-John Perse, edited by Henry, Publications de la Fondation Saint-John Perse, no. 3 (Paris: Gallimard, 1983);

Nocturne . . . , edited by Henry, Publications de la Fondation Saint-John Perse, no. 5 (Paris: Gallimard, 1985).

Editions in English: *Two Addresses,* bilingual edition, Bollingen Series, no. 86 (New York: Pantheon, 1966)—comprises "On Poetry," translated by W. H.

Auden, and "Dante," translated by Robert Fitzgerald;

Birds by Saint-John Perse, translated by J. Roger Little (Durham, U.K.: North Gate Press, 1967);

St.-John Perse: Collected Poems, bilingual edition, translated by Auden and others, Bollingen Series, no. 87 (Princeton: Princeton University Press, 1971).

Saint-John Perse is chiefly remembered for his antiphonal, psalmodic celebration of a vitalist natural religion founded on the principle of the *coincidentia oppositorum* (coincidence of opposites). Perse specialists have long recognized that he embodies the perspective of a Janus-like seer with "la reconnaissance du sacré et de sa fondamentale ambiguïté . . . le caractère équivoque de la réalité" (the recognition of the sacred and its fundamental ambiguity . . . the equivocal character of reality), in the words of Henriette Levillain in her 1977 monograph. Response to the *versets* (verses) of this latter-day "dieu bifront" (two-faced god) has accordingly registered a high degree of ambiguity and wonder, even mystification. The resolutely "pagan" sense of divinity basic to Perse's writings understandably has not invited unqualified assent from traditionalist Christian readers—"Mais *Dieu* est un mot que Saint-John Perse évite . . . religieusement" (But *God* is a word that Saint-John Perse avoids . . . religiously), as Paul Claudel observes in his contribution to the festschrift *Honneur à Saint-John Perse* (In Honor of Saint-John Perse, 1965). Nor, again any less understandably, has Perse's staunch resistance to the dead-end of unbelief, such as he found exemplified in Friedrich Nietzsche's *Ecce Homo* (Behold the Man, 1908), encouraged attention or endorsement from readers of a postmodern or deconstructionist persuasion. Certainly, the aristocratic diction and sense of hierarchy that Perse's poetry sustains have worked to limit both its popular and critical appeal.

Marie-René Alexis Saint-Leger Leger was born 31 May 1887, on the islet of Saint-Leger-les-Feuilles, Guadeloupe, to Françoise-Renée Saint-Leger Leger (née Dormoy), heiress to coffee and sugar plantations carved out by émigrés to the West Indies in the early 1800s, and to her husband, Amédée Saint-Leger Leger, a lawyer from an old Antillean family with roots in seventeenth-century Bourgogne. As the only son, Alexis Saint-Leger Leger enjoyed an idyllic boyhood on the family estates of La Joséphine and Le Bois-Debout, reveling in swimming, riding, and sailing, even as his private tutors, a retired naval officer and the Reverend Father Antoine Duss, author of *Flore phanérogamique des Antilles* (Flowering Plants of the Antilles, 1896), found him a ready student of astronomy, mathematics, botany, and Latin. Alexis continued to excel during his three years of study at the Lycée de La Pointe-à-Pitre, winning a prize for proficiency in the natural sciences in 1899. That same year, consequent to a sharp decline in the West Indies economy, and with a view to assuring the best possible future education for their son, Amédée and Françoise-Renée Saint-Leger Leger departed with their four children for France, where they established a materially much reduced yet still comfortable household in the resort town of Pau.

Again, Alexis Leger benefited from his opportunity to advance in learning. Prizewinning achievement at the Lycée de Pau, in French composition and rhetoric, Latin and Greek, paved the way to his enrollment, in 1904, in the Faculty of Law at the Université de Bordeaux. Leger performed brilliantly there, supplementing his major program with courses ranging from classical philology to the natural sciences. He completed his degree in 1910, the progress of his formal studies having been delayed by a year of compulsory military service (1905–1906), then by the need to attend to immediate family responsibilities on the sudden death of his father in 1907. Sailing excursions in the North Atlantic and annual summer holidays in the Pyrenees provided some relief from the pressure of those responsibilities.

The period of Leger's studies at Bordeaux was marked by a bourgeoning of his interest in the life of art and philosophy. He familiarized himself with writings in the counter-rationalist tradition extending from Anaxagoras and Heraclitus to Ralph Waldo Emerson and Henri Bergson, established friendships with such authors as Francis Jammes, Jacques Rivière, Gabriel Frizeau, and Claudel, translated Pindar's *Epinikia,* and launched his own poetic career with the composition of "Images à Crusoé" (Images of Crusoe), written in 1904 and first published in *Nouvelle Revue française* (August 1909); "Pour fêter une enfance" (For Celebrating a Childhood), written in 1907; "Ecrit sur la porte" (Written on the Door), written in 1908; and eighteen poems written in 1908 and first published in *Nouvelle Revue française* (June 1911) as "Eloges" (Praises). It was only reluctantly, however, and at the insistence of André Gide, that Leger consented to the publication in book form of these Pindaric-style odes, which appeared together in the volume *Eloges* (1911) under the imprint of Editions de la Nouvelle Revue Française. He almost immediately came to regret having done so, on practical as well as philosophical grounds, as he was now acting as head of the family and was naturally concerned with the material well-being of his mother and sisters. He remarked to Valery Larbaud in 1911, so the latter reported to Léon-Paul Fargue in a letter dated 6 April of that year, that the publication of verse in a highbrow review has no more genuinely practical value than does playing the piano for tourists on a luxury cruise ("c'est jouer du piano sur le pont d'un paquebot"). Nor did Leger's sense, at this time, of the substantial limitation of art entice him to make his mark as a poet. Since "l'art n'étant qu'*ellipse* et l'ellipse tendant au silence" (art is only

Perse in Mongolia while he was serving with the French legation in Beijing (1916–1921)

ellipsis and ellipsis tends only toward silence), Leger explained to Larbaud, "mieux vaut ne rien écrire, et simplement goûter la vie" (it is better not to write, and simply to savor life). So convinced, he resolved to set aside the work of creative writing in favor of pursuing a career in the diplomatic service.

For all its logical cogency, though, young Leger's position on the invincible shortcoming of art, that, as he put it in a July 1909 letter to Gustave-Adolphe Monod, "l'essentiel ne se dit pas, et bien plus, n'a jamais désiré se dire" (the essential is not said, and what is more, it has never wished to be said), seems to have been held quite ambiguously. The poet of *Eloges* could no less affirm, as he did in a 10 December 1908 letter to Claudel, the "l'esprit libérateur" (the liberating spirit) he found exemplified, for instance, in "maître" (master) Emerson's practice of a philosophy of contradiction; or what he called, in a December 1913 letter to Claudel, "la joie créatrice" (the creative joy) he found in Claudel's play *Protée* (published 1914). Paradoxically, yet consistently enough, indications are that Leger's sense of the logically negative value of art did nothing to slow his participation in literary circles in the years immediately following the publication of his first book of poetry. He readily joined company with Larbaud, Edmund Gosse, and Gide in the John Donne Club, whimsically chartered in London (where Leger visited for six months during 1912) by American lady of letters Agnes Tobin, had extended close conversations with Claudel, Paul Valéry, and Joseph Conrad, resolved to translate Rabindranath Tagore's *Gitanjali* (Song Offerings, 1910), and visited with G. K. Chesterton, Gide, William H. Hudson, Hilaire Belloc, and Arthur Symons, even as he undertook those studies in economics and the social sciences that prepared his successful competing for a position with the Department of Foreign Affairs in 1916. Shortly before taking up his first posting, to the French Legation at Beijing as second secretary in the fall of that year, Leger met with Valéry, who took the occasion to justify his decision to make a living with his pen by showing the tyro diplomat his work-in-progress, published as *La Jeune Parque* (The Young Fate, 1917).

Distance and the press of professional duties naturally curtailed Leger's literary contacts during his five-year tenure in Beijing. Most of his personal letters from China were addressed to his mother. But he did find time to maintain a correspondence with Valéry and Conrad, with whom he shared his now fully settled belief in the coincidence of opposites as the generative principle of art as of life—as he put it in a 27 February 1909 letter to Frizeau, contradictions are "génératrices, ou révélatrices, de chances nouvelles pour l'esprit"(generators, or revealers, of new chances for the spirit). Leger's letter of 2 September 1917 to Valéry indicates something of the force of his finding for "l'absurde" (the absurd) or "surrationalisme" (suprarationalism) as "une incitation légitime de l'esprit" (a legitimate incitement of the spirit), over the machine-thinking epitomized by the "lamentable positivisme d'Auguste Comte" (lamentable positivism of Auguste Comte). Writing in much the same vein to Conrad on 26 February 1921, he recalls "for the most perfect aristocrat and truest friend I have ever known" their conversation, some ten years before, on "l'esprit des grandes aventures"(the spirit of great adventures) embodied in tales by "les meilleurs auteurs de mer" (the best writers of the sea), such as Herman Melville, and, even more spiritedly, Leger's recitation of some of the nonsense lyrics of Edward Lear's long poem "The Jumblies," from his *Nonsense Songs* (1870). Substantially formed by the time of the publication of *Eloges,* the spirit of high adventure—as much beyond as against reason— that Leger shared with such writers as Conrad and Lear served as the impelling principle and ruling theme of Leger's subsequent poetry.

Leger also found sufficient respite from his duties in Beijing to trek across desert regions in Manchuria and Mongolia by car and to visit an abandoned Taoist temple. He documented his response to those sites of natural sublimity, ancient military adventure, and archaeological discovery in his lyrical yet lapidary epic *Anabase* (1924; translated as *Anabasis,* 1930). Richly informed by readings in Xenophon, the Old Testament (Exodus, Psalms, and Ecclesiastes in particular), and Conradian narratives of "Eastern logic" as "an intimate alliance of contradictions" (from *Under Western Eyes,* 1911) Perse's first long poem highlights "Hommes" (men) as "flaireurs de signes" (trackers of signs), following the most enigmatic of traces across spaces of obscurity and along "les voies du silence" (the paths of silence), and bespeaks "le délice du large" (the grand joy) of adventure shared by voyagers across "les ténèbres . . . les frontières . . . de l'esprit" (the shadows . . . the frontiers of the spirit) in their quest after the truth of their dreams in a world rife with wonder: "la terre enfante des merveilles" (the world gives birth to marvels). The Gobi Desert—described by Leger in his 1921 letter to Conrad as "un Océan de poussière au vent" (an Ocean of dust blown by the wind)—represents a "restless mirror of the Infinite," an element of unremitting ambiguity and a stage for the "mystery play" of travail and joy, defeat and triumph that is life.

His roundabout return voyage to France in 1921, which included a sailing cruise in the Caribbean and a leisurely excursion along the American seaboard from Mexico to Maine, afforded Leger the occasion to add refining touches to *Anabase.* On his return to Paris after a five-year absence, Leger discovered, much to his surprise and apparent displeasure, that readers of *Eloges* had installed him in the vanguard of artists for the "modernity" and "lyrical exaltation" of his poetry. Guillaume Apollinaire, Rainer Maria Rilke, Marcel Proust, Louis Chadourne, and some of the Surrealists had cited his poetry to celebratory effect, while composers Louis Durey and Darius Milhaud had set parts of *Eloges* to music performed in London and Brussels. Nor did Leger's consenting to the publication of *Anabase* in 1924—first in the periodical *Nouvelle Revue française* and then in book form by Librarie Gallimard—do much to stem the subsequent growth of his reputation as an artist. Translations of *Anabase,* including G. Adamovitch and G. Ivanoff's 1926 Russian version, Bernard Groethuysen and Walter Benjamin's 1929 German version, T. S. Eliot's 1930 English version, Giuseppe Ungaretti's 1931 Italian version, Ion Pillat's 1932 Romanian version, and Arthur Lundkvist's 1939 Swedish version, established the author's place of honor among the elite of international literature. Ever polite, expressing himself with proper obliquity, Leger advised admirers and translators of his poetry that his reservations regarding the practical efficacy of high-literary endeavor had not been dispelled. Apparently with a view to separating the career diplomat from the poet, the author of *Anabase* signed himself "Saint-John Perse," the bilingual pseudonym he used for all of his published poetry after 1924.

Those works, though, were not soon in coming. For almost two decades after *Anabase* appeared Perse published no poetry. Although he did continue to find

Perse in his office at the Quai d'Orsay, circa 1930, when he served under Aristide Briand, minister of foreign affairs

time to compose in the spirit of élan vital (there is evidence that the Gestapo in 1940 confiscated manuscripts of some five long Perse poems now unlikely to be found), the main force of his energies was taken up with the business of a high-ranking civil servant. During the period from 1924 to 1939 Perse served as cabinet director under "Great Peacemaker" Aristide Briand, the minister of foreign affairs, helped negotiate the Briand-Kellogg Pact of 1928, participated in The Hague Conference of 1930, held the position of ambassador and secretary-general in the government of Edouard Daladier, and personally negotiated the French-Soviet Pact of 1935. His growing opposition to a policy of peacemaking by appeasement notwithstanding, Perse maintained his position as secretary-general under Daladier in the late 1930s. But matters came to a head after Germany invaded France in 1940. Denounced as a "belliciste" (warmonger) by a regime in a hurry to conclude an armistice, Perse fled to England, where he had private meetings with the prime minister, Winston Churchill; the British foreign secretary, Edward Frederick Lindley, first Earl of Halifax; and British secretary of state for the colonies, George Ambrose Lloyd, first

Baron Lloyd of Dolobran. Perse then departed for the United States, arriving there on 14 July 1940. Three months later the Vichy government revoked his French citizenship, stripped him of the rank of Grand Officier de La Légion d'Honneur, and ordered the confiscation of all his property. Although his rights were restored after the war, for now Perse's career as civil service mandarin was effectively over.

Yet again, Perse profited from loss, since his flight to exile in the United States resulted in his return to public literary endeavor. The Eliot translation of *Anabase* having established his American credentials, Perse was received as a distinguished man of letters; and in 1941, thanks to the good offices of Librarian of Congress Archibald MacLeish, he was assured a modest income as literary adviser to the Library of Congress in Washington, D.C. MacLeish lent additional aid by promoting and writing an introduction for a bilingual edition of *Eloges,* eventually published by W. W. Norton & Co. in 1944. Now relatively at leisure and stimulated by his new situation, Perse responded with a burst of poetic production. In New Jersey in 1941 he wrote *Exil* (Exile), which was first published in the March 1942 issue of the Chicago review *Poetry,*

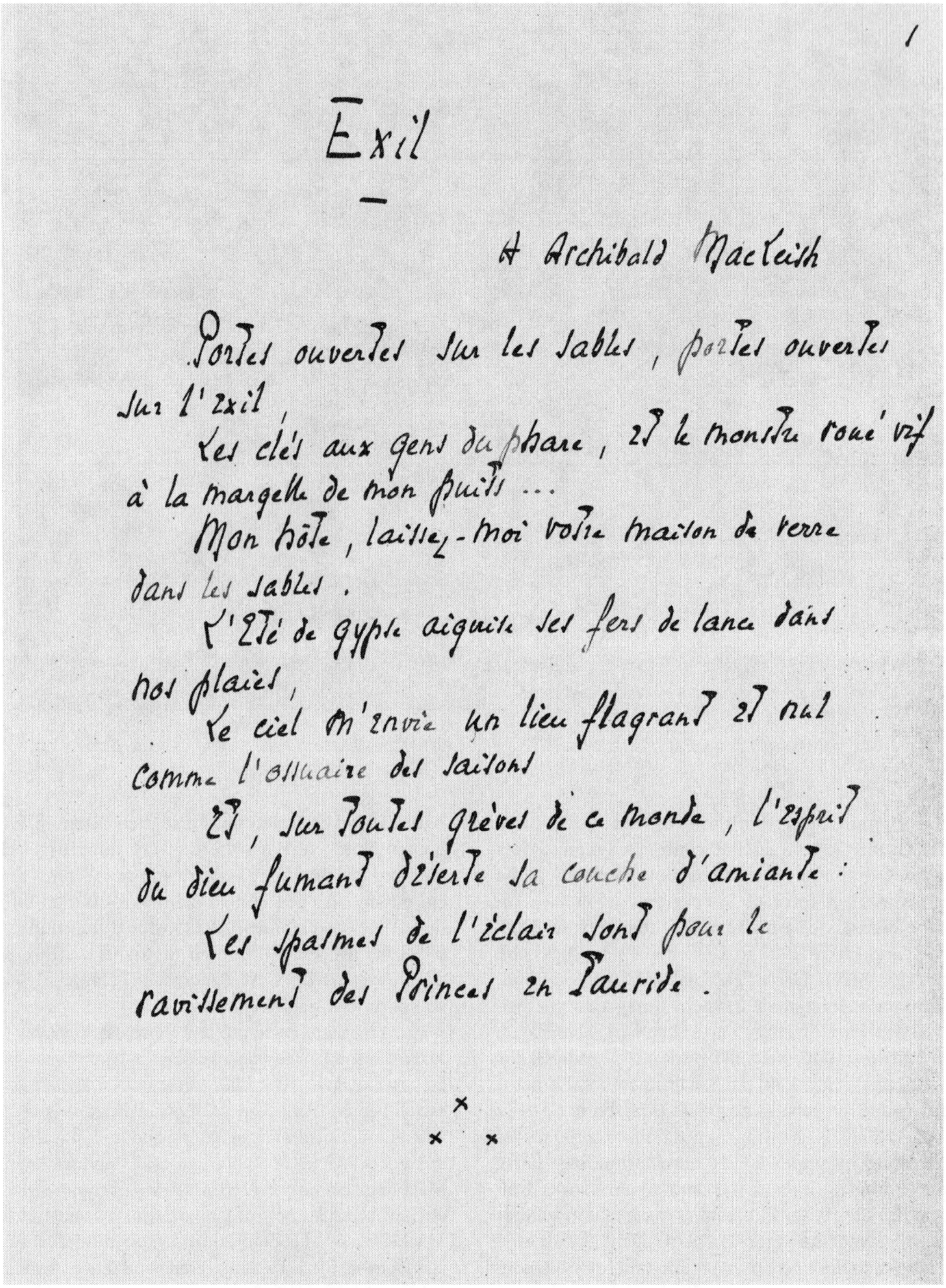

1

Exil

—

À Archibald MacLeish

Portes ouvertes sur les sables, portes ouvertes
sur l'exil,
    Les clés aux gens du phare, et le monstre roué vif
à la margelle de mon puits ...
    Mon hôte, laissez-moi votre maison de verre
dans les sables.
    L'Été de gypse aiguise ses fers de lance dans
nos plaies,
    Le ciel m'envie un lieu flagrant et nul
comme l'ossuaire des saisons
    Et, sur toutes grèves de ce monde, l'esprit
du dieu fumant déserte sa couche d'amiante :
    Les spasmes de l'éclair sont pour le
ravissement des Princes en Tauride.

×
× ×

*First page from the manuscript for the long poem Perse wrote in 1941, while he was living in New Jersey after
the German conquest of France (Fondation Saint-John Perse, Cité du Livre, Aix-en-Provence)*

reprinted in the May 1942 issue of *Cahiers du Sud* in Marseilles (which also published the poem as a limited edition, without Perse's corrections), and then published in the July 1942 issue of the Buenos Aires review *Les Lettres françaises;* the first authorized publication in book form, with Perse's corrections, was by Les Editions Lettres Françaises in 1942. *Poème à l'étrangère* (Poem to a Foreign Lady) was written in 1942, after Perse had moved to Washington D.C., and was first published in the Summer 1943 issue of the New York review *Hémisphères.* Perse wrote *Pluies* (Rains) during a 1943 visit to Savannah, Georgia, and *Neiges* (Snows) in New York the following year; the latter first appeared in the July 1944 issue of *Les Lettres françaises,* and the former was published in book form by Les Editions des Lettres Françaises in 1944. Later that year Les Editions des Lettres Françaises published a collective edition of these poems, *Quatre poèmes, 1941–1944* (Four Poems, 1941–1944), shortly thereafter published in France as *Exil, suivi de Poème à l'étrangère, Pluies, Neiges* (1945; translated as *Exile and Other Poems,* 1949).

Appointed "Ambassadeur en disponibilité" by the new French government in 1944, Perse found the practical demands of his diplomatic role presented no impediment to his continuing literary enterprise. In 1945 he composed the epic hymn *Vents* (translated as Winds, 1953), had it published by Gallimard the following year, and in 1946 signed a contract with the Bollingen Foundation for the production of his complete works in English translation. Nor is there any indication that Perse objected to his placement as the only living poet cited in Gide's *Anthologie de la poésie française* (Anthology of French Poetry, 1949).

For all the creative energy that it liberated, however, Perse's dramatically altered situation neither encouraged nor produced any notable shift in his spiritual perspective. Indications are that the remarkably high level of lyrical intensity sustained in his poetry from the 1940s owed its provenance as much to his perseverant holding to a philosophy of reasoned nonsense as it did to his faith in abiding change for the sake of vitality. The absurdist, mystical logic figured in the coincidence of light and shade in his first volume, *Eloges,* "Pour voir, se mettre à l'ombre. Sinon, rien" (To see, to place onself in shadow. If not that, nothing), and rehearsed in his 1924 collection, *Anabase,* "l'ombre et la lumière alors étai[en]t plus près d'être une même chose" (the shadow and the light then are very close to being the same thing), shows itself again in the 1941 poem, *Exil,* which reinscribes the world as an inscrutable text, "le monde" (the world) is like a "seule et longue phrase sans césure à jamais inintelligible" (single long phrase without pause always unintelligible), composed from a grammar that naturally signs itself doubly, like forked lightning: "Syntaxe de l'éclair! ô pur langage de l'exil" (Syntax of lightning! O pure language of exile). And the sense of enigma conveyed by the secular mystic "poète

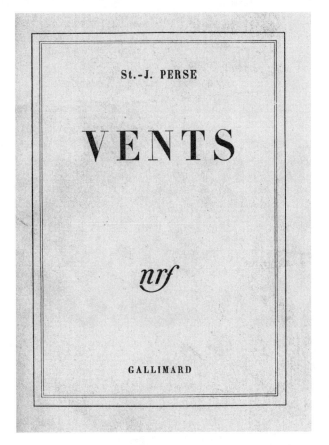

Cover for Perse's 1946 epic poem, a "hymne de force et de splendeur" (hymn of force and splendor) to the power of the wind (Perkins Library, Duke University)

bilingue" (bilingual poet) of the 1945 poem *Vents,* "homme parlant dans l'équivoque" (man speaking in ambiguity) and "lecteur de gazettes au soleil de minuit" (reader of newspapers under the midnight sun), substantially accords with the riddling spirit of *Pluies* (composed two years earlier)—"les pluies sont lourdes de l'énigme" (the rains are heavy with enigma)—as much as it does with the motif of wonder sung by the "ode du silence" (ode of silence), the 1944 poem *Neiges:* "l'abîme enfante ses merveilles!" (the abyss gives birth to marvels).

Perse's longest poem, *Amers* (1957; translated as *Seamarks,* 1958), is a homage to "la mer" (the sea). In this work Perse again further strikes his dominant note: "un grand poème hors de raison" (a great poem outside of reason), it stands as an "hommage à la diversité divine" (homage to the divine diversity), to the intimate alliance of contradictions, "les ombres lumineuses" (the luminous shadows) reflected in the mirror of sea in which, analogically figured in "l'Obscur" (the Obscure) that he reads in himself, Perse finds himself immersed: "Ô multiple et contraire! . . . Ô Mer plénière de l'alliance et de la mésentente!" (O many and contrary! . . . O plenary Sea of union and of strife!). *Amers* was published in a bilingual

Perse and his wife, Dorothy Milburn Russell Saint-Leger
Leger, in 1960 (photograph by Dalmas)

edition in the United States in 1958, the same year that Perse was married, in Washington, D.C., to Dorothy Russell (née Milburn).

The Persean praises of creation from *Eloges* to *Amers* harmonize together so closely as to seem but one composition. The comparatively slight body of poems he wrote for publication after *Amers–Chronique* (1959; translated, 1961), *L'Ordre des oiseaux* (The Order of Birds, 1962; translated as *Birds*, 1966), *Chanté par celle qui fut là* (1969; translated as *Sung By One Who was There*, 1970), and *Chant pour un équinoxe* (1975; translated as *Song for an Equinox,* 1977)—indicates Perse's abiding in the lively spirit of praise, high adventure, and nonsense he had embraced some half-century before.

What truth there was for Perse in the old Virgilian adage that *Audentis Fortuna iuvat* (Fortune favors the Bold) was additionally confirmed by the many honors and distinctions that came his way in the three remaining decades of his life after *Exil*. Salient items in the long record of those tributes include the special act of Congress admitting him to the status of "permanent resident in the United States" in 1949; the international "hommages à Saint-John Perse" in a special number of the *Cahiers de la Pléiade* (September–October 1950) and the first issue of the *Berkeley Review* (1956); the twice-repeated offer, first in 1946 and again in 1952, of the Charles Eliot Norton Chair of Poetry at Harvard University; the publication in Paris in 1953 of the first collected edition of his poems (suspended after publication of the first volume and resumed in 1959); the setting of *Anabase* to music, first by Alan Hovhannes in

1954, then by Karl-Birger Blomdahl in1955; the gift, in 1957, of a house on the Giens Peninsula from American friends and admirers; the conferring of honorary membership in the Modern Language Association (his election companioned with that of Eliot, Jorge Guillen, Albert Camus, and Jean-Paul Sartre); the conferring of an honorary doctorate from Yale, and the awarding of the French Grand Prix National des Lettres–all in 1959; the Nobel Prize in literature (1960); dinners in his honor at the White House, then in Marseilles, with Les Bibliophiles de Provence, in 1962; the display of Perse manuscripts mounted by France at the 1967 World Exposition in Montréal; and, most enduringly momentous for the enshrining of his name in French literature, the inclusion of *Œuvres Complètes: Saint-John Perse* in the prestigious series Bibliothèque de la Pléiade in 1972, some three years before his death on 20 September 1975. More tributes followed in the late 1970s, with a spate of books on his life and writing, consecrating him as one of the greatest poets of twentieth-century France.

Oddly enough, though, the main body of commentary devoted to the so-consecrated Perse has worked to diminish the sense of vitality and the youthful spirit of liberty that are basic to his writings. Readings of his work as a palimpsest bible from a latter-day Paraclete, a book of new commandments made for veneration, have naturally had an idolizing and consequently freezing effect on its reception. Such an altogether serious solemnifying of Perse may seem somewhat out of place, given the repeated indications of his affinity with "la liberté d'esprit" he found epitomized in the venturesome Conrad and "le cher Edward Lear" (dear Edward Lear), whom he described as "seul poète d'une race qui me semble la race même poétique" (a very embodiment of the species poet) to Gide in a 7 December 1912 letter. A letter written by Perse to one of his American admirers, Mina Curtiss, on 9 September 1958, almost a half-century later, lists Conrad and Lear among the main spirits "haunting" his new home on the Giens Peninsula. Appropriately enough, the mortal remains of Marie-René Alexis Saint-Leger Leger lie buried in "le petit cimetière marin" (the small marine cemetery for sailors) on that peninsula, just a short day's sail from Lear's resting place at San Remo and within sight of the spot where the adventurous old pagan hero and returned exile of Conrad's last completed novel, *The Rover* (1923), met his death at sea.

Letters:

Letters: St.-John Perse, translated and edited by Arthur J. Knodel, Bollingen Series, no. 87 (Princeton: Princeton University Press, 1979);

Perse and Rosalía Sánchez Abreu, *Lettres à l'étrangère,* edited by Mauricette Berne (Paris: Gallimard, 1987);

Correspondance Saint-John Perse–Jean Paulhan: 1925–1966,
 edited, with an introduction and notes, by Joëlle
 Gardes-Tamine, Cahiers Saint-John Perse, no. 10
 (Paris: Gallimard, 1991);

*Alexis Léger, Dag Hammarskjöld–Correspondance: 1955–
1961,* edited, with an introduction, by Marie-
 Noëlle Little, Cahiers Saint-John Perse, no. 11
 (Paris: Gallimard, 1993);

Lettres d'Alexis Léger à Gabriel Frizeau: 1906–1912, edited,
 with an introduction and notes, by Albert Henry
 (Brussels: Académie Royale de Belgique, 1993);

Correspondance 1942–1945: Roger Caillois, Saint-John Perse,
 edited, with an introduction, by Gardes-Tamine,
 Cahiers Saint-John Perse, no. 13 (Paris: Gallimard, 1996);

*Courrier d'exil: Saint-John Perse et ses amis américains, 1940–
1970,* edited and translated, with an introduction,
 by Carol Rigolot, Cahiers Saint-John Perse, no.
 15 (Paris: Gallimard, 2001).

Bibliographies:

Ruth S. Freitag, "Saint-John Perse: A List of His Writings in the Collections of the Library of Congress," in Pierre Emmanuel's *Saint-John Perse:
 Praise and Presence* (Washington, D.C.: Library of
 Congress, 1971), pp. 25–80;

Roger Little, *Saint-John Perse: A Bibliography for Students of
 His Poetry* (London: Grant & Cutler, 1971);

"Bibliographie sélective," in *Œuvres Complètes: Saint-John
 Perse,* Bibliothèque de La Pléiade, no. 240 (Paris:
 Gallimard, 1972), pp. 1347–1392;

René Galand, "Saint-John Perse," in *A Critical Bibliogra-
 phy of French Literature,* edited by Richard A.
 Brooks, volume 6, *The Twentieth Century,* edited by
 Douglas W. Alden and Brooks, part 2, *Principally
 Poetry, Theater, and Criticism before 1940, and Essay*
 (Syracuse, N.Y.: Syracuse University Press, 1980),
 pp. 1024–1059.

References:

Marcelle Achard-Abell, "Heidegger et la poèsie de
 Saint-John Perse: Un rapprochement," *Revue de
 métaphysique et de morale,* 71 (July–September
 1966);

Roger Caillois, *Poétique de Saint-John Perse* (Paris: Gallimard, 1954);

Mechthild Cranston, *Enfance mon amour: La Rêverie vers
 l'enfance dans l'œuvre de Guillaume Apollinaire,*

Saint-John Perse et René Char (Paris: Debresse,
 1970);

Christian Doumet, *Les Thèmes aériens dans l'oeuvre de
 Saint-John Perse* (Paris: Minard, 1976);

Yves-Alain Favre, *Saint-John Perse: Le Langage et le sacré*
 (Paris: José Corti, 1977);

Wallace Fowlie, "The Poetics of Saint-John Perse,"
 Poetry (Chicago), 82 (September 1953);

René Galand, *Saint-John Perse* (New York: Twayne,
 1972);

Roger Garaudy, *D'un réalisme sans rivages: Picasso,
 Saint-John Perse, Kafka* (Paris: Plon, 1963);

Pierre Guerre, *S.-J. Perse et l'homme* (Paris: Gallimard,
 1955);

Albert Henry, *"Amers" de Saint-John Perse: Une Poésie de
 mouvement* (Neuchâtel, Switzerland: Editions de La
 Baconnière, 1963);

Honneur à Saint-John Perse (Paris: Gallimard, 1965);

Arthur J. Knodel, *Saint-John Perse: A Study of His Poetry*
 (Edinburgh: Edinburgh University Press, 1966);

Camille R. La Bossière, "The Monumental Nonsense
 of Saint-John Perse," *Folio,* 18 (February 1990);

Henriette Levillain, *Le Rituel poétique de Saint-John Perse*
 (Paris: Gallimard, 1977);

Roger Little, *Etudes sur Saint-John Perse* (Paris: Klincksieck, 1984);

Little, *Saint-John Perse* (London: Athlone, 1973);

Little, "Saint-John Perse, poète anglais," *Revue de Littérature Comparée,* 46 (1972);

Archibald MacLeish, "The Living Spring," *Saturday
 Review,* 32 (16 July 1949), pp. 8–9;

Charles Moeller, *L'Homme moderne devant le salut: Sartre,
 T. S. Eliot, Kafka, Saint John / Perse, Claudel, Péguy*
 (Paris: Editions Ouvrières, 1965);

C. E. Nelson, "Saint-John Perse and T. S. Eliot," *Western Humanities Review,* 17 (Spring 1963);

Erika Ostrovsky, *Under the Sign of Ambiguity: Saint-John
 Perse/Alexis Leger* (New York: New York University Press, 1985);

Georges Poulet, "Saint-John Perse," in his *Etudes sur le
 temps humain* (Paris: Plon, 1964), pp. 160–186;

Kathleen Raine, "St. John Perse: Poet of the Marvellous," in her *Defending Ancient Springs* (London:
 Oxford University Press, 1968), pp. 176–192;

Jorge Zalamea, *La Poesía ignorada y olvidada* (Bogota: Ediciones de la Nueva Prensa, 1965).

Jacques Prévert

(4 February 1900 – 11 April 1977)

Malcolm McGoldrick
University of Regina

SELECTED BOOKS: *La Crosse en l'air, feuilleton* (Paris: Editions Soutes, 1937);

Paroles (Paris: Editions du Point du Jour, 1945; revised and enlarged, 1947);

Histoires, by Prévert and André Verdet (Paris: Le Pré aux Clercs, 1946); enlarged as *Histoires et d'Autres histoires* (Paris: Gallimard, 1963);

Contes pour enfants pas sages, illustrated by Elsa Henriquez (Paris: Editions du Pré-aux-Cleres, 1947);

Spectacle (Paris: Gallimard, 1951);

Grand bal du printemps (Lausanne, Switzerland: La Guilde du Livre, 1951);

Lumières d'homme (Paris: Editions G.L.M., 1955);

La Pluie et le beau temps (Paris: Gallimard, 1955);

Images, preface by René Bertelé (Paris: Maeght, 1957);

Fatras (Paris: Gallimard, 1966);

Arbres (Paris: Editions de la Galerie d'Orsay, 1967; republished, with illustrations by Georges Ribemont-Dessaignes, Paris: Gallimard, 1976);

Choses et autres (Paris: Gallimard, 1972);

Hebdromadaires, by Prévert and André Pozner (La Chapelle-sur-Loire: Guy Authier, 1972; revised and enlarged edition, Paris: Gallimard, 1982);

Soleil de nuit (Paris: Gallimard, 1980);

La Cinquième saison, edited by Arnaud Laster and Danièle Gasiglia-Laster (Paris: Gallimard, 1984);

Œuvres complètes, 2 volumes, edited by Laster and Gasiglia-Laster, Bibliothèque de la Pléiade, nos. 388 and 427 (Paris: Gallimard, 1992, 1996).

Collection: *Anthologie Prèvert,* edited by Christiane Mortelier (London: Methuen Educational, 1981);

Edition in English: *Selections from Paroles by Jacques Prévert,* edited and translated by Lawrence Ferlinghetti (San Francisco: City Lights Books, 1968).

PRODUCED SCRIPTS: *Souvenirs de Paris ou Paris-Express,* motion picture, 1928;

L'Affaire est dans le sac, motion picture, Pathé-Cinéma, 1932;

Ciboulette, motion picture, Cipar-Films, 1933;

Jacques Prévert (photograph by Ilse Bing)

Le Crime de Monsieur Lange, motion picture, by Prévert and Jean Renoir, Films Obéron, 1935;

Jenny, motion picture, by Prévert and Jacques Constant, dialogue by Prévert, Réalisations d'Art Cinématographique, 1936;

Drôle de Drame, motion picture, Productions Corniglion-Molinier, 1937;

Quai des Brumes, motion picture, Ciné-Alliance, 1938;

Le Jour se lève, motion picture, by Jacques Viot, adapted by Prévert, dialogue by Prévert, Sigma, 1939;

Remorques, motion picture, by Prévert, Roger Vercel, Charles Spaak, dialogue by Prévert, MAIC, 1939–1941;

Les Visiteurs du Soir, motion picture, by Prévert and Pierre Laroche, dialogue by Prévert, André Paulvé, 1942;

Adieu Léonard, motion picture, by Jacques Prévert and Pierre Prévert, dialogue by Jacques Prévert, Essor Cinématographique français, 1943;

Les Enfants du Paradis, motion picture, Pathé-Cinéma, 1943–1945;

Aubervilliers, motion picture, commentary and lyrics by Prévert, Ciné-France, 1945;

Les Portes de la nuit, motion picture, adapted by Prévert from the ballet *Le Rendez-vous* by Prévert, Joseph Kosma, and Roland Petit, dialogue by Prévert, songs by Kosma and Prévert, Pathé-Cinéma, 1946.

Jacques Prévert exemplified the twentieth-century "popular" poet. His work expressed the joys and frustrations of the average man contending with the forces of oppression that seek to overwhelm him. His poetry often takes the form of a scathing attack on organized religion, complacency, lies, social injustice, false ideologies, and war. Colored by the interwar years and their aftermath, Prévert denounced the totalitarianism of Francisco Franco, Benito Mussolini, Adolf Hitler, and what he saw as their henchmen—the intellectual and right-wing establishment of the Third and Fourth Republics, the Pope and the Catholic Church, and all those who would seek to prevent the man in the street from achieving personal fulfillment. His is a vitriolic attack against the cynical, hypocritical, jingoistic, nationalist, capitalist, conformist, militarist society in which he lived, but his negativism is tempered by his defense of the downtrodden and oppressed, often represented by children, animals, and birds.

Because Prévert champions the cause of the common man, the language of his poetry most typically rests on an oral and nonliterary tradition, expressive in its very simplicity of the language and culture of the masses. He uses wit and irony, as well as neologisms and spoonerisms, to create poetry that is sometimes marked by black humor but that also possesses a musical and incantatory value, which was underscored when it was set to music by Joseph Kosma and sung in renditions by such performers as Yves Montand, Marianne Oswald, and Juliette Gréco. Prévert's poetry earned him wide renown. *Paroles* (Words, 1945) attests to the power of his image-making, already evidenced by his success as a writer of screenplays and director of experimental movies. Cinematographic techniques account in no small measure for the visual impact of his poetry, while the black humor found in his work derives from his ties with Surrealism.

Another sign of the influence of Surrealism is Prévert's interest in the associations and implications of words, not just their literal significance. And yet, his writings also show the power of language as an instrument of its own destruction. The triteness of a cliché is expressed through satire. The quality of people's lives is revealed through the way they talk. So too, his disjointed and disconnected word lists have antecedents among the Surrealists. Finally, Surrealism left another, more indelible mark on Prévert, one that he deftly communicates to the reader through children and those richly endowed with imagination—the sense of magic imparted through language, glimpses of the extraordinary perceived through and beyond the ordinary phenomena of creation.

Jacques-Henri-Marie Prévert was born at Neuilly-sur-Seine on 4 February 1900, the second of three sons. Jean, the eldest, died in 1915 of typhoid fever at the age of seventeen, and Pierre, the youngest, later became a renowned motion-picture director. Pierre remained close to Jacques throughout their lives. The parents, André and Suzanne Prévert, lived in straitened circumstances but lavished affection upon their children. André Prévert found work with a charitable organization that provided help for the needy, and he would take Jacques with him on his rounds, awakening in him a love of city streets and a sympathy for the underprivileged.

Prévert was unhappy in school, left early, and was called up for military service in 1920. While in Lunéville he met Yves Tanguy, the future Surrealist painter, and shortly after, as an infantry corporal in Constantinople, Prévert met Marcel Duhamel, a translator of American detective novels. From 1924 on, the three of them lived at 54 rue du Château in Montparnasse in an old house, rented by Duhamel, which became a venue for Surrealist painters and poets, including André Breton. All three were enthralled by the early cinema, the era of the silent movie. Jacques developed an interest in scriptwriting, which led to a documentary titled *Souvenirs de Paris ou Paris-Express* (Recollections of Paris or Paris-Express). On 30 April 1925 Prévert married Simone Dienne; the marriage was later dissolved.

Differences of opinion led to a parting of the ways in 1928 with Breton, the founder and theorist of the Surrealist movement. It is uncertain whether Prévert was excluded from the group or left it voluntarily, but he did begin his satirical writing in 1930 with "Mort d'un monsieur" (Death of a Gentleman), a contribution to the anti-Breton pamphlet *Un cadavre* (A Corpse). He did not entirely sever his ties with Surrealism, however, and remained on cordial terms with the group.

(Comfortably installed on his cloud ship, God the Father, of the firm God father son Holy Ghost, Inc., heaves a huge sigh of contentment, two or three junior little clouds immediately burst forth with obsequiousness and God the Father exclaims: "Praised be me, blessed be my holy corporate name, my beloved son has the cross, my firm is launched!")

As befits his vacuous calling, the first person of the Trinity is punningly depicted as being installed not on his "vaisseau amiral," or flagship, but on his "nuage amiral" (cloud ship). There is also, in French, an equivocal pun on "Dieu le père" (God the Father) and "Dieu père," which means "God senior"—the senior partner in a business. The "cross" referred to may also be construed as the cross of the Légion d'Honneur or the croix de guerre, rather than the sacred cross of Calvary, and the participle "lancée" evokes the noun "lance," an allusion to the spear that pierced Jesus' side in the Johannine account of the Crucifixion. The trivializing of Christianity and its dogma is a constant in Prévert's work.

"Tentative de description d'un dîner de têtes à Paris-France" describes a fancy-dress banquet attended by the callous bourgeois whom Prévert hated. The poem begins characteristically with the itemizing of the people targeted by his satire. The thirty-three-line anaphora allows Prévert to vent his antireligious, antipatriotic, antibourgeois, and antimilitaristic fury. The costume party is interrupted by the arrival of an interloper, who bursts upon the scene. He has crashed the party in order to exhort the leisured class to see how the proletariat live in the slums, hinting at the coming revolution. The guests are dismayed, feel threatened, and someone throws a pitcher at him, which strikes him in the forehead. The interloper is carried away on a stretcher and dies. The rambling poem ends as it begins, with an inventory. But this time, in a poignant recitation of the martyrdom of the masses, for whom the interloper stands as a kind of secular Messiah, actual occupations are listed. Reproduced in the later collection *Paroles,* the two poems are the mainstay of the themes that appear in that and later collections.

Prévert's social commitment came to the fore again in the 1930s, bolstered by the economic crisis, which solidified his ties to the proletariat. From 1932 to 1936, he belonged to le Groupe Octobre, a theater troupe sponsored by the Fédération du Théâtre Ouvrier Français. Taking its name from the Russian Revolution of 1917, the group was clearly communist in allegiance; it played before Moscow audiences in 1933, performing sketches, protest songs, ballads, pantomimes, a farcical play *La Bataille de Fontenoy* (The Battle of Fontenoy), and a *chœur parlé* (spoken chorus) by Prévert, "Citroën." In 1936 he published another poem

Prévert in a bistro, 1930 (photograph by Roger-Viollet)

From the 1930s onward, Prévert's activities expanded to include cinema, poetry, song, and collective theater. His satirical poem "Souvenirs de famille ou l'ange garde-chiourme" (Family Recollections or the Guardian Angel) was published in the journal *Bifur* in December 1930, followed in the quarterly pamphlet *Commerce* by a long, satirical piece of invective called "Tentative de description d'un dîner de têtes à Paris-France" (An Attempt to Describe a Dinner of Heads at Paris-France). "Souvenirs de famille" is a vitriolic satire that portrays Christianity in an unfavorable light. God is depicted in worldly terms, as a company boss:

Confortablement installé sur son nuage amiral, Dieu le père, de la maison Dieu père fils Saint-Esprit et Cie, pousse un immense soupir de satisfaction, aussitôt deux ou trois petits nuages subalternes éclatent avec obséquiosité et Dieu père s'écrie: 'Que je sois loué, que ma sainte raison sociale soit bénie, mon fils bien aimé a la croix, ma maison est lancée!'"

that later appeared in *Paroles*, "Le temps des noyaux" (Cherry Stone Time). The title of the poem, which first appeared in *Soutes* in February, is derived from the expression "le temps des cerises" (cherry time), a popular, nostalgic, pre–World War I song celebrating the brevity of youth and the carefree quality of love. Prévert coined the term "le temps des noyaux" to intimate that the stone, or pit, would be all that would remain once the fruit of the cherry had been consumed. It is a vitriolic, antimilitaristic piece aimed at the old generation of men, who willingly sacrificed their sons in the sacred cause of war. Prévert warns that a new generation is coming of age that will no longer brook unquestioning sacrifice.

In October 1936, the first part of "La Crosse en l'air" (The Crozier in the Air) appeared in *Soutes*. The poem was published in its entirety as a small book in 1937. Unlike Prévert's previous endeavors, which expressed strongly held feelings impersonally, the poem is a ferocious, personal attack on Pope Pius XI. It opens with the spectacle of a drunken bishop:

Rassurez-vous braves gens
ce n'est pas un appel à la révolte
c'est un évêque qui est saoul et qui met sa crosse en l'air.

(Don't worry good people
this isn't a call to revolt
it's a bishop who's drunk and who's putting his crozier in the air).

As well as designating the bishop's crook, or crozier, "la crosse" is also the butt of a rifle, and the idiom "mettre la crosse en l'air" means "to mutiny," or "to refuse to bear arms." The bishop staggers along the rue de Rome, in Paris, then rolls in the gutter, where he vomits. His miter, which, along with his crozier, is the symbol of his episcopal office, falls from his head and is retrieved by a dog who makes off with it and proceeds to a large gathering of fellow canines, where he satirizes the clergy. At this point a night watchman, who, like the gate-crasher in "Tentative de description," is a spokesman for the working class, stirs from his sleep after dreaming about Rome, and repeats a line from Pierre Corneille's *Horace* (1641) that sums up his feelings about the Eternal City: "Rome l'unique objet de mon ressentiment" (Rome the single subject of my resentment). He then sets off for the Vatican to berate the Pope. Then the Pope appears at the balcony:

sérieux comme un pape
paraît le pape
entouré de ses sous-papes

(As sober as a judge
appears the Pope
surrounded by his Vice-Popes).

"Sérieux comme un pape"–literally "As serious as a pope"–is an idiom used first figuratively, then literally in the line that follows, in reference to Pius XI. Prévert also makes jocular use of the homophonous "sous- papes" (Vice-Popes) and "soupapes" (valves), linking animate and inanimate entities. A similar use of alliteration occurs a few lines later. The Pope's father is with him in the Vatican, smoking a pipe, which detail leads to the punch line: "la pipe au papa du pape Pie pue" (the pipe of the papa of Pope Pius pongs). The drunken bishop arrives on the scene: "mais tous les ruisseaux mènent à Rome / et voilà l'évêque qui surgit en agitant sa crosse" (but all streams lead to Rome / and lo and behold the bishop appears from nowhere, waving his crozier). The expression "tous les chemins mènent à Rome" (all roads lead to Rome) is also associated with the watchman's journey to Rome. In the case of the bishop, however, mention of "ruisseaux" (streams, but also meaning gutters) conjures up the image of the man's heaving in the gutter and of its unsavory detritus, flowing by association all the way to the See of Rome. The Pope rebukes the bishop for his inebriation, to which the bishop replies: "Dans tous les cas si je suis saoul c'est pas avec ce que tu m'as payé . . . tout pape que tu es . . . " (In any case, if I'm drunk, it's not with what you paid me . . . Pope though you may be . . .). This remark is all the more outrageous because of its *tutoiement* (use of the familiar "tu" instead of "vous").

The diminished stature of the Pope resulting from the lack of deference on the part of the bishop is further eroded as the Pope endures a litany of further terms of abuse and has his infallibility called into question by the bishop. The scene then gives way to a kind of newsreel in which the Pope is further described in abusive terms,

cette grande tête avec toutes les marques
de la déformation professionnelle
la dignité l'onction l'extrême onction la cruauté la
roublardise la papelardise
et tous ces simulacres
toutes ces mornes et sérieuses pitreries
toutes ces vaticaneries . . . ces fétiches . . . ces gris-gris . . .
ce luxe . . .

(this big head with all the signs
of job conditioning
dignity unction Extreme Unction cruelty
craftiness suaveness
and all these pretenses
all this dreary and solemn clowning around
all these Vaticaneries . . . these fetishes . . . these charms
this luxury . . .)

By this stage the reader is uncertain whether these remarks are authorial ones or are to be attributed to the bishop or the newsreel. The stream of invective is a constant one, and the satire of the appurtenances and

Cover by Brassaï for Prévert's 1945 collection of poetry (from Yves Courrière, Jacques Prévert en vérité, *2000)*

the language of the Pope is at its most biting. "Papelardise," which is incidentally jocular but etymologically unrelated to the papacy, is twinned by the rhyming suffix "ise" with the derogatory "roublardise," and "pitreries," in turn rhymes with the nonce word "vaticaneries." The listing of nouns conjoined by adjectival pronouns has the effect of linking Catholicism to superstitious objects such as fetishes and magic charms, likening it to African witchcraft or voodoo.

The footage of the Pope concludes and the newsreel continues with coverage of the bombing of an Abyssinian village by the Italian military, which allows Prévert to satirize the delight of Italian Catholics in the barbarity of the war waged by the Fascist dictator Mussolini against Ethiopia and its negus, Haile Selassie. The night watchman gains entrance to the Vatican, knocks over Premier Pierre Laval (who, together with the British government, was prepared to settle the Ethiopian dispute by ceding a large part of that country to Italy), engages in conversation in an antechamber with Mussolini, then appears before the Pope. The watchman is present as the Pope meets a delegation of prelates of the Catholic Church of Spain who had been burned to

death by the Popular Front and who now appear before the Sovereign Pontiff in a resurrected state. They relate the atrocities they suffered at the hands of the barbarians. At the stroke of noon a rumbling of the prelates' stomachs sends them scurrying to the great banquet hall. In keeping with the Surrealistic tenor of the passage, Prévert has them relate:

il y avait des fruits sauvages
nous les avons apprivoisés . . . baptisés
et puis nous les avons mangés

(there were some wild fruits
we tamed . . . we baptised them
and then we ate them)

The passage occurs immediately after details of the atrocious death by crucifixion suffered by these prelates, followed by their resurrection, interpreted in the most optimistic light, as the work of "Dieu qui fait bien ce qu'il fait" (God who does well what he does), which attitude recalls the sanguine disposition of Voltaire's Candide. The pun on "sauvage" leads ironically, and absurdly, to the fruits being tamed and baptized to eat, hinting once again at a linkage between Christian rites and sacraments and the pagan practices exemplified here by cannibalism.

Following the departure of the prelates, the Pope believes himself to be alone. Prévert itemizes the things the Pope does to while away the time, which do not reflect highly on the dignity of his office; then the Pope becomes aware of the watchman's presence and asks "Quel bon vent vous amène mon ami?" (What good wind brings you, my friend?). The watchman takes all of thirteen lines before answering: "Je suis venu à pied le vent était mauvais" (I came on foot, the wind was bad). Taking the Pope's question with a naive and paralyzing literalism, he alludes in his reply to the stench of the Vatican. He proceeds to berate the Pope at length as an absurd anomaly. The Pope eventually goes into convulsions, rolls on the floor, and gets up screaming. Prévert diagnoses his ailment as follows: "il a reçu un éclat de rire dans l'oeil" (he received a splinter of laughter in his eye).

The watchman leaves the Vatican and is approached by an alley cat that leads him to a wounded bird that has fallen from the sky. The bird's song was so beautiful that the cat had resisted the temptation to eat it. The symbolism of the bird becomes apparent at the end of the poem. The bird's injuries were inflicted by the depredations incurred in Fascist Italy with its reactionary Pope and in the midst of the Spanish Civil War. The bird recounts its meeting with a pretty girl of spring, depicted as bellicose as well as bucolic. She wears on her shoulder a bright red flower, representing the cause of freedom and revolution in Spain, and she also holds dynamite in her hand. The poem ends on an allegorical note: the night watchman sets off with the delirious bird in the hollow of his hand, while the alley cat holds his lantern, lighting the way for them.

In the 1930s Prévert began making a name for himself in cinema: he wrote the script and dialogue for *L'Affaire est dans le sac* in 1932; *Le Crime de Monsieur Lange* (with Jean Renoir) in 1935; *Drôle de Drame* in 1937; *Quai des Brumes* in 1938; and *Les Enfants du Paradis* between 1943 and 1945. He also wrote the dialogue to *Le Jour se lève* in 1939, and the script (with Pierre Laroche) to *Les Visiteurs du Soir* in 1942. *L'Affaire est dans le sac* was directed by Pierre Prévert, *Le Crime de Monsieur Lange* by Renoir, and the other motion pictures by Marcel Carné.

The first edition of *Paroles* consolidated the reputation Prévert had acquired through his work in cinema and theater and through the adaptation of his poems to music, which included many poems compiled in *Paroles* itself. Seventy-nine poems appeared in the collection published in 1945, a number increased to ninety-five in the definitive edition. Many of the poems had circulated orally and were familiar to Parisians. Prévert's collection depicts authority in all its perversity, as it destroys the individual. The most insidious examples of the abuse of power are to be found in the nation state, government, army, church, school, and the family. Children are coerced and constrained by teachers and parents. The poem "Page d'écriture" (Notebook Page) attests to the power of the child's imagination when faced with the stultifying discipline of rote learning. A schoolmaster imposes the learning and repeating of addition tables upon his class. A lyrebird distracts the attention of a child, who pleads with it to come and play. It does so and gains the attention of the whole class, sparking the collective imagination. The resulting hubbub drowns out the schoolmaster's call for order, and anarchy results. All the objects associated with school revert to their original substance:

> . . . les murs de la classe
> s'écroulent tranquillement.
> Et les vitres redeviennent sable
> l'encre redevient eau
> les pupitres redeviennent arbres
> la craie redevient falaise
> le porte-plume redevient oiseau.
>
> (. . . the walls of the classroom
> quietly collapse.
> And the windows become sand again
> ink becomes water
> desks become trees
> chalk becomes cliff
> the pen-holder becomes a bird).

Through the help of a bird–the symbol of freedom–the children, who are referred to only as "enfants," never as "écoliers" (pupils), while their teacher is mentioned only by the language of his professional calling as "maître"(master) and "professeur" (teacher), are freed from the tyranny of school as the institution is magically transformed into images of sand, water, tree, cliff, and bird. The synergy of the bird's freedom and the child's imagination results in liberation from the confinement of the classroom. In five other poems of *Paroles:* "Les oiseaux du souci" (Birds of Care), "Chanson de l'oiseleur" (Song of the Bird-Catcher), "Pour faire le portrait d'un oiseau" (To Paint the Portrait of a Bird), "Quartier libre" (Free Sector), and "Au hasard des oiseaux" (Birds as I Find Them), the bird is also used as symbol.

Prévert sides with another victim of the school system in "Le cancre" (The Dunce), who says no with his head to the schoolmaster and yes with his heart to what he likes. While being grilled by the schoolmaster, he succumbs to an attack of uncontrollable laughter, erases everything on the blackboard, and with chalks of every color "sur le tableau noir du malheur / il dessine le visage du bonheur" (on the blackboard of unhappiness / he draws the face of happiness).

"La chasse à l'enfant" (The Hunt for the Child), set to music by Kosma and sung by Oswald as a protest song, recounts the search for a child who is on the loose from a reformatory. When he protested that he had had enough, the wardens broke his teeth with their keys. The boy flees and is hunted down like an animal by a righteously indignant mob.

"Familiale" (Family Life) shows Prévert's criticism of the robotic nature of people's lives, against which they do not rebel. It tells of a mother who knits, a father who conducts business, and a son who goes to war and loses his life. The poem is a bitter comment on the couple's placid acceptance of their loss as being in the natural order of things, and on the morality of a society that sends its young to war. The internal rhyme that links the words mère / guerre / père / affaires / cimetière (mother / war / father / business / cemetery) is made into a maddening refrain that is a disturbing comment on the mechanistic acceptance of a status quo that has destroyed the family unit.

"La lessive" (The Wash) depicts a horrific act of revenge. A girl, who is going to have an illegitimate child, is put into the family washtub and pummeled as though she were washing. In a ritual cleansing meant to remove the "tache" (stain) that has sullied them, the whole family plunges the girl beneath the waters of the tub. She is trampled on and dies by drowning. There is an ironic play on words between the reference to the father of the unborn child, whom the

Prévert, his wife, Janine, and their daughter, Michèle, at Saint-Paul-de-Vence, Provence, 1950 (photograph by Izis)

daughter has refused to divulge, and the Holy Father, the first of the vertices of the Trinity, who is invoked in a collective plea that, through this settling of accounts *en famille,* the family honor remain intact: "on ne connaît pas le nom du père / au nom du père et du fils / au nom du . . . Saint-Esprit / Que tout ceci ne sorte pas d'ici . . ." (We don't know the name of the father / in the name of the father and of the son / in the name of the . . . Holy Ghost / Let none of this get beyond these four walls . . .). The proverb "il faut laver son linge sale en famille" (don't wash your dirty linen in public), would normally be understood figuratively. Here it is invoked to justify the revenge wrought by this family. The exhortation: "il ne faut pas que le nouveau-né / sorte d'ici" (the newborn must

not / get out of here) is also acted upon with a murderous literalism. The poem ends with the father returning to his office with feet red with blood, but wearing well-polished shoes, in illustration of the closing line of the poem: "Il vaut mieux faire envie que pitié" (It's better to be envied than pitied).

Another poem, "L'orgue de Barbarie" (The Barrel Organ), hints that violence is acquired and passed on in a self-perpetuating cycle by children who imitate the example of their elders. Against the backdrop of cruelty and depravity, Prévert depicts with tenderness people who persevere against all odds. His sympathies are extended to those who are the victims of war and conflict. "Barbara," which, like "La chasse à l'enfant," was set to music by Kosma, is a case in point. The poem comprises a series of reminiscences based upon a fleeting smile exchanged between the author and a girl, drenched with rain, who was walking in the street. A man sheltering from the rain called out her name, "Barbara," and she ran and threw herself into his arms. Prévert speculates about this couple whose happiness was probably curtailed by war, which is denounced in the only didactic line of the poem: "Quelle connerie la guerre" (what a bloody waste war is). The rain beneath which Barbara appeared "souriante / Epanouie ravie ruisselante" (smiling / Radiant joyful streaming wet) is turned by war into ". . . cette pluie de fer / De feu d'acier de sang" (. . . this downpour of iron / of fire of steel of blood), and after the destruction of Brest "c'est une pluie de deuil terrible et désolée" (it's a terrible desolate rain of bereavement).

The poem is an apostrophe to the eponymous Barbara, whose name, together with the accusative form of the second person "tu" are dotted through the poem as a lyric refrain, disappearing toward the end because of the vicissitudes of time. The transitoriness of the encounter is cherished and invested with a poignant lyricism. Ironically, Barbara—a stranger with whom Prévert exchanged nothing more than a smile—is the only woman in *Paroles* who is given a name.

Love is a dominant leitmotif of *Paroles,* portrayed as erotic passion and longing in poems such as "Dans ma maison" (Into My House), "La rue de Buci maintenant" (Buci Street Now), "Alicante," "Paris at night," and "Le Jardin" (The Garden). Sometimes the relationship between a couple is a disharmonious one. "Rue de Seine" (Seine Street) is, again, a poem with a street setting. At ten thirty one night, a woman harries an evasive partner to be truthful in revealing something that he has chosen to hide from her. Pierre squirms with guilt in the face of her onslaught, but, although trapped, he continues to writhe with a contorted smile. The poem depicts the inadequacy of language as a vehicle for communication within a dysfunctional relationship.

Another poem whose subject is the breakdown of communication between the sexes is "Déjeuner du matin" (Morning Breakfast). The poem depicts a breakfast table scene that portrays a man absorbed in the minutiae of putting coffee in his cup, followed by cream, then sugar, stirring it with the little spoon, and carrying out, in all, thirteen gestures that, after the smoking of a cigarette, conclude with putting his hat on his head, putting on his raincoat, and leaving. It is only when the reader reaches the eleventh line of the poem that he or she becomes aware of the presence of a second person, who relates the story, and who is ignored by the man. At this point one should realize that this persona is not a detached observer, but someone—probably a woman—with close ties to the man, who is treated by him as an object. She becomes the subject of the last three lines of the poem:

> Et moi j'ai pris
> Ma tête dans ma main
> Et j'ai pleuré.
>
> (And I put
> My head in my hand
> And I cried).

The poem is marked by economy of words, which suggest the highly charged emotional undercurrent of this breakfast table scene but concentrate exclusively on gestures. It possesses the character of a cinema "take." Its dramatic effect is assured by its ending, which catches the reader by surprise. The anonymity of the couple gives representative value to the drama that unfolds, for they could be any couple. The paucity of explanatory detail heightens the dramatic effect and obliges the reader to reinterpret the robotic gestures of the man in the light of the woman's reaction. In this poem, as in "Rue de Seine" and many others, Prévert places the reader *in medias res,* in the continuum of an unfolding drama whose origin and outcome are unknown. "Le Message" (The Message) also imparts an aura of mystery and suspense, and is subtly suggestive.

Many of the poems of *Paroles* were set to music by the composer Kosma, with whom Prévert shared a lifelong collaboration, which had begun in 1933. "Familiale," "La chasse à l'enfant," "L'orgue de Barbarie," "La pêche à la baleine" (The Whale Hunt), were among the songs included in the repertoire of such performers as Oswald and Agnès Capri in the 1930s. Gréco later immortalized "Barbara" and "Les Feuilles mortes" (Dead Leaves), which was originally written for Marlene Dietrich, but was also sung by Edith Piaf and became the theme music to Robert Aldrich's motion picture *Autumn Leaves.* Montand popularized "Sables mouvants" (Moving Sands), which is a love song from the movie *Les Visiteurs du Soir.* Many of his humorous songs were recorded by the group Frères Jacques. Later, Joan Baez popularized "Chanson dans le sang" (Song in the Blood), on her record album *Baptism. A Journey Through Our Time* (1968).

In April 1946 the poetry collection *Histoires* (Stories) appeared. It did not have the same success as *Paroles* had had the previous December, and it has been considerably less anthologized than *Paroles.* But it does include many of Prévert's customary themes. Contempt for the establishment is expressed in "Les clefs de la ville" (The Keys to the City) and for the Shah of Iran in "Voyage en Perse" (Journey to Persia). In "Baptême de l'air" (First Flight) Prévert decries the changing of street names to honor dead heroes, using as his example *la rue du Luxembourg* (Luxembourg Street), which was altered to *la rue Guynemer,* in honor of the World War I ace Georges-Marie Guynemer, and questions whether the Jardin du Luxembourg (Luxembourg Garden), with its trees, birds, and children, is better served by the name of a dead aviator. In "Harlem" he criticizes the insensitivity of whites toward a black shoeshine boy.

Children, too, receive their customary attention. In "Jour de fête" (Birthday) repressive parents try to stop their child from going out in the rain with flowers to celebrate a frog's birthday. The child is commended in "En sortant de l'école" (Upon Leaving School) for taking an imaginary journey around the world. "L'Enfance" (Childhood) chronicles the stifling influence old people have on children.

Love also plays a prominent role in *Histoires*. In "Adrien" it is once again portrayed as dysfunctional. In "Les Ombres" (Shadows) lovers are depicted as incompatible because they are dogged by each other's shadow. Compassion for the dispossessed is portrayed in "A la belle étoile" (Under the Stars), for a loved one in "Vieille chanson" (Old Song) who committed suicide by drowning. Compassion for humanity–together with contempt for the priesthood–is depicted in a deathbed scene in "Toile de fond" (Backdrop), and antireligious sentiment in "La nouvelle saison" (The New Season), where, in an earthly paradise, there is no place for God.

Prévert's artistic production continued throughout the 1940s. He collaborated with photographers, worked on animated cartoons, pantomime, and ballet, and exhibited collages. He married Janine Tricotet on 4 March 1947. Their only daughter, Michèle, was born in 1946, and this event prompted Prévert to write books for children. His *Contes pour enfants pas sages* (Tales for Children Who Misbehave) was published in 1947. In 1948, while working in a sound studio, he fell one story to the sidewalk, and was in a coma for several weeks. He moved to Saint-Paul de Vence in Provence to recover, and returned permanently to Paris only in 1955.

Published in 1951, *Spectacle* (Show) comprises mainly dramatic sketches meant to be enacted in short theatrical productions. The excoriation of authority depicted earlier in *Paroles* and *Histoires* again can be seen in this volume, as Prévert paints a world inhabited by exploiters and exploited, haves and have-nots, heroes and villains.

"Aubervilliers" is representative of his solidarity with the proletariat. This poem in three parts had been used by Kosma, who composed the songs for the motion picture of the same name that had been produced by Elie Lotar and Prévert in 1945. Aubervilliers is a poor Parisian suburb where factory workers toil and live in squalid conditions. Only the youth of the town are spared the harsh reality of the adult world. The water running along the gutters of the town heads toward the countryside, there to tell the rivers, woods, and meadows of the workers' dream of escaping from Aubervilliers.

"Chanson des sardinières" (Song of the Girls Working in the Sardine Canneries) is in the same vein. Originally a protest song composed for le Groupe Octobre, it tells of the bad fairies who come to the cribs of the daughters of fishermen and farmers, predicting lives of hardship, with many children, for them. The poem "Los olvidados" is a tribute to the director Luis Buñuel and his motion picture of the same name, produced in 1950 (released in English as *The Young and the Damned*). The motion picture chronicles corruption and cruelty in youths growing up amid the slums of Mexico City. Sympathy for the outcast is also expressed in "L'Enfant abandonné" (The Abandoned Child), for the oppressed in "On" (One), and for dispossessed children from broken homes in "La belle vie" (What a Life). The theme of love is portrayed in "Le balayeur" (The Street Sweeper), the title character of which finds his true love when he jumps into the river at the behest of the Guardian Angel to rescue a drowning girl. Passionate love is portrayed in "Sanguine" (Blood Orange) and exploitative love in "Il a tourné autour de moi" (He Turned Around Me).

As elsewhere, militarism is targeted here, typically in "Rue de Rivoli" (Rivoli Street). This poem sarcastically depicts the chain of command that prevents anyone in the police or the military from avenging his honor except by picking on someone of lower standing. A policeman whose wife was seduced by the sergeant vents his frustration by kicking a tramp in the stomach, for which he is reprimanded. He beats his wife and disembowels his dog. At the end of the poem, in response to the rhetorical question "Where is he going?" the reader is told that only God knows:

> Lui qui a créé toutes choses
> et en particulier
> les grandes Ecoles de guerre
> d'où l'on sort Officier de paix.

> (He who has created all things
> and in particular
> the military academies
> from which one passes out as an Officer of the peace).

The paradox of military academies (literally "war schools") turning out officers of the peace is an ironic comment on the military and the police as well as on the idiosyncratic properties of language.

Prévert in Paris, 1955 (photograph © Robert Doisneau/Rapho)

"Sur le champ" (In the Field) portrays a raw recruit, a pacifistic soul with no war-like proclivities whatsoever. He wanders onto the parade ground at noon, like a sleepwalker, staggering along like a drunk man. The major utters the mocking comment: "Tiens un revenant" ("Hello stranger" or "Long time no see"). The captain chips in with the observation that this must be a "réfractaire" (draft dodger), and the major quips about the proper dress code for draft evaders in time of war:

Pour un réfractaire
un costume de planches
c'est l'habit réglementaire

dit le commandant
Une grande planche dessus
une grande planche dessous
une plus petite du côté des pieds
une plus petite du côté de la tête
tout simplement.

(For a draft evader
a suit made of planks
is the regulation dress
says the major
A large plank on top
a large plank underneath
a smaller one on the side facing the feet
a smaller one on the side facing the head
quite simply).

The symbolism of the planks is quite apparent from idiomatic expressions such as "quand il sera entre quatre planches"–literally, "when he's between four planks," the equivalent of "when he's six feet under."

Upon hearing this remark the recruit apologizes, saying that he was just passing by and naively admits that he was asleep when reveille sounded. The major then gives the order:

> Donnez-lui un cheval une hache un canon un lance-
> flammes un cure-dents un tournevis
> Mais qu'il fasse son devoir sur le champ.
>
> (Give him a horse an ax a cannon a flame-
> thrower a bayonet a screwdriver
> But make him do his duty in the field).

"Sur le champ" meaning "in the field," or figuratively "at once," plays on both meanings simultaneously to create jocular ambiguity here, and, of course, in the title of the poem. Similar confusion is elicited by the talkative recruit's reply:

> Je n'ai jamais su faire mon devoir
> je n'ai jamais su apprendre une leçon
> Mais donnez-moi un cheval
> je le mènerai à l'abreuvoir
> Donnez-moi aussi un canon
> je le boirai avec les amis
> Donnez-moi . . .
> et puis je ne vous demande rien
> je ne suis pas réglementaire
> le casse-pipe n'est pas mon affaire.
>
> (I have never been able to do my duty
> I have never been able to learn a lesson
> But give me a horse
> I'll take it to the watering hole
> Give me a glass too
> I'll drink it with my friends
> Give me . . .
> I'm not asking you for anything
> I'm not for rules and regulations
> war isn't my business).

The major's enumeration of the implements of war strikes a responsive chord in the recruit. The "Donnez-lui" of the order is eagerly taken up in the thrice-repeated "Donnez-moi" in the recruit's eager reply. He willingly accepts the responsibility of watering a horse, and it is obvious that, construed as a simple farm animal, it holds no bellicose associations for him whatsoever. "Canon" is likewise dissociated from any military application, as the recruit happily envisages the chance to "boire un canon" (drink a glass).

Similarly, a moment after alluding to "casse-pipe" in its figurative meaning of "war," the loquacious recruit mentions his epicurean liking for "une petite pipe en terre / en terre réfractaire" (a small, clay pipe / of fireproof clay). Prévert's raw recruit insists on the quality of his pipe "en terre réfractaire." The equivocal pun "réfractaire"–meaning "refractory" or "resistant to heat"–divested of its military connotation of "deserter," shows how blissfully ignorant the conscript is of the concerns of the military. The poem ends as the pipe that he demands to be allowed to smoke morning and night becomes an antiwar symbol:

> Je ne suis pas réglementaire
> Sur le sentier de votre guerre
> je fume
> mon petit calumet de paix
> Inutile de vous mettre en colère
> je ne vous demande pas de cendrier.
>
> (I cannot be subject to rules and regulations
> Along the path of your war
> I'm smoking
> my little pipe of peace
> There's no need to get angry
> I'm not asking you for an ashtray).

The symmetrically placed "war" and "peace" (the possessive adjectives draw out the antithesis between "your war" and "my peace") highlight the coup of the morally triumphant recruit as he has the last word.

"La guerre," also an antiwar poem, shows environmental sensitivity to the problem of indiscriminate deforestation. In "L'Enseignement libre" (Denominational education) Prévert again takes aim at the education system. The poem relates the dream of a diffident schoolboy:

> En entendant parler
> d'une société sans classes
> l'enfant rêve
> d'un monde buissonnier
>
> (Upon hearing about
> a classless society
> the child dreams
> of a world of skipping classes).

The term "classless society" heard in school conjures up in the schoolboy's mind a world in which he would not have to attend school. He adapts "faire l'école buissonnière" (to play hooky) and makes out of it an idiom of his own that sums up his dreamed-of world of escape to "un monde buissonnier."

Subtle satire documents the schoolboy's disaffection from the authoritarianism of the school system. When the boy is told by "le professeur de Vive la France" (the teacher of Long Live France) that he is at the bottom of the class–"le dernier des derniers" (the last of the last)–and that he should be ashamed of himself, in response to the rebuke he musters a smile of appreciation for the truth of a lesson learned from religious instruction:

> Ne m'avez-vous pas dit vous-même
> et il n'y a pas si longtemps
> Les derniers seront les premiers
> Alors j'attends.

> (Did you yourself not say to me
> and not so long ago
> The last shall be the first
> So I'm waiting).

The poem "Un beau jour . . . " (One Fine Day . . .) tells of a verger, enmeshed in a variety of unsavory dealings, who attempts to put things right by appealing to divine intervention; however, he mistakes a confessional for a telephone booth, is blind drunk, and shows poor timing as he tries to get help in the middle of high mass, disrupting the service. He tries first of all to get through to God the Father, but the line appears to be engaged. He next tries to call Louis XVI and is cut off, then calls Complaints and a variety of agencies:

> Donnez-moi la Sainte Chapelle la Sainte Trinité l'Incarnation la Rédemption la Police Judiciaire le Palais de Justice la Grande Chartreuse Saint-Emilion
> Allo Allo
> Donnez-moi Lourdes la Basilique
> Donnez-moi l'Absolution.

> (Give me the Holy Chapel the Holy Trinity the Incarnation the Redemption the Central Intelligence Agency the Law Courts the Grande-Chartreuse Saint-Emilion.
> Hello Hello
> Give me Lourdes the Basilica
> Give me Absolution).

"Donnez-moi" is used ambiguously, firstly in the idiomatic sense of an instruction to a telephone operator to "be put in contact with"; secondly in the sense of "grant me" when applied to Redemption or Absolution or (sacrilegiously) to Incarnation. Mention of "La Sainte-Chapelle," a building within the precincts of the Law Courts of Paris, followed by the Holy Trinity, has the effect of reducing the latter to a listing in a telephone directory. The indiscriminate lumping together of buildings and terms of theology turns the verger's enumeration into gobbledygook, and the equating of the spiritual power of the church with temporal and judicial authority has the effect of trivializing it. The enumeration assumes a zany twist when "la Grande Chartreuse" is mentioned. The ecclesiastical Grande-Chartreuse, a monastery, evokes associations of "chartre" (prison), linking it both to the law and the discipline of monastic life. But the liqueur

Cover for Prévert's 1966 book, which includes aphorisms and poems (from Jacques Prévert, Œuvres complètes, edited by Arnaud Laster and Danièle Gasiglia-Laster, 1996)

"chartreuse" would seem to be uppermost in the mind of the drunken official, as the next item on the list is "Saint-Emilion," the red wine harvested in the Bordeaux region.

Prévert's fondness for enumerations that often contain hyphenated or double-barreled names, particularly when used by those who are drunk, snobs, or illiterate, often leads to linguistic anarchy. This anarchy forces the reader to reappraise the literal and figurative uses of language.

La Pluie et le beau temps (One Thing and Another) was published in 1955. The collection includes some dramatic sketches, along with songs and poems, most of them fairly short. The volume bears the hallmark of Prévert's stay in Saint-Paul de Vence, on the French Riviera. "Itinéraire de Ribemont" (Ribemont's Itinerary) pays tribute to a friend, Georges Ribemont-Dessaignes, a landscape artist whose illustrations later adorned Prévert's volume *Arbres* (Trees, 1967). In "Tant de forêts . . . " (So Many Forests . . .) a newfound environmental awareness leads Prévert to remark that billions of newspapers draw their readers' attention every year to the danger of woods and forests being stripped of trees. The tone of "Vignette pour les vignerons" (Vignette for the vine-growers) is, by contrast, one of Bacchanalian revelry. The poem celebrates the wine harvest at Saint-Jeannet, near Vence:

La nature a horreur des bouteilles vides
mais de même elle a horreur des bouteilles pleines
quand elles ne sont pas débouchées
Et saute le bouchon!

(Nature abhors empty bottles
But it similarly abhors full bottles
when they are not uncorked
so pop the cork!)

Prévert makes a jocular quip out of the scientific dictum that "la nature a horreur du vide" (nature abhors a vacuum) to express nature's generosity on the occasion of an abundant wine harvest.

"Cagnes-sur-Mer" is a disconcerting poem whose setting is the resort town on the *Côte d'Azur,* which holds Youth and Peace Festivals during the winter months. A festive occasion is turned into preparation for war, since peace can only be maintained by resort to belligerence, according to the wise doctors "du monde occis-mental"—wordplay on "le monde occidental" (the western world), with the adjective pulverized into "occis" from the archaic verb *occire* (to kill) and linked by hyphen to the ratiocinative "mental," which for Prévert held associations of war and intellectuals. Modern-day executioners have substituted newspapers and radio outposts for classical bards, in order to herald the "New Europe." This term harks back to "L'Ordre nouveau" (The New Order), a poem in *Paroles* that uses the words of Marshal Philippe Pétain in various radio addresses to the French nation after signing the armistice with Germany. In "Cagnes-sur-Mer" Prévert attacks the new Franco-German rapprochement as vociferously as he did the Vichy one:

le drapeau dieu blanc rouge
flotte sur le chantier
que l'Europe nouvelle est en train de nous fabriquer
Allô allô laissez-nous travailler en paix
et bientôt l'Afrance et la Lemagne
amies héréditaires soeurs latines ignorées
trop longtemps divisées mais enfin retrouvées
marqueront le pas de l'oie du vaillant coq gaulois
sous l'Arc de Triomphe

(the god-white-and-blue flag
fluttering over the site
that the New Europe is busy constructing for you
Hello hello let us work in peace
and soon frAnce and gerMany

hereditary friends and Latin sisters ignored by all
too long divided but finally reunited
will goose-step in celebration of the valiant French cockerel
under the Arc de Triomphe).

The *humour noir* (black humor) of the French *tricolore*—"le drapeau bleu blanc rouge" (the blue white and red flag)—having its *bleu* changed to *dieu* (god) is an expression of Prévert's violent antipathy to the alliance of God and Country in all its manifestations. Similar animus is present in the exhortation voiced a little further on in the poem: "Epée sur la terre aux hommes de bonne volonté" (Sword on earth to men of good will), with "Epée" replacing "Paix" (peace).

La Pluie et le beau temps also has its share of dysfunctional couples. In "Comme cela se trouve!" (As Things Turn Out!) a husband and wife, separated by death, each express contradictory feelings—hilarity mingled with grief, indifference with sadness. The dead woman exclaims: "Mon mari m'a perdue, qui jamais ne m'avait trouvée!" (My husband has lost me, he who had never found me!). The loss is caused by death, but the paradoxical statement that he "had never found me" calls in question the meaning of the bond of marriage. Marriage in "J'attends" (I'm Waiting) is seen as a fatality from which one can only escape by being widowed.

Children are abused here too. In the ambiguously titled "Le beau langage" (Fine Language), a father berates his son for threatening someone with the words "je vais te casser la gueule" (I'm going to bash your face in), and as punishment for using such vulgar language bashes his face in. He tells the boy that he will go to bed without supper, then, changing his mind, informs him that, instead, he will be dining in the company of a well-mannered guest—a "Gueule Cassée" (the term denotes a war veteran with severe face injuries).

"Petite tête sans cervelle" (Impulsive Bird Brain) recounts a little boy's theft of a bicycle on which he is making his getaway, with the bicycle owner in hot pursuit. The boy is run over and killed when he fails to stop at a train crossing. Anticlerical sentiment is present in "Et que faites-vous, Rosette, le dimanche matin?" (And What Do You Do, Rosette, on a Sunday Morning?), to which a maid replies, among other things, that she and her consort sometimes tune into a radio broadcast of Mass, and recalls a sermon on concupiscence, broken up by the preacher into its component parts: conque, huppe, Is, Hans. According to the preacher, these units signify, respectively: spiral shell, hoopoe bird, a Celtic city Is or Ys that disappeared beneath the waves, and the name of the sailor, Hans, who betrayed Is to the sea. They hardly constitute the stuff of a ser-

JACQUES PRÉVERT

Arbres

Gravures de
Georges Ribemont-Dessaignes

nrf

GALLIMARD

Frontispiece and title page for the second edition of Prévert's 1967 poetry collection (Collection of Malcolm McGoldrick)

mon on the lusts of the flesh and show how disconnected the preacher is from reality.

Histoires was republished in an enlarged edition as *Histoires et d'Autres Histoires* (Stories and Other Stories) in 1963. This edition collects the prose collection *Contes pour enfants pas sages,* as well as excerpts from *Arbres,* and other poems.

Published in 1966, *Fatras* (Jumble) is a mixture of sayings, poems, extracts from newspapers and books, and dramatic fragments, with fifty-seven pictures provided by the author. It has been treated as a poor excuse for a book and elicited poor reviews. However, some of its dictums are pithy and humorous. The miscellany is organized around the themes of love, war, and religion.

With keen ecological sensitivity, Prévert takes up the subject of the tree, and society's dependence on it for survival, in his 1967 book, *Arbres*. He also sounds

the alarm at mankind's continuing to make war, and war against nature, in particular. He decries arsonists who destroy trees as well as the ghoulish appetite of tourists who flock to a site of devastation. At the end of the book Prévert imagines a revolt fomented by trees uprooting themselves to form barricades in order to prevent humans from getting past. From the beginning, sensitivity had been the hallmark of children, but it is lost as the child is influenced by the world of adults. At the end of *Arbres,* in a world riven by war, with evocations of Pascal's "espaces infinis" (eternal spaces) striking fear into people's hearts, two lovers carve interlocked hearts with their names inside on a poplar tree and are saved.

The title of *Hebdromadaires* (Weekly Dromedaries, 1972) is a neologism made from *hebdomadaire*–a weekly magazine–and *dromadaire,* a dromedary. The volume consists of interviews conducted with Prévert, and in an augmented edition published a decade later, included notations about André Malraux, Breton, and Søren Kierkegaard.

Choses et autres (Things and Others, 1972) is the last work published during Prévert's lifetime. This collection comprises less textual unity than some previous ones, comprising fewer poems and more prose pieces, songs, and aphorisms. "Enfance" (Childhood), with which the collection begins, is a poetic narrative that recounts Prévert's early years in Neuilly, Toulon, and Paris. This text is dated 1972 but appeared in the magazine *Elle* in 1959.

Prévert's career ended with his death from lung cancer. A compulsive smoker—a myriad of camera shots captured his trademark cigarette dangling from his lips—he succumbed to "la très douce sorcière Nicotine" (The sweet sorceress Nicotine; in the words of a title of one of his collages in *Images*) on 11 April 1977 at Omonville-la-petite, a small village in the Cotentin to which he had retired in 1972. He was heralded for the unparalleled diversity of his contribution to different media and as a poet who never lost the common touch.

Two posthumous volumes attest to the poet's prolific output. *Soleil de nuit* (Night Sun), a collection of poems, was published in 1980, and *La Cinquième saison* (Fifth Season), which comprises mostly brief dramatic sketches, in 1984. These books express, in the same vein as earlier collections, Prévert's preoccupations and concerns, assuaged by love.

Jacques Prévert's world is the site of a struggle between the forces of good and evil. Good, on the one hand, is represented by beings and things expressive of spontaneity and beauty: nature, flowers, the sun, a beautiful girl, a bird, or a child. Evil, on the other hand, is depicted by all that is construed as negative: the family, old age, the fatherland, civilization, religion, duty, knowledge, and ideas. Although distrust of ideas is the basis for the invective he unleashes in "Tentative de description . . . " and "La Crosse en l'air," Prévert refuses to theorize. He takes up the cudgels on behalf of working-class people and the dispossessed everywhere, but his vitriol is never elevated to the status of a system. Instead, all that is alien gives rise to negative satire, while spontaneity elicits from him a reaction of love. Prévert's poetry thus depicts an exuberance that is in itself a form of social cohesion.

Interview:

Madeleine Chapsal, "Entretien avec Jacques Prévert," *L'Express,* 14 March 1963.

Biographies:

Marcel Duhamel, *Raconte pas ta vie* (Paris: Mercure de France, 1972);

René Gilson, *Des mots et merveilles, Jacques Prévert* (Paris: Pierre Belfond, 1990);

Marc Andry, *Jacques Prévert* (Paris: Editions de Fallois, 1994);

Danièle Gasiglia-Laster, *Jacques Prévert, "celui qui rouge de cœur,"* revised edition (Paris: Séguier, 1994);

Alain Rustenholz, *Prévert, inventaire* (Paris: Seuil, 1996);

Michel Rachline, *Jacques Prévert,* revised edition (Paris: Editions Olbea, 1999);

Yves Courrière, *Jacques Prévert en vérité* (Paris: Gallimard, 2000).

References:

Andrew S. Allen, "The Syntax of Word Formation in Satirical Language," in *Proceedings of the XVth International Congress of Linguists* (Québec: Université Laval, 9–14 August 1992); pp. 245–248;

William E. Baker, *Jacques Prévert* (New York: Twayne, 1967);

Andrée Bergens, *Jacques Prévert* (Paris: Editions Universitaires, 1969);

Daniel Bergez, "Etude d'un poème de Jacques Prévert: 'Le désespoir est assis sur un banc,'" *L'Information littéraire,* 31, no. 1 (1979): 37–42;

Gaston Bouthoul, "Jacques Prévert et un siècle de poésie martiale," *Lettres Nouvelles,* 56 (1958): 91–101;

Régis Boyer, "Mots et jeux de mots chez Prévert, Queneau, Boris Vian, Ionesco. Essai d'étude méthodique," *Studia neophilologica* (Uppsala), 40 (1968): 317–358;

Lucienne Cantaloube-Ferrieu, "La parole surréaliste de Jacques Prévert," in *Dada-Surrealismo: Precursores, Marginales y Heterodoxos. Cádiz del 19 al 22 de Noviembre de 1985* (Cádiz: Servicio de Publicaciones, Universidad de Cádiz, 1986), pp. 189–192;

Georges-Emmanuel Clancier, "Prévert, poète insoumis," in his *Dans l'aventure du langage* (Paris: Presses Universitaires de France, 1987); pp. 44–53;

Anna E. S. Creese, "L'oiseau dans *Paroles* de Prévert. Symbolisme et structure," *Chimères,* 19, no. 2 (1988): 61–80;

Kazimierz Derylo, "Fonctions sociales de néologismes dans l'œuvre poétique de Jacques Prévert," in *La Pensée sociale dans la littérature française: Actes du colloque de Katowice-Sosnowiec, 22–24 mai 1980,* edited by Aleksander Abłamowicz (Katowice, Poland: Universytet Slaski Katowice, 1981), pp. 140–144;

Pierre Descaves, "Jacques Prévert: *Spectacle*," *Revue du Caire,* 144 (1951): 321–326;

Jacques Doucet, "Deux poèmes de Jacques Prévert" ['Pour faire le portrait d'un oiseau'; 'Chanson dans le sang'], *Etudes classiques,* 18 (1950): 209–216;

Pierre Dumayet, "Prévert et l'optimisme," *Poésie, 46,* 33 (1946): 102–104;

Europe, special Prévert issue, nos. 748 and 749 (August–September 1991);

Eliot G. Fay, "The Bird Poems of Jacques Prévert," *Modern Language Journal,* 33 (1949): 450–457;

Albert Gaudin, "La poésie de Jacques Prévert," *French Review,* 20 (1947): 423–438;

Anne Hyde Greet, *Jacques Prévert's Word Games* (Berkeley & Los Angeles: University of California Press, 1968);

Greet, "Negation and Affirmation in Prévert's Word Games," *Wisconsin Studies in Contemporary Literature,* 7 (1966): 131–141;

Léon-Gabriel Gros, "De l'expérience à l'artifice," *Cahiers du Sud,* 309 (1951): 311–318;

Arnaud Laster, "Ecrits de Prévert, écrits sur Prévert, de 1978 à 1992," in *Œuvres et critiques* XVIII, 1–2 (1993): *Treize ans d'études sur le surréalisme,* edited by Dominique Baudouin (Tübingen: Gunter Narr, 1993), pp. 153–158;

Laster, "L'Humour complice de l'amour chez Jacques Prévert," *Mélusine,* 10 (1988): 159–170;

Laster, *Paroles: Analyse critique* (Paris: Hatier, 1972);

Laster, "Un poète du siècle," *Magazine littéraire,* 155 (December 1979): 8–16;

Marie-Louise Lentengre, "Une écriture dramatique: trois poèmes de Jacques Prévert," in *Miscellanea in onore di Liano Petroni. Studi e ricerche sulle letterature di lingua francese,* edited by Ruggero Campagnoli (Bologna: Cooperativa Libraria Universitaria Editrice Bologna, 1996), pp. 365–372;

Paul Miclau, "Le Français parlé dans les poésies de Prévert," *Beiträge zur Romanischen Philologie,* 5, no. 1 (1966): 120–133;

Christian Moncelet, "'Page d'écriture' de Prévert: la répétition ou la mort punie," in *La Répétition,* edited by Slaheddine Chaouachi and Alain Montandon (Clermont-Ferrand: Assocation des Publications de la Faculté des Lettres et Sciences Humaines de Clermont-Ferrand, 1994), pp. 191–201;

Christiane Mortelier, *Paroles de Jacques Prévert* (Paris: Hachette, 1976);

Alvio Patierno, "Lecture comparée: 'Barbara' et 'Le dernier poème,'" *Micromégas* (Rome), 19 (1992): 23–48;

Jacques Poujol, "Jacques Prévert ou le langage en procès," *French Review,* 31 (1958): 387–395;

Jan Prokop, "La voix anonyme de Prévert," *Kwartalnik Neofilologiczny* (Warsaw), 16 (1969): 349–357;

Jacques Thomas, "Grammaire et poésie: 'Le message' de Jacques Prévert," *Français moderne,* 26 (1958): 124–128;

Jennifer Waelti-Walters, "Femmes de *Paroles,*" in *Trois fous du langage: Vian, Queneau, Prévert: Actes du colloque Vian-Queneau-Prévert, Université de Victoria (Canada),* edited by Marc Lapprand (Nancy: Presses universitaires de Nancy, 1993), pp. 171–177;

Pierre Weisz, "Langage et Imagerie Chez Jacques Prévert," *French Review,* 43, special issue, no. 1, (Winter 1970): 33–43;

A. J. A. van Zoest, "Analyse structurale d'un poème narratif: Prévert, 'Quartier libre,'" *Neophilologus,* 54 (1970): 347–368.

Raymond Queneau

(21 February 1903 – 25 October 1976)

André and Jean-François Leroux
University of Ottawa

See also the Queneau entry in *DLB 72: French Novelists, 1930–1960.*

BOOKS: *Le Chiendent* (Paris: Gallimard, 1933); translated by Barbara Wright as *The Bark-Tree (Le Chiendent): A Novel* (London: Calder & Boyars, 1968); translation republished as *The Bark Tree (Le Chiendent): A Novel* (New York: New Directions, 1971);

Gueule de Pierre (Paris: Gallimard, 1934);

Les Derniers jours (Paris: Gallimard, 1936); translated by Wright as *The Last Days* (Elmwood Park, Ill.: Dalkey Archive Press, 1990; London: Atlas, 1990);

Chêne et chien (Paris: Denoël, 1937);

Odile (Paris: Gallimard, 1937); translated by Carol Sanders as *Odile* (Elmwood Park, Ill.: Dalkey Archive Press, 1988);

Les Enfants du limon (Paris: Gallimard, 1938); translated by Madeleine Velguth as *Children of Clay* (Los Angeles: Sun & Moon Press, 1998);

Un rude hiver (Paris: Gallimard, 1939); translated by Betty Askwith as *A Hard Winter* (London: Lehmann, 1948);

Les Temps mêlés; Gueule de pierre, II, roman (Paris: Gallimard, 1941);

Pierrot mon ami (Paris: Gallimard, 1943); translated by J. McLaren Ross as *Pierrot: A Novel* (London: Lehmann, 1950);

Les Ziaux (Paris: Gallimard, 1943);

Loin de Rueil (Paris: Gallimard, 1944); translated by H. J. Kaplan as *The Skin of Dreams* (Norfolk, Conn.: New Directions, 1948; London: Atlas, 1987);

Bucoliques (Paris: Gallimard, 1947);

Exercices de style (Paris: Gallimard, 1947; revised, 1947); translated by Wright as *Exercises in Style* (London: Gaberbocchus, 1958); French version revised and enlarged (Paris: Gallimard, 1963); translation republished (New York: New Directions, 1981);

Raymond Queneau, 1943 (photograph by Roger Parry)

On est toujours trop bon avec les femmes traduit de l'irlandais par Michel Presle, as Sally Mara (Paris: Editions du Scorpion, 1947); translated by Wright as *We Always Treat Women Too Well* (London: Calder, 1981; New York: New Directions, 1981);

L'Instant fatal: Poèmes (Paris: Gallimard, 1948);

Saint Glinglin: précédé d'une nouvelle version de Gueule de Pierre; et de Les Temps mêlés (Paris: Gallimard, 1948); translated James Sallis as *Saint Glinglin* (Normal, Ill.: Dalkey Archive Press, 1993);

Rendez-vous de juillet, by Queneau and Jean Quéval (Paris: Chavane, 1949);

Joan Miró, ou le poète préhistorique, Les trésors de la peinture française, XXe siècle (Geneva: Editions d'Art Albert Skira, 1949);

Vlaminck: ou le vertige de la matière, Les trésors de la peinture française (Paris: A. Skira, 1949);

Bâtons, chiffres et lettres (Paris: Gallimard, 1950; revised and enlarged, 1965);

Journal intime, as Mara (Paris: Editions du Scorpion, 1950);

Petite cosmogonie portative: Poème (Paris: Gallimard, 1950);

Le Dimanche de la vie: Roman (Paris: Gallimard, 1951); translated by Wright as *The Sunday of Life* (London: Calder, 1976; New York: New Directions, 1977);

Si tu t'imagines, 1920–1951 (Paris: Gallimard, 1952); revised as *Si tu t'imagines, 1920–1948* (Paris: Gallimard, 1968);

Le Chien à la mandoline (Verviers: Temps Mêlés, 1958; enlarged edition, Paris: Gallimard, 1965);

Sonnets (Paris: Editions Hautefeuille, 1958);

Zazie dans le métro (Paris: Gallimard, 1959); translated by Wright as *Zazie* (London: Bodley Head, 1960; New York: Harper, 1960);

Cent mille milliards de poèmes (Paris: Gallimard, 1961); translated by John Crombie as *One Hundred Million Million Poems* (Paris: Kickshaws, 1983);

Zoneilles: Scénario, by Queneau, Michel Arnaud, and Boris Vian (Paris: Collège de Pataphysique, LXXXIX [i.e., 1962]);

Entretiens avec Georges Charbonnier (Paris: Gallimard, 1962);

Les Œuvres complètes de Sally Mara (Paris: Gallimard, 1962);

Bords: Mathématiciens, précurseurs, encyclopédistes (Paris: Hermann, 1963);

Les Fleurs bleues (Paris: Gallimard, 1965); translated by Wright as *Between Blue and Blue: A Sort of Novel* (London: Bodley Head, 1967); translation republished as *The Blue Flowers* (New York: Atheneum, 1967); French version republished, edited by Wright (London: Methuen, 1971);

Une histoire modèle (Paris: Gallimard, 1966);

Courir les rues (Paris: Gallimard, 1967);

Battre la campagne (Paris: Gallimard, 1968);

Le Vol d'Icare (Paris: Gallimard, 1968); translated by Wright as *The Flight of Icarus* (London: Calder & Boyars, 1973; New York: New Directions, 1973);

Chêne et chien, suivi de Petite cosmogonie portative (éd. rev. et corr.) et de Le Chant du Styrène (Paris: NRF/Gallimard, 1968); translated by Madeleine Velguth as *Raymond Queneau's Chene et Chien: A Translation with Commentary* (New York: Peter Lang, 1995);

Fendre les flots (Paris: Gallimard, 1969);

Raymond Queneau en verve, edited by Jacques Bens (Paris: Horay, 1970);

De quelques langages animaux imaginaires et notamment du langage chien dans Sylvie et Bruno (Paris: L'Herne, 1971);

Le Voyage en Grèce (Paris: NRF/Gallimard, 1973);

Morale élémentaire (Paris: Gallimard, 1975);

Contes et propos, preface by Michel Leiris (Paris: Gallimard, 1981); translated by Marc Lowenthal as *Stories & Remarks* (Lincoln: University of Nebraska Press, 2000);

Journal 1939–1940, suivi de Philosophes et voyous, edited by Anne Isabelle Queneau and Jean-José Marchand (Paris: Gallimard, 1986);

Œuvres complètes, 3 volumes projected, 1 volume to date, edited by Claude Debon, Bibliothèque de la Pléiade, volume 358 (Paris: Gallimard, 1989–   );

Traité des vertus démocratiques, edited by Emmanuel Souchier (Paris: Gallimard, 1993);

Journaux: 1914–1965, edited by Anne Isabelle Queneau (Paris: Gallimard, 1996).

Editions in English: *The Trojan Horse & At the Edge of the Forest,* translated by Barbara Wright (London: Gaberbocchus, 1954);

Raymond Queneau: Poems, translated by Teo Savory (Santa Barbara, Cal.: Unicorn, 1971);

Pounding the Pavements; Beating the Bushes; and Other Pataphysical Poems, translated by Savory (Greensboro, N.C.: Unicorn, 1985);

Pierrot mon ami, translated by Wright (Elmwood Park, Ill.: Dalkey Archive Press, 1987; London: Atlas, 1988);

OuLiPo Laboratory: Texts from the Bibliothèque oulipienne, Prefaced by Two Manifestos by François Le Lionnais, by Queneau and others, translated by Harry Mathews, Iain White, and Warren Motte Jr. (London: Atlas, 1995).

PRODUCED SCRIPTS: *Monsieur Ripois,* motion picture, screenplay by Queneau, René Clément, and Hugh Mills, Transcontinental Films, 1953;

Le Mort en ce jardin, motion picture, screenplay by Queneau, Luis Alcoriza, Gabriel Arout, Luis Buñuel, and José-André Lacour, Dismage, 1956;

Un couple, motion picture, screenplay by Queneau and Jean-Pierre Mocky, Balzac Films, 1960;

La Grande frousse, motion picture, dialogue contributed by Queneau, Attica, 1964;

Le Dimanche de la vie, motion picture, screenplay by Queneau, Olivier Hussenot, and Georges Richard, Doxa-Film, 1967.

OTHER: "Dédé," in *Un cadavre,* by Queneau, Jacques Baron, Georges Bataille, J.-A. Boiffard, Robert

Desnos, Michel Leiris, Georges Limbour, Max Morise, Jacques Prévert, Georges Ribemont-Dessaignes, and Roger Vitrac (Paris, 1930);

Edgar Wallace, *Le Mystère du train d'or,* translated by Queneau (Paris: Gallimard, 1934);

Maurice O'Sullivan, *Vingt ans de jeunesse,* translated by Queneau (Paris: Gallimard, 1936);

Sinclair Lewis, *Impossible ici,* translated by Queneau (Paris: Gallimard, 1937);

George du Maurier, *Peter Ibbetson, avec une introduction par sa cousine Lady X ("Madge Plunket"),* translated by Queneau (Paris: Gallimard, 1946);

Alexandre Kojève, *Introduction à la lecture de Hegel: Leçons sur La phénoménologie de l'esprit, professées de 1933 à 1939 à l'Ecole des hautes-études,* edited by Queneau (Paris: Gallimard, 1947); translated by James H. Nichols Jr. as *Introduction to the Reading of Hegel, by Alexandre Kojève: Lectures on the Phenomenology of Spirit Assembled by Raymond Queneau,* edited by Allan Bloom (New York: Basic Books, 1969);

Gustave Flaubert, *Bouvard et Pécuchet: Avec une présentation nouvelle de la deuxième partie,* introduction by Queneau (Paris: Editions du Point du Jour, 1947);

Amos Tutuola, *L'Ivrogne dans la brousse,* translated by Queneau (Paris: Gallimard, 1953);

Anthologie des jeunes auteurs, edited by Queneau (Paris: Editions J.A.R., 1955);

Alfred Jarry, *L'Amour fou, précédé Le vieux de la montagne et de l'autre Alceste,* commentaries by Queneau and others (Paris: Mercure de France, 1964).

SELECTED PERIODICAL PUBLICATIONS–UNCOLLECTED: "Récit de rêve," *Révolution Surréaliste,* no. 3 (15 April 1925): 5;

"Texte surréaliste," *Révolution Surréaliste,* no. 5 (15 October 1925): 3–4;

"Sur quelques aspects relativement peu connus du verbe en français," *Surréalisme Révolutionnaire,* no. 1 (1948): 36;

"Philosophes et voyous," *Temps Modernes,* no. 63 (January 1951): 1193–1205;

"Zazie dans son plus jeune âge," *Lettres Nouvelles,* new series 2 (1959): 5–7;

"Premières confrontations avec Hegel," *Critique,* nos. 195–196 (August–September 1963): 694–700;

"L'analyse matricielle du langage," *Etudes de Linguistique Appliquée,* no. 3 (1964): 37–50.

Raymond Queneau's work is difficult to classify. Set to music by the Frères Jacques, his *Exercices de style* (1947; translated as *Exercises in Style,* 1958) earned him a reputation as something of a comedian. That reputation was confirmed by the appearance of the highly popular, highly zany *Zazie dans le métro* (Zazie on the Subway, 1959; translated as *Zazie,* 1960), for which Queneau won the Prix de l'Humour Noir (Black Humor Prize). Although less well known, his substantial œuvre in verse shows that if Queneau is habitually jocose, his antics are meant in deadly earnest. Combining metaphysical high jinks with mathematical, linguistic, and stylistic experimentation, ignorance with learning, high with low, tradition with invention, Queneau's wit belongs to the baroque tradition of *serio ludere* (comic seriousness) descending from Samuel Taylor Coleridge through Lewis Carroll (Charles Lutwidge Dodgson) to Alfred Jarry. Though Queneau's poetry typically takes on the lineaments of classicism and Romanticism, on closer inspection it often reveals an awareness of human limitations; its tone is ironic, reflecting the growing pessimism and skepticism of his age. In Queneau's poetry Romantic spirituality becomes jeux d'esprit. Poetry for him is a spectacle, an artifice or trompe l'oeil, concealing inanity.

"Je nacqui au Havre un vingt et un février / en mil neuf cent et trois. / Ma mère était mercière et mon père mercier" (I was born in Le Havre one 21 February / in 1903 / My mother was a haberdasher and so was my father), Queneau writes in *Chêne et chien* (Oak and Dog, 1937). He decided early that traveling was not for him: his father, Auguste, had served in the army in Asia and Africa and returned home with chronic hepatitis; his maternal grandfather, a ship's captain, had been shipwrecked. Queneau remained in France most of his life, taking his vacations in provincial towns. (He did, however, travel to Greece in 1932; to the northeastern United States in 1950; to Finland, Sweden, and Austria in 1945; to Belgium and again to Greece in 1952; to Mexico in 1955; to the Soviet Union in 1956; and to Sicily in 1963.) Five years older than her husband, Queneau's mother, Josephine Mignot Queneau, brought her family's talent for commerce to the relationship and frequently reminded Auguste that it was their petit-bourgeois marriage that had elevated him from farmer's son to businessman. Queneau was their only child.

Though of fragile health, Queneau was a good student at the lycée. He read extensively; was fascinated by mathematics; catalogued his collections of rocks, coins, and so forth; and inventoried all the Charlie Chaplin movies he saw. By fifteen he had read the *Dictionnaire Larousse* from *A* to *Z.* He also wrote highly imaginative novels. While still in secondary school, he renounced Catholicism.

Queneau obtained his *baccalauréat* (secondary-school leaving certificate) in 1920, with a prize in philosophy. A year later his parents sold the family business and moved to Epinay-sur-Orge, a short train ride from Paris, and Queneau began the study of philosophy and mathematics at the Sorbonne. He twice failed

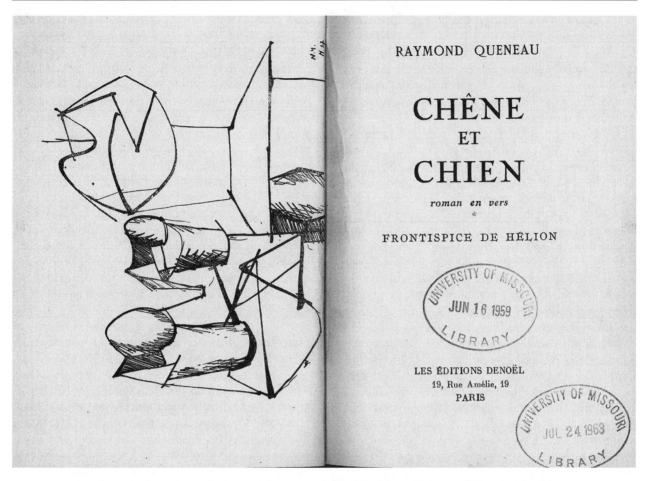

RAYMOND QUENEAU

CHÊNE
ET
CHIEN

roman en vers

FRONTISPICE DE HÉLION

LES ÉDITIONS DENOËL
19, Rue Amélie, 19
PARIS

Frontispiece and title page for Queneau's first poetry collection (Ellis Library, University of Missouri–Columbia)

the examination for a license to teach mathematics, and his first attempt at publication, a study of Gustave Le Bon, was refused by the *Mercure de France*. In 1923 he obtained his certificate in general philosophy and logic from the Sorbonne but again failed the licensing examination. The following year he was granted certificates in the general history of philosophy and psychology. Also in 1924 Queneau met André Breton and became part of the Surrealist milieu, which was then in full effervescence in Paris. He contributed a poem and two examples of automatic writing to the journal *La révolution surréaliste* and signed the Surrealist manifesto *Déclaration du 27 janvier 1925* (Declaration of 27 January 1925). The tract affirmed that the movement had "rien à voir avec la littérature" (nothing to do with literature) and explained: "Nous sommes des spécialistes de la Révolte. Il n'est pas un moyen d'action que nous ne soyons capables au besoin d'employer" (We are revolutionary specialists. There is no means of action that we are incapable of using). Queneau also participated in demonstrations to disrupt official conferences and

signed the manifesto *La Révolution d'abord et toujours* (Revolution Now and Forever), signifying the group's rapprochement with the Communist Party.

In 1926 Queneau finally received the *licence ès lettres*. That year he was called up for his compulsory eighteen-month military service in the Zouaves, a regiment referred to by other soldiers as "les fillettes à Lyautey" (the little girls of Lyautey), after Louis Hubert Gonzalve Lyautey (colonial administrator in Algeria and Morocco), because of its reputation for avoiding combat. Queneau's service took him to the outskirts of the War of the Rif in northern Africa, first to Batna and then to Algiers and Morocco. His duties consisted of guarding prisoners and gathering rocks for the construction of roads and walls until he was made a secretary at the military post in Fez. He later recorded his impressions in *Odile* (1937; translated, 1988): he felt that he was participating in a war without fighting, whiling away his days at useless tasks between drinking binges. His education and intelligence seemed irrelevant, given the tasks he was assigned, and the absurdity

357

of the situation was amplified by the incompetence of his commanding officers.

On his return home Queneau worked briefly at the Comptoir National d'Escompte (a bank) and as a paper-tablecloth salesman. His new friends included Jacques Prévert and the other members of the Surrealist group at 54 de la rue du Château.

In October 1927 Queneau signed "Hands off Love," an editorial in *La Révolution surréaliste* defending Chaplin's unconventional sex life, and published the poem "Le tour de l'ivoire" (Around the Ivory) in the same issue. Collected in his *L'Instant fatal* (The Fatal Moment, 1948), the poem ends with the slogan "DÉFENSE DE NE PAS RÊVER" (NO NOT DREAMING). The following year he "kidnapped," then married, Janine Kahn, the sister of Simone Breton, thus alienating her husband, André Breton; he added salt to the wound by questioning the Surrealists' support of Joseph Stalin after the purging of Leon Trotsky from the Soviet leadership in 1926, as well as by publishing "Dédé" in *Un cadavre* (A Corpse, 1930), a vehemently anti-Breton pamphlet co-written by Prévert, Jacques Baron, Georges Bataille, J.-A. Boiffard, Robert Desnos, Michel Leiris, Georges Limbour, Max Morise, Georges Ribemont-Dessaignes, and Roger Vitrac. The intimate form of André, "Dédé" is reminiscent of the men's past closeness; but the text is anything but friendly, including, as it does, a reference to Breton's "trou du cul" (asshole).

Caused by personal, temperamental, and, ultimately, theoretical differences, the rupture with the Surrealists left Queneau in limbo. He recalled in *Bâtons, chiffres et lettres* (Sticks, Figures and Letters, 1950; revised and enlarged, 1965): "C'est ce qui arrive, je crois, à tous ceux qui s'excluent ou sont exclus de groupes fortement constitués. Je ne savais que faire et je me suis réfugié à la Bibliothèque Nationale où je me suis mis à étudier les fous littéraires" (That is what happens to those who are excluded or exclude themselves from tightly knit groups. I did not know what to do; I took refuge in the National Library, where I began to study literary madmen). The result of this research was his Jarry-like "Encyclopédie des science inexactes" (Encyclopedia of Inexact Sciences), unpublished except in his 1938 novel *Les Enfants du limon* (Children of the Earth; translated as *Children of Clay,* 1998), where it figures as an otherwise unpublishable encyclopedia that is to be published in a novel by a character named Raymond Queneau, "un binoclard d'une trentaine d'années" (a bespectacled man of some thirty years) who works at the *Nouvelle Revue française.*

From 1931 to 1933 Queneau belonged to Boris Souvarine's circle of Communist outcasts and former Surrealists and was a reviewer for their journal, *La Cri-* *tique sociale.* Despite the publication of a verse novel, *Le Chiendent* (The Twitch; translated as *The Bark-Tree,* 1968), in 1933, this period was difficult for Queneau. Married and soon to be a father—he and his wife had a son, Jean-Marie, in 1934—he saw himself as a man without a vocation or social status. His six-year course of psychoanalysis is recorded in his first collection of poetry, *Chêne et chien.* (For *psychoanalysis* he invents the compound "psychanasouillis," suggesting that his work is the excrement thereof.) Like the rest of the works of this decade, *Chêne et chien* is mainly autobiographical. Canto one, comprising thirteen poems, recounts Queneau's first thirteen years. In his esoteric numerology, however, thirteen is not just the unlucky number it is in the popular mind; rather, it is the number that presides over his "essais de sauver l'existence / en naviguant les enfers" (attempts to save existence / by navigating Hades). *Hades* here stands for the inwardly turbulent times before World War I, particularly his first five years, "cet avant-hier, / caverne et souterrains, angoisses et pénitence, / ignorance et mystère" (that predawn, / cavern and underground, anguish and penitence, / ignorance and mystery), from which he inherited his decadent "goût pour l'ordure et la crasse" (taste for filth and muck) and "les désastres" (disasters). Queneau's narration of his "cure" leads one to suspect that his integration into society and emergence as an author rests less on a resolution of the conscious or unconscious conflicts that afflicted him than on an ironic artistic channeling of them. Surrealism, from under whose shadow he was just emerging, had already prepared the way for such an approach. In response to the "coups du sort" (hard knocks) of existence, Queneau began to formulate his own personal mythology, so that both the epigraph from Nicolas Boileau-Despréaux that precedes the classically structured first canto in alexandrines and octosyllables and the one from the pietistic poet-writer Thomas Traherne that heads up the second seem incongruous.

Queneau's treatment of "le soleil maternel" (the maternal sun) as "un excrément noir" (a black excrement) and consequent "inversion" of many of the traditional associations of Western culture may recall for some readers the work of Charles Baudelaire and other *poètes maudits* (accursed [that is, brilliant, self-destructive, and misunderstood] poets) such as Bataille, Jarry, and Antonin Artaud: "Méduse qui tires la langue, / c'est donc toi qui m'aurais châtré" (Medusa wagging your tongue / it is you, then, who has emasculated me). Inversion and invention, however, always presuppose tradition. Where Boileau-Despréaux writes a confessional poem in epistolary form, Queneau writes a confessional novel in verse. From the death of Medusa (standing for petrified con-

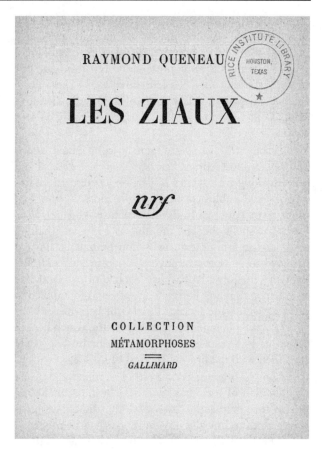

RAYMOND QUENEAU

LES ZIAUX

nrf

COLLECTION
MÉTAMORPHOSES
═══
GALLIMARD

Cover and title page for Queneau's 1943 poetry collection (Fondren Library, Rice University)

vention, the mother tongue) son and song are born; as the last poem in the second canto implies, taking up thesymbolthatgivesQueneau'scollectionitstitle,languageis a labyrinth of meanings and myths from which one cannot escape:

> Chêne et chien voilà mes deux noms,
> étymologie délicate:
> comment garder l'anonymat
> devant les dieux et les démons?
>
> (Oak and dog these are my two names,
> delicate etymology:
> how to keep anonymity
> before the gods and the demons?)

Queneau is the embodiment of the contraries signified by the Norman-Picard origins of his name. On the one hand, the dog (*quenot*) represents his instinctual, most basic nature:

> L'animal dévore et nique
> telles sont ses deux qualités;
> il est féroce et impulsif,
> on sait où il aime mettre son nez.

> (The animal devours and bites
> these are his two characteristics;
> he is ferocious and impulsive,
> we know where he likes to stick his nose).

On the other hand, the oak (*quesne*) carries the opposite connotations of strength and nobility. What unites them, symbolically, is that they stand on the threshold of knowledge: the oak as the tree of the knowledge of good and evil, with all its taboos, and as the Cross of the Passion; the dog as Cerberus, the guardian of the pagan underworld descended from Medusa. But the tree, though it soars upward and perdures, is also fixed, immobile, and, as is well known, the dog's victim. More dog than oak, Queneau is not chary about attacking the most sacred associations of Western culture: "Symboles œuvres individuelles, / vous ne méritez que cela: / vous êtes commes moi mortels / et celui qui vivra verra" (Individual symbols works, / you deserve nothing more: / you who are like me mortal / and who lives will see). As evidenced by the title of another of his poetic works, *Le Chien à la mandoline* (The Dog at the Mandolin, 1958; enlarged, 1965), the dog becomes a persona or mask in Queneau's later poetry, representing his desire to celebrate, imaginatively and comically, that "mélange de l'ordure et de l'innocence / que présentait la Création" (mixture of ordure and innocence / that the Creation presented). The third and last canto of *Chêne et chien*, "La fête au village" (The Village Festival), depicts a celebration in honor of a fictitious saint, Saint Glinglin, whose name in everyday French means "never."

From 1937 to 1940 Queneau contributed essays and reviews to Georges Pelorson's journal *Volontés* and served, along with Henry Miller, on its editorial board. The journal published pieces of the most diverse, and often avowedly contradictory, nature and purpose. Queneau spent the last months of 1939 and half of 1940 in the army—again as a noncombatant: he was assigned to an administrative position in Paris. He left the army in July 1940 with the rank of corporal. He was active on many literary committees and dabbled at painting with some success. In 1941 he became *Secrétaire général* of the Gallimard publishing house, which he had joined in 1938 as a reader of English manuscripts. He remained with the firm for the rest of his life.

Les Ziaux appeared in 1943. The title is a punning combination of *yeux* (eyes) and *eaux* (waters). Including poems that date as far back as 1920, the collection is much more technically accomplished than its predecessor. The poems in the first section, of which "Idées" (Ideas) and "Iris" are the finest specimens, are of symbolist-Parnassian inspiration. The puns and anagrams in the second section reflect the poet's search for a "neofrançais," a French mediating between *la langue* (the French of the Renaissance, formalized by grammarians) and *la parole* (spoken French). The mediation between learned and popular culture required by Queneau is effected in the third section by a return to the simple lyricism of the baroque "poètes de la mort" (poets of death) of the late sixteenth century such as Théodore-Agrippa d'Aubigné, Jacques Davy du Perron, Jean de Sponde, and Jean Baptiste Chassignet. A long memento mori on the evanescence of earthly things, this section looks forward, thematically, to Queneau's mature poetry, particularly *L'Instant fatal*. The theme of mortality is already implicit, however, in many of the poems in the previous sections, such as "A partir du désert" (Leaving the Desert), "Il pleut" (It Is Raining), and "Les joueurs de manille" (The Players of Manila), which are characterized by an increasingly elaborate use of anaphora, alliteration, counterpoint, repetition, and parataxis. The final section of *Les Ziaux* offers what appear to theoretical reflections, beginning with "L'explication des métaphores" (The Explication of Metaphors). But Queneau's explanation is not one: he holds that to explain or unfold metaphor is impossible because it is the intractable stuff of which human beings are made. The human being, "ni dieu ni démon" (neither god nor demon), can only express himself or herself imperfectly or metaphorically—that is, express one thing by another. The title poem of the collection is a feat of baroque mirror-play relying on homophony, neologism, repetition, alliteration, antithesis, and the use of nouns as verbs.

After 1944 Queneau was a public figure; he was linked to many literary associations and publishing articles on Hegelian philosophy, contemporary painting, and cinematography. His most important and representative work of poetry, *L'Instant fatal,* was published in 1948. The title refers to the fatal instant that awaits one not only at the end of life but also every day, undercutting one's illusions and dreams. As in *Les Ziaux,* the first part of the collection includes early poems of Surrealist ("L'aube évapore le nouveau-né" [The Dawn Evaporates the Newborn]), "Materia garrulans") and symbolist ("Phaéton," "Les Thermopyles," "Robinson," "Cygnes" [Swans]) inspiration. In other poems, such as "Maigrir" (To Grow Thin) and "La pendule" (The Pendulum), which were both later set to music, Queneau plays on the phonetic spelling of words and removes *e* whenever it is the first or only vowel in a word. The second part of the collection offers more recent poems that are filled with puns, guided by the notion that the poet must take pleasure in his use of diction, even to the extent of creating apparent paralogisms. This belief is carried into the third part, "Pour un art poétique" (For an *Ars Poetica*), which must not be taken too seriously, in spite of its title; as in "L'explication des métaphores" in *Les Ziaux,* Queneau's ostensible efforts to elaborate an *ars poetica* explain nothing but consist of a series of exercises in paradox that mock the very idea of doing so, whether through the Romantic notion of inspiration or through the more modern one of technique:

> Prenez un mot, prenez en deux
> Faites les cuire comme des oeufs
> Prenez un petit bout de sens
> Puis un grand morceau d'innocence
> Faites chauffer à petit feu
> Au petit feu de la technique
> Versez la sauce énigmatique
> Saupoudrez de quelques étoiles
> Poivrez et puis mettez les voiles
> Où voulez-vous donc en venir
> A écrire?
> Vraiment? A écrire?
>
> (Take a word, take two
> Cook them like eggs
> Take a little bit of sense
> And a chunk of innonence
> Cook them on a slow burner
> The slow burner of technique

Queneau and his wife, Janine Kahn Queneau, 12 March 1951

Pour in the enigmatic sauce
Powder with a few stars
Pepper and then cover
What do you expect to achieve
In writing?
Really? A poem?)

Emotion is derived from words, not from sentiment; poetry is the work of a juggler, an artisan—not a sage. All one needs is a pen, some paper, a few rules, and a vast vocabulary. But is this recipe really poetry? All of Queneau's poetry asks this rhetorical question. Here and in other poems he takes aim at conventional definitions of poetry's essence, which tend to focus either on form or subject matter, and purpose, which is usually directed by the notion of posterity or of creating an oeuvre. For Queneau, who is in many ways a traditionalist, that essence or "mystère poétique" (poetic mystery) can never be defined or captured in a work; it can

only approximated through practice: "un poème c'est bien peu de chose" (a poem is hardly nothing), and yet, "ça a toujours kékchose d'extrême" (it always has something extreme in it). That is because poetry is inseparable from life and its lurking contrary, death. Thus, the section that bears the title of the book reverts to Queneau's perennial subject, the universal themes of lyrical poetry: melodramatic and tragic meditations on death and aging, the passing of time, and the vanity of human wishes. A representative poem in this section is "Saint-Ouen's blues":

Des cheveux en avalanche
Des yeux non c'est des pervenches
Belles filles de Paris

Ma tristesse qui s'épanche
La fleur bleue ou bien la blanche
Et mon cœur qu'en a tant pris

Et mon cœur qu'en a tant pris
A Saint-Ouen près de Paris

(Hair cascading
Eyes no they are periwinkles
Beautiful girls of Paris

My sadness pours out
The blue flower or the white
And my heart which has borne so much

And my heart which has borne so much
In Saint-Ouen near Paris).

Based on Lucretius's classic *De rerum natura* (On the Nature of Things, first century B.C.), *Petite cosmogonie portative* (Small Portable Cosmogony, 1950) is a poetic history of the universe comprising 1,386 alexandrines grouped into six cantos. The work is extremely difficult; a complete understanding of it would require abundant annotations. But the erudition evinced in it is most often mock erudition. Queneau's method is poetic, not scientific. His juxtapositions of diverse things are contingent on their sound. Words, for Queneau, are tactile objects with smell and taste:

... les mots pour lui saveur ont volatile
la violette et l'osmose on la même épaisseur
l'âme et le wolfram on des sons acoquinés
cajole et kaolin assonance usées
souffrant et sulfureux sont tous deux adjectifs
le choix s'étend des pieds jusqu'au septentrion
du nadir à l'oreille et du radar au pif

(... words for him have a volatile flavor
the violet and osmosis have the same thickness
the soul and the wolfram have promiscuous sounds
Cajole and kaolin worn-out assonance
suffering and sulfurous are both adjectives
the choice extends from the feet up to the North
from the nadir to the ear and from the radar to the snout).

Like the poetry of Stéphane Mallarmé and Raymond Roussel, Queneau's work is sometimes so hermetic as to conceal its meaning from all, perhaps, but the author himself.

The pseudoscientific *Petite cosmogonie portative* may be read as a product of the Collège de la Pataphysique, a movement of leftist thinkers, philosophers, poets, and artists that Queneau joined around the time he wrote the work. Founded on the theory of equivalences, or "the truth of contradictions and exceptions," the "college" was a "société de recherches savantes et inutiles" (society of scholarly and useless investigations) inspired by Jarry's *Gestes et opinions du docteur Faustroll, pataphysicien: Roman néo-scientifique* (1911; translated as *Exploits & Opinions of Doctor Faustroll, Pataphysician: A Neo-Scientific*

Novel, 1996). Other members of the group included Prévert, Eugène Ionesco, Boris Vian, René Clair, Leiris, and Jean Dubuffet. The college's aim was to foster a "science des solutions imaginaires" (science of imaginary solutions) that would not only surpass all other sciences "comme la métaphysique dépasse la physique" (as metaphysics surpasses physics) but would also subvert them. (At one point Queneau attempted to integrate wind speed into the proof that two plus two equals four.) Queneau was the college's "Transcendent Satrape" and "Grand Conservateur de l'Ordre de la Grande Gidouille" (Great Keeper of the Order of the Great Spiral), the emblem for Pataphysic's circular unreason.

In 1951 Queneau was elected to the prestigious Académie Goncourt. The following year he gathered most of the poetry he had written to that time in *Si tu t'imagines, 1920–1951* (If You Think, 1920–1951). Written in the carpe diem mode and made into a hit song, the title poem epitomizes Queneau's marrying of the popular and the learned, tradition and innovation, in a proverbial wisdom rooted in quotidian existence:

Si tu t'imagines
si tu t'imagines
fillette fillette
si tu t'imagines
xa va xa va xa
va durer toujours
. . . .
. . . .
saison des amours
ce que tu te goures
fillette fillette
ce que tu te goures

(If you imagine
if you imagine
my girl my girl
if you imagine
that this that this
will last forever
. . . .
. . . .
the season of
the season of love
my girl my girl
then you are sadly mistaken).

Queneau spent the next seventeen years in a variety of literary activities. For Gallimard he directed the first three volumes (1955–1958) in the prestigious *Encyclopédie de la Pléiade* series. The aim of the *Encyclopédie,* Queneau says in his preface to the first volume, *Littératures anciennes, orientales et orales* (Ancient, Oriental, and Oral Literatures), is to present "pas un entassement de faits" (not a heap of facts) but a series of "tendances . . .

synthèses . . . perspectives . . . méthodes" with which to "apprendre à apprendre . . . savoir s'orienter" (learn to learn . . . know how to orient oneself). So dogged are Queneau's attempts to lead the reader, through various "rapprochements," to a just apprehension of "l'unité de la littérature universelle" (the unity of universal literature) that he is jocosely brought to point out in a note to the index of the volume that it contains "tous les noms cités dans le texte, y compris par exemple celui d'Argos, le chien d'Ulysse" (all the names cited in the text, including for example that of Argos, Ulysses' dog). In an early essay, "Richesse et limite" (Wealth and Limit), he had declared that "Une Encyclopédie *vraie* est actuellement une absurdité" (A *true* Encyclopedia is presently an absurdity). In his 1973 preface to *Le Voyage en Grèce* (The Voyage to Greece), in which that essay is republished along with others written between 1931 and 1939, he concedes: "On s'étonnera peut-être . . . de me voir qualifier d'absurde l'établissement de nos jours d'une Encyclopédie, alors que je dirige celle de la Pléiade; je répondrai: à coeur vaillant, rien d'impossible" (Some may wonder to see me characterize as absurd at this time the establishing of an Encyclopedia, while I am overseeing that of the Pléiade; to which I would respond: where there is a will, there is a way). By the logic of Pataphysics, the work of undermining and building could go hand in hand.

Queneau sat on the jury for the Cannes Film Festival in 1952; wrote scripts for Alain Resnais's *Le chant du styrène* (Ode to Plastic, 1952), René Clément's *Monsieur Ripois* (1954), the French version of Federico Fellini's *La strada* (1954), and Luis Buñuel's *La Mort en ce jardin* (1956); had a cameo role in Claude Chabrot's *Landru* (1962); and was the commentator in Pierre Kast's short *Arithmétique* (1951), which was conceived as the first part of a motion-picture encyclopedia but never got beyond the letter *A*. Several of his novels were made into movies: *Zazie dans le métro* by Louis Malle in 1960; *Le Dimanche de la vie* (1951; translated as *The Sunday of Life*, 1976) by Jean Herman in 1965; *On est toujours trop bon avec les femmes* (1947; translated as *We Always Treat Women Too Well*, 1981) by Michel Boisrond in 1970; and *Pierrot mon ami* (1943; translated, 1950) by François Leterrier in 1978.

In the early 1960s Queneau and François Le Lionnais founded OuLiPo, an acronym for "Ouvroir de littérature potentielle" (Workshop for Potential Literature). Dedicated to self-conscious experimentation, OuLiPo began as part of a subcommission of the College of Pataphysics. *Cent mille milliards de poèmes* (1961; translated as *One Hundred Million Million Poems*, 1983) is Queneau's contribution to this endeavor. The book consists of ten sonnets, each cut into fourteen strips; by combining the lines in various ways, the reader can theoretically create one hundred million million different sonnets. According to Queneau, the experiment is an attempt to reintroduce an element of restraint that is lacking in much contemporary literature, where spontaneity and genius have been elevated to guiding principles.

In 1965 Queneau published an enlarged version of *Le Chien à la mandoline*. The first part is an intimate diary spanning the previous fifteen years. In spite of its mundane subject matter, the collection is aesthetically and thematically a continuation of *L'instant fatal*–the poem "Mort mobile" (Mobile Death) returns to the ever-lurking theme of death; "Terre meuble" (Land Furniture) is a wordplay on death; and in "L'existence tout de même quel problème" (Existence In Any Case What a Problem) the poet succinctly expresses the existential dilemma that confronts him:

J'en ai assez de vivre et non moins de mourir
Que puis-je faire alors? sinon mourir ou vivre
Mais l'un n'est pas assez et l'autre c'est moisir
Aussi me peut-on voir errer plus ou moins ivre

C'est un faite je pourrais écrire un bien beau livre
Où je saurais bêler en me voyant mourir

(I've had enough of living and no less of dying
What can I do? Except to live or die
But one is not enough and the other is rotting
Hence you see me drifting more or less drunk

It's a fact I could write a very beautiful book
Where I would groan while dying).

The second part of the volume comprises forty-nine sonnets, many of which, such as "Magie noire" (Black Magic) and "Magie blanche" (White Magic), had appeared in previous collections. Queneau experiments with new rules of sonnet versification, such as replacing the number of syllables with the number of words and replacing rhyme with alliteration. These moves are not made lightly: Queneau calls the sonnet "la suprême combine" (the supreme combination) and strives to demonstrate that the alexandrine verse line that is its building block survives even in free verse if one takes caesura, hiatus, and feminine rhyme into account.

During this period Queneau was the subject of biographies, radio and television programs, and newspaper articles. A special number of the literary review *L'Arc* was devoted to his life and work in 1966. In 1967, 1968, and 1969 appeared, successively, *Courir les rues* (Pounding the Pavement), *Battre la campagne* (Beating the Bushes), and *Fendre les flots* (Cleaving the Waves). The triptych comprises the monument Queneau leaves

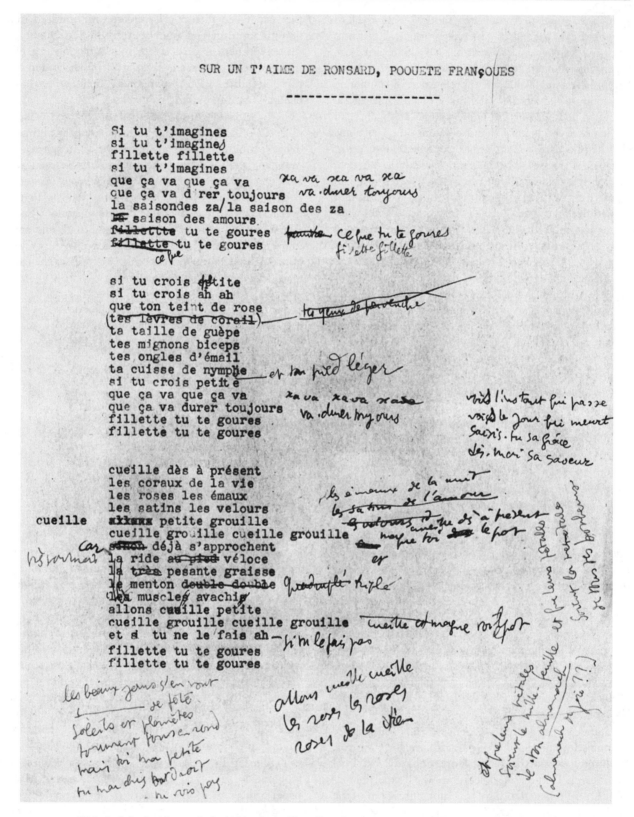

Early draft for the title poem in the 1952 collection Si tu t'imagines, *1920–1951* *(Bibliothèque Nationale, Paris)*

to posterity, as is suggested by "La rhétorique des marées" (The Rhetoric of the Tides) in *Fendre les flots:*

San rature et mouvant
il mène son poème à bonne fin
sans cesse élaborant son alphabet de pierres
au rythme des marées incurvant sa grammaire

(Without erasure and moving
he leads his poem to a good end
incessantly elaborating his alphabet of stones
to the rhythm of the tides curving his grammar in).

The infinitives in the titles of the three collections and of many of the individual poems convey the poet's struggle to find the perfect form for each work. Queneau places *Courir les rues* and *Battre la campagne* in the tradition of satire going back through Boileau to Horace and Martial; they are literary medleys in which allusions to authors as diverse as Breton, Prévert, Gustave Flaubert, Marcel Proust, Guillaume Apollinaire, Paul Verlaine, Gérard de Nerval, Pierre de Ronsard, Alfred de Vigny, William Shakespeare, and Paul Valéry have been detected. Queneau's Homeric odyssey in *Fendre les flots* seeks to complete that eminently literary survey by charting a circular voyage back to its mythic origin and final destination:

Allons c'est le réveil il faut de la rature
ressouder les deux bord en la seule nature
d'un voyage obstiné vers un azur plus pur

(Come it is the awakening we must of the erasure
Solder again the two sides in the one nature
of an obstinate voyage toward an azure more pure).

Queneau recurs to his age-old theme of time's erosion and life as vanity of vanities most conspicuously in the poem "Ces mois" (These Months). But the theme is sharpened now, as in "Tempête sous un crâne" (Tempest in a Skull), by his awareness of the approach of his own death and his desire to assure the survival of his poetry:

Un rai soudain vient à pâlir
l'oiseau s'envole et puis revient
apportant le brin de laurier
qui rend à l'eau sa verdeur primitive
mais le navire est-il sauvé?

(A ray suddenly comes to wane
the bird takes flight and then returns
bringing the slender stalk of laurel
which renders to the water its primal greenness
but is the vessel saved?)

Queneau dedicated *Le Voyage en Grèce* to the memory of his wife, who died in 1972. Raymond Queneau died on 25 October 1976.

Letters:

Correspondance Raymond Queneau–Elie Lascaux (Verviers: Temps Mêlés, 1979);

Une Correspondance: Raymond Queneau–Boris Vian (Levallios-Perret: Association des Amis de Valentin Brû, 1982);

Lettres Croisaees, 1949–1976: Andre Blavier, edited by Jean-Marie Klinkenberg (Brussels: Labor, 1988).

Bibliographies:

Wolgang Hillen, *Bibliographie des études sur l'homme et son oeuvre* (Cologne: Gemini, 1981);

Claude Rameil, Bibliography of Queneau's writings, *Les Amis de Valentin Brû,* no. 23 (1983).

References:

L'Arc, special Queneau issue, no. 28 (February 1966);

Renée Baligand, *Les Poèmes de Raymond Queneau* (Montreal, Paris & Brussels: Didier, 1972);

Jacques Bens, *Queneau* (Paris: Gallimard, 1962);

Andrée Bergens, *Raymond Queneau* (Geneva: Droz, 1963);

Cahiers Raymond Queneau, 1– (1986–   );

Jean-Marie Catonné, *Queneau* (Paris: Pierre Belfond, 1992);

Jean-Pierre Dauphin, ed., *Raymond Queneau plus intime* (Paris: Gallimard, 1978);

Europe, special Queneau issue, no. 650–651 (June–July 1983);

Paul Gayot, *Raymond Queneau* (Paris: Editions Universitaires, 1967);

Jacques Guicharnaud, *Raymond Queneau* (New York: Columbia University Press, 1965);

Jane Alison Hale, *The Lyric Encyclopedia of Raymond Queneau* (Ann Arbor: University of Michigan Press, 1989);

L'Herne, special Queneau issue, no. 29 (December 1975);

Magazine Littéraire, special Queneau issue, no. 94 (November 1975);

Jean Queval, *Essai sur Raymond Queneau* (Paris: Seghers, 1960);

Temps Mêlés: Documents Raymond Queneau (Paris: Argon, 1978);

Allen Thiher, *Raymond Queneau* (Boston: Twayne, 1985).

Papers:

Raymond Queneau's publications and criticisms of his work are in a special collection supervised by André Blavier at the Bibliothèque Municipale, Verviers, Belgium.

Pierre Reverdy
(13 September 1889 – 17 June 1960)

Paul Robichaud
University of Toronto

BOOKS: *Poèmes en prose* (Paris: Birault, 1915);
La Lucarne ovale (Paris: Birault, 1916);
Quelques poèmes (Paris: Birault, 1916);
Le Voleur de Talan (Paris: Ruillière, 1917);
Les Ardoises du toit (Paris: Birault, 1918);
Les Jockeys camouflés (Paris: Birault, 1918);
La Guitare endormie (Paris: Editions Nord-Sud, 1919);
Self defense: Critique, esthétique (Paris: Imprimerie littéraire, 1919);
Etoiles peintes (Paris: Editions Kra, 1921);
Cœur de chêne (Paris: Galérie Simon, 1921);
Cravates de chanvre (Paris: Editions Nord-Sud, 1922);
Les Epaves du ciel (Paris: Editions de la Nouvelle Revue Française, 1924); enlarged as *Plupart du temps: Poèmes, 1915–1922* (Paris: Gallimard, 1945);
Ecumes de la mer (Paris: Editions de la Nouvelle Revue Française, 1925);
Grande nature (Paris: Editions des Cahiers Libres, 1925);
La Peau de l'homme (Paris: Editions de la Nouvelle Revue Française, 1926);
Le Gant de crin (Paris: Plon, 1927);
La Balle au bond (Paris: Editions des Cahiers du Sud, 1928);
Flaques de verre (Paris: Editions de la Nouvelle Revue Française, 1929);
Sources du vent (Paris: Maurice Sachs, 1929);
Pierres blanches (Carcassonne: Jordy, 1930);
Risques et périls (Paris: Gallimard, 1930);
Ferraille (Brussels: Cahiers du Journal des poètes, 1937);
Plein verre (Nice: Editions des Isles de Lérins, 1940);
Visages (Paris: Editions du Chêne, 1946);
Le Livre de mon bord: Notes 1930–1936 (Paris: Mercure de France, 1948; revised according to the author's corrections and enlarged with previously unpublished fragments, 1989);
Le Chant des morts (Paris: Tériade, 1948);
Main d'œuvre: Poèmes, 1913–1949 (Paris: Mercure de France, 1949; revised according to the author's corrections, 1989);
Pierre Reverdy: Œuvres choisies, fac-similés, portraits, dessins et documents, edited by Jean Rousselot, with an essay

Pierre Reverdy, 1930 (photograph by R. P. Agaesse)

by Michel Manoll, Poètes d'aujourd'hui, no. 25 (Paris: Seghers, 1951);
Au Soleil du plafond (Paris: Editions Verve, 1955);
En Vrac: Notes (Monaco: Editions du Rocher, 1956);
La Liberté des mers (Paris: Maeght, 1960);
Sable mouvant (Paris: Louis Broder, 1966);
Pablo Picasso, par Pierre Reverdy; suivi de Marcoussis, par Jean Cassou; Jacques Lipchitz, par Roger Vitrac; Marcel Gromaire, par Jean Cassou; Gino Severini, par Jacques Maritain (Paris: Mercure de France, 1999).

Editions and Collections: *Œuvres complètes,* edited by Etienne-Alain Hubert, Maurice Saillet, and Stanislaus Fumet, 15 volumes projected, 12 volumes to date (Paris: Flammarion, 1967–   )—comprises *Plupart du temps* (1967); *Le Voleur de Talan: Roman* (1967); *Le gant de crin: Notes* (1968); *La peau de l'homme: Roman et conte* (1968); *Flaques de verre* (1972); *Risques et périls: Contes, 1915–1928* (1972); *Note éternalle du présent: Ecrits sur l'art 1923–1960* (1973); *Cette émotion appelée poésie: Ecrits sur la poésie (1932–1960)* (1974); *Nord-Sud, Self-defence et autres écrits sur l'art et la poésie 1917–1926* (1975); *La liberté des mers; Sable mouvant, et autres poèmes* (1978); *Au soleil du plafond et autres poèmes* (1980); *En vrac: Notes; Suivi de Un morceau de pain noir* (1989);

Plupart du temps, 1915–1922, 2 volumes, preface by Hubert Juin, Collection Poésie, nos. 50 and 51 (Paris: Gallimard, 1969);

Sources du vent, précédé de La Balle au bond, preface by Michel Deguy (Paris: Gallimard, 1971);

La Liberté des mers, Sable mouvant et autres poèmes (Paris: Flammarion, 1978);

Au Soleil du plafond et autres poèmes (Paris: Flammarion, 1980);

Ferraille, Plein verre, Le Chant des morts, Bois vert, suivi de Pierres blanches (Paris: Gallimard, 1981).

Editions in English: "Henri Laurens: The Silent Sculpture," translated by Walter Pach, in *Henri Laurens: Stone, Bronze, Terracotta. Catalogue of an Exhibition Held at the Buchholz Gallery, New York, 29 September–18 October, 1947* (New York: Buchholz Gallery, 1947), pp. 1–3;

Reverdy, translated by Anne Hyde Greet (Santa Barbara, Cal.: Unicorn Press, 1968);

Selected Poems, bilingual edition, translated by Kenneth Rexroth (New York: New Directions, 1969); republished as *Selected Poems: Bilingual Edition* (London: Cape, 1973);

Pierre Reverdy, translated by Vivienne Finch (London: X Press, 1978);

Roof Slates and Other Poems of Pierre Reverdy, translated by Mary Ann Caws and Patricia Terry (Boston: Northeastern University Press, 1981);

Freedom of the Seas: Nineteen Prose Poems, translated by Michael Bullock (London: Oasis, 1988);

Selected Poems, selected by Caws, translated by Caws, Terry, and John Ashbery, edited by Timothy Bent and Germaine Brée (Newcastle upon Tyne, U.K.: Bloodaxe, 1991);

Reverdy Translations, translated by Martin Bell, foreword by Peter Porter, introductory essay by John Pilling (Reading, U.K.: Whiteknights, 1997).

OTHER: *Pablo Picasso: Vingt-six reproductions de peintures et dessins précédées d'une étude critique par Pierre Reverdy; de notices biographiques et documentaires et d'un portrait inédit de l'artiste dessiné par lui-même et gravé sur bois par G. Aubert,* Les Peintres français nouveaux, no. 16 (Paris: Editions de la Nouvelle Revue Française, 1929);

Antoine Tudal, *Souspente,* preface by Reverdy (Paris: Godet, 1945);

George Braque, *Un Aventure méthodique,* preface by Reverdy (Paris: Mourlot, 1949);

Nord Sud: Revue littéraire, edited with contributions by Reverdy, facsimile reprint (Paris: Jean-Michel Place, 1980).

Pierre Reverdy's importance for twentieth-century French poetry lies in his innovative application of Cubist theories to the writing of verse; his theory of the image, which was taken up by André Breton and the Surrealists; and his editorship of the literary journal *Nord-Sud* (North-South), a catalyst for French avant-garde writers. Formally, Reverdy favored free verse and the prose poem. Central to his poetics is the idea of the image, "une création pure de l'esprit" (a pure creation of the spirit) that discloses a spiritual, poetic reality different from everyday life. Reverdy's favorite images are those of voyages, rooms, and barriers, which are often allegories of the poetic process; feelings of alienation and frustration are tempered by a sense of wonderment.

In addition to poetry, Reverdy wrote experimental fiction such as the novel *Le Voleur de Talan* (The Thief of Talan, 1917) and important reviews of Cubist painters that helped establish the movement in France. He converted to Roman Catholicism in 1921, and in 1926 he retreated to the monastic village of Solesmes. Although he lost his faith in 1928, he remained in virtual seclusion in Solesmes with his wife until his death in 1960. His isolation and the paucity of original work published in his later life contributed to the decline of Reverdy's reputation. Scholarly interest revived in the 1980s, and translators such as Mary Anne Caws, Patricia Terry, and John Ashbery have made Reverdy's poetry more widely available to English-speaking audiences.

Henri Pierre Reverdy was born on 13 September 1889 in Narbonne and abandoned by his parents. When he was six, it was legally established that his father was Henri Pierre Reverdy, a wine merchant, and the surname was added to his birth certificate. He then went to live in Toulouse with his mother, Jean Rose Esclopiér, a haberdasher; his parents finally married in 1897. Shame about his illegitimacy led Reverdy in later life to be notoriously reticent about his biography, and details about his early life—including who raised him and what surname he used

Frontispiece by Juan Gris and title page for Reverdy's collection of poetry about the elusiveness of creative inspiration (William T. Young Library, University of Kentucky)

before his father acknowledged his paternity—remain a mystery.

Reverdy dropped out of the Collège Victor Hugo in Narbonnes in 1905. In 1910 he moved to Paris, where he became friends with the experimental painters Pablo Picasso, George Braque, Juan Gris, and Henri Laurens; they had a profound effect on Reverdy's aesthetics, as did his poet friends Guillaume Apollinaire and Max Jacob. Reverdy shows these influences in his emphasis on the appearance of his poems on the page; punctuation is frequently absent, and syntax is often determined by the visual arrangement of words and phrases.

Reverdy married Henriette Charlotte Bureau on 8 September 1914. During World War I he enlisted in the auxiliary forces, but he was exempt from combat because of a heart condition.

Reverdy's first book, *Poèmes en prose* (Poems in Prose), appeared in 1915, with illustrations by Gris and Laurens. Most of the poems take the form of a series of paragraphs, with scenes or imagery shifting from one to the next. The juxtaposition of various aspects of vividly imagined situations reveals the impact of Reverdy's relationship with the Cubist artists. Often, as in "Les Poètes" (The Poets), the

imagery is the stuff of nightmare, showing the figure of the artist as alienated and fearful:

> Sa tête s'aritait craintievement sous l'abat-jour de la lampe.
> Il est vert et ses yeux sont rouges. Il y a un musicien qui ne bouge
> pas. Il dort; ses mains coupées jouent du violon pour lui faire
> oublier sa misère.

> (His head sheltered fearfully under the shade of the lamp.
> He is green and his eyes are red. There is a musician who does not move
> at all. He sleeps; his severed hands play on the violin so he can
> forget his misery).

Reverdy's unnatural use of color and the image of detached hands evoke the Cubist challenge to mimetic representation, and the disquieting mood of the poem is one that is frequently conveyed in contemporary experimental painting. The sleeping musician's detached hands suggest a separation between the artist and his art that came to be a typical feature of modernist poetry and painting.

Reverdy, Pablo Picasso, Jean Cocteau, and Brassaï,
1944 (photograph by Brassaï)

Poèmes en prose also engages with the realities of the world war that was raging at the time of its publication. Though a noncombatant, in "Fronts de bataille" (Battlefronts) Reverdy expresses a surprisingly powerful and evocative sense of the horror experienced on the western front:

Sur le rempart où tremblent des ruines on entend un écho
de tambours. On les avait crevés. Ceux d'hier se répon-
dent
encore.
La nuit finie, le bruit dissipe les rêves et les fronts
découverts où saigne une blessure.

(On the rampart where the ruins tremble is heard an echo
of a drum. They had been burst. Those of yesterday
respond to one another
again.
The night ends, more noise dissipates the dreams and the
uncovered foreheads
where a wound bleeds).

This aspect of Reverdy's early work is easily overlooked or assimilated to his more explicitly aesthetic

concerns, but it situates his poetry in its immediate historical context.

La Lucarne ovale (The Oval Garrett Window, 1916) and *Quelques poèmes* (Some Poems, 1916) move away from the prose poem to more conventional vers libre. One of the most autobiographical of Reverdy's collections, *La Lucarne ovale* includes many poems that evoke the time he spent living in a Paris garret, such as the following isolated lyric from an untitled poem. For example:

Aux premières lueurs du jour je me suis levé
lentement. Je suis monté à l'échelle du mur et,
par la lucarne, j'ai regardé passer les gens qui
s'en allaient.

(At the first light of day, I got up
slowly. I climbed up the ladder on the wall and,
by the garret window, I watched the people
who were passing by).

The poet is a perpetual outsider who can obtain a vantage point unavailable to the people passing by on their daily business, people whom he is able to transform into material for his art.

In 1917 Reverdy founded the semi-monthly review *Nord-Sud* as an outlet for avant-garde writing and the promotion of experimental movements in the other arts. *Nord-Sud* was sponsored by Jacques Doucet, a wealthy friend of Jacob's, and may also have received the patronage of Apollinaire. Contributors to the journal included such important figures as Breton, Louis Aragon, Tristan Tzara, and Phillipe Soupault. In addition to introducing a new generation of writers, *Nord-Sud* provided Reverdy a forum in which to present his own aesthetic theories, which had a seminal influence on later developments in the arts. In his essay "Sur le cubisme" (On Cubism), published on 15 March 1917 and republished in the collection *Nord-Sud, Self-defence et autres écrits sur l'art et la poésie 1917–1926* (North-South, Self-Defense, and Other Writings on the Art of Poetry 1917–1926, 1975), Reverdy characterizes Cubism as "un art éminemment plastique; mais un art de création et non de reproduction ou d'interprétation" (an eminently plastic art; but an art of creation and not of reproduction or interpretation). This characterization also applies to poetry. By refusing merely to replicate existing objects, art can achieve an existence that adds to reality: "l'Art d'aujourd'hui est un art de grand réalité" (the Art of today is an art of great reality). Reverdy's observations on Cubist art illuminate his early poetry, which transforms objects into poetic images and explores potential relationships within the imaginative space of the poem.

The most important of Reverdy's *Nord-Sud* essays for modern French poetry is "L'Image" (The Image), published on 16 March 1918, which provided Breton with a theory of the image that he developed in his first *Manifeste du surréalisme* (Manifesto of Surrealism, 1924). According to Reverdy, the poet creates "une forte image, neuve pour l'esprit, en rapprochant sans comparaison deux réalités distantes don't *l'esprit seul* a saisi les rapports" (a strong image, new for the spirit, in reconciling without comparison two distant realities of which *the spirit alone* has grasped the relationship). This kind of poetry is "une *poésie de création*" (a *poetry of creation*) in which a new reality, "une *réalité poétique*" (a *poetic reality*), is made. In rejecting comparison as a basis for poetry Reverdy also rejects such common poetic devices as the simile and the more obvious kinds of metaphor. Modern poetry is to follow the example of Cubism, which rejects imitation to disclose a reality that is purely artistic and relational.

Also in 1917 Reverdy published *Le Voleur de Talan*, an autobiographical poetic novel based on his souring relationship with Jacob, who was notoriously suspicious that other artists had designs on his ideas and work. The novel received little critical attention. In 1918 Reverdy published two volumes of poetry: one of his most important collections, *Les Ardoises du toit* (The Roof Slates), and *Les Jockeys camouflés* (The Camouflaged Jockeys). The eighty-one poems of *Les Ardoises du toit* demonstrate Reverdy's preoccupation with the spatial arrangement of words on the page. The reader plays an active role in the creation of meaning by forging the connections usually made by punctuation and conventional syntactic arrangements, as in "Départ" (Departure):

> L'horizon s'incline
>   Les jours sont plus longs
>   Voyage
> Un cœur saute dans une cage
>
>   (The horizon slants
>   The days are longer
>   Journeying
>   A heart jumps in its cage).

The slanting of the horizon is depicted in the marginal slant of the first and fourth lines. A syntactic connection is suggested by the grouping together of lines 2 and 3, implying that "The days are longer" while one is "journeying," but the subject of *voyage* remains open; there is no necessary link between the days' lengthening and the journey. The relationship between these three lines and the fourth is unclear. Whose heart leaps in a cage? A reader may decide that it is the traveler's, but it may also be that of the bird in lines 5 and 6: "Un oiseau chante / Il va mourir" (A bird sings / He will die). By refusing to offer definite meanings, Reverdy's poems convey a sense of evocative mystery and suggest an imaginative reality that they can neither fully express nor exhaust.

Reverdy on the terrace of the Aiglon café in Paris, 1947 (photograph by Brassaï)

Reverdy published two books in 1919: *La Guitare endormie* (The Sleeping Guitar), a volume of poems, and *Self defense* (Self Defense), a collection of aphorisms on aesthetics. Illustrated by Gris, *La Guitare endormie* is dominated by the theme, suggested by the title, of the elusiveness of creative inspiration. The bleakness of Reverdy's vision is haunted in "En Attendant" (Waiting) by a fear of creative failure in which "Toute s'évapore et sèche" (Everything evaporates and dries up), which could be regarded as a prophesy of the poet's later years of silence.

Self defense, in contrast, is an affirmation of Reverdy's faith in the spiritual motivation of art: "Il n'y a pas de *réalité artistique* sans esprit" (There is no *artistic reality* without spirit). Stéphane Mallarmé is identified as an important influence on modern poetry because he taught the importance of "*Vocabulaire, syntaxe, choix et limitations des éléments*" (*Vocabulary, syntax, choice and limitation of elements*).

Having helped to launch the careers of a generation of avant-garde writers, *Nord-Sud* ceased publication after a year. The demise of the journal marks the end of the most innovative and dynamic phase of Reverdy's poetic career, which was part of the explosion of artistic activity in Paris at the time of World War I. Jacob, who had converted to Roman Catholicism and was living in retirement at the abbey in Sainte-Benoît-sur-Loire, persuaded Reverdy and his wife to join the church on 2 May 1921. Conversion did not have the effect on Reverdy's poetry that it did on the work of converts such as Charles Péguy and Paul Claudel. The prose poems of *Etoiles peintes* (Painted Stars, 1921) explore a thoroughly disorienting and threatening landscape. In "Tumulte" the poet is tormented by the image of a mob: "La foule descendait plus vite et en criant. Ils venaient tous du fond, de derrière les arbres, de derrière le bois du cadre, de la maison" (The mob descends quickly and crying. They come through the forest, from behind the trees, from behind the wood frame, from the house). The themes of alienation and imaginative desolation continue through *Cœur de chêne* (Heart of Oak, 1921) and *Cravates de chanvre* (Hemp Neckties, 1922). Reverdy followed these collections with two volumes of selections from his earlier Paris days, *Les Epaves du ciel* (Chips from Heaven, 1924) and *Ecumes de la mer* (Sea Foam, 1925). A book of new poems, *Grande nature* (Great Nature, 1925), expresses a sense of human insignificance before the vast impersonal forces of the natural world. The poems are unpunctuated, creating syntactic ambiguity. In "Ce Souvenir" (This Souvenir) Reverdy presents nature as utterly overwhelming: "Le ciel tenait tout le fond tout l'espace / Un peu de terre en bas qui brillait au soleil / Encore un peu de place / Et la mer" (The sky occupies all the background all the space / A bit of earth below which shines with the sun / Again a little place / And the sea).

In 1926 Reverdy and his wife retreated to the abbey in Solesmes. That year Reverdy published *La Peau de l'homme* (The Skin of Humanity), a collection of short stories and a novella—his first book of fiction since *La Voleur de Talan* in 1917. Another prose work, *Le Gant de crin* (The Horsehair Glove, 1927), is a collection of aphorisms on faith and art that acknowledge the need to submit to the will of God. This apparent certainty of faith is contradicted by the poems of *La Balle au bond* (The Rebounding Ball, 1928), which explore a state of profound spiritual disquiet. Images of hope and comfort are threatened with extinction, as in "L'Angoisse" (Anguish): "De la rue, monte un murumure paisible. Le soir est tiède. Alors l'espoir renaît. Mais les murs trop étroits se serrent" (From the street rises a peaceful murmur. The evening is tepid. Then hope is reborn. But the too-narrow walls contract). Such lines suggest that Reverdy's openness to peace and hope is relentlessly challenged by darker, constricting psychic forces. Later that year, disappointed and bitter, Reverdy left the Catholic faith.

In 1929 Reverdy published two quite different collections. The prose poems of *Flaques de verre* (Pools of Glass), such as "Ça" (That), explore the ominous, hallucinatory world that was by this time familiar to Reverdy's readers: "Les quelques raies qui raccourcissent le mur sont des indications pour la police. Les arbres sont des têtes, ou les têtes des arbres, en tout cas les têtes des arbres me men-

acent" (The few rays that foreshorten the wall are signs for the police. The trees are heads, the heads trees—in any case, the heads of the trees threaten me). Heads and trees are indistinguishable but menacing, evoking a natural world at once unknowable and in constant flux. *Sources du vent* (Sources of the Wind) gives voice to despair and isolation in more conventional vers libre and reflects Reverdy's sense of hopelessness following the failure of his spiritual search, as in "Lumière rousse" (Russet Light):

Personne dans la marge
Plus rien sur le trottoir
Le ciel est plein d'orages
Ma tête sans espoir

(Person in the margin
Nothing on the sidewalk
The sky is full of thunderstorms
My head without hope).

This sense of emptiness, of a hostile environment, and of hopelessness testifies to the poet's deepening psychological troubles, lending the poems an aspect of almost visceral pain. Significantly, *Sources de vent* is Reverdy's amplest book of poems, which suggests the depth of his disquietude.

Pierres blanches (White Stones, 1930) is haunted by the poet's fear of his own death, as in "Il devait en effet faire bien froid" (It must have been very cold indeed), which features a grim vantage point: "De la tapisserie où mon corps s'aplatait de / profil" (From the tapestry where my body reclines in / profile). That same year Reverdy published another collection of short fiction, *Risques et périls* (Risks and Perils).

Seven years of silence followed before Reverdy produced his next collection, a slim volume of twenty-six poems titled *Ferraille* (Scrap Iron). The nadir of Reverdy's psychological disintegration finds expression in these poems, accompanied by an heroic recognition of the need to continue and to endure. In "Reflux" (Ebb) Reverdy recognizes his mental state as an obstacle to be overcome: "Il faut remonter du plus bas de la mine, de la terre épassier par l'humus du malheur . . . dans les tempêtes sans tendresse de l'égoïsme et les décisions tranchantes de l'esprit" (I must climb back up from the very bottom of the mine, from the earth thickened by the soil of unhappiness . . . in egoism's storms without tenderness and the cutting decisions of the spirit). There is a resolve here to overcome the limits of egoism, as well as the spiritual crisis of the previous ten years. *Plein verre* (Full Glass, 1940), a brief collection, further explores the poet's acceptance of his situation. In 1945 Reverdy produced a major collection of his poetry written up to 1922, *Plupart du temps* (Most of the Time).

Manuscript for "Chemin perdu," included in Reverdy's 1948 collection, Le Chant des morts
(from Luc Decaunes, ed., Hommage à Pierre Reverdy, *1961)*

*Title page for a collection of the pessimistic poetry Reverdy
published after World War II (from Maurice Saillet,*
Pierre Reverdy, 1889–1960, *1962)*

written over a period of thirty years; his views show little change. His final publication during his lifetime, *La Liberté des mers* (The Freedom of the Seas, 1960), comprises poems written mostly during his dynamic years in Paris.

Pierre Reverdy died in Solesmes on 17 June 1960. He is remembered as a galvanizing force during the formative years of French modernism. In the bleakness of his vision and in his spiritual torments and failings, Reverdy reveals his fundamental humanity before the existential and historical terrors of the twentieth century.

Letters:

Lettres à Jean Rousselot / Pierre Reverdy. Suivies de, Pierre Reverdy romancier, ou, Quand le poète se dédouble, edited by Jean Rousselot (Mortemart: Rougerie, 1973).

Bibliographies:

Michael Bishop, *Pierre Reverdy: A Bibliography* (London: Grant & Cutler, 1976);

Etienne-Alain Hubert, *Bibliographie des écrits de Pierre Reverdy* (Paris: Minard, 1976).

References:

Peter Brunner, *Pierre Reverdy: De la solitude au mystère* (Zurich: Juris, 1966);

Mary Ann Caws, *La Main de Pierre Reverdy* (Geneva: Droz, 1979);

Michel Collot and Jean-Claude Mathieu, eds., *Reverdy aujourd'hui: Actes du colloque des 22, 23, 24 juin 1989; suivis de notes de Pierre Reverdy transcrites et présentées par François Chapon et Etienne-Alain Hubert* (Paris: Presses de l'Ecole normale supérieure, 1991);

Luc Decaunes, ed., *Hommage à Pierre Reverdy* (Subverie: Rodez, 1961);

Robert Greene, *The Poetic Theory of Pierre Reverdy* (Berkeley: University of California Press, 1967);

Mortimer Guiney, *La Poésie de Pierre Reverdy* (Geneva: Georg, 1966);

Yvan LeClerc and Georges Cesbron, eds., *Le Centenaire de Pierre Reverdy (1889–1960): Actes du colloque d'Angers, Sablé-sur-Sarthe, Solesmes, du 14 au 16 septembre 1989* (Angers: Presses de l'Université d'Angers, 1989);

Michel Manoll, *Pierre Reverdy,* edited by Jean Rousselot, Poètes d'aujourd'hui no. 25 (Paris: Seghere, 1951);

Anthony Rizzuto, *Style and Theme in Reverdy's "L'Ardoises du toit"* (University: University of Alabama Press, 1971);

Andrew Rothwell, *Textual Spaces: The Poetry of Pierre Reverdy* (Amsterdam: Rodopi, 1989);

Maurice Saillet, *Pierre Reverdy, 1889–1960* (Paris: Mercure de France, 1962).

Three years later Reverdy published *Le Chant des morts* (Song of the Dead). As the title suggests, the poems are preoccupied with mortality; but they also reflect on the fate of Western civilization in the aftermath of World War II, as in "Le Poids des hommes" (The Weight of Men): "Il n'y a plus rien dans notre hémisphere / Rien à boire / Rien à dire / Rien à voir" (There is nothing in our hemisphere / Nothing to drink / Nothing to say / Nothing to see). Reverdy's pessimism and proclivity for psychological self-destruction need to be understood, in part, as symptomatic of the twentieth-century Europe in which he lived and worked. *Le Livre de mon bord* (My Logbook), also published in 1948, includes prose meditations from the 1930s that bear witness to the poet's tortured state of mind during that period. *Main d'œuvre* (Manpower, 1949) includes an early unpublished collection, "Cale sèche" (Dry Dock); Reverdy's published volumes from 1925 to 1946; and "Bois vert" (Green Woods), written between 1946 and 1949. His efforts to make all of his previous work available continued with *Au Soleil du plafond* (In the Sun of the Ceiling, 1955), comprising poems written during his *Nord-Sud* period. In *En Vrac: Notes* (In Bulk: Notes, 1956) Reverdy presents his aesthetic positions in a series of notes

Jules Supervielle
(16 January 1884 – 17 May 1960)

Kenneth W. Meadwell
University of Winnipeg

BOOKS: *Brumes du passé* (N.p., 1901);

Comme des voiliers, illustrated by Fernand Sabatté (Paris: La Poétique, 1910);

Les Poèmes de l'humour triste, illustrated by André Favory, André Lhote, and André Dunoyer de Segonzac (Paris: A la Belle Edition, 1919);

Poèmes: Voyage en soi, Paysages, Les Poèmes de l'humour triste, Le Goyavier authentique, preface by Paul Fort (Paris: Eugène Figuière, 1919);

Débarcadères: La Pampa, Une Paillotte au Paraguay, Distances, Flotteurs d'alarme (Paris: Editions de la Revue de l'Amérique Latine, 1922; revised and enlarged edition, Maastricht, Paris & Brusses: A. A. Stols, 1934);

L'Homme de la pampa (Paris: Editions de la Nouvelle Revue Française, 1923);

Gravitations: Poèmes (Paris: Gallimard, 1925; revised, 1932);

Le Voleur d'enfants (Paris: Gallimard, 1926); dramatized as *Le Voleur d'enfants, comédie en 3 actes et un épilogue* (Paris: Gallimard, 1949); original novel translated by Alan Pryce-Jones as *The Colonel's Children* (London: Secker & Warburg/Sidgwick & Jackson, 1950);

Oloron-Sainte-Marie, with a portrait by Lhote (Marseilles: Cahiers du Sud, 1927);

La Piste et la mare (Paris: Les Exemplaires, 1927);

Saisir, with a portrait by Borès, Collection Une œuvre, un portrait (Paris: Editions de la Nouvelle Revue Française, 1928);

Le Survivant (Paris: Editions de la Nouvelle Revue Française, 1928); translated by John Russell as *The Survivor* (London: Secker & Warburg/Sidgwick & Jackson, 1951);

Uruguay, with a frontispiece by Jean-Gabriel Daragnès (Paris: Editions Emil-Paul, 1928);

Trois mythes (Madrid, Paris & Buenos Aires: Agrupación de Amigos del Libro de Arte en España y América, 1929)—comprises "L'Enfant de la haute mer," "La Sirène 825," and "Les Boiteux du ciel";

Jules Supervielle, 1939 (photograph by Giselle Freund)

Bolivar et les femmes (nouvelle historique) (Paris: Printed by Allard, Chatelard, 1930);

Le Forçat innocent (Paris: Gallimard, 1930);

L'Enfant de la haute mer (Paris: Gallimard, 1931); translated by Darsie Jaap and Norah Nicolls as *Along the Road to Bethlehem,* illustrated by Mary Adshead (New York: Dutton, 1933); translation republished as *Souls of the Soulless* (London: Methuen, 1933);

La Belle au bois, pièce en trois actes (Paris: Gallimard, 1932); revised and enlarged as *La Belle au bois* (Buenos

374

Aires: Lettres Françaises, 1944; Paris: Gallimard, 1947); revised and enlarged, with *Robinson ou l'amour vient de loin* (Paris: Gallimard, 1953);

Boire à la source: Confidences de la mémoire et du paysage (Paris: Corrêa, 1933); new edition, enlarged with *Journal d'une double angoisse, Le Temps immobile, Les Bêtes* (Paris: Editions de la Nouvelle Revue Française, 1952);

Les Amis inconnus (Paris: Editions de la Nouvelle Revue Française, 1934);

Phosphorescences: Gravures d'Herbert Lespinasse, interprétées par Jules Supervielle (Paris: Librairie de France, 1936);

Bolivar: Pièce en trois actes et onze tableaux; La première famille: Farce en un acte (Paris: Gallimard, 1936; revised, 1955);

La Fable du monde (Paris: Gallimard, 1938);

L'Arche de Noé (Paris: Gallimard, 1938);

Poèmes de la France malheureuse (1939–1941), Collection des Amis des Lettres Françaises, no. 2 (Buenos Aires: Editions des Lettres Françaises, 1941); enlarged as *Poèmes de la France malheureuse (1939–1941): suivi de Ciel et Terre,* Collection des Cahiers du Rhône, no. 6 (Neuchâtel, Switzerland: Editions de La Baconnière, 1942);

Le Petit bois, et autres contes, illustrated by Ramón Gaya, Renaissance, no. 2 (Mexico City: Ediciones Quetzal, 1942; Paris: Jacques & René Wittmann, 1947);

Choix de poèmes (Buenos Aires: Editorial Sudamericana, 1944; Paris: Gallimard, 1947);

Une Métamorphose ou l'époux exemplaire (Montevideo: La Galatea, 1945);

1939–1945, Poèmes (Paris: Gallimard, 1946);

Orphée et autres contes, Collection du Fleuron, no. 4 (Neuchâtel, Switzerland & Paris: Ides et Calendes, 1946);

Dix-huit poèmes (Paris: Seghers, 1946);

A la nuit, afterword by Albert Béguin (Neuchâtel, Switzerland: Editions de la Baconnière / Paris: Editions du Seuil, 1947);

La Création des animaux, nouvelle (Paris: Editions du Pavois, 1947); enlarged, with illustrations by Jacques Noël, as *La Création des animaux* (Paris: Presses du Livre Français, 1951);

Robinson: Comédie en trois actes (Paris: Gallimard, 1948);

Schéhérazade: Comédie en trois actes (Paris: Gallimard, 1949);

Oublieuse mémoire, Collection Métamorphoses, no. 37 (Paris: Gallimard, 1949);

Les B.B.V., Nouvelles Originales, no. 7 (Paris: Editions de Minuit, 1949);

Premiers pas de l'univers: Contes, (Paris: Gallimard, 1950);

Naissances: Poèmes; suivis de, En songeant à un art poétique (Paris: Gallimard, 1951); edited and translated by Philip Cranston as *Naissances = Births: A Bilingual Edition* (Potomac, Md.: Scripta Humanistica, 1992);

Le Jeune homme du dimanche, illustrated by Elie Lascaux (Paris: Gallimard, 1952); enlarged as *Le Jeune homme du dimanche et des autres jours: Roman* (Paris: Gallimard, 1955);

L'Escalier, nouveaux poèmes (Paris: Gallimard, 1956)– includes revised versions of *A la nuit, Débarcadères,* and *Les Poèmes de l'humour triste;*

Le Corps tragique: Poèmes (Paris: Gallimard, 1959);

Les Suites d'une course; suivi de L'Etoile de Séville (Paris: Gallimard, 1959).

Editions and Collections: *L'Enfant de la haute mer,* illustrated by Pierre Roy (Paris: Editions de la Nouvelle Revue Française, 1946);

Poèmes choisis, French and Spanish edition (Montevideo: Academia Nacional de Letras, 1959);

Gravitations; précédé de Débarcadères, preface by Marcel Arland, Collection Poésie, no. 9 (Paris: Gallimard, 1966);

L'Enfant de la haute mer, illustrated by Jacqueline Duheme (Paris: Editions G.P., 1978);

La Fable du monde; suivi de, Oublieuse mémoire, preface by Jean Gaudon, Collection Poésie, no. 219 (Paris: Gallimard, 1987);

Œuvres poétiques complètes: Jules Supervielle, edited by Michel Collot and others, Bibliothèque de la Pléiade, no. 426 (Paris: Gallimard, 1996).

Editions in English: *The Ox and the Ass at the Manger,* translated by Naomi Royde Smith and illustrated by Muriel Broderick (London: Hollis & Carter, 1945);

Selected Writings of Jules Supervielle (New York: New Directions, 1967)–includes translations from *Débarcadères, Gravitations, Le Forçat innocent, Les Amis inconnus, La Fable du monde, 1939–1945,* and *Oublieuse mémoire;*

Supervielle, translated by Teo Savory (Santa Barbara, Cal.: Unicorn Press, 1967);

The Horses of Time: Poems of Jules Supervielle, translated by Geoffrey Gardner (Syracuse, N.Y.: Tamarack Editions, 1985);

Selected Poems and Reflections on the Art of Poetry, translated by George Bogin (New York: SUN, 1985).

SELECTED PLAY PRODUCTIONS: *La Belle au bois,* Brussels, 24 December 1931;

Bolivar, pièce en trois actes et onze tableaux, Paris, Comédie-Française, 1 March 1936; revised, Paris, Opéra, 12 May 1950;

Shéhérazade, comédie en trois actes, Avignon, Palais des
　　Papes, 17 July 1948;
Le Voleur d'enfants, comédie en trois actes et un épilogue, Paris,
　　Théâtre de l'Œuvre, 15 October 1948;
Robinson, ou, l'Amour vient de loin, Paris, Théâtre de
　　l'Œuvre, 6 November 1952.

Prolific poet, dramatist, fabulist, essayist, and
novelist Jules Supervielle occupies a singular place in
modern French literature by virtue of his simple yet
highly evocative poetic style. Remarkable as a chronicle
of his frequent travels between France and Uruguay,
lands that he envisaged with affection and loyalty, his
poetry is also resonant with voices that evoke seas,
pampas—vast and treeless South American plains—
yearnings for self-discovery, and ultimately, the need to
understand the passing of time and one's place in an
evolving world.

　　Born in Montevideo, Uruguay, on 16 January
1884, to Jules Supervielle *père,* descendant of Béarnais
stock (from the Béarn region of the French Pyrénées)
and partner with his brother, Bernard Supervielle, in
the banking firm of Supervielle of Montevideo, and
Maria Munyo, of Basque origin, Supervielle began
what became a truly peripatetic life by sailing to
Marseilles with his parents at the age of eight months.
What was meant to have been a reunion of both families proved to be the most tragic event in the young
Supervielle's life, for soon after arriving in the south of
France, his mother and father died from cholera, having drunk polluted water from a street tap. Thus began
the poet's existence: orphaned at a tender age and
adopted by his father's brother, Bernard, and his
mother's sister, Marie-Anne Munyo, who were husband and wife, he began a life of constant travel by ship
between South America and Europe, eventually nam-
ing himself a "bicontinental." With the help of friends
he mastered the Spanish language during his early
years, spoke French at home in Montevideo, while at
the same time attending an English school. At the age of
six he began to write poetry, and at nine, fables. At this
time he learned that his uncle and aunt were not his
parents, that his cousins were not his siblings. Henceforth, death inhabited the psyche of the young Supervielle: that of his parents as well as the abstraction of
death. His personal grief engendered a desire to com-
prehend the meaning and nature of death on a philosophical level, a longing that he says was constantly
present in his heart after learning of the loss of his parents.

　　At the age of ten Supervielle was sent as a boarder
to the Lycée Janson-de-Sailly in Paris, where he continued his education in what was believed to be a more
rigorous and disciplined academic environment. Such

*Supervielle in Montevideo, Uruguay, circa 1887–1888 (from
Ricardo Paseyro,* Jules Supervielle, *1987)*

nineteenth-century French poets as Leconte de Lisle,
Victor Hugo, Alfred de Musset, and Alfred de Vigny,
all somewhat conventional in their esthetics, were
Supervielle's inspiration. Other poets who exercised
much greater freedom in poetic form and thematics,
such as Arthur Rimbaud and Stéphane Mallarmé, for
example, were scarcely known to Supervielle. After
receiving his *baccalauréat* (high-school diploma) in 1902,
Supervielle completed his military service in France
before commencing a *licence-ès-lettres* (bachelor of arts
degree) in Spanish at the Sorbonne, which he completed in 1906. His military service had a deleterious
effect on his health by aggravating what later became a
serious cardiac condition. His first small collection of
poetry, *Brumes du passé* (Mists from the Past) had been
privately published in 1901 when he was still a teenager. A young sensibility in that early collection evokes
themes that came to characterize Supervielle's later
works: loss of parents, underprivileged individuals,
human suffering, dream-filled lovers. The epigraph of
the work, "Mon coeur a trop saigné aux épines des
roses"(My heart has bled too much on the rose thorns),
renders a melancholy curious in a soul so young, but
also epitomizes the primordial and simple imagery that
structures much of his poetry: heart, thorn, rose. The

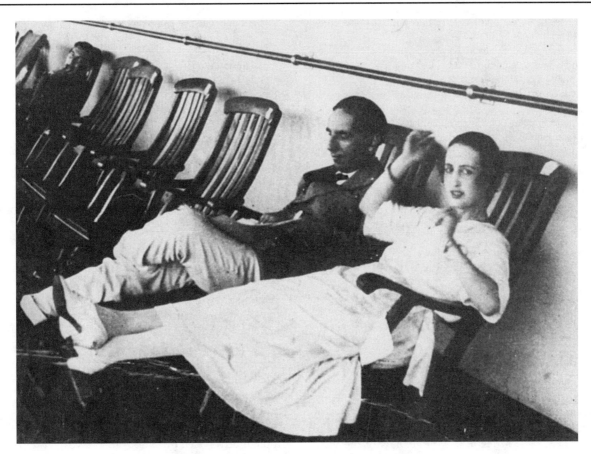

Supervielle and his wife, Pilar Saavedra Supervielle, during their 1924 voyage to South America
(from Ricardo Paseyro, Jules Supervielle, *1987)*

human body and flora are recurring motifs that underline a fundamental aspect of his esthetics, for his poetry is profoundly visual, striving to create clearly defined imagery that invites the reader's appreciation and understanding of the ambient world.

Supervielle's love for Pilar Saavedra, whom he had met during a vacation in Montevideo, resulted in their marriage on 18 May 1907 in Uruguay and colored with affection and earnestness his next collection, *Comme des voiliers* (Like Sailboats), published in 1910 and dedicated to her. The first of their children, Henri, was born in Uruguay.

With the outbreak of World War I in 1914, Supervielle, who was already in France, was mobilized with the auxiliary service, but his poor health kept him out of combat. However, his proficiency in English, Spanish, Italian, and Portuguese was of significant use to the French forces, and at the end of war he held the rank of corporal. For much of the next twenty-five years he lived comfortably in his Paris apartment, surrounded by his growing family; the Supervielles had five more children in the postwar period. In 1919 Supervielle published *Poèmes: Voyage en soi, Paysages, Les*

Poèmes de l'humour triste, Le Goyavier authentique (Poems: Travels within Oneself, Landscapes, Poems of Sad Humor, The Authentic Guava Tree), dedicated to his mother. In this work he paints vivid pictures of landscapes and seascapes, trees, plains, and mountains as they compel the attention of the poet-traveler.

Débarcadères: La Pampa, Une Paillotte au Paraguay, Distances, Flotteurs d'alarme (Landing Stages: The Pampas, A Straw Hut in Paraguay, Distances, Alarm Signal Floaters), which appeared in 1922 and was dedicated to Supervielle's cousin Louis, whom he viewed as a brother, refers to sea travel, departures, and returns, and is comprised of poems in free verse, in contrast to the preceding collection, which consists of poems following regular meters. The themes of the two works are similar, however, and underline the yearning for the South American landscape that had fascinated the young child. One of the more eloquent pieces of this collection, "Retour à l'Estancia" (Return to the Estancia), conveys a return to the past:

Le petit trot des gauchos me façonne,
les oreilles fixes de mon cheval m'aident à me situer.

Je retrouve dans sa plénitude ce que je n'osais plus envis-
    ager,
même par une petite lucarne,
toute la pampa étendue à mes pieds comme il y a sept ans.
O mort! me voici revenu.
J'avais pourtant compris que tu ne me laisserais pas revoir
    ces terres,
une voix me l'avait dit qui ressemblait à la tienne et tu ne
    ressembles qu' à toi-même,
Et aujourd'hui, je suis comme ce hennissement qui ne sait
    pas que tu existes,

(The jog trot of the gauchos shapes me,
the pricked up ears of my horse help me to place myself.
I find again in its plenitude what I no longer dared to
    envisage,
even through a little garret window—
all the pampa spread out at my feet as though it was seven
    years ago.
Oh Death, here I am back again!
It was my understanding, though, that you would not let
    me see these lands again.
A voice resembling yours told me so and you resemble
    only yourself
and today I am like this neighing which does not know
    you exist).

The poet's return to the sweeping expanse of land of
the *estancia,* in essence an immense ranch, rekindles the
poet's memories of death, but the fullness of the vista
and the senses also sparks a defiance toward death:

je trouve comique d'avoir tant douté de moi et c'est de toi
    que je doute ô surfaite,
même quand mon cheval enjambe les os d'un bœuf pro-
    prement blanchis par les vautours et par les aigles,
ou qu'une odeur de bête farouchement écorchée, me tord
    le nez quand je passe.
Je fais corps avec la pampa qui ne connaît pas la mytholo-
    gie,
avec le désert orgueilleux d'être le désert depuis les temps
    les plus abstraits,
il ignore les Dieux de l'Olympe qui rythment encore le
    vieux monde.
Je m'enfonce dans la plaine qui n'a pas d'histoire et tend
    de tous côtés sa peau dure de vache qui a toujours
    couché dehors
et n'a pour toute végétation que quelques *talas, ceibos, pitas,*
qui ne connaissent le grec ni le latin,
. . . .
Je me mêle à une terre qui ne rend de comptes à personne
    et se défend de ressembler à ces paysages manufacturés
    d'Europe, saignés par les souvenirs. . . .

(I find it amusing to have doubted myself so much and it is
    you whom I really doubt, Oh overrated one,
even when my horse leaps over the bones of a steer
    cleanly whitened by the vultures and the eagles,
or when the odor of a freshly-skinned animal puckers my
    nose when I pass.

I am one with the pampa which knows nothing of mythol-
    ogy,
with the desert proud of being the desert from the most
    abstract times—
it is unaware of the Gods of Olympus who still rhythm the
    old world.
I bury myself in the plain which has no history and
    spreads out on all sides its tough cowhide which has
    always slept outdoors
and has for vegetation only some *talas, ceibos,* and *pitas*
which know neither Greek nor Latin,
. . . .
I mingle with a land which answers to no one and forbids
    itself to resemble those landscapes manufactured in
    Europe, bloodied by memories. . . .).

The striking images of whitened steer bones and the
exotic names of the vegetation of the pampas draw a
stark contrast between this natural landscape and those
"paysages manufacturés d'Europe," darkened with
blood, and artificial. This example of Supervielle's writing clearly shows that he was not a practitioner of Surrealist poetry nor an adherent of that school, but rather
he practiced a poetic art that was inspired by *le quotidien*
(life's routine experiences), transforming such experiences into the universal, accessible and anecdotal, without masking them in nightmarish imagery.

    From 1919 to 1939 Supervielle lived in Paris,
though he traveled every four to five years to Uruguay,
where he continued his writing. During this period he
became involved in the Paris literary scene, establishing
friendships with André Gide, Paul Valéry and Henri
Michaux. In *Le Forçat innocent* (The Innocent Prisoner,
1930) Supervielle displays a maturity of style that
prompted a widespread appreciation of his poetic
rhythms, rhymes, assonances, and generally more controlled versification. In "Cœur" (Heart), dedicated to
his wife, Pilar, the poet attempts a reconciliation
between physical reality–his heart–and abstract reality–his uneasiness with his physical being. The first
lines are: "Il ne sait pas mon nom / Ce cœur dont je suis
l'hôte, / Il ne sait rien de moi / Que des régions sauvages." (It does not know my name / This heart of
which I am host / It knows of me nothing but untamed
regions). A prisoner of his body, incessantly reminded
of his mortality by his physical frailty, Supervielle,
grave yet perceptive, takes stock of experiences with
death–his own imagined death, that of his parents and,
of course, death created by war–in order to understand
and accept its omnipresence, since he himself is, as suggested by the title, an "innocent prisoner" of death.

    When World War II broke out in 1939, Super-
vielle was once again in Montevideo, where he had
traveled with Pilar to celebrate the wedding of his son
Henri. He suffered greatly from the German occupation of France, considering himself, a French citizen, to

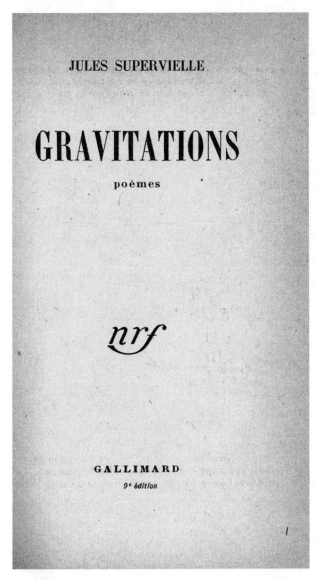

Title page for Supervielle's 1925 poetry collection (Thomas Cooper Library, University of South Carolina)

be in forced exile. Furthermore, his health had deteriorated because of a severe case of influenza, compounded by his cardiac troubles, which had led to tuberculosis, for which he was confined to a sanatorium. His poetry written at this time is profoundly melancholic, and works in *1939–1945, Poèmes* (1945) attest to the haunting presence of death, as in "Tu disparais" (You Disappear): "La lune qui te suit prend tes dernières forces / Et te bleuit sans fin pour ton ultime jour" (The moon that follows you takes your last strength / And turns you endlessly blue for your last day). This imagery, and which is characteristic of Supervielle's work, flows from his conception of life as a construct of time and space, air and water, light and dark. The moon that pursues the poet is a menacing presence, one

that illuminates the darkness, but that also casts an inhuman color on the poet's fragile body.

Following the failure of the Supervielle family bank in Montevideo, Supervielle, Pilar, and their youngest daughter sailed back to France in July 1946. Supervielle, his health continuing to fail, would have found himself in financial difficulty had he not been appointed by Uruguay, which allowed dual citizenship, to the post of honorary cultural attaché in Paris, which position came with a housing allowance. His *Oublieuse mémoire* (Forgetful Memory, 1949) is a lucid and contemplative work in which the poet remains faithful to his primordial imagery, as in the title poem: "Pâle soleil d'oubli, lune de la mémoire, / Que draines-tu au fond de tes sourdes contrées? / Est-ce donc là ce peu que tu donnes à boire, / Ces gouttes d'eau, le vin que je te confiai?" (Pale sun of forgetfulness, moon of memory / What do you drain from the bottom of your silent landscapes? / Is that really the little that you give to drink, / Those drops of water, the wine that I entrusted with you?) Memory and forgetfulness, sun and moon, water and wine: such antitheses serve to underline the basic sensibility that structures Supervielle's world, perceived through the filter of memory.

Naissances: Poèmes; suivis de, En songeant à un art poétique (Births: Poems; with, Reflections on the Art of Poetry) was first published in 1951 and republished in the United States in 1992, with translations by Philip Cranston, as *Naissances = Births: A Bilingual Edition*. A momentous work, *Naissances* offers a vision of the world that is rich in mature perspective and tranquillity of tone, reminiscent of the landscapes and seascapes making up Supervielle's physical world. He speaks in "Insomnie" (Insomnia) of his chronic sleeplessness, of "chevaliers de la nuit blanche" (horsemen of the sleepless night), and in the poem "Paris" of the constant beckoning in his psyche of the city of lights, while he was in South America: "Que de fois je regardai par la fenêtre en Amérique / Dans l'espoir que vînt à moi un paysage de France" (How many times in America I looked through a window / In the hope that to me would appear a landscape from France). The familiar expanses of the pampas, the seascape of his endless travels, the stone of the Cathedral of Notre Dame: these are points of reference in the topography of his poetry and of his affections. *Naissances* was published with *En songeant à un art poétique,* an essay in which Supervielle affirms his belief in creating poetry that is accessible:

. . . le poète peut aspirer à la cohérence, à la plausibilité de tout le poème dont la surface sera limpide alors que le mystère se réfugiera dans les profondeurs. Je compte sur mon poème pour ordonner et faire chanter juste les

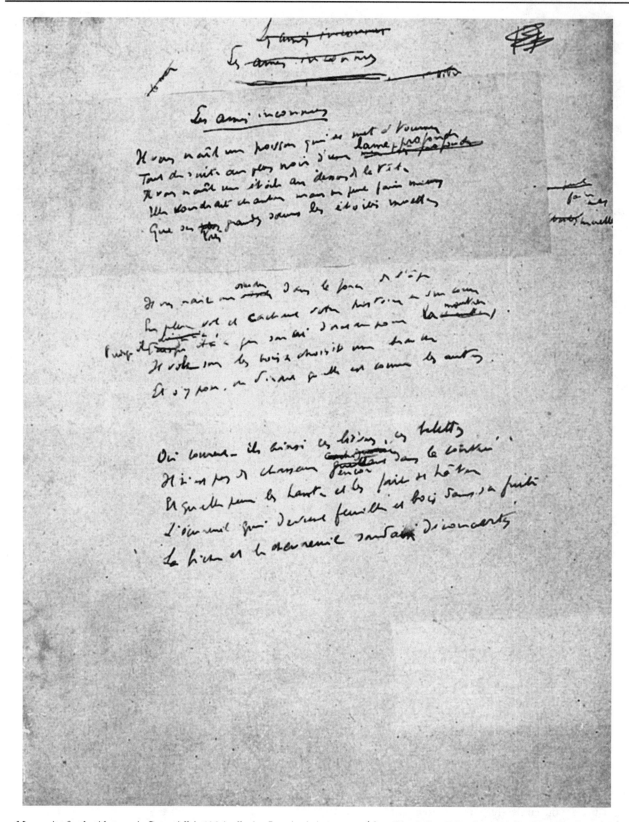

Manuscript for the title poem in Supervielle's 1934 collection, Les Amis inconnus *(from Claude Roy,* Jules Supervielle: Une Etude, *1949)*

images. Comme il baigne dans le rêve intérieur je ne crains pas de lui faire prendre parfois la forme d'un récit. La logique du conteur surveille la rêverie divagante du poète. La cohésion de tout le poème loin d'en détruire la magie en consolide les assises.

(... the poet can aspire to coherence, to the plausibility of the whole poem whose surface is limpid while the mystery hides in the depths. I count on my poem to organize the images and make them sing true. Since the poem bathes in the interior dream, I do not hesitate to make it take now and then a narrative form. The story-teller's logic oversees the poet's wandering reverie. Far from destroying its magic, the cohesion of the entire poem strengthens its foundations).

Supervielle's poetics is that of an individual who strives to express personal truths that affect all human-kind–from the mystery of the passing of time and the radiant beauty of flora and fauna to the devastation of human suffering, individual and collective. His poetry does indeed include a narrative thread, one that guides the reader from image to image, from scent to texture, and in so doing celebrates the richness of human existence. Ultimately, his poetry is evidence of an esthetic that respects his own idiosyncratic vision of the world, one that does not bow to fashion and that in a fundamental way communicates evocatively and sincerely epiphanic moments, which, in all their fullness, become engraved upon the reader's imagination.

Recognition of that breadth of vision soon came: in 1955, upon the unanimous recommendation of the Académie Française, Supervielle received its Grand Prix de la Littérature. In 1957 he shared the Etna-Taormina International Prize in Poetry with the Italian poet Camillo Sbarbaro, and in 1960 he was named *prince des poètes* (prince of poets) by the French review *Nouvelles littéraires*.

The death of Jules Supervielle on 17 May 1960 in his Paris apartment on the Quai Louis-Blériot marked the end of a truly remarkable literary career. Supervielle continues to cast a benevolent shadow on the world of contemporary poetry; the loss of his parents before the age of one, the agony of two world wars and of his own frail health, and an unceasing love of magical seascapes, sweeping expanses of the pampas, and elegant Paris landscapes are the elements from which his poetry derives its simplicity of form and meaning and upon which rests his prolific and varied literary production.

Letters:
Jules Supervielle–Etiemble: Correspondence 1936–1959, edited, with an introduction and notes, by Jeannine Etiemble (Paris: Société d'Edition d'Enseignement Supérieur, 1969).

Biography:
Ricardo Paseyro, *Jules Supervielle: Le Forçat volontaire* (Monaco: Editions du Rocher, 1987).

References:
Louis Allen, "Magic as Art: The Work of Jules Supervielle," *Durham University Journal,* new series 21 (March 1960): 70–86;

Dorothy S. Blair, *Jules Supervielle, a Modern Fabulist* (Oxford: Blackwell, 1960);

Sabine Dewulf, *Jules Supervielle, ou, La Connaissance poétique: Sous le "soleil d'oubli,"* 2 volumes (Paris: L'Harmattan, 2000);

René Etiemble, *Supervielle,* second edition, Pour une Bibliothèque Idéale, no. 1 (Paris: Gallimard, 1968);

Yves-Alain Favre, *Supervielle, la rêverie et le chant dans Gravitations* (Paris: Nizet, 1981);

Tatiana Wolff Greene, *Jules Supervielle* (Geneva: Droz / Paris: Minard, 1958);

James A. Hiddleston, *L'Univers de Jules Supervielle* (Paris: José Corti, 1965);

Louisa E. Jones, *Poetic Fantasy and Fiction: The Short Stories of Jules Supervielle* (The Hague: Mouton, 1973);

Jacques Robichez, *Gravitations de Supervielle: Commentaires* (Paris: Société d'Edition d'Enseignement Supérieur, 1981);

Claude Roy, *Jules Supervielle: Une Etude,* sixth edition, Collection Poètes d'Aujourd'hui, no. 15 (Paris: Seghers, 1970);

Christian Sénéchal, *Jules Supervielle, poète de l'univers intérieur* (Paris: Jean Flory, 1939);

Paul Viallaneix, *Le Hors-Venu; ou, Le Personnage poétique de Supervielle* (Paris: Klincksieck, 1972).

Papers:
Collections of Jules Supervielle's correspondence are held at the Bibliothèque Municipale, Vichy; the Bibliothèque Littéraire Jacques Doucet, Paris; the Bibliothèque Municipale, La Chaux-de-Fords, Switzerland; and the Archivo Literario, Biblioteca Nacional, Montevideo.

Paul Valéry

(31 October 1871 – 20 July 1945)

Charles Chadwick
Aberdeen University

SELECTED BOOKS: *La Conquête allemande (1897)* (Paris: Mercure de France, 1915); republished, with a revised introduction by Valéry, as *Une Conquête méthodique (1897),* Les Amis d'Edouard, no. 74 (Paris: E. Champion, 1924);

La Jeune Parque (Paris: Editions de la Nouvelle Revue Française, 1917);

Introduction à la méthode de Léonard de Vinci (Paris: Editions de la Nouvelle Revue Française, 1919); translated by Thomas McGreevy as *Introduction to the Method of Leonardo da Vinci* (London: Rodker, 1929);

La Soirée avec M. Teste (Paris: Editions de la Nouvelle Revue Française, 1919); translated by Ronald Davis as *An Evening with Mr. Teste,* with a new introduction by Valéry (Paris: R. Davis, 1925);

Album de vers anciens (Paris: Monnier, 1920);

Le Cimetière marin (Paris: Emile Paul, 1920); translated by Emlen Pope Etting as *The Graveyard by the Sea,* bilingual edition (Philadelphia: Centaur Press, 1928);

Odes de Paul Valéry, illustrated by Paul Véra (Paris: Editions de la Nouvelle Revue Française, 1920); republished as *Odes: Compositions de D. Galanis,* illustrated by Démétrius Emmanuel Galanis (Paris: Aux Aldes, 1926)—comprises "Aurore," "La Pythie," and "Palme";

Charmes; ou, Poèmes (Paris: Editions de la Nouvelle Revue Française, 1922); revised as *Charmes* (Paris: Gallimard, 1926); revised again as *Charmes: Poems de Paul Valéry,* with commentary by Alain (Paris: Gallimard, 1928);

Eupalinos; ou, L'Architecte, précédé de L'Ame et la Danse (Paris: Editions de la Nouvelle Revue Française, 1923)—comprises *Eupalinos; ou, L'Architecte,* translated, with a preface, by William McCausland Stewart as *Eupalinos; or, The Architect* (London: Oxford University Press/H. Milford, 1932); and *L'Ame et la Danse,* translated by Dorothy Bussy as *Dance and the Soul* (London: Lehmann, 1951); French original enlarged as *Eupalinos, L'Ame et la danse, Dialogue de l'arbre* (Paris: Gallimard, 1944);

Paul Valéry

B. 1910 (Paris: E. Champion, 1924); republished as *Cahier B 1910* (Paris: Gallimard, 1926);

Fragments sur Mallarmé (Paris: R. Davis, 1924);

Situation de Baudelaire (Monaco: Imprimerie de Monaco, 1924; Paris: Chez Madame Lesage, 1924);

Variété, 5 volumes (Paris: Gallimard, 1924–1944);

Durtal (Paris: E. Champion, 1925); republished as *Durtal; ou, Les Points d'une conversion* (Paris: M. Sénac, 1927);

Discours de la diction des vers: Prononcé par Paul Valéry au dîner annuel de la Revue critique le XXVII mai

M.CM.XXVI (Paris: Société d'Edition Le Livre, 1926); enlarged as *De la diction des vers* (Paris: Emile Chamontin, 1933);

Analecta ex. Mss. Pauli Ambrosii Valerii ad usum amicorum eius qui a septemtrione habitant: I (The Hague: Stols, 1926); enlarged French version published as *Paul Valéry: Analecta* (Paris: Gallimard, 1935);

M. Teste, Société des médecins bibliophiles, no. 8 (Paris: Les Arts et le Livre, 1926)–comprises *La Soirée avec monsieur Teste,* "Lettre d'un ami," "Lettre de madame Emile Teste," and "Extraits du log-book de monsieur Teste"; enlarged as *Monsieur Teste* (Paris: Gallimard, 1946)–comprises "La Soirée avec Teste," "Lettre de madame Émilie Teste," "Extraits du log-book de monsieur Teste," "Lettre d'un ami," "La Promenade avec monsieur Teste," "Pour un portrait de monsieur Teste," "Quelques pensées de monsieur Teste," and "Fin de monsieur Teste";

Propos sur l'intelligence, Collection La Porte étroite, no. 10 (Paris: A l'Enseigne de La Porte Etroite, 1926);

Le Retour de Hollande: Descartes & Rembrandt (Maastricht, The Netherlands: Stols, 1926); republished as *Le Retour de Hollande,* illustrated by Pierre Guastalla (Paris: M. Darantière, 1933); enlarged as *Le Retour de Hollande: Suivi de fragment d'un Descartes,* illustrated by Jean-Eugène Bersier (Paris: Compagnie Française des Arts Graphiques, 1946);

Rhumbs (notes et autres), Les Soirées du Divan, no. 21 (Paris: Le Divan, 1926);

Autres Rhumbs de Paul Valéry (Paris: Editions de France, 1927);

Maîtres et amis, illustrated by Jacques Beltrand (Paris: Beltrand, 1927);

Discours prononcé le 10 novembre 1927 à l'occasion de l'inauguration du monument Emile Verhaeren (Paris: E. Champion, 1927); republished as *Discours sur Emile Verhaeren* (Brussels & Maastricht, The Netherlands: Stols, 1928);

Discours de réception à l'Académie française (Paris: Gallimard, 1927);

Poësie: Essais sur la poétique et le poète (Paris: Bertrand Guégan, 1928);

Littérature (Paris: Adrienne Monnier à la Maison des Amis des Livres, 1929; enlarged edition, Paris: Gallimard, 1930);

Poésies (Paris: Gallimard, 1929; revised, 1931, revised and enlarged, 1942);

Remarques extérieures, illustrated by L. J. Soulas (Paris: Editions des Cahiers Libres, 1929);

Choses tues: Cahier d'impressions et d'idées, Collection Les Images du temps, no. 10 (Paris: Editions Lapina,

1930); republished as *Choses tues* (Paris: Gallimard, 1932);

Suite (Paris: P. Hartmann, 1930; enlarged edition, Paris: Gallimard, 1934);

Variation sur une "Pensée," annotée par l'auteur (Liège: Editions du Balancier, 1930);

Amphion: Mélodrame (Paris: Rouart, Lerolle, 1931);

Les Divers essais sur Léonard de Vinci de Paul Valéry: Commentés et annotés par lui-même (Paris: Editions du Sagittaire, 1931)–includes "Note et digression," Introduction à la méthode de Léonard de Vinci, and "Léonard et les philosophes, lettre à Léo Ferrero";

Moralités: Paul Valéry (Paris: Adrienne Monnier à la Maison des Amis des Livres, 1931);

Œuvres de Paul Valéry, 12 volumes (volumes 1–2, Paris: Editions du Sagittaire, 1931; volumes 3–12, Paris: Editions de la Nouvelle Revue Française, Gallimard, 1933–1951)–includes volume 2, *L'Ame et la danse; Eupalinos: ou, L'Architecte; Paradoxe sur l'architecte* (1931), and volume 12, *Ecrits divers sur Stephané Mallarmé* (1951);

Regards sur le monde actuel (Paris: Stock, 1931); revised and enlarged as *Regards sur le monde actuel & autres essais* (Paris: Gallimard, 1945); enlarged edition translated by Francis Scarfe as *Reflections on the World Today* (London: Thames & Hudson, 1951);

Pièces sur l'art (Paris: Maurice Darantiere, 1931; enlarged edition, Paris: Gallimard, 1934; enlarged again, 1936);

Discours prononcé à l'occasion de la distribution solennelle des prix du lycée Janson-de-Sailly (grand lycée) le treize juillet 1932 (Paris: Les Presses Modernes, 1932);

L'Idée fixe, ou, Deux hommes à la mer (Paris: Les Laboratoires Martinet, 1932; revised edition, Paris: Editions de la Nouvelle Revue Française, 1933); republished as *L'Idée fixe* (Paris: Gallimard, 1934);

Discours prononcé par Paul Valéry à la Maison d'Education de la Légion d'Honneur de Saint-Denis à la distribution des prix le 11 juillet 1932 (Melun: Imprimerie Administrative, 1933);

Sémiramis (Paris: Gallimard, 1934);

Etat de la vertu: Rapport à l'Academie française (Paris: L. Pichon, 1935);

Degas, danse, dessin (Paris: A. Vollard, 1936); translated by Helen Burlin as *Degas Dance Drawing* (New York: Lear, 1948);

L'Homme et la coquille, illustrated by Henri Mondor (Paris: Gallimard, 1937); translated by Ralph Manheim as *Sea Shells,* foreword by Mary Oliver (Boston: Beacon, 1998);

Discours aux chirurgiens (Paris: Gallimard, 1938);

Introduction à la poétique (Paris: Gallimard, 1938);

*Valéry in 1889, when he began his compulsory military service
with a regiment garrisoned in Montpellier*

Existence du Symbolisme (Maastricht, The Netherlands: Stols, 1939);

Poésie et pensée abstraite, The Zaharoff Lecture, 1938 (Oxford: Clarendon Press, 1939);

La Cantate du Narcisse, photographs by Laure Albin-Guillot (Paris: Artra, 1941);

Etudes pour Mon Faust, illustrated by Pierre Bouchet (Paris: Le Cent Une, 1941);

Mélange (Paris: Gallimard, 1941);

La Politique de l'esprit, notre souverain bien, introduction by Lucy Leveaux (Manchester: University of Manchester Press, 1941);

Tel Quel, 2 volumes (Paris: Gallimard, 1941, 1943);

Mauvaises pensées et autres (Marseille: Les Cahiers du Sud / Paris: José Corti, 1941; enlarged edition, Paris: Gallimard, 1942);

Dialogue de l'arbre (Paris: Firmin-Didot, 1943);

Au sujet de Nerval (Paris: Textes Pretextes, 1944);

Un Poète inconnu, La Porte étroite, no. 3 (Buenos Aires: Letters Françaises/Editions SUR, 1944);

Voltaire, discours prononcé le 10 décembre 1944 en Sorbonne, Collection Au Voilier, no. 1 (Paris: Domat-Montchrestien, 1945);

Henri Bergson: Allocution prononcée à la séance de l'Académie du jeudi 9 janvier 1941, Collection Au Voilier, no. 2 (Paris: Domat-Montchrestien, 1945);

Mon Faust (Paris: Gallimard, 1945); republished as *Mon Faust—Ebauches* (Paris: Gallimard, 1946)—comprises *Lust, ou, La Demoiselle de cristal: Comédie* and *Le Solitaire, ou, Les Malédictions d'univers: Féerie dramatique;*

L'Ange (Paris: Editions de la Nouvelle Revue Française, 1946);

Souvenirs poetiques: Paul Valéry; recueillis par un auditeur au cours d'une conférence prononcée à Bruxelles le 9 janvier 1942 (Paris: Le Prat, 1947);

Vues, illustrated by Gilbert Poilliot, Collection Le Choix, no. 9 (Paris: La Table Ronde, 1948);

Histoires brisées (Paris: Gallimard, 1950);

Agathe (Paris: A. Tallone, 1956);

Les Cahiers de Paul Valery, 29 volumes, preface by Louis de Broglie, facsimile edition (Paris: Centre National de la Recherche Scientifique, 1957–1961); abridged as *Abeille spirituelle: Poème inconnu et art poétique de Paul Valéry,* edited by André Nadal (Nîmes: Privately printed, 1968);

Douze poèmes, edited by Octave Nadal, illustrated by Jean Cocteau (Paris: Les Bibliophiles du Palais, 1959);

Cahiers de Paul Valéry, 2 volumes, edited by Judith Robinson, Bibliothèque de la Pléiade, nos. 242 and 254 (Paris: Gallimard, 1973, 1974); translated by Paul Gifford and others as *The Cahiers/Notebooks of Paul Valéry,* 2 volumes, edited by Brian Stimpson, Gifford, and Robert Pickering (New York & Frankfurt: Peter Lang, 2000).

Editions and Collections: *Le Cimetière marin,* edited by Henri Mondor and L. J. Austin (Grenoble: Roissard, 1954);

Œuvres, 2 volumes, edited by Jean Hytier, Bibliothèque de la Pléiade, nos. 127 and 148 (Paris: Gallimard, 1957, 1960);

Charmes ou Poèmes, edited, with an introduction in English, by Charles G. Whiting (London: Athlone, 1973);

Cahiers 1894–1914: Paul Valéry, edited by Nicole Celeyrette- Pietri, Judith Robinson-Valéry, and Pickering (Paris: Gallimard, 1987–)—includes volume 1, *1894–1898,* edited by Celeyrette-Pietri and Robinson-Valéry (1987); volume 2, *1897–1899,* edited by Celeyrette-Pietri and Robinson-Valéry (1989); volume 3, *1898–1900,* edited by Celeyrette-Pietri and Robinson-Valéry (1990); volume 4, *1900–1901,* edited by Celeyrette-Pietri (1992);

volume 5, *1902–1903,* edited by Celeyrette-Pietri (1994); volume 6, *1903–1904,* edited by Celeyrette- Pietri (1997); volume 7, *1904–1905,* edited by Celeyrette-Pietri and Pickering (1999); and volume 8, *1905–1907,* edited by Celeyrette-Pietri and Pickering (2001).

Poésies: Paul Valéry, edited by Michel Décaudin (Paris: Imprimerie Nationale, 1992).

Editions in English: *Variety,* translated by Malcolm Cowley (New York: Harcourt, Brace, 1927);

An Evening with Monsieur Teste, translated by Merton Gould (London: Besant, 1936);

Variety: Second Series, translated by William Aspenwall Bradley (New York: Harcourt, Brace, 1938)– includes translations from volumes 2 (1930) and 3 (1936) of *Variété;*

The Graveyard by the Sea/Le Cimetière Marin, bilingual edition, translated by C. Day Lewis (London: Secker & Warburg, 1946);

The Collected Works of Paul Valéry, 15 volumes, edited by Jackson Matthews (volumes 3–5, 7, 10, 12, and 13, New York: Pantheon, 1956–1965; volumes 1, 2, 6, 8, 9, 11, 14, and 15, Princeton: Princeton University Press, 1968–1975; volumes 1–15, London: Routledge & Kegan Paul, 1958–1975)–comprises volume 1, *Poems: Paul Valéry; On Poets and Poetry: Selected and Translated from the Notebooks,* translated by David Paul and James R. Lawler (1971); volume 2, *Poems in the Rough,* translated by Hilary Corke, with an introduction by Octave Nadal (1969); volume 3, *Plays,* translated by Paul and Robert Fitzgerald, with an introduction by Francis Fergusson and a memoir by Igor Stravinsky (1960); volume 4, *Dialogues,* translated by William McCausland Stewart, with prefaces by Wallace Stevens (1956, 1957); volume 5, *Idée fixe: Paul Valéry,* translated by Paul, with an introduction by Philip Wheelwright (1965); volume 6, *Monsieur Teste,* translated, with an introduction, by Matthews (1973); volume 7, *The Art of Poetry,* translated by Denise Folliot, with an introduction by T. S. Eliot (1958); volume 8, *Leonardo, Poe, Mallarmé,* translated by Cowley and Lawler (1972); volume 9, *Masters and Friends,* translated by Martin Turnell, with an introduction by Joseph Frank (1968); volume 10, *History and Politics,* translated by Folliot and Matthews, with a preface by François Valéry and an introduction by Salvador de Madariaga (1962, 1963); volume 11, *Occasions,* translated by Roger Shattuck and Frederick Brown (1970, 1971); volume 12, *Degas, Manet, Morisot,* translated by Paul, with an introduction by Douglas Cooper (1956, 1960); volume 13, *Aesthetics,* translated by Ralph Manheim,

with an introduction by Herbert Read (1964); volume 14, *Analects: Paul Valéry,* translated by Stuart Gilbert, with an introduction by W. H. Auden (1970); and volume 15, *Moi,* translated by Marthiel Mathews and Jackson Mathews (1975);

Le Cimetière Marin, The Graveyard by the Sea, bilingual edition, translated, with commentary, by Graham Martin (Edinburgh: University Press, 1971; Austin: University of Texas Press / Edinburgh: University Press, 1972);

Paul Valéry, An Anthology, selected, with an introduction, by Lawler (London: Routledge & Kegan Paul, 1977; Princeton: Princeton University Press, 1977);

Paul Valéry, La Jeune Parque, translated by Alistair Elliot, bilingual edition (Newcastle upon Tyne, U.K.: Bloodaxe, 1997).

PLAY PRODUCTIONS: *Amphion,* libretto by Valéry and music by Arthur Honegger, Paris, L'Opéra, 23 June 1931;

Semiramis, libretto by Valéry and music by Honegger, Paris, L'Opéra, 11 May 1934;

Cantate du Narcisse, libretto by Valéry and music by Germaine Taillefere, Paris, Conservatoire, 14 January 1939.

Paul Valéry is the last great representative of the late nineteenth-century symbolist movement in French poetry, prolonging into the first half of the twentieth century the forms and themes of such predecessors as Charles Baudelaire and, more particularly, Stéphane Mallarmé, whom he knew and admired.

Ambroise-Paul-Toussaint-Jules Valéry was born on 31 October 1871 some eighty miles west of Marseilles in the small seaport of Sète on the Mediterranean coast of France. His father, Barthélémy Valéry, a customs officer, was Corsican by birth, and his mother, Fanny Valéry (née de Grassi), was Italian. In 1884 his family moved to the nearby town of Montpellier. His school days were unremarkable, as were his unenthusiastic studies of law at the university in Montpellier, where he matriculated in 1888. He interrupted his studies to perform a year of compulsory military service in 1889–1890, with a regiment garrisoned in Montpellier. During the course of his service he met the writer Pierre Louÿs, who subsequently introduced him to such literary figures as André Gide and Mallarmé.

Valéry had begun writing poetry as early as the age of thirteen, and his facility was such that by the age of nineteen he is said to have composed more than two hundred poems, only a few of which were published at the time, in various magazines. But at the age of twenty-one, Valéry virtually abandoned poetry, largely because

Valéry with his daughter, Agathe, his mother, Fanny de Grassi Valéry, his wife, Jeanne Gobillard Valéry, and his eldest son, Claude, in 1910

strands of knowledge. At about the same time, he wrote *La Soirée avec M. Teste* (translated as *An Evening with Mr. Teste*, 1925), which was published in the periodical *Le Centaure* (1896) and then in book form in 1919. In this piece, the first of a cycle of short prose works that were collected in *M. Teste* (1926), he created the character of M. Teste, whose name is related, significantly, to *tête* (head). M. Teste discovers "des lois de l'esprit que nous ignorons" (laws of the mind of which we are ignorant); in a striking metaphor Valéry writes, "son âme se fait une plante singulière dont la racine, et non le feuillage, pousserait vers la clarté" (his soul is like some strange plant whose roots rather than its foliage push toward the light). Yet, M. Teste, like Valéry himself, has another side to his character; in "Lettre de Mme Emilie Teste," a later part of the Teste cycle, Mme. Emilie Teste says of her husband

> Quand il me revient de la profoundeur, il a l'air de me découvrir comme une terre nouvelle! Je lui apparais inconnue, neuve, nécessaire. Il me saisit aveuglément dans ses bras, comme si j'étais un rocher de vie et de présence réelle, où ce grand génie incommunicable se heurterait, toucherait, s'accrocherait, après tant d'inhumains silences monstrueux.

> (When he returns to me from the depths, it is as if he has discovered me like a strange land. I seem to him to be unknown, new, necessary. He seizes me blindly in his arms as if I were a solid rock of life and of real substance, which this great and solitary genius would touch and feel and clasp after so long a period of monstrous and inhuman silence).
> (translation by Charles Chadwick)

In 1900 Valéry took a job as a private secretary to Edouard Lebey, the director of Agence Havas (a news agency). That same year Valéry married Jeannie Gobillard, the niece of the well-known painter Berthe Morisot. The couple subsequently had three children, Claude, Agathe, and François. Valéry's "return from the depths," his renewed desire to make fresh contact with the world of the senses and the emotions after his long years of intellectual activity, began to make itself felt in 1912, when he was persuaded by his friend Gide to gather together some of his early poems with a view to publication. The revision of these lines written some twenty years before was begun with reluctance and even with a feeling of hostility toward something he now regarded as completely alien to him, but he was gradually recaptured by the pleasure of writing poetry. Although this pleasure was, in a sense, a renewal of the creative urge of his adolescence and early youth, there was a difference in that Valéry's second, conscious, intellectual self, assiduously developed over so many years, could now stand

he saw it as an emotional activity and preferred instead to cultivate the intellectual side of his nature. Architecture, mathematics, physics, and music were among the many subjects that his restless, inquiring mind explored during this period in his life; however, rather than the subjects themselves, in none of which he ever attained any specialized knowledge, it was the relationships between them that fascinated him as manifestations of the workings of the human mind. In the fall of 1892 he moved to Paris, where he was better able to pursue these interests. He wrote works on commission and worked at various jobs, including a stint in the London office of Cecil Rhodes in 1896, before he found a job as a clerk in the French Ministry of War, where he was employed from 1897 to 1900. In the 15 August 1895 issue of *La Nouvelle Revue* he published an essay titled *Introduction à la méthode de Léonard de Vinci* (translated as *Introduction to the Method of Leonardo da Vinci,* 1929), which was published in book form in 1919. In this essay he expresses his admiration for da Vinci's capacity for patiently and persistently pursuing various

back and watch his unconscious, emotional self at work. This conscious awareness of the activities of the unconscious forms the fundamental theme of the poem, at first intended to be a mere thirty or forty lines long, which Valéry began to write in 1912 to add to his early verse and which slowly grew, as he worked on it over the course of the next four or five years, to a length of more than five hundred lines.

The title of this work, which was finally published in 1917, was originally to have been the simple and more or less self-explanatory one of "Psyché" (Psyche), but since this title had already been chosen by his friend Louÿs for a novel he was writing, Valéry chose instead the title *La Jeune Parque* (The Young Fate). Valéry's title refers to Clotho, the youngest of the three Fates, whose task is to spin the thread of life, and in the poem Valéry explores the complex web of the intimate thoughts and feelings that have woven the destiny of the poet and weave the destiny of man in general. Her awakening to the realization that within her "une secrète sœur brûle" (a hidden sister smoulders) can be equated, whatever the wider implications of this involved and difficult poem may be, with Valéry's own awakening to the fact that within him a sensitive poet still existed: the temptations and hesitations she experiences no doubt reflect the poet's own uncertainties during the years when he was searching for a way forward in life; and her willingness, at the end of the poem, to face the wind, the sea, and the sun (which Valéry so vividly remembered from his younger days at Sète) and to experience the "doux et puissant retour du délice de naître" (sweet and powerful return of the delight of being born) has its equivalent in his decision to abandon the exclusively intellectual ambitions of M. Teste and to make a place, as well, for the world of the senses.

Unsurprisingly, the fifteen poems (increased to twenty in later editions) that Valéry selected from among his considerable amount of early verse to make up the slim volume titled *Album de vers anciens* (Collection of Early Verses, 1920) reflect the two sides of his nature that, he now realized, had always been present in him subconsciously and that he now wished consciously to emphasize. The opening poem of the collection, and probably the best and best-known, "La Fileuse" (The Girl at the Spinning Wheel), written in 1891, may originally have been meant as a simple poem about a girl falling asleep at her spinning wheel, which nevertheless continues to turn, so that the thread mysteriously continues to be spun without her conscious participation. But the poem acquired an added depth of meaning for Valéry after *La Jeune Parque,* once he had realized that the rational processes of the conscious mind were not, after all, capable of achieving

everything and that the potentialities of the unconscious had to be acknowledged, as well.

Similarly, "Narcisse parle" (Narcissus speaks) is ostensibly about the commonplace subject of Narcissus trying, and failing, to grasp his own reflection, with which image he is obsessed, but it can also be seen as a metaphorical representation of the failure of Valéry's intellectual introspection. "Orphée" (Orpheus) tells how the magical sound of Orpheus's music caused rocks to move of their own accord and to build themselves into a temple; on a deeper level, however, it is about the way in which forms can take shape without the conscious intervention of the creative artist. "Naissance de Vénus" (The Birth of Venus) may have been conceived as a conventional set piece on another well-known classical subject, but it can also be seen as a further manifestation of Valéry's preoccupation with the theme of spontaneous creation. "Baignée" (The Bather) has a similar theme, depicting the figure of a girl partly submerged in the sea so that the shape of the upper half of her body is clearly defined while that of the lower half, blurred by the water, seems not yet fully formed. In "Féerie" (Fairy) yet another female figure is again on a frontier, but this time between night and day, moonlight and sunlight, and, by implication, death and life. In "Même Féerie" (Same Fairy), however—a different version of the same poem—the heroine yields to the "inexorable charme de la nuit" (the irresistible magic of the night) and takes pleasure in her solitude. "Hélène" (Helen) also deals with life and death as the ghost of Helen of Troy returns from the grave to enjoy once again the pleasures she had known in life. A further variation on this constant theme of some kind of frontier between two worlds is to be found in "Au Bois dormant" (The Sleeping Beauty), in which the stock female figure is about to be awakened from her innocent dreams by the pleasures of the sense. "Episode" (Episode) too depicts a young girl experiencing the first promptings of sensuality. Although the autocratic Assyrian queen in "Air de Sémiramis" (The Song of Semiramis), who is reputed to have created the hanging gardens of Babylon, resists the temptations of love, she has nevertheless briefly experienced them. "Eté" (Summer) and "Anne" are two other poems that depict female figures trying, not altogether successfully, to remain impervious to the demands of the sensual world. "César" (Caesar) seems at first sight exceptional in its praise of the cool and calculating authority that the Roman emperor proudly wielded:

César, calme César, le pied sur toute chose,
Les poings durs dans la barbe, et l'œil sombre peuplé
D'aigles et des combats du couchant contemplé,
Ton cœur s'enfle et se sent toute-puissante cause.

(Caesar, calm Caesar, with the world beneath your feet,
your clenched fist under your china and your sombre gaze
filled with eagles and the battles you contemplate at sunset,
your heart swells with pride and you feel an all-powerful
       god).
(translations by Chadwick)

However, two lines take on a particular significance in their criticism of Caesar's total insensitivity to the emotional appeal of the landscape around him: "Le lac en vain palpite et lèche son lit rose / En vain d'or précieux brille le jeune blé" (The waves of the lake in vain wash the rosy sand / the precious gold of the wheat fields gleams in vain).

As is to be expected in work dating from Valéry's youth, most of the poems of the *Album de vers anciens* are not of the highest quality. But they are important in that they give a foretaste of his later work as regards both content and form. The heroine of *La Jeune Parque* can already be perceived in the all-too-frequent female figures hesitating between the sensual and the nonsensual worlds, and the conflict between the two is the subject of the most celebrated of Valéry's later poems, *Le Cimetière marin* (translated as *The Graveyard by the Sea*, 1932), first published in June 1920 in the *Nouvelle Revue Française*, published separately in a small volume by the firm of Emile Paul Frères later that same year, and later collected in *Charmes; ou, Poèmes* (Charms; or, Poems, 1922). As regards the techniques Valéry uses in the *Album de vers anciens*, the poems may often fail to maintain a high level of poetic quality throughout, but many of them nevertheless include memorable lines making that audacious use of assonance and alliteration that became a particular feature of Valéry's mature poetry. The opening lines of "La Fileuse" are a good example:

Assise, la fileuse au bleu de la croisée
Où le jardin mélodieux se dodeline,
Le rouet ancien qui ronfle l'a grisé

(As she sits spinning at the window by the blue of the sky
where the flowers of the garden nod gently in tune
the whispering wheel sends her softly to sleep).

The first two lines of "Au bois dormant" achieve a similar effect by similar means: "La princesse, dans un palais de rose pure, / Sous les murmures, sous la mobile ombre dort" (The princess, in a palace of purest rose, / among the murmurs and the shifting shadows sleeps). The last line of "César" admirably conveys a sense of the emperor's immense power "Quel fondre s'amasse au centre de César" (What thunderbolts gather in Caesar's soul).

The revision of these early poems and the composition of *La Jeune Parque* inspired Valéry to write several new poems expressing the ideas that had matured in his mind by 1920 as he approached the age of fifty. These twenty-one new poems were published in 1922 under the intriguing title *Charmes,* which can be taken simply in its etymological sense of *poems* or *songs* (from the Latin *carmina*), but which also suggests, through its literal meaning of *charms,* that some magical process, lying outside the domain of the conscious mind, has contributed both to their composition and their effect. From the outset, then, Valéry gives an indication of the motif recurrent in these poems, though it has many variations. Since the poems revolve around the same basic subject, their order is of no particular significance; Valéry, in fact, rearranged them in the course of the first few editions. By 1928, however, a definitive order had been decided upon.

In "Aurore" (Dawn) Valéry describes himself waking from sleep and taking conscious control of the ideas that have been slowly forming in his mind during the night:

Nous étions non éloignées,
Mais secrètes arraignées
Dans les ténèbres de toi

(We did not desert you,
but were like secret spiders
in the darkness within you).
(translations by Chadwick)

The poet then marshals and modifies these half-formed ideas in a fruitful alliance of the conscious and the unconscious.

"Au Platane" (To the Plane Tree) is unusual in that it is concerned with poetic impotence, for which the tree, firmly rooted in the earth and unable to soar upward, is a symbol. This subject is one that is usually associated with Mallarmé rather than Valéry, and it may be that the latter's captive plane tree is a variant on the former's captive swan in his celebrated sonnet "Le vierge, le vivace et le bel aujourd'hui" (This Untouched Day Dawning Lively and Lovely, 1884).

The well-known "Cantique des colonnes" (The Song of the Columns) returns to a typically Valérian theme: a row of marble columns is depicted as a line of female figures. In a series of delightful and ingenious images, human features are detected in them:

Pour affronter la lune,
La lune et le soleil,
On nous polit chacune
Comme ongle de l'orteil!

(To face up to the moon,
the moon and the sun,
we are each of us polished

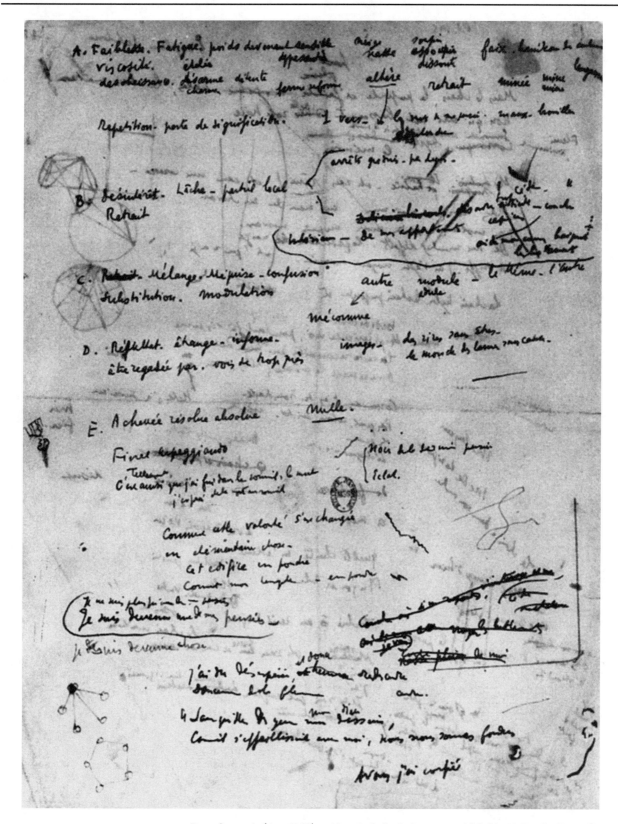

Pages from early (circa 1915) and late drafts for the long poem published in 1917 as La Jeune Parque
(Bibliothèque Nationale, Paris)

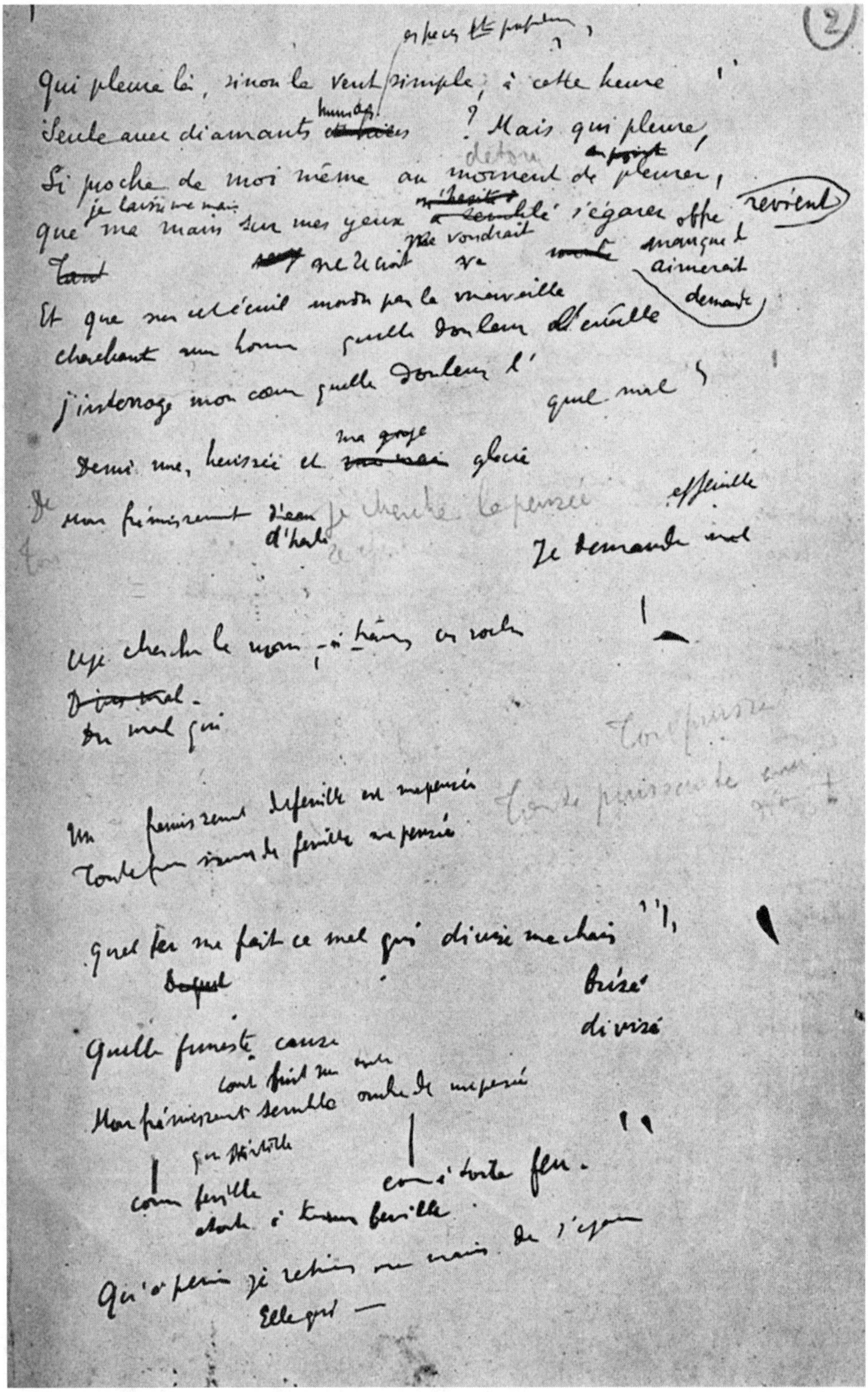

as if we were toenails!)

The flawless stone of the identical columns is equated with the purity of soul possessed by sisters whose pleasures remain entirely innocent, despite the touch of sensuality symbolized by the burning rays of the sun from which they are only partly sheltered:

Incorruptibles sœurs,
Mi-brûlantes, mi-fraîches,
Nous prîmes pour danseurs
Brises et feuilles sèches . . .

(Incorruptible sisters,
half in sunlight, half in shadow,
our sole dancing partners
are breezes and dry leaves . . .).

The sonnet "L'Abeille" (The Bee) seems, at first sight, to be not only shorter but much less complicated, since it is apparently concerned simply with a woman asking to be stung on the breast by a bee. There is, however, a fairly obvious second level of meaning in the clearly sexual connotations of this image. When the poem is read in the light of Valéry's other poems, moreover, a third level of meaning can be perceived, one related to his desire to be awakened from intellectual detachment and stung into action; in other words, the poem is about the creative act in a poetic rather than a sexual sense:

Quelle, et si fine et si mortelle,
Que soit ta poite, blonde abeille,
Je n'ai, sur ma tendre corbeille,
Jeté qu'un songe de dentelle.

Pique du sein la gourde belle,
Sur qui l'Amour meurt ou sommeille,
Qu'un peu de moi-même vermeille
Vienne à la chair ronde et rebelle . . .

(However fine, however fatal
may be your sting, golden bee,
across my tender bosom I have
flung no more than a wisp of lace.

Prick the beautiful bowl of the breast
where love lies dying or dormant,
let at least a droplet of my blood
break through the round rebellious flesh . . .).

The poem can also be seen as expressing a slightly different but equally typical Valérian theme–the need for poetic inspiration, for the unconscious mind to make its contribution to the creative process.

Yet, another aspect of the creative process is dealt with in "Poésie" (Poetry), which features a maternal figure (the muse of poetry) with a child (the poet) feeding at her breast. The flow of milk, however, is halted and the poet expresses his surprise and sorrow, asking:

Dis, par quelle crainte vaine,
Par quelle ombre de dépit,
Cette merveilleuse veine
A mes lèvres se rompit?

(Tell me through what groundless fear,
through what touch of spite,
this marvelous flow
has been closed off from my lips?)

The answer given by the muse is that the poet has tried to force inspiration instead of waiting patiently for it to flow of its own accord: "–Si fort vous m'avez mordue / Que mon cœur s'est arrêté!"(–You have pressed me so hard / that my heart has stopped beating!).

"Les Pas" (The Footsteps) is also on the subject of poetic inspiration, but from a rather different angle. Again there is a surface layer of imagery of a sexual nature, as the poet waits for a woman to come to him, but it is to the thoughts in his mind that this symbolic figure is finally to provide nourishment, and here he prefers to prolong the process of creation rather than hasten its completion:

Si, de tes lèvres avancées,
Tu prépares pur l'apaiser,
A l'habitant de mes pensées,
La nourriture d'un baiser,

Ne hâte pas cet acte tendre,
Douceur d'être et de n'être pas,
Car j'ai vécu de vous attendre
Et mon cœur n'était que vos pas.

(If, with your approaching lips,
you are about to bring peace
to what is forming in my mind
through the encouragement of a kiss,

do not hasten this tender act and thus end
the pleasure of suspending the gift of life,
for awaiting your coming has kept me alive
and my heartbeat has followed your footsteps).

If, in "Les Pas," Valéry is calmly confident of his ability to carry the creative act through to a successful conclusion in his own good time, the next poem, "La Ceinture" (The Belt), expresses a different view using different imagery. Inspiration is now compared to a belt or band of cloud at sunset surrounding a shadowy, moving shape in the sky, which slips from his grasp. Whereas in the preceding poem he had delighted in the period of suspense between creation and noncreation–"Douceur d'etre et de n'être pas"–in "La Ceinture" the same suspense between the absence and presence of

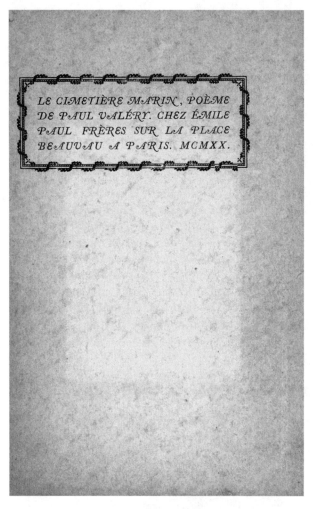

Cover for Valéry's 1920 poem, which opens with the speaker contemplating the Mediterranean from the seaside cemetery at Sète (Yale University Library)

inspiration means uncertainty and leads ultimately to failure. So the poem ends with the elusive band of cloud becoming a shroud covering him in his loneliness: "Absent, présent . . . Je suis bien seul, / Et sombre, ô suave linceul" (Absent, or present? . . . I am left alone / and in somber mood with a silken shroud).

"La Dormeuse" (The Sleeping Girl) seems at first sight to be a piece from the *Album de vers anciens,* with its portrait of a girl lying asleep. But the point Valéry emphasizes is that even while the subject is asleep an intense activity is going on within her: "Quels secrets dans son cœur brûle ma jeune ami" (What secrets burn in the heart of my young friend). He refers to the "rayonnement d'une femme endormie" (the radiance of a sleeping woman) so that, although she is asleep, paradoxically she is awake and observing the poet as much as he is observing her: "ta forme veille, et mes yeux sont ouverts" (your body is watching, and my eyes are fixed on you). Far more deliberately, therefore, than in the poems of the *Album de vers anciens,* "La Dormeuse" is concerned with the alliance between the conscious contribution of the poet and the unconscious contribution of his subject.

"Fragments du Narcisse" (Fragments from the Narcissus Theme) has much closer links with the *Album de vers anciens* since it is a more extended treatment of the subject dealt with in "Narcisse parle." Again Narcissus visits a pool at night so as to contemplate obsessively his own reflection: "Nulle des nymphes, nulle amie, ne m'attire / Comme tu le fais sur l'onde, inépuisable Moi!" (None of the nymphs, no woman attracts me like / the reflection in the water of my inexhaustible self). The end result is the same as in the earlier version: Narcissus leans over the pool to kiss his adored reflection, but in so doing he shatters the image of himself in the water. Introspection ends in failure.

"La Pythie" (The Pythoness) introduces an entirely new symbol. The Pythoness was the name given to the Delphic priestess who, possessed by some demonic force in the shape of a serpent, at first struggled against it but finally accepted her fate and imposed on her initially delirious outpourings an ordered form: "Belles chaines en qui s'engage / Le dieu dans la chair égaré (Fine chains within which is confined / the god let loose in her flesh). Despite the much different imagery and the much more violent forces involved, "La Pythie" is clearly related to "Aurore," where Valéry takes control of the ideas that have become half-formed in his mind during sleep.

"Le Sylphe" (The Sylph) is also reminiscent of a previous poem, "La Ceinture," in that, as the title suggests, it too is concerned with the elusive nature of poetry. It is, however, a much more lighthearted piece, comparing inspiration to a passing perfume, asking whether a poem, completed in an instant, is the result of chance or genius, wondering whether it will be neither read nor understood, teasing future critics about the errors of interpretation that they will make, and ending, typically, with a sexual image, suggesting that fleeting inspiration is like the tantalizing glimpse of a woman's breast.

"L'Insinuant" (The Seducer), like "La Pythie," features a serpent; not, however, the Pythoness, but the serpent of the Garden of Eden patiently seducing Eve, though neither of the protagonists is actually named, perhaps because they are merely symbols of inspiration slowly and deviously leading the poet toward his goal. The poem is therefore much different from "Le Sylphe" and is linked to "Les Pas" by the way in which the insidious process of seduction is enjoyed by the serpent and the final consummation is held back:

O Courbes, méandre,
Secrets du menteur,
Est-il art plus tendre
Que cette lenteur? . . .

O Courbes, méandre,
Secrets du menteur,
Je veux faire attendre
Le mot le plus tendre.

(As I weave and meander,
a secret deceiver,
is there an art more tender
than this slow patience? . . .

As I wave and meander
a secret deceiver,
I take care to delay
the last tender word).

If "L'Insinuant" and "Les Pas" are concerned with the slow coming of unconscious inspiration, the next poem, "La Fausse Morte" (The Living Corpse), by contrast, symbolically depicts the poet's persistent return to a poem as he works to perfect it. There are times when he gives up the struggle, but as soon as he does so, the "corpse" of the abandoned poem comes to life again and demands that he continue to work on it.

"Ebauche d'un serpent" (Sketch of a Serpent), so titled because, although it is one of the longest poems in *Charmes,* Valéry intended to give the subject an even more extended treatment, is related to "L'Insinuant" in that it too deals with the seduction of Eve from the point of view of the serpent. This time, however, the protagonists are named, and the poem goes into much greater detail over the course of more than three hundred lines grouped in verses of ten lines. Its purpose, too, is quite different, since it is concerned not with inspiration but with such philosophical and theological issues as God's motives for creating the universe, the serpent's reasons for seducing Eve and, most importantly, the consequences of that seduction. In the first part of the poem the serpent contends that ". . . l'univers n'est qu'un défaut / Dans la pureté du Non-être" (. . . the universe is but a flaw / in the purity of Non-existence). God's vanity, it is argued, explains his creation of the universe, of which the first element was, of course, Lucifer:

Mais, le premier mot de son Verbe,
MOI! . . . Des astres le plus superbe
Qu'ait parlés le fou créateur.

(But the first word he spoke created
ME! . . . the most brilliant of the stars
that the foolish creator brought into being).

Because man was then made in God's image, Lucifer has an intense hatred for these docile creatures, and it is this hatred that explains his determination, in the guise of the serpent, to seduce Eve, the vivid details of the seduction occupying the central section of the poem. The poem ends with a return to the philosophical question and with the paradoxical conclusion that Eve's grasping of the fruit of the tree of knowledge endows her with a kind of grandeur. Man's disobedience may have brought as its first fruits "death into the world and all our woe," as John Milton put it in his *Paradise Lost* (1667), but in Valéry's view it also means that man became an independent being, able to come to terms with the realities of life rather than remaining entirely sheltered from them. This point links "Ebauche d'un serpent" with M. Teste's return from his sheltered intellectual existence, Clotho's embracing of the sensual world at the end of *La Jeune Parque,* and Valéry's own abandonment of his exclusively intellectual pursuits once he had returned to writing poetry. This point is also one that Valéry later made, in a much more personal way and without the biblical symbolism, in *Le Cimetière marin.*

A quite different fruit of knowledge is the subject of the next poem, "Les Grenades" (Pomegranates). The resemblance between the structure of a pomegranate, with its cluster of seeds set in a reddish pulp inside a hard outer shell, and that of the brain enclosed within the skull, leads Valéry to see an analogy between the ripening of the pomegranate and the ripening of ideas within the human mind. This analogy is a further variation in the manner of "Poésie," "Les Pas," and "L'Insinuant," on the theme of the coming of inspiration.

"Le Vin perdu" (The Lost Wine) looks at inspiration from yet another angle, using yet another image. A little wine is flung into the sea, which, after becoming momentarily tinged with red, recovers its transparency. The wine seems to have disappeared, but then magical figures suddenly spring up from the surface. In poetic terms, this image means that the poet abandons an idea, which then apparently completely disappears from his mind, and yet, at some later date, has a quite unexpected fertilizing effect:

Perdu ce vin, ivres les ondes! . . .
J'ai vu bondir dans l'air amer
Les figures les plus profondes . . .

(The wine was gone, the waves were drunk! . . .
Then I suddenly saw leap into the salt air
figures springing up from the depths of the sea).

"Intérieur" (Interior), made up of a mere eight lines, is the shortest poem in *Charmes* and is the only one whose superficial subject seems not to conceal a deeper meaning. It may be no more than a gently teasing trib-

*Valéry when he was inducted into the Academie Française,
23 June 1927*

ute to a maidservant, or perhaps to Valéry's wife, depicted in the opening line as "Une esclave aux longs yeux chargés de molles chaînes" (A slave whose long eyes are laden with gentle chains), an oriental slave whose bondage, however, weighs lightly upon her and who is occupied with domestic duties, "Elle met une femme au milieu de ces murs"(she provides the gentleness of a woman between these walls), leaving him free to reflect and ponder on his work: "Qui, dans ma rêverie errant avec décence / Passe entre mes regards sans briser leur absence" (Who, moving quietly to leave my reverie undisturbed / passes across my faraway gaze without interrupting it). But it is possible that Valéry may be referring to that capacity of the human mind to undertake menial tasks automatically while still continuing to concentrate on other more important matters: "Comme passe le verre au travers du soleil / Et de la raison pure épargne l'appareil" (as a piece of glass passes across a ray of sunlight / and lays no burden on the workings of my mind).

By way of contrast, *Le Cimetière marin* is one of the longest and most profoundly thoughtful poems in

Charmes, along with "Ebauche d'un serpent," with which it has some similarities. It is headed by an epigraph from the Greek poet Pindar—"Do not, my soul, seek eternal life, but confine yourself to what is possible"—and is an analysis of the way in which Valéry had succumbed to the temptation to detach himself from the realities of existence only to recognize that, like the heroine of his *La Jeune Parque* and mankind in general in his "Ebauche d'un serpent," he had to come to terms with life as it is.

The first seven verses depict the poet contemplating the still waters of the Mediterranean from the vantage point of the cemetery at Sète: "Ce toit tranquille, où marchent des colombes, / Entre les pins palpite, entre les tombes" (This peaceful roof, where doves are walking, / shimmers between the pine trees and the tombs). The poetic persona has become hypnotized by the glittering expanse of the sea, "La scintillation sereine sème / Sur l'altitude un dédain souverain" (The serene sparkle gives me a sense, / as I look down, of supreme disdain). He has the impression of having a foretaste of immortality.

As he sits facing the fullness of the sun and refracting its light, however, he is suddenly struck by the thought that a reflecting surface necessarily has a dark underside: ". . . Mais rendre la lumière / Supose d'ombre une morne moitié (. . . But an object which reflects light / must have another sad side in shadow). The mood of the poem now changes. He turns his gaze away from the sea toward the cemetery and thinks no longer of his soul and his immortality but of his body and his mortality: "Quel corps me traîne à sa fin paresseuse, / Quel front l'attire à cette terre osseuse?" (What body drags me to a useless end, / what forehead pulls it to this bony earth?) He recovers, however, from his initial despondency and recognizes that death is part of a cycle; men die and are buried but the cemetery is nonetheless alive with blooms: "L'argile rouge a bu la blanche espèce, / Le don de vivre a passé dans les fleurs!" (the red clay has absorbed their white bodies, / the gift of life has passed into the flowers!).

This realization leads into the final philosophical section of the poem, where Valéry admits that he had at one time accepted the theory of the Greek philosopher, Zeno of Elea, that because an arrow is stationary at any given moment in its flight, movement, and consequently the passage of time, are illusory:

Zénon! Cruel Zénon! Zénon d'Elée!
M'as-tu percé de cette flèche aileée
Qui vibre, vole, et qui ne vole pas!

(Zeno! Cruel Zeno! Zeno of Elea!
How you once pierced me with your winged arrow
which twangs and flies and yet does not fly!)

He now recognizes, on the contrary, that man cannot remain motionless and unchanging and that it is the intimation of immortality, described so evocatively at the beginning of the poem, which is illusory. There then comes the vigorous and optimistic conclusion to the poem:

> Brisez, mon corps, cette forme pensive!
> Buvez, mon sein, la naissane du vent!
> Une fraîcheur, de la mer exhalée,
> Me rend mon âme . . . O puissance salée!
> Courons à l'onde en rejaillir vivant! . . .
> Le vent se lève! . . . Il faut tenter de vivre!
>
> (Let my body break free from this reflective mind!
> Let my lungs breathe in the new-born wind!
> A freshness, sweeping in from the sea
> gives back to me my soul . . . O strong salt air!
> Let us run into the waves and re-emerge alive! . . .
> The wind is rising! . . . Life must be lived!)

The poem finally comes full circle in the last two lines, where the breaking waves shatter the tranquility of the roof of the opening line and the peaceful doves are revealed as boats with their triangular sails dipping up and down: "Rompez, vagues! Rompez d'eaux réjouies / Ce toit tranquille où picoraient des focs!" (Break up, waves! Break up with joyful waters / this tranquil roof where jibs pecked!)

If *Le Cimetière marin* is one of the most complex poems of *Charmes*, "Ode secrète" (Secret Ode) is one of the most enigmatic, which perhaps explains its title. It is concerned with some kind of victory after a long and exhausting struggle. As it was written in November 1918, critics have suggested that it was inspired by the armistice that ended World War I. There is, however, no specific reference to this particular victory, nor to any other, in the poem. It seems therefore more likely that Valéry is trying to convey the overwhelming sense of triumph that accompanies the successful conclusion of any task and that gives the victor the impression of having achieved immortality and of having written his name among the various constellations that are named in the course of the poem.

"Le Rameur" (The Oarsman) too is concerned with a long and exhausting struggle but of a much simpler kind, since it describes in some detail a man rowing steadfastly upstream and refusing to be distracted by the charms of the landscape through which he is passing. There is, however, little doubt that this image is yet another symbol of the poet sticking firmly to his task.

It seems appropriate that "Le Rameur," the penultimate poem in *Charmes*, should emphasize the conscious effort that the poet must make, and doubly appropriate that the final poem, "Palme," should emphasize, on the contrary, the arbitrary nature of poetic inspiration, for whose fruits the poet must patiently wait. The volume therefore ends as it began, by recognizing the contribution that both the conscious and the unconscious mind have to make to the poetic process.

Valéry extends his fusion of these two forces into the domain of form as well as content. There is no doubt that, as has been said, he was a naturally gifted poet, capable of composing verses with little conscious effort. With regard to "La Fileuse," he claimed that the opening line—"Assise, la fileuse au bleu de la croisée"—had come to him in his sleep and that he had then developed the rest of the poem from this starting point. "La Pythie," as well, he said, had begun from a single unconscious line—"Pâle, profondément mordue"—around which the poem had then been constructed. He contended in his 1938 Zaharoff Lecture that *Le Cimetière marin,* for its part, had begun simply as a rhythm, that of the decasyllabic line divided into two groups of four and six syllables, which suggested itself to him before he had any conception of the subject of the poem. There is no doubt, however, that, following his return to poetry with the achievement of *La Jeune Parque,* he became one of the supreme practitioners of conscious artistry. Whereas in the *Album de vers anciens* his verse had flowed easily into largely conventional molds—more than half of the poems are in traditional sonnet form and three quarters of them use the standard twelve-syllable alexandrine—he exercises a much greater technical virtuosity in *Charmes*. An unusual and elaborate pattern of ten-line stanzas is adopted in four long and important poems, "Aurore," "Palme," "La Pythie," and "Ebauche d'un serpent," the first two being in seven-syllable lines and the last two in eight-syllable lines. The decasyllabic lines of *Le Cimetière marin* are grouped in stanzas of six lines, and the critic Bernard Vannier suggests, in an article in *Modern Language Notes* (1972), that the consequent sixty syllables in each stanza and the twenty-four stanzas in the poems as a whole were deliberately chosen to match the poet's concern with the passage of time. "Cantique des colonnes" is in short six-syllable lines, appropriate to the lightness of touch with which Valéry treats the subject, whereas the much weightier theme of "Le Rameur" is dealt with in ponderous alexandrines. It is true that there are half a dozen sonnets in *Charmes,* but they show considerable variety: "La Dormeuse" being in conventional alexandrines; "Le Sylphe" in pentasyllabic lines; and "L'Abeille," "La Ceinture," "Les Grenades," and "Le Vin perdu" in octosyllabic lines, each with a different rhyme scheme. In fact, only the first and last poems of *Charmes,* "Aurore" and "Palme," have precisely the same form, perhaps in order to give an impression of

Valéry in 1937

balance in the volume. The remaining nineteen poems all differ from one another in line length, verse length, rhyme scheme, or overall length.

As with *Charmes* as a whole, there is ample evidence within individual poems of the patient and subtle craftsmanship that Valéry must have exercised in order to give his poetry its wealth of connotations. One example of this craftsmanship is the shift from the languorous rhythm and the feminine rhymes of the quatrains in "L'Abeille" to the thrusting rhythm and the masculine rhymes of its tercets, which adds to the sexual overtones of the poem and, beyond that, to the urgency of the appeal for a creative stimulus:

> J'ai grand besoin d'un prompt tourment:
> Un mal vif et bien terminé
> Vaut mieux qu'un supplice dormant!
>
> Soit donc mon sens illuminé
> Par cette infime alerte d'or
> Sans qui l'amour meurt ou s'endort!

(I greatly need a prompt torment:
a sharp and soon finished pain
is better than slow torture!

So let my senses be lit
by this tiny golden sting
without which love dies or sleeps!)

Another example of Valéry's poetic craftsmanship is "Les Grenades." The title is generally agreed as referring not only to the principal image of ripe pomegranates but also to the subsidiary images of grenades and the palace of the Alhambra in the Spanish city of Granada, which are woven through the poem by way of several words evocative of war and royalty, thus reinforcing the theme of ideas exploding from a powerful mind conveyed by the extraordinary accumulation of harsh *r* sounds and plosives:

> Dures grenades entr'ouvertes
> Cédant à l'excès de vos grains,
> Je crois voir des fronts souverains
> Eclatés de leurs découvertes
>
> (Hard pomegranates splitting open
> yielding under the increase of your seeds,
> I seem to see the heads of great men
> bursting with their discoveries).

Individual lines also bear witness to Valéry's skill at matching, to use his own terms, "vers donnés" (given lines) with "vers calculés" (calculated lines). Among the latter must no doubt be classed those many lines in which, putting into practice his definition of poetry, elucidated in *Tel Quel* (As Such, 1941) as "cette hésitation prolongée entre le son et le sense" (that lengthy hesitation between sound and sense), he makes an extensive use of assonance and alliteration. The hissing of the serpent, for example, can be heard throughout "Ebauche d'un serpent," in the constantly repeated *s* sounds of such lines as "Quel silence battu d'un cil! Mais quel souffle sous le sein sombre." In "La Dormeuse" the description of a sleeping girl: "Dormeuse, amas doré d'ombres et d'abandons," with its *m* consonants and nasal vowels, means that the sound of the words is as important as their sense in giving an impression of sleep. The short, sharp vowel sounds in the line "L'insecte net gratte la sécheresse," in *Le Cimetière marin,* convey the image of an insect scratching the dry earth of the cemetery as much as do the dictionary meanings of the words. The dramatic opening of *La Jeune Parque* is another well-known example of lines that make their impact felt through their sound as much as their sense and that cannot therefore be adequately translated:

Qui pleure là, sinon le vent simple, à cette heure
Seule avec diamants extrêmes? . . . Mais qui pleure,
Si proche de moi-même au moment de pleurer?
(Who weeps, if not simply the wind, at this
lonely hour with the distant stars? . . . But who weeps,
so close to me as I too am about to weep?)

With such poetry it is as impossible to distinguish between what has been consciously worked out and what has been unconsciously suggested as it is to distinguish between its intellectual and its emotional appeal. The earlier conflict between the two sides of Valéry's nature has been resolved and has produced in *La Jeune Parque* and *Charmes* poetry of an extraordinarily rich and complex nature, both in its origins and in its effects.

No sooner had Valéry completed *Charmes* than his financial circumstances suddenly changed. For more than twenty years he had been supported by Lebey, who had employed him as a secretary but had allowed him ample time to devote himself to his literary work. In 1922 Lebey died and Valéry was obliged to think of ways of earning a living. The obvious method, which he promptly adopted, was to capitalize on the enormous reputation he had acquired over the course of the last few years, especially with the publication of *La Jeune Parque, Introduction a la methode de Léonard da Vinci,* and *Le Cimetière marin.* In 1925 he was elected to membership in the prestigious Académie Française; in 1933 he was made chief administrator of the Centre Universitaire Méditerranéen at Nice; and in 1937 he became professor of poetry at the Collège de France. He had, indeed, already begun the endless round of lectures and speeches and the vast output of essays, articles, and extracts from his *cahiers* (notebooks) that occupied the remainder of his life. But although these works take up many hundreds of pages in his collected works, they are not of the same importance as the far fewer pages devoted to his poetry, despite the perceptiveness of many of his remarks. One might naturally be tempted to assume that Valéry, who frequently complained about the new life as a public figure into which he was plunged, was prevented by force of circumstances from devoting himself to poetry, though he continued to write the occasional poem that he sometimes included in one of his many volumes of prose or, more often, left unpublished. But one can also, perhaps, take the view that these multiple activities fall into place as part of the pattern of Valéry's life. Given his recognition that the mind cannot remain turned into itself, but must turn outward to the world, it seems both logical and inevitable that he should have put this principle into practice. The latter part of Valéry's life could therefore be considered as complementary to the earlier part and even as a response to the closing lines of *La Jeune Parque* and

to the injunction given in *Le Cimetière Marin:* "il faut tenter de vivre" (life must be lived).

His work after 1922 is not, however, entirely unrelated to what had preceded it; on the contrary, he was still concerned with the same fundamental issues. This continuity of concern can be seen in four dialogues. The first two were published together in *Eupalinos; ou, L'Architecte, précédé de L'Ame et la Danse* (1923). The first of these dialogues, *Eupalinos; ou, L'Architecte* (translated as *Eupalinos; or, The Architect,* 1932), a commissioned piece, is clearly linked to the lifelong interest in architecture evidenced in an essay written thirty years before, *Paradoxe sur l'architecte,* for which the sonnet "Orphée"(republished in *Album de vers anciens*) served as an epilogue. First published in *L'Ermitage* (March 1891), this essay was actually republished with the first two dialogues, in volume 2 (1931) of the Editions du Sagittaire / Editions de la Nouvelle Revue Française *Œuvres de Paul Valéry* (1931–1951). The theme of *Eupalinos* is the alliance of the conscious and the unconscious, the mind and the body, work and inspiration, and it rises to a climax in the final prayer of Eupalinos:

Mon intelligence . . . ne cessera, cher corps, de vous appeler à soi désormais . . . Nous agissions chacun de notre côté. Vous viviez, je rêvais . . . Mais cette œuvre que maintenant je veux faire . . . puisse-t-elle surgir uniquement de notre entente.

(My mind, dear body, will henceforth never cease to call you to its aid. So far we have each operated independently. You lived while I dreamed. But the work which I now wish to do, may it arise solely from the understanding between us).
(translation by Chadwick)

The second dialogue, *L'Ame et la Danse* (translated as *Dance and the Soul,* 1951), is a hymn in praise of movement as a means of combating "l'ennui de vivre" (the boredom of living), which clearly echoes the concluding verses of *Le Cimetière marin.* The third dialogue, *L'Idée fixe; ou, Deux hommes à la mer* (The Fixed Idea; or, Two Men By the Seaside, 1932), published nine years later, though written in a humorous vein, revolves around themes borrowed from *Charmes*—that the mind is engaged in a constant and intense activity, that it has a fixation with ideas in general rather than with one particular idea and that man is "à la fois capable de raisonnement minutieux . . . et d'autre part sujet aux impulsions" (at one and the same time capable of rigorous reasoning and yet also subject to sudden impulses). Finally, in the *Dialogue de l'arbre* (Dialogue of the Tree), which was written in 1943 and was included in *Eupalinos, L'Ame et la Danse, Dialogue de l'arbre* (1944), Lucrèce,

Valéry's grave in the cemetery at Sète. The epitaph is from his Le Cimetière marin.

for whom the tree of the title is a pretext for speculative ideas, and Tityre, the simple shepherd whose love of the tree is deep but uncomplicated, decide to join forces in a manner typical of Valéry: "Faisons entre nous l'échange de ta connaissance de cet Arbre avec l'amour et la louange qu'il m'inspire" (Let us exchange between us your knowledge of this tree with the love and praise which it inspires in me).

In 1931 Valéry collaborated with the composer Arthur Honegger to produce a short opera-ballet, *Amphion,* whose theme is the same as that of his early sonnet "Orphée": Amphion is another figure from Greek mythology gifted with the power to move stones with the sound of his music and build them into a temple. Three years later Valéry collaborated with Honegger a second time in the production of another short opera-ballet, *Sémiramis* (published 1934), which, as the title indicates, deals with the same subject as the "Air de Sémiramis" in the *Album de vers anciens.* A third and final collaboration with another composer, Germaine Taillefer, gave rise in 1938 to *Cantate du Narcisse* (published 1939), yet another treatment of the Narcissus theme that had figured in both the *Album de vers anciens* and *Charmes.*

Two unfinished plays, *Le Solitaire; ou, La Demoiselle de cristal* (The Solitary; or, The Crystal Lady), twenty pages long, and *Lust; ou, Les Malédictions d'univers* (Lust, or, The Maledictions of the Universe), five times that length, that Valéry rapidly sketched out in

1940 on the theme of Dr. Faustus also reveal that his thoughts still ran along the same lines. Some scenes from the plays were published in *Etudes pour Mon Faust* (Studies for My Faust, 1941); longer versions are included in *Mon Faust,* a limited edition of 123 copies published on 15 February 1945 by Gallimard, which was republished in a large edition on 30 April of the following year as *Mon Faust–Ebauches* (My Faust–Sketches). The choice of subject–a man who aspires to universal knowledge–recalls Valéry's early admiration for da Vinci and his fictive M. Teste; just as the latter, in "Lettre de Mme Emilie Teste," emerges from his meditations and clings to his wife as if to a "rocher de vie et de présence réelle," so Faustus turns toward the heroine, Lust, and in a moving hymn to life declares that: "Le moindre regard, la moindre sensation, les moindres actes et fonctions de la vie me deviennent de la même dignité que les desseins et les voix intérieures de ma pensée . . . C'est un état suprême, où tout se résume en vivre" (The slightest glance, the slightest sensation, the slightest acts and functions of life are of the same worth to me as the projects and inner voices of my thoughts . . . It is a supreme state of being in which everything is summed up in living).

Valéry therefore remained convinced of the need to maintain that reconciliation of thought and action, of the mind and the senses, of the inner world and the outer world, which, after the earlier period of conflict between the two, he had achieved between the years

1912 and 1922 and that had formed the subject of *La Jeune Parque, Album de vers anciens,* and *Charmes* during that productive decade.

Paul Valéry died of a heart ailment on 20 July 1945. Even on the occasion of his death the two worlds might be said to have been reconciled. He was given a lavish state funeral in Paris attended by thousands of mourners, but he was then buried in the quiet cemetery by the sea in Séte, where his modest tombstone is inscribed with two lines from *Le Cimetière marin:* "O récompense après une pensée / Qu'un long regard sur le calme des dieux."

Letters:

Lettres à quelques-uns (Paris: Gallimard, 1952);

André Gide-Paul Valéry, Correspondance 1890–1942, edited by Robert Mallet (Paris: Gallimard, 1955); abridged and translated by June Guicharnaud as *Self-Portraits, the Gide/Valéry Letters, 1890–1942* (Chicago: University of Chicago Press, 1966);

Paul Valéry and Gustave Fourment, Correspondance 1887–1933, edited by Octave Nadal (Paris: Gallimard, 1957);

Lettres inédites: Pierre Louÿs et Paul Valéry, edited by Pierre Borel, Les Œuvres libres, new series no. 147 (Paris: Fayard, 1958).

Bibliographies:

Georges Karaïskakis and François Chapon, *Bibliographie des œuvres de Paul Valéry publiées de 1889 à 1965* (Paris: Auguste Blaizot, 1976);

A. James Arnold, "Paul Valéry," in *A Critical Bibliography of French Literature,* edited by Richard A. Brooks, volume 6, *The Twentieth Century,* edited by Douglas W. Alden and Brooks, part 2, *Principally Poetry, Theater, and Criticism before 1940, and Essay* (Syracuse, N.Y.: Syracuse University Press, 1980), pp. 943–1023.

References:

Christine M. Crow, *Paul Valéry, and the Poetry of Voice* (Cambridge & New York: Cambridge University Press, 1982);

Paul Gifford, *Paul Valéry, Charmes,* Glasgow Introductory Guides to French Literature, no. 30 (Glasgow: University of Glasgow French and German Publications, 1995);

Henry A. Grubbs, *Paul Valéry* (New York: Twayne, 1968);

Jean Hytier, *La Poétique de Valéry* (Paris: Armand Colin, 1953); translated by Richard Howard as *The Poetics of Paul Valéry* (Garden City, N.Y.: Doubleday, 1966);

W. N. Ince, *The Poetic Theory of Paul Valéry* (Leicester: Leicester University Press, 1961);

Michel Jarrety, *Paul Valéry* (Paris: Hachette, 1992);

James R. Lawler, *Lecture de Valéry, une étude de Charmes* (Paris: Presses Universitaires de France, 1963);

Lawler, *The Poet as Analyst: Essays on Paul Valéry* (Berkeley, Los Angeles & London: University of California Press, 1974);

Agnes Ethel Mackay, *The Universal Self: A Study of Paul Valéry* (London: Routledge & Kegan Paul, 1961);

Octave Nadal, *Paul Valéry, La Jeune Parque, étude critique* (Paris: Le Club du Meilleur Livre, 1957);

Francis Scarfe, *The Art of Paul Valéry: A Study in Dramatic Monologue* (London: Heinemann, 1954);

Brian Stimpson, *Paul Valéry and Music: A Study of the Techniques of Composition in Valéry's Poetry* (Cambridge & New York: Cambridge University Press, 1984);

Alastair W. Thomson, *Valéry,* Writers and Critics, no. 45 (Edinburgh: Oliver & Boyd, 1965);

Bernard Vannier, "Horlogerie," *Modern Language Notes,* special Valéry issue, 87 (1972): 539–681;

Charles G. Whiting, *Paul Valéry* (London: Athlone, 1978).

Papers:

A substantial collection of Paul Valéry's manuscripts and correspondence, mostly compiled by Julien-Pierre Monod, is at the Bibliothèque Jacques Doucet, Paris; another collection, which includes many of his notebooks, was donated by his heirs to the Bibliothèque Nationale de France in 1972.

Books for Further Reading

Alden, Douglas W., and Richard A. Brooks. *A Critical Bibliography of French Literature,* volume 6. *The Twentieth Century.* Parts 1 and 3. Syracuse, N.Y.: Syracuse University Press, 1980.

Alyn, Marc. *La Nouvelle poésie française.* Mane: R. Morel, 1968.

Aragon, Louis. *Chroniques du bel canto.* Geneva: Skira, 1947.

Aragon. *Journal d'une poésie nationale.* Lyon: Ecrivains Réunis, 1954.

Aspel, Alexander, and Donald Justice. *Contemporary French Poetry: Fourteen Witnesses of Man's Fate.* Ann Arbor: University of Michigan Press, 1965.

Barthes, Roland. *Le Degré zéro de l'écriture, suivi de Nouveaux essais critiques.* Paris: Seuil, 1972. Translated by Annette Lavers and Colin Smith as *Writing Degree Zero.* London: Cape, 1967.

Bédouin, Jean-Louis. *La Poésie surréaliste.* Paris: Seghers, 1964.

Bernard, Suzanne. *Le Poème en prose de Baudelaire jusqu'à nos jours.* Paris: Nizet, 1959.

Bersani, Jacques, Michel Autrand, Jacques Lecarme, and Bruno Vercier. *La Littérature en France depuis 1945.* Paris: Bordas, 1970.

Bishop, Michael. *The Contemporary Poetry of France. Eight Studies.* Amsterdam: Rodopi, 1985.

Bishop, ed. *The Language of Poetry: Crisis and Solution; Studies in Modern Poetry of French Expression, 1945 to the Present.* Amsterdam: Rodopi, 1980.

Bohn, Willard. *The Aesthetics of Visual Poetry, 1914–1928.* Cambridge: Cambridge University Press, 1986.

de Boisdeffre, Pierre. *Une Anthologie vivante de la littérature d'aujourd'hui: La Poésie française de Baudelaire à nos jours.* Paris: Librairie Académique Perrin, 1966.

Bonnefoy, Yves. *Une Autre époque de l'écriture.* Paris: Mercure de France, 1988.

Bosquet, Alain. *Verbe et vertige. Situations de la poésie.* Paris: Hachette, 1961.

Brée, Germaine. *Le XXe siècle: II, 1920–1970.* Paris: Librairie Arthaud, 1978.

Bremond, Henri. *La Poésie pure, avec un débat sur la poésie par Robert de Souza.* Paris: Bernard Grasset, 1926.

Brindeau, Serge. *La Poésie contemporaine de langue française depuis 1945.* Paris: St. Germain des Prés, 1973.

Broome, Peter, and Graham Chesters. *The Appreciation of Modern French Poetry, 1850–1950.* Cambridge: Cambridge University Press, 1976.

Caws, Mary Ann, *The Poetry of Dada and Surrealism.* Princeton: Princeton University Press, 1970.

Caws, ed. *About French Poetry from Dada to "Tel Quel."* Detroit: Wayne State University Press, 1974.

Chiari, Joseph. *Contemporary French Poetry.* Manchester: Manchester University Press, 1952.

Chiari. *Symbolisme from Poe to Mallarmé.* Foreword by T. S. Eliot. New York: Macmillan, 1956.

Cornell, Kenneth. *The Post-Symbolist Period: French Poetic Currents, 1900–1920.* New Haven: Yale University Press, 1958.

Darras, Jacques, ed. *Arpentage de la poésie contemporaine.* Amiens: Trois Cailloux, 1987.

Décaudin, Michel, ed. *Anthologie de la poésie française du XXe siècle, de Paul Claudel à René Char.* Preface by Claude Roy. Collection Poésie. Paris: Gallimard, 1983.

Deluy, Henri. *Poésie en France 1983–1988: Une Anthologie critique.* Paris: Flammarion, 1989.

Gibson, Robert. *Modern French Poets on Poetry.* Cambridge: Cambridge University Press, 1979.

Hubert, Renée Riese. *Surrealism and the Book.* Berkeley, Los Angeles & Oxford: University of California Press, 1988.

La Charité, Virginia A. *Twentieth-Century French Avant-Garde Poetry, 1907–1990.* Nicholasville, Ky.: French Forum Publishers, 1992.

Lagarde, André, and Laurent Michard. *XXe siècle: Les Grands auteurs français.* Paris: Bordas, 1962.

Little, Roger. *The Shaping of Modern French Poetry: Reflections on Unrhymed Poetic Form 1840–1990.* Manchester, U.K.: Carcanet / Paris: Alyscamp Press, 1995.

Matthews, J. H. *Surrealist Poetry in France.* Syracuse, N.Y.: Syracuse University Press, 1969.

Onimus, Jean. *La Connaissance poétique: Introduction à la lecture des poèmes modernes.* Paris: Desclée de Brouwer, 1966.

Oulipo. *La Littérature potentielle: Créations, re-créations, récréations.* Paris: Gallimard, 1973.

Raymond, Marcel. *De Baudelaire au surréalisme.* Paris: José Corti, 1966.

Richard, Jean-Pierre. *Onze Etudes sur la poésie moderne.* Paris: Seuil, 1964.

Roubaud, Jacques. *La Viellesse d'Alexandre.* Paris: Maspéro, 1978.

Sabatier, Robert. *Histoire de la poésie française.* Volume 9. Paris: Albin Michel, 1989.

Sartre, Jean-Paul. *Qu'est-ce que la littérature?* Paris: Gallimard, 1948.

Souriau, Etienne. *La Poésie française et la peinture.* London: Athlone Press, 1966.

Tzara, Tristan. *Le Surréalisme et l'après-guerre.* Paris: Nagel, 1947.

Walzer, Pierre-Olivier. *Le XXe siècle: I, 1896–1920.* Paris: Librairie Arthaud, 1975.

Williams, Adelia M. *The Double Cipher: Encounter between Word and Image in Bonnefoy, Tardieu and Michaux.* New York: Peter Lang, 1990.

Contributors

Frank A. Anselmo . . . . *Louisiana State University*

Margaret M. Bolovan . . . .

Camille René La Bossière . . . . *University of Ottawa*

James Bunzli . . . . *Central Michigan University*

Charles Chadwick . . . . *Aberdeen University*

Joseph A. DiLuzio . . . . *St. Joseph's University*

Toby Garfitt . . . . *University of Oxford*

Karen Humphreys . . . . *Trinity College*

Rhona Justice-Malloy . . . . *Central Michigan University*

Kevin Karlin . . . . *University of Washington*

Van Kelly . . . . *University of Kansas*

André Leroux . . . .

Jean-François Leroux . . . . *University of Ottawa*

Malcolm McGoldrick . . . . *University of Regina*

Kenneth W. Meadwell . . . . *University of Winnipeg*

Craig Monk . . . . *University of Lethbridge*

Adrian Morfee . . . . *Université Lumière Lyon 2*

Glenn Moulaison . . . . *University of Lethbridge*

Mary Anne O'Neil . . . . *Whitman College*

Catherine Perry . . . . *University of Notre Dame*

David Rampton . . . . *University of Ottawa*

J. M. Reibetanz . . . . *University of Toronto*

Jean-Xavier Ridon . . . . *University of Nottingham*

Paul Robichaud . . . . *University of Toronto*

Paul Matthieu St-Pierre . . . . *Simon Fraser University*

David LeHardy Sweet . . . . *Columbia University*

Cumulative Index

Dictionary of Literary Biography, Volumes 1-258
Dictionary of Literary Biography Yearbook, 1980-2001
Dictionary of Literary Biography Documentary Series, Volumes 1-19
Concise Dictionary of American Literary Biography, Volumes 1-7
Concise Dictionary of British Literary Biography, Volumes 1-8
Concise Dictionary of World Literary Biography, Volumes 1-4

Cumulative Index

DLB before number: *Dictionary of Literary Biography,* Volumes 1-258
Y before number: *Dictionary of Literary Biography Yearbook,* 1980-2001
DS before number: *Dictionary of Literary Biography Documentary Series,* Volumes 1-19
CDALB before number: *Concise Dictionary of American Literary Biography,* Volumes 1-7
CDBLB before number: *Concise Dictionary of British Literary Biography,* Volumes 1-8
CDWLB before number: *Concise Dictionary of World Literary Biography,* Volumes 1-4

C

L

M

Q

T

Cumulative Index

ISBN 0-7876-5252-0

90000